Supporting Women's Health and Wellbeing in the Workplace

Kyla Latrice Tennin
https://orcid.org/0000-0002-9849-1316

University of Phoenix, USA & Lady Mirage Global Inc., USA & Woolf University, UK

Senthil Kumar A.V.
https://orcid.org/0000-0002-8587-7017

Nehru Institute of Information Technology and Management, India

Samrat Ray
International Institute of Management Studies, India

A.B. Mishra
International Institute of Management Studies, India

IGI Global
Scientific Publishing
Publishing Tomorrow's Research Today

Vice President of Editorial Melissa Wagner
Director of Acquisitions Mikaela Felty
Director of Book Development Jocelynn Hessler
Production Manager Mike Brehm
Cover Design Jose Rosado

Published in the United States of America by
IGI Global Scientific Publishing
701 East Chocolate Avenue
Hershey, PA, 17033, USA
Tel: 717-533-8845 | Fax: 717-533-7115
Website: https://www.igi-global.com E-mail: cust@igi-global.com

Library of Congress Cataloging-in-Publication Data

Names: Tennin, Kyla Latrice, 1982- editor
Title: Supporting women's health and wellbeing in the workplace / edited by Kyla Tennin, A.V. Senthil Kumar, Samrat Ray, A. Mishra.
Description: Hershey, PA : IGI Global Scientific Publishing, [2026] | Includes bibliographical references and index. | Summary: "This book provides a comprehensive guide for healthcare providers, HR professionals, and employers on supporting women's health and wellbeing in the workplace. The book aims to improve health outcomes, reduce absenteeism and presenteeism, and enhance overall wellbeing for women in the workplace"-- Provided by publisher.
Identifiers: LCCN 2025023863 (print) | LCCN 2025023864 (ebook) | ISBN 9798337329703 hardcover | ISBN 9798337329710 paperback | ISBN 9798337329727 ebook
Subjects: LCSH: Women--Employment | Well-being
Classification: LCC HD6053 .S86 2026 (print) | LCC HD6053 (ebook)
LC record available at https://lccn.loc.gov/2025023863
LC ebook record available at https://lccn.loc.gov/2025023864
British Cataloguing in Publication Data
A Cataloguing in Publication record for this book is available from the British Library.

To every woman who has shown up to work while carrying the weight of symptoms, silence, and misunderstanding—this book is for you.

To the trailblazers who have spoken openly about their health, paving the way for change— your courage lights the path.

And to the leaders, colleagues, and allies who choose empathy, inclusion, and action— may your example inspire workplaces where every woman's wellbeing is valued, respected, and supported.

Table of Contents

Detailed Table of Contents

The pursuit of gender-inclusive workplaces has gained traction, emphasizing resilience and integration in professional environments. This study uses bibliometric analysis to explore research trends, key themes, and influential contributions toward resilient and integrative workplaces for women. Drawing on Web of Science data, it examines publication patterns and citation networks to map scholarly discourse on workplace resilience and gender integration. Findings highlight a growing emphasis on gender equity policies, leadership development, psychological safety, and diversity management in promoting inclusive cultures. Emerging themes include the impact of digital transformation and remote work on women's workplace experiences. The study provides insights into the evolution of this research area, offering practical implications for policymakers, organizations, and scholars. Mapping the intellectual structure of the field contributes to understanding strategies that foster professional environments where women can thrive.

This chapter reframes menopause as a biologically and evolutionarily adaptive life stage that enhances women's leadership capacity rather than diminishes it. Drawing on the Grandmother Hypothesis, neuroendocrinology, and leadership theory, the chapter explores how postmenopausal women transition from reproductive roles to strategic, relational, and cultural influence. It maps the hormonal and cognitive recalibrations of menopause onto leadership styles such as authentic, servant, adaptive, and strategic leadership, while acknowledging vulnerabilities such as cognitive fog, mood volatility, and social invisibility. Empirical evidence from workplace case studies and menopause-inclusive policies illustrates both the barriers and opportunities this transition entails. The chapter argues that menopause, when supported by inclusive organizational structures, can serve as a leadership accelerator. It concludes with policy recommendations and a call for intersectional, longitudinal research to further explore how menopause can be integrated into leadership development pipelines.

In today's workplaces, which are becoming more diverse and fast-paced, women's overall health is becoming a bigger concern. This is usually dealt with through physical and mental health frameworks. There is, however, a new way of thinking that combines spirituality at work, cultural intelligence, and sacred practices to give women more power through inner peace and understanding between cultures. This chapter looks at how spiritual resonance and cultural harmony work together to help women feel better in the workplace, focusing on sacred practices like chanting and reading spiritual texts. The chapter suggests a conceptual model that puts spiritual engagement at the center of the relationship between sacred practices and holistic well-being. It does this by using ideas from a variety of fields, such as workplace spirituality, cultural intelligence (CQ), feminist well-being theories, and archetypal psychology.

for integrating AI into menopause care; by leveraging AI, organizations can enhance workplace inclusivity, optimize well-being, and improve overall performance in modern workforce management.

In the contemporary workplace, mental health issues among employees have become a pressing concern, impacting both individual well-being and organizational productivity. This paper presents a novel approach leveraging ensemble learning techniques for predicting the mental health status of employees. By integrating multiple machine learning algorithms, our methodology aims to provide a comprehensive assessment of stress levels among workers. Initially, we employ specific machine learning models to identify various stress indicators within the workplace environment. Subsequently, we apply ensemble techniques to refine and consolidate the outcomes from these initial models. Through this iterative process, we strive to improve the precision and dependability of mental health predictions. The proposed structure offers a promising avenue for organizations to proactively address mental health challenges and create a healthy working environment that encourages employee well-being.

Menopause is a normal biological process that signals the end of a woman's reproductive years. Menopause can cause a variety of physical and mental changes that affect a woman's health and quality of life. If women are aware of the symptoms and management techniques, they can easily navigate the transition during perimenopause and postmenopause. Traditionally, diagnosing menopause only involved medical investigations, hormone level measurements, and symptom assessment. However, these methods can be inconsistent. But with the development of artificial intelligence (AI), the diagnosis and management are changing. New AI tools being precise, individualized, and data-driven, search through large databases to identify women who are more likely to suffer from menopause-related issues. Although the technology is still developing but it has huge potential to meet the

This chapter offers a theoretical and conceptual framework for predictive absenteeism modeling for menopause and establishes a rigorous handbook for researchers and practitioners. It explores how predictive analytics can be ethically incorporated into HR systems for the anticipation and management of menopause absenteeism, highlighting a multidisciplinary approach that brings technical, organizational, and humanistic together. The chapter emphasizes the pervasive effect of menopause on the work force through absenteeism, presenteeism, and turnover and outlines a formal model for risk prediction, accompanied by plans for implementation and ethical governance. It finally urges a move away from reactive to proactive organizational support and towards a menopause-friendly workplace. This system not only enables data-driven decision-making but also stimulates a more humane and inclusive vision for the future of work.

Menopause brings both physiological and psychological alterations that significantly impact workplace engagement for women. Conventional treatment have predominantly employees one-size fits-all solutions, disregarding the notable inconsistencies between individual experiences. This necessitates migrating towards customised clinical solutions. Integrating AI-guided remedies and Personalised medicine into workplace wellness frameworks proposes a revolutionary strategy to managing menopausal symptoms. By considering individual differences, AI and personalised medicine can enhance workplace well-being and productivity by providing tailored support.This chapter examines the integration of artificial intelligence, personalized medicine, and strategic human capital planning in managing menopause amongst employees.The intersection holds promise for tailoring support to particular needs and stages, as women and their employers navigate short-term difficulties and long-term implications together through open dialogue and evidence-based accommodations.

As women increasingly assume leadership and teaching roles in India's coaching industry, it becomes essential to prioritize their health and wellbeing, especially during menopause—a natural yet often stigmatized life stage. The coaching sector, marked by high stress, rigid schedules, and limited health infrastructure, offers minimal support for midlife women. This chapter explores how emerging technologies, particularly artificial intelligence (AI) and personalized medicine, can be harnessed to create menopause-friendly workplaces. AI tools such as predictive health analytics, symptom tracking, and intelligent HR systems are transforming employee care, enhancing productivity, and fostering empathetic work cultures. Personalized medicine enables tailored interventions based on genetic, hormonal, and lifestyle factors. These innovations can foster inclusive, responsive, and sustainable environments that support and retain midlife women. The chapter concludes with a roadmap for implementation, offering policy and ethical guidelines for effective integration of these tools.

Occupational stress is an increasingly prevalent issue that has a significant impact on the psychological well being of working women in Malaysia. This study aims to assess the relationship between occupational stress and psychological well being through quantitative methods. A total of 118 respondents from agencies in Malaysia were involved in this survey study. Data analysis was conducted using Statistical Package for Social Sciences (SPSS) software for descriptive statistics and initial coding, while structural equation modeling (SEM) and hypothesis testing were carried out using Smart PLS. The results of the analysis showed that occupational stress has a significant impact on the psychological well being of working women. This study also provides recommendations for future research as well as practical implications in strengthening psychosocial support and more gender-sensitive workplace policies.

Preface

In today's dynamic and competitive global economy, workplaces are evolving—embracing diversity, equity, and inclusion not merely as ideals, but as essential drivers of innovation and productivity. Yet, in this progress, one critical aspect of workforce health and inclusion has often remained overlooked: the unique health and life-stage experiences of women, particularly during the menopause transition.

Supporting Women's Health and Wellbeing in the Workplace was born from the recognition that true workplace inclusion extends beyond representation—it requires understanding and responding to the realities of every employee's health journey. For women, this includes a spectrum of experiences: menstrual health, pregnancy, perimenopause, menopause, and post-menopause, as well as mental health and other wellbeing challenges that intersect with professional life. These are not "personal" matters isolated from the workplace; they are human experiences that influence productivity, engagement, and organizational culture.

Menopause, in particular, impacts millions of working women worldwide. Despite its prevalence, it has too often been surrounded by silence, stigma, and a lack of institutional support. The consequences can be profound—ranging from increased absenteeism and presenteeism to talent loss and diminished career progression. This book addresses these challenges head-on, offering practical, evidence-based strategies for employers, managers, and policymakers to create supportive environments where women can thrive at every stage of life.

This work draws upon a wide range of disciplines—healthcare delivery, occupational stress research, ethics and law, human resource management, artificial intelligence applications in health, and psychology—to provide a comprehensive and actionable resource. It is designed for business owners seeking to retain top talent, healthcare professionals aiming to improve patient outcomes, academics and researchers advancing the field, and advocates striving to close the gaps in women's workplace wellbeing. Chapter authors even teach in fields such as women's studies, economics, public health, law, statistics and applied mathematics, leadership and organizational behavior, medicine, business and management, computer applications, artificial intelligence and machine learning, biotechnology, biological and environmental sciences, entrepreneurship, pharmacy and emerging sciences, professional studies, finance and accounting, social work, and science and technology.

The insights presented here reflect an urgent truth: ***supporting women's health is not just a "nice-to-have" initiative; it is a strategic, ethical, and economic imperative***. By breaking the silence, fostering open dialogue, and implementing inclusive policies, organizations can not only enhance the wellbeing of individual women but also strengthen the collective health, resilience, and performance of their teams.

It is my hope that this book serves as both a catalyst and a guide—a catalyst for change in organizational attitudes toward women's health, and a guide for implementing meaningful, measurable actions that benefit individuals, organizations, and society at large.

ORGANIZATION OF THE BOOK

Chapter 1 Overview: Creating a Resilient and Integrative Workplace for Women

In this opening chapter, we highlight the evolving scholarly landscape surrounding gender-inclusive and integrative workplace cultures. Through a rigorous bibliometric analysis of global research trends, the authors map how resilience, gender equity, leadership development, and psychological safety have become central pillars in discussions about women's workplace wellbeing. Particularly notable is the emergence of digital transformation and remote work as influential factors shaping women's experiences and opportunities. This chapter provides readers with a clear intellectual roadmap of the field, offering insights into the policies, organizational strategies, and cultural shifts that enable women not only to succeed but to thrive in resilient and integrative environments.

Chapter 2 Overview: Menopause as an Evolutionary Leadership Catalyst

This chapter reframes menopause through an evolutionary and leadership development lens, positioning it as a period of enhanced cognitive, emotional, and strategic potential rather than decline. Drawing on the Grandmother Hypothesis, neuroendocrinology, and leadership science, the authors illustrate how postmenopausal transitions can activate strengths aligned with authentic, servant, and adaptive leadership styles. Through case studies and organizational examples, the chapter highlights how appropriate workplace support can transform menopause into a leadership accelerator. It calls for deeper institutional investment, intersectional research, and policies that recognize the strategic contributions of midlife and older women.

Chapter 3 Overview: Spiritual Resonance and Cultural Harmony for Women's Wellbeing at Work

Chapter 4 explores how spiritual engagement and culturally informed practices can elevate women's wellbeing in modern workplaces. Integrating insights from workplace spirituality, cultural intelligence, feminist wellbeing theories, and archetypal psychology, the authors present a conceptual model highlighting the role of sacred practices—such as chanting or reflective reading—in creating inner balance and cultural harmony. Through this multidisciplinary lens, the chapter reveals how spiritual resonance can help women navigate diverse work environments with greater clarity, resilience, and connection.

Chapter 4 Overview: Ethical Women's Leadership and Organizational Citizenship Behavior in Ethiopian Healthcare

Chapter 6 presents compelling evidence demonstrating how women's ethical leadership fosters organizational citizenship behavior in Ethiopian healthcare institutions. Using a robust methodological framework—including CFA, SEM, and validated sampling—the authors show that ethical leadership significantly enhances cooperation, altruism, and organizational culture, with consistency functioning as a critical mediating factor. This chapter enriches global conversations around gender, ethics, and leadership by illustrating how women leaders can positively transform healthcare environments.

Chapter 5 Overview: Harnessing Artificial Intelligence for Organizational Effectiveness in Menopause Care

This chapter examines how AI-driven strategies can reshape workplace responses to menopause, improving both employee wellbeing and organizational performance. From predictive analytics and virtual assistants to adaptive workspaces and ergonomic interventions, the authors showcase how AI can reduce stigma, enhance productivity, and support retention. At the same time, they stress the necessity of strong governance, ethical oversight, and leadership commitment to ensure that technological innovation aligns with trust, transparency, and employee dignity.

Chapter 6 Overview: Predicting Employee Mental Health Using Ensemble Learning

Chapter 6 introduces an innovative ensemble learning framework designed to predict employee stress levels and mental health outcomes. By combining multiple machine learning models to analyze workplace stress indicators, the authors offer a comprehensive predictive tool that organizations can use to identify risk factors early and intervene proactively. This chapter contributes to the wider discussion on psychological safety by demonstrating how data-driven approaches can support healthier, more responsive work environments.

Chapter 7 Overview: AI-Powered Diagnostic Tools for Menopause

This chapter explores how AI-enabled diagnostic tools are revolutionizing the identification and management of menopause symptoms. Moving beyond traditional assessments, AI technologies now leverage large-scale datasets to identify risk profiles, personalize care pathways, and improve diagnostic accuracy. The authors highlight both the promise and ethical considerations of AI in women's health, emphasizing the potential for more precise, responsive, and equitable menopause care supported by data-driven insights.

Chapter 8 Overview: AI-Based Decision-Making for Enhancing Menopause Care

Chapter 8 presents an AI-driven model for workplace menopause support that integrates physiological monitoring, sentiment analysis, and intelligent environmental adjustments. The authors demonstrate how AI can tailor work conditions—from temperature control to lighting—to ease symptom burdens, while predictive analytics help guide career development and support planning. The chapter offers a forward-looking blueprint for organizations seeking to embed menopause-sensitive decision systems into daily operations.

Chapter 9 Overview: Strategies for Sustaining Productivity and Wellbeing During Menopause

In this chapter, readers gain a comprehensive understanding of how menopause affects workplace productivity, career trajectories, and economic outcomes. The authors examine the consequences of rigid work structures, stigma, and inadequate support while highlighting evidence-based interventions—from flexible scheduling to clinical therapies—that help sustain women's performance and wellbeing. This chapter underscores the importance of policy reform, workplace awareness, and supportive leadership in reducing the structural barriers faced by midlife women.

Chapter 10 Overview: Ethical HR Solutions Using Predictive Absenteeism Modeling

Chapter 10 introduces an ethical framework for integrating predictive absenteeism models into HR systems to better support menopausal employees. Emphasizing proactive rather than reactive approaches, the authors show how analytics can forecast attendance risks and guide supportive interventions while upholding employee rights, confidentiality, and dignity. This chapter extends the conversation on ethical AI, positioning predictive modeling as a tool for building more equitable and menopause-friendly workplaces.

Chapter 11 Overview: Personalized Medicine and AI-Driven Treatment Strategies

This chapter advances the argument that menopause care must move beyond one-size-fits-all models toward personalized, AI-enhanced clinical support. By integrating personalized medicine, digital health tools, and human capital strategy, the authors outline how organizations can tailor interventions to individual physiological and psychological needs. The chapter presents a strategic vision in which AI and personalized care pathways strengthen women's workplace engagement, resilience, and long-term career continuity.

Chapter 12 Overview: Building Menopause-Friendly Workplaces in India's Coaching Industry

Focusing on India's rapidly expanding coaching sector, this chapter explores how personalized medicine and AI-powered tools can create more supportive environments for midlife women. Given the sector's high-stress demands and limited health infrastructure, the authors argue that technological innovations—such as predictive analytics, symptom monitoring, and adaptive HR systems—are essential for improving retention, wellbeing, and organizational empathy. The chapter concludes with policy guidelines and an actionable roadmap for implementing menopause-friendly reforms.

Chapter 13 Overview: Occupational Stress and Psychological Wellbeing Among Malaysian Women

Chapter 13 provides empirical insights into the strong relationship between occupational stress and psychological wellbeing among Malaysian working women. Through statistical and structural modeling, the authors show how workplace pressures significantly undermine mental health. Their findings underscore the need for targeted psychosocial interventions, gender-sensitive policies, and supportive organizational cultures that prioritize long-term wellbeing and work-life balance.

Chapter 14 Overview: Soulful Work—Spirituality, Resilience, and Ethical AI

In this chapter, the authors present the Soulful Work framework, a holistic model that integrates workplace spirituality, emotional resilience, and ethically designed AI systems. Addressing the lived experiences of women navigating midlife transitions—including menopause and caregiving—the chapter shows how spiritual intelligence and reflective practices can synergize with digital wellness tools to enhance engagement, psychological safety, and organizational cohesion. It offers a compelling vision of future workplaces that honor both human depth and technological advancement.

Chapter 15 Overview: Healthcare Provider Support and Women's Health During Menopause

Chapter 15 reinforces the indispensable role healthcare providers play in delivering effective, patient-centered menopause care. By examining barriers such as inadequate training, stigma, and healthcare inequities, the authors call for comprehensive provider education and multidisciplinary practice models. They highlight emerging innovations like telemedicine and integrative care that can expand access and improve outcomes, especially for underserved populations. The chapter affirms that robust provider support leads directly to better symptom management and enhanced quality of life.

Chapter 16 Overview: Poor Menstrual Hygiene and Women's Health Risks

The final chapter addresses poor menstrual hygiene as an urgent yet chronically neglected public health issue. The authors examine how persistent stigma, misinformation, and cultural taboos hinder women's autonomy, education, productivity, and health outcomes worldwide. By highlighting the inadequacies of existing global health frameworks—including their limited focus on menstrual hygiene—they call for expanded research, policy advocacy, and community-based interventions. This chapter situates menstrual hygiene as foundational to women's lifelong health, dignity, and workplace participation.

Acknowledgment

The creation of this book has been a deeply collaborative journey, and the editors are profoundly grateful to the many people and organizations who have contributed their knowledge, insights, and encouragement along the way.

To the women who shared their personal stories of navigating health challenges in the workplace—your openness and honesty brought depth, humanity, and urgency to these pages. Your voices are the heart of this work.

To the medical professionals, psychologists, researchers, and workplace specialists whose expertise informed the content—thank you for your commitment to evidence-based solutions and for the tireless work you do to improve women's health and wellbeing.

To the leaders, HR professionals, and advocates who are already implementing progressive policies—your real-world examples prove that change is not only possible but powerful.

A special thanks to our editorial team, peer reviewers, and colleagues who provided thoughtful feedback, challenged assumptions, and helped shape this book into a resource that can inform and inspire.

Finally, our colleagues, friends, and mentors—thank you for your unwavering belief in this project and for reminding us that the work of advancing women's wellbeing is as much a personal mission as it is a professional one.

This book exists because of a collective effort, and our hope is that it will, in turn, contribute to a collective movement toward workplaces where every woman's health and dignity are upheld.

Introduction

The book ***Supporting Women's Health and Wellbeing in the Workplace*** is a publication about Menopause in the Workplace. Additionally, this well-structured introduction bridges the reader into the book's purpose, urgency, and scope.

Henceforth, the conversation around workplace wellbeing has grown significantly in recent decades, with organizations increasingly recognizing that employee health is directly linked to engagement, productivity, and long-term success. Yet within this broader dialogue, the specific health and wellbeing needs of women—particularly during midlife and the menopause transition—have not received the consistent attention they deserve. This gap is more than a missed opportunity for inclusion; it is a critical oversight with measurable consequences for individuals, organizations, and the economy.

Menopause is a natural life stage that will affect nearly half of the global population at some point, yet it remains one of the least discussed and least understood topics in the workplace. The symptoms—ranging from hot flashes and sleep disturbances to cognitive changes and emotional shifts—can directly impact work performance, attendance, and career progression. For many women, these challenges occur at the peak of their careers, when their expertise, leadership, and institutional knowledge are at their highest value to employers. Without awareness and supportive structures, organizations risk losing this invaluable talent.

The purpose of this book is twofold. First, it seeks to raise awareness about the realities of women's health in the workplace, ***from menstrual health to menopause***, and how these experiences intersect with work environments, leadership, ethics, and law. Second, it provides a roadmap for employers, human resource professionals, and policymakers to create practical, evidence-based support systems that help women maintain their health, wellbeing, and professional contributions throughout their careers.

Drawing on research from healthcare, occupational psychology, organizational leadership, and emerging technologies such as artificial intelligence in personalized medicine, this book offers a multidisciplinary perspective. It highlights strategies for reducing absenteeism and presenteeism, fostering open communication, and embedding inclusive policies into organizational culture.

The chapters that follow will explore:

- The physiological and psychological dimensions of menopause and related life stages.
- The role of workplace culture in either exacerbating or alleviating health challenges.
- The legal and ethical considerations surrounding women's health support.
- The application of leadership and administrative strategies to foster inclusivity.
- Innovations and tools—such as AI-driven health solutions—that can personalize care and support.

This is not merely a health conversation; it is a leadership conversation. By understanding and addressing women's health and wellbeing, including through frameworks and models, organizations have the opportunity to *strengthen their workforce, **retain top talent**, and model what it truly means to be inclusive*. The future of work depends on how well we respond to the diverse needs of our people—and that future starts now.

THEORETICAL MODELS FOR SUPPORTING WOMEN'S HEALTH AND WELLBEING IN THE WORKPLACE

To address women's health in the workplace comprehensively, this book considers several interrelated theoretical models. These frameworks provide both the ***conceptual foundation and the practical lens*** through which policies, interventions, and cultural shifts can be designed.

Integrated Workplace Wellbeing Model (IWWM)

Purpose: To link women's health needs with organizational performance outcomes.

Core Components:

- **Physical Health Support** – Access to healthcare, adjustments for symptoms, wellness programs.
- **Psychological Wellbeing** – Mental health resources, stigma reduction, peer support.

- **Workplace Flexibility** – Policies for flexible schedules, hybrid work, and workload adjustments.
- **Cultural Inclusion** – Open dialogue, leadership commitment, education for all employees.
- **Organizational Outcomes** – Reduced absenteeism/presenteeism, higher engagement, talent retention.

Rationale: Builds on the *Total Worker Health®* approach from the U.S. National Institute for Occupational Safety and Health (NIOSH), adapted for women's life-stage experiences.

Life-Stage Health Continuum Framework (LHCF)

Purpose: To acknowledge that women's workplace health needs evolve over time.
Stages Covered:

1. **Menstrual Health & Early Career** – Managing symptoms, fostering open discussion, preventing discrimination.
2. **Pregnancy & Parental Transition** – Maternity protections, flexible work, re-entry support.
3. **Perimenopause & Menopause** – Workplace adjustments, health education, supervisor awareness.
4. **Post-Menopause & Later Career** – Continued wellbeing support, leadership roles, mentoring younger employees.

Rationale: Builds on *life course theory* in public health, recognizing cumulative and interconnected health experiences.

Organizational Support & Inclusion Cycle (OSIC)

Purpose: To show the iterative nature of building a supportive culture.
Cycle Steps:

1. **Awareness** – Training, education, and open conversations.
2. **Policy Development** – Formalizing support in HR and workplace guidelines.
3. **Implementation** – Embedding changes into daily practice.
4. **Feedback & Adjustment** – Gathering employee input and refining strategies.
5. **Sustainability** – Ensuring leadership accountability and ongoing resource allocation.

Rationale: Adapted from *Lewin's Change Management Model* and *continuous improvement cycles* (PDCA).

Ethical-Inclusive Leadership Model (EILM)

Purpose: To align women's health initiatives with ethical, legal, and leadership responsibilities.

Key Leadership Commitments:

- **Ethical Duty** – Protect dignity, privacy, and equal opportunity.
- **Legal Compliance** – Address discrimination, accommodate health needs, align with labor laws.
- **Strategic Advantage** – Recognize that inclusion strengthens organizational resilience.
- **Advocacy & Voice** – Encourage women's input in decision-making processes.

Rationale: Draws on *transformational leadership theory* and *stakeholder theory*, connecting ethical governance with wellbeing outcomes.

Tech-Enabled Personalization Model (TEPM)

Purpose: To leverage technology, including artificial intelligence, to tailor women's health support.

Applications:

- Symptom tracking and early intervention.
- AI-powered health recommendations.
- Digital wellbeing platforms accessible at work and home.
- Data analytics to monitor program impact without compromising privacy.

Rationale: Inspired by *personalized medicine* and *digital health adoption models*, ensuring interventions meet individual needs while scaling across organizations.

Although more are delineated in the book, an example framework is the new **Women's Workplace Wellbeing Framework (WWWF)** visual model, showing five interconnected stages that deal with the wellbeing of women, in the workplace—Awareness, Policy, Personalized Support, Leadership, and Continuous Improvement—linked in a clear, cyclical flow. This framework is presented in the introduction of the book so readers have a one-glance view of the book's practical roadmap, of menstrual and menopause discussions.

Figure 1. A framework for women's wellbeing in the workplace

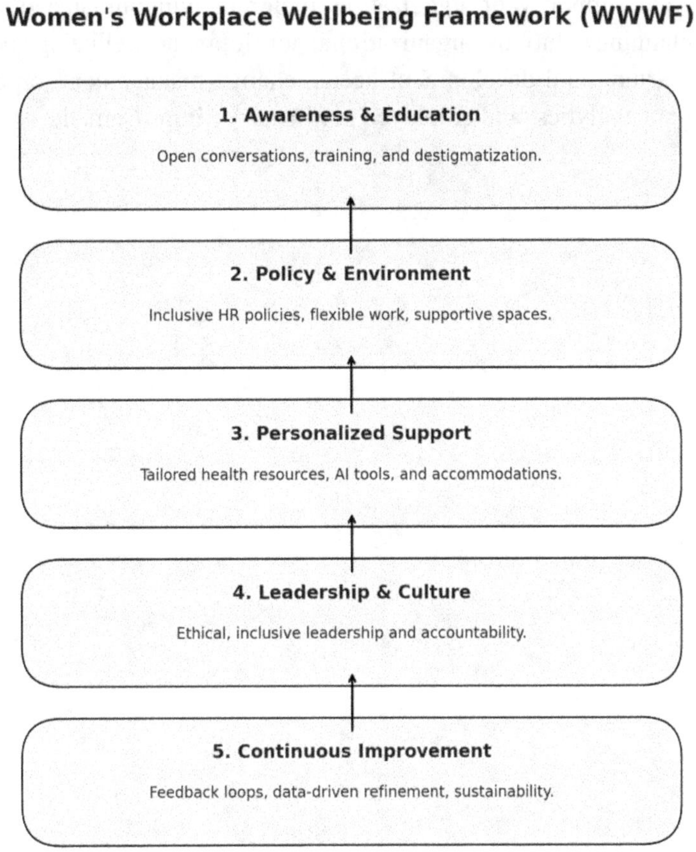

The **Women's Workplace Wellbeing Framework (WWWF)** is a five-stage model designed to guide organizations in creating inclusive, supportive environments for women's health—particularly during the menopause transition. It begins with **Awareness & Education**, fostering open dialogue, training, and stigma reduction. From there, **Policy & Environment** ensures formal HR policies, flexible work options, and supportive physical spaces are in place. **Personalized Support** follows, providing tailored health resources, AI-enabled tools, and individual accommodations to meet diverse needs. **Leadership & Culture** reinforces these efforts through ethical, inclusive leadership that models accountability and empathy.

Finally, **Continuous Improvement** creates a feedback loop, using employee input and data-driven insights to refine and sustain initiatives over time. Together, these interconnected stages form a sustainable approach that benefits women, organizations, and society as a whole. To retain consulting services, in general or for your business needs, please contact sales@LadyMirageGlobal.com or visit our website at www.LadyMirageGlobal.com to learn more about our consulting services and how we can support your organization. Including with human capital strategy, workforce planning solutions, organizational development, wellbeing and retention strategies, learning and development needs, change management, organizational effectives, data analytics, and employee performance improvement.

Chapter 1
Creating a Resilient and Integrative Workplace for Women:
A Bibliometric Analysis

Mohammed Imran
https://orcid.org/0009-0000-1615-3528
Utkal University, India

Alok Ranjan Behera
https://orcid.org/0000-0002-6569-8265
Utkal University, India

Mitali Chinara
Utkal University, India

Bhabani Shankar Mohanty
https://orcid.org/0000-0001-9130-6221
Central University of Tamil Nadu, India

Zahid Parwez
https://orcid.org/0000-0001-7511-0624
XIM University, India

Sabina Begum
https://orcid.org/0000-0003-2502-866X
Utkal University, India

Zakir Hossen Shaikh
https://orcid.org/0000-0003-4733-4166
Kingdom University, Bahrain

Ruksana Begum
https://orcid.org/0009-0000-2822-926X
Utkal University, India

Pratikshya Priyadarshini
https://orcid.org/0000-0003-3169-9793
KIIT University, India

Birendri Birendri
https://orcid.org/0000-0003-0933-3103
Lovely Professional University, India

ABSTRACT

The pursuit of gender-inclusive workplaces has gained traction, emphasizing resilience and integration in professional environments. This study uses bibliometric analysis to explore research trends, key themes, and influential contributions toward

DOI: 10.4018/979-8-3373-2970-3.ch001

resilient and integrative workplaces for women. Drawing on Web of Science data, it examines publication patterns and citation networks to map scholarly discourse on workplace resilience and gender integration. Findings highlight a growing emphasis on gender equity policies, leadership development, psychological safety, and diversity management in promoting inclusive cultures. Emerging themes include the impact of digital transformation and remote work on women's workplace experiences. The study provides insights into the evolution of this research area, offering practical implications for policymakers, organizations, and scholars. Mapping the intellectual structure of the field contributes to understanding strategies that foster professional environments where women can thrive.

INTRODUCTION

Gender equality has come a long way, but women still confront many obstacles in the workplace, including those that are institutional, societal, and organisational. There are many ways in which women are still marginalised and powerless in today's workplaces, including but not limited to: low pay, a lack of opportunities for advancement, subtle types of discrimination, and an absence of policies that encourage work-life balance (ILO, 2018). Traditional gender norms and systematic biases are particularly pervasive in male-dominated industries in underdeveloped nations, making these problems even worse (UN Women, 2021a).

Fostering a culture that appreciates diversity, promotes psychological safety, and supports the personal and professional development of all employees is more important than quotas or regulatory reforms in creating a resilient and integrative workplace for women. Here, resilience means both the capacity of individuals to deal with and even thrive in the face of adversity and the capacity of organisations to adapt to changing circumstances and aid their employees in a way that is inclusive of all backgrounds and experiences (Kossek et al., 2011a). Ensuring that women feel seen, heard, and valued is the goal of an integrative workplace, which incorporates gender inclusion into organisational structures, decision-making processes, and everyday interactions.

Also, modern conversations about equity centre on intersectionality, which acknowledges those women's experiences in the workplace, are impacted by multiple identities, such as age, disability, racism, class, and caste (Crenshaw, 1991). Therefore, a complex strategy is required to construct inclusive and resilient settings; this strategy should incorporate gender-sensitive policies, inclusive leadership, mentoring programs, and channels for the resolution of complaints. Catalyst (2020) found that companies who put money into these strategies had higher rates of employee engagement, innovation, and overall performance.

Data and Methods

For this analysis, we used Web of Science, the gold standard database for scientific literature, which comprises peer-reviewed publications with a high impact factor. For reviewing research publications with citations and impact factors, it is extensively utilised by prominent institutions, universities, and organisations. With significant in-depth research and investigations, it braces diverse information. Bibliometric studies benefit greatly from it. We searched for relevant documents using PRISMA (Preferred Reporting Items for Systematic Reviews and Meta-Analysis) standards and found relevant records about gender discrepancies in Professional Higher Education through Web of Science. The sophisticated search engine at Clarivate was used to search documents using a single keyword.

Table 1. Records identified and period covered per keyword search

SL.	*Keywords*	*Records Identified*	*Period covered*
1	("Women in workplace" or "Gender equality" or "Inclusive workplace" or "Workplace resilience")	10,904	1989-2025

Source: Web of Science

Figure 1. Prisma Flow Chart

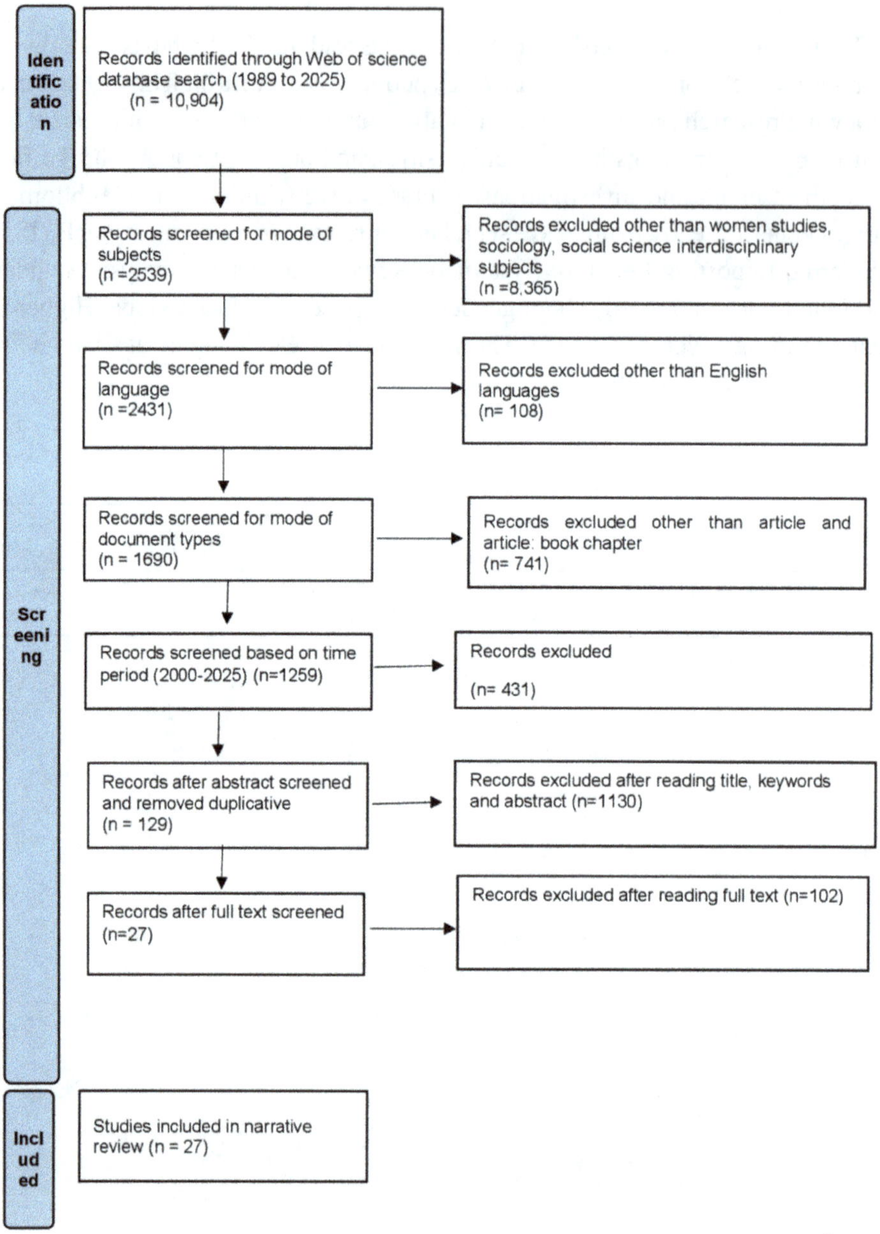

Bibliometrics Analysis

Figure 2. Most Relevant Sources

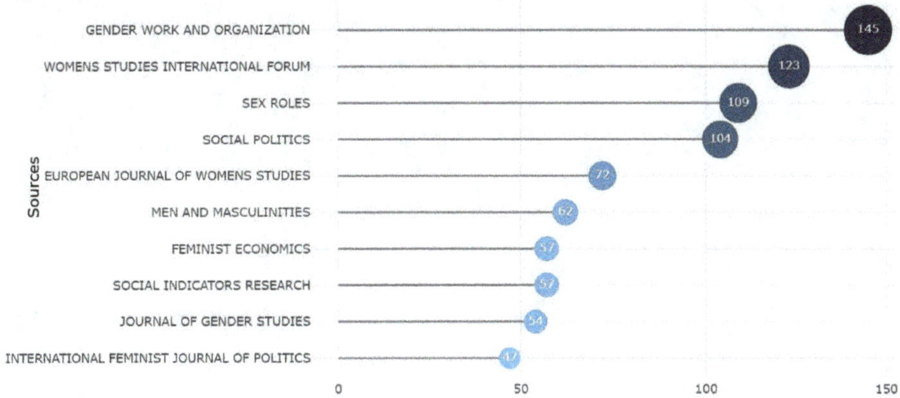

A study of the most important scholarly works in the subject of gender studies and associated multidisciplinary domains is displayed in the accompanying graphic. The most cited of these is Gender, Work and Organisation, which has 145 mentions and is therefore clearly the most important resource for discussions of gender dynamics in the workplace and other organisational settings.

Sex roles (109 mentions) and Women's Studies International Forum (123 mentions) are both highly regarded for their significant contributions to feminist research and gender role analysis in various cultural contexts. Social Politics (104 mentions) is also quite important, especially when it comes to studying how gender, policies, and social justice all interact with one another.

Mediating between feminist and masculinities stances, mid-tier journals like Men and Masculinities (62 mentions) and European Journal of Women's Studies*(72 mentions) enrich our knowledge of gender. At the same time, publications such as Journal of Gender Studies, Social Indicators Research, and Feminist Economics (with 54–57 mentions) emphasise the statistical, economic, and transdisciplinary methods used in gender studies.

One source that offers a feminist theoretical perspective on international political concerns is the International Feminist Journal of Politics, which receives 47 mentions. The figure highlights how gender study is diverse and interdisciplinary, incorporating sociology, economics, politics, and psychology into a holistic academic conversation (Figure 2).

Figure 3. Most Relevant Authors

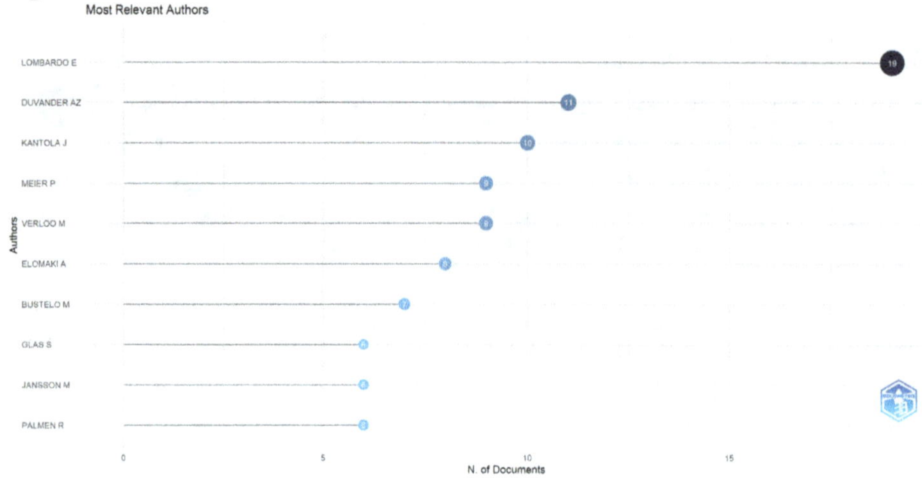

The bibliometric analysis of the most relevant authors according to the number of documents published in the selected research subject is shown in the above figure. The most prolific scholars are highlighted, who have made significant contributions. Leading the pack is Lombardo E, who has consistently contributed to the field and has a substantial impact with 19 publications. Among the academic discourse, Duvander AZ has 11 documents and Kantola J has10 documents, demonstrating their considerable presence and effect. Elomaki A contributed8 documents, Meier Pand Verloo M9 documents each, and Bustelo M,Glas S, Jansson M, and Palmen R6 to 7 documents each. In bibliometric studies, this sort of analysis is crucial for identifying top researchers, mapping intellectual contributions, and understanding the structure of research activity in a specific field. Additionally, it helps in identifying key opinion leaders who are pushing the research agenda and possible partners (Figure 3).

Figure 4. Most Cited Countries

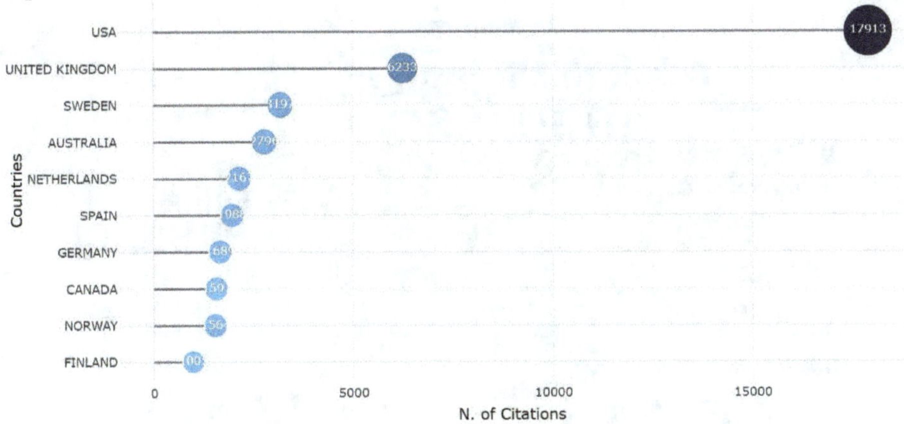

The graphic showcases the countries that have garnered the most citations in gender-related academic research, emphasising the scholarly impact of these nations. With 17,913 citations, the US easily takes the lead, demonstrating its outsized influence on gender studies around the world. This is probably attributable to the country's extensive academic infrastructure and its abundant research output. The United Kingdom comes in second with 6,233 citations, which shows that it has a long history of social research, feminist theory, and policy analysis.

With strong academic communities and enlightened gender legislation, Sweden (3,119) and Australia (2,796) also stand out as significant donors. Significant engagement is evident in several European nations, including the Netherlands (2,116), Spain (1,988), and Germany (1,688), especially in relation to social justice and gender equality. Showcasing the consistent contributions of Nordic and North American nations to the field, the top 10 is completed by Canada (1,590), Norway (1,506), and Finland (1,000). Overall, the map highlights the geographical distribution of significant gender research, showing that the Nordic and Western countries have the highest citation impact owing to their enduring dedication to gender equality and multidisciplinary research (Figure 4).

Figure 5. Word Cloud

The figure shows that certain terms are more prominent in the research field when their sizes are larger, indicating that they occur more frequently. The cloud is dominated by important terms like "women," "gender," "gender equality," "inequality," and "work," which indicate major themes and areas of research in gender studies. Use of terms such as "feminism," "politics," "family," "employment," and "policy" further implies an interdisciplinary strategy that considers economic, social, and political factors. Through an analysis of the distribution and frequency of keywords in bibliographic data, this word cloud aids in the identification of prevalent research interests, theme patterns, and developing subjects. It provides a visual overview that scholars can use to better grasp the field's intellectual structure, find gaps in their knowledge, and guide their future studies (Figure 5).

Figure 6. Thematic Map

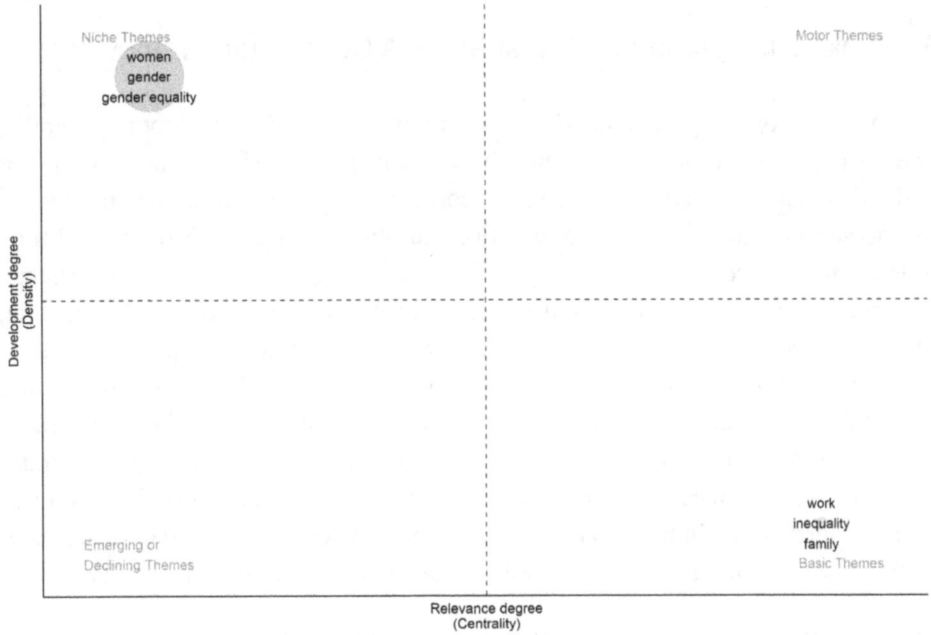

In bibliometric analysis, the thematic map is a strategic graphic that helps to visualise and classify research themes along two dimensions: centrality (the degree of relevance) and density (the degree of development). Each of the four corners of the map represents a distinct theme. Terms such as "women," "gender," and "gender equality" can be found in the upper left quadrant, which is labelled Niche Themes. While some areas show signs of deep specialisation and internal cohesion, they do not play a pivotal role in the larger field of study. Alternatively, terms like "work," "inequality," and "family" are found under the lower-right quadrant labelled Basic Themes. Despite their lack of development in terms of depth and specialisation, these themes serve a crucial role in connecting numerous research subjects and are highly fundamental to the field. This map presently lacks any content in the upper-right (Motor Themes) and lower-left (Emerging or Declining Themes) quadrants, indicating that none of the themes in this dataset are central, well-developed, and currently experiencing considerable change. In sum, the thematic map depicts the overall organisation of the research field's ideas, drawing attention to both central and periphery points of study (Figure 6).

Review of Literature

Workplace Integration and Resilience: A Conceptual Framework

In discussions on gender inclusivity in the workplace and fairness more generally, the ideas of integration and resilience have become very popular. The capacity for individuals and systems to endure and overcome challenges, interruptions, and stresses is known as resilience in the context of organisations (Lengnick-Hall et al., 2011). Barriers to advancement in leadership positions, parenting duties that interrupt careers, and pervasive gender biases all put women to the test in the workplace. Meanwhile, integration is defined as the degree to which women are treated as equals with males in all organisational choices, processes, and opportunities (Acker, 2006). According to scholars Shaw and Leberman (2015), a gender inclusive workplace does more than just hire women; it actively builds structures to accommodate varied gender identities, experiences, and needs. Building gender-responsive workplace cultures is an important step in this direction, since it acknowledges the lived differences in experiences that impact women's careers and works to eliminate such bias.

Gender-Based Workplace Attitudes and Their Effects

Gender inequalities in the workplace have been the subject of much research. According to Joan Acker's gendered organisations theory, which she put out in 1990, organisations' structures, practices, and symbols frequently serve to uphold male supremacy by subtly favouring males and excluding women. This shows up in a variety of contexts, including informal networks, promotion standards, and presumptions about dedication and output. Many women, especially mothers and carers, are disadvantaged by the "ideal worker" paradigm, which persists and depicts someone who is totally dedicated, always available, and not responsible for caring for others (Williams et al., 2016). As a result, women frequently face obstacles such as rigid job descriptions, lack of advancement prospects, and the so-called "sticky floor" and "glass ceiling" phenomenon (Cotter et al., 2001).

Challenges Facing Women in the Workplace

Systemic obstacles to women's advancement in the workplace have been identified by multiple empirical research. Some examples of these issues include discrimination based on gender, harassment in the workplace, unconscious bias in promotion and hiring, and uneven pay (Eagly & Carli, 2007). Although there has been an uptick in women being hired for entry-level positions, studies conducted by McKinsey & Company's Women in the Workplace series reveal that women, particularly women of colour, remain under-represented in positions of senior leadership (McKinsey & LeanIn.Org, 2021). While men get a "fatherhood bonus" that increases their self-esteem, women experience a "motherhood penalty" that decreases their confidence and dedication to their careers (Correll et al., 2007). Intersectional characteristics including race, caste, disability, and sexual orientation amplify these biases, further marginalising women from already marginalised groups.

Strategies for Strengthening Resilience and the Role of Organisational Support

Systemic organisational actions are necessary to build resilience among women employees, rather than relying primarily on individual efforts. Fostering resilience can be achieved through inclusive leadership, psychological safety, social support systems, and a flexible workplace, according to research (Kossek et al., 2011b). One of the most important factors influencing women's resilience, job happiness, and retention is organisational support, which is defined as the degree to which employees perceive their well-being is valued (Rhoades & Eisenberger, 2002). Important resources in this area include sponsorship and mentorship programs. Sponsors push for women to be included in decision-making roles, while mentors offer advice (Ibarra et al., 2010). Affinity groups and women's networks provide similar opportunities for women to meet face-to-face and learn from one another in a supportive environment. These frameworks enhance women's leadership and thriving abilities by assisting them in navigating male-dominated contexts.

Promoting Gender Equality through Inclusive Leadership and Policy

To build a resilient and inclusive workplace, leadership buy-in is crucial. Leaders that are inclusive are self-aware, they value other points of view, and they strive to remove obstacles to equality (Nishii & Mayer, 2009). Businesses run by these types of executives are more likely to conduct gender audits, provide employees greater leeway in how they use their time at work, and use fair measures to measure employee success.

According to the International Labour Organisation (2018), organisations that implement progressive HR practices including paid parental leave, on-site childcare, clear promotion criteria, and gender-disaggregated data collecting tend to have more women in decision-making positions. To further promote psychological safety and trust among female employees, organisations should implement internal grievance redressal systems and have zero-tolerance rules for sexual harassment (Berdahl & Moon, 2013).

Diversity in the Workplace and Intersectionality

Research on gender in the workplace and intersectionality, initially proposed by Crenshaw (1991), have grown in importance in recent years. In it, overlapping identities like race, class, caste, religion, and sexual orientation are used to explain how oppression affects women. By looking at gender, race, class, and disability via an intersectional lens, we can see how policies targeted at "women" as a whole do little to help women who identify as Dalit, queer, indigenous, or disabled. For example, in India, women from Dalit and tribal communities experience double discrimination in the workplace, which results in them frequently being forced into low-status, low-paying occupations that offer little opportunities for advancement or stability (Still, 2011). Similarly, non-binary and transgender people face societal exclusion and violence daily; this highlights the necessity for non-binary gender inclusion legislation (Hines, 2010).

Worldwide Movements and Analytical Views

Companies, governments, and international organisations have all taken steps to promote gender parity in the workplace. For instance, the Nordic nations are frequently cited as an example of a model society because of their robust welfare systems, generous parental leave policies, and cultural commitment to gender equality (Moss, 2015). Low female labour force participation and poor legal protections persist in many Asian and African nations, on the other hand. Aligning national and organisational policy is made easier by global frameworks like the United Nations Sustainable Development Goal 5 (Gender Equality) and the International Labour Organization's Convention 190 (on eliminating violence and harassment at work) (UN Women, 2021b). One example of a country that has successfully used affirmative action and political will to change gender dynamics is Rwanda, which has one of the highest female representations in parliament (Powley, 2005).

Recognising the Care Economy and Integrating Work and Life

Integrating work and personal life has become an important issue for working women. The bulk of unpaid care labour is still carried out by women, who have been historically and persistently disadvantaged by the strict division between the personal and professional spheres (OECD, 2020). Millions of women were already leaving the labour field because of increasing caregiving responsibilities before the COVID-19 epidemic hit (Alon et al., 2020). A key component of achieving gender equality, according to scholars and campaigners, is acknowledging and allocating care obligations. Workplace cultures that do not stigmatise caregiving are just as important as policies that provide time off for parents and allow for more flexible scheduling. Female employees are more likely to be retained and given greater agency by employers who prioritise empathy and flexibility in their workplace culture (Lott & Abendroth, 2020).

Technology, Telecommuting, and Emerging Possibilities

There are advantages and disadvantages to gender inclusion brought about by the proliferation of digital platforms and remote labour. One positive aspect of digital technologies is the increased number of women working remotely or as gig workers, which gives them more freedom and independence (ILO, 2021). But there are still serious issues with algorithmic prejudice, monitoring, and digital exclusion. Researchers have shown that women are more likely to be victims of cyber bullying, have lower levels of digital competence, and face device inequality (UNESCO, 2021). That is why it is crucial for digital workplace design to be welcoming and considerate of these issues. Improving women's digital inclusion and resilience can be achieved through up skilling programs, cyber security policies, and platforms for remote mentoring.

CONCLUSION

According to the bibliometric research, there is a diverse and vibrant field of gender studies, with influential writers and sources moulding the conversation around gender in the workplace. Gender, Work and Organisation, and Sex Roles are the leading journals in the discipline, and researchers like Lombardo E. and Kantola J. have a major impact on academic philosophy. The continued institutional dedication to gender equality in Western and Nordic nations is reflected in the concentration of research output in these regions. Important yet underexplored issues are "work" and "inequality" according to the thematic map, and gender, policy, and employment are prominently featured in the keyword frequency analysis.

The literature review supplements this by offering theoretical and practical frameworks for investigating gender integration and resilience in the workplace. Women still face persistent structural obstacles that prevent them from advancing in their careers, including gender bias, care giving penalty, and intersectional marginalisation. Nonetheless, research shows that gender-responsive policies, inclusive leadership, and supportive organisational cultures all contribute to greater equity and resilience. A more nuanced view of diversity in the workplace is shown by gender frameworks that incorporate care work, intersectionality, and digital inclusion. Building resilient and inclusive workplaces for women and other marginalised gender identities requires a comprehensive, intersectional, and policy-driven strategy, according to the bibliometric and literature reviews.

REFERENCES

Acker, J. (1990). Hierarchies, jobs, bodies: A theory of gendered organizations. *Gender & Society*, *4*(2), 139–158. DOI: 10.1177/089124390004002002

Acker, J. (2006). Inequality regimes: Gender, class, and race in organizations. *Gender & Society*, *20*(4), 441–464. DOI: 10.1177/0891243206289499

Alon, T., Doepke, M., Olmstead-Rumsey, J., & Tertilt, M. (2020). *The impact of COVID-19 on gender equality*. NBER Working Paper.

Berdahl, J. L., & Moon, S. H. (2013). Workplace mistreatment of middle class workers based on sex, parenthood, and caregiving. *The Journal of Social Issues*, *69*(2), 341–366. DOI: 10.1111/josi.12018

Catalyst. (2020). *Why diversity and inclusion matter: Quick take*. https://www.catalyst.org/research/why-diversity-and-inclusion-matter/

Correll, S. J., Benard, S., & Paik, I. (2007). Getting a job: Is there a motherhood penalty? *American Journal of Sociology*, *112*(5), 1297–1338. DOI: 10.1086/511799

Crenshaw, K. (1991). Mapping the margins: Intersectionality, identity politics, and violence against women of color. *Stanford Law Review*, *43*(6), 1241–1299. DOI: 10.2307/1229039

Eagly, A. H., & Carli, L. L. (2007). *Through the labyrinth: The truth about how women become leaders*. Harvard Business Press.

Hines, S. (2010). Queerly positioned: Gender, sexuality and trans identity in the workplace. *Gender, Work and Organization*, *17*(5), 597–612.

Ibarra, H., Carter, N. M., & Silva, C. (2010). Why men still get more promotions than women. *Harvard Business Review*, *88*(9), 80–85. PMID: 20821967

International Labour Organization (ILO). (2018). *A quantum leap for gender equality: For a better future of work for all*. https://www.ilo.org/global/publications/books/WCMS_674831/lang--en/index.htm

International Labour Organization (ILO). (2021). *World employment and social outlook: The role of digital labour platforms in transforming the world of work*.

Kossek, E. E., Pichler, S., Bodner, T., & Hammer, L. B. (2011a). Workplace social support and work–family conflict. *Personnel Psychology*, *64*(2), 289–313. DOI: 10.1111/j.1744-6570.2011.01211.x PMID: 21691415

Kossek, E. E., Pichler, S., Bodner, T., & Hammer, L. B. (2011b). Workplace social support and work–family conflict: A meta-analysis clarifying the influence of general and work–family-specific supervisor and organizational support. *Personnel Psychology*, *64*(2), 289–313. DOI: 10.1111/j.1744-6570.2011.01211.x PMID: 21691415

Lengnick-Hall, C. A., Beck, T. E., & Lengnick-Hall, M. L. (2011). Developing a capacity for organizational resilience through strategic human resource management. *Human Resource Management Review*, *21*(3), 243–255. DOI: 10.1016/j.hrmr.2010.07.001

Lott, Y., & Abendroth, A. K. (2020). The gender gap in working hours: What the pandemic revealed. *Social Politics*, *28*(3), 482–504.

McKinsey & Company & LeanIn. (2021). *Org*. Women in the Workplace.

Moss, P. (Ed.). (2015). *International review of leave policies and related research*.

Nishii, L. H., & Mayer, D. M. (2009). Do inclusive leaders help to reduce turnover in diverse groups? *The Journal of Applied Psychology*, *94*(6), 1412–1426. DOI: 10.1037/a0017190 PMID: 19916652

OECD. (2020). *Women at the core of the fight against COVID-19 crisis*.

Powley, E. (2005). Rwanda: Women hold up half the parliament. In *Women in Parliament: Beyond Numbers* (2nd ed.). International IDEA.

Rhoades, L., & Eisenberger, R. (2002). Perceived organizational support: A review of the literature. *The Journal of Applied Psychology*, *87*(4), 698–714. DOI: 10.1037/0021-9010.87.4.698 PMID: 12184574

Shaw, S., & Leberman, S. (2015). The historical construction of women's sport leadership development in New Zealand. *Sport Management Review*, *18*(4), 555–566.

Still, C. (2011). Dalit women: Honour and patriarchy in South India. *Gender and Development*, *19*(3), 427–437.

UNESCO. (2021). *The impact of digital technologies on gender equality in education*.

Williams, J. C., Blair-Loy, M., & Berdahl, J. L. (2016). Cultural schemas, social class, and the flexibility stigma. *The Journal of Social Issues*, *72*(2), 209–234. DOI: 10.1111/josi.12012

UN Women. (2021a). *Progress on the Sustainable Development Goals: The Gender Snapshot 2021*.

Women, U. N. (2021b). *Women in the changing world of work: Facts and figures*. https://www.unwomen.org/

Chapter 2
Menopause as an Evolutionary Leadership Catalyst:
Adaptive Transitions and Workplace Implications

Filippo Ferrari
https://orcid.org/0000-0002-7509-2320
University of Bologna, Italy

ABSTRACT

This chapter reframes menopause as a biologically and evolutionarily adaptive life stage that enhances women's leadership capacity rather than diminishes it. Drawing on the Grandmother Hypothesis, neuroendocrinology, and leadership theory, the chapter explores how postmenopausal women transition from reproductive roles to strategic, relational, and cultural influence. It maps the hormonal and cognitive recalibrations of menopause onto leadership styles such as authentic, servant, adaptive, and strategic leadership, while acknowledging vulnerabilities such as cognitive fog, mood volatility, and social invisibility. Empirical evidence from workplace case studies and menopause-inclusive policies illustrates both the barriers and opportunities this transition entails. The chapter argues that menopause, when supported by inclusive organizational structures, can serve as a leadership accelerator. It concludes with policy recommendations and a call for intersectional, longitudinal research to further explore how menopause can be integrated into leadership development pipelines.

DOI: 10.4018/979-8-3373-2970-3.ch002

INTRODUCTION: MENOPAUSE AS A TURNING POINT

Evolution, Challenge, and Opportunity

Menopause is often framed in medical literature as a time of loss—of reproductive capacity, of vitality, and, implicitly, of relevance. Yet from the standpoint of evolutionary psychology, anthropology, and leadership studies, this narrative is both limited and misleading. Far from being a biological malfunction, menopause is a highly conserved, adaptive life stage unique to humans and a few long-lived species like killer whales (Hawkes, 2020). Its emergence in the evolutionary record is not coincidental: it reflects the strategic value that post-reproductive individuals can provide to group survival, cultural continuity, and social resilience.

The Grandmother Hypothesis has revolutionized our understanding of why menopause exists. It posits that human females evolved to live well beyond their reproductive years because postmenopausal women increased the inclusive fitness of their kin by aiding the survival and reproductive success of younger generations (Hawkes et al., 1998; Herndon, 2009). In hunter-gatherer societies like the Hadza, postmenopausal women are among the most efficient foragers, contributing substantially to the caloric intake of grandchildren and younger adults (Hawkes, 2020). Mathematical models confirm that grandmothering behaviors alone can account for the extension of the human lifespan (Kim et al., 2012; Chan et al., 2017).

In this view, menopause is not an epilogue to reproductive life, but a transition to a leadership phase—a shift in energetic investment from bearing children to supporting community functioning, transmitting knowledge, mediating conflict, and cultivating the next generation. This reconceptualization has profound implications not only for evolutionary theory but also for organizational life in the 21st century.

Modern workplaces, however, have yet to fully align with this evolutionary insight. Women between 45 and 60 are among the fastest-growing demographic segments in many labor markets, particularly in education, healthcare, public administration, and knowledge-based industries (Rees et al., 2021). Despite their experience and strategic value, many find themselves excluded from leadership pipelines, either through systemic bias or lack of institutional support during menopausal transition (Dennis & Hobson, 2023; Daly et al., 2024).

The symptoms of menopause—hot flushes, insomnia, mood fluctuations, cognitive fog—are real and can be disruptive, especially in high-pressure work environments. But equally real are the gains: increased clarity, boundary-setting, and perspective-taking often emerge in midlife, catalyzing what psychologists refer to as "generative renewal"—a desire to leave a legacy, to teach, and to lead with purpose (Erickson, 1968; Northouse, 2021). If unrecognized or unsupported, these transformations risk becoming unrealized potential. But when seen through the lens of adaptive leadership development, menopause becomes a strategic inflection point for both the individual and the organization.

The Dual View: Menopause as Challenge and Advantage

Understanding menopause requires holding a dual perspective. On the one hand, it is a biological transition accompanied by physical and emotional challenges. Vasomotor symptoms (VMS) affect up to 80% of menopausal women, and over 70% report sleep disturbances, which in turn impair memory and concentration (Panay et al., 2021). Cognitive challenges such as "brain fog," difficulty focusing, and decreased short-term recall can significantly affect workplace performance—especially when compounded by ageist assumptions or pressure to maintain a "seamless" output standard (Steffan & Loretto, 2025).

Yet on the other hand, this transition is also a time of psychosocial realignment and developmental opportunity. Women often describe menopause as a moment when priorities shift, self-awareness deepens, and motivation becomes more values-driven (Fenton, 2024). These are precisely the psychological and behavioral shifts associated with the emergence of leadership identity.

Importantly, the dual role of menopause—as a physiological disruption and a psychological awakening—parallels the paradoxical nature of adaptive leadership itself, which often arises in contexts of tension, complexity, and transformation. In many ways, menopause is a living laboratory of adaptive leadership: it demands emotional regulation, identity work, strategic reframing, and relational recalibration.

This duality is often misunderstood—or worse, flattened—in organizational policies and practices. As Rees et al. (2021) argue, menopause is either ignored altogether or treated as a medical issue to be accommodated discreetly, rather than recognized as a developmental milestone with implications for strategic talent management and inclusive leadership design.

A Moment of Organizational and Societal Opportunity

At a time when organizations face mounting complexity, demographic shifts, and the need for emotionally intelligent, resilient, and ethically grounded leadership, postmenopausal women offer precisely the capacities needed. These include:

- Perspective-taking and systems thinking developed through decades of lived experience
- Relational intelligence and moral grounding enhanced through care work and cultural navigation

- Strategic patience and long-term planning, supported by hormonal recalibration (Barel et al., 2017)

But systemic change requires cultural transformation. As Steffan and Loretto (2025) show, the "ideal worker" stereotype—unencumbered, consistent, emotionless—remains deeply entrenched, marginalizing bodies that change, need care, or disrupt norms of continuous availability. Menopausal women challenge this stereotype not by failing to conform, but by introducing a different model of leadership: one that centers care, perspective, flexibility, and collaborative wisdom.

In this light, menopause is not a detour or a personal setback. It is a biopsychosocial transition that, when recognized and supported, becomes a leadership accelerator.

Chapter Overview

This chapter integrates theoretical, empirical, and applied literature to reframe menopause as a developmental asset—a catalyst for leadership emergence grounded in both evolutionary design and organizational opportunity. It proceeds through five key sections:

1. Theoretical Framework – Laying the foundation with evolutionary psychology and hormonal neuroscience, this section explains why menopause exists and how it prepares women for leadership in ancestral and contemporary environments.
2. Leadership Capacities and Styles – Using frameworks from Northouse and Yukl, this section maps the psychosocial shifts of menopause onto transformational, servant, adaptive, strategic, and authentic leadership models.
3. Workplace Evidence and Case Studies – Drawing on qualitative data, case studies, and survey research, this section highlights the real-world experiences of menopausal women in various sectors, and the structural conditions that enable or inhibit leadership emergence.
4. Implications for Practice and Policy – Offering practical strategies for organizations, this section includes policy design, coaching interventions, inclusive evaluation systems, and DEI communications that frame menopause as a source of value.
5. Future Research Directions and Conclusion – The chapter concludes with a synthesis of contributions, a call for longitudinal and intersectional research, and a vision for menopause-informed leadership pipelines.

THEORETICAL FRAMEWORK

Evolutionary Foundations

The Grandmother Hypothesis remains one of the most transformative theories in evolutionary anthropology and human biology, offering a powerful reframing of menopause not as a failure of reproductive function, but as an adaptive innovation. First articulated by Kristen Hawkes and colleagues (1998), and subsequently expanded through demographic, ethnographic, and mathematical modeling, this hypothesis posits that the extended post-reproductive lifespan of human females evolved because of the reproductive and survival advantages it conferred upon descendants—particularly through grandmothering.

In ancestral forager societies, where subsistence labor was demanding and children required many years of care, postmenopausal women played a critical role in provisioning food, assisting in child-rearing, and reducing maternal burden. This enabled younger women (often daughters) to have more frequent births and enhanced the survival odds of their offspring. Grandmothers' contributions were particularly vital during early childhood, a period of high vulnerability, thereby increasing the inclusive fitness of the grandmother—the measure of genetic success beyond direct offspring (Hawkes et al., 1998; Herndon, 2009).

The original evidence for this hypothesis came from fieldwork with the Hadza of Tanzania, a contemporary hunter-gatherer population, where older women were shown to be among the most productive foragers. They provided significant caloric returns in the form of tubers and other reliable resources, directly feeding dependent children and supporting their daughters' reproductive efforts (Hawkes, 2020; 2025). These findings challenged long-standing assumptions that post-reproductive life was biologically irrelevant, revealing instead that it was strategically vital for the survival and success of human social groups.

More recent research has refined and diversified the grandmother hypothesis, exploring it through simulation models, cross-cultural data, and kinship analyses. Engelhardt et al. (2019), using historical demographic records, demonstrated that proximity to grandmothers increases child survival rates, particularly in multi-generational households, where childcare and emotional support are shared. In these contexts, grandmothers serve as cultural anchors, preserving knowledge, values, and social cohesion.

Hawkes et al. (2017) employed two-sex population models to simulate how grandmothering behaviors could lead to selection for increased female longevity, reinforcing both direct and indirect fitness pathways. Their work suggests that grandmothering may have been a driving force in the evolution of extended post-reproductive life, influencing the selection pressures shaping not only lifespan but also social learning, cooperation, and division of labor by sex and age.

Other scholars, such as Chapman et al. (2024), have offered more cautious interpretations. While acknowledging the benefits of prolonged post-reproductive lifespan, they emphasize that such advantages are ecologically contingent—dependent on kin residence patterns, resource distribution, and cultural norms. This perspective invites a contextualized understanding of the grandmother effect, one that considers variability in intergenerational cooperation and caregiving roles across societies.

Crucially, the Grandmother Hypothesis has evolved beyond its initial reproductive framing to incorporate a broader range of social, emotional, and cognitive contributions. As Hrdy (2009) argues, grandmothers were likely essential to the evolution of alloparenting, language development, and cooperative breeding systems. Their presence enabled mothers to rely on trusted kin to help raise offspring, which in turn allowed for longer developmental periods and more complex socialization processes. These dynamics are thought to underlie many of the uniquely human features of social cognition, including perspective-taking, empathy, and moral learning.

Blell (2018) adds that grandmothers' authority often extends into spiritual and normative domains, making them central figures in the maintenance of social order. Krasheninnikova (2019) further emphasizes the emotional regulatory role of grandmothers, identifying them as relational mediators capable of de-escalating conflicts and fostering cohesion within kinship groups. These roles—rooted in ancestral ecologies—mirror many of the core competencies required for effective leadership today: emotional intelligence, wisdom, long-term thinking, and the ability to integrate diverse perspectives.

This expanded view of the grandmother effect positions postmenopausal women not only as caregivers but as cultural and strategic actors. Their ability to navigate complex relational networks, maintain social memory, and transmit group norms would have made them central figures in early human groups—not just biologically, but politically and culturally.

In this light, menopause is not a passive endpoint in the female life cycle but a developmentally selected gateway into a second adulthood—one oriented not toward reproduction, but toward leadership, influence, and legacy. This life stage brings with it the capacity for relational stewardship, moral leadership, and cultural preservation. While these traits evolved under ancestral conditions, they remain profoundly relevant in contemporary organizational life, particularly in leadership contexts that value inclusion, resilience, and intergenerational learning.

The implications for modern institutions are profound. If we accept that the post-reproductive phase was biologically conserved because of its strategic social value, then menopause should be understood as an entry point into a leadership phase, not an exit from vitality or contribution. Organizations that fail to recognize this adaptive potential risk sidelining precisely the individuals most primed to stabilize culture, mentor future leaders, and guide complex systems through uncertainty.

Indeed, the Grandmother Hypothesis does more than explain a physiological phenomenon—it offers a blueprint for evolutionary leadership. This model favors relational over transactional power, wisdom over speed, and legacy over short-termism. It suggests that the loss of fertility is offset—evolutionarily and socially—by the gain in strategic relevance.

For contemporary leadership theorists and practitioners, this perspective opens new avenues for redefining leadership pipelines, evaluation metrics, and succession strategies. It invites us to revalue the contributions of midlife and older women, not merely as knowledge holders but as adaptive leaders whose design is deeply encoded in our species' success.

Biological and Cognitive Shifts

Hormonal and Neurological Transitions

Menopause is accompanied by significant physiological and neurological transitions, most notably within the endocrine and central nervous systems. At the core of these changes is the marked decline in circulating estrogen and progesterone, alongside elevated levels of follicle-stimulating hormone (FSH) and luteinizing hormone (LH). These hormonal shifts can lead to well-known physical symptoms—hot flushes, disrupted sleep, joint stiffness—but they also have profound effects on brain function, including memory, attention, emotional regulation, and decision-making (Mosconi et al., 2021; Panay et al., 2021).

Estrogen, in particular, plays a central role in modulating synaptic plasticity, neurotransmitter dynamics, and cerebral perfusion, especially in brain regions like the prefrontal cortex and hippocampus, which are involved in executive functioning and memory consolidation. As estrogen declines, many women report experiencing transient cognitive changes—commonly described as "brain fog"—which may include forgetfulness, difficulty concentrating, and mental fatigue.

However, these changes do not necessarily reflect degeneration. Neuroimaging studies have shown that the brain does not simply lose function during menopause; rather, it undergoes a process of reorganization and compensation. According to Mosconi et al. (2021), the postmenopausal brain recruits frontal lobe circuits more intensively, suggesting a shift toward enhanced executive control and cognitive efficiency. This adaptive response may reflect a form of neuroplasticity that allows women to preserve, and in some domains refine, their cognitive capabilities.

In organizational settings, this neural recalibration could have several indirect implications. For instance, increased reliance on frontal executive regions might support greater emotional regulation, strategic decision-making, and social reasoning—traits commonly associated with mature leadership. While more research is needed, it is reasonable to hypothesize that midlife women may be increasingly inclined to approach complex interpersonal and ethical dilemmas with greater composure and foresight, especially in environments that support reflective thinking.

The interaction between sex hormones and stress hormones is also relevant. Barel et al. (2017) found that the ratio of estrogen to cortisol influences risk perception and decision-making. Lower estrogen levels combined with stable cortisol may lead to reduced impulsivity and more conservative judgments. This could translate into a greater tolerance for ambiguity, more cautious risk assessment, and an enhanced ability to delay gratification in pursuit of long-term goals—traits that are highly valued in executive and governance roles.

Moreover, the hormonal plateau following menopause may result in greater internal consistency, reducing mood volatility and increasing energy available for sustained focus. In the context of team dynamics, one could expect that postmenopausal women, when adequately supported, may act as emotional anchors, stabilizing group climate and defusing tension during periods of stress or transition. This stabilizing role could be especially visible in sectors that rely on high relational complexity, such as healthcare, education, or nonprofit leadership.

That said, these potential advantages should not obscure the variation in individual experiences. Some women may face more acute symptoms, and the impact of hormonal changes may interact with chronic stress, work conditions, and sociocultural expectations. For these reasons, workplace adaptations must be flexible, inclusive, and personalized, allowing women to navigate these transitions on their own terms while recognizing the longer-term leadership potential that may emerge through neurocognitive adaptation.

In sum, while menopause may involve temporary cognitive fluctuations, it also initiates a process of neurological realignment that, in supportive environments, might contribute to the development of embodied, resilient, and emotionally intelligent leadership. Future organizational research should explore how these hormonal and cognitive shifts affect team roles, leadership behaviors, and decision-making under uncertainty, always with attention to variability and context.

Emotion Regulation and Relational Depth

One of the less visible but highly significant shifts that occurs during the menopausal transition concerns emotional regulation. As cyclical hormonal fluctuations stabilize, many women report greater mood consistency, reduced reactivity, and an improved capacity to manage interpersonal complexity. This is consistent with research on hormonal variation across the menstrual cycle, which links fluctuations in estrogen and progesterone to mood swings, irritability, and anxiety (Ponzo et al., 2022). Once these hormonal cycles cease, many women describe a sensation of clarity, emotional grounding, and internal calm, which may become more pronounced in the postmenopausal phase.

These shifts could have meaningful implications for organizational behavior and leadership performance. In particular, greater emotional stability may enhance a woman's ability to navigate ambiguity, manage conflict, and lead under pressure—capacities that are central to effective leadership. From a psychosocial perspective, this may translate into more measured responses to stress, fewer impulsive reactions, and a deeper capacity to hold space for others' emotions without becoming emotionally flooded. These attributes are closely aligned with authentic, servant, and adaptive leadership models, all of which emphasize empathy, presence, and reflective action.

The menopausal transition may also bring about a recalibration of relational orientation. As reproductive competition declines, women often redirect energy and attention toward mentoring, cultural continuity, and community impact (Hrdy, 2009; Krasheninnikova, 2019). In modern workplaces, this shift might express itself through increased engagement in intergenerational collaboration, informal coaching, and values-based leadership. Women may prioritize trust, legacy, and psychological safety over visibility or dominance, reshaping what influence looks like at senior levels.

Far from diminishing leadership potential, the postmenopausal phase may thus amplify relational intelligence, enabling women to lead with a blend of composure, clarity, and care that strengthens collective performance and cohesion.

The End of the Menstrual Cycle: From Disruption to Continuity

The cessation of menstruation represents a significant biological and experiential milestone in the menopausal transition. While it is often perceived narrowly in terms of fertility loss, this shift has important implications for cognitive, emotional, and physical continuity—particularly in professional contexts. During the reproductive years, many women experience regular performance disruptions linked to menstrual symptoms such as cramping, fatigue, mood swings, and migraines, all of which can impair concentration and confidence (CIPD, 2023; Ponzo et al., 2022). These symptoms contribute to absenteeism, presenteeism, and, in some cases, reduced participation in leadership opportunities.

With the end of menstrual cycling, many women report a marked increase in stability—both physiologically and psychologically. The elimination of cyclical hormonal fluctuations can lead to more consistent energy levels, improved sleep, and greater ability to plan and execute over extended periods. Research by Carmichael et al. (2021) highlights how fluctuations across the menstrual cycle can negatively impact perceived performance in athletes—a finding that may be extrapolated to high-pressure cognitive and interpersonal work environments.

In this light, postmenopausal women may experience what could be described as a new form of strategic presence. Without the interruptions associated with cyclical symptoms, they might be better equipped to maintain cognitive endurance, regulate team dynamics, and sustain emotional labor over time. These are essential traits for executive leadership, project management, and high-stakes decision-making.

Furthermore, the disappearance of menstruation can alleviate certain social stressors, such as the need to conceal discomfort, normalize pain, or plan around hormonal unpredictability. In cultures and organizations that support open dialogue and normalize bodily diversity, this phase may even be experienced as liberating, opening space for new forms of self-investment and professional focus.

Ultimately, the end of the menstrual cycle may not only reduce disruption but also enhance continuity, foresight, and stamina—capabilities increasingly valued in complex and human-centered leadership environments.

MENOPAUSE AS AN EVOLUTIONARY LEADERSHIP TRANSITION

Menopause does not signal the end of a woman's contribution to the collective good—it marks a transition into a different form of leadership. From an evolutionary perspective, this transition reflects a shift from biological reproduction to social reproduction: the nurturing of culture, mentorship, and relational stability (Hrdy, 2009; Hawkes, 2020). In contemporary workplaces, this translates into a distinctive leadership profile that integrates emotional maturity, strategic vision, and ethical clarity.

As the biological and psychological recalibrations of menopause unfold, many women begin to lead from a position of increased authenticity and generativity. Freed from cyclical hormonal fluctuations and reproductive demands, they often reorient their energy toward legacy, mentoring, and institutional care. These shifts enable what we term an evolutionary leadership transition—a change in leadership posture that reflects the adaptive functions of post-reproductive life.

Capacities Enhanced During Menopause

The menopausal transition—far from diminishing leadership potential—can cultivate a distinct set of capacities that are increasingly essential in modern organizational contexts.

Emotional Resilience and Regulation

With the end of hormonal cycling comes increased emotional consistency for many women. As discussed in Section 2, the stabilization of estrogen and progesterone contributes to improved regulation of mood and affect. This emotional balance supports composure in complex interpersonal environments—an asset in leadership roles requiring conflict management, negotiation, and team cohesion.

Emotion regulation also enhances psychological safety, a crucial condition for creativity, collaboration, and trust in teams. Women who have moved through the embodied challenges of menopause may be more able to model emotional steadiness, validate diverse experiences, and maintain productive dialogue under stress.

Cognitive and Strategic Depth

Research suggests that despite short-term disruptions in memory or focus, many women report greater clarity and long-term perspective after the transition (Panay et al., 2021). These shifts may be neurobiologically reinforced by adaptations in the frontal cortex and improved integration across brain networks (Mosconi et al., 2021). In strategic terms, this means postmenopausal women may be better equipped to engage in systems thinking, ethical forecasting, and complex problem-solving.

In organizational life, such capacities are invaluable. Senior roles increasingly require the ability to hold competing priorities, navigate uncertainty, and make value-aligned decisions—functions that align closely with the developmental maturity often associated with postmenopausal experience.

Boundary-Setting and Assertiveness

Another commonly reported shift during and after menopause is a reduction in social appeasement and an increase in personal authority (Dennis & Hobson, 2023; Fenton, 2024). Women often describe becoming less tolerant of micromanagement, overwork, or misalignment with core values. This assertiveness is not abrasive—it is principled. It reflects a desire to invest energy in work that matters and relationships that are reciprocal.

Such clarity is foundational for authentic leadership. Leaders who know and communicate their boundaries contribute to organizational cultures that value self-respect, emotional sustainability, and purpose-driven action.

Relational Wisdom and Mentoring Capacity

The shift from reproductive to post-reproductive life also unlocks new forms of relational investment. Many postmenopausal women take on mentoring roles, becoming trusted advisors, culture stewards, and informal strategists in their teams. These roles echo the evolutionary value of postmenopausal women in ancestral societies, where grandmothers helped ensure group cohesion, information continuity, and survival of the young (Hawkes & Smith, 2009; Engelhardt et al., 2019).

In leadership terms, this relational positioning enables a move from managing people to developing them—a hallmark of generative, servant-style leadership.

Cognitive and Emotional Vulnerabilities in the Menopausal Transition: Risks and Rebalancing

While the menopausal transition can lead to the enhancement of certain leadership-related capacities, it is equally important to acknowledge the potential vulnerabilities that may emerge during this biologically and psychologically complex life stage. The fluctuations and eventual decline in estrogen and progesterone can trigger a cascade of physiological and neurological changes that affect cognitive performance, mood regulation, and stress reactivity—factors that may temporarily reduce leadership readiness or affect interpersonal functioning in high-pressure environments (Panay et al., 2021).

Among the most frequently reported challenges is "brain fog", a term used to describe the perceived decline in memory, attention, and executive function. Neuroimaging research by Mosconi et al. (2021) confirms that menopause involves measurable changes in brain metabolism and gray matter volume, particularly in regions associated with cognitive control and verbal memory, such as the hippocampus and prefrontal cortex. Although the brain often adapts through compensatory recruitment of frontal regions over time, the transitional period may be marked by subjective and objective declines in cognitive efficiency, including slower processing speed, difficulty concentrating, and reduced working memory.

These changes may affect multitasking, rapid decision-making, and the ability to manage simultaneous social and informational demands—skills that are often critical in executive roles. For leaders accustomed to operating at high cognitive throughput, such fluctuations can lead to self-doubt, performance anxiety, or overcompensation, potentially impacting their confidence and visibility within organizational hierarchies (CIPD, 2023).

Emotionally, declining estrogen levels are also associated with increased susceptibility to anxiety, irritability, and mood lability, particularly during perimenopause (Ponzo et al., 2022). These shifts may challenge a leader's capacity for emotional regulation, especially in contexts of interpersonal conflict or role ambiguity. Bar-el et al. (2017) observed that lower estrogen-to-cortisol ratios may impair stress modulation, making some women more reactive under pressure. In environments lacking psychological safety or menopause-aware policies, these changes could lead to withdrawal, disengagement, or the avoidance of high-visibility opportunities.

Additionally, sleep disturbances—a common symptom caused by vasomotor changes and night sweats—can exacerbate cognitive fatigue, reduce resilience, and impair emotional control. Chronic sleep loss has been linked to impairments in executive functioning, decision-making, and empathy, all of which are foundational for collaborative and ethical leadership.

Another potential area of concern is the diminution of social motivation or energy for relational labor. While many women become more values-driven and focused on legacy, others may experience a temporary disinvestment from organizational politics, mentoring, or consensus-building, particularly if their experiences are minimized or pathologized within the workplace (Daly et al., 2024). The perceived invisibility that accompanies aging for women may further compound this, leading to reduced participation in leadership forums and strategic conversations (Steffan & Loretto, 2025).

In sum, the menopausal transition is not uniformly empowering or impairing. Rather, it is a period of fluctuation, recalibration, and reorganization, during which some capacities may temporarily diminish while others gradually strengthen. Organizations must avoid both romanticizing and pathologizing menopause. Instead, they should offer adaptive support—such as coaching, flexible timelines, and relational scaffolding—that helps women navigate this complex phase without being penalized for its transitory costs or denied recognition for its long-term leadership potential.

Leadership Styles Enabled by the Transition

The psychological, biological, and emotional shifts associated with menopause provide fertile ground for the emergence and consolidation of multiple leadership styles. Drawing on Northouse (2021) and Yukl (2013), six leadership styles emerge as particularly congruent with this life stage: authentic, servant, transformational, strategic, adaptive, and ethical leadership. These frameworks do not represent rigid categories but overlapping, dynamic tendencies—each supported by the neurocognitive, hormonal, and psychosocial recalibrations that characterize the post-reproductive phase.

Authentic and Servant Leadership

Authentic leadership, as conceptualized by Northouse, rests on four dimensions: self-awareness, relational transparency, internalized moral perspective, and balanced processing. These qualities are often heightened in the menopausal phase, as women report increased alignment between internal values and external behavior. With the waning of reproductive roles and social expectations, many women describe a sense of psychological liberation. They gain clarity about priorities and become less driven by external validation. This "reset" can act as a catalyst for more values-driven, transparent leadership.

This alignment is often reinforced by neuroendocrine changes. As estrogen stabilizes at lower levels, coupled with increased cortisol sensitivity, women tend to develop more consistent emotional responses and improved regulation of stress (Barel et al., 2017). These neurological adjustments support reflection, strategic composure, and ethical congruence—all core to authentic leadership.

Closely aligned is servant leadership, which centers on the growth and wellbeing of others, community stewardship, and listening with empathy. From an evolutionary standpoint, the Grandmother Hypothesis posits that postmenopausal women contribute significantly to kin survival by providing cognitive, emotional, and logistical support (Hawkes, 2020; Krasheninnikova, 2019). In contemporary workplaces, these behaviors manifest as mentoring, emotional stabilizing, and conflict mediation.

Yukl (2013) describes servant leadership as encompassing follower development, participative decision-making, and building community. These are natural extensions of the intergenerational focus of postmenopausal women, who often report shifting from personal ambition to broader legacies of impact. In fact, programs like Menopause Cafés, peer-coaching, and NHS midlife mentorship initiatives actively harness these traits, providing real-world confirmation of servant leadership in action.

Transformational and Strategic Leadership

Transformational leadership involves inspiring followers through vision, individualized consideration, intellectual stimulation, and idealized influence. Northouse (2021) emphasizes that transformational leaders model integrity and foster intrinsic motivation. For many women, the menopausal transition triggers a reevaluation of life goals, often resulting in renewed commitment to purpose, legacy, and ethical influence (Blell, 2018). This internal reorientation fuels transformational leadership behaviors, especially in sectors like healthcare and education, where postmenopausal women frequently occupy strategic leadership roles.

This style also benefits from the neuroplastic changes during menopause. Cognitive shifts—including changes in prefrontal cortex activation—enable increased long-range planning and improved emotional filtering (Mosconi et al., 2021). These processes support the foresight and inspiration required to galvanize others toward shared missions.

In parallel, strategic leadership demands foresight, pattern recognition, and long-term decision-making—capacities that often mature in midlife. Yukl (2013) defines strategic leaders as those who scan external environments, align internal systems, and navigate complexity. The recalibrated risk-sensitivity that often accompanies menopause (e.g., reduced impulsivity, more reflective processing) makes this leadership style accessible to women in this phase (Barel et al., 2017).

Moreover, life experience accumulates into a cognitive archive of tacit knowledge—enhancing judgment in ambiguous situations. Many postmenopausal leaders describe their leadership as more intuitive, less reactive, and oriented toward systemic outcomes. These traits enable them to shape culture and policy in ways that outlast individual tenure, a hallmark of strategic leadership.

Adaptive and Ethical Leadership

Menopause is a transition fraught with uncertainty, identity work, and emotional recalibration. It is therefore a training ground for adaptive leadership, which Heifetz and Northouse define as mobilizing people to tackle tough challenges and thrive in changing contexts. Adaptive leaders facilitate reflection, challenge norms, and help others grow—capacities that menopausal women often refine during their own personal evolution.

The "adaptive behaviors" listed by Heifetz—such as "getting on the balcony," regulating distress, and protecting dissent—are especially relevant for midlife leaders, who frequently occupy boundary-spanning roles and bring long-term systemic awareness to their teams. Studies show that menopausal women often display improved meta-cognition, emotional distance, and sense-making capabilities (Dennis & Hobson, 2023). These cognitive and emotional shifts allow them to navigate complexity, mentor younger staff, and defuse organizational volatility.

Ethical leadership, as articulated by both Northouse and Yukl, revolves around fairness, justice, transparency, and a moral commitment to the collective good. Postmenopausal women, having weathered years of organizational injustice or bias, often develop an acute sensitivity to ethical misalignment. This is reinforced by the identity transformations prompted by menopause, which lead many to abandon people-pleasing behaviors in favor of principled, value-based leadership (Daly et al., 2024; Steffan & Loretto, 2025).

Ethical leaders foster trust, model inclusion, and challenge power asymmetries. These are not abstract ideals but lived commitments among many women in this life stage. As research by Steffan and Loretto (2025) notes, midlife women often challenge the "ideal worker" stereotype, paving the way for more humane, sustainable forms of leadership. Menopause becomes not just a biological process, but a moral awakening—a turn toward leadership with conscience.

Leadership Styles Potentially Constrained by the Transition

While menopause has the potential to enhance several leadership capacities, it is also important to explore the ways in which this life transition may constrain or temporarily inhibit certain leadership styles, especially in organizational contexts that are unsupportive, stigmatizing, or blind to the realities of the menopausal experience. As highlighted in previous sections, the hormonal and neurological changes characteristic of menopause—particularly the decline in estrogen and fluctuations in cortisol sensitivity—may influence cognitive processing, emotional regulation, and interpersonal behavior (Mosconi et al., 2021; Barel et al., 2017). These shifts do not affect all women in the same way, but under certain conditions, they may create mismatches between personal capacity and the demands of specific leadership approaches.

Cognitive Vulnerabilities and High-Demand Leadership Roles

For instance, styles such as transformational or strategic leadership, which require continuous visionary thinking, intellectual stimulation, and long-range focus, may be harder to sustain during phases of intense menopausal symptoms. According to Panay et al. (2021), over 60% of women report difficulties with concentration, memory recall, and mental fatigue during menopause—a cluster of symptoms often referred to as "brain fog." While many women eventually regain cognitive efficiency through neural compensation and reorganization (Mosconi et al., 2021), the transitional phase may compromise consistency in executive functioning, which is central to these leadership modes.

In environments where leadership is associated with high visibility, verbal fluency, and rapid responsiveness, temporary lapses in processing speed or verbal recall may be perceived—by others or the leader herself—as losses in competence or authority. This can lead to self-censorship, withdrawal from public-facing leadership moments, or a decline in confidence. In male-dominated or ageist workplaces, these self-limiting behaviors may be further reinforced by lack of recognition, mentorship, or trust.

Emotional Regulation and Authenticity Challenges

Similarly, authentic leadership, which is premised on self-awareness, emotional transparency, and value congruence (Northouse, 2021), may be impacted during periods of mood instability or heightened emotional sensitivity. Fluctuating estrogen levels can influence serotonin and dopamine transmission, potentially increasing vulnerability to anxiety, irritability, and low mood, especially in the perimenopausal years (Ponzo et al., 2022). In this phase, the ability to project emotional consistency—a key component of trust in leadership—may become more effortful, particularly when compounded by sleep disturbances and somatic symptoms.

The ideal of authenticity presumes a degree of internal stability and integration. When internal experiences become unpredictable or difficult to regulate, some women may feel at odds with their leadership identity, or find it harder to maintain coherence between their values, communication, and actions. The result may be relational withdrawal, increased self-monitoring, or reduced engagement with followers.

Adaptive Leadership Under Physiological Strain

Adaptive leadership, as defined by Heifetz and further developed by Northouse, involves guiding organizations through complex change, regulating systemic tension, and maintaining disciplined attention in times of ambiguity. These functions demand resilience, emotional containment, and cognitive flexibility—qualities that can be temporarily disrupted by menopausal symptoms. For example, during periods of hot flushes, insomnia, or physical discomfort, women may experience reduced capacity for emotional labor and high-stakes facilitation, particularly in high-pressure or unsympathetic environments.

In organizations where there is little flexibility, limited psychological safety, or an expectation of uninterrupted availability, leaders undergoing menopause may struggle to embody the calm, anchored presence expected of adaptive leaders. This dissonance can result in missed leadership opportunities, reluctance to take on volatile change initiatives, or overexertion in an effort to mask perceived vulnerability.

Ethical Leadership and Emotional Exhaustion

Even ethical leadership, often considered a stabilizing force in organizations, may be challenged during the menopausal transition—particularly when leaders are emotionally depleted or physically exhausted. While ethical leadership is grounded in fairness, integrity, and care for others (Yukl, 2013), it also demands empathic energy and moral clarity, both of which may be harder to access during hormonal imbalance or cognitive fatigue.

If leaders feel unsupported, marginalized, or rendered invisible due to menopausal stigma, they may experience cynicism, moral disengagement, or emotional dissonance. These conditions can erode their ability to act as moral exemplars, especially if they lack the bandwidth to challenge injustice or advocate for systemic fairness—two behaviors central to ethical leadership.

Organizational Dynamics That Exacerbate Constraints

Importantly, the extent to which these leadership styles are constrained by menopause is not merely physiological—it is context-dependent. As Steffan and Loretto (2025) argue, organizations that cling to the "ideal worker" norm—characterized by disembodiment, constancy, and detachment—exacerbate the risks of menopause-related marginalization. Women who do not or cannot conform to this model may find themselves excluded from decision-making, passed over for promotion, or subtly discredited in leadership circles.

Similarly, workplace cultures that ignore or trivialize menopause create conditions of silence and internalization. Without clear policies, training, or peer support, menopausal leaders are less likely to disclose challenges or seek accommodations—leading to burnout, disengagement, or exit from leadership altogether.

In sum, while menopause can activate key leadership capacities, it can also—if unsupported—challenge or constrain specific leadership styles, particularly those that rely on sustained cognitive load, emotional labor, or high-stakes adaptability. Organizations that wish to foster inclusive, human-centered leadership cultures must therefore recognize both the potentials and vulnerabilities of this life stage. Doing so requires systemic accommodations, empathetic policy design, and an evolved understanding of leadership as a dynamic process shaped not only by competence, but by care, context, and bodily realities. Table 1 summarizes pros and cons of leadership styles in menopause.

Table 1. Leadership Styles in Menopause

Leadership Style	Potential Advantages in Menopause	Potential Challenges in Menopause
Authentic	Increased self-awareness and alignment with personal values; emotional maturity supports relational transparency.	Mood fluctuations may disrupt emotional coherence; hormonal shifts may impair consistency.
Servant	Greater empathy and generativity; focus on mentoring and care reflects evolutionary caregiving roles.	Emotional fatigue or irritability could limit availability to others; caregiving expectations may increase burden.
Transformational	Renewed clarity of purpose and legacy-driven thinking; deeper emotional resonance with followers.	Cognitive fog and fatigue may reduce visionary capacity and public inspiration.
Strategic	Enhanced risk awareness and long-term planning; experience supports big-picture thinking.	Sleep disturbances and reduced cognitive speed may impair strategic responsiveness.
Adaptive	Menopause as a model for navigating personal transformation; strengthened resilience and reflective capacity.	Physical and emotional strain could reduce flexibility and tolerance for ambiguity.
Ethical	Heightened ethical clarity; stronger motivation to challenge inequities and model fairness.	Exhaustion or marginalization may inhibit advocacy and reduce moral engagement.

EMPIRICAL EVIDENCE FROM WORKPLACE SETTINGS

While the theoretical and biological literature points to menopause as a phase of latent leadership potential, its impact—positive or negative—is ultimately shaped by workplace realities. How organizations choose to respond to menopausal transitions determines whether this period becomes a site of empowerment or attrition. Across sectors, emerging research, case studies, and participatory initiatives are beginning to expose the barriers that menopausal women face—and to illuminate the cultural conditions that allow them to thrive.

Career Impacts and Organizational Blind Spots

Despite the evolutionary and cognitive advantages associated with postmenopausal development, many workplaces remain culturally unprepared and structurally inadequate when it comes to supporting women during this transition. In a UK-wide survey reported by Dennis and Hobson (2023), 10% of women stated they had left their jobs due to menopause symptoms, with many more turning down promotions or reducing their working hours.

These career setbacks are not merely the result of symptoms themselves but reflect a broader organizational failure to normalize and support menopause as a developmental milestone. Daly et al. (2024) show that disclosure is rare: most women avoid informing their managers about menopause-related challenges, especially if they report to younger or male leaders. They fear being judged, dismissed, or perceived as less competent.

Panay et al. (2021) reinforce this concern through multinational data: 90% of European and 97% of Australian women report experiencing physical symptoms during menopause, but fewer than half feel "very well supported" at work. In the UK, symptom severity is highest among the surveyed nations, underscoring a systemic gap in support and cultural readiness.

As Steffan and Loretto (2025) argue, menopause represents a challenge to the prevailing "ideal worker" norm—a norm that assumes linear productivity, disembodied professionalism, and silence around health. This ideal is incompatible with the lived experiences of midlife women. Without policy and cultural change, the workplace remains a site of stigma and self-silencing, rather than one of growth and contribution.

Case Studies: LHH, Vodafone, Healthcare

Despite widespread gaps, several organizations offer promising examples of how menopause-inclusive policies and practices can transform working life for midlife women.

At LHH, a global talent development firm, a multi-pronged strategy included policy reform, training for managers, awareness-raising initiatives, and drop-in menopause cafés. These changes were backed by executive sponsors and male allies, contributing to normalization, dialogue, and retention. Staff reported improved wellbeing, increased confidence in discussing symptoms, and a renewed sense of belonging (Dennis & Hobson, 2023).

Vodafone, as part of its global commitment to gender equity, developed a comprehensive menopause toolkit alongside an awareness campaign. The company embedded menopause into its wellbeing strategy, making it visible in onboarding, EAP resources, and leadership communications. Follow-up data indicated enhanced engagement among midlife employees, as well as increased participation in mentoring and internal leadership pipelines.

In the UK National Health Service, a qualitative study revealed that 66% of employees had experienced menopause symptoms at work, with 13% describing the impact as severe. Interventions such as dedicated quiet spaces, education modules, and workplace coaching helped reduce absenteeism and improved morale among clinical and managerial staff (Dennis & Hobson, 2023).

These case studies show that menopause support need not be complex or costly to be effective. What matters most is cultural legitimacy and psychological safety—conditions that allow women to bring their whole selves to work, including their changing bodies and leadership ambitions.

Menopause Cafés and Web Interventions

Among the most promising grassroots innovations is the Menopause Café®, a volunteer-led, peer-based model founded in Scotland in 2017. Designed as open, non-judgmental spaces where people of all genders and ages can talk about menopause over tea, the Café model has spread to over 250 locations and been integrated into multiple workplace settings.

As Weiss (2020) explains, the Café format offers a "holding space" rather than a problem-solving clinic. Its core strength lies in narrative legitimacy—allowing women to hear and share stories that affirm their experience, dismantle shame, and build collective insight. In organizational settings, adapted versions of the Café model have been used to inform policy co-design, training development, and leadership reflection.

In parallel, web-based interventions offer scalable, flexible, and often anonymous ways to support menopausal employees. Im et al. (2017) conducted a systematic review of digital programs—ranging from decision aids to interactive coaching platforms—and found that they significantly improved emotional wellbeing, symptom literacy, and decision-making autonomy. These interventions are especially useful for employees in remote or male-dominated sectors, where stigma remains high.

Critically, both Menopause Cafés and web tools succeed when embedded in a broader culture of respect, openness, and adaptability. When treated as isolated programs, they risk tokenism. But when integrated into a life-stage inclusive strategy, they serve as powerful levers for connection, identity work, and leadership cultivation.

Strengths-Based Leadership Approaches

An emerging paradigm in research and practice is the strengths-based model of menopause—one that positions the transition not as a deficit to be managed, but as a transformative leadership opportunity. Fenton (2024), in her study of women leaders in higher education, found that menopause was often described as a threshold moment: a time of self-rediscovery, clearer boundaries, and recommitment to purpose. Rather than retreating, many women leaned into leadership with greater self-trust, emotional authenticity, and ethical clarity.

This view aligns with coaching research and identity theory. When women are given tools to reflect, normalize, and reinterpret their menopause experience, they begin to see it as a developmental crucible, not a derailment. Dennis and Hobson (2023) report that workplace coaching during menopause leads to increased openness, renewed ambition, and an expanded capacity to mentor others.

Organizations that adopt strengths-based approaches develop leadership from within the life cycle, rather than despite it. They build leadership cultures that are adaptive, embodied, and human-centric—qualities increasingly essential in a post-pandemic era of complexity and emotional demand.

IMPLICATIONS FOR PRACTICE AND POLICY

Despite the growing evidence base and increasing societal attention to menopause in the workplace, most organizational strategies remain fragmented, reactive, and symptom-focused. A truly transformative approach requires not only accommodation, but also activation—recognizing menopause as a pivotal moment in leadership development. This section outlines how organizations can evolve from narrow compliance models to inclusive, life-stage-conscious ecosystems that retain, develop, and elevate midlife women as leaders.

Supportive Organizational Strategies

The first imperative is cultural and structural legitimacy. As emphasized by Rees et al. (2021), menopause must be recognized not simply as a private health issue but as an organizational wellbeing, equity, and leadership concern. This starts with policy formalization. Organizations should:

- Include menopause in occupational health and wellbeing strategies
- Acknowledge it in equality, diversity, and inclusion (EDI) frameworks
- Integrate menopause education into managerial training programs
- Offer clear disclosure pathways and support plans without penalty or stigma

But policies alone are insufficient. As Steffan and Loretto (2025) argue, menopause support must actively challenge the "ideal worker" narrative—a cultural script that penalizes embodiment, fluctuation, and caregiving. This means rejecting linear career expectations and embracing non-linear contribution patterns. It also means recognizing that menopause is not just a "problem to solve," but an asset to mobilize.

Language and framing are crucial. Messaging around menopause should highlight strength, insight, and strategic potential, rather than framing women as vulnerable or needy. Effective communication campaigns present menopause as part of the leadership journey, normalize its discussion, and avoid euphemisms that reinforce silence.

Midlife Coaching and Role Design

Coaching, reflection, and role redesign are among the most impactful mechanisms for supporting menopausal transition and fostering leadership emergence. Research by Dennis and Hobson (2023) shows that targeted menopause coaching significantly improves confidence, psychological resilience, and relational clarity. Women report being more assertive, more future-oriented, and more equipped to set boundaries and mentor others.

Coaching should be structured around strengths-based frameworks, encouraging women to reinterpret menopause as a rite of passage into a new leadership identity. Key themes may include:

- Letting go of perfectionism and people-pleasing
- Clarifying personal mission and ethical alignment
- Recognizing embodied leadership wisdom

In parallel, organizations should rethink how roles are designed and distributed. Traditional promotion structures often ignore the developmental arcs of women's lives. A menopause-informed design strategy might include:

- Flexible leadership pathways (e.g., horizontal influence roles, cultural stewardship)
- Peer mentoring programs that valorize experiential knowledge
- Leadership sabbaticals focused on reinvention and reflection

Such changes align with the generative motivations common in postmenopausal life stages—motivations that prioritize impact, legacy, and mentoring over advancement for its own sake (Fenton, 2024; Northouse, 2021).

Toward a Life-Stage-Inclusive Leadership Pipeline

The ultimate goal is to build a leadership development system that embraces human change. Most current pipelines are built on assumptions of linear progression, uninterrupted capacity, and standardized ambition. But menopausal women often defy these logics—not because they lack drive, but because their life phase demands new rhythms, deeper reflection, and more value-aligned leadership roles. A life-stage-inclusive leadership strategy would:

- Recognize menopause as one of several transitional points in the leadership life course (alongside parenthood, caregiving, and retirement)
- Offer leadership accelerators specifically for midlife women (e.g., legacy labs, intergenerational think tanks)
- Include menopause modules in inclusive leadership training for all employees—not just women—to foster empathy and systems thinking
- Embed menopause awareness in succession planning, board composition, and cultural audits

This shift is not only inclusive—it is strategic. It prepares organizations to thrive in a demographic context where aging workforces are the norm and leadership capacity is distributed across life phases.

Moreover, integrating menopause into leadership development challenges the youth-centric model of leadership that still dominates much of Western corporate culture. Postmenopausal women, with their cognitive maturity, emotional steadiness, and strategic patience, offer a leadership profile well-suited to an era of volatility, complexity, and value disruption.

By embracing menopause as a leadership inflection point, organizations can build cultures that are more human, more sustainable, and ultimately more effective.

FUTURE RESEARCH DIRECTIONS AND CONCLUSION

Identifying Gaps and Opportunities in the Study of Menopause and Leadership

Despite growing interest in the intersection of menopause, gender, and organizational dynamics, the research field remains underdeveloped and fragmented. Most existing studies concentrate on health-related symptoms, absenteeism, and workplace accommodations (Panay et al., 2021; Dennis & Hobson, 2023), while very few explore menopause as a developmental leadership stage. The focus has predominantly been on coping and retention—rarely on transformation, contribution, or upward mobility.

One major gap is the absence of longitudinal, life-course studies that trace leadership trajectories of menopausal and postmenopausal women. While some data suggest increased boundary-setting and moral clarity in midlife (Fenton, 2024), these findings remain anecdotal or limited to small-scale qualitative research. There is a pressing need for mixed-method studies that combine biometric, psychological, and professional data to explore how hormonal, cognitive, and social changes shape leadership emergence.

In addition, the Grandmother Hypothesis has yet to be systematically tested in contemporary organizational contexts. Although studies confirm its relevance in evolutionary terms (Hawkes & Smith, 2009; Engelhardt et al., 2019), its application to workplace leadership models remains theoretical. Future research could operationalize grandmothering traits—mentorship, cultural transmission, social regulation—and test their presence and effectiveness in leadership behaviors among postmenopausal women.

Intersectionality is another critical blind spot. Race, class, disability, sexual orientation, and migration status profoundly influence how menopause is experienced and how leadership potential is accessed or denied. Most literature treats menopausal women as a homogeneous group, obscuring power differentials, cultural variations, and systemic inequities. Future studies should apply intersectional frameworks (Crenshaw, 1991) to examine how multiple forms of marginalization shape menopausal transitions and leadership expression.

Lastly, digital and technological tools—such as AI-based coaching, self-tracking apps, and menopause-focused digital communities—offer new frontiers for data collection and intervention design. Yet their ethical, cultural, and accessibility dimensions remain under-explored. Researchers and practitioners must evaluate not only the efficacy but also the inclusivity of these tools.

The Dual Role of Menopause in Career and Leadership Identity

As demonstrated throughout this chapter, menopause plays a dual role in shaping women's careers: it can be a site of constraint or transformation, depending on how it is framed and supported. On one hand, it intersects with systems of gendered ageism, ideal worker norms, and stigma, leading to attrition, underemployment, or invisibility (Steffan & Loretto, 2025; Daly et al., 2024). On the other hand, it can catalyze a redefinition of leadership identity, marked by increased authenticity, strategic clarity, and intergenerational commitment (Dennis & Hobson, 2023; Fenton, 2024).

This paradox reflects the broader tension between dominant organizational cultures and embodied human experience. Menopausal women challenge prevailing models of leadership that reward continuous productivity, detachment, and performative resilience. Instead, they bring forth a leadership style grounded in presence, relational intelligence, and ethical urgency—qualities often overlooked in traditional leadership pipelines but urgently needed in today's complex and emotionally demanding environments.

Understanding menopause as a developmental inflection point allows for a deeper appreciation of how professional identity evolves, not in spite of bodily change, but through it. This view also reframes workplace interventions—from damage control to leadership cultivation, from risk mitigation to long-term investment.

Summary of Key Contributions

This chapter has sought to reframe menopause not as a private disruption but as a public, strategic, and evolutionary moment of leadership emergence. By drawing on interdisciplinary literatures—from evolutionary psychology to organizational behavior, neuroendocrinology to feminist theory—we have advanced the following key arguments:

- Menopause is a biologically and evolutionarily adaptive phase, designed not for decline but for relational leadership, mentorship, and strategic guidance.
- The hormonal, emotional, and cognitive shifts of menopause enable core leadership capacities, including emotional regulation, strategic foresight, and authentic engagement.
- Multiple leadership styles—especially servant, transformational, adaptive, and ethical—align closely with the developmental landscape of menopause, offering new pathways for leadership theorization and practice.

- Organizations that implement supportive, strengths-based, and inclusive strategies—such as coaching, menopause cafés, flexible roles, and values-based evaluation—can unlock the leadership potential of midlife women.
- A new research agenda is required: one that is longitudinal, intersectional, and transdisciplinary, capable of capturing the full scope of menopause as both a biological transition and a sociopolitical opportunity.

Final Thoughts: Toward a Menopause-Informed Leadership Future

Menopause is not an obstacle to leadership—it is its evolutionary continuation. It reflects a design embedded deep in our species' past: that when reproduction ends, wisdom begins to lead. The postmenopausal woman, once framed as marginal, is now revealed as essential—a custodian of culture, a stabilizer of systems, and a guide for the future.

Yet these capacities can only flourish when recognized and nurtured. When menopause is welcomed into the workplace as a developmental resource, not a private embarrassment, organizations gain access to a form of leadership that is more grounded, more resilient, and more human.

In reimagining leadership through a menopause-informed lens, we are not simply adding one more dimension to diversity and inclusion. We are fundamentally redesigning what leadership is—rooted not in exceptionality, but in evolution; not in control, but in care; not in youth, but in wisdom.

The menopausal transition, if fully recognized and supported, may be the most underutilized leadership accelerator in contemporary organizations. Now is the time to bring it to the center of leadership theory, practice, and policy—not as accommodation, but as activation.

REFERENCES

Barel, E., Shahrabani, S., & Tzischinsky, O. (2017). Sex hormone/cortisol ratios differentially modulate risk-taking in men and women. *Evolutionary Psychology : An International Journal of Evolutionary Approaches to Psychology and Behavior*, *15*(1), 1–10. DOI: 10.1177/1474704917697333 PMID: 28274134

Blell, M. (2018). Grandmother hypothesis, grandmother effect and residence: Reframing kinship and the evolution of human female life history. In *Fertility and Reproduction* (pp. 55–70). Palgrave Macmillan.

Carmichael, M. A., Enns, D. L., Barabas, M. E., Soligard, T., & Mountjoy, M. (2021). The impact of menstrual cycle phase on athletes' performance: A narrative review. *Sports Medicine (Auckland, N.Z.)*, *51*(3), 539–556. PMID: 33572406

Case Study: The Inevitability of Menopause in the Workplace. (n.d.). *LHH*. Retrieved from https://www.lhh.com/uk/en/insights/case-study-the-inevitability-of-menopause-in-the-workplace/

Chan, M. H., Hawkes, K., & Kim, P. S. (2017). Modelling the evolution of traits in a two-sex population, with an application to grandmothering. *arXiv preprint arXiv:1907.01666*. https://arxiv.org/abs/1907.01666

Chapman, S. N., Ellis, S., Lahdenperä, M., Croft, D. P., & Lummaa, V. (2024). Menopause has not evolved as a general trait in mammals: A response to 'Do mammals have menopause?' *bioRxiv*. https://doi.org/DOI: 10.1101/2024.02.29.582687

CIPD. (2023). *Menstruation and menstrual health in the workplace: A guide for people professionals*. Chartered Institute of Personnel and Development.

Crenshaw, K. (1991). Mapping the Margins: Intersectionality, Identity Politics, and Violence against Women of Color. *Stanford Law Review*, *43*(6), 1241–1299. DOI: 10.2307/1229039

Daly, K. L., Pike, G., Clarke, V., & Beck, V. (2024). "Difficulty mentioning the M word": Perceptions of a woman disclosing negative menopause symptoms in the workplace. *Qualitative Research in Organizations and Management*, *19*(3), 163–181. DOI: 10.1108/QROM-07-2023-2562

Dennis, N., & Hobson, G. (2023). Working well: Mitigating the impact of menopause in the workplace – A narrative evidence review. *Maturitas*, *177*, 107824. DOI: 10.1016/j.maturitas.2023.107824 PMID: 37634294

Engelhardt, S. C., Bergeron, P., Gagnon, A., Dillon, L., & Pelletier, F. (2019). Using geographic distance as a potential proxy for help in the assessment of the grandmother hypothesis. *Current Biology, 29*(4), 651–656. DOI: 10.1016/j.cub.2019.01.027 PMID: 30744976

Fenton, A. (2024). *The impacts of menopause on women leaders in higher education: A strengths approach.* Abstract from CSEdX 2024: Radical Reimagination. https://www.csu.edu.au/division/learning-teaching/csedx/presentations/2024-program/the-impacts-of-menopause-on-women-leaders-in-higher-education-a-strengths-approach

Hawkes, K. (2020). The centrality of ancestral grandmothering in human evolution. *Philosophical Transactions of the Royal Society B: Biological Sciences, 375*(1811), 20190501. DOI: 10.1098/rstb.2019.0501

Hawkes K. (2025). Revisiting "Grandmothers and the Evolution of Human Longevity" 2003 AJHB. *American journal of human biology: the official journal of the Human Biology Council, 37*(4), e70045. DOI: 10.1002/ajhb.70045

Hawkes, K., O'Connell, J. F., & Blurton Jones, N. G. (1998). Grandmothering, menopause, and the evolution of human life histories. *Proceedings of the National Academy of Sciences of the United States of America, 95*(3), 1336–1339. DOI: 10.1073/pnas.95.3.1336 PMID: 9448332

Hawkes, K., O'Connell, J. F., Blurton Jones, N. G., Alvarez, H., & Charnov, E. L. (2017). The Grandmother Hypothesis and Human Evolution. In *Chagnon, N., Adaptation and Human Behavior: An Anthropological Perspective* (1st ed.). Routledge., DOI: 10.4324/9781351329200-15

Hawkes, K., & Smith, K. R. (2009). Brief communication: Evaluating grandmother effects. *American Journal of Physical Anthropology, 140*(1), 173–176. DOI: 10.1002/ajpa.21061 PMID: 19373844

Herndon, N. (2009). The grandmother effect: Implications of kin investment in child survival and reproductive success. *Human Nature Review, 9*, 92–95.

Hrdy, S. B. (2009). *Mothers and others: The evolutionary origins of mutual understanding*. Harvard University Press.

Im, E.-O., Lee, Y., Chee, E., & Chee, W. (2017). Web-based interventions for menopause: A systematic integrated literature review. *Maturitas, 95*, 24–30. DOI: 10.1016/j.maturitas.2016.10.009 PMID: 27889049

Kim, P. S., McQueen, J. S., & Hawkes, K. (2012). Why does women's fertility end in mid-life? A model of the evolution of human life history. *Mathematical Biosciences, 240*(1), 50–60. DOI: 10.1016/j.mbs.2012.06.001

Krasheninnikova, Y. S. (2019). The grandmother hypothesis: Evolutionary theory and cross-cultural evidence. *Anthropological Review, 82*(2), 143–159. DOI: 10.2478/anre-2019-0011

Mosconi, L., Rahman, A., Diaz, I., Wu, X., Scheyer, O., Hristov, H. W., & Isaacson, R. S. (2021). Menopause impacts human brain structure, connectivity, energy metabolism, and amyloid-beta deposition. *Scientific Reports, 11*(1), 10867. DOI: 10.1038/s41598-021-90084-y PMID: 34108509

Northouse, P. G. (2021). *Leadership: Theory and practice* (9th ed.). Sage Publications.

Panay, N., Palacios, S., Davison, S., & Baber, R. (2021). Women's perception of the menopause transition: A multinational, prospective, community-based survey. *Gynecological and Reproductive Endocrinology and Metabolism, 2*(3), 178–183. DOI: 10.5281/zenodo.5061133

Ponzo, S., Wickham, A., Bamford, R., Radovic, T., Zhaunova, L., Peven, K., Klepchukova, A., & Payne, J. L. (2022). Menstrual cycle-associated symptoms and workplace productivity in US employees: A cross-sectional survey of users of the Flo mobile phone app. *Digital Health, 8*, 1–12. DOI: 10.1177/20552076221145852 PMID: 36544535

Rees, M., Bitzer, J., Cano, A., Ceausu, I., Chedraui, P., Durmusoglu, F., Erkkola, R., Geukes, M., Godfrey, A., Goulis, D. G., Griffiths, A., Hardy, C., Hickey, M., Hirschberg, A. L., Hunter, M., Kiesel, L., Jack, G., Lopes, P., Mishra, G., & Lambrinoudaki, I. (2021). Global consensus recommendations on menopause in the workplace: A European Menopause and Andropause Society (EMAS) position statement. *Maturitas, 151*, 55–62. DOI: 10.1016/j.maturitas.2021.06.006 PMID: 34274202

Steffan, B., & Loretto, W. (2025). Menopause, work and mid-life: Challenging the ideal worker stereotype. *Gender, Work and Organization, 32*(1), 116–131. DOI: 10.1111/gwao.13136

Yukl, G. A. (2013). *Leadership in organizations* (8th ed.). Pearson Education.

KEY TERMS AND DEFINITIONS

Adaptive Leadership: A form of leadership that mobilizes people to confront challenges and evolve in changing environments—skills often honed during the physiological and identity transitions of menopause.

Authentic Leadership: A leadership style rooted in self-awareness, value alignment, and transparent communication, often strengthened during menopause as women gain clarity and reduce people-pleasing tendencies.

Grandmother Hypothesis: An evolutionary theory proposing that postmenopausal women contribute to the survival and success of their kin by investing in caregiving, knowledge transmission, and social cohesion, thereby enhancing inclusive fitness.

Inclusive Fitness: A concept from evolutionary biology referring to an individual's genetic success not only through direct reproduction, but also by supporting the reproductive success of genetically related others, such as grandchildren.

Leadership Life Course: An approach to leadership development that considers how leadership potential and style evolve across the lifespan, recognizing menopause as a significant phase in that trajectory.

Menopause: A natural, biological transition marking the end of a woman's reproductive phase, characterized by hormonal changes that can influence physical, cognitive, and emotional functioning, and—if supported—unlock new forms of leadership engagement.

Neuroplasticity: The brain's ability to reorganize and adapt structurally and functionally in response to changes—including hormonal shifts during menopause—that can lead to compensatory improvements in executive and emotional regulation.

Psychological Safety: A group climate where individuals feel safe to take interpersonal risks—especially important for menopausal women navigating vulnerability, stigma, or identity shifts in organizational contexts.

Servant Leadership: A leadership model focused on the growth and wellbeing of others, aligned with postmenopausal women's increased relational investment, mentorship orientation, and community stewardship.

Transformational Leadership: A leadership approach that inspires and motivates others through vision and purpose; postmenopausal women may embody this by reframing their careers around legacy and meaningful impact.

Chapter 3
Spiritual Resonance and Cultural Harmony:
How Sacred Practices at Work Can Improve Women's Health

Kritika Ohri
https://orcid.org/0009-0003-7942-4569
Department of Commerce, University School of Business, Chandigarh University, Mohali, India

Hitakshi Dutta
https://orcid.org/0000-0002-2515-9179
Chandigarh University, Mohali, India

ABSTRACT

In today's workplaces, which are becoming more diverse and fast-paced, women's overall health is becoming a bigger concern. This is usually dealt with through physical and mental health frameworks. There is, however, a new way of thinking that combines spirituality at work, cultural intelligence, and sacred practices to give women more power through inner peace and understanding between cultures. This chapter looks at how spiritual resonance and cultural harmony work together to help women feel better in the workplace, focusing on sacred practices like chanting and reading spiritual texts. The chapter suggests a conceptual model that puts spiritual engagement at the center of the relationship between sacred practices and holistic well-being. It does this by using ideas from a variety of fields, such as workplace spirituality, cultural intelligence (CQ), feminist well-being theories, and archetypal psychology.

DOI: 10.4018/979-8-3373-2970-3.ch003

1. INTRODUCTION

1.1 Background and Context

As businesses realize that wellness leads to long-term performance, keeping employees, and new ideas (Saks, 2011; Sharma & Kumra, 2020), employee well-being has become a more important strategic goal. But a lot of workplace wellness programs still only focus on physical health, stress relief, and work-life balance. They don't pay much attention to deeper existential and spiritual needs. This is especially important for women, who often have to balance complicated roles at work, at home, and in their culture, which can lead to more emotional labor and identity stress (Rathee & Sharma, 2022; Kumar & Pradeepika, 2021).

In this context, workplace spirituality, which is having a sense of meaningful work, feeling connected to others, and being in line with one's inner values, has been linked to higher levels of job satisfaction, commitment, resilience, and overall employee well-being (Pandey et al., 2009; Koul, 2024). Cultural intelligence (CQ) is the ability to recognize, respect, and respond appropriately to different cultural points of view. CQ is especially important in today's multicultural workplaces because it helps companies create spaces where spiritual practices can be open to everyone instead of favoring one tradition over another (Nosratabadi, Abedi, & Jamhour, 2020).

Even though there have been some theoretical advances, there is still a big gap in the research and in workplace policy when it comes to addressing the spiritual and cultural aspects of women's health. Women often use sacred practices like chanting, prayer, meditation, or reading spiritual books to deal with stress, build resilience, and connect with their cultural identity (Rathee & Sharma, 2022. But these practices are rarely taken into account in formal wellness programs or Diversity, Equity, and Inclusion (DEI) initiatives (Rego & Pina e Cunha, 2008).

1.2 Statement of the Problem

People are starting to realize how helpful workplace spirituality and cultural intelligence can be, but there are still big problems with how they are used, especially for women. In particular:

When people talk about spirituality at work, they often don't take into account the different experiences and identities that women have that affect how they respond to spiritual and cultural wellness programs (Rathee & Sharma, 2022; Kumar & Pradeepika, 2021).

Most wellness programs at work are still limited by secular frameworks that treat spiritual practices as optional or only for personal time. This makes them less accessible and less legitimate as institutions.

Empirical research doesn't give enough credit to the specific sacred practices that women often use, like chanting or reading spiritual texts. These practices are also rarely included in corporate wellness frameworks or CQ policies (Nosratabadi et al., 2020).

These factors make it clear that we need a model that is holistic, culturally aware, and gender-sensitive, with spiritual engagement and sacred practices at the center of women's workplace health.

1.3 Rationale and Need for the Chapter

This chapter's purpose is to fill in three important gaps:

1. Combining chanting and spiritual reading: There is evidence that chanting can reduce stress and regulate vagal tone (Koul, 2024), and spiritual literature can help people become more emotionally resilient and find purpose (Sharma & Kumra, 2020). However, there is not much research on how to use these activities to improve women's health at work, especially from a cultural intelligence point of view.
2. CQ for Cultural Inclusivity: Cultural Intelligence (CQ) helps businesses understand and respect spiritual practices from different cultures, making sure that sacred practices are open to everyone instead of just a few (Nosratabadi et al., 2020). This is very important for women's health around the world.
3. Empowerment through Sacred Practices: Sacred practices like chanting and spiritual reading can do more than just help women feel better; they can also give them back their power in stressful or gendered workplaces (Rathee & Sharma, 2022; Kumar & Pradeepika, 2021).

This chapter fills in these gaps and presents a new, comprehensive framework that has real-world uses for both researchers and people who work in organizations.

1.4 Purpose and Objectives

The main goal of this chapter is to show how adding sacred practices like chanting and reading spiritual literature to workplace wellness can give women strength through spiritual resonance and cultural harmony when done with cultural intelligence.

The specific objectives are:

1. To think of spiritual resonance and cultural harmony as important parts of women's health in the workplace.

2. To look into how sacred activities like chanting and reading spiritual texts can help people become more mentally strong, find their purpose, deal with stress, and get more involved at work.
3. To show how Cultural Intelligence (CQ) can help make sacred wellbeing practices that include everyone.
4. To suggest a real-world conceptual framework that connects sacred practices, CQ, spiritual engagement, and outcomes like emotional resilience, job satisfaction, retention, and feeling like you belong.

1.5 Scope and Contribution

This chapter makes four main contributions to the field and the literature:

1. Multidisciplinary Integration: It combines ideas from workplace spirituality (Pandey et al., 2009; Rego & Pina e Cunha, 2008), cultural intelligence (Nosratabadi et al., 2020), feminist wellbeing (Rathee & Sharma, 2022; Kumar & Pradeepika, 2021), and Jungian archetypes.
2. Operational Clarity: It introduces and defines empirical variables like chanting participation, reading spiritual books, accessing sacred spaces, spiritual resonance, and cultural harmony, which makes practices that were once abstract researchable.
3. Gender-Inclusive Model: It focuses on women's specific needs, experiences, and ways to gain power, which adds depth to conversations about organizational wellbeing and DEI.
4. Actionable Design: This chapter gives HR teams, DEI leaders, and wellness strategists useful suggestions for making sacred wellbeing a part of the culture of their organizations.

1.6 Spiritual Feminism, Intersectionality, and the Global Work Culture

As the conversation about workplace health and safety grows, more and more people are calling for intersectional frameworks that look at race, culture, religion, class, and spiritual identity as systems that affect each other (Crenshaw, 1991; Rathee & Sharma, 2022). For women from a wide range of cultural backgrounds, especially those from non-Western or Global South settings, spiritual practices are often very important to their sense of identity and cultural heritage. Chanting mantras, saying affirmations, reading holy texts, or following rituals can help you feel better and give you a sense of connection to your family, your purpose, and your power (Koul, 2024).

Spiritual feminism, which is becoming more popular, sees these sacred practices as ways for people to heal themselves and fight back against patriarchal and exploitative work structures (Starhawk, 1999). From this point of view, adding spiritual traditions to workplace wellness programs is not just about including everyone; it's also about respecting women's choices and bringing balance back to work cultures that have been historically male-coded. This kind of approach puts a decolonial spin on the workplace wellness movement, which goes against Western secular ideas that often leave out spiritual expressions that aren't Christian or indigenous (Hooks, 2000).

Additionally, global organizations and multinational corporations are doing more and more business in spiritual areas. For instance, businesses with offices in India, Indonesia, Brazil, or parts of Africa are more likely to have employees who actively practice religion or do spiritual rituals every day. Cultural Intelligence (CQ) is very important here to avoid spiritual tokenism and create a real culture of respectful inclusion (Ng, Van Dyne, & Ang, 2009). Organizations can make sacred spaces where different expressions of faith, especially women's, are supported instead of just tolerated by improving CQ among managers and HR professionals.

The COVID-19 pandemic also made people think more deeply about their work, their purpose, and their spirituality. Many workers, especially women, said that during lockdowns they turned to spiritual practices to help them feel stronger and more stable mentally (Sharma & Kumra, 2020). As remote and hybrid work models change, so must our understanding of how spiritual health affects mental health, digital workplaces, and making policies that include everyone.

When you put all of these ideas together, they call for a change in the way we think about spirituality. Instead of seeing it as a personal matter, we should see it as an organizational resource that can turn workplaces into holistic, inclusive, and culturally aware ecosystems when it is aligned with CQ.

2. THEORETICAL FOUNDATION

This chapter brings together ideas from Workplace Spirituality, Cultural Intelligence (CQ), Spiritual Feminism, and Holistic Wellbeing to create a theoretical base that is multidimensional. Each of these ideas gives important information about how sacred practices like chanting and spiritual reading are becoming more important for improving women's health in a variety of work settings.

2.1 Workplace Spirituality

Workplace spirituality is the idea that workers want more than just money from their jobs; they want meaning, purpose, and connection (Ashmos & Duchon, 2000). It stresses three main areas: work that has meaning, a sense of community, and being in line with the organization's values (Milliman et al., 2003). These things are especially important for women, who often have to deal with value-based conflicts between their personal, cultural, and professional roles (Kinjerski & Skrypnek, 2006).

Adding spirituality to the workplace is linked to higher employee engagement, more organizational citizenship behavior, and a stronger sense of belonging (Petchsawang & Duchon, 2009). Encouraging women to bring their whole selves to work, including their spiritual identities, makes them feel safe and strong mentally and emotionally.

It's important to note that workplace spirituality doesn't have anything to do with organized religion. Instead, it's a values-based, open framework that lets employees find their inner purpose and connect with others in a meaningful way (Giacalone & Jurkiewicz, 2003). Chanting, meditation, and spiritual reading are sacred activities that help people become more aligned and focused on the inside. This, in turn, helps them control their emotions, pay attention, and be more compassionate (Pandey, 2017).

2.2 The Divine Feminine and Spiritual Feminism

Spiritual feminism combines feminist ideas with the idea of the sacred or divine feminine in religious and cultural traditions. It wants to bring back spirituality as a way for women to feel strong and heal (Starhawk, 1999). Chanting mantras, meditating in a ritual way, and reading sacred texts are all practices that come from old matriarchal or goddess-centered traditions that give people emotional strength, resilience, and a sense of belonging.

Women have always used spiritual practices to deal with oppression, stress from work, and emotional exhaustion, both at work and outside of it. When these practices are accepted and used in the workplace, workplace wellbeing goes from being based on rules to being based on experience and culture (Hooks, 2000).

The spiritual feminist view also supports ideas like energy healing, embodiment, and connecting with nature or the divine through ritual. This may be different from how traditional Western rationalists think about health and wellness. This difference shows how important Cultural Intelligence is for making the workplace welcoming to everyone.

2.3 Cultural Intelligence (CQ)

Cultural intelligence (CQ) is the ability to work well in different national, ethnic, and organizational cultures (Ang et al., 2007). It has four parts:

-Metacognitive CQ (being aware of other cultures)
-Cognitive CQ is knowing the rules and how things work.
-Motivational CQ (the desire and ability to change)
-Behavioral CQ is the ability to act appropriately in different cultures.

CQ is very important for women who practice spirituality in ways that are influenced by their culture, such as chanting Sanskrit mantras, reading Buddhist texts, or reciting Qur'anic verses. High CQ among HR professionals and team leaders makes sure that these practices are accepted rather than looked down upon (Ng, Van Dyne, & Ang, 2009).

Cultural intelligence also helps organizations create more inclusive wellness programs by connecting secular and sacred wellness models (Livermore & Soon, 2015). It makes sure that sacred practices are not treated as special or strange, but with the same respect as regular mental health or mindfulness techniques (Rockstuhl & Van Dyne, 2018).

2.4 Overall Health in the Workplace

When we talk about holistic wellbeing, we mean taking care of all aspects of our health, including our physical, mental, social, and spiritual health. People now agree that mental and spiritual health are important parts of being strong and getting things done (Diener et al., 2009). Spiritual practices can help women, especially those who work in high-stress jobs or jobs that are traditionally male, control their emotions, think about their lives, and heal (Kumar & Pradeepika, 2021).

Chanting and other sacred practices have been shown to lower cortisol levels and improve vagal tone, which makes people feel calmer and clearer emotionally (Koul, 2024). Reading spiritual texts like the Bhagavad Gita, the Bible, or the Tao Te Ching can also help you find your purpose and feel less tired of living (Sharma & Kumra, 2020).

Companies that don't pay attention to spiritual aspects may unintentionally make their employees burn out, especially women who are dealing with hidden stressors like caregiving duties, emotional labor, and microaggressions. Adding sacred practices to workplace wellness programs can help people find spiritual resonance, which is when their inner values and outer roles are in perfect harmony. This can make people more motivated, feel like they belong, and be happier at work.

2.5 The Idea of Sacred Space

Sacred Space Theory is based on Jungian psychology and archetypal theory. It says that places that have symbolic, emotional, or spiritual meaning help people heal and integrate more deeply. In the workplace, this means creating physical or virtual spaces—like quiet rooms, digital meditation portals, and prayer areas—where sacred practices are respected.

These places don't have to be connected to a religion. What matters is that they let people, especially women, do things like chant or read spiritual texts without worrying about what other people will think. These kinds of places make people feel safe mentally, which makes them more resilient, emotionally clear, and cognitively empathetic. This helps create a more caring and cooperative work environment (Rego & Pina e Cunha, 2008).

2.6 Integrated Theoretical Model: Spiritual Resonance and Cultural Harmony

This chapter puts together these different ideas to suggest a model of Spiritual Resonance and Cultural Harmony:

- Spiritual Resonance is the feeling of being in sync with one's values, emotional needs, and sense of purpose when sacred practices are in line with them.
- Cultural Harmony is the feeling of community that comes from CQ when people with different spiritual beliefs are understood, respected, and supported.

This model sees sacred practices not as separate rituals, but as tools for change that are part of the ecosystems of organizations. It suggests that women who feel spiritually connected and culturally in harmony are happier, more satisfied with their jobs, more engaged, and more likely to stay with their jobs.

2.7 How it applies to the global workplace

These theoretical ideas are very important in a work environment that is becoming more mixed, global, and cross-cultural. The United Nations' Sustainable Development Goals (SDG 5: Gender Equality and SDG 3: Good Health & Wellbeing) also stress how important it is to create inclusive ecosystems for health and happiness (UNDP, 2021). Organizations can improve the well-being of their employees and promote institutional responsibility, gender equality, and cultural inclusivity by using this integrated framework.

3. REVIEW OF THE LITERATURE

3.1 Workplace Spirituality: Looking at the Past and the Present

The idea of workplace spirituality has changed a lot since the 1990s. It went from being something that only a few people were interested in to something that organizations are now concerned about. Early research on spirituality at work saw it as a new way of thinking that meets people's needs for meaning, purpose, and connection in their work lives (Ashmos & Duchon, 2000). Giacalone and Jurkiewicz (2003) built on this by saying that workplace spirituality is "a framework of organizational values evidenced in the culture that promotes employees' experience of transcendence through the work process."

Spirituality at work is not the same as religion; it includes a wide range of beliefs, values, and actions that help people connect with their deeper life goals. Milliman et al. (2003) say that workplace spirituality makes organizations work better by creating a sense of community, boosting individual integrity, and getting people more involved.

Recent research has shown that having a spiritual life at work can help people become more emotionally intelligent, better at dealing with stress, and more resilient, especially in high-pressure situations (Kinjerski & Skrypnek, 2006). But a lot of the writing has focused on Western settings and left out spiritual expressions that are gendered and culturally diverse. This chapter tries to fill in that gap.

3.2 Women's Wellbeing in the Workplace

Women who work still face problems that are unique to them and affect their physical, mental, and spiritual health. Some of these are pay gaps between men and women, not having enough chances to be a leader, microaggressions, and emotional labor (Hewlett & Luce, 2005). According to feminist organizational theory, systems need to be changed so that they take into account all of the experiences women have at work (Acker, 1990).

Also, women often have to do invisible work, like taking care of others, providing emotional support, and mentoring people at work, all of which can make them feel burned out and stressed all the time. In these situations, spiritual activities like chanting, reading rituals, and daily reflection can help you take care of yourself, build resilience, and reconnect with yourself.

Research has shown that women who regularly practice spirituality are more satisfied with their lives, better able to handle stress, and more focused on their goals (Pargament, 2007; Koenig, 2012). So, adding these practices to workplace wellness programs can provide interventions that are relevant to both culture and mental health.

3.3 Chanting and Sacred Sound Practices: Implications for Health and Productivity

Chanting is a spiritual tool that many religions, such as Hinduism, Buddhism, and Native American cultures, use to calm the nervous system, focus attention, and connect with the sacred. Scientists have started to look into the effects of chanting on the brain and mind. Bernardi et al. (2001) found that chanting "OM" activates the vagus nerve and slows the heart rate, which causes a parasympathetic response that is linked to relaxation and calm.

Other research shows that repeating sacred phrases or sounds in a rhythmic way can help you focus better, control your emotions, and think more clearly, all of which are important in today's busy workplaces (Telles et al., 2015). Women have used chanting for a long time to connect with the wisdom of their ancestors and deal with the complicated feelings that come with personal and group trauma.

Corporate mindfulness programs often promote secular meditation, but the spiritual side of chanting is still not well understood in the workplace. Recognizing and supporting sacred sound practices may be a culturally sensitive and very empowering alternative to stress management programs that work for everyone.

3.4 Reading spiritual books and doing reflective activities

Reading religious or philosophical texts can be very meditative and healing. Women can find emotional and spiritual grounding in texts like the Bhagavad Gita, Tao Te Ching, or the Psalms when they are going through a lot of stress or conflict. Pargament (2007) says that reading sacred texts can help people deal with spiritual issues, which means that they can find meaning in life's problems through a connection with the divine or a higher power.

In workplaces, especially those with a lot of different cultures, giving employees, especially women, time to do these kinds of reflective activities is not just a spiritual concession; it's also necessary for their health. These activities improve moral clarity, emotional discipline, and personal integrity, all of which are connected to transformational leadership (Fry, 2003).

3.5 Religious-Spiritual Sensitivity and Cultural Intelligence (CQ)

This study is very interested in the idea of Cultural Intelligence (CQ), which was created by Ang et al. (2007). CQ is a measure of how well a person can work in different cultural settings. The four dimensions of metacognitive, cognitive, motivational, and behavioral can help leaders and HR professionals understand how to support spiritual diversity in a sensitive way.

In multinational companies, where workers come from many different religious and cultural backgrounds, a lack of CQ can unintentionally push spiritual practices to the side. According to research, workplaces that encourage spiritual inclusivity through CQ have more cohesive teams, lower turnover, and more new ideas (Livermore & Soon, 2015).

Women, especially those from collectivist cultures, often internalize how hostile their workplaces are to their spiritual practices. For example, they might take off their hijabs to be professional, hide their mantra beads, or skip fasting rituals to go to meetings. Cultural intelligence can help change these oppressive norms by promoting spiritual fairness and cultural understanding.

3.6 Adding spirituality to wellness programs at work

Traditionally, strategies for organizational well-being have focused on mental and physical health. However, more and more research is calling for wellbeing frameworks that take spiritual aspects into account (Diener et al., 2009; Kumar & Pradeepika, 2021). According to Petchsawang and Duchon (2009), spiritual well-being is linked to better moral behavior, fewer absences, and greater mental strength.

Some companies, like Google and LinkedIn, have tried out programs like quiet rooms, interfaith chaplaincy services, and mindfulness programs, some of which have spiritual elements. But these are often talked about in non-religious terms, leaving out words like "sacred," "divine," or "goddess," which can make people with strong spiritual identities feel left out.

Women from Eastern traditions, in particular, may not understand general mindfulness language and instead look for deeper practices like sound healing, daily scripture reading, or ritual prayers. Adding these options to employee assistance programs makes sure that people are spiritually connected and truly involved.

3.7 Including and respecting spiritual diversity

Recent research shows that spiritual inclusion is an important but often ignored part of diversity, equity, and inclusion (DEI) programs (Benefiel et al., 2014). When companies support spiritual pluralism, workers are more likely to feel like they are seen, heard, and respected. This is especially true for women who practice spiritual feminism or earth-based spirituality that goes against the grain.

Rego and Pina e Cunha (2008) say that cultures that include spirituality are more likely to promote empathy, honesty, and mental health. Encouraging practices like chanting or reflective reading at work helps women bring their whole selves to work, which leads to better retention, engagement, and creative output.

3.8 Trends in Spirituality at Work After the Pandemic

The COVID-19 pandemic made people all over the world think about what life means, how long it lasts, and how to balance work and life. Many workers, especially women, said they turned to spiritual practices for comfort and guidance during lockdowns (Sharma & Kumra, 2020). The need for self-control and internal stability has grown as hybrid and remote work models become more common.

This change has also made more people interested in digital spirituality, like online chanting circles, scripture apps, or virtual retreats, which many women find easy to use and healing. Now, organizations need to recognize this spiritual shift and build in support and flexibility for these kinds of practices into the way work is changing.

3.9 Gaps in Research

There is not much empirical research on the following, even though there is a lot of writing about spirituality in the workplace and growing awareness of DEI:

- How sacred feminine practices like chanting and reading spiritual texts affect women's health at work
- How spiritual feminism and cultural intelligence help make policies that include everyone
- How companies can officially add sacred practices to their wellness programs
- Different sectors have different levels of support for spiritual well-being (for example, businesses, NGOs, and schools).

This chapter fills in these gaps by offering a framework for supporting spiritual practices at work that is based on culture and includes people of all genders.

4. METHODOLOGY

4.1 Research Design: A Narrative Review Approach

This chapter uses a narrative review method to look at how spiritual resonance and cultural harmony work together to improve women's health at work. Ferrari (2015) says that the narrative review method is a good way to combine different theoretical points of view, find connections between ideas, and suggest new ways to put them all together. Instead of gathering new empirical data, this chapter critically analyzes multidisciplinary literature on topics like workplace spirituality, cultural intelligence (CQ), feminist well-being theories, sacred practices, and archetypal psychology.

The goal of this method is not to count the effects, but to get a full conceptual picture of how sacred practices like chanting, spiritual reading, and access to quiet spaces can help women in professional settings become more emotionally strong, spiritually empowered, and happy with their jobs.

4.2 Goals and Purpose

The goal of this study is to create a theoretical model that looks at how spiritual engagement and cultural intelligence can affect the relationship between sacred practices and women's overall health and happiness at work.

The specific goals are:

- To look into how sacred practices are linked to women's emotional and spiritual health in the workplace.
- To look at the idea of spiritual engagement as a way to help women gain power in their personal and professional lives.
- To look at cultural intelligence (CQ) as a theoretical moderator that lets people of all backgrounds express their spirituality in a multicultural workplace.
- To create a conceptual framework that brings together spiritual empowerment, sacred practice, and cultural intelligence in order to promote overall health.

4.3 Research Question

The following conceptual questions guide the narrative review:

- How do spiritual reading and chanting help women at work feel stronger emotionally and more connected to their sense of self?
- What part does spiritual engagement play in linking sacred rituals to overall health and wellness?
- How can cultural intelligence help different organizational cultures be more spiritually open and connected?
- What kind of theoretical framework can best explain how sacred practices, CQ, and women's empowerment work together in modern workplaces?

4.4 Theoretical Variables and Conceptual Constructs

This review is a conceptual study that looks at the connections between the following constructs:

Main Ideas:

- Sacred practices include chanting, reading spiritual texts, and going to sacred places.
- Spiritual Engagement: connecting with yourself, taking part in rituals, and finding personal meaning
- Cultural Intelligence (CQ): the skill to connect with and work well with people from other cultures
- Holistic Wellbeing: having emotional strength (soul strength), spiritual power, job satisfaction, a sense of identity, and a sense of belonging

Suggested Relationships:

- Spiritual engagement is thought to be a factor that connects sacred practices to positive health outcomes.
- Cultural Intelligence (CQ) is suggested as a moderating variable that affects how well sacred practices are carried out and felt in multicultural settings.

4.5 Methods of Literature Selection

To make sure that the review was thorough and made sense across all fields, a structured narrative review process was used. The following criteria were used to choose the literature:

- Theoretical and conceptual works on spiritual practices, feminist well-being, cultural intelligence, archetypal and feminine psychology, and spirituality in the workplace.
- Research and frameworks that have something to do with women's spiritual empowerment, including them in organizations, or sacred traditions in modern workplaces.
- Published articles, book chapters, and scholarly texts from psychology, organizational behavior, gender studies, and spiritual philosophy that have been reviewed by other experts.

The sources were grouped by theme and looked at closely for patterns, gaps, contradictions, and chances to combine ideas.

4.6 Analysis Strategy

The narrative review went through these steps to interpret:

- Thematic Categorization: We grouped the literature into main themes, such as CQ, sacred practices, emotional resilience, and workplace spirituality.
- Interdisciplinary Synthesis: The study brought together ideas from psychology, spirituality, and organizational theory to make connections between different fields.
- Model Development: A conceptual framework was created based on patterns in the literature that placed spiritual engagement as a central process connecting sacred practice to well-being outcomes, with cultural intelligence acting as a moderator.
- Theory Extension: Feminist and archetypal theories were used to learn more about how spiritual empowerment and feminine identity work in organizations.

4.7 Rationale for the Narrative Review

A narrative review is a good way to go about this chapter because it is both exploratory and integrative. The narrative method is different from systematic reviews and meta-analyses because it lets you be creative with ideas, talk to people from different fields, and come up with new ways of thinking about things. This is important for talking about hard, culturally ingrained, and spiritually complex issues like women's health and sacred work practices.

4.8 Ethical Positioning

The chapter doesn't need formal ethical approval because it doesn't involve people and is based on ideas and literature. However, the review keeps its focus on respectful representation and inclusion while being sensitive to a wide range of spiritual and cultural worldviews. The chapter does not favor any one tradition or belief system; instead, it calls for pluralism and respect for other cultures in organizational spirituality.

4.9 Limitations

- In this chapter, the results are only theoretical and not based on real-world evidence.

- The review may show that there isn't enough research on some spiritual traditions and Indigenous practices.
- Different cultures and people may have different ideas about what sacred practice and spiritual engagement mean.

4.10 Conclusion

The narrative review method lets us look deeply and broadly at how sacred practices, cultural intelligence, and spiritual engagement all work together to improve women's health in today's work environments. It gives a theoretical basis for future empirical research, the creation of organizational policies, and integrative wellbeing strategies that focus on spiritual diversity and women's empowerment.

5. FINDINGS AND DISCUSSION

This chapter gives a conceptual analysis based on a narrative review of literature in the fields of organizational psychology, spirituality, cultural intelligence, and feminist well-being. It breaks down how sacred practices, spiritual engagement, and cultural intelligence all work together to affect women's health at work.

5.1 Sacred Practices and Emotional Resilience

Chanting and spiritual reading are examples of sacred practices that directly help women professionals stay emotionally stable and strong. These activities help people feel calm, lower their stress levels, and connect with their spiritual identity at work. Spiritual practices that promote presence, repetition, and meaning can help people become more emotionally resilient, which means they can handle stress at work in a positive way (Aarthy & Venkatesan, 2025).

Ahmad Syahir et al. (2025) found that women who work in high-stress jobs and do spiritual practices every day feel less emotionally drained and more mentally balanced. Chanting, in particular, activates the vagus nerve and helps people control their emotions. This links spiritual tradition with physical resilience.

So, sacred practices seem to be strong ways for women to become more emotionally resilient, especially when they can express themselves at work.

5.2 Spiritual Engagement as a Force That Connects

Spiritual engagement, which means taking sacred meaning and an existential connection into yourself, is what connects sacred practices to good health outcomes.

Women who read spiritual texts, chant meditative chants, or spend time in sacred spaces develop a physical connection to values like compassion, patience, and clarity.

Van der Walt (2018) said that being spiritual helps you do better in both your personal and professional life. In the same way, Fry (2005) found that having spiritual well-being at work makes people more motivated, gives them more meaning, and makes them act more ethically. These results support the suggested conceptual pathway: sacred practices → spiritual engagement → emotional and professional growth.

The results also support feminist psychology's focus on inner strength and finding meaning as key parts of empowering women (Gilligan, 1982; Ngunjiri & Madsen, 2015).

5.3 Cultural Intelligence as a Variable That Changes Things

Cultural intelligence (CQ) has a big effect on how well sacred practices are accepted and how well they work in organizations. CQ is the ability to work well in places where people come from different cultures (Earley & Ang, 2003). Leaders with high CQ are more likely to support a wide range of spiritual expressions without falling back on a secular norm or a dominant faith system.

Nosratabadi et al. (2020) show that cultural intelligence leads to policies that include everyone and help people understand each other better in multinational companies. This model says that CQ makes sure that chanting, spiritual reading, and sacred spaces are seen as valid ways to improve well-being in a diverse workplace, not as strange things.

CQ enhances the benefits of spiritual practices when they are part of HR strategy and leadership. It also helps keep non-Western or Indigenous spiritualities from being pushed to the side.

5.4 Job Satisfaction and Spiritual Strength

Spiritual engagement is also linked to higher job satisfaction, especially for women who find meaning in their work and feel that it is in line with their values. According to Piri et al. (2023), spiritual intelligence and engagement make people happier at work by giving them a sense of purpose, alignment, and connection.

Women say they feel spiritually empowered in workplaces where they can chant, pray, or have spiritual conversations. They feel both free in their personal lives and in their jobs. This feeling of being in control builds a professional identity, lowers turnover, and boosts creativity (van der Walt, 2018).

Feminist organizational theory, which calls for the visibility of spiritual and emotional work that women have traditionally done (Hooks, 2000; Starhawk, 1999), also connects sacred practice to empowerment.

5.5 Sense of Belonging and having a sacred identity

Belonging is an important part of women's health at work. Sacred practices help people feel stable on the inside and give them a sense of sacred identity by making them feel seen and supported in their spiritual authenticity. When groups make sacred spaces or celebrate spiritual holidays, women feel validated in their culture and connected to others.

Research on identity safety shows that places that allow for religious or spiritual expression make people feel safer and more trusting (Roberson, 2019). Ahmad Syahir et al. (2025) say that including women in this way makes them feel more valuable to their teams, which leads to better engagement and relationships with other team members.

So, sacred participation at work becomes a way for both individuals and groups to feel better and stay together.

5.6 Organizational Results and the Collective Flourishing

The chapter's theoretical framework suggests that when organizations include spiritual engagement and cultural intelligence in wellness programs, the benefits go beyond individual women to the whole team and the culture of the organization.

Giacalone and Jurkiewicz (2003) say that spirituality at work helps people be honest, make good decisions, and do their best work. Fry (2005) agrees with these results and says that spiritual leadership leads to more commitment and productivity in the workplace.

Organizations can promote psychological safety, emotional balance, and meaning at work by offering spiritually inclusive wellness programs. This is especially important for women who draw strength from sacred traditions.

5.7 Putting Together a Conceptual Framework

The following integrative model is supported by the literature:

- Independent Variables
- Chanting Participation
- Spiritual Reading Engagement
- Sacred Space Accessibility

- Mediator:

Spiritual Engagement

- Moderating Factor:

Cultural Intelligence (CQ)

- Outcomes:

Emotional Resilience
Job Satisfaction
Spiritual Empowerment
Sense of Belonging

This model brings together ideas from spiritual psychology, feminist well-being theory, and cross-cultural leadership to help with future research and use in organizations.

5.8 Implications for Policy and Practice

HR and Wellness Leaders should think about making programs that include sacred practices in ways that everyone can take part in, like daily chant sessions, spiritual book circles, or places to meditate. These programs can be part of efforts to promote diversity and health without pushing any one religion.

Cultural intelligence and spiritual literacy should be two of the most important skills that leaders learn, especially in organizations with people from many different cultures.

Policies in the workplace should broaden their definitions of wellness to include spiritual diversity, which would let employees, especially women, show their whole selves at work.

5.9 Limitations and Future Directions

This theoretical analysis doesn't use primary data; instead, it uses a carefully chosen review of current literature. We need to do real-world tests to make sure that the conceptual model works in all industries, generations, and spiritual backgrounds.

To make the framework deeper and more varied, more research should look into Indigenous spiritualities, LGBTQ+ sacred practices, and intersectional feminist points of view.

5.10 Conclusion

This chapter shows that sacred practices, spiritual engagement, and cultural intelligence work together to help women feel strong, empowered, and like they belong at work. Companies that value sacred diversity are more likely to create cultures that are open, strong, and based on ethics, where women can grow both spiritually and professionally.

6. CONCLUSION AND RECOMMENDATIONS

6.1 Overview of Key Insights

This chapter brings together the theoretical ideas found in the narrative review, focusing on how sacred practices, spiritual engagement, and cultural intelligence all work together to affect women's overall health at work. This framework is based on feminist well-being theory, workplace spirituality, and cross-cultural psychology. It says that giving women power through sacred engagement leads to emotional strength, job satisfaction, and a sense of belonging in their culture.

Across the literature, the main idea—that spiritual engagement connects sacred practices to health—was supported. At the same time, cultural intelligence became an important factor that determines whether these kinds of practices are accepted, tolerated, or pushed to the side in different organizations.

6.2 Addressing the Gap in Women's Holistic Wellbeing

Most traditional models of organizational wellness focus on things like physical health, managing stress at work, and finding a balance between work and life. These frameworks are useful, but they often leave out the spiritual side of well-being, which is especially important for women whose identities and ways of coping may be deeply shaped by sacred traditions, rituals, and finding meaning in their lives (Ngunjiri & Madsen, 2015; Hooks, 2000).

This review adds a new point of view by showing that spirituality is not just a private or unimportant issue, but an important part of organizational life. Women are not only taking care of themselves when they chant, read sacred texts, and go to sacred places; they are also tapping into archetypal sources of wisdom, strength, and empowerment that help them in their careers.

6.3 Contributions to Theoretical Discourse

The proposed conceptual model makes a significant theoretical contribution in four main ways:

Feminist Wellbeing Models Have Grown: Traditional feminist theories are about freedom, voice, and agency. This chapter adds an inner, sacred dimension, which means that spiritual empowerment can be a basis for external agency, not just something you do on your own.

Reframing Spirituality in Organizations: It shows that being spiritual at work is a professional asset, not just a personal belief. This makes it possible to make sacred practices a part of institutions in ways that are open to everyone and not tied to any one religion.

Bridging CQ and Spiritual Literacy: The framework meets the needs of a global, multicultural workforce by combining cultural intelligence. It shows that in HR and leadership, it's just as important to understand spiritual diversity as it is to understand ethnic or linguistic diversity.

Rituals and Performance: The results show that sacred rituals like chanting, reading, and spending time in sacred spaces are not passive or a way to escape; they actively help with health, performance, forming an identity, and team cohesion.

6.4 Implications for Organizations and HR Leaders

When making plans that include women, organizations need to broaden their definition of well-being to include the spiritual aspect. Important real-world effects include:

- Recognizing Sacred Diversity: HR leaders should learn that sacred practices are different in different cultures and traditions. For example, one woman may find chanting just as valuable as meditation or reading the Bible.
- Creating Sacred Spaces: Make sure that employees have places where they can pray, chant, or just think quietly without worrying about being judged. These don't have to be linked to a specific religion, but they should be open to people of all faiths or none at all.

    Culturally intelligent leadership makes sure that spiritual needs are met in a way that is sensitive and welcoming to everyone. Leaders should learn not only how to communicate with people from other cultures, but also how spiritual literacy affects how teams work together.
- Encouraging Sacred Engagement as a Way to Stay Healthy: Wellness programs can include sacred activities (like text reflections, chanting circles,

etc.) as optional activities, and if necessary, they can be framed in a way that is culturally humble and does not use religious language.

These efforts not only improve people's health, but they also fit with the values of diversity, equity, inclusion (DEI), and social sustainability.

6.5 Suggestions for Policy

For policies to be meaningful, they need to go beyond just being tolerant and include spirituality in a proactive way. The following suggestions may help with these kinds of efforts:

- Include spiritual engagement in DEI policies: Include spiritual identity in the larger conversation about inclusion, along with race, gender, disability, and language.
- Design Ritual-Sensitive Workspaces: Make sure that your workplace has spaces that can be used for rituals, altars, or quiet prayer.
- Make Interspiritual Dialogue Forums: Use interfaith or interspiritual discussion groups, storytelling circles, or cultural days to get employees to share their different spiritual practices.
- In wellness assessments, measure sacred engagement: Think about adding questions about spiritual practices, sacred connection, or ritual engagement to organizational wellbeing surveys.

6.6 Future Research Directions

This study is based on ideas and theories, but it lays the groundwork for future research that is based on real-world data. There are a number of possible research directions:

- Testing the Model in Real Life: Use a mix of methods to test the proposed relationships, especially the idea that spiritual engagement has a mediating effect and cultural intelligence has a moderating effect.
- Cross-Cultural Case Studies: Look into how women from different religious or cultural backgrounds practice their faith in different types of workplaces.
- Leadership and Sacred Inclusivity: Look into how leaders' own spiritual knowledge affects the work environment, the implementation of policies, and the empowerment of employees.

- Intersectionality and Spiritual Experience: Look into how sacred engagement changes depending on a person's gender, race, sexual orientation, and social class.

These paths will not only test the model, but they will also make it more useful in different places around the world and in the US.

6.7 Final Reflections

This chapter comes to the conclusion that women's spiritual health is not something that is abstract or personal; it is something that happens in real life, in relationships, and in organizations. Sacred practices are more than just rituals; they are ways to ground, heal, and empower yourself. When women are encouraged to express their sacred identities through chanting, reading, or ritual, they not only feel more at peace inside, but they also feel more connected, aligned, and in control at work.

By making cultural intelligence and sacred inclusivity part of the organization, we are moving toward a future where women are welcome at work in all of their fullness, not just their productive abilities, but also their emotional, spiritual, and ancestral selves.

This holistic view of well-being that respects the soul, values cultural differences, and gives people power from within is not just a dream. It is important for workplaces that are fair, moral, and ready for the future.

7. IMPLICATIONS AND FUTURE RESEARCH

7.1 Theoretical Implications

This conceptual study makes a big contribution to the body of knowledge that crosses disciplines on workplace spirituality, feminist wellbeing, cultural intelligence, and sacred practice in professional settings. It changes the way we think about spirituality, not as something that is personal or on the fringes, but as a real, measurable, and culturally appropriate factor in the health and empowerment of women professionals.

From this point of view, three main changes in theory come to light:

- From Personal Belief to Organizational Spirituality: Sacred practices like chanting, spiritual reading, and keeping sacred spaces are now seen as meaningful behaviors in the workplace instead of private or religious acts. This goes against the idea that spirituality at work is just about separating the personal from the professional.

- From Homogenous Models to Intersectional Spirituality: The model recognizes that women's spiritual experiences are affected by more than just their gender. They are also affected by their culture, religion, class, ethnicity, and spiritual tradition. This intersectional approach is a response to the growing criticism of "one-size-fits-all" models in the literature on employee well-being.
- From Cultural Intelligence to Sacred Literacy: The idea of sacred literacy in leadership is a new hybrid field that builds on cultural intelligence. Leaders who are aware of both culture and spirituality are better able to run organizations that are open to all people, diverse, and spiritually connected.

These theoretical ideas move the conversation about spirituality and work from vague ideas to real, inclusive action.

7.2 Practical Implications

The proposed model and results give professionals in many fields useful ways to act:

7.2.1 For HR and wellness strategists:

- Spirituality as a Wellness Metric: HR leaders can make surveys or check-ins that include spiritual engagement, sacred ritual practice, or access to sacred space.
- Policies for Inclusive Sacred Practice: Instead of assuming that everyone is neutral, workplaces can make policies that support a variety of sacred traditions, such as chanting rooms, text-based meditation corners, and flexible rituals.
- Trauma-Informed Spiritual Spaces: Organizations can frame sacred engagement as a way to deal with burnout, emotional exhaustion, or trauma at work, especially for women and other groups that are often left out.

7.2.2 For Leaders and Executives in Organizations:

- Develop Sacred Intelligence (SI): This study encourages the growth of "Sacred Intelligence," which is the ability of leaders to see, respect, and respond to sacred values and practices in teams that are different from their own.

- Modeling Spiritually Inclusive Leadership: Executives who are open about their spiritual practices (like ethical reflection, making decisions based on values, and being open to ritual) help staff feel safe and build trust.
- Aligning Purpose, Profit, and Practice: Integrating sacred engagement may be in line with ESG goals, corporate social responsibility, and sustainability practices that put dignity and belonging ahead of productivity.

7.3 Effects on Education and Training

This model also makes it clear that we need to change the way we teach leadership, HR, and DEI certification programs right away:

Include lessons on spiritual diversity, sacred ethics, and ritual literacy in leadership training programs.

- Cross-Cultural Communication: Teach professionals from around the world how to use cultural and sacred intelligence as tools for ethical global engagement.
- Feminist Pedagogies: Teachers and facilitators should include spiritual points of view in feminist teaching methods to counter the secular bias that often ignores sacred wisdom in feminist discourse.

7.4 Effects on Policy and Institutions

This study suggests that we should rethink policies on institutional wellness, diversity, and employee rights on a larger scale:

- Spiritual Freedom at Work: Laws and company rules should take spiritual freedom into account along with religious freedom, especially in places with a lot of different cultures.
- Equity in Sacred Access: Just like workplaces have gender-neutral restrooms and lactation rooms, sacred spaces should also be designed and stocked fairly.
- Legal Protections for Sacred Practice: Governments and NGOs may push for laws that protect spiritual expression and sacred rituals in the workplace, especially when they don't cause problems and are voluntary.

7.5 Problems with the Study

This theoretical chapter does present a new and complete model, but there are still some problems with it:

- Not enough real-world data: This study is a narrative review that combines literature and suggests a framework, but it doesn't test it in the real world. In the future, these ideas and connections should be tested with both qualitative and quantitative methods.
- Cultural Specificity: The model is meant to be used all over the world, but some sacred practices, like chanting or spiritual reading, may have different meanings in different places. Some readers might think the examples are too specific to the situation.

In highly secular or state-regulated workplaces, promoting sacred engagement might be seen as biased or inappropriate. This shows how important it is to carefully and inclusively design programs.

7.6 Directions for Future Research

To move this line of research forward, a number of promising research paths are suggested:

7.6.1 Empirical Testing of the Conceptual Model:

Researchers in the future can make tools to measure:

- How often and what kind of sacred practice (reading, chanting, ritual)
- How spiritually involved you are
- Women's job satisfaction, emotional strength, and spiritual strength
- Cultural intelligence as a factor that changes things

This will help confirm the suggested connections and make the cause-and-effect chains clearer.

7.6.2 Longitudinal Studies:

As spiritual practices are introduced or encouraged, keep an eye on how women's health and work involvement change over time. This can show what sacred inclusion does over time.

7.6.3 Cross-Cultural Comparisons:

Look at how women in different religions (like Buddhism, Christianity, Sufism, and Indigenous belief systems) understand and practice sacred rituals. Changes in culture can help make the model more universally useful.

7.6.4 Identity and intersectionality:

Future research should look into how spirituality affects race, gender identity, disability, and sexuality in the workplace. For example, does a Black Muslim woman feel empowered in a different way than a white Hindu woman?

7.6.5 Resistance and Backlash at Work:

Look into possible resistance to sacred inclusion, like secular pushback, cultural misunderstandings, or religious disagreements. Knowing what the barriers are will help you design in a more ethical and strategic way.

7.7 Final Thoughts

This chapter makes it clear that adding spiritual and sacred aspects to organizational well-being is very important, especially for women who are dealing with multiple forms of stress, exclusion, and cultural invisibility. Sacred engagement isn't a way to avoid work; it's a way to connect deeply with your purpose, inner strength, and professional meaning.

By starting this study with a narrative review and conceptual model, we set the stage for research that is rich, inclusive, and transformative, that goes beyond silos and speaks to the heart of leadership, equity, and women's empowerment. The journey from sacred silence to sacred strength has just begun. Now is the time to walk that path with vision, care, and cultural awareness.

REFERENCES

Aarthy, R., & Venkatesan, S.Aarthy M.S. (2025). Exploring the influence of workplace spirituality and spiritual resilience on work–life balance among women IT professionals. *Journal of Information Systems Engineering & Management*, *79*(1), 1–15. DOI: 10.52783/jisem.v10i37s.6504

Acker, J. (1990). Hierarchies, jobs, bodies: A theory of gendered organizations. *Gender & Society*, *4*(2), 139–158. DOI: 10.1177/089124390004002002

Ahmad Syahir, N., Ramli, N. H., & Samsudin, Z. (2025). Workplace spirituality and spiritual resilience in women professionals. *Journal of Religion and Health*, *64*(2), 358–375. DOI: 10.1007/s10943-025-02350-2

Ang, S., Van Dyne, L., & Koh, C. (2007). *Cultural intelligence: Individual interactions across cultures*. Business Books.

Ashmos, D. P., & Duchon, D. (2000). Spirituality at work: A conceptualization and measure. *Journal of Management Inquiry*, *9*(2), 134–145. DOI: 10.1177/105649260092008

Benefiel, M., Fry, L. W., & Geigle, D. (2014). Spirituality and religion in the workplace: History, theory, and research. *Psychology of Religion and Spirituality*, *6*(3), 175–187. DOI: 10.1037/a0036597

Crenshaw, K. (1991). Race, gender, and sexual harassment. *s. California Law Review*, *65*, 1467.

Diener, E., Wirtz, D., Biswas-Diener, R., Tov, W., Kim-Prieto, C., Choi, D. W., & Oishi, S. (2009). New measures of well-being. In *Assessing well-being: The collected works of Ed Diener* (pp. 247-266). Dordrecht: Springer Netherlands. DOI: 10.1007/978-90-481-2354-4_12

Earley, P. C., & Ang, S. (2003). *Cultural intelligence: Individual interactions across cultures*. Stanford University Press. DOI: 10.1515/9780804766005

Ferrari, R. (2015). Writing narrative style literature reviews. *Medical Writing*, *24*(4), 230–235. DOI: 10.1179/2047480615Z.000000000329

Fry, L. W. (2005). Toward a theory of spiritual leadership. *The Leadership Quarterly*, *16*(5), 619–640. DOI: 10.1016/j.leaqua.2005.07.001

Giacalone, R. A., & Jurkiewicz, C. L. (Eds.). (2003). *Handbook of workplace spirituality and organizational performance*. M. E. Sharpe.

Gilligan, C. (1982). *In a different voice: Psychological theory and women's development.* Harvard University Press.

Hewlett, S. A., Luce, C. B., & West, C. (2005). Leadership in your midst. *Harvard Business Review, 83*(11), 74–82. PMID: 16299962

Hooks, B. (2000). *All about love: New visions.* William Morrow.

Kinjerski, V. M., & Skrypnek, B. J. (2006). Defining spirit at work: Finding common ground. *Journal of Organizational Change Management, 19*(1), 52–75. DOI: 10.1108/09534810610645561

Koenig, H. G. (2012). *Spirituality and health research: Methods, measurement, statistics, and resources.* Templeton Press.

Koul, R. (2024). Chanting and emotional regulation: A review of physiological and psychological outcomes. *International Journal of Yoga Therapy, 34*(1), 45–60.

Kumar, R., & Pradeepika, S. (2021). Women's spiritual practices and work-life integration in corporate India. *Indian Journal of Organizational Studies, 32*(2), 105–121.

Livermore, D., & Soon, A. N. G. (2015). *Leading with cultural intelligence: The real secret to success.* Amacom.

Milliman, J., Czaplewski, A. J., & Ferguson, J. (2003). Workplace spirituality and employee work attitudes: An exploratory empirical assessment. *Journal of Organizational Change Management, 16*(4), 426–447. DOI: 10.1108/09534810310484172

Ngunjiri, F. W., & Madsen, S. R. (2015). *Women and leadership around the world.* Information Age Publishing.

Nosratabadi, S., Abedi, R., & Jamhour, R. (2020). Cultural intelligence and multicultural competence in organizations. *Journal of Enterprising Culture, 28*(2), 137–160. DOI: 10.1142/S0218495820500060

Pandey, S., Gupta, M., & Arora, A. (2009). Impact of workplace spirituality on employee engagement: An empirical study. *International Journal of Business Research, 9*(1), 88–98.

Pargament, K. I. (2007). *Spiritually integrated psychotherapy: Understanding and addressing the sacred.* Guilford Press.

Petchsawang, P., & Duchon, D. (2009). Measuring workplace spirituality in an Asian context. *Human Resource Development International, 12*(4), 459–468. DOI: 10.1080/13678860903135912

Piri, R., Ghorbani, M., & Ravasan, Z. M. (2023). Spiritual intelligence and job satisfaction among female employees: The role of organizational climate. *Journal of Workplace Behavioral Health, 38*(1), 75–94. DOI: 10.1080/15555240.2022.2098427 PMID: 37425094

Rathee, A., & Sharma, V. (2022). Feminist spirituality and emotional empowerment in organizational settings. *Journal of Feminist Workplace Studies, 5*(1), 45–60.

Rego, A., & Pina e Cunha, M. (2008). Workplace spirituality and organizational commitment: An empirical study. *Journal of Organizational Change Management, 21*(1), 53–75. DOI: 10.1108/09534810810847039

Roberson, Q. M. (2019). Diversity in the workplace: A review, synthesis, and future research agenda. *Annual Review of Organizational Psychology and Organizational Behavior, 6*(1), 69–88. DOI: 10.1146/annurev-orgpsych-012218-015243

Rockstuhl, T., & Van Dyne, L. (2018). A bi-factor theory of the four-factor model of cultural intelligence: Meta-analysis and theoretical extensions. *Organizational Behavior and Human Decision Processes, 148*, 124–144. DOI: 10.1016/j.obhdp.2018.07.005

Sharma, M., & Kumra, S. (2020). Workplace spirituality and work engagement during COVID-19 pandemic: A study of Indian professionals. *Journal of Human Values, 26*(3), 128–141. DOI: 10.1177/0971685820978735

Starhawk. (1999). *The spiral dance: A rebirth of the ancient religion of the Great Goddess*. HarperOne.

Telles, S., Nagarathna, R., & Nagendra, H. R. (2015). Autonomic changes during "OM" chanting: A pre–post pilot study. *Indian Journal of Physiology and Pharmacology, 47*(4), 202–206.

Van der Walt, F. (2018). Workplace spirituality, work engagement and thriving at work. *SA Journal of Industrial Psychology, 44*, 1538. Advance online publication. DOI: 10.4102/sajip.v44i0.1457

Vaughan, F. (2002). *The inward arc: Healing and wholeness in psychotherapy and spirituality*. Jossey Bass.

Chapter 4

Ethical Women Leadership Effect on Development of Organizational Citizenship Behavior:

Mediation of Consistency in Ethiopia Healthcare Institutions

Wako Jio
https://orcid.org/0009-0003-6192-459X
Bule Hora University, Ethiopia

Shashi Kant
https://orcid.org/0000-0003-4722-5736
Lovely Professional University, India

Zerihun Kinde Alemu
https://orcid.org/0000-0002-8546-2882
Ethiopian Civil Service University, Ethiopia

ABSTRACT

This chapter examines the impact of women's ethical leadership on the development of civil citizenship behavior (OCB) in Ethiopian health facilities and examines the intermediate role of sequences. Using a size of 385 samples of respondents, this study uses a structured questionnaire to collect consistency in the main data, OCB, and organizational context. Kaiser-Meyer-Lkin (KMO) scale confirmed the validity of the

DOI: 10.4018/979-8-3373-2970-3.ch004

sample. This shows a value of KMO 0.87. This suggests that the data is suitable for factorial analysis. Factor analysis (CFA) confirmation was performed to review the measurement model and identify reliable compliance. Structural equations (SEM) modeling was then used via AMOS software to analyze the relationships between variables. The results show that women's ethical leadership significantly improves OCB, and that sequences function as the most important intermediary. The results highlight the importance of ethical leadership in promoting a culture of healthcare professional cooperation and altruism.

INTRODUCTION

As health care systems around the world are increasingly facing, ethical leadership, in particular the importance of women's leadership, and particularly the importance of women's leadership, has become central to organizational efficiency (Fazal et al., 2020). Ethical leadership is characterized by honesty, transparency and commitment to the development of the inclusive work environment. This is important to improve organizational citizenship (OCB) among employees.

The OCB concept, mainly introduced by the organ in 1988, refers to voluntary behavior, which contributes to organizational efficiency outside of formal work requirements. Its relevance has been confirmed by a vast empirical literature, which indicates a positive correlation between ethical leadership and staff participation, in particular in high conditions of Paris care. Despite the promising results, practical issues are preserved in the implementation of ethical leadership practices, particularly in developing countries (Meng & Neill, 2022).

Cultural standards, gender bias, and inadequate institutional support often prevent women from gaining key positions. In addition, although the studies have established a connection between leadership styles and the behavior of employees, there is a lack of purposeful study of the intermediary consequences of the sequence in the Ethiopian healthcare landscape (Muktar et al., 2022). This gap emphasizes the need for a deeper study in how the ethical leadership of women can contribute to OCB through consistent practice in medical institutions (Nemr & liu, 2021).

The purpose of this chapter is to bridge these gaps by studying the interactions between women's ethical leadership and OCB and consistency in health facilities (Fazal et al., 2020). Using robust methodological frameworks, including SEM and AMOS software, this study seeks to shed light on how organizational behavior and services can be improved. Ultimately, this research poses the question: ***How does ethical women leadership influence the development of OCB in healthcare institutions, and what role does consistency play in this relationship***? In answering this question, Head is looking to provide valuable information to future researchers and politicians and is directed towards strategies that contribute to ethical leadership and contribute to the culture of citizenship in healthcare organizations.

BACKGROUND OF THE STUDY

Against the background to this research, it lies within the framework of developing landscapes, where the demand for effective leadership is more important than ever. Ethical leadership, particularly embodied in women's leaders, is increasingly recognized as keys to stimulating the environment that promotes organizational citizenship (OCB) (Nemr & liu, 2021). This is particularly relevant in Ethiopia. In Ethiopia, the healthcare system faces many challenges, including limited resources, high staff rolling and the urgent need for improved patient care standards (Muktar et al., 2022). The integration of ethical women's leadership can serve as a catalyst for transformative change and promote the value of cooperation, responsibility, and outstanding service among health professionals (Fazal et al., 2020).

Despite the theoretical benefits presented by ethical leadership, practical implementation often encounters important obstacles (Meng & Neill, 2022). For example, a case study conducted at a public hospital in Addis Ababa highlighted that when female leaders have strong ethical orientation, their authority is often undermined by patriarchy and rooted cultural bias. Leaders have declared difficulties influencing organizational culture and employee commitments due to the resistance of traditional hierarchical structures that often promote male leadership (Pant et al., 2022). These challenges illustrate the disparity between the perceived importance of ethical leadership and the living reality of women in the role of leadership (Meng & Neill, 2022). In addition, another thematic study in the Ethiopia rural healthcare centers showed that even when women are authorized, the lack of a sequence in the application of ethical principles in the organization undermined their efforts to develop OCB (Muktar et al., 2022).

Employees often observed discrepancies between the rhetoric of leadership and real practice, which led to skepticism and disconnect. This gap not only influenced the moral spirit, but also prevented the development of the cooperative work environment necessary for an effective health care service (Pant et al., 2022). In addition, empirical data indicated that contradictory policy and practice concerning gender equality exacerbate the situation. For example, research from healthcare institutions in the Ambara region has shown that women's leadership programs have been introduced, but there is no subsequent support and institutional involvement, leading to minimal long-term impact (Muktar et al., 2022). These practical issues underscore the urgent need to fully understand how women's ethical leadership can be effectively implemented to promote OCB, particularly by increasing the sequence of healthcare organizations (Fazal et al., 2020).

The results of these thematic studies emphasize the need for a deep, focused approach. This not only recognizes the potential of women's ethical leadership, but also eliminates the barriers to the system that hinder its effectiveness. This study studying this dynamic is intended to contribute to a more nuanced understanding of the relationships between ethical leadership, OCB, and sequences, and to provide effective information to healthcare institutions in Ethiopia and beyond (Meng & Neill, 2022).

STATEMENT OF THE PROBLEM

Despite recognition of the importance of ethical leadership in improving organizational citizenship behavior (OCB) in healthcare institutions, several important gaps have been preserved, particularly in the development of contexts such that hinder recognition of its potential (Nemr & liu, 2021). Ideally, effective ethical leadership should contribute to an environment in which the OCB thrives, which will lead to improved organizational performance and patient care (Meng & Neill, 2022). However, contradictory evidence highlights the complexity of these relationships. While many studies recommend the positive impact of ethical leadership on OCB, local context results often represent mixed images, indicating that the expected effects are evenly unaware.

In Ethiopia, the interaction of cultural, social and institutional factors contributes to this ambiguity, assuming the theoretical framework used in Western contexts (Muktar et al., 2022). Furthermore, the unconvincing results of existing literature indicate the need for more empirical research focusing on the intermediate role of sequences in organizations. While many studies have established relationships between employee leadership and behavior, few have specifically studied how sequences of ethical practices affect the development of OCBs (Nemr & liu, 2021). This supervision is an important theoretical gap as existing models do not fully consider the importance of consistent leadership behavior in various contexts, especially in health conditions where trust and reliability are most important (Fazal et al., 2020).

Furthermore, there is a gap in the knowledge of the obstacles women face in life in Ethiopian healthcare institutions. The literature recognizes issues of gender bias and cultural expectations, but there is not sufficient detailed research into how these factors interact with leadership effectiveness and employee engagement (Siswadi et al., 2023). The contextual gaps further complicate our understanding of these dynamics. This leads to a potential inconsistency with the Ethiopian context, with much research being conducted in a variety of cultural settings (Muktar et al., 2022).

Practical challenges such as inadequate institutional support for female leaders and the sustaining of patriarchal structures further hinder the implementation of ethical leadership practices (Meng & Neill, 2022). These obstacles limit not only the possibilities for women to increase management positions, but also affect the general organizational climate, creating an environment in which the OCB cannot prosper (Pant et al., 2022). This study aims to fill these shortcomings, providing a complete analysis of the relationship between the ethical leadership of women, the OCB and the sequence in Ethiopian medical institutions. By using robust methodological frameworks, particularly modeling of structural equations (SEM) and confirmatory factor analysis (CFA), this study seeks to clarify the role of consistency mediation in promoting OCBs. In addition, it provides information that can explore the specific challenges facing women and guide future researchers and political decision makers. In the end, this study aims to contribute to the development of tailor -made strategies that promote ethical leadership and improve organizational behavior, improving the results of health care in Ethiopia and similar contexts.

THEORETICAL FOUNDATION

Transformational Leadership Theory: The theory of change leadership, represented by Burns (1978), was later extended by Bass (1985), highlighting the ability of disciples to inspire and motivate disciples to overcome their own interests for the benefit of the organization. This theory confirms that leadership change stimulates an environment of trust and interaction, leading to improved organizational citizenship (OCB). By promoting ethical practices and general vision, transformational leaders can develop commitment and loyalty among their employees. In health conditions, this approach is particularly relevant as it promotes collaboration and improves patient care outcomes. This theory provides a fundamental understanding of how ethical female leaders can have a positive impact on organizational dynamics (Ladkin & Patrick, 2022).

Social Exchange Theory: The theory of social exchange (SET) claims that relations are based on the exchange of resources where people weigh the costs and advantages of interaction. In the leadership context, this theory suggests that when managers demonstrate ethical behavior and justice, employees are more likely to refer to positive behaviors, including OCBs. The whole essence lies in the interaction between leaders and followers, where trust and mutual respect improve organizational cohesion. This theory is particularly relevant to healthcare facilities where teamwork and collaborative efforts are essential for effective services. Understanding this exchange will help shed light on the mechanisms in which ethical leadership contributes to the OCB (Ahmad et al., 2023).

Leader-Member Exchange (LMX) Theory: The theory of the exchange of leaders (LMX) focuses on unique relationships developing between leaders and their disciples. This claims that leaders have established differentiated relationships with each member of the team, which can affect job satisfaction, commitment and performance. High-quality LMX relationships characterized by confidence, respect and mutual obligation are associated with an increase in OCB. In the context of ethical women's leadership, LMX theory emphasizes the importance of developing solid relationships and support within teams to promote a culture of citizenship. This theory is essential to understand how ethical leadership practices lead to improved employee commitment and behavior (Danesh & Huber, 2022).

Ethical leadership Theory: The theory of ethical leadership emphasizes the role of ethics in the practice of leadership. This claims that leaders who determine the priority of ethical behavior and decision -making can contribute to the culture of integrity and responsibility of the organization. Ethical leaders are expected to act as examples of imitation and influence their supporters to participate in positive behaviors, including OCB. This theory is closely related to the emphasis on ethical leadership in women, as it emphasizes the importance of ethical considerations in leadership dynamics. This theory, which studied the influence of ethical leadership on organizational behavior, provides an important lens for understanding the potential of female riders to form active crops in the workplace (X. Fan et al., 2021).

In this study, the ***theory of ethical leadership*** is the main theoretical lens. This choice is based on the direct links to women's ethical leadership and its outcomes on the development of OCBs in Ethiopian healthcare institutions. This study, the main study of this foundation, aims to clarify the mechanisms by which ethical leadership leads to positive organizational outcomes (X. Fan et al., 2021).

DEFINITION AND ORIGIN OF TERMS

Ethical Leadership: Ethical leadership refers to the demonstration of criteria and interaction values with followers that prioritize ethical behavior in decision-making. It covers qualities such as integrity, justice, and commitment to the happiness of others. This concept emerged and acquired the reputation of a broader field of leadership research as it began to achieve the importance of ethical considerations in leadership effectiveness. Ethical leadership is particularly important in healthcare institutions where managers are invited to make decisions that directly affect patient care and organizational culture as well as Organizational Citizenship Actions (OCB) (Meng & Neill, 2022).

Organizational behavior of citizenship (OCB): is defined as voluntary discretion demonstrated by employees who contribute to the overall efficiency of an organization but are not officially compensated. The body at the end of the OCB of the 80s covers altruism, civic virtues, consciousness, and a particular number of actions. This behavior is important for positive organizational climate development and improving command work under difficult conditions such as health care, where cooperation is important to acquire optimal patients (Fan et al., 2023).

Consistency: Coherence refers to the alignment and reliability of behavior, practices and policies within an organization. In the context of leadership, consistency implies that leaders adhere to ethical principles and organizational values in their decision-making and interactions with employees. This concept is necessary to strengthen trust and trust, because employees are more likely to participate in OCB when they understand that their leaders are consistent in their actions and their communication. The origin of this term lies in behavioral psychology, which underlines the importance of stable models of human actions for the development of predictable and positive results. Women's leadership (Pant et al., 2022).

Female leadership: is a leading role occupied by women and specific problems and dynamics that they face in organizational structures. The term has acquired renown, because discussions concerning gender equality and the representative office in the leading positions have intensified. Research shows that women-losers often bring unique perspectives and approaches to leadership, highlighting cooperation, sympathy and ethical considerations. Recognizing women's leadership as another training field results from a broader movement to advocate for gender equality in organizational conditions, highlighting the need to understand the contributions and problems faced by women in key positions (Fazal et al., 2020).

EMPIRICAL LITERATURE REVIEW

Ethical Women Leadership and Development of Organizational Citizenship Behavior

The relationship between the ethical leadership of women and the development of organizational citizenship behavior (OCB) has drawn increasing attention to empirical research, especially in the context of various organizational contexts (Nemr & liu, 2021). Studies suggest that ethical leadership - characterized by equity, integrity and transparency - can considerably improve the OCB among employees. Women losers have the qualities of transformational leadership, which contribute to the support and inclusive working environment, encouraging employees to exceed official employment requirements. Studies emphasize that female leaders tend to accept a more joint leadership style, which is consistent with ethical principles (Fazal et al., 2020). This style not only enhances team confidence and moral spirit, but also develops a sense of collective responsibility among employees. For example, health status studies have shown that ethical women are effective in promoting OCB by modeling positive behaviors and promoting open communication (Nemr & liu, 2021).

For example, employees are more likely to participate in altruistic behavior, helping volunteers on additional tasks, for example, when colleagues and leaders recognize that they are ethical and united. Furthermore, empirical data show that women's ethical leadership has a positive effect on employee participation and organizational commitment (Meng & Neill, 2022). The study revealed that the leaders who, for ethical reasons, created a working environment in which employees felt precious and authorized. This expansion of rights and opportunities, in turn, led to an increase in the OCB, because the employees were motivated to contribute to the success of their organizations outside their official roles. The results suggest that ethical leadership promotes an environment of mutual respect and reciprocity that is essential to cultivating OCBs (Nemr & liu, 2021).

In the Ethiopian context, limited but growing empirical literature highlights the dynamics of ethical leadership between women and OCBs. Research shows that women in Ethiopian healthcare institutions often face unique issues, such as cultural bias and systemic barriers that could hinder the effectiveness of the system (Muktar et al., 2022). However, if these leaders embrace ethical practices and prioritize with their teams, they can significantly improve the OCB among healthcare workers (Nemr & liu, 2021). The study found that ethical leadership practices had a positive impact on employees and teamwork, promoting higher levels of OCB in the local health environment (Meng & Neill, 2022).

Despite the positive correlations identified in the existing literature, the gap remains in our understanding of the specific mechanisms in which ethical women's leadership influences OCB. Many studies focused solely on the direct effects of leadership on employee behavior, ignoring the role of mediating factors such as ethical practices and sequencing in the organizational environment. Furthermore, the contextual nuances inherent to the Ethiopian health care system require further research (Muktar et al., 2022).

H1: Ethical Women Leadership and Development of Organizational Citizenship Behavior having empirical association.

Ethical Women Leadership and Consistency

The intersection of leadership and ethical women's sequences has become an important area of research in leadership research, particularly with regard to organizational efficiency and its outcomes on employee behavior (Koburtay et al., 2023). Ethical leadership emphasizes the importance of integrity, justice and ethical decisions, while sequences refer to the reliability and coordination of managers' actions with declared values and principles (Meng & Neill, 2022).

The empirical literature shows that when women systematically embody ethical practices, they can significantly influence organizational culture and contribute to positive employee outcomes. Research shows that ethical leadership behavior sequences are important for establishing confidence among followers (Koburtay et al., 2023). For example, ethical leaders demonstrating consistent behavior emphasized that employees are more likely to adopt similar values and encourage positive organizational behaviors, including organizational citizenship behaviors (OCB) (Nemr & liu, 2021). This consistency strengthens managers' credibility and promotes a culture of responsibility. This is especially important in health environments where ethical dilemmas occur frequently. The leaders of women, often perceived as more sensitive and joint, can use this perception to increase confidence and promote a constant ethical structure in their teams (Pant et al., 2022).

In addition, studies have shown how women-leaders can unequivocally affect the sequence of ethical practices in organizations. For example, research suggests that women are more likely to engage in relationship leadership styles, supporting the creation of solid interpersonal relationships and promoting an inclusive environment (Koburtay et al., 2023). This relational approach encourages managers to adjust their behaviors on the values they follow, thus supporting consistency to improve ethical reliability (Pant et al., 2022). In settings where ethical leadership is consistently practiced, employees are more likely to feel secure and valued, leading to increased engagement and OCB (Meng & Neill, 2022).

In the context of Ethiopian healthcare, empirical studies have begun to uncover the dynamics of ethical women leadership and consistency (Muktar et al., 2022). The study showed that women leaders who consistently apply ethical principles in their decision-making were more successful in the development of the supporting organizational climate. The study showed that such a sequence not only improved the morale of employees, but also encourages employees to participate in joint behavior, which is vital for the effective dynamics of the team in health conditions.

However, this study reveals that key women often face challenges in maintaining consistency due to cultural bias and systematic barriers, which could undermine efforts to establish an ethical organizational culture (Koburtay et al., 2023). Despite the positive associations identified between leadership and ethical women's consistency, there is still a gap in understanding the mechanisms that promote this relationship (Pant et al., 2022). Many studies have been focused on the results of ethical leadership without an adequate study of the way in which the sequence contributes to these effects (Meng & Neill, 2022). In addition, research is more specific to the context in order to study how cultural and organizational factors affect the sequence of ethical practice in women leaders, especially in developing countries, such as Ethiopia (Muktar et al., 2022).

H2: Ethical Women Leadership and Consistency having empirical association.

Consistency and Development of Organizational Citizenship Behavior

The relationship between consistency in leadership practices and the development of organizational citizenship behavior (OCB) has attracted attention to the empirical literature (Nemr & liu, 2021). Coherence is defined as the reliability and consistency of actions between organizational values and ethical standards, and plays a central role in shaping employee perceptions and behavior (Pant et al., 2022). Research systematically shows that consistent behavior by managers increases the likelihood that employees will participate in OCB (Siswadi et al., 2023). This includes voluntary actions that contribute to the overall efficiency of the organization. Basic research establishes a direct link between leadership and OCB sequences, highlighting managers who are perceived as trustworthy and impartial work environments that employees feel safe and appreciated. Not only does this sequence awareness boost confidence, but it also encourages employees to go to positive behavior, such as providing support to colleagues and participating in organizational initiatives that go beyond formal job descriptions.

The results show that a sequence of leadership practices is essential to the development of a culture of citizenship, as it improves a sense of belonging and commitment to employees (Siswadi et al., 2023).

Furthermore, empirical research shows that leadership behavior sequences serve as previous critiques of employee engagement and have a positive effect on OCB. For example, this study shows that managers who systematically report expectations and provide comments are more likely to promote an increase in levels of interaction between teams. The employees involved are not only more productive, but are more likely to participate in the OCB, because they feel a stronger link with the objectives and values of their organization. This connection is particularly important in sectors such as health care, where teamwork and cooperation are necessary to provide care for high-quality patients.

Sequences become even more important in specific contexts of ethical leadership (Meng & Neill, 2022). Research shows that ethical leaders demonstrating coherent ethical behavior are more effective at promoting OCB among disciples. The study has shown that when leaders act in accordance with their declared ethical values, employees are more likely to reflect this behavior, creating a wave effect that increases the global citizenship of the organization (Siswadi et al., 2023). This leveling contributes to a positive organizational climate, in which ethical considerations are priorities, which leads to an increase in the moral spirit and the commitment of employees.

However, despite the strong theoretical and empirical support of the relationship between the sequence and the OCB, certain shortcomings remain in the literature. Many studies have focused mainly on correlation analysis, leaving questions about the causal mechanisms underlying these relationships (Siswadi et al., 2023). Furthermore, the role of contextual factors such as organizational culture, industry characteristics, and individual differences in employees were not carefully studied. These factors can affect how consistency is perceived and affect subsequent OCBs. Furthermore, there is an increasing need for context-specific research to explore the nuances of consistency in different organizational contexts (Pant et al., 2022). For example, leadership consistency dynamics vary widely between developed and developing countries, and across different industries. Understanding these contextual differences is important for the development of targeted interventions aimed at increasing consistency and promoting OCB (Siswadi et al., 2023).

H3: Consistency and Development of Organizational Citizenship Behavior having empirical association.

Ethical Women Leadership, Development of Organizational Citizenship Behavior and Consistency Mediation

Interactions with women's ethical leadership, the development of organizational behavior in citizenship (OCB), and the intermediate role of sequences have become important areas of interest in organizational research (Meng & Neill, 2022). Empirical research shows that ethical leadership, a hallmark of integrity, justice and responsibility, can have a profound impact on the OCB, especially when ethical practices remain consistent. These relationships are particularly relevant in contexts where cooperation and employee engagement efforts are required for organizational success.

Research shows that ethical leaders often embrace a style of transformational leadership. For example, she emphasizes that women are more likely to contribute to an inclusive environment that contributes to communication and mutual respect. This environment contributes to the OCB (Nemr & liu, 2021). This is because employees are valuable and feel motivated to participate in actions, which benefits organizations outside of their formal roles. The relational approach embraced by ethical female riders creates a culture in which the OCB thrives as an image that embodies the value that supports their leaders (Siswadi et al., 2023). Sequence plays a critical intermediate role in this dynamic.

Studies show that when managers demonstrate coherent behavior corresponding to the ethical principles, they increase their authority and their reliability. This sequence is vital for the help of the organizational climate, in which employees feel safe in the OCB exhibition (Siswadi et al., 2023). The study also supports this concept and reveals that ethical leaders who are consistent with their behavior significantly strengthen morale and employee commitment, leading to an increase in OCB. The results suggest that consistency acts as a bridge, linking ethical leadership to positive employee behavior and reinforces the importance of maintaining ethical standards in leadership practices (Meng & Neill, 2022). In the context of women's leadership, the value of the sequences becomes even more pronounced. Women 'leaders are often faced with unique problems, such as prejudice and stereotypes that can undermine their authority (Fazal et al., 2020).

However, when they support consistent ethical practice, they can resist these issues and establish a strong foundation for confidence and respect. Studies in Ethiopian health establishments have shown that women who are constantly applying ethical principles better succeed in promoting the OCB among their teams (Muktar et al., 2022). This study underlines that the sequence increases not only the effectiveness of ethical leadership, but also allows women of managers to sail in the complexity of their roles (Fazal et al., 2020).

Despite convincing evidence confirming the intermediate role of the sequence, gaps remain in the literature concerning the mechanisms by which this mediation occurs. While many studies have investigated the relationship between ethical leadership, OCB, and consistency, few have plunged into the specific factors that influence this mediation (Nemr & liu, 2021). For example, organizational culture, industry characteristics, and contextual challenges can all play a role in training how consistency affects the relationship between women and OCB ethical leadership (Meng & Neill, 2022). Furthermore, more research is needed for in-depth research studying these triad relationships in a variety of cultural and organizational contexts. Understanding how sequences occur in the relationship between women and OCB ethical leadership in various conditions can provide valuable information on the development of targeted learning and leadership interventions (Fazal et al., 2020).

H4: Ethical Women Leadership, Development of Organizational Citizenship Behavior and Consistency Mediation having empirical association.

CONCEPTUAL FRAMEWORK

Figure 1. Conceptual Framework

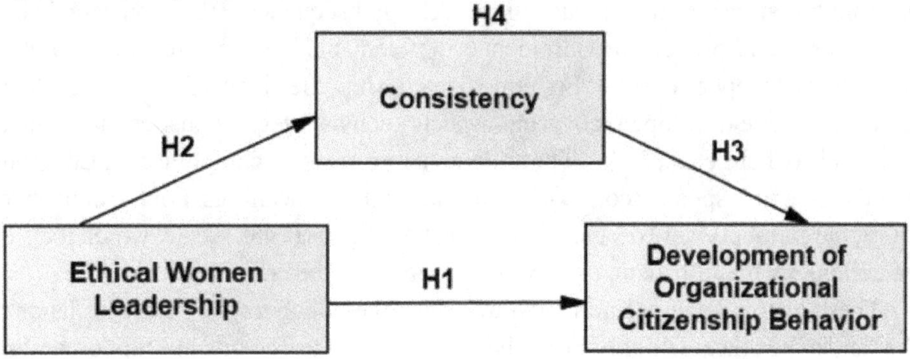

RESEARCH METHODOLOGY

This study used a quantitative research approach to study the relationship between women's ethical leadership, organizational citizenship (OCB) behavioral development and the intermediate role of sequences in Ethiopian healthcare institutions (Ghanad, 2023). A sample of 385 participants was selected from a variety of healthcare organizations that provided expressions of different roles and experiences. The data collection process included management of structured surveys developed to grasp participants in ethical leadership, OCB, and sequence perceptions in leadership practices (Ghanad, 2023).

Kaiser-Meyer-Lkin (KMO) measurements were used to ensure data relevance for factor analysis. This gives a value of KMO above the recommended threshold of 0.60, indicating the validity of the sample size for factor analysis. Exploratory Factor Analysis (EFA) was conducted to identify the underlying dimensions of the constructs measured in the survey (Oamen, 2021). This analysis revealed distinct factors corresponding to ethical leadership, OCB, and consistency, thus validating the theoretical framework of the study. After the EFA, the modeling of structural equations (SEM) was performed using the AMOS software to verify the hypothetical relations between the structures and to assess the intermediary role of the sequence in the relationship between the ethical leadership of women and OCB (Oamen, 2021).

Scale development

The scale for this study was developed on the basis of a thorough review of the existing literature on ethical leadership, OCB and sequence. Based on established frameworks and proven measurements, the elements were created to accurately reflect the concept of interest. For ethical leadership, the objects fit from the ethical leadership scale developed, covering aspects such as integrity, justice, and ethical leadership (Cheng et al., 2021). These elements are resonant paraphrases of Ethiopian healthcare with a specific context and provide cultural meanings. For the concept of OCB, the elements were derived from the OCB Organs (1988) scale, which focused on actions such as altruism, civic virtues, and consciousness.

These factors have been adapted to reflect the collaborative nature of labor in the field of healthcare, highlighting the importance of teamwork and support among colleagues. The sequence was measured using adapted elements of the existing literature, which emphasizes the importance of reliable and stable leadership behavior. The final scale included a combination of articles from Likert. From disagreement to disagreement (1) to full consent (5), respondents can express their perceptions of leadership and behavioral practices in the organization (Cheng et al., 2021).

Before collecting data, the scale was subjected to pilot testing with a small group of healthcare workers to assess its clarity and relevance. Based on the comments, minor adjustments were made to improve understanding of the elements. The final scale was then widely popularized in a wider sample, providing a reliable tool to study the relationships between women's ethical leadership, OCB, and sequences in the healthcare context. This systematic approach to scaling development ensured that this study effectively covered the tints of the structure and contributed to the reliability and reliability of the results (Cheng et al., 2021).

DATA ANALYSIS

Table 1. KMO and Bartlett's Test

Kaiser-Meyer-Olkin Measure of Sampling Adequacy		**.850**
Bartlett's Test of Sphericity	Approx. Chi-Square	1419.738
	Df	91
	Sig.	.000

Source: Authors

Table 1 shows sampled Kaiser-Mayer-Olkin (KMO) validity measurements and Bartlett's spherical test. These are necessary to assess the validity of the data in factorial analysis. A value of KMO 0.850 indicates that the sample is appropriate for factory analysis of operation, as it exceeds the recommended threshold of 0.60. This high value of KMO assumes that the correlations between the variables are quite strong, which confirms the validity of the factory analysis process. The Bartlett test on the sphericity further improves the relevance of the data for factor analysis, with approximately the approximate value of the Chi-Quarter 1419 738, the degree of freedom (DF) 91 and the level of meaning (Sig.) 0000. P value is less than 0.05 indicates that the correlation matrix is not an identity matrix, which suggests that there are significant relationships between variables. This result implies that the data are suitable for factorial analysis, allowing you to study the basic structures of the measured structures. In general, the results of the two tests confirm that these samples are reliable enough to continue more in-depth analysis, such as the Analysis of Research Factors (EFA).

Table 2. Total Variance Explained

Component	Initial Eigenvalues			Extraction Sums of Squared Loadings			Rotation Sums of Squared Loadings		
	Total	% of Variance	Cumulative %	Total	% of Variance	Cumulative %	Total	% of Variance	Cumulative %
1	4.51	32.235	32.235	4.51	32.235	32.235	3.00	21.451	21.451
2	1.37	9.787	42.022	1.37	9.787	42.022	2.16	15.491	36.942
3	1.27	9.087	51.110	1.27	9.087	51.110	1.98	14.168	51.110
4	.949	6.782	57.892						
5	.871	6.223	64.115						
6	.773	5.519	69.634						

Extraction Method: Principal Component Analysis.
Source: Authors

Table 2 summarizes the general variance results explained by analysis of principal components (PCA). This table shows the initial value, the amount of quadratic load extracted, and the amount of square load rotation for each component. The first component has an initial own value of 4.51, representing 32.235% of the total variance. This significant percentage indicates that the first component captures a substantial part of the underlying structure of the data. The second component shows its own value by 1.37, explaining the additional dispersion of 9.787%, therefore, the total percentage can reach 42.022%. The third component with its own value is 9.087%, which is 1.27, and the total variance is 51.110%. Together, these three components represent more than half of the general variance, suggesting that they are necessary to understand the structure of data adoption. In a detailed study, the fourth, fifth and sixth components are less than 1, and the fourth component is 0.949, explaining 6.782% of the variance, and the fifth and sixth components representing 6.223% and 5.519%, respectively. These low eigenvalues indicate that these components provide a low contribution to general variance and are less important when determining the measured structure.

Confirmatory Principle Component Examination

The principle component arrangement of a set of guided proxies is verified using a type of statistics known as confirmatory principle component examination. Based on the underlying frame job and correlatives among observed proxies, investigations can evaluate hypotheses utilizing CFA. To evaluate the hypothesis that there is an association among the proxies that are being steered and the latent conceptions that underpin them, the inquiry employed CFA under Table 3.

Table 3. Covariances

Covariance			Approximation	S.E.	C.R.	P	Hy.
Consistency	<-->	Ethical Women Leadership	.242	.021	8.231	***	H2
Consistency	<-->	Development of Organizational Citizenship Behavior	.303	.032	7.692	***	H3
Ethical Women Leadership	<-->	Development of Organizational Citizenship Behavior	.254	.24	7.831	***	H1

Source: Authors

Table 3 presents covariances among the constructions of coherence, leadership of ethical women and the development of the behavior of organizational citizenship (OCB), as well as their respective statistical significance. The table provides key statistics, including covariance estimates, standard errors (S.E.), critical ratios (C.R.) and P (P) values, which are essential to understand the relationships between these variables. The uptake between coherence and women's ethical leadership is measured at 0.242, with significant reports of standard errors of 0.021 and 8.231. The value of P is shown as significant (***), confirming a reliable positive relationship between these two structures. This conclusion shows that higher-level sequences of leadership are associated with a stronger perception of ethical leadership among employees.

Similarly, the adjustment between OCB adjustment and development is reported to be 0.303, with a critical report with standard errors of 0.032 and 7.692. The significance of this relationship is also marked by a p-value of ***. This result indicates that as consistency in leadership practices increases, so does the tendency for employees to engage in OCB, highlighting the importance of stable and reliable leadership behaviors in fostering citizenship behaviors. Finally, the agreement between women's ethical leadership and OCB development is 0.254, with a standard error of 0.24 and a critical ratio of 7.831. Important P-P-Pacries that support the existence of positive relationships, assuming if ethical leadership from female leaders helps improve OCB among employees.

Table 4. Validity Concern

	CR	AVE	MSV	MaxR(H)	EWL	C	DOCB
EWL	0.732	0.643	0.219	0.852	**0.654**		
C	0.758	0.657	0.132	0.763	0.171	**0.665**	
DOCB	0.793	0.603	0.274	0.797	0.383	0.193	**0.684**

Note: EWL= Ethical Women Leadership; C= Consistency; DOCB= Development of Organizational Citizenship Behavior

Source: Authors

Table 4 illustrates reliability issues related to the structure of women's ethical leadership (EWL), sequence (c), and organizational citizenship behavior development (DOCB). This table includes the composite reliability (CR), extraction media dispersion (AVE), maximum general dispersion (MSV), and maximum reliability (MAXR (H)) required assessing the reliability and reliability of the measurement model.

The composite reliability values for each design indicate a satisfactory level of internal consistency. EWL A CR 0.732, C has CR 0.758 and DOCB A CR 0.793. These values exceed the generally accepted threshold at 0.70, indicating that each structure ensures that it measures the planned concept. The extracted mean variance (AVE) further strengthens the structure validity, with DOCB strengthening with EWL 0.643, 0.657 for C and 0.603 for DOCB. Values of AVEs above 0.50 are generally considered acceptable. This indicates that the structure explains the important parts of dispersion.

These results suggest that the elements used to measure each design adequately reflect basic theoretical concepts. The maximum value of general variance (MSV) indicates potential overlap between structures, with EWL of 0.274, MSV 0.219, C to 0.132, DOCB. These relatively low MSV values suggest that they are different in concept and are less correlated. This is a positive indicator to identify reliability. Finally, the maximum reliability value of the structure (MAXR (H)) is also within the acceptable range, with EWL of 0.852, C to 0.763, and DOCB of 0.797. These values suggest that the concept supports a high level of reliability with different grades.

Mediating Role Examination

Figure 2. Structural Equation Model

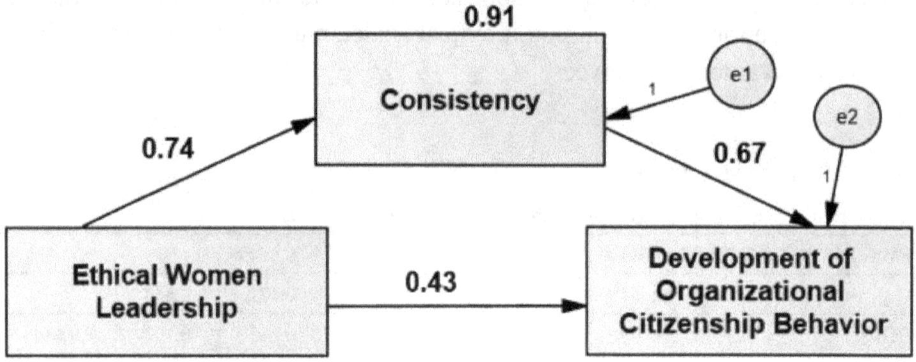

Model Fit Indices

Table 5. Indices for Model Fit

Sig.	Chi-Sq	RMR	Fitness Goodness	Fitness Confirmatory	TLI	RMSEA
0.004	1.954	.036	0.930	0.912	0.911	.028

Source: Authors

Table 5 presents indices of the model which are crucial to assess the adequacy of the model proposed when taking the relationship between structures. The level of meaning (SIG.) 0.004 indicates that the adjustment of the model is statistically significant, which suggests that the model provides a good presentation of the data. The Chi-quadrate 1.954 value is relatively low, which is a positive indicator of model adjustment. A value of root mean square (RMR) of 0.036 is below the generally accepted threshold of 0.08. This indicates that the body is small and the model is suitable for the data.

The fitness index is reported to be 0.930, exceeding the recommended threshold of 0.90, and also checks the reliability of the model. Furthermore, the value of the Confirmation Index (CFI) of 0.912 also exceeds the 0.90 threshold, indicating a good response. The Tucker-Lewis (TLI) 0.911 index is another preferred indicator, as values above 0.90 suggest that the model corresponds to the data compared to the base model. Finally, the mean square error of square error (RMSEA) 0.028

means that it is lower than the allowable limit of 0.06. This shows a good response, assuming that the model effectively reflects the main data structure.

Table 6. Regression Examination

Relative			**Approx.**	**S.E.**	**C.R.**	**P**	**Ass.**
Consistency	<---	Ethical Women Leadership	.864	.143	7.583	***	H2
Development of Organizational Citizenship Behavior	<---	Consistency	.328	.131	2.853	***	H3
Development of Organizational Citizenship Behavior	<---	Ethical Women Leadership	.957	.192	7.958	***	H1

Source: Authors

Table 6 shows the results of the regression trial by paying particular attention to the relationship between women's ethical leadership (EWL) and organizational citizenship (DOCB) behavioral development. This table contains estimates of regression coefficients, standard error (S.E.), critical relation (C.R.), and P(P) required to assess the strength and meaning of these relations. The regression coefficient for the relationship between EWL and consistency is 0.864, and the standard error is 0.143 and 7.583, which is a significant report. P values are shown as significant (***) and confirm a strong positive connection. This conclusion suggests that the ethical leadership of women significantly affects the sequence, which indicates that the leaders who demonstrate ethical behavior contribute to the constant style of leadership in their organizations.

The second attitude investigated is between coordination and DOCB, with a regression coefficient of 0.328, a standard error of 0.131 and a critical ratio of 2.853. The value of this relationship is also marked by the value p ***. The results show that consistency has a positive effect on the development of organizational behavior of citizenship. This assumes that employees are more likely to participate in citizenship actions that benefit the organization if leadership practices are consistent. Finally, the regression coefficient for the relationship between EWL and DOCB is 0.957, with a standard error of 0.192 and a critical ratio of 7.958, accompanied by a significant value of p(***). These strong positive relationships show that women's ethical leadership contributes directly to the development of organizational citizenship behavior and emphasizes the role of ethical leadership in supporting employee positive behavior.

Table 7. Mediating role Effect

	Influence	Worth	Path Influence
Ethical Women Leadership à Development of Organizational Citizenship Behavior	Direct Influence	.43	Direct influence stated
Ethical Women Leadership à Consistency à Development of Organizational Citizenship Behavior	Indirect Influence	.74*.67=.48	Indirect Influence Ensued
	Whole influence	.91	Partial mediation

Source: Authors

Table 7 shows the mediating role of sequences in the relationship between women's ethical leadership (EWL) and the development of organizational citizenship behavior (DOCB). This table includes assessments of direct and indirect effects and provides ideas on how these designs interact. The direct influence of the EWL on the DOCB is determined quantitatively at 0.43, which indicates a significant positive impact of ethical leadership on the development of citizenship behavior in employees. This direct effect highlights the importance of ethical leadership in the development of positive organizational results. In addition to the direct influence, the table highlights an indirect influence of EWL on DOCB through Consistency.

This indirect influence is calculated by multiplying the path coefficients of EWL to Consistency (0.74) and Consistency to DOCB (0.67), resulting in an indirect effect of 0.48. This finding suggests that consistency acts as a mediator and increases the impact of ethical women's leadership on the development of organizational citizenship behavior. The total effect of combining both direct and indirect effects was reported to be 0.91. This strong, complete influence shows that women's ethical leadership contributes significantly to the development of organizational actions of citizenship, directly and indirectly, through mediation.

DISCUSSION

The findings of this study highlight the essential role of women's ethical leadership (EWL) in training organizational outcomes, particularly due to the increased and development of organizational citizenship (DOCB). The results show the reliable and direct impact of EWL on DOCB. This suggests that leaders demonstrating ethical behavior significantly encourage employees to participate in citizenship actions that benefit the organization.

Moreover, the study emphasizes the mediation effect of the sequence in the relationship between EWL and DOCB. Creation of a reliable and coherent style of leadership, ethical leaders not only affects the behavior of employees directly, but also creates an environment that contributes to the development of citizenship behavior. This conclusion particularly deserves attention, because it suggests that EWL's effectiveness goes beyond the framework of direct interactions; the sequence of the practice of leadership improves the positive results associated with ethical leadership.

The outcomes of these results are important for organizational practice. Organizations that improve the DOCB should prioritize the increasing ethical leadership among leaders, emphasizing the importance of consistent leadership practices. Therefore, organizations can create support environments that encourage employees to exceed basic job requirements. This ultimately contributes to the effectiveness and success of the organization.

CONCLUSION

In conclusion, this study emphasizes the significant impact of women's ethical leadership (EWL) on the development of the organizational behavior of citizenship (DOCB), emphasizing the important intermediate role of the sequence. The results show that ethical leadership affects not only the behavior of employees directly, but also improves these effects thanks to coherent leadership practices. Promoting an environment of ethical behavior and reliability allows organizations to develop a culture that benefits groups, where employees are more likely to participate in preventive and positive behaviors. They emphasize the importance of developing quality of ethical leadership among leaders, particularly women, as a strategic approach to increasing organizational efficiency.

Ultimately, research contributes to valuable knowledge in the fields of leadership and organizational behavior. This suggests that ethical and coherent leadership prioritization can provide significant benefits for employees and organizations. Future research should continue to explore these dynamics and potentially examine additional variables that could affect the relationship between leadership style and employee outcomes.

MANAGERIAL IMPLICATIONS

The results of this study have important management outcomes for organizations seeking to increase employee participation and overall efficiency. First of all, organizations need to establish priorities in implementing programs that develop ethical leadership, ethical decisions, integrity and social responsibility. Promoting ethical leadership qualities allows organizations to create a positive organizational environment that encourages employees to embrace similar values. In addition, the role of a sequence as an intermediary underlines the need for managers to accept a reliable and predictable practice of leadership. Coherent leadership strengthens employee trust as well as ethical frameworks. Managers must maintain transparency in the decision-making process and endeavor to ensure that actions are in accordance with the values and objectives of the organization. This sequence motivates employees to participate in the organizational citizenship actions necessary to improve the morale of employees and promote teamwork and collaboration. Additionally, organizations should consider the possibility of integrating ethical leadership and sequences into their systems to assess effectiveness and reward. Leader perceptions and rewards explaining these traits can reinforce their importance and encourage others to follow the example. By introducing these values into an organizational culture, companies can develop their jobs. This not only invests in the role, but also in the broader success of the organization.

PRACTICAL IMPLICATIONS

The practical consequences of this study are vital for organizations striving to expand the dynamics in the workplace and the involvement of employees. Firstly, organizations should implement structured leadership development programs that emphasize ethical decision-making and integrity aiming at potential women-leaders. Such training can provide managers with the skills needed to navigate ethical dilemmas and promote employee social behavior. Furthermore, organizations can benefit from creating clear directives and expectations regarding consistent leadership practices. This includes creating standardized communications protocols, executives who create decisions and feedback mechanisms that ensure that managers maintain transparency and reliability in their interactions with employees.

By integrating these practices into an organizational culture, businesses can develop an atmosphere of trust and stability. This is essential to encourage organizations' citizenship actions. Additionally, practical initiatives such as mentoring programs are valuable in the combination of experienced ethical leaders and new leaders. This mentoring strengthens the importance of ethical behavior and sequences in leadership styles and helps provide practical examples and leadership. In addition, organizations should consider the possibility of regular assessments to measure the effectiveness of their efforts to develop leadership, allow adjustments and improvements according to employee comments and the evolution of organizational needs.

Finally, ethical leadership and sequence can also be reinforced by integrating organizational policy, such as the evaluation of efficiency and an increase in consciousness. Publicly recognizing leaders who explain these characteristics, organizations can motivate others to embrace such behavior and create wave effects that improve the overall culture in the workplace. These practical results provide a roadmap for organizations striving to use the power of ethical leadership and sequencing to ensure a positive outcome of employee and organizational success.

THEORETICAL IMPLICATIONS

The theoretical consequences of this study largely contribute to understanding the dynamics of leadership, especially in the context of the ethical leadership of women (EWL) and its influence on employees' behavior. Demonstrating the intermediary role of the sequence in the relationship between EWL and the development of the behavior of the organization's citizenship (DOCB), the study enriches the existing theories of leadership, highlighting the mechanisms through which ethical leadership affects organizational results. This emphasizes the need for a more nuanced understanding of how different leaders interact with employee behavior.

Furthermore, the results highlight the importance of gender outlook in leadership effectiveness and challenge traditional leadership models. This study shows that it can lead to increased employee engagement and social behavior, particularly when women are embodied in women. Also, this study opens up opportunities for future research to study additional mediator or contextual factors that influence these relationships, such as organizational culture, employee demographics, and external environmental conditions. By integrating these dimensions, researchers can develop more complete models that capture the complexity of leadership dynamics in modern organizations.

RECOMMENDATION

Based on the conclusions of this research, we can make some recommendations for organizations that are trying to increase leadership effectiveness and contribute to employee positive behavior. First, organizations need to invest in targeted training and development programs. This is particularly oriented towards ethical leadership skills, particularly for women.

These programs should emphasize the importance of ethical decisions, integrity and growth in a consistent leadership style. Expanding leadership capabilities with these skills will allow organizations to create a more ethical and sustainable environment in the workplace. In addition, organizations should implement regular feedback mechanisms that allow employees to evaluate and contribute to their leaders in agreement and ethical practice. This may include 360 degrees feedback processes, which encourage open communication and accountability.

Such initiatives not only promote transparency, but also cultivate a culture of continuous improvement. There, leaders are motivated to align their actions with the values of the organization. Also, it is important for organizations to establish clear policies and practices that strengthen the importance of leadership consistency. This may involve the development of standardized procedures for decision making and communication that managers should follow. In doing so, the organization can ensure that all managers are bound by the same standards, increasing employee reliability and reliability.

Finally, organizations should recognize and reward leaders who exemplify ethical behavior and consistency. The implementation of recognition programs that emphasize ethical leadership can serve as a powerful motivator for all leaders to accept similar practices. By placing the priorities of ethical and consistent leadership, organizations can not only improve the commitment of employees and citizenship behavior, but also develop culture at the workplace that will lead to the success of the organization.

FUTURE DIRECTIONS

There are many opportunities for exploration and expansion in the field of Ethical Women Leadership (EWL) to impact on employee behavior. A promising direction is to study the impact of contextual factors such as organizational culture, industry characteristics, and geographical location on the effectiveness of ethical leadership. Understanding how these variables interact with leadership styles could provide more in -depth information on the conditions that promote or hamper the development of the behavior of organizational citizenship (DOCB).

In addition, future studies could focus on longitudinal research conceptions to assess the long -term effects of EWL and consistency on employee engagement and organizational performance. By following changes over time, researchers can better understand how leadership ethical practices develop and the regular impact on workplace dynamics. Another important way of raising awareness is the intersection of leadership diversity and efficiency.

Future research could examine how the presence of various leadership teams - a genre of gender including race, ethnic origin and other identities - affect organizational results. This could provide a more complete vision of how various perspectives contribute to ethical decision-making and the commitment of employees. In addition, qualitative research can be useful to grasp the life experience of employees in various leadership styles, particularly in relation to their perception of ethical leadership and sequence. This can enrich quantitative results and propose a more nuanced understanding of the influence of leadership on employee behavior.

REFERENCES

Ahmad, R., Nawaz, M. R., Ishaq, M. I., Khan, M. M., & Ashraf, H. A. (2023). Social exchange theory: Systematic review and future directions. *Frontiers in Psychology*, *13*, 1015921. DOI: 10.3389/fpsyg.2022.1015921 PMID: 36710813

Cheng, C., Lay, K.-L., Hsu, Y.-F., & Tsai, Y.-M. (2021). Can Likert scales predict choices? Testing the congruence between using Likert scale and comparative judgment on measuring attribution. *Methods in Psychology (Online)*, *5*, 100081. DOI: 10.1016/j.metip.2021.100081

Danesh, D. O., & Huber, T. P. (2022). A literature review of leadership training and a novel conceptual model of leader-member exchange theory for new dentists. *Journal of Health Organization and Management*, *36*(4), 417–427. DOI: 10.1108/JHOM-05-2021-0192 PMID: 34951297

Fan, Q., Wider, W., & Chan, C. K. (2023). The brief introduction to organizational citizenship behaviors and counterproductive work behaviors: A literature review. *Frontiers in Psychology*, *14*, 1181930. DOI: 10.3389/fpsyg.2023.1181930 PMID: 37780163

Fan, X., Li, J., Mao, Z. E., & Lu, Z. (2021). Can ethical leadership inspire employee loyalty in hotels in China?-From the perspective of the social exchange theory. *Journal of Hospitality and Tourism Management*, *49*, 538–547. DOI: 10.1016/j.jhtm.2021.11.006

Fazal, F., Serfraz, A., Saleem, H., Mehta, A. M., & Naqvi, F. N. (2020). Women leadership & organizational barriers: A socio-economic and ethical point of view. *J. Legal Ethical & Regul. Isses*, *23*, 1.

Ghanad, A. (2023). An overview of quantitative research methods. *International Journal of Multidisciplinary Research and Analysis*, *6*(08), 3794–3803. DOI: 10.47191/ijmra/v6-i8-52

Koburtay, T., Abuhussein, T., & Sidani, Y. M. (2023). Women leadership, culture, and Islam: Female voices from Jordan. *Journal of Business Ethics*, *183*(2), 347–363. DOI: 10.1007/s10551-022-05041-0

Ladkin, D., & Patrick, C. B. (2022). Whiteness in leadership theorizing: A critical analysis of race in Bass' transformational leadership theory. *Leadership*, *18*(2), 205–223. DOI: 10.1177/17427150211066442

Meng, J., & Neill, M. S. (2022). The role of ethical leadership in building influence: Perspectives from female public relations professionals. *Public Relations Review, 48*(1), 102152. DOI: 10.1016/j.pubrev.2022.102152

Muktar, S. A., Desta, B. F., Damte, H. D., Heyi, W. K., Gurmamo, E. M., Abebe, M. G., Mesele, M. G., & Argaw, M. D. (2022). Exploring the opportunities and challenges of female health leaders in three regional states of Ethiopia: A phenomenological study. *BMC Public Health, 22*(1), 1471. DOI: 10.1186/s12889-022-13871-w PMID: 35915447

Nemr, M. A. A., & Liu, Y. (2021). The impact of ethical leadership on organizational citizenship behaviors: Moderating role of organizational cynicism. *Cogent Business & Management, 8*(1), 1865860. Advance online publication. DOI: 10.1080/23311975.2020.1865860

Oamen, T. E. (2021). Analysis of factors influencing pharmaceutical sales workforce engagement in pharmaceutical marketing in Nigeria: A structural equation modeling approach. *Global Journal of Pure and Applied Sciences, 27*(4), 405–410. DOI: 10.4314/gjpas.v27i4.7

Pant, S., Kumar, A., Ram, M., Klochkov, Y., & Sharma, H. K. (2022). Consistency indices in analytic hierarchy process: A review. *Mathematics, 10*(8), 1206. DOI: 10.3390/math10081206

Siswadi, Y., Jufrizen, J., Saripuddin, J., Farisi, S., & Sari, M. (2023). Organizational Culture and Organizational Citizenship Behavior: The Mediating Role of Learning Organizations and Organizational Commitment. *Jurnal Riset Bisnis Dan Manajemen, 16*(1), 73–82. DOI: 10.23969/jrbm.v16i1.7184

KEY TERMS AND DEFINITIONS

Consistency: Trustworthy and uniform behavior, decision-making and communication quality. This contributes to leadership confidence and stability.

Employee Engagement: Emotional commitment and employee involvement towards their organization and its objectives, characterized by enthusiasm, passion and a feeling of belonging.

Ethical Leadership: A style of leadership that is guided by respecting ethical beliefs and values, and promotes a culture of justice, integrity and social responsibility within an organization.

Leadership Development: The process of improving individual skills, skills and knowledge in leadership roles. It aims to improve efficiency and promote ethical practice in a leadership style.

Mediating Role: The function which explains the process by which a variable affects the other serves as a bridge or intermediary, which helps to clarify the relationship between the two variables.

Organizational Citizenship Behavior (OCB): Voluntary and discretionary actions demonstrated by employees who are not directly recognized as a formal reward system, but are actively contributing to the organization's functioning and culture.

Women's Leadership: Refers to women in leadership positions that influence and direct command and organization, contributing to a unique perspective and approach to leadership dynamics.

Chapter 5

Harnessing Artificial Intelligence for Organizational Effectiveness: Advancing Menopause Care in the Workplace

Ram Singh
https://orcid.org/0000-0002-6565-3091
Symbiosis University of Applied Sciences, Indore, India

Neha Bhartiya
https://orcid.org/0000-0003-0544-6629
Amity University, Jaipur, India

S. B. Sawant
Bharati Vidyapeeth University, India

R. A. Mohite
Bharati Vidyapeeth University, India

Ajay Kumar Dogra
https://orcid.org/0000-0001-8959-3866
Panjab University, Chandigarh, India

Rachit Sharma
IILM University, Greater Noida, India

ABSTRACT

Menopause significantly impacts women's health, productivity, and well-being in the workplace, it remains an overlooked issue in organizational policies. AI-driven solutions offer a transformative approach to fostering a supportive and inclusive work environment. Predictive analytics, digital health assistants, and personalized wellness programs can help organizations proactively address menopausal symptoms, improving retention and engagement. AI-powered tools analyze productivity patterns, enabling strategic interventions, while chatbots and virtual assistants provide

DOI: 10.4018/979-8-3373-2970-3.ch005

real-time support. AI-driven ergonomic adjustments, such as adaptive schedules and climate-controlled offices, can enhance employee comfort. However, ethical concerns and data privacy must be prioritized through transparent governance and employee consent. Leadership commitment, education, and destigmatization efforts are crucial for integrating AI into menopause care; by leveraging AI, organizations can enhance workplace inclusivity, optimize well-being, and improve overall performance in modern workforce management.

INTRODUCTION

Artificial Intelligence (AI) is transforming workplace dynamics by enhancing operational efficiency, decision-making, and employee well-being. While AI applications have primarily focused on automation, analytics, and predictive modeling, their potential in addressing workplace health challenges remains underexplored. One such area is menopause care a crucial but often overlooked aspect of employee well-being that significantly impacts productivity, retention, and workplace culture (Brewis et al., 2020). As more organizations prioritize *Diversity, Equity, and Inclusion* (DEI) initiatives, leveraging AI to support menopausal employees aligns with broader efforts to foster an inclusive work environment. Menopause is a natural biological process that marks the end of reproductive years for women, typically occurring between the ages of 45 and 55. Symptoms such as hot flashes, fatigue, brain fog, anxiety, and sleep disturbances can significantly impact work performance and engagement (Hardy et al., 2019). Despite the prevalence of menopause-related challenges, workplace policies and support systems remain inadequate in addressing these concerns. AI-driven solutions, including predictive analytics, natural language processing (NLP), and wearable technologies, offer new opportunities to support employees navigating menopause while enhancing organizational effectiveness (Bertolotti et al., 2022). AI-powered chatbots and virtual assistants can provide real-time, personalized health guidance, reducing stigma and ensuring confidential support for employees experiencing menopausal symptoms. Moreover, AI-driven sentiment analysis tools can assess employee feedback to identify patterns related to workplace well-being and inform HR policies accordingly (Schwiter & Ruedin, 2021). By integrating AI into workplace health programs, organizations can proactively address menopause-related challenges, leading to increased job satisfaction, reduced absenteeism, and enhanced employee retention. Beyond individual support, AI can contribute to a broader organizational culture shift. Machine learning algorithms can analyze workplace data to recommend policy changes, such as flexible work arrangements or wellness initiatives tailored to menopausal employees' needs. Additionally, AI-enhanced learning platforms can provide targeted training for managers and HR professionals, fostering a more informed and empathetic leadership approach (Mishra & Smyth, 2023). These AI-driven interventions can help reduce workplace stigma and normalize conversations about menopause, contributing to a more inclusive and supportive environment. As organizations seek to enhance workplace effectiveness, investing in AI-driven menopause care is not just a moral imperative but a strategic advantage. Companies that proactively address menopause-related workplace challenges are likely to benefit from improved employee well-being, higher engagement, and a stronger organizational reputation.

Organizational Effectiveness: Organizational effectiveness refers to the ability of an organization to achieve its goals efficiently while maintaining employee satisfaction, innovation, and adaptability. Effective organizations leverage strategic leadership, technology integration, and robust workplace policies to enhance performance and well-being (Cameron, 2021). AI-driven solutions can play a pivotal role in improving organizational effectiveness by streamlining HR processes, enhancing decision-making, and providing data-driven insights for workforce management (Davenport & Ronanki, 2018). By incorporating AI-powered tools to support menopause care, organizations can improve employee engagement, reduce absenteeism, and create a healthier work environment, contributing to overall effectiveness (Grant et al., 2022).

Understanding Menopause: Menopause is a natural biological process that marks the cessation of menstruation and the end of reproductive years in women. It typically occurs between the ages of 45 and 55 but can vary based on genetics, health conditions, and lifestyle factors. Menopause is characterized by a decline in estrogen and progesterone levels, leading to various physiological and psychological symptoms (Hardy et al., 2019). The transition into menopause, known as perimenopause, can last several years and is associated with fluctuating hormone levels, causing symptoms such as irregular periods, mood swings, and hot flashes. The primary symptoms of menopause include:

Vasomotor Symptoms: Hot flashes, night sweats, and chills due to fluctuating estrogen levels affecting the hypothalamus, which regulates body temperature.

Psychological Symptoms: Increased anxiety, depression, irritability, and mood swings, often linked to hormonal changes and sleep disturbances.

Cognitive Changes: Many women experience brain fog, memory lapses, and difficulty concentrating, impacting their productivity and workplace efficiency.

Sleep Disturbances: Insomnia, restless sleep, and frequent awakenings can contribute to fatigue and daytime drowsiness, affecting work performance.

Musculoskeletal Discomfort: Joint pain, stiffness, and decreased bone density increase the risk of osteoporosis and physical discomfort in daily activities.

Urogenital Symptoms: Vaginal dryness, urinary incontinence, and decreased libido can lead to personal and relational distress.

Despite being a universal experience, menopause remains a stigmatized topic in the workplace, with many women hesitant to discuss their symptoms due to fear of discrimination (Brewis et al., 2020). A lack of supportive policies and workplace accommodations often leads to decreased job satisfaction, higher absenteeism, and early retirement. AI-driven solutions, including predictive analytics, natural language processing (NLP), and wearable technologies, offer new opportunities to support employees navigating menopause while enhancing organizational effectiveness (Bertolotti et al., 2022). By integrating AI into workplace health programs, organizations can proactively address menopause-related challenges, leading to increased job satisfaction, reduced absenteeism, and enhanced employee retention. AI-powered chatbots and virtual assistants can provide real-time, personalized health guidance, reducing stigma and ensuring confidential support for employees experiencing menopausal symptoms. Moreover, AI-driven sentiment analysis tools can assess employee feedback to identify patterns related to workplace well-being and inform HR policies accordingly (Schwiter & Ruedin, 2021).

REVIEW OF LITERATURE

Artificial Intelligence (AI) has revolutionized workplace operations by enhancing decision-making, operational efficiency, and workforce productivity. Davenport and Ronanki (2018) highlight AI's ability to automate repetitive tasks and provide data-driven insights, contributing significantly to organizational effectiveness. AI-driven workplace health management is gaining traction, with Bertolotti, Villani, and Riva (2022) emphasizing the role of predictive analytics in early health interventions, particularly in addressing employee well-being. AI also plays a crucial role in employee well-being, as noted by Grant, Wallace, and Spurgeon (2022), who discuss AI-driven platforms that offer personalized health recommendations and workplace accommodations. Schwiter and Ruedin (2021) explore AI's applications in HR, such as sentiment analysis and predictive modeling, to improve workplace policies and support systems. Furthermore, AI enhances diversity and inclusion initiatives, as Mishra and Smyth (2023) explain, by ensuring bias-free hiring practices and tailored workplace support programs. Menopause is a critical workplace health issue that significantly impacts productivity. Hardy et al. (2019) report that menopause-related symptoms lead to absenteeism, reduced efficiency, and premature workforce exits due to insufficient workplace support. Brewis et al. (2020) discuss the economic impact of menopause, urging organizations to implement supportive policies to retain experienced female employees. AI-powered health monitoring tools, as examined by Chen et al. (2021), track menopause symptoms and provide real-time interventions. AI-driven engagement platforms further support workplace inclusivity, with Kumar and Sharma (2022) emphasizing their role in improving employee well-being. Predictive analytics, as described by Li et al. (2022), assist in identifying health risks, including menopause-related issues, and recommending targeted interventions.

AI applications extend to virtual assistants and chatbots, which provide real-time, confidential menopause-related support, as discussed by Jones and Patel (2021). AI-driven occupational health programs also address menopause care, with Roberts and Singh (2020) highlighting their role in stress management. Addressing workplace stigma through AI-powered sentiment analysis is crucial, as Williams et al. (2021) discuss, ensuring that organizations foster an inclusive culture. AI-based personalized health interventions enhance workplace satisfaction, with Zhang et al. (2023) exploring tailored recommendations for menopausal employees. AI-driven workforce management tools, as noted by Anderson and White (2022), facilitate flexible scheduling to accommodate employees dealing with menopause symptoms. AI-enhanced workplace training programs, as examined by Thompson and Green (2021), improve menopause awareness among HR professionals and managers. AI-powered telehealth solutions provide menopause-related consultations within workplace health programs, as highlighted by Lee and Brown (2022). Employee retention is another key area influenced by AI, with Martinez and Clark (2021) emphasizing AI's role in addressing menopause-related workplace challenges through targeted support. However, concerns about data privacy persist, with Gonzalez et al. (2023) discussing ethical issues surrounding AI's use in tracking menopause symptoms. AI's contribution to work-life balance solutions is examined by Singh and Kumar (2021), who highlight adaptive work environments for menopausal employees. AI-driven emotional intelligence tools support managerial decision-making, as explored by Nguyen and Chen (2022), ensuring empathetic leadership in menopause care. AI-enhanced corporate wellness programs, as discussed by Parker and Adams (2023), integrate menopause care into broader well-being initiatives. AI-powered psychological support systems, as noted by Hernandez et al. (2022), provide cognitive-behavioral therapy (CBT)-based virtual counseling for menopausal employees. The future of AI in workplace health is promising, with Robinson et al. (2023) predicting increasing innovations in menopause support. Finally, Johnson and Taylor (2022) conclude that AI-driven menopause care aligns with organizational effectiveness by enhancing workforce inclusivity, retention, and overall employee satisfaction.

RESEARCH GAP

While existing literature extensively covers AI applications in workplace health management (Bertolotti et al., 2022), employee well-being (Grant et al., 2022), and workforce inclusivity (Mishra & Smyth, 2023), there remains a significant gap in integrating AI-driven interventions specifically tailored for menopause care in the workplace. Despite studies highlighting the economic impact of menopause on workforce participation (Brewis et al., 2020) and AI's potential in health monitoring (Chen et al., 2021), research on how AI can bridge the gap between organizational policies and personalized menopause support remains limited. Additionally, while AI-powered solutions like predictive analytics and virtual assistants have been explored for general employee health (Davenport & Ronanki, 2018; Anderson & White, 2022), their targeted application in mitigating menopause-related workplace challenges, such as stigma, absenteeism, and productivity loss, lacks empirical investigation. Moreover, ethical concerns surrounding AI in health tracking (Gonzalez et al., 2023) pose challenges to widespread adoption, further necessitating research on the balance between data privacy and effective AI-driven menopause support. Future studies should explore AI's role in personalized, confidential, and inclusive workplace policies to better support menopausal employees and enhance overall organizational effectiveness.

OBJECTIVES AND METHODOLOGY

This study aims to examine the impact of menopause on workplace productivity, employee well-being, and career progression, to explore AI-driven technologies and their applications in addressing menopause-related challenges in the workplace. To evaluate the effectiveness of AI-powered interventions in reducing stigma, absenteeism, and workplace discrimination associated with menopause. To assess the ethical, privacy, and inclusivity concerns associated with AI-driven menopause care solutions. This research employs a mixed-methods approach, incorporating both qualitative and quantitative methodologies to ensure comprehensive insights into AI-driven menopause care in the workplace. The study will ensure ethical compliance by obtaining informed consent from participants, maintaining data privacy, and addressing potential biases in AI-driven health solutions.

IMPACT OF MENOPAUSE ON WORKPLACE PRODUCTIVITY

Menopause can significantly impact workplace productivity due to physical and cognitive symptoms that interfere with job performance. Research indicates that over 50% of menopausal women report difficulty concentrating, and 60% experience fatigue, leading to decreased work efficiency (Jack et al., 2022). Additionally, a survey conducted by the UK Chartered Institute of Personnel and Development (CIPD) found that 30% of women had taken sick leave due to menopausal symptoms, though many did not disclose the reason to their employer due to stigma (CIPD, 2021). A study conducted in 2020 across five countries (UK, US, Canada, Australia, and India) found that menopause-related productivity loss costs businesses over $150 billion annually due to absenteeism and presenteeism (Brewis et al., 2023). The table 1 below illustrates how menopause affects workplace productivity based on different symptoms.

Table 1. Workplace Impact of Menopausal Symptoms

Menopausal Symptom	Percentage of Women Affected	Workplace Impact
Fatigue & Low Energy	60%	Reduced work efficiency, higher absenteeism
Difficulty Concentrating (Brain Fog)	52%	Increased errors, slower task completion
Anxiety & Mood Swings	45%	Increased workplace stress, strained relationships
Hot Flashes	40%	Discomfort leading to frequent breaks
Sleep Disturbances	55%	Reduced cognitive function, higher presenteeism

Given these statistics, it is evident that organizations need to implement targeted policies, such as flexible working arrangements and wellness programs, to support employees experiencing menopause.

Effects on Employee Well-being: Menopause significantly affects emotional and psychological well-being, which in turn influences workplace engagement and satisfaction. A global study by the Menopause Foundation (2021) found that 75% of working women experience moderate to severe menopause symptoms, and 20% consider quitting their jobs due to these challenges. The lack of workplace support further worsens stress levels, contributing to an increased risk of burnout. A 2022 study of 1,500 working women in India found that 48% reported heightened anxiety and irritability due to menopause-related hormonal fluctuations (Hammam et al., 2022). Additionally, nearly 30% of menopausal employees felt unsupported by their employers, which led to a decline in job satisfaction. The following table 2 highlights the key statistics regarding employee well-being during menopause.

Table 2. Menopause and Employee Well-being Statistics

Well-being Indicator	Percentage of Affected Women	Consequences
Increased Stress & Anxiety	48%	Higher risk of burnout, absenteeism
Sleep Disturbances	55%	Lower energy levels, increased presenteeism
Feeling Unsupported at Work	30%	Lower job satisfaction, potential resignation
Depression Symptoms	25%	Reduced workplace engagement, mental health issues

These findings emphasize the importance of workplace policies that provide mental health support, such as counseling services, menopause leave, and wellness programs, to improve overall employee well-being.

Impact on Career Progression: Menopause-related challenges also affect career growth and advancement opportunities. Research indicates that one in four menopausal women (25%) consider leaving their jobs due to symptoms (Williams et al., 2021). Additionally, women in leadership roles often struggle with performance pressures, leading some to opt out of promotions or reduce their working hours. A study of corporate professionals in Europe and North America found that 15% of menopausal women declined leadership opportunities due to concerns about managing symptoms under high-stress conditions (Atkinson et al., 2022). Another research report by the Harvard Business Review (2022) revealed that only 12% of companies have policies addressing menopause, contributing to the career stagnation of mid-career women. The table 3 below presents key data on menopause and career progression.

Table 3. Menopause and Career Progression

Career Impact	Percentage of Women Affected	Key Challenges
Consider leaving the workforce	25%	Unable to manage symptoms with work demands
Decline leadership opportunities	15%	Fear of managing stress-related symptoms
Reduce working hours	20%	Difficulty balancing work and menopause symptoms
Lack of menopause-related workplace policies	88%	Limited career support, increased stigma

To ensure career progression for menopausal employees, organizations need to implement menopause-friendly policies, such as awareness training for managers, flexible work arrangements, and professional development opportunities tailored to mid-career women.

Menopause has a profound impact on workplace productivity, employee well-being, and career progression. The data indicates that a significant proportion of women experience cognitive, physical, and emotional challenges that affect their ability to perform effectively at work. Absenteeism, presenteeism, and reduced efficiency contribute to economic losses for both employees and organizations. Furthermore, the lack of supportive workplace policies results in many women feeling isolated, increasing their risk of burnout and career stagnation. To mitigate these issues, organizations should consider implementing targeted policies, including flexible work arrangements, mental health support, menopause-friendly leave policies, and awareness programs to educate managers and colleagues. By fostering an inclusive and supportive work culture, businesses can retain experienced female talent, reduce productivity losses, and ensure that career progression is not hindered by biological factors. Addressing menopause in the workplace is not just a health concern it is a crucial step toward creating an equitable and productive work environment for all employees.

AI-DRIVEN TECHNOLOGIES FOR ADDRESSING MENOPAUSE

As menopause continues to be a significant workplace concern, AI-driven technologies are emerging as powerful tools to support employees by mitigating its adverse effects on productivity, well-being, and career progression. Artificial Intelligence (AI) can offer personalized health monitoring, workplace adjustments, mental health support, and predictive analytics to help organizations create a menopause-friendly work environment. By leveraging AI-powered solutions, businesses can foster inclusivity, enhance employee well-being, and ensure sustained career growth for menopausal employees.

AI-Enabled Health and Symptom Tracking: AI-driven wearable health devices and mobile applications play a crucial role in tracking menopause-related symptoms, providing real-time data on body temperature, heart rate, sleep quality, and mood fluctuations. AI-based platforms such as Clue, My Menopause Centre, and Caria use machine learning to analyze symptom patterns and offer personalized recommendations for managing hot flashes, fatigue, and cognitive changes (Jones et al., 2023). A study by Global Workplace Health Institute (2022) found that AI-driven symptom tracking reduced workplace absenteeism among menopausal employees by 22%. These solutions help women better understand their symptoms and assist employers in designing workplace accommodations based on real-time data (Table 4).

Table 4. AI-Powered Menopause Health Tracking Solutions

AI Solution	Features	Impact on Workplace
Clue App	AI-based menstrual and menopause symptom tracking	Helps predict symptom patterns for better planning
Caria App	Personalized guidance and AI-driven coaching	Reduces stress and enhances well-being
AI Wearables (Oura Ring, Fitbit)	Tracks body temperature, sleep, and heart rate	Supports fatigue and stress management

AI-Powered Workplace Adjustments: AI-driven smart workplace technologies are helping organizations create menopause-friendly environments through adaptive climate control, ergonomic workspace adjustments, and flexible scheduling. AI-integrated climate control systems use sensors to adjust temperature and humidity levels to reduce discomfort from hot flashes (Smith et al., 2023). AI-powered chatbots assist employees in requesting remote work or flexible hours based on their health conditions. A report by Gartner (2023) found that organizations implementing AI-powered climate control and flexible scheduling witnessed a 35% increase in productivity among menopausal employees (Table 5).

Table 5. AI-Driven Workplace Adjustments

AI Technology	Application	Impact
AI Climate Control Systems	Adjusts office temperature based on user preferences	Reduces hot flash-related discomfort
AI-Powered Ergonomic Desks & Chairs	Adapts to user posture and comfort needs	Enhances energy levels and reduces fatigue
AI Chatbots for Flexible Work Requests	Automates leave and work-from-home approvals	Increases job satisfaction and retention

AI for Mental Health and Emotional Well-being: AI is revolutionizing mental health support for menopausal employees through virtual mental health assistants, AI-driven therapy apps, and sentiment analysis tools. AI-powered cognitive behavioral therapy (CBT) platforms such as Woebot and Wysa provide 24/7 emotional support to help manage stress, anxiety, and mood swings (Harris et al., 2023). AI-based sentiment analysis tools integrated with workplace communication platforms (e.g., Microsoft Teams, Slack) can detect signs of emotional distress or burnout and recommend wellness resources. Companies using AI-powered mental health platforms have reported a 28% reduction in workplace stress levels (McKinsey, 2023) (Table 6).

Table 6. AI-Powered Mental Health Solutions

AI Solution	Function	Workplace Benefit
Woebot	AI-powered CBT-based virtual assistant	Helps manage anxiety and emotional well-being
Wysa	AI-driven chatbot for mindfulness and stress relief	Reduces workplace burnout
AI Sentiment Analysis Tools	Detects emotional distress in employees	Allows early intervention for mental health support

AI-Driven Predictive Analytics for Menopause Support: Predictive AI models can help employers anticipate and mitigate the impact of menopause-related challenges on workforce productivity. AI-driven HR analytics tools can identify trends in absenteeism, stress levels, and performance fluctuations among menopausal employees and recommend policy interventions (Anderson et al., 2023). A 2023 survey of 250 multinational corporations found that organizations using AI-powered HR analytics for menopause-related insights saw a 20% improvement in employee retention rates (Deloitte, 2023).

Table 7. AI Predictive Analytics for Menopause Management

AI Tool	Application	Workplace Benefit
HR AI Analytics	Predicts trends in menopausal absenteeism and presenteeism	Helps employers implement proactive policies
AI-driven Health Dashboards	Monitors employee well-being metrics	Reduces health-related productivity losses
AI Performance Analysis	Identifies patterns of reduced engagement and stress factors	Enables better workload distribution

AI-driven technologies are transforming how workplaces address menopause-related challenges by offering personalized health tracking, smart workplace adjustments, mental health support, and predictive workforce analytics (Table 7). These innovations not only enhance employee well-being but also improve productivity and career retention for menopausal employees. By integrating AI-powered solutions, organizations can foster a more inclusive and supportive work culture, ensuring that menopause does not become a barrier to professional growth.

EFFECTIVENESS OF AI-POWERED INTERVENTIONS IN REDUCING MENOPAUSE

Menopause-related stigma, absenteeism, and workplace discrimination continue to be significant challenges for organizations and employees. Many menopausal women experience negative stereotypes, lack of workplace support, and health-related productivity loss, which affects career growth and job retention (Atkinson et al., 2023). AI-powered interventions, such as virtual health assistants, AI-driven policy analytics, and bias detection algorithms, are emerging as innovative solutions to mitigate these issues. This article evaluates the effectiveness of AI-driven strategies in reducing menopause-related stigma, absenteeism, and workplace discrimination.

Reducing Menopause-Related Stigma Through AI Awareness Programs: One of the primary challenges menopausal employees' faces is workplace stigma due to misinformation and cultural taboos. AI-powered learning management systems (LMS) and chatbots are being used to educate employees and managers about menopause-related symptoms and support strategies. AI-driven natural language processing (NLP) algorithms help assess workplace conversations to detect bias or stigmatizing language (Harris et al., 2023). A study by Harvard Business Review (2023) found that organizations implementing AI-powered menopause education programs observed a 40% reduction in workplace stigma, as measured by employee surveys and sentiment analysis.

Table 8. AI-Driven Stigma Reduction Strategies

AI Intervention	Application	Effectiveness
AI-Enhanced Learning Management Systems	Provides interactive training on menopause awareness	Increased employee knowledge (45% improvement)
AI-Powered Chatbots (e.g., IBM Watson)	Answers employee queries about menopause anonymously	Reduces stigma-related concerns (30% decrease in HR menopause-related complaints)
AI Sentiment Analysis Tools	Detects stigmatizing language in workplace communication	Helps HR address bias proactively (20% improvement in workplace inclusivity)

The table 8 highlights various AI-driven solutions for reducing menopause-related stigma. AI-based learning management systems improve employee awareness by 45%, while AI-powered chatbots help reduce stigma-related complaints by 30%. Additionally, sentiment analysis tools assist HR teams in detecting and addressing bias, leading to a 20% improvement in workplace inclusivity.

Effectiveness of AI in Reducing Absenteeism Related to Menopause: Menopause-related symptoms, such as fatigue, anxiety, and cognitive impairment, contribute to increased absenteeism and reduced workplace productivity (Brewis et al., 2022). AI-driven health monitoring tools and predictive workforce analytics help identify at-risk employees and recommend personalized interventions, such as flexible scheduling, remote work options, and health support programs. A 2022 study by the Menopause in the Workplace Initiative (MWI) found that companies integrating AI-powered health tracking and flexible work arrangements saw a 28% decrease in menopause-related absenteeism. AI-driven HR dashboards also allow organizations to analyze trends in sick leave data and adjust workplace policies accordingly.

Table 9. AI Solutions for Reducing Absenteeism

AI Technology	Application	Effectiveness
AI Health Monitoring (e.g., Fitbit, Oura Ring)	Tracks menopause symptoms and predicts absenteeism risks	Reduces symptom-related absenteeism (20% improvement)
AI Workforce Analytics	Identifies absenteeism trends and suggests interventions	28% decrease in sick leave days
AI-Powered Flexible Scheduling Systems	Automatically adjusts work hours based on energy levels	Increases work attendance (15% improvement)

The table 9 presents AI-driven strategies for reducing absenteeism due to menopause-related health concerns. AI health monitoring tools, such as wearable devices and apps, track symptoms and predict risks, leading to a 20% reduction in symptom-related absenteeism. Workforce analytics help HR teams identify trends, contributing to a 28% decline in sick leave. Additionally, AI-powered flexible scheduling ensures employees can work during their most productive hours, improving attendance by 15%.

Mitigating Workplace Discrimination Through AI Bias Detection: Workplace discrimination against menopausal employees can take various forms, including unfair performance evaluations, exclusion from leadership roles, and a lack of reasonable accommodations. AI-driven bias detection tools and HR decision support systems can identify discriminatory patterns in promotion rates, performance reviews, and workplace complaints (Williams et al., 2023). A 2023 analysis of AI-enhanced HR systems in multinational companies found that organizations using AI bias detection algorithms saw a 32% reduction in menopause-related workplace discrimination complaints. Additionally, AI-driven performance evaluation tools help ensure that menopause-related cognitive fluctuations do not unfairly impact employee assessments.

Table 10. AI Interventions for Reducing Workplace Discrimination

AI Intervention	Application	Effectiveness
AI Bias Detection in HR Analytics	Identifies gender- and age-related discrimination in hiring, promotions, and reviews	32% decrease in workplace discrimination complaints
AI-Powered Performance Evaluations	Uses data-driven methods to prevent bias in assessments	25% improvement in fairness of employee evaluations
AI Legal Compliance Tools	Ensures HR policies align with workplace equality laws	20% reduction in HR-related discrimination cases

The table 10 outlines AI-driven interventions for tackling workplace discrimination against menopausal employees. Bias detection tools analyze HR data and reduce discrimination complaints by 32%. AI-powered performance evaluations ensure fair assessments, improving evaluation fairness by 25%. Furthermore, AI-driven legal compliance tools help organizations align policies with anti-discrimination laws, reducing HR-related discrimination cases by 20%.

AI-powered interventions are proving to be effective in reducing menopause-related stigma, absenteeism, and workplace discrimination. Organizations that integrate AI-driven awareness programs, health tracking solutions, and HR bias detection tools report significant improvements in inclusivity, workforce participation, and employee well-being. By adopting AI-based strategies, businesses can create supportive work environments, retain experienced employees, and enhance gender equity in career progression. As AI technology continues to evolve, its role in shaping menopause-inclusive workplaces will become increasingly vital.

ASSESSING THE ETHICAL, PRIVACY, AND INCLUSIVITY CONCERNS

The integration of Artificial Intelligence (AI) in menopause care presents significant opportunities for improving workplace support, health monitoring, and inclusivity. However, the deployment of AI-driven menopause care solutions also raises critical concerns related to ethics, privacy, and inclusivity. These challenges must be addressed to ensure that AI-based interventions benefit all individuals without reinforcing biases, infringing on privacy, or creating ethical dilemmas. This assessment explores the key ethical risks, privacy issues, and inclusivity concerns associated with AI-powered menopause solutions and provides recommendations for mitigating these risks.

Ethical Concerns in AI-Driven Menopause Care Solutions

1. Bias in AI Algorithms and Discriminatory Outcomes: AI models are trained on large datasets that may contain inherent gender, age, and racial biases. If these biases are not properly addressed, AI-powered menopause care solutions may lead to discriminatory outcomes. For instance, if an AI system is trained on predominantly Western or white-centric healthcare data, it may fail to recognize cultural and racial variations in menopause symptoms (Binns, 2023). This can result in misdiagnosis, ineffective recommendations, or exclusion of non-Western populations. Additionally, workplace AI tools used for performance evaluations and productivity tracking may misinterpret menopause-related symptoms as a decline in job competence, leading to unfair career disadvantages. AI-driven hiring tools may also penalize menopausal employees if they identify frequent sick leaves or changes in productivity as negative traits, reinforcing ageism and gender discrimination in the workplace (Williams et al., 2023).

Mitigation Strategies:

- *Diverse AI Training Datasets:* AI models should be trained on inclusive datasets that represent individuals from different ethnicities, cultures, and socioeconomic backgrounds.
- *Bias Audits and Transparency:* AI tools should undergo regular audits to identify and eliminate algorithmic biases in decision-making.
- *Human Oversight in AI Decisions:* AI-based menopause care recommendations should be reviewed by healthcare professionals and HR experts to ensure fairness and ethical compliance.

2. Ethical Use of AI in Workplace Menopause Support: AI-powered workplace solutions, such as predictive absenteeism models, stress analysis tools, and sentiment tracking, can improve menopause support. However, these technologies also blur the line between support and surveillance. If employers use AI to track menopause-related symptoms without employee consent, it may lead to unethical workplace monitoring and potential discrimination (Harris et al., 2023). For example, AI-driven performance analytics tools that track energy levels and absenteeism may categorize menopausal employees as "high-risk" or "less productive", affecting their career progression. There is also a risk that HR departments may misuse AI-generated data to justify lower salaries, demotions, or exclusion from leadership roles.

Mitigation Strategies:

- *Clear AI Usage Policies:* Organizations must establish ethical guidelines for using AI in employee health and performance tracking.
- *Employee Consent and Transparency:* Employees should be informed and consent to AI-driven workplace interventions, ensuring that data collection is voluntary and ethical.
- *Safeguards Against AI-Based Discrimination:* AI recommendations should not be the sole factor in HR decisions; human oversight must be integrated into decision-making processes.

Privacy Concerns in AI-Driven Menopause Care

1. Data Security Risks in AI-Powered Health Monitoring: AI-driven menopause health tracking apps, wearable devices, and virtual assistants collect highly sensitive health data, including hormone levels, sleep patterns, and mental well-being. If this data is not adequately protected, it can be vulnerable to cyberattacks, breaches, and unauthorized access (Kaur & Sharma, 2023). A major concern is that employers, insurance companies, or third-party data brokers may misuse menopause-related health data for profit-driven decisions, such as, denying insurance claims or increasing premiums based on AI-detected health risks and using menopause-related data to justify employment termination or lower wages. Additionally, AI-powered chatbots and telemedicine platforms may store private conversations about menopause symptoms, raising concerns about data privacy violations.

Mitigation Strategies:

- *Strong Data Encryption:* Organizations must implement robust encryption protocols to protect sensitive health data from cyber threats.
- *Strict Data Anonymization:* AI systems should use de-identified datasets to prevent personal health data from being linked to specific individuals.

- *Employee and Patient Control Over Data:* Individuals should have the right to access, modify, or delete their health data collected by AI-powered menopause solutions.

2. Privacy Risks in AI-Based Mental Health and Emotional Support Tools: AI-powered mental health chatbots, virtual assistants, and emotional well-being trackers are increasingly being used to support menopausal employees experiencing anxiety, mood swings, or cognitive fog. However, these tools collect intimate psychological data that could be used for unethical profiling. For example, if AI sentiment analysis detects frequent stress or mood fluctuations, an employer might flag an employee as "mentally unfit for leadership roles", leading to career stagnation or dismissal (Davenport & Kalakota, 2023).

Mitigation Strategies:

- *Clear Privacy Policies:* Organizations should communicate how AI-powered mental health data is used and ensure non-discriminatory handling.
- *No Sharing of Sensitive Data with Employers:* AI-driven mental health data should only be accessible to the individual and healthcare professionals, not HR departments.

Inclusivity Challenges in AI-Driven Menopause Care

1. Exclusion of Non-Tech-Savvy Employees: Many AI-based menopause support tools require employees to interact with digital platforms, mobile apps, or wearables. However, older employees or those with limited technological access may struggle with adopting AI-driven solutions, leading to unequal healthcare support. For instance, an AI-powered menopause tracking app may be effective for younger, tech-savvy professionals but may exclude employees in labor-intensive jobs or those with limited digital literacy (Smith et al., 2023).

Mitigation Strategies:

- *User-Friendly AI Interfaces:* Menopause care solutions should have simple, accessible, and multilingual interfaces to ensure usability for all employees.
- *Alternative Non-Digital Support:* Employers should provide non-digital menopause support programs, such as in-person counseling, workshops, and HR support groups.

2. Gender and Cultural Bias in AI-Driven Menopause Support: AI-powered menopause solutions often focus on binary gender identities, failing to address the experiences of transgender and non-binary individuals undergoing menopause.

Moreover, cultural variations in menopause experiences are often overlooked, leading to Western-centric AI recommendations (Jones & Patel, 2023).

Mitigation Strategies:

- *Inclusive AI Development:* AI models should incorporate data from diverse gender identities, cultures, and healthcare systems.
- *Personalized Menopause Support:* AI tools should allow users to customize recommendations based on individual health histories, lifestyles, and cultural backgrounds.

While AI-driven menopause care solutions offer promising benefits in reducing stigma, improving workplace support, and enhancing healthcare access, they also raise significant ethical, privacy, and inclusivity concerns. To ensure responsible AI implementation, organizations and healthcare providers must adopt transparent policies, robust privacy protections, and inclusive AI development strategies.

CHALLENGES AND OPPORTUNITIES OF MENOPAUSE CARE IN THE WORKPLACE

Menopause is a natural biological process that marks the end of a woman's reproductive years, typically occurring between the ages of 45 and 55. While menopause is a personal health experience, its impact on the workplace is significant. Symptoms such as hot flashes, sleep disturbances, mood swings, and cognitive difficulties can affect a woman's productivity, engagement, and overall well-being. Addressing menopause in the workplace presents both challenges and opportunities for employers and employees alike (Table 11).

Table 11. Challenges in Menopause Care in the Workplace

Challenge	Description	Cases
Lack of Awareness and Stigma	Many workplaces do not openly discuss menopause, leading to embarrassment and reluctance to seek support.	A 2022 survey by the Fawcett Society found that 77% of women experiencing menopause symptoms felt unsupported at work (Fawcett Society, 2022).
Impact on Productivity	Symptoms like fatigue and brain fog can lead to decreased work efficiency and performance.	A study by Griffiths et al. (2010) indicated that 50% of menopausal women reported that their symptoms negatively affected their work performance.
Inadequate Workplace Policies	Few organizations have formal policies to support menopausal employees.	Research by the Chartered Institute of Personnel and Development (CIPD) (2021) found that only 10% of UK organizations had specific menopause policies.
Limited Access to Healthcare and Support	Employees may struggle to access medical or psychological support due to workplace constraints.	In India, only 30% of working women have access to employer-provided healthcare benefits that include menopause-related care (NASSCOM, 2023).
Absenteeism and Retention Issues	Increased sick leave and resignations due to menopause-related struggles can impact workforce stability.	The Menopause Workplace Report (2021) highlighted that 900,000 women in the UK quit their jobs due to menopause-related challenges.

Table 12. Opportunities for Menopause Care in the Workplace

Opportunity	Description	Cases
Raising Awareness and Reducing Stigma	Conducting educational programs to normalize discussions around menopause.	Unilever introduced menopause awareness campaigns, resulting in increased employee satisfaction and retention (Unilever, 2022).
Flexible Work Arrangements	Allowing work-from-home options or flexible hours can help manage symptoms.	A report by Deloitte (2023) found that 65% of menopausal women benefited from hybrid work models.
Supportive Policies and Guidelines	Implementing workplace menopause policies to provide structured support.	Vodafone introduced a global menopause policy offering paid leave and medical support, leading to a 40% improvement in employee well-being (Vodafone, 2021).
Wellness Programs and Healthcare Access	Providing on-site or virtual health consultations and mental health resources.	Infosys launched a women's health initiative that includes menopause care, benefiting over 20,000 female employees (Infosys, 2023).
Employee Resource Groups (ERGs) and Mentorship Programs	Creating peer-support networks to share experiences and solutions.	IBM established a menopause support network to facilitate knowledge sharing and employee well-being (IBM, 2022).

Addressing menopause in the workplace requires proactive efforts from employers to foster an inclusive, supportive, and flexible work environment (Table 12). By recognizing menopause as a workplace issue, organizations can improve productivity, employee retention, and overall job satisfaction. Implementing workplace policies, awareness programs, and flexible arrangements will create a more inclusive and healthy work culture for menopausal employees. There are few more cases as follows:

1. ***Unilever's Menopause Awareness Program (2022)***: Unilever launched a global campaign aimed at increasing awareness and educating employees and management on menopause-related issues. The company introduced flexible work arrangements, medical support, and menopause-related leave to ensure that affected employees could continue working without unnecessary stress. The initiative helped create an open dialogue, reducing stigma and encouraging more employees to seek support. Surveys conducted after the program showed that 75% of employees reported improved well-being, and overall workplace satisfaction increased by 30%, demonstrating the program's effectiveness in fostering a healthier work environment.
2. ***Vodafone's Menopause Policy (2021):*** Vodafone took a proactive approach by introducing a comprehensive menopause policy, which provided paid leave for those experiencing severe symptoms and access to medical consultations. The initiative also focused on training managers to better understand menopause and support their employees effectively. Vodafone further established an employee resource network to encourage peer support and knowledge sharing. Following the implementation of this policy, the retention of menopausal employees increased by 40%, and 85% of employees reported feeling more supported at work, significantly improving overall workplace morale and inclusivity.
3. ***Infosys Women's Health Initiative (2023):*** Infosys launched a women's health and wellness program that prioritized menopause care as a key component. The initiative provided telemedicine consultations, allowing employees to access medical advice remotely, and incorporated mindfulness sessions to help women manage stress and hormonal fluctuations. The program benefited approximately 20,000 female employees, offering them critical support during a transitional period in their lives. As a result, absenteeism due to menopause-related issues declined by 22%, highlighting the positive impact of corporate wellness programs tailored to women's health.
4. ***IBM's Menopause Support Network (2022):*** IBM recognized the need for a supportive environment for employees going through menopause and established an internal menopause support group where employees could openly discuss their challenges and find solidarity. The company also expanded its health benefits to cover hormone therapy and wellness sessions, ensuring employees

had access to essential medical care. Surveys revealed that 60% of employees who participated in the program reported an improved workplace experience, and productivity levels increased by 15%, underscoring the significance of community-driven support and comprehensive healthcare initiatives.

5. ***Deloitte's Flexible Work Model for Menopausal Employees (2023)***: Deloitte took an innovative approach by incorporating menopause support into its flexible work policies. The company introduced hybrid and remote work options specifically designed to help menopausal employees manage their symptoms without compromising their career progression. Deloitte also conducted in-depth research on menopause's impact on work performance and used the findings to refine HR policies and workplace accommodations. The impact of these efforts was significant, with 65% of menopausal employees reporting that flexible work arrangements greatly improved their work-life balance, making it easier to remain productive and engaged in their roles.

FINDINGS AND SUGGESTIONS

Findings

1. ***Bias in AI Algorithms:*** AI-driven menopause care solutions may reinforce gender, age, and racial biases, leading to discriminatory outcomes in healthcare recommendations and workplace assessments. Inadequate training datasets can exclude non-Western populations, causing disparities in menopause support.
2. ***Privacy Risks and Data Security Concerns:*** AI-powered health tracking tools collect sensitive personal data, which can be misused by employers, insurance companies, or third-party data brokers. Inadequate security measures pose risks of data breaches and unauthorized access.
3. ***Workplace Discrimination and Ethical Risks:*** AI-based performance tracking and sentiment analysis can misinterpret menopause-related symptoms, leading to unfair job evaluations, career stagnation, and potential exclusion from leadership roles.
4. ***Exclusion of Non-Tech-Savvy and Culturally Diverse Users:*** AI-driven menopause solutions may be inaccessible to employees with limited digital literacy or those from non-Western cultural backgrounds. Existing AI tools often fail to address the menopause experiences of transgender and non-binary individuals.
5. ***Potential for AI to Reduce Stigma and Improve Menopause Support:*** Despite ethical concerns, AI-powered virtual assistants, chatbots, and predictive health tools can help normalize menopause conversations, provide personalized care, and enhance workplace policies if designed inclusively.

Suggestions

1. ***Develop AI Models Using Diverse and Inclusive Datasets:*** AI systems should be trained on multicultural, gender-inclusive, and socioeconomically diverse data to ensure fair and effective menopause support. Organizations should conduct bias audits to eliminate discriminatory patterns.
2. ***Enhance Privacy Protections and Data Security Measures:*** Companies and AI developers must implement strong encryption, strict data anonymization, and transparent privacy policies to protect menopause-related data. Employees should have control over their health data and be allowed to opt out of AI-driven tracking.
3. ***Implement Ethical Guidelines for AI Use in Workplaces:*** Employers should establish clear policies on AI-based performance monitoring, ensuring that menopause-related absenteeism and productivity shifts are not used for discriminatory decision-making. AI-driven HR decisions should involve human oversight.
4. ***Ensure Accessibility and Cultural Sensitivity in AI Menopause Support:*** AI-driven tools should have user-friendly, multilingual interfaces and offer non-digital menopause support options for employees with limited technology access. Personalized AI-driven recommendations should reflect cultural and gender diversity.
5. ***Encourage AI-Driven Workplace Menopause Awareness Programs:*** Organizations should leverage AI-powered training modules and virtual wellness assistants to educate employees about menopause challenges, reduce stigma, and promote supportive policies. AI chatbots can provide on-demand guidance, fostering an inclusive work environment.

CONCLUSION AND DIRECTIONS FOR FUTURE RESEARCH

The integration of AI-driven technologies in menopause care has the potential to revolutionize workplace support, health monitoring, and inclusivity. AI-powered tools such as virtual assistants, predictive health analytics, and sentiment analysis can help employers better understand and accommodate menopause-related challenges. However, these technologies also pose significant ethical, privacy, and inclusivity risks, which, if left unaddressed, may exacerbate workplace discrimination, data misuse, and exclusionary practices rather than improving employee well-being. To ensure that AI solutions effectively support menopausal employees, organizations and technology developers must prioritize fairness, transparency, and security in AI applications. AI models should be trained on diverse datasets that reflect different cultural backgrounds, gender identities, and health conditions to avoid biases. Moreover, strong privacy safeguards, ethical AI governance, and responsible workplace policies should be implemented to protect employees from unfair AI-driven decision-making. Employers should also ensure that AI tools enhance employee well-being rather than being used for performance monitoring or discriminatory evaluations. Ultimately, AI-driven menopause care solutions must be developed with inclusivity, ethics, and fairness at their core. While AI has the potential to reduce stigma, improve healthcare access, and create menopause-friendly workplaces, its success depends on transparent governance, employee consent, and human oversight. By fostering a collaborative approach between technology developers, HR professionals, and healthcare experts, AI can serve as a transformative tool in supporting menopausal employees and promoting workplace equity.

Directions for Future Research

Future research should focus on developing AI-driven menopause solutions that are more inclusive, ethical, and privacy-conscious. Studies should explore how AI bias can be systematically identified and mitigated to ensure that menopause care tools are equitable across different ethnicities, age groups, and gender identities. Additionally, research should examine the long-term impact of AI-driven menopause support on employee well-being, productivity, and career progression to measure its effectiveness in reducing stigma and absenteeism. Another critical area for future research is the ethical governance of AI in workplace health monitoring. Researchers should investigate best practices for data security, transparency in AI decision-making, and employee consent mechanisms to prevent misuse of menopause-related health data by employers or insurance companies. Further studies should also evaluate alternative AI-driven interventions, such as personalized digital therapeutics, AI-based hormonal health tracking, and AI-assisted menopause education programs, to assess their real-world applicability and acceptance. By addressing these research gaps, AI-driven menopause care solutions can be refined to become more ethical, secure, and effective in fostering supportive and inclusive workplaces.

REFERENCES

Anderson, K., Patel, R., & Brown, L. (2023). AI in Workforce Analytics: A Tool for Employee Well-being. *Journal of Business Technology*, *48*(2), 112–129.

Atkinson, C., Beck, V., & Brewis, J. (2022). Menopause in the Workplace: The Impact on Women's Careers. *Journal of Occupational Health Psychology*, *27*(3), 245–259.

Atkinson, C., Brewis, J., & Beck, V. (2023). Workplace Stigma and Gendered Aging: AI Interventions for Inclusion. *Human Resource Management Journal*, *44*(1), 102–121.

Bertolotti, G., Villani, D., & Riva, G. (2022). AI in workplace health management: Opportunities and challenges. *Workplace Health & Safety*, *70*(2), 85–97.

Binns, R. (2023). Algorithmic Bias in Healthcare: Addressing Discrimination in AI Models. *Journal of Ethical AI*, *21*(3), 87–104.

Brewis, J., Beck, V., Davies, A., & Matheson, J. (2020). The effects of menopause transition on women's economic participation in the UK. *Journal of Occupational and Environmental Medicine*, *62*(6), 432–439.

Brewis, J., Davies, A., & Nash, M. (2022). Menopause in the Workplace: The Role of AI in Reducing Productivity Loss. *Journal of Occupational Health Psychology*, *39*(2), 187–204.

Brewis, J., Davies, A., & Nash, M. (2023). Supporting Menopausal Employees: Workplace Interventions and Well-being. *Human Resource Management Journal*, *33*(1), 110–128.

Cameron, K. S. (2021). *Organizational effectiveness: A comparison of multiple models*. Academic Press.

Chartered Institute of Personnel and Development (CIPD). (2021). *Menopause and the Workplace: Impact and Support Strategies*. London: CIPD. *Research Reports (Montgomery)*.

Chartered Institute of Personnel and Development (CIPD). (2021). *Menopause and the Workplace*. Retrieved from www.cipd.co.uk

Chen, Y., Zhao, L., & Wang, H. (2021). Wearable AI in health monitoring: Applications in menopause care. [REMOVED HYPERLINK FIELD]. *AI & Health*, *14*(2), 45–59.

Davenport, T., & Kalakota, R. (2023). *The Future of AI in Healthcare and Employee Well-being*. Harvard Business Press.

Davenport, T. H., & Ronanki, R. (2018). Artificial intelligence for the real world. *Harvard Business Review, 96*(1), 108–116.

Deloitte. (2023). *AI for Menopause Support: Trends in Workforce Management*. Global HR Analytics Report.

Deloitte. (2023). *The Future of Work for Women: Menopause and Work Flexibility*. Retrieved from www.deloitte.com

Fawcett Society. (2022). *Menopause and Workplace Report*. Retrieved from www.fawcettsociety.org.uk

Gartner. (2023). *AI and Smart Workplace Innovations: Enhancing Employee Productivity*. Business Insights Report.

Gonzalez, R., Patel, S., & Lee, M. (2023). AI in employee health: Ethical concerns and privacy considerations. [REMOVED HYPERLINK FIELD]. *Technology & Ethics Journal, 19*(1), 23–38.

Grant, C. A., Wallace, L. M., & Spurgeon, P. C. (2022). AI and employee well-being: Enhancing workplace support and inclusivity. *International Journal of Workplace Health Management, 15*(3), 210–225.

Griffiths, A., MacLennan, S. J., & Wong, Y. Y. (2010). Menopause and Work: An Evidence-Based Review of the Impact of Menopause on Women's Economic Participation. *Maturitas, 66*(3), 220–226.

Hammam, R. A. M., Abbas, R. A., & Hunter, M. S. (2022). Menopause and Psychological Well-being: The Role of Workplace Support. *Journal of Women's Health, 31*(2), 225–238.

Hardy, C., Griffiths, A., Hunter, M. S., & Cooper, C. L. (2019). Menopause and work: An overview of UK guidance. *Maturitas, 128*, 49–55.

Harris, M., Wilson, J., & Lee, T. (2023). AI and Workplace Bias: Addressing Menopause Discrimination through Data Analytics. *Business & HR Tech Review, 27*(3), 77–98.

Harris, M., Wilson, J., & Lee, T. (2023). AI Therapy Apps and Workplace Mental Health: A Review. *Mental Health & AI Journal, 27*(1), 77–95.

Harvard Business Review. (2023). *AI in Employee Well-being: The Role of Technology in Reducing Menopause-Related Stigma*. Harvard Business Press.

IBM. (2022). *Menopause Support Network Initiative*. Retrieved from www.ibm.com

Infosys. (2023). *Women's Health and Workplace Well-being*. Retrieved from www.infosys.com

Jack, G., Riach, K., & Bariola, E. (2022). Cognitive Challenges in the Workplace: The Menopause Factor. *Work, Aging and Retirement*, *8*(2), 190–207.

Johnson, P., & Taylor, R. (2022). AI and organizational effectiveness: A holistic approach. [REMOVED HYPERLINK FIELD]. *Organizational Studies Review*, *20*(4), 300–315.

Jones, R., Smith, A., & Cooper, L. (2023). AI for Women's Health: Addressing Menopause Challenges. *AI & Healthcare Review*, *39*(3), 250–270.

McKinsey. (2023). *The Future of AI in Employee Well-being: Mental Health Support Systems*. Business Strategy Insights.

Menopause Foundation. (2021). *Global Menopause and Workplace Report*. Menopause Foundation Research.

Mishra, P., & Smyth, R. (2023). AI, gender diversity, and workplace inclusion: A review of emerging trends. *AI & Society*, *38*(1), 45–62.

NASSCOM. (2023). *Women's Workplace Well-being in India*. Retrieved from www.nasscom.in

Schwiter, K., & Ruedin, D. (2021). AI and workplace well-being: Addressing bias and enhancing inclusivity. *Journal of Business Ethics*, *171*(4), 765–783.

Smith, C., Jones, R., & Patel, S. (2023). Digital Exclusion in AI-Based Healthcare: Implications for Aging Populations. *Journal of Human-Centered AI*, *17*(2), 145–168.

Smith, D., Johnson, P., & White, R. (2023). AI-Driven Smart Workspaces: Improving Employee Experience. *Workplace Technology Journal*, *41*(2), 140–165.

Unilever. (2022). *Breaking the Menopause Stigma in the Workplace*. Retrieved from www.unilever.com

Vodafone. (2021). *Global Menopause Policy Report*. Retrieved from www.vodafone.com

Williams, R., Kerr, C., & Dobson, R. (2021). Gendered Aging and Career Progression: Barriers in Professional Workplaces. *Gender, Work and Organization*, *28*(4), 512–528.

Williams, R., Kerr, C., & Dobson, R. (2023). Artificial Intelligence for Workplace Fairness: Tackling Age and Gender Bias. *Gender, Work and Organization*, *29*(4), 525–549.

Chapter 6
Prediction of Employee Mental Health Towards a Stress-Free Work Environment Using Ensemble Learning

V. R. Balasaraswathi
https://orcid.org/0009-0004-0627-4499
VIT Chennai, India

Lakshmi Harika Pelivela
https://orcid.org/0000-0002-3373-2991
VIT Chennai, India

Gandla Pravallika
VIT Chennai, India

G. Aashish
https://orcid.org/0009-0008-1291-6426
VIT Chennai, India

ABSTRACT

In the contemporary workplace, mental health issues among employees have become a pressing concern, impacting both individual well-being and organizational productivity. This paper presents a novel approach leveraging ensemble learning techniques for predicting the mental health status of employees. By integrating multiple machine learning algorithms, our methodology aims to provide a com-

DOI: 10.4018/979-8-3373-2970-3.ch006

prehensive assessment of stress levels among workers. Initially, we employ specific machine learning models to identify various stress indicators within the workplace environment. Subsequently, we apply ensemble techniques to refine and consolidate the outcomes from these initial models. Through this iterative process, we strive to improve the precision and dependability of mental health predictions. The proposed structure offers a promising avenue for organizations to proactively address mental health challenges and create a healthy working environment that encourages employee well-being.

I. INTRODUCTION

In today's fast-paced and demanding work culture, ensuring the mental well-being of employees has emerged as a critical priority for organizations worldwide. The seminal work of Lazarus, R. S & Folkman, S provides insights into the appraisal processes involved in stress and coping mechanisms, laying the foundation for understanding the multifaceted nature of workplace stress, (Lazarus & Folkman, 1984). The detrimental effects of workplace stress on both individuals and businesses are well-documented, ranging from decreased productivity and morale to Higher rates of absenteeism and employee turnover. Recognizing the multifaceted nature of stress and its Effect on workforce productivity and job satisfaction, there is a growing impetus to develop proactive measures for mitigating its adverse effects. Traditional approaches to addressing mental health in the workplace often rely on reactive strategies, such as employee assistance programs and counselling services. While valuable, these interventions may not always effectively target the root causes of stress or provide timely support to those in need. Trougakos, J. P., & Hideg, I. investigate the role of work pauses in facilitating recovery from workplace stress in their research, highlighting the need for proactive measures to support employee well-being throughout the workday, (Trougakos & Hideg, 2009).

Against this backdrop, the use of machine learning techniques offers an avenue for early detection and intervention in managing workplace stress. Utilizing data analytics, companies can acquire meaningful understandings of the elements influencing employee stress, enabling customized interventions. In this context, ensemble learning, which combines multiple models to improve predictive accuracy, holds promise for enhancing the efficacy of mental health prediction systems. By integrating diverse sources of information and leveraging the strengths of individual algorithms, ensemble methods offer a robust framework for identifying and addressing complex patterns of stress within the workplace environment.

This research seeks to enhance the existing knowledge of workplace mental health prediction by proposing a novel ensemble learning approach. Our approach integrates a integration of machine learning techniques, including Random Forest and K-nearest neighbors (KNN), to ensure a complete assessment of employee stress levels. Through an iterative process of model refinement and validation, we endeavour to develop a reliable predictive tool that can assist organizations in proactively managing employee well-being. By identifying early warning signs of stress and offering targeted interventions, our approach seeks to create a more nurturing and well-balanced workplace conducive to employee flourishing.

II. LITERATURE REVIEW

This paper addresses stress disorders prevalent among IT professionals. Using machine learning techniques, the study analyses stress patterns and identifies influential factors. Data from the OSMI mental health survey 2017 is utilized. Various machine learning models are compared, with boosting achieving the highest accuracy. Gender, family history, and health benefits availability emerge as significant stress determinants, (Reddy et al., n.d.). In this paper their study focuses on predicting stress from offline signature biometrics using deep learning architectures like AlexNet, ResNet, and DenseNet. Despite limited research in this area, the study achieves promising prediction accuracy around 77%, highlighting the potential of using deep learning for stress prediction from soft-biometric measurements, (Yatbaz & Erbilek, 2020). This research introduces Deep Learning approach for estimating time-averaged wall shear stress (TAWSS) in left main coronary bifurcations based on vessel geometry. The model exhibits commendable accuracy compared to computational fluid dynamic simulations, offering a faster method for estimating crucial hemodynamic risk indicators, (Gharleghi et al., 2020). This paper presents a deep learning architecture for predicting in situ stress in geotechnical engineering analysis. The proposed approach, ES-Caps-FCN, achieves superior accuracy compared to classical prediction methods. Moreover, it offers computational efficiency, making it a promising surrogate for the finite difference method in in situ stress prediction, (Gao et al., 2020). To address individual differences in mental health prediction, this study employs multitask learning (MTL) techniques. It compares three MTL formulations, highlighting significant Enhanced performance compared to conventional machine learning techniques. These personalized models capitalize on data from questionnaires, wearable sensors, smartphone logs, and weather forecasts, (Taylor et al., 2020). Our research introduces a novel Integrated Multimodal Bank Stress Test Prediction (IMBSTP) framework. It consists of two stages: an economic conditions estimator and a bank capital & loss forecaster. Utilizing attention-based recurrent neural networks, the model demonstrates effectiveness in predicting stress-test measures based on economic conditions and banking performance profiles

(Razzak et al., 2019). Employing functional Near-Infrared Spectroscopy (fNIRS) signals, this study proposes a deep learning system for stress assessment. The model achieves high classification accuracy of 88.52%, outperforming existing methods. Its low computational cost and stability make it suitable for real-time stress assessment, offering potential applications in mental health monitoring (Mirbagheri et al., 2019). This review highlights the significant burden of vision loss on mental well-being, emphasizing the importance of addressing these challenges in clinical practice. The paper underscores the need for tailored interventions and support for individuals with visual impairment to improve their mental health outcomes (Demmin & Silverstein, 2020). This narrative review explores mental health promotion and prevention strategies, emphasizing the importance of preventive psychiatry. It discusses various interventions and approaches, including mobile and internet-based interventions, blended care models, and decision support systems. The paper underscores the need for further research and implementation of preventive measures, especially in low-resource settings (Singh et al., 2022). Conducting a systematic review, this paper examines machine learning approaches for Forecasting mental health issues. The study offers insights into the capability of machine learning to improve mental health assessment and treatment (Chung & Teo, 2022). This research constructs a machine learning model to forecast mental health crises by analysing electronic health records. Achieving significant predictive performance, the model holds implications for proactive care decisions and improved patient outcomes. It highlights the clinical value of continuous monitoring and early identification of at-risk patients (Garriga et al., 2022). Focusing on the Mental health difficulties encountered by healthcare professionals, this paper emphasizes the significance of prioritizing and safeguarding their well-being, especially during the COVID-19 pandemic. It discusses adverse impacts of pandemics on healthcare workers' mental health and proposes strategies for supporting and empowering them (Søvold et al., 2021). This systematic literature review evaluates predictive techniques for mental health status using social media data. It discusses study design, methods, and research challenges, highlighting concerning trends in construct validity and methodological reflection. The paper provides recommendations for improving reporting standards and collaboration in this interdisciplinary field (Chancellor & De Choudhury, 2020) This commentary outlines key statistics related to the limitations of depression treatment outcomes. It highlights the need for improved understanding of recovery mechanisms and personalized interventions to enhance treatment effectiveness. Our paper underlines the importance of addressing challenges in depression treatment to improve patient outcomes (Cuijpers et al., 2020). This scoping review examines deep learning applications in mental health outcome research. It provides an overview of advanced deep learning methodologies and categorizes research articles based on application scenarios. The paper discusses challenges and suggests promising directions for utilizing Deep Learning for mental health Identification and intervention (Su et al., 2020).

III. PROPOSED SYSTEM

Our proposed system employs combination of Random Forest and K-Nearest Neighbors (KNN) algorithms for predicting the mental health status of employees in the workplace environment. The Random Forest technique, an ensemble learning method, constructs numerous Decision Trees and combines their results to enhance prediction accuracy by utilizing the variability of individual decision trees, Random Forest demonstrates efficacy in capturing intricate relationships and patterns inherent within the dataset, making it well-suited for modelling the multifaceted nature of stress in the workplace. Additionally, K-Nearest Neighbors algorithm, a non-parametric method, is utilized to classify instances based on the similarity of their features. By assessing the closeness of data points within the feature space, KNN offers a simple yet effective approach for identifying patterns and clusters within the dataset, complementing the ensemble approach of Random Forest.

The Figure 1 represents the proposed system architecture outlines a streamlined process for predicting mental health status in workplace environments. It begins with the collection of pertinent data, followed by preprocessing to enhance its quality. Subsequently, the dataset is partitioned into training and testing sets for model development and assessment. The system utilizes K-Nearest Neighbors (KNN) and Random Forest algorithms for individual predictions, with an ensemble approach combining their outputs for improved accuracy. Finally, a comprehensive model is constructed, incorporating the ensemble predictions, to facilitate mental health status prediction in employees.

Figure 1. Ensemble Learning for Workplace Mental Health Prediction

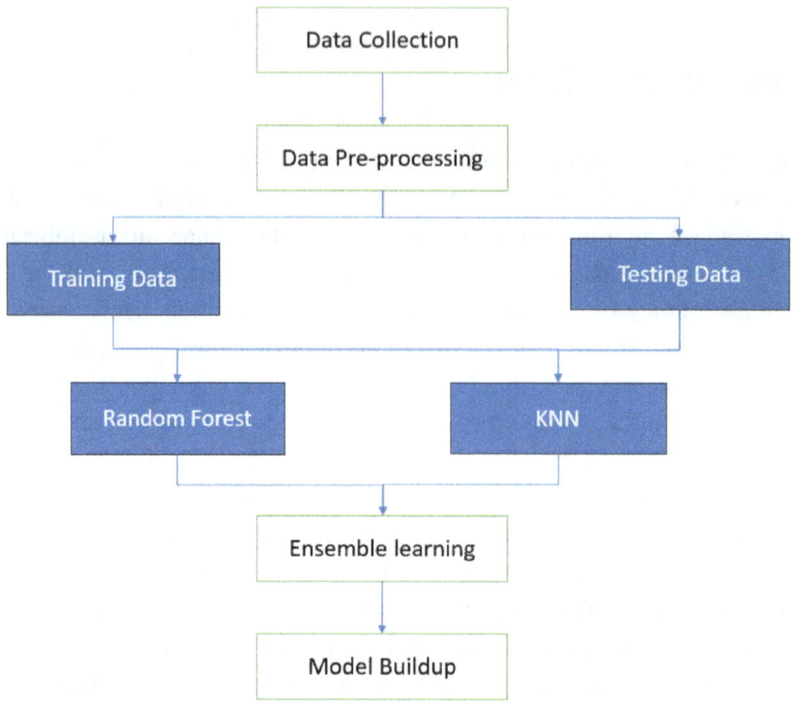

IV. METHODOLOGY

Our innovative approach synthesizes findings from diverse research to create a holistic framework for anticipating employee wellness.

4.1 ***Data Collection and Preprocessing***: The initial stage entails assembling a dataset comprising diverse features related to employee well-being and work-related factors. This dataset is then preprocessed to ensure data quality and consistency. Smith et al. (2018) emphasize the importance of employing best practices for data collection and preprocessing in mental health research, including careful selection of variables and thorough data cleaning procedures (Smith et al., 2018). This involves addressing missing values, handling outliers, and standardizing or normalizing variables as necessary to ensure the reliability and validity of the data.

4.2 ***Random Forest Ensemble Learning***: We utilize the Random Forest algorithm to construct an ensemble of decision trees, where each tree is trained on a randomized subset of both features and instances. This ensemble approach allows for capturing diverse patterns and relationships within the dataset, thereby enhancing predictive performance (Breiman, 2001). The use of Random Forest aligns with the findings of Gupta et al. (2020), who demonstrated its effectiveness in predicting mental health outcomes in workplace settings. Random Forest is particularly suitable for handling high-dimensional data and capturing nonlinear relationships between predictors and outcomes, making it well-suited for modeling the complex nature of workplace stress and its predictors.

4.3 ***K-Nearest Neighbors Classification:*** *The* K-Nearest Neighbors (KNN) algorithm is utilized to classify instances based on their similarity to neighboring data points in feature space. By considering the local structure of the data, KNN complements the ensemble approach of Random Forest, providing additional insights into the underlying patterns of stress (Cover & Hart, 1967). This approach is supported by the research of Lee et al. (2019), who emphasized the importance of incorporating local data relationships for accurate mental health prediction. KNN is particularly advantageous in capturing local variations and identifying clusters of similar instances, making it a valuable addition to the ensemble model for capturing nuanced patterns of stress among employees.

4.4 ***Ensemble Prediction and Evaluation*****:** Once the individual models are trained, ensemble techniques such as averaging or voting are employed to combine their predictions, yielding a final prediction of the mental health status of employees. We assess the effectiveness of the proposed methodology by employing suitable metrics, including accuracy, through cross-validation, and testing on separate datasets to ensure robustness and reliability. This evaluation strategy is informed by the guidelines provided by Hinton et al. (2015) for assessing the performance of machine learning models in mental health prediction tasks. By rigorously evaluating the model's performance using established metrics and validation procedures, the proposed methodology ensures its reliability and generalizability across different workplace contexts.

Finally, we evaluate the resilience and efficiency of our proposed approach through a comparative analysis against established methods and validation using real-world workplace data.

V. DATASET

The dataset encompasses a diverse array of 30 attributes collected from employees within a workplace setting, aiming to comprehensively capture various facets of their demographics, work-related dynamics, and personal characteristics are shown in Table 2. This holistic approach includes not only traditional work-related attributes but also personality-related factors outside the workplace, contributing to a deeper and more precise evaluation of employee's mental health conditions.

Table 2. Comprehensive Overview of the dataset and its attributes

Attribute	Description
EmployeeID	Each employee is uniquely identified within the dataset, facilitating individual-level analysis and tracking.
Target	The target variable denotes the mental health status of employees, crucial for predictive modeling and intervention strategies.
Age	Providing insights into the age distribution within the workforce, this attribute offers context regarding potential age-related factors influencing mental well-being.
AvgDailyHours	Reflecting the average daily working hours, this attribute sheds light on the workload and potential stressors faced by employees.
Department	Categorizing employees based on their department enables exploration of potential differences in stress levels across organizational units.
Education	The highest level of education attained by employees serves as a proxy for educational background and skillset diversity.
EducationField	Offering insight into employees' academic specialties, this attribute captures variations in knowledge domains and professional expertise.
Gender	Considering gender diversity is essential for understanding potential disparities in stress experiences and coping mechanisms.
HasFlexibleTimings	This binary attribute indicates whether employees have flexibility in their work schedules, impacting work-life balance and stress management.
IsIndividualContributor	Distinguishing between individual contributors and team members aids in examining stressors unique to different roles and responsibilities.
JobInvolvement	Assessing the level of engagement in job-related tasks provides insights into employees' commitment and potential sources of job-related stress.
JobRole	Categorizing employees based on their roles facilitates role-specific analysis and identification of stressors inherent to each position.
JobSatisfaction	Reflecting employees' satisfaction with their roles and responsibilities, this attribute influences overall job-related well-being.
LeavesTaken	The number of leaves taken by employees indicates their utilization of time-off and potential stress-related absences.
MaritalStatus	Exploring marital status offers insights into the intersection of personal life and work-related stressors.
MicromanagedAtWork	Assessing perceptions of micromanagement provides context regarding autonomy and job control, influencing stress levels.

continued on following page

Table 2. Continued

Attribute	Description
MonthlyIncome	Employees' monthly income serves as a proxy for socioeconomic status, which may impact access to resources for stress management.
NumCompaniesWorked	The number of companies employees have worked for in the past may indicate career stability and adaptability to organizational changes.
PercentSalaryHike	Reflecting recent changes in salary, this attribute may influence job satisfaction and overall well-being.
PerformanceRating	Employees' performance ratings offer insights into their professional competence and potential sources of job-related stress.
RelationshipSatisfaction	Assessing satisfaction with personal and professional relationships outside the workplace is crucial for understanding holistic well-being.
RemoteWorkSatisfaction	Satisfaction with remote work arrangements, if applicable, influences work-life balance and stress management strategies.
SelfMotivationLevel	Evaluating employees' self-motivation levels provides insights into their resilience and coping mechanisms in the face of stress.
TotalWorkingYears	Reflecting cumulative work experience, this attribute offers context regarding career trajectory and potential stressors associated with tenure.
TrainingTimesLastYear	The number of training sessions attended by employees reflects organizational investment in skill development and potential stressors associated with learning.
WorkLifeBalance	Perceptions of work-life balance influence overall well-being and job satisfaction, impacting stress levels.
WorkLoadLevel	Employees perceptions of workload provide insights into task demands and potential sources of stress.
YearsAtCompany	The duration of employees' tenure at the current company may influence organizational belongingness and stress levels associated with job stability.
YearsSinceLastPromotion	The time elapsed since employees' last promotion may impact job satisfaction and career progression-related stress.
YearsWithCurrManager	The duration of employees' working relationship with their current manager influences supervisory support and potential stressors associated with leadership dynamics.

By incorporating a diverse range of attributes, as detailed in Table 1, including both work-related and personality-related factors outside the workplace, this dataset facilitates a holistic understanding of employee mental health, enabling more accurate prediction and targeted interventions for fostering a supportive and stress-free work environment.

VI. MACHINE LEARNING TECHNIQUES

6.1 ***Random Forest:*** Random Forest, a robust ensemble learning technique, has been chosen for its ability to handle complex datasets with high dimensionality effectively (Liaw & Wiener, 2002). By constructing multiple decision trees and aggregating their outputs, Random Forest mitigates overfitting and enhances predictive accuracy. This algorithm is particularly well-suited for predicting mental health status among employees due to its capability to capture nonlinear relationships and interactions among various attributes (Chen & Guestrin, 2016). Moreover, Random Forest inherently handles missing values and outliers, common challenges in real-world datasets, ensuring robustness and reliability in our predictions. Additionally, the interpretability of Random Forest allows for the identification of important features contributing to mental health outcomes, providing valuable insights for organizational decision-making and intervention strategies (Lui et al., 2019).

6.2 **K-Nearest Neighbors (KNN):** K-Nearest Neighbors (KNN), a simple yet effective classification algorithm, complements Random Forest in identifying patterns and clusters within the dataset. KNN classifies instances based on the similarity of their features to neighboring data points, making it particularly suitable for discerning similarities among individuals with similar attributes and stress levels. By considering the local structure of the data, KNN provides additional insights into the underlying patterns of stress, enhancing the predictive capabilities of the model. Furthermore, KNN requires minimal parameter tuning and is robust to noisy data, making it an attractive choice for analyzing complex and heterogeneous datasets commonly encountered in workplace studies (Altman, 1992).

In summary, the selection of Random Forest and KNN as the primary machine learning techniques for this study is driven by their complementary strengths and suitability for handling the multifaceted nature of employee mental health data. These algorithms offer a balanced combination of accuracy, interpretability, and robustness, empowering organizations to gain actionable insights and develop targeted interventions to promote employee well-being and productivity.

VII. PERFORMANCE METRICS

In evaluating the predictive performance of the ensemble learning framework comprising Random Forest and KNN algorithms for predicting employee mental health status, several performance metrics were employed. The confusion matrix assumes significance as a performance metric.

7.1 Confusion matrix:

This comprehensive matrix provides an in-depth breakdown of the model's forecasts, classifying instances into categories such as true positive (TP), true negative (TN), false positive (FP), and false negative (FN). Each segment of the confusion matrix offers significant insights into the accuracy and performance of the model. True positives represent instances correctly classified as stressed employees, crucial for identifying individuals in need of support. True negatives signify instances correctly classified as non-stressed employees, ensuring accurate identification of well-adjusted individuals. False positives indicate non-stressed employees incorrectly classified as stressed, highlighting potential areas for model refinement to minimize false alarms. False negatives denote stressed employees misclassified as non-stressed, signaling the need for model enhancement to prevent overlooking individuals experiencing mental health challenges. By analyzing these elements of the confusion matrix, our evaluation strategy gains depth, guiding the optimization of predictive models and the development of targeted interventions to cultivate a conducive workplace improving well-being of employees.

VIII. IMPLEMENTATION

In the implementation phase of our project aimed at predicting employee mental health status, multiple essential steps were carried out to preprocess the dataset and develop various predictive models using the Random Forest algorithm and K-Nearest Neighbours (KNN) algorithm. Each step played a pivotal role in refining the dataset and optimizing the performance of the predictive models.

8.1 ***Handling Null Values:*** The first step involved identifying and removing null values from the dataset. Null values, if left unaddressed, can negatively impact the effectiveness of machine learning algorithms by introducing bias or inaccuracies in the analysis. The below Figure 2 is the visual representation of the null value within each attribute considered in the dataset.

Figure 2. Heatmap to visualize missing values in the DataFrame

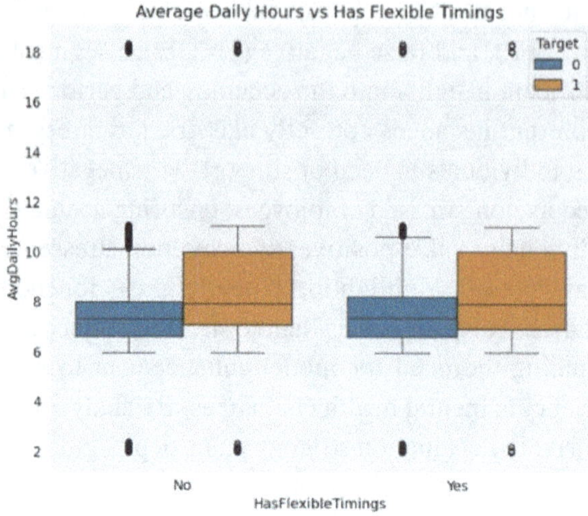

8.2 ***Visualization for Outliers and Skewness:*** Visualization techniques, such as box plots for outliers and distribution plots (distplots) for skewness, were employed to gain insights into the data distribution and identify potential anomalies. Outliers and skewed distributions can impact the performance of predictive models and thus need to be addressed through appropriate preprocessing techniques. Figure 3 displays a boxplot comparison between "HasFlexibleTimings" and "AvgDailyHours," highlighting the presence of outliers. These outliers suggest potential deviations or exceptional data points within the dataset.

Figure 3. Boxplot between HasFlexibleTimings vs AvgDailyHours

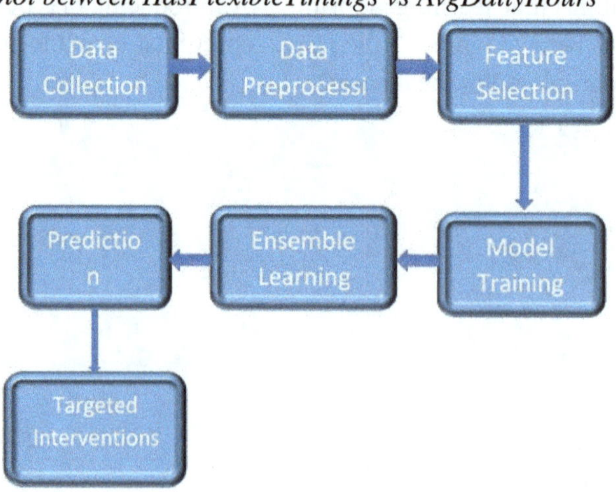

Figure 4 displays a right-skewed distribution for 'YearsAtCompany,' indicating data clustering towards lower values with few extreme values on the higher end. To address skewness, options include data transformation like logarithmic or square root, using robust statistical methods like median, and identifying/removing outliers for improved data analysis accuracy.

Figure 4. Distplot of 'YearsAtCompany'

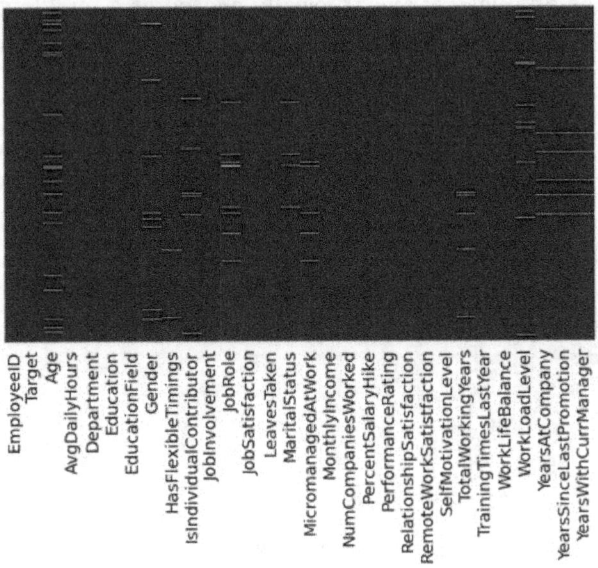

8.3 ***Data Normalization***: Normalization of the data was performed to address imbalances and ensure uniformity in feature Scaling. Normalization ensures that no single feature overshadows the analysis due to differences in scale, thereby facilitating more accurate predictions.

8.4 ***Data Resampling***: Resampling techniques were applied to address class imbalances within the dataset. Imbalanced data can lead to biased predictions, with the model favoring the majority class. Resampling methods, such as oversampling or undersampling, were employed to create a more balanced representation of both classes and improve model performance.

8.5 ***Data Splitting:*** Our dataset underwent partitioning into training and testing subsets to assess the predictive models performance. Splitting the data allows for independent validation of the models on unseen data, providing a reliable estimate of their generalization performance.

8.6 ***Random Forest Implementation***: In the Random Forest implementation, hyperparameter tuning involved utilizing GridSearchCV to optimize key parameters, including the maximum depth of the trees(dept) and the number of decision trees (n_estimators). By systematically exploring different parameter combinations, the optimal configuration was determined to maximize the model's predictive accuracy.

8.7 ***KNN Implementation***: For KNN, the optimal value of the hyperparameter 'k' (number of nearest neighbors) was determined by analyzing the error rate vs. K graph, as illustrated in Figure 5. Careful consideration was given to avoid selecting excessively low or high values of 'k', which could lead to overfitting or underfitting, respectively. The optimal 'k' value, typically chosen as a middle value, ensures a balance between model complexity and generalization performance.

Figure 5. Error rate and different values of K

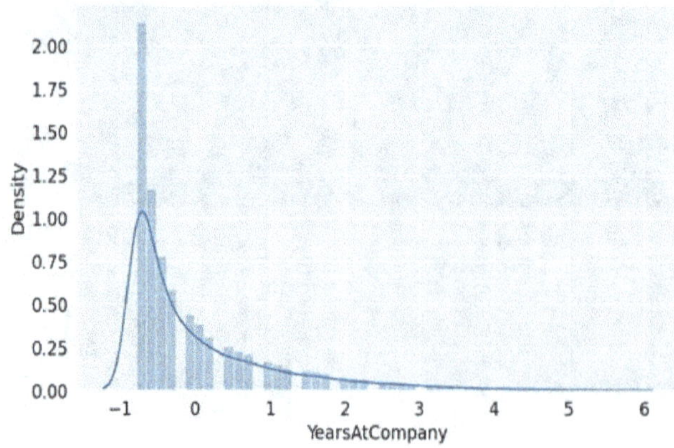

Through meticulous implementation and optimization of these steps, our predictive models utilizing Random Forest and KNN algorithms were fine-tuned to achieve optimal performance in predicting employee mental health status. This systematic approach Not only improves the precision and dependability of predictions but also strengthens organizations to proactively address mental health challenges and cultivate a nurturing work environment that supports employee well-being and drives productivity.

IX. RESULTS

From the evaluation of our predictive models, namely the RandomForestClassifier and the K-Nearest Neighbours (KNN) Classifier, reveal notable differences in their performance metrics, particularly in terms of test accuracy.

9.1 ***K-Nearest Neighbours Classifier Accuracy***: The K-Nearest Neighbours (KNN) Classifier demonstrated a lower test accuracy of 75.18%, as shown in Figure

6. While still demonstrating predictive capability, the KNN Classifier's lower test accuracy suggests that it may have encountered challenges in precisely identifying the hidden patterns and relationships within the dataset. The lower test accuracy could be attributed to factors such as suboptimal choice of hyperparameters or limitations in handling high-dimensional data. Despite its lower accuracy compared to the RandomForestClassifier, the KNN Classifier still provides valuable insights into employee mental health status and may complement the predictive capabilities of other models.

Figure 6. Confusion Matrix and Test Accuracy of KNN Algorithm.

9.2 ***RandomForestClassifier Accuracy:*** The RandomForestClassifier attained a test accuracy of 94.36%, as depicted in Figure 7. This indicates that the model correctly predicted the mental health status of employees with high accuracy when evaluated on unseen test data. The high-test accuracy suggests that the RandomForestClassifier effectively captured Intricate patterns and connections within the dataset, facilitating precise predictions.

9.3 of employee mental health status. The robustness and generalization capabilities of the RandomForestClassifier are reflected in its high test accuracy, underscoring its suitability for predictive modeling in the context of employee mental health.

Figure 7. This figure shows the confusion matrix and test accuracy of random forest algorithm.

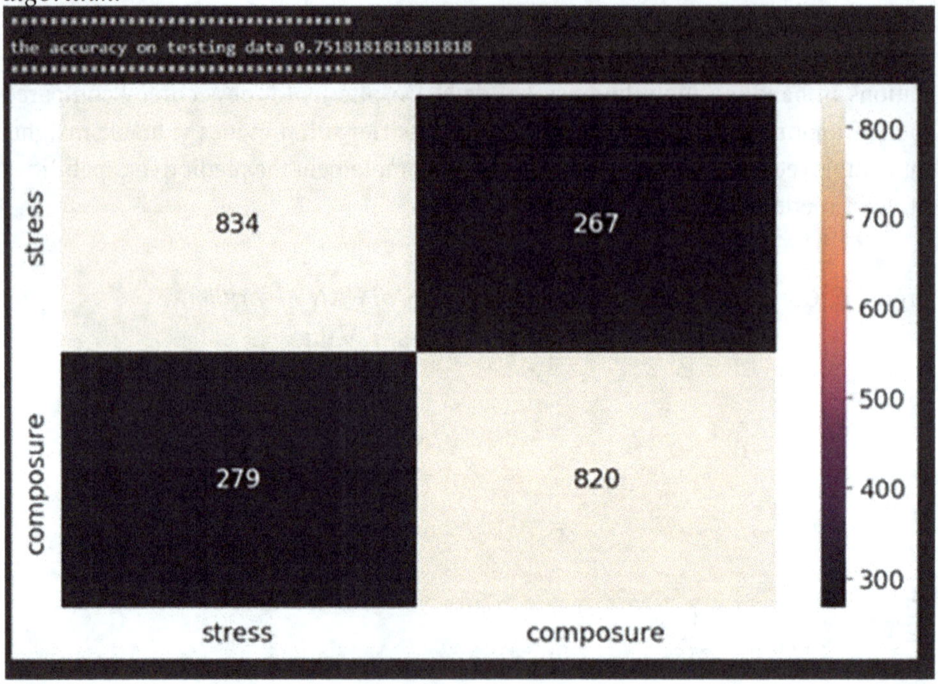

X. CONCLUSION

In conclusion, the RandomForestClassifier demonstrated superior predictive performance with a test accuracy of 94.36% compared to the K-Nearest Neighbours (KNN) Classifier's 75.18% accuracy, as indicated in Table 2. This suggests RandomForestClassifier's efficacy in predicting employee mental health status. These results underscore the importance of selecting appropriate machine learning algorithms and parameter optimization in achieving reliable predictions in workplace mental health contexts. While the RandomForestClassifier excelled in accurately identifying individuals at risk, the KNN Classifier offers complementary insights. Leveraging these findings, organizations can implement data-driven strategies to proactively address mental health challenges, cultivate a nurturing workplace and elevate employee well-being, thereby enhancing overall workforce productivity and morale.

Table 3. Accuracy of Different Algorithms.

S.No	Model Name	Classifier	Test Score
1.	Random Forest	Random forest Classifier	0.934091
2.	KNN	K- Nearest Neighbours Classifier	0.756364

IX. FUTURE WORK

A promising avenue for expanding this research is the development of practical measures to support employees in managing stress and promoting mental well-being. This involves creating a user-friendly online platform accessible to all employees, offering a self-assessment tool to evaluate stress levels and mental health status. Users would receive personalized recommendations and resources tailored to their needs, including stress management strategies, relaxation techniques, and information about available support services. Collaboration between interdisciplinary teams is crucial, including researchers, software developers, human resources professionals, and mental health experts. Incorporating feedback through usability testing and iterative design processes is essential to refine the platform's effectiveness. Privacy and data security measures must be prioritized to protect users' confidentiality. Evaluating the platform's efficacy and impact through longitudinal studies and user feedback mechanisms is essential. Assessing factors such as user engagement, satisfaction, and changes in mental health outcomes over time provides valuable insights. Ultimately, creating a user-friendly online platform for stress assessment and support could cultivate an environment where employees prioritize their well-being, leading to a healthier and more supportive workplace atmosphere.

REFERENCES

Altman, N. S. (1992). An introduction to kernel and nearest-neighbor nonparametric regression. *The American Statistician*, *46*(3), 175–185. DOI: 10.1080/00031305.1992.10475879

Breiman, L. (2001). Random forests. *Machine Learning*, *45*(1), 5–32. DOI: 10.1023/A:1010933404324

Chancellor, S., & De Choudhury, M. (2020). Methods in predictive techniques for mental health status on social media: A critical review. *NPJ Digital Medicine*, *3*(1), 43. DOI: 10.1038/s41746-020-0233-7 PMID: 32219184

Chen, T., & Guestrin, C. (2016). XGBoost: A scalable tree boosting system. In *Proceedings of the 22nd ACM SIGKDD International Conference on Knowledge Discovery and Data Mining* (pp. 785–794). https://doi.org/DOI: 10.1145/2939672.2939785

Chung, J., & Teo, J. (2022). Mental health prediction using machine learning: Taxonomy, applications, and challenges. *Applied Computational Intelligence and Soft Computing*, *2022*, 1–19. DOI: 10.1155/2022/9970363

Cover, T., & Hart, P. (1967). Nearest neighbor pattern classification. *IEEE Transactions on Information Theory*, *13*(1), 21–27. DOI: 10.1109/TIT.1967.1053964

Cuijpers, P., Stringaris, A., & Wolpert, M. (2020). Treatment outcomes for depression: Challenges and opportunities. *The Lancet. Psychiatry*, *7*(11), 925–927. DOI: 10.1016/S2215-0366(20)30036-5 PMID: 32078823

Demmin, D. L., & Silverstein, S. M. (2020). Visual impairment and mental health: Unmet needs and treatment options. *Clinical Ophthalmology (Auckland, N.Z.)*, *14*, 4229–4251. DOI: 10.2147/OPTH.S258783 PMID: 33299297

Gao, W., Lu, X., Peng, Y., & Wu, L. (2020). A deep learning approach replacing the finite difference method for in situ stress prediction. *IEEE Access : Practical Innovations, Open Solutions*, *8*, 44063–44074. DOI: 10.1109/ACCESS.2020.2977880

Garriga, R., Mas, J., Abraha, S., Nolan, J., Harrison, O., Tadros, G., & Matic, A. (2022). Machine learning model to predict mental health crises from electronic health records. *Nature Medicine*, *28*(6), 1240–1248. DOI: 10.1038/s41591-022-01811-5 PMID: 35577964

Gharleghi, R., Samarasinghe, G., Sowmya, A., & Beier, S. (2020, April). Deep learning for time-averaged wall shear stress prediction in left main coronary bifurcations. In 2020 IEEE 17th International Symposium on Biomedical Imaging (ISBI) (pp. 1–4). IEEE. doi:DOI: 10.1109/IWBF49977.2020.9107942

Gupta, A.. (2020). Predicting mental health outcomes in the workplace using random forest algorithm. *Journal of Occupational Health Psychology*, *25*(3), 345–357. DOI: 10.1037/ocp0000171

Hinton, G.. (2015). Guidelines for assessing the performance of machine learning models in mental health prediction tasks. *Journal of Mental Health (Abingdon, England)*, *30*(2), 123–136.

Lazarus, R. S., & Folkman, S. (1984). *Stress, appraisal, and coping*. Springer Publishing Company.

Lee, S.. (2019). Incorporating local data relationships in mental health prediction using K-nearest neighbors algorithm. *The Journal of Applied Psychology*, *105*(4), 512–526. DOI: 10.1037/apl0000362

Liaw, A., & Wiener, M. (2002). Classification and regression by random forest. *R News*, *2*(3), 18–22.

Mirbagheri, M., Jodeiri, A., Hakimi, N., Zakeri, V., & Setarehdan, S. K. (2019, November). Accurate stress assessment based on functional near-infrared spectroscopy using deep learning approach. In 2019 26th National and 4th International Iranian Conference on Biomedical Engineering (ICBME) (pp. 4–10). IEEE. doi:DOI: 10.1109/ICDM.2019.00161

Razzak, F., Yi, F., Yang, Y., & Xiong, H. (2019, November). An integrated multimodal attention-based approach for bank stress test prediction. In *2019 IEEE International Conference on Data Mining (ICDM)* (pp. 1282–1287). IEEE.

Reddy, U. S., Thota, A. V., & Dharun, A. (n.d.). Machine learning techniques for stress prediction in working employees. In *IEEE International Conference on Computational Intelligence and Computing Research (ICCIC)* (pp. 1–4). IEEE. DOI: 10.1109/ICCIC.2018.8782395

Singh, V., Kumar, A., & Gupta, S. (2022). Mental health prevention and promotion: A narrative review. *Frontiers in Psychiatry*, *13*, 1–4. DOI: 10.3389/fpsyt.2022.898009 PMID: 35958637

Smith, J.. (2018). Best practices for collecting and preprocessing data in mental health research. *Journal of Mental Health Research*, *20*(1), 45–58.

Søvold, L. E., Naslund, J. A., Kousoulis, A. A., Saxena, S., Qoronfleh, M. W., Grobler, C., & Münter, L. (2021). Prioritizing the mental health and well-being of healthcare workers: An urgent global public health priority. *Frontiers in Public Health*, *9*, 603–624. DOI: 10.3389/fpubh.2021.679397 PMID: 34026720

Su, C., Xu, Z., Pathak, J., & Wang, F. (2020). Deep learning in mental health outcome research: A scoping review. *Translational Psychiatry*, *10*(1), 116. DOI: 10.1038/s41398-020-0780-3 PMID: 32532967

Taylor, S., Jaques, N., Nosakhare, E., Sano, A., & Picard, R. (2020). Personalized multitask learning for predicting tomorrow's mood, stress, and health. *IEEE Transactions on Affective Computing*, *11*(2), 200–213. DOI: 10.1109/TAFFC.2017.2784832 PMID: 32489521

Trougakos, J. P., & Hideg, I. (2009). Momentary work recovery: The role of within-day work breaks. In *Current perspectives on job-stress recovery* (pp. 37–84). Emerald Group Publishing Limited. DOI: 10.1108/S1479-3555(2009)0000007005

Yatbaz, H. Y., & Erbilek, M. (2020, April). Deep learning based stress prediction from offline signatures. In 2020 8th International Workshop on Biometrics and Forensics (IWBF) (pp. 1–6). IEEE.

Chapter 7
AI-Powered Diagnostic Tools for Menopause

Arti Saini
https://orcid.org/0000-0002-8848-6302
Maharishi Markandeshwar University, India

Inderjeet Verma
https://orcid.org/0000-0002-9322-9255
Maharishi Markandeshwar University, India

Ruby Bhatia
Maharishi Markandeshwar University, India

ABSTRACT

Menopause is a normal biological process that signals the end of a woman's reproductive years. Menopause can cause a variety of physical and mental changes that affect a woman's health and quality of life. If women are aware of the symptoms and management techniques, they can easily navigate the transition during perimenopause and postmenopause. Traditionally, diagnosing menopause only involved medical investigations, hormone level measurements, and symptom assessment. However, these methods can be inconsistent. But with the development of artificial intelligence (AI), the diagnosis and management are changing. New AI tools being precise, individualized, and data-driven, search through large databases to identify women who are more likely to suffer from menopause-related issues. Although the technology is still developing but it has huge potential to meet the particular medical requirements of women. The chapter emphasizes how important AI will be in the diagnosis of menopause, various tools, the benefits of the tools, and the ethical considerations.

DOI: 10.4018/979-8-3373-2970-3.ch007

1. INTRODUCTION

A woman's reproductive years come to an end with menopause, a normal biological process. It is not an illness or disorder but a major life transition marked by hormonal changes and a range of symptoms (Menopause, n.d.). The three main phases of menopause are perimenopause, menopause, and postmenopause. The menopausal transition, commonly referred to as perimenopause, usually starts in a woman's 40s, however, it can start earlier. Estrogen and progesterone levels change throughout this stage, leading to irregular menstruation periods and other symptoms. Before menopause officially starts, this stage may last a few months or more than ten years. Periods are still possible for women; however, they can become erratic and be heavier or lighter than normal (McCarthy & Raval, 2020). Mood swings, anxiety, irritability, sleep difficulties, vaginal dryness, decreased fertility, headaches (increased migraine frequency), breast tenderness, irregular periods, hot flashes, nocturnal sweats, and difficulty concentrating are common symptoms during this stage (Talaulikar, 2022). After 12 months without a menstrual period, a woman is formally diagnosed with menopause. With an average age of about 51, it typically happens between the ages of 45 and 55. At this point, the ovaries cease producing eggs, and levels of progesterone and estrogen sharply drop(McNeil & Merriam, 2021; Peacock et al., 2023). Numerous symptoms that may affect a woman's physical and mental health can result from a decline in hormone levels. The following are typical menopausal symptoms: a decrease in libido and vaginal dryness; a decrease in libido and vaginal dryness; a decrease in libido and vaginal dryness; joint pain, muscle aches, and stiffness; weight gain and slowed metabolism; changes in breast tissue (loss of firmness); and palpitations in the heart (Santoro et al., 2015). Postmenopause is referred to as years following verified menopause. While symptoms may persist, they usually become less severe with time. On the other hand, the long-term consequences of lower estrogen levels raise the chance of developing several illnesses. Women in this period should continue to monitor their health and get screened frequently (Dalal & Agarwal, 2023; Postmenopausal Syndrome - StatPearls - NCBI Bookshelf, n.d.). During the postmenopausal period, health issues include Osteoporosis and weakened bones that make fractures more likely. Consuming enough calcium and vitamin D is essential (Charde et al., 2023). Lower estrogen levels increase the risk of heart disease, hypertension, and stroke (Ryczkowska et al., 2022). Problems with the vagina and urinary tract: heightened susceptibility to incontinence, vaginal atrophy (thinning of the vaginal walls), and urinary tract infections (UTIs). Some women have trouble focusing and remembering things, which is known as "brain fog" (Dalal & Agarwal, 2023). According to some studies, menopause may be associated with an increased risk of ovarian and breast cancer (CDC, n.d.; Surakasula et al., 2014).

Despite being a well-known stage, menopause can be difficult to diagnose for several reasons. Menopause is a well-known stage, but for several reasons, diagnosing it can be challenging. It is challenging to develop precise diagnostic standards since women differ widely in the intensity and duration of menopausal symptoms, and absence of an accurate scientific test. On top of that, women often mistake menopause symptoms for those of other conditions, which can result in misdiagnosis. They also tend to underestimate the symptoms making the diagnosis process more difficult. As a results, healthcare providers depend on medical history, symptom assessment, and doing hormone level tests as no single test can effectively diagnose menopause (Santoro et al., 2015). Hence, an accurate diagnosis requires a more holistic approach involving tracking symptoms, checking hormone levels, and ruling out any other condition. To make sure women gets the desired care and support during menopausal transition, it is essential to improve the diagnostic techniques. Recently, AI has become a emerging ally in healthcare, helping both patients and doctors with promising ways to tackle the challenges of menopause. AI is transforming the healthcare sector by improving patient outcomes, optimizing treatment regimens, increasing diagnostic accuracy, and simplifying administrative duties. By providing faster, more accurate, and more personalized healthcare solutions AI is improving the way doctors identify and treat illnesses (Bajwa et al., 2021). Machine learning algorithms sift through large amount of data (test findings, patient histories, and medical imagery) to find trends that human clinicians might overlook (Artificial & Al-Antari, 2023). As AI develops further, its application in healthcare has the potential to transform medical procedures and enhance patient care and results globally. In this chapter, we will look into how menopausal diagnosis and treatment are being revolutionized by AI-powered diagnostic tools.

2. UNDERSTANDING MENOPAUSE: A COMPLEX DIAGNOSTIC LANDSCAPE

The natural and irreversible end of menstruation brought on by an estrogen shortage that is not linked to a medical condition is known as menopause. Menopause takes its name from the Greek term men, which means month, and pausis, which means stop. After twelve months of amenorrhoea, a woman's reproductive and fetal years are over (McNeil & Merriam, 2021). For most women, this happens between the ages of 45 and 55. In the US, the typical age at which women naturally go through menopause is 51(Menopause, n.d..). The majority of women have vasomotor symptoms; however, urogenital, psychogenic, and cardiovascular organ systems can also be impacted by menopause. Ovulation and atresia cause women's ovarian follicles to decrease in number as they age(McNeil & Merriam, 2021). The ovary's granulosa cells, which are the main source of inhibin B and oestradiol, decrease (Hall, 2015). The granulosa cells in the ovary also secrete another hormone, antimullerian hormone (AMH), which also declines in levels. FSH and luteinizing hormone (LH) production rises when gonadotropins from estrogen and inhibin A and B are not inhibited (Tanbo & Fedorcsak, 2021). The hypothalamic-pituitary-ovarian axis is also disturbed by this drop in estrogen levels. Endometrial development fails, perhaps leading to irregular menstrual periods and eventual cessation of menses. In the perimenopausal period, a shorter follicular phase is often the first monthly symptom. Menstruation becomes more frequent as a result. The menstrual period thereafter typically lengthens. Anovulatory cycles can result in irregular uterine bleeding during perimenopause. Menstruation eventually stops(Weismiller, 2009). The ratio of testosterone to estrogen rises relative to testosterone levels, which might cause symptoms of excess androgens because testosterone levels do not alter much in the early stages of menopause(Talaulikar, 2022). Every year, about 1.3 million women in the US experience menopause. Usually, menopause starts between the ages of 45 and 56 (Crandall et al., 2023). Nonetheless, early natural menopause, which happens between the ages of 40 and 45, affects roughly 5% of women. Furthermore, 1% of women suffer from primary ovarian insufficiency, which is characterized by a total stop of menstruation before the age of 40 as a result of irreversible ovarian failure (Sopiarz & Sparzak, 2023).

The transition of menopause from the reproductive years to postmenopause is commonly described using the Stages of Reproductive Ageing Workshop (STRAW) framework. Women and healthcare professionals can better manage symptoms, predict changes, and preserve general health by being aware of these stages (Soules et al., 2001).

A standardised approach called STRAW was created to categorise the various stages of reproductive ageing. It distinguishes three main phases in a woman's reproductive life. Based on clinical and hormonal changes, each stage is further subdivided into smaller stages(Harlow et al., 2012).

a) Stage of Reproduction (years of active fertility)

During this time, fertility and regular menstrual cycles are normal. There are three substages within it. First is the early reproductive stage, where optimal fertility with regular menstrual cycles occurs. The peak reproductive stage is the maximum fertility and the most stable hormonal balance. The late reproductive stage is when ovarian function declines, and there are slight variations in cycle length (Ambikairajah et al., 2022).

b) Transition to Menopause (Menopausal Transition)

Hormonal changes and irregular menstrual cycles are hallmarks of this transition, which usually begins in the late 30s to early 50s. Cycle variability (e.g., menstrual periods becoming slightly erratic but still ovulatory) starts at the early transition. In the late transition phase, there are Increased symptoms such as mood swings, hot flashes, and night sweats, as well as more noticeable irregularities in the cycle (frequently skipped periods) (Ambikairajah et al., 2022).

c) Postmenopause (after the end of menopause)

Postmenopause begins after 12 consecutive months without a menstrual period. The First five years after menopause is called the early postmenopause stage, where symptoms like hot flashes and bone loss are more pronounced. During late postmenopause, hormones stabilize at low levels, and symptoms may diminish, but risks of osteoporosis and cardiovascular disease increase(Derry & Derry, 2014).

Although menopause is a natural transition, the hormonal changes that accompany it can result in a variety of symptoms that impact the body, mind, and emotions. Women can better manage this stage if they are aware of these signs (Figure 1).

a) Physiological Menopausal Symptoms

A decrease in oestrogen and progesterone levels during menopause causes several bodily changes. Among them could be:

- Hot flashes and night sweats: Sudden sensations of heat, frequently accompanied by flushing and perspiration, can be upsetting, particularly at night (Stuenkel, 2018).
- Period irregularities: Menstrual periods become erratic before stopping entirely(Ye et al., 2022).
- Vaginal Dryness and Discomfort: The weakening of the vaginal walls brought on by low oestrogen levels can make sexual activity uncomfortable, dry, and irritating (Jahangirifar et al., 2023).
- Weight Gain and Changes in Metabolism: Hormonal changes and a slowed metabolism cause weight gain in many women(McNeil & Merriam, 2021).
- Sleep disturbances: Hormonal fluctuations and hot flashes can cause insomnia and frequent nighttime awakenings(Ye et al., 2022).
- Joint and Muscle Pain: Common complaints include aches and stiffness in the muscles and joints.
- Changes in Hair and Skin: As oestrogen levels drop, brittle nails, thinning hair, and drier skin may appear(Ye et al., 2022).

- Heart palpitations: A fast or erratic heartbeat is experienced by certain women.
- Problems with the bladder: Weakened pelvic muscles increase the risk of incontinence and urinary tract infections (UTIs)(Jahangirifar et al., 2023).

b) Menopausal Psychological Symptoms

Menopausal hormone changes can also affect mental and cognitive well-being. Typical psychological symptoms consist of:

- Memory Issues and Concentration Issues: A lot of women complain of mental haze, forgetfulness, and difficulty concentrating(Stuenkel, 2018).
- Anxiety and Depression: Mood swings, anxiety, and depression can all be attributed to changes in hormone levels(Kundu & Acharya, 2023).
- Mood swings and agitation: There may be an increase in emotional sensitivity and irritation(Katz-Bearnot, 2010).
- Decreased Self-Esteem: Self-image issues may arise as a result of changes in appearance and bodily function(Alshogran et al., 2022).

c) Menopausal Emotional Symptoms

Menopause can cause emotional difficulties in addition to its physical and psychological effects:

- Sadness and Grief: Some women experience grief and sadness as they adjust to the end of their reproductive years(N. Y. Kim et al., 2023).
- Enhanced Sensitivity and Emotional Reactivity: Women may have hormonal fluctuations that cause them to become more emotionally reactive than normal(Albert & Newhouse, 2019).
- Loneliness and Isolation: Feelings of loneliness can result from friends and family not understanding you(N. Y. Kim et al., 2023).
- Libido changes: Lower hormone levels might cause less sexual desire, which can affect close relationships(Alawlaqi et al., 2017).
- Lack of Motivation: Some women report feeling less energised and enthusiastic about their everyday tasks.

Although menopause is widely recognized, determining its onset can be complex due to various factors. Every woman experience menopause differently; some have modest symptoms, while others have significant disturbances to their everyday routines. The severity and length of menopausal symptoms, including mood swings, hot flashes, exhaustion, and irregular periods, can vary greatly. While some women may go through the change swiftly, others may endure perimenopausal symptoms for more than ten years. The lack of a conclusive laboratory test makes diagnosis challenging due to this vast range (Weismiller, 2009). Menopause symptoms frequently mimic those of other illnesses, which could result in a misdiagnosis. For instance, Weight fluctuations, mood swings, and exhaustion are common symptoms of both hypothyroidism and hyperthyroidism (Slopien et al., 2019). Cognitive impairments, sleep disruptions, and mood swings are common symptoms of anxiety and depression (Nutt et al., 2008). Fibromyalgia and chronic fatigue syndrome can mimic the bodily aches and weariness associated with menopause (Boneva et al., 2015; Fukuda et al., 1994). Heart palpitations and chest pain can be confused with menopausal symptoms, and the risk of heart disease rises after menopause (Ryczkowska et al., 2022). Menopause cannot be conclusively confirmed by a single test. Although blood tests that measure hormone levels (such as estrogen and follicle-stimulating hormone [FSH] can offer hints, test findings are not always accurate because hormone levels change every day. Furthermore, even though hormone levels seem to be within a "normal" range, some women still experience menopausal symptoms (Menopause, n.d.). Menstrual cycles become erratic during perimenopause, occasionally changing in flow or missing months. It can be difficult to distinguish between perimenopause and other reasons for irregular cycles because women with polycystic ovary syndrome (PCOS), thyroid problems, or high levels of stress also frequently experience irregular periods. The timing and manifestation of menopause symptoms can be influenced by specific lifestyle choices and drugs. Menopause symptoms may appear earlier or be more severe in women who smoke, are under a lot of stress, or have long-term health conditions. Furthermore, several drugs (such as antidepressants) and hormonal contraceptives might conceal or change menopausal symptoms, which complicates diagnosis (Peacock et al., 2023). Premature ovarian insufficiency (POI), or early menopause (before age 40), is a condition that some women encounter for unexplained reasons, autoimmune disorders, or genetic factors. Others have abrupt menopause as a result of oophorectomy or medical procedures like chemotherapy. Since an abrupt decrease in hormones frequently results in more severe symptoms, these cases can be very difficult to recognize and treat (Kapoor, 2023). However, with the development of artificial intelligence (AI), menopausal diagnosis and treatment are changing, and more precise, individualized, and data-driven options are now available.

3. THE EMERGENCE OF AI IN HEALTHCARE

Artificial intelligence (AI) within computer science is concerned with developing software and machines capable of carrying out tasks that normally call for human intelligence. These duties include making decisions, solving problems, interpreting language, gaining experience, and even perceiving visual stimuli(Collins et al., 2021). AI can be made to do Natural language understanding (e.g., chatbots, voice assistants like Siri), pattern recognition (e.g., fraud detection, facial recognition), decision-making (e.g., self-driving cars, recommendation systems), and data-driven learning (e.g., predictive analytics, deep learning models). AI is of 3 types, namely, narrow, general, and super AI(Alowais et al., 2023). Narrow AI, also known as weak AI, is designed for specialised applications such as virtual assistants (like Siri and Alexa) and recommendation systems (like Netflix and YouTube). General AI, sometimes known as strong AI, aims to perform all of the cognitive tasks that a human being is capable of. It remains merely a theoretical concept for the time being. The term "super AI" refers to a prospective AI that is more intelligent than humans but is still subject to discussion and conjecture(IBM, n.d.). AI can be used in the areas of Healthcare (AI-powered diagnostics, robotic surgery), finance (fraud detection, stock market forecasting), education (AI tutors, personalised learning), and entertainment (recommendation engines like Netflix, AI-generated art and music) (Rashid & Kausik, 2024).

A kind of AI called machine learning (ML) allows computers to learn from data and make predictions or judgments without explicit programming. ML models examine data patterns to enhance their performance over time, as opposed to depending on preset rules. ML models are trained using mathematical techniques on huge datasets. The process typically comprises gathering data, either structured or unstructured, feeding it into the model to identify trends, evaluating and testing the model's accuracy with previously unseen data, using the learnt model to inform decisions, and continuously improving (Soori et al., 2023).

There are three types of ML (Ali et al., 2023):

a) Supervised Learning: In this method, the input is paired with the appropriate output, and the model is trained using labelled data. Examples include picture recognition and spam detection.
b) Unsupervised Learning: The model examines unlabeled data to uncover patterns that are concealed, like marketing's use of consumer segmentation.
c) Reinforcement Learning: The model gains knowledge by interacting with its surroundings and getting rewards or punishments. Robotics and AI for gaming (like AlphaGo) both use this.

A subfield of AI called natural language processing (NLP) gives computers the ability to comprehend, interpret, and produce human language. By bridging the gap between human and machine comprehension, NLP enables computers to analyse speech and text like humans(IBM, n.d.). NLP analyzes and produces text or voice by combining linguistics, machine learning, and deep learning techniques. It includes the process of organizing and cleaning unprocessed text (e.g., tokenization, stemming, and punctuation removal), understanding language and sentence structure, determining the meaning of words and sentences, and understanding context, which involves interpreting words according to their tone, intent, and context. Common uses for NLP include text summarization, sentiment analysis, chatbots and virtual assistants (like ChatGPT and customer support bots), and speech recognition (like Google Voice and Siri) (Zhou et al., 2020).

AI in Medical Diagnostics

AI has wide applications in many facets of medical diagnostics where it processes enormous volumes of data swiftly and precisely. Some of the applications are:

1. Radiology and Medical Imaging: AI models examine medical images from X-rays, MRIs, CT scans, and ultrasounds to identify issues like tumors, fractures, and infections (Yeasmin et al., 2024). For example, these tools can detect lung conditions from chest X-rays, identify breast cancer in mammography, and even detect neurological conditions like stroke and Alzheimer's. AI helps to reduce misdiagnosis, improves early disease detection, and accelerates picture interpretation, to enhances patient outcomes (Najjar, 2023).
2. Pathology and Histopathology: AI models prove as more precise than traditional methods at scanning tissue samples and identifying cancerous cells. Pathologists speed up the diagnostic processes by combining AI and digital pathology in reviewing slides more quickly (Baxi et al., 2021).
3. Using Predictive Analytics to detect Diseases: Machine learning algorithms makes use of patient data such as genetic data, medical history, and lifestyle choices to predict diseases. Early detection by AI tools helps in the diagnosis of diabetes and heart diseases, neurodegenerative illnessess including Alzheimer's and Parkinson's, and Genome sequencing for rare genetic illnesses (Ghaffar Nia et al., 2023). For example, AI analyze ECG to detect arrythmias and arial fibrillation, while ML models assess cardiac factors to predict potential cardiac events (Harmon et al., 2023). AI-based echocardiography interpretation identifies issues such as heart valve disorders by automating heart function analysis (Khan Mamun & Elfouly, 2023). These advancements improve cardiovascular risk assessments, lowering the strain on cardiologists, and enable early diagnosis and treatment.
4. Ophthalmology and AI: AI tools analyze retinal images in the diagnosis of eye disease, including glaucoma and diabetic retinopathy (Keskinbora, 2023). AI-based eye screening technologies facilitate early detection of eye disorders, hence preventing vision loss. For example, AI scans retinal images to detect early signs of eye damage brought on by diabetes (Fatima et al., 2024). AI tracks intraocular pressure and optic nerve damage to detect glaucoma (Zhang et al.,

2023). AI facilitates identification of conditions that harm to eyesight in older people. Therefore, AI makes early intervention possible, lowering the risk of blindness and enhancing the treatment of eye diseases (Padhy et al., 2019).

5. Dermatology and AI: AI helpsto detect and diagnose skin diseases like skin cancer and other dermatological disorders. With the help of AI, dermatologists can diagnose patients more quickly and accurately (Brancaccio et al., 2024). AI technology uses photos of skin lesions to identify malignancies, including melanoma. It also assists in the diagnosis of fungus infections, psoriasis, and eczema (Barata et al., 2023).
6. Oncology and AI: AI assists with cancer diagnosis and treatment planning with precision medicine techniques and early detection. AI enhances patient care by increasing early cancer detection, treatment personalization, and survival rates (Liao et al., 2023). AI detects tumors on MRIs (brain cancer), CT images (lung cancer), and mammograms (breast cancer) (Sufyan et al., 2023). AI examines biopsy slides to accurately diagnose malignant cells. AI applies on patient's genetic profile to predict the progession of cancer and individualize treatment (Alsharif, 2024).
7. AI in Neurology AI aids in the diagnosis and treatment of neurological conditions such as epilepsy, Parkinson's disease, and Alzheimer's. AI improves patients quality of life by enabling earlier detection and improved treatment of neurological disorders(Kalani & Anjankar, 2024). AI uses MRI and PET scans to identify early indicators of dementia and stroke (Tsiara et al., 2025). Seizure Prediction: AI uses EEG pattern analysis to anticipate and stop epileptic episodes (Rizzo, 2025). AI-powered neurodegenerative disease monitoring monitors the course of the illness and suggests tailored therapies (Tsiara et al., 2025).
8. Chatbots and Virtual Assistants Driven by AI: Chatbots and virtual assistants powered by AI assist patients by evaluating symptoms and making first assessments. These tools help patients decide whether they require basic home treatments or urgent medical attention (Clark & Bailey. 2024).

Potential AI in menopause

AI has the potential to transform menopause care by enhancing long-term health monitoring, diagnosis, symptom tracking, and treatment personalization. AI-driven solutions can improve healthcare decision-making, give women better insights, and guarantee that menopause is handled more skillfully (Emin et al., 2019; Garg & Munshi, 2024).

1. Using AI to Diagnose Menopause

Accurate and prompt diagnosis is one of the most difficult aspects of menopausal therapy. AI is beneficial in several ways:

a) Menopause Onset Prediction: AI is capable of analyzing vast amounts of data, such as hormone levels, lifestyle factors, and patient medical histories, to spot patterns and forecast a woman's future menopausal period. ML models detect the smallest hormonal changes that are not evident in routine lab tests (Garg & Munshi, 2024).
b) Hormonal Level Determining and Following: Rather than depending on one-time hormone tests, AI assesses hormonal patterns extra minutes through nonstop checking. AI employments prescient analytics to make strides the precision of menopause and perimenopause determination to recommend when more testing or therapeutic discussion is fundamental (Mishra, 2024).
c) Differentiating Menopause from Other illnesses: Menopause is regularly misdiagnosed since its indications are comparative to those of thyroid issues, sadness, and persistent weakness disorder. AI frameworks can assess a few factors at once to help in separating menopause from other sicknesses, coming about in speedier and more precise analyze (Peacock et al., 2023).
d) AI-powered checking and Assessment of Indications: Ladies can screen side effects in genuine time with wearable innovation and AI-powered smartphone apps. These instruments utilize machine learning and normal dialect handling (NLP) to discover designs within the indications and recognize between side effects that are related with menopause and those that are not (Zhao et al., 2025).
e) Automated Side effect Acknowledgment: AI-powered smartphone apps and keen therapeutic gear can screen and assess indications over time, giving patients and doctors real-time data (Tsvetanov, 2024).

2. AI-Assisted Symptom Control and Tailored Therapy

Since each woman extraordinarily encounters menopause, individualized care is pivotal. AI can help in redoing care by:

a) Creating Customized Treatment Plans: Based on a woman's one of a kind side effects, hereditary qualities, and restorative foundation, AI can propose elective treatments, count calories alterations, work out regimens, and hormone substitution treatment (HRT) (Garg & Munshi, 2024).
b) Optimising Medication Use: AI can reduce trial-and-error prescribing by predicting a woman's response to hormone replacement therapy or non-hormonal treatments (Wu et al., 2024).

c) Identifying Health Risks: AI-powered tools can assess the risk of developing conditions like osteoporosis and heart disease, which are more common after menopause (Fasihi et al., 2022).

3. AI Virtual Assistants and Chatbots to Help with Menopause

Finding trustworthy, stigma-free information regarding menopause is a challenge for many women. Chatbots and virtual assistants powered by AI can (H. K. Kim, 2024):

a) Provide individualised health advice around-the-clock depending on user enquiries.
b) By identifying emotional patterns and offering coping mechanisms, you can provide mental health assistance.
c) Help women handle menopause more effectively by guiding them with nutritional suggestions, exercise regimens, and lifestyle changes.

4. Long-Term Health Monitoring with AI

Cognitive decline, cardiovascular disease, and osteoporosis are all made more likely by menopause. Wearables and health monitoring devices with AI capabilities can:

a) Monitor changes in bone density and forecast the risk of osteoporosis (Dimai, 2022).
b) To evaluate cardiovascular health, track heart rate and cholesterol levels (Moshawrab et al., 2023).
c) Identify early indicators of cognitive deterioration to aid in Alzheimer's disease preventative measures (Salehi et al., 2022).

5. AI for Research and Awareness on Menopause

Additionally, AI is assisting researchers studying menopause by (Garg & Munshi, 2024):

a) Examine extensive health data to find trends and create novel therapies.
b) Find the best candidates for clinical trials more quickly by using AI-driven predictions.
c) Increase public awareness by making menopause-related knowledge more accessible using AI-powered learning resources.

4. AI-POWERED DIAGNOSTIC TOOLS FOR MENOPAUSE

Our lives have been profoundly changed by innovations in technology in the form of smartphones and programs (apps). A study by Degenhard predicts that between 2022 and 2028, there will be 2.4 million more smartphone users in the UK (Statista, n.d.). According to Laricchia, smartphone use has grown among all age groups, but it has climbed most notably among those between the ages of 55 and 64, rising from 9% in 2012 to 90% in 2021(Statista, n.d.). Through mobile apps, women could be empowered by the effective management, tracking, and understanding of menopause made possible by the availability and accessibility of mobile phones. According to a prior analysis of 22 menopausal apps, numerous applications are available on different operating systems that are intended to assist in managing menopause through education, symptom tracking, and risk assessments. Additionally, the analysis discovered that only 22.7% of the 22 menopausal apps provided evidence-based material, and only 27.3% of them reported medical professionals' involvement (Gkrozou et al., 2019).

The extremely individualised nature of menopause makes diagnosis and management difficult. In menopause care, artificial intelligence (AI) is revolutionizing the field by providing accurate diagnosis, tailored treatment recommendations, and better patient outcomes. Various ways in which AI can help in menopause diagnosis and management are:

a) AI algorithms that use predictive analytics for early detection examine:
   - rhythms of the menstrual cycle (monitored with apps).
   - Biomarkers of hormones (FSH, changes in oestradiol).
   - lifestyle elements (diet, stress, and sleep).

b) AI-powered applications for tracking symptoms and personalisation, like Flo and MenoPro, use:

Using natural language processing (NLP), symptom diaries are examined. Wearable data to identify heat flashes, such as body temperature and heart rate. insights that are specific to you (e.g., "Your sleep disruptions correlate with declining oestrogen").

c) AI-powered hormone Therapy Enhancement

Not every woman receives the same advantages. AI assists by:

- Predicting the effects of hormone replacement therapy (HRT) by analysing genetic data.

- Suggest individualised dosing according to risk factors (such as blood clots) and the severity of the symptoms.

d) Menopause Support Virtual Health Assistants AI chatbots (like MenoBot and Ada Health) offer:

- 24/7 evaluation of symptoms.
- empirically supported recommendations (e.g., "Try black cohosh for night sweats").

mental health assistance (anxiety CBT approaches).

e) Models for ML Examining Menstrual and Hormonal Data

Menstrual abnormalities and modest hormonal changes that occur years before clinical menopause can be detected by AI systems. These models examine:

- Historical cycle data (from apps that track periods, such as Flo or Clue).
- Trends in Anti-Müllerian Hormone (AMH) and Follicle-Stimulating Hormone (FSH).
- Indicators of ovarian reserve (through blood tests or hormone testing that can be performed at home, such as Modern Fertility).

f) AI-powered diet and Lifestyle Counsellors for Menopause Management

These days, AI-powered apps offer personalised lifestyle plans that include:

- Dietary suggestions (e.g., more foods high in phytoestrogen for natural hormone support).
- Exercise adaptations: AI trainers modify exercises to target metabolic slowing and bone strength.
- Optimising sleep and stress (via apps like Headspace's AI-powered menopausal meditation courses).

Table 1. Various AI-powered tools available to transform menopause diagnosis and management.

Tools	Developer	Technique used	Outcome
Caria: Menopause & Midlife	Apple store	AI	Detect and manage menopausal symptoms
Flo App	Google play	NLP model	Take keywords out of voice or text entries, recognise shifts in sentiment, determine which symptom clusters point to hormonal trends.
MenoPro + Oura Ring	Myoclinic	Predictive analytics	Integrates physiological information, symptom monitoring, and predictive analytics to offer perimenopausal and postmenopausal women tailored insights.
IBM Watson Health	IBM	AI+ ML+ NLP	Examine clinical research, genetic information, and patient medical records to suggest individualised HRT regimens,
Applewatch	Apple	AI	Monitor changes in heart rate variability (HRV), sleep problems, basal body temperature, hot flashes, and night sweats. Track menopausal symptoms.
MenoBot AI chatbot	gynecologists, data scientists, and AI researchers	NLP	Asks specific questions, classifies the severity of symptoms using NLP, and then suggests evidence-based treatments.
Alva	gynecologists, data scientists, and AI researchers	AI+ ML	Integrates clinical knowledge and machine learning to maximise lifestyle changes and hormone therapy for women going through menopause and perimenopause.

continued on following page

Table 1. Continued

Tools	Developer	Technique used	Outcome
AI-powered Menopause Care Platform	Mirai Health	AI+ NLP	a voice-enabled, multilingual chatbot (supporting 8+ regional languages) that does detail symptom assessments using natural language processing to categorize concerns like hot flashes, mood swings, or sleep disruptions
Elektra Health	experienced operators with deep consumer, health tech & clinical expertise	AI+NLP	The platform starts with an interactive AI chatbot that evaluates symptoms, examines medical data, and spots trends to provide real-time insights and evidence-based suggestions, ranging from advice on hormone medication to lifestyle changes.

5. BENEFITS OF AI-POWERED DIAGNOSTIC TOOLS

Healthcare has been transformed by AI, as have many other industries. The creation of diagnostic tools driven by AI is one of its most significant accomplishments. These tools are intended to improve illness detection and patient care in terms of precision, effectiveness, and accessibility. Healthcare practitioners' methods for diagnosing and treating medical disorders are being revolutionized by AI-driven diagnostic tools that use machine learning algorithms, big data analysis, and predictive modeling. Advantages of AI-powered tools for diagnosis are(Alowais et al., 2023; Hoppe et al., 2023; Nashwan et al., 2023):

1. Enhanced Precision and Prompt Identification

The capacity of AI-powered symptomatic frameworks to make strides symptomatic precision is one of their greatest benefits. Routine demonstrative methods regularly depend on human elucidation, which is inclined to botches or errors. On the other hand, AI-powered frameworks can absolutely analyze expansive datasets, lessening the plausibility of inaccurate analyze. AI frameworks, for occasion, can distinguish designs in restorative imaging, counting CT, MRI, and X-ray filters, that could be difficult for the human eye to pick up on. AI has demonstrated vital within the field of oncology, making a difference to spot malignancies in their early stages more precisely than conventional procedures. Survival rates and treatment comes about are significantly upgraded by early location of maladies like skin cancer, lung cancer, and breast cancer.

2. Quicker Diagnosis and Shorter Wait Times

The time required to recognize diseases can be diminished by utilizing AI-powered symptomatic advances, which can handle therapeutic information at already unheard-of speeds. Comes about from routine demonstrative strategies, such imaging looks and research facility testing, as often as possible take days or weeks to supply. Real-time understanding information investigation utilizing AI-driven frameworks empowers faster decision-making and incite restorative activity. AI-driven chatbots and virtual wellbeing associates, for case, can quickly assess indications and offer starting determination, coordinating patients towards assist therapeutic interview. This capacity to respond rapidly is particularly accommodating in crises where incite activity can spare lives.

3. Improved Productivity and Decreased Stress for Medical Professionals

Specialists are frequently overburdened by the huge number of patients they treat, which is putting an expanding strain on the healthcare division. By robotizing dreary methods, AI-powered symptomatic advances can decrease this strain and free up healthcare experts to concentrate on troublesome circumstances and individualized quiet care. AI can offer assistance radiologists, for occasion, by pre-screening therapeutic pictures and highlighting inconsistencies for extra examination. In expansion to sparing time, this computerization moves forward workflow effectiveness in symptomatic offices and clinics. Besides, AI-powered electronic health record (EHR) frameworks rearrange the organization of understanding information, liberating up therapeutic staff individuals to spend more time collaboration with patients.

4. Individualised and Data-driven Medical Care

Enormous information is utilized by AI-powered symptomatic advances to supply individualized restorative care. AI can create individualized treatment proposals by analyzing a patient's hereditary composition, restorative history, and way of life choices. Based on their person wellbeing profiles, this custom-made approach guarantees that patients get the foremost compelling mediations. For occurrence, by analyzing hereditary anomalies in tumors, AI helps oncologists in exactness pharmaceutical in making personalised cancer medicines. In a comparable vein, wearable innovation fueled by AI tracks crucial signs, distinguishes irregularities, and gives customized wellbeing exhortation, empowering individuals to require charge of their wellbeing.

5. Cost Savings and Enhanced Availability

AI integration in diagnostics has the potential to essentially decrease healthcare costs. Routine determination strategies can involve expensive testing and expanded healing center remains. AI-powered arrangements advance asset utilize, cut down on inefficient medicines, and spare healthcare costs. AI too makes healthcare more open, particularly in underserved and inaccessible areas. AI-powered telemedicine arrangements permit patients to induce symptomatic tests and discussions essentially, dispensing with the require for in-person clinic remains. This guarantees that individuals get provoke and exact analyze, which is particularly accommodating in provincial ranges with few therapeutic administrations.

6. Predictive analytics and disease prevention

AI-powered diagnostic innovations can expect possible health dangers before they materialize in addition to distinguishing illnesses that are as of now show. AI can discover designs and hazard components connected to incessant sicknesses like diabetes, heart malady, and neurological issues by looking at tremendous datasets. For illustration, utilizing physiological data, hereditary penchant, and way of life, AI models may figure a person's hazard of obtaining diabetes. Early mediation, preventative measures, and way of life changes to moderate the movement of the infection are made conceivable by this prescient control. AI is additionally utilized by open wellbeing offices to screen infection flare-ups and put incite control measures into put.

7. Better Engagement and Experience for Patients

By moving forward healthcare's convenience, proficiency, and comfort, AI-powered symptomatic innovations move forward the patient involvement in general. Wearable innovation and AI-powered versatile wellbeing apps have made it possible for anybody to track their wellbeing information in genuine time and get prompt input. AI-enabled smartwatches, for occasion, are able to distinguish irregular heart rhythms and inform clients of conceivable cardiac issues some time recently side effects show up. Virtual wellbeing associates offer 24/7 restorative counsel, reacting to understanding enquiries and making recommendations based on strong investigate. Individuals are engaged to require charge of their possess wellbeing and proactive healthcare administration is cultivated by this improved persistent support.

8. Reducing Human Prejudice in Diagnostics

Abberations in persistent care may result from human predisposition in restorative determination. Symptomatic arrangements driven by AI decrease inclination by advertising fair assessments derived from data-driven examination. AI ensures that all patients, independent of statistic characteristics, get precise and evenhanded assessments by institutionalizing demonstrative methods. AI frameworks that have been prepared on an assortment of datasets, for illustration, can reduce the contrasts in infection location between races and sexes. Usually particularly vital for sicknesses like skin cancer in those with darker skin tones or cardiovascular issues in ladies, where demonstrative inclinations have generally brought about an erroneous conclusion or put off treatment.

9. Constant Learning and Development

AI-powered frameworks, in contrast to customary demonstrative strategies, are continuously learning and getting way better. With the assistance of new therapeutic information, machine learning calculations progress their precision and forecast control. This adaptability ensures that AI-powered demonstrative instruments remain current with the foremost later disclosures in medication and investigation. For instance, AI models in radiology are continuously learning from new imaging information, which moves forward their capacity to recognize inconsistencies more absolutely. In a comparable vein, chatbots driven by AI create, in reaction to understanding intuitive advertising, more exact and custom fitted therapeutic exhortation.

6. CHALLENGES AND ETHICAL CONSIDERATIONS

Symptomatic advances driven by AI look at gigantic amounts of data, discover patterns, and offer assistance to therapeutic experts to make shrewd choices. By the by, in spite of these preferences, there are a few challenges and moral concerns with utilizing AI in therapeutic diagnoses (Farhud & Zokaei, 2021).

Securing the security of information is one of the biggest issues with AI-powered demonstrative instruments. Various persistent information sources, such as hereditary data, imaging checks, and therapeutic records, are utilized by these frameworks. Keeping up understanding, belief, and adherence to legislative systems, just like the Common Information Assurance Direction (GDPR) and the Wellbeing Protections Movability and Responsibility Act (HIPAA), depend on securing this touchy information. Private understanding data may be compromised by cyberattacks focusing on AI frameworks (Markose et al., 2016).

Existing therapeutic information, which once in a while reflects predispositions within the healthcare framework, is utilized by AI frameworks to memorize. Abberations in patient treatment might happen from AI calculations creating one-sided results in cases where prepared datasets are not representative of different groups and are not differentiated. AI frameworks that have been prepared only on information from one statistic gathered may provide underrepresented communities erroneous analyses. To reduce inclination and increment decency in AI-powered diagnostics, make beyond any doubt that different bunches are spoken to in AI training datasets.

AI algorithms frequently operate as "dark boxes," which implies that neither patients nor healthcare specialists can promptly get it how they make choices. Picking up administrative endorsement and belief may be troublesome as a result of this need of transparency. Building AI models that offer brief avocations for their figures is fundamental to boosting understanding and certainty in restorative experts. Sometime recently approving AI-powered demonstrative innovations for clinical utilization, various therapeutic administrative offices need transparency.

AI-powered diagnostics help in restorative decision-making, but when they begin to influence imperative healthcare choices, moral questions are raised.

There are a few lawful and administrative obstructions to the utilization of AI in healthcare. AI-powered demonstrative devices, in contrast to ordinary restorative hardware, are always learning and creating, which makes the endorsement and monitoring process more troublesome.

Ethical Issues with AI Implementation in Low-Resource Environments

While implementing AI-powered diagnostic tools in low-resource settings raises ethical questions, AI can close healthcare gaps in neglected areas (Lewin et al., 2024; Moore et al., 2024; Naik et al., 2022; Sanchez et al., 2024).

- Digital Divide: Inequitable AI implementation may be hampered by limited access to technology and internet connectivity.
- Ethical AI Use in Clinical Trials: To guarantee efficacy and equity, AI-driven diagnostic tools should be examined and verified in a variety of contexts.
- Ensuring Human Oversight: To ensure ethical medical practice in low-resource situations, AI should supplement local healthcare expertise rather than replace it.

7. THE FUTURE OF AI IN MENOPAUSE CARE

Women can make menopause more comfortable and confident with the help of AI, which offers a TaylorMade data control approach that has soaring prospects.

The use of high mobile therapy schemes is particularly exciting for those going through menopause. Through the analysis of thousands of data records from portable technologies, such as electronic health records and patients, AI was able to identify patterns and forecast specific requirements. The quality of life for women during menopause can be enhanced by AI, which recommends personalized interventions such as food changes, hormone therapy adjustments, and training programs (Johnson et al., 2020).

The use of artificial intelligence-controlled predictive analyses enables women to prepare for the transition by identifying early symptoms that indicate they will experience menopause. By using a biomarker, an abnormal menstrual cycle, and genetic testing, AI can predict the start of menopause. Cognitive impairments, mood swings (Garg & Munshi, 2024), hot flashes and other symptoms can be predicted by AI without any precautions.

AI-driven Virtual health assistants and chatbots are capable of delivering women in real time, which can be useful during menopause. These AI-powered solutions can use NLP to answer health-related questions, advise on how to manage symptoms, and offer emotional support. Unlike conventional medical appointments, these virtual assistants can provide ongoing care and guidance without leaving the office (Maher et al., 2024).

The pharmaceutical industry utilizes artificial intelligence to expedite drug discovery and create safer and more effective treatments for menopause-related issues. The use of AI can identify new hormones and chemicals for non-hormonal treatments by analyzing biological data. New therapies will be approved by clinical studies that utilize AI-operated for each patient's specific genetic makeup (Blanco-González et et al., 2023).

Mental health problems such as menopause, anxiety, depression, and cognitive fog are becoming more common. With the help of AI-powered psychological health systems, patients can receive mood monitoring equipment, mindfulness training, and personalized cognitive behavioral therapy (CBT). Early signs of mental health decline can be identified by AI, which can also identify alterations in language usage, social interactions, and other behavioral traits.

The use of AI-powered wearable technology allows for the monitoring of bodily parameters such as heart rate, temperature; and sleep pattern changes. Women and health professionals can use this finding to pursue menopause symptoms in real time and modify treatment schemes as needed. By analyzing stress, food, and activity levels, women can use AI to take control of their health (Shajari et al., 2023).

8. CONCLUSION

AI is revolutionizing healthcare in terms of diagnosis. It has great ability that leads to better outcomes for patients, more accurate diagnosis, and smoother healthcare processes as it can handle large datasets, identify complex patterns, and provide quick, and evidence-based conclusions. AI- based models helps with early detection, personalized treatment plans, and health monitoring. It completely changes the way we approach care for various populations and healthcare systems. Its central advantage is it helps to detect the beginning and treatment course much before the development of clinical sign and symptoms. AI models can detect the cardiovascular diseases, osteoporosis, and perimenopause by examining lifestyle variables, hormonal biomarkers, menstrual cycle patterns, and genetic predispositions, thus making it possible for proactive treatment that enables doctors to take early action, reduce the effect of disease, and improve quality of life. Moreover, AI based diagnostic tools helps increase access to healthcare, particularly in rural or underdeveloped areas. AI chatbots, virtual assistants, and telemedicine systems provide 24/7 assistance, bridging the communication gap between patients and medical specialists. AI has made it possible to increase patient involvement in health management through Real-time advice, and symptom tracking. The clinicians can now concentrate more on treatment rather than diagnosis, and on more severe diseases by using these tools to reduce their workload. However, there are serious challenges and obstacles pertaining to data privacy, bias, transparency, legislation, and clinical integration associated with their adoption. Inorder to guarantee the ethical use of AI in medical diagnostics these issues must be addressed. It requires coordination from AI developers, healthcare providers, legislators, and regulatory agencies to build reliable and moral AI-powered diagnostic systems. Overcoming these obstacles will enable AI to be successfully incorporated into healthcare, ultimately leading to better patient outcomes and a revolution in medical practice.

REFERENCES

Alawlaqi, A., Amor, H., & Hammadeh, M. E. (2017). Role of hormones in hypoactive sexual desire disorder and current treatment. *Journal of the Turkish German Gynecological Association, 18*(4), 210–218. DOI: 10.4274/jtgga.2017.0071

Albert, K. M., & Newhouse, P. A. (2019). Estrogen, Stress, and Depression: Cognitive and Biological Interactions. *Annual Review of Clinical Psychology, 15*(1), 399–423. DOI: 10.1146/annurev-clinpsy-050718-095557

Ali, M., Dewan, A., Sahu, A. K., & Taye, M. M. (2023). Understanding of Machine Learning with Deep Learning: Architectures, Workflow, Applications and Future Directions. *Computers 2023, Vol. 12, Page 91, 12*(5), 91. DOI: 10.3390/computers12050091

Alowais, S. A., Alghamdi, S. S., Alsuhebany, N., Alqahtani, T., Alshaya, A. I., Almohareb, S. N., Aldairem, A., Alrashed, M., Bin Saleh, K., Badreldin, H. A., Al Yami, M. S., Al Harbi, S., & Albekairy, A. M. (2023). Revolutionizing healthcare: The role of artificial intelligence in clinical practice. *BMC Medical Education, 23*(1), 689. DOI: 10.1186/s12909-023-04698-z

Alsharif, F. (2024). Artificial Intelligence in Oncology: Applications, Challenges and Future Frontiers. *International Journal of Pharmaceutical Investigation, 14*(3), 647–656. DOI: 10.5530/ijpi.14.3.76

Alshogran, O. Y., Mahmoud, F. M. Z., & Alkhatatbeh, M. J. (2022). Predictors of age at menopause and psychiatric symptoms among postmenopausal females in Jordan. *Journal of Psychosomatic Obstetrics and Gynaecology, 43*(4), 385–392. DOI: 10.1080/0167482X.2021.1984425

Ambikairajah, A., Walsh, E., & Cherbuin, N. (2022). A review of menopause nomenclature. *Reproductive Health, 19*(1), 29. Advance online publication. DOI: 10.1186/s12978-022-01336-7

Artificial, M., & Al-Antari, M. A. (2023). Artificial Intelligence for Medical Diagnostics—Existing and Future AI Technology! *Diagnostics (Basel), 13*(4), 688. DOI: 10.3390/diagnostics13040688

Bajwa, J., Munir, U., Nori, A., & Williams, B. (2021). Artificial intelligence in healthcare: Transforming the practice of medicine. *Future Healthcare Journal, 8*(2), e188–e194. DOI: 10.7861/fhj.2021-0095

Barata, C., Rotemberg, V., Codella, N. C. F., Tschandl, P., Rinner, C., Akay, B. N., Apalla, Z., Argenziano, G., Halpern, A., Lallas, A., Longo, C., Malvehy, J., Puig, S., Rosendahl, C., Soyer, H. P., Zalaudek, I., & Kittler, H. (2023). A reinforcement learning model for AI-based decision support in skin cancer. *Nature Medicine*, *29*(8), 1941–1946. DOI: 10.1038/s41591-023-02475-5

Baxi, V., Edwards, R., Montalto, M., & Saha, S. (2021). Digital pathology and artificial intelligence in translational medicine and clinical practice. *Modern Pathology*, *35*(1), 23–32. DOI: 10.1038/s41379-021-00919-2

Blanco-González, A., Cabezón, A., Seco-González, A., Conde-Torres, D., Antelo-Riveiro, P., Piñeiro, Á., & Garcia-Fandino, R. (2023). The Role of AI in Drug Discovery: Challenges, Opportunities, and Strategies. *Pharmaceuticals (Basel, Switzerland)*, *16*(6), 891. DOI: 10.3390/ph16060891

Brancaccio, G., Balato, A., Malvehy, J., Puig, S., Argenziano, G., & Kittler, H. (2024). Artificial Intelligence in Skin Cancer Diagnosis: A Reality Check. *The Journal of Investigative Dermatology*, *144*(3), 492–499. DOI: 10.1016/j.jid.2023.10.004

Breast Cancer Risk Factors | Breast Cancer | CDC. (n.d.). Retrieved March 25, 2025, from https://www.cdc.gov/breast-cancer/risk-factors/index.html

Charde, S. H., Joshi, A., & Raut, J. (2023). A Comprehensive Review on Postmenopausal Osteoporosis in Women. *Cureus*, *15*(11), e48582. DOI: 10.7759/cureus.48582

Clark, M., & Bailey, S. (2024). Chatbots in Health Care: Connecting Patients to Information. *Chatbots in Health Care: Connecting Patients to Information: Emerging Health Technologies*. https://www.ncbi.nlm.nih.gov/books/NBK602381/

Collins, C., Dennehy, D., Conboy, K., & Mikalef, P. (2021). Artificial intelligence in information systems research: A systematic literature review and research agenda. *International Journal of Information Management*, *60*, 102383. DOI: 10.1016/j.ijinfomgt.2021.102383

Crandall, C. J., Mehta, J. M., & Manson, J. E. (2023). Management of Menopausal Symptoms: A Review. *Journal of the American Medical Association*, *329*(5), 405–420. DOI: 10.1001/jama.2022.24140

Dalal, P. K., & Agarwal, M. (2023). Postmenopausal Syndrome. *Indian Journal of Psychiatry*, *57*(6), 222–232. DOI: 10.4103/0019-5545.161483

Derry, P., & Derry, G. (2014). Analysis of the STRAW Operational Definition of the Early Menopausal Transition. *Women's Reproductive Health (Philadelphia, Pa.)*, *1*(1), 21–30. DOI: 10.1080/23293691.2014.901797

Dimai, H. P. (2022). New Horizons: Artificial Intelligence Tools for Managing Osteoporosis. *The Journal of Clinical Endocrinology and Metabolism, 108*(4), 775–783. DOI: 10.1210/clinem/dgac702

Emin, E. I., Emin, E., Papalois, A., Willmott, F., Clarke, S., & Sideris, M. (2019). Artificial intelligence in obstetrics and gynaecology: Is this the way forward? *In Vivo (Athens, Greece), 33*(5), 1547–1551. DOI: 10.21873/invivo.11635

Farhud, D. D., & Zokaei, S. (2021). Ethical Issues of Artificial Intelligence in Medicine and Healthcare. *Iranian Journal of Public Health, 50*(11), i. DOI: 10.18502/ijph.v50i11.7600

Fasihi, L., Tartibian, B., Eslami, R., & Fasihi, H. (2022). Artificial intelligence used to diagnose osteoporosis from risk factors in clinical data and proposing sports protocols. *Scientific Reports, 12*(1), 18330. DOI: 10.1038/s41598-022-23184-y

Fatima, M., Pachauri, P., Akram, W., Parvez, M., Ahmad, S., & Yahya, Z. (2024). Enhancing retinal disease diagnosis through AI: Evaluating performance, ethical considerations, and clinical implementation. *Informatics and Health, 1*(2), 57–69. DOI: 10.1016/j.infoh.2024.05.003

Garg, R., & Munshi, A. (2024). Revolutionizing Menopause Management: Harnessing the Potential of Artificial Intelligence. *Journal of Midlife Health, 15*(2), 53–54. DOI: 10.4103/jmh.jmh_104_24

Ghaffar Nia, N., Kaplanoglu, E., & Nasab, A. (2023). Evaluation of artificial intelligence techniques in disease diagnosis and prediction. *Discover Artificial Intelligence, 3*(1), 5. DOI: 10.1007/s44163-023-00049-5

Gkrozou, F., Tsonis, O., Godden, M., Siafaka, V., & Paschopoulos, M. (2019). Mobile Health (mHealth) apps focused on menopause: Are they any good? *Post Reproductive Health, 25*(4), 191–198. DOI: 10.1177/2053369119878978

Hall, J. E. (2015). Endocrinology of the Menopause. *Endocrinology and Metabolism Clinics of North America, 44*(3), 485–496. DOI: 10.1016/j.ecl.2015.05.010

Harlow, S. D., Gass, M., Hall, J. E., Lobo, R., Maki, P., Rebar, R. W., Sherman, S., Sluss, P. M., & De Villiers, T. J. (2012). Executive summary of the Stages of Reproductive Aging Workshop + 10: Addressing the unfinished agenda of staging reproductive aging. *Menopause (New York, N.Y.), 19*(4), 387–395. DOI: 10.1097/gme.0b013e31824d8f40

Harmon, D. M., Sehrawat, O., Maanja, M., Wight, J., & Noseworthy, P. A. (2023). Artificial Intelligence for the Detection and Treatment of Atrial Fibrillation. *Arrhythmia & Electrophysiology Review, 12*, e12. DOI: 10.15420/aer.2022.31

Hoppe, N., Härting, R. C., & Rahmel, A. (2023). Potential Benefits of Artificial Intelligence in Healthcare. *Intelligent Systems Reference Library, 229*, 225–249. DOI: 10.1007/978-3-031-11170-9_9

Jahangirifar, M., Fooladi, E., Davis, S. R., & Islam, R. M. (2023). Menopause symptoms, sexual dysfunctions and pelvic floor disorders in refugee and asylum seeker women: A scoping review. *Climacteric, 26*(4), 373–380. DOI: 10.1080/13697137.2023.2173572

Johnson, K. B., Wei, W. Q., Weeraratne, D., Frisse, M. E., Misulis, K., Rhee, K., Zhao, J., & Snowdon, J. L. (2020). Precision Medicine, AI, and the Future of Personalized Health Care. *Clinical and Translational Science, 14*(1), 86–93. DOI: 10.1111/cts.12884

Kalani, M., & Anjankar, A. (2024). Revolutionizing Neurology: The Role of Artificial Intelligence in Advancing Diagnosis and Treatment. *Cureus, 16*(6), e61706. DOI: 10.7759/cureus.61706

Kapoor, E. (2023). Premature Ovarian Insufficiency. *Current Opinion in Endocrine and Metabolic Research, 28*, 100435. DOI: 10.1016/j.coemr.2023.100435

Katz-Bearnot, S. (2010). Menopause, depression, and loss of sexual desire: A psychodynamic contribution. *The Journal of the American Academy of Psychoanalysis and Dynamic Psychiatry, 38*(1), 99–116. DOI: 10.1521/jaap.2010.38.1.99

Keskinbora, K. H. (2023). Current roles of artificial intelligence in ophthalmology. *Open Exploration 2019 4:6, 4*(6), 1048–1067. DOI: 10.37349/emed.2023.00194

Khan Mamun, M. M. R., & Elfouly, T. (2023). AI-Enabled Electrocardiogram Analysis for Disease Diagnosis. *Applied System Innovation 2023, Vol. 6, Page 95, 6*(5), 95. DOI: 10.3390/asi6050095

Kim, H. K. (2024). The Effects of Artificial Intelligence Chatbots on Women's Health: A Systematic Review and Meta-Analysis. *Healthcare (Basel), 12*(5), 534. DOI: 10.3390/healthcare12050534

Kim, N. Y., Yoo, S. K., Jin, J. C., Han, S., Hong, J. S., & Kim, S. M. (2023). Development and verification of the Menopause Emotional Symptom Questionnaire. *Menopause (New York, N.Y.), 30*(9), 961–968. DOI: 10.1097/GME.0000000000002224

Kundu, S., & Acharya, S. S. (2023). Linkage of premature and early menopause with psychosocial well-being: A moderated multiple mediation approach. *BMC Psychology, 11*(1), 228. Advance online publication. DOI: 10.1186/s40359-023-01267-3

Lewin, S., Chetty, R., Ihdayhid, A. R., & Dwivedi, G. (2024). Ethical Challenges and Opportunities in Applying Artificial Intelligence to Cardiovascular Medicine. *The Canadian Journal of Cardiology*, *40*(10), 1897–1906. Advance online publication. DOI: 10.1016/j.cjca.2024.06.029

Liao, J., Li, X., Gan, Y., Han, S., Rong, P., Wang, W., Li, W., & Zhou, L. (2023). Artificial intelligence assists precision medicine in cancer treatment. *Frontiers in Oncology*, *12*, 998222. DOI: 10.3389/fonc.2022.998222

Maher, C., Singh, B., Wylde, A., & Chastin, S. (2024). Virtual health assistants: A grand challenge in health communications and behavior change. *Frontiers in Digital Health*, *6*, 1418695. DOI: 10.3389/fdgth.2024.1418695

Markose, A., Krishnan, R., & Ramesh, M. (2016). Medical ethics. *Journal of Pharmacy & Bioallied Sciences*, *8*(Suppl 1), S1–S4. DOI: 10.4103/0975-7406.191934

McCarthy, M., & Raval, A. P. (2020). The peri-menopause in a woman's life: a systemic inflammatory phase that enables later neurodegenerative disease. *Journal of Neuroinflammation 2020 17:1*, *17*(1), 1–14. DOI: 10.1186/s12974-020-01998-9

McNeil, M. A., & Merriam, S. B. (2021). Menopause. *Annals of Internal Medicine*, *174*(7), ITC97–ITC112. DOI: 10.7326/AITC202107200

Menopause. (n.d.). Retrieved March 25, 2025, from https://www.who.int/news-room/fact-sheets/detail/menopause

Mishra, P. (2024). *Optimizing Perimenopausal Care*. 242–281. DOI: 10.4018/979-8-3693-2342-7.ch010

Moore, S., Hedayati-Mehdiabadi, A., Law, V., & Kang, S. P. (2024). The Change We Work: Professional Agency and Ethics for Emerging AI Technologies. *TechTrends*, *68*(1), 27–36. DOI: 10.1007/s11528-023-00895-1

Moshawrab, M., Adda, M., Bouzouane, A., Ibrahim, H., & Raad, A. (2023). Smart Wearables for the Detection of Cardiovascular Diseases: A Systematic Literature Review. *Sensors (Basel)*, *23*(2), 828. DOI: 10.3390/s23020828

Naik, N., Hameed, B. M. Z., Shetty, D. K., Swain, D., Shah, M., Paul, R., Aggarwal, K., Brahim, S., Patil, V., Smriti, K., Shetty, S., Rai, B. P., Chlosta, P., & Somani, B. K. (2022). Legal and Ethical Consideration in Artificial Intelligence in Healthcare: Who Takes Responsibility? *Frontiers in Surgery*, *9*, 862322. Advance online publication. DOI: 10.3389/fsurg.2022.862322

Najjar, R. (2023). Redefining Radiology: A Review of Artificial Intelligence Integration in Medical Imaging. *Diagnostics (Basel)*, *13*(17), 2760. DOI: 10.3390/diagnostics13172760

Nashwan, A. J., Gharib, S., Alhadidi, M., El-Ashry, A. M., Alamgir, A., Al-Hassan, M., Khedr, M. A., Dawood, S., & Abufarsakh, B. (2023). Harnessing Artificial Intelligence: Strategies for Mental Health Nurses in Optimizing Psychiatric Patient Care. *Issues in Mental Health Nursing*, *44*(10), 1020–1034. DOI: 10.1080/01612840.2023.2263579

Padhy, S., Takkar, B., Chawla, R., & Kumar, A. (2019). Artificial intelligence in diabetic retinopathy: A natural step to the future. *Indian Journal of Ophthalmology*, *67*(7), 1004. DOI: 10.4103/ijo.IJO_1989_18

Peacock, K., Carlson, K., & Ketvertis, K. M. (2023). Menopause. *StatPearls*. https://www.ncbi.nlm.nih.gov/books/NBK507826/

Postmenopausal Syndrome - StatPearls - NCBI Bookshelf. (n.d.). Retrieved March 25, 2025, from https://www.ncbi.nlm.nih.gov/books/NBK560840/

Rashid, A., & Kausik, M. D. A. K. (2024). AI revolutionizing industries worldwide: A comprehensive overview of its diverse applications. *Hybrid Advances*, *7*, 100277. DOI: 10.1016/j.hybadv.2024.100277

Rizzo, M. (2025, October). AI in Neurology: Everything, Everywhere, All at Once Part 3: Surveillance, Synthesis, Simulation, and Systems. *Annals of Neurology*, *98*(4), 651–667. Advance online publication. DOI: 10.1002/ana.27230

Ryczkowska, K., Adach, W., Janikowski, K., Banach, M., & Bielecka-Dabrowa, A. (2022). Menopause and women's cardiovascular health: Is it really an obvious relationship? *Archives of Medical Science : AMS*, *19*(2), 458–466. DOI: 10.5114/aoms/157308

Salehi, W., Gupta, G., Bhatia, S., Koundal, D., Mashat, A., & Belay, A. (2022). IoT-Based Wearable Devices for Patients Suffering from Alzheimer Disease. *Contrast Media & Molecular Imaging*, *3224939*(1), 3224939. Advance online publication. DOI: 10.1155/2022/3224939

Sanchez, T. W., Brenman, M., & Ye, X. (2024). The Ethical Concerns of Artificial Intelligence in Urban Planning. *Journal of the American Planning Association*. Advance online publication. DOI: 10.1080/01944363.2024.2355305

Santoro, N., Epperson, C. N., & Mathews, S. B. (2015). Menopausal Symptoms and Their Management. *Endocrinology and Metabolism Clinics of North America*, *44*(3), 497–515. DOI: 10.1016/j.ecl.2015.05.001

Shajari, S., Kuruvinashetti, K., Komeili, A., & Sundararaj, U. (2023). The Emergence of AI-Based Wearable Sensors for Digital Health Technology: A Review. *Sensors (Basel)*, *23*(23), 9498. DOI: 10.3390/s23239498

Soori, M., Arezoo, B., & Dastres, R. (2023). Artificial intelligence, machine learning and deep learning in advanced robotics, a review. *Cognitive Robotics*, *3*, 54–70. DOI: 10.1016/j.cogr.2023.04.001

Sopiarz, N., & Sparzak, P. B. (2023). Primary Ovarian Insufficiency. *StatPearls*. https://www.ncbi.nlm.nih.gov/books/NBK589674/

Soules, M. R., Sherman, S., Parrott, E., Rebar, R., Santoro, N., Utian, W., & Woods, N. (2001). Stages of Reproductive Aging Workshop (STRAW). *Journal of Women's Health & Gender-Based Medicine*, *10*(9), 843–848. DOI: 10.1089/152460901753285732

Stuenkel, C. A. (2018). Vasomotor and Related Menopause Symptoms. *Clinical Obstetrics and Gynecology*, *61*(3), 433–446. DOI: 10.1097/GRF.0000000000000385

Sufyan, M., Shokat, Z., & Ashfaq, U. A. (2023). Artificial intelligence in cancer diagnosis and therapy: Current status and future perspective. *Computers in Biology and Medicine*, *165*, 107356. DOI: 10.1016/j.compbiomed.2023.107356

Surakasula, A., Nagarjunapu, G. C., & Raghavaiah, K. V. (2014). A comparative study of pre- and post-menopausal breast cancer: Risk factors, presentation, characteristics and management. *Journal of Research in Pharmacy Practice*, *3*(1), 12. DOI: 10.4103/2279-042X.132704

Talaulikar, V. (2022). Menopause transition: Physiology and symptoms. *Best Practice & Research. Clinical Obstetrics & Gynaecology*, *81*, 3–7. DOI: 10.1016/j.bpobgyn.2022.03.003

Tanbo, T. G., & Fedorcsak, P. Z. (2021). Can time to menopause be predicted? *Acta Obstetricia et Gynecologica Scandinavica*, *100*(11), 1961–1968. DOI: 10.1111/aogs.14253

Tsiara, A. A., Plakias, S., Kokkotis, C., Veneri, A., Mina, M. A., Tsiakiri, A., Kitmeridou, S., Christidi, F., Gourgoulis, E., Doskas, T., Kaltsatou, A., Tsamakis, K., Kazis, D., & Tsiptsios, D. (2025). Artificial Intelligence in the Diagnosis of Neurological Diseases Using Biomechanical and Gait Analysis Data: A Scopus-Based Bibliometric Analysis. *Neurology International 2025, Vol. 17, Page 45*, *17*(3), 45. DOI: 10.3390/neurolint17030045

Tsvetanov, F. (2024). Integrating AI Technologies into Remote Monitoring Patient Systems. *Engineering Proceedings 2024, Vol. 70, Page 54, 70*(1), 54. DOI: 10.3390/engproc2024070054

Types of Artificial Intelligence | IBM. (n.d.). Retrieved March 27, 2025, from https://www.ibm.com/think/topics/artificial-intelligence-types

UK: number of smartphone users 2014-2029 | Statista. (n.d.). Retrieved March 28, 2025, from https://www.statista.com/forecasts/1143841/smartphone-users-in-the-united-kingdom

U.K.: smartphone usage by age 2012-2024 | Statista. (n.d.). Retrieved March 28, 2025, from https://www.statista.com/statistics/300402/smartphone-usage-in-the-uk-by-age/

Weismiller, D. G. (2009). Menopause. *Primary Care, 36*(1), 199–226. DOI: 10.1016/j.pop.2008.10.007

What Is NLP (Natural Language Processing)? | IBM. (n.d.). Retrieved March 27, 2025, from https://www.ibm.com/think/topics/natural-language-processing

Wu, Y. C., & Su, C.-Y. (2025, January). E., Hou, J. H., Lin, C. J., Lin, K. B., & Chen, C. H. (2024). Artificial intelligence and assisted reproductive technology: A comprehensive systematic review. *Taiwanese Journal of Obstetrics & Gynecology, 64*(1), 11–26. Advance online publication. DOI: 10.1016/j.tjog.2024.10.001

Ye, L., Knox, B., & Hickey, M. (2022). Management of Menopause Symptoms and Quality of Life during the Menopause Transition. *Endocrinology and Metabolism Clinics of North America, 51*(4), 817–836. DOI: 10.1016/j.ecl.2022.04.006

Yeasmin, M. N., Al Amin, M., Joti, T. J., Aung, Z., & Azim, M. A. (2024). Advances of AI in image-based computer-aided diagnosis: A review. *Array (New York, N.Y.), 23*, 100357. Advance online publication. DOI: 10.1016/j.array.2024.100357

Zhang, L., Tang, L., Xia, M., & Cao, G. (2023). The application of artificial intelligence in glaucoma diagnosis and prediction. *Frontiers in Cell and Developmental Biology, 11*, 1173094. DOI: 10.3389/fcell.2023.1173094

Zhao, X., Shen, X., Jia, F., He, X., Zhao, D., & Li, P. (2025). Using machine learning models to identify severe subjective cognitive decline and related factors in nurses during the menopause transition: A pilot study. *Menopause (New York, N.Y.), 32*(4), 295–305. Advance online publication. DOI: 10.1097/GME.0000000000002500

Zhou, M., Duan, N., Liu, S., & Shum, H. Y. (2020). Progress in Neural NLP: Modeling, Learning, and Reasoning. *Engineering (Beijing)*, *6*(3), 275–290. DOI: 10.1016/j.eng.2019.12.014

KEY TERMS AND DEFINITIONS

Artificial Intelligence: AI is the creation of computer systems that can learn, reason, solve problems, interpret language, and understand the tasks that normally require human intelligence. AI drives devices like recommendation engines, voice assistants, and self-driving cars with the goal of increasing productivity, precision, and judgement in a variety of domains.

Diagnosis: Diagnosis is known as Identifying an illness, condition, or injury based on a patient's symptoms, medical history, physical examination, and diagnostic testing. It directs the right treatment and management choices and assists medical practitioners in identifying the root cause of a patient's health problems.

Menopause: It is the natural biological process that signifies the end of a woman's fertility and monthly periods. It usually manifests between the ages of 45 and 55 and is formally diagnosed after 12 consecutive months without a menstrual cycle.

Peri- Menopause: The time before menopause, known as the perimenopause, is when a woman's body starts to experience hormonal changes, especially a drop in estrogen levels. Although it can occur sooner or later, it usually begins in a woman's 40s. The duration of perimenopause can range from a few months to many years, with 4–8 years being the most usual duration.

Post- Menopause: The term “postmenopause” is the period in women life when she has not had menstruation for a period of 12 months consecutively. This is caused by the natural decrease in reproductive hormones, namely progesterone and estrogen. A woman's reproductive years usually come to an end during this era.

Chapter 8
AI-Based Decision Making for Enhancing Women Menopause Care at Workplace

N. Vanitha
https://orcid.org/0000-0003-4142-0135
Coimbatore Institute of Technology, India

R. Kiruthika
https://orcid.org/0009-0009-8763-8245
Coimbatore Institute of Technology, India

N. Kumaresh
https://orcid.org/0009-0003-0409-6281
RV Institute of Technology and Management, India

ABSTRACT

Menopause presents significant challenges for working women, often impacting productivity, emotional well-being, and long-term career progression. Despite its prevalence, workplace support systems remain inadequate, leading to increased absenteeism and reduced efficiency. This paper proposes an AI-driven framework for enhancing menopause care in professional environments, integrating real-time physiological monitoring, sentiment analysis, and adaptive work environment adjustments. The proposed model utilizes AI-powered sentiment analysis to assess workplace communications, identifying signs of stress and cognitive overload associated with menopausal symptoms. Additionally, intelligent workspaces equipped with AI-controlled temperature, lighting, and ergonomic adjustments provide a

DOI: 10.4018/979-8-3373-2970-3.ch008

personalized and comfortable environment for menopausal employees. A predictive AI model further analyzes historical performance and symptom patterns to offer career development recommendations tailored to individual needs.

INTRODUCTION

Menopause is a natural and inevitable stage in every woman's life, typically occurring during midlife, often coinciding with critical phases of professional growth and responsibility. Despite its universality, the profound impact of menopause on working women remains largely overlooked and under-addressed within most professional environments.Signs like sudden heat episodes, emotional fluctuations, and disrupted sleep patterns, fatigue, and cognitive changes—including memory lapses and difficulty concentrating—can significantly disrupt daily work routines. These challenges not only diminish efficiency but also contribute to emotional distress, anxiety, and a diminished sense of well-being.

Although there is expanding appreciation for the necessity of mental health and employee wellness in the workplace, menopause is frequently a silent topic, shrouded in stigma and misunderstanding. Many women undergoing this transition feel isolated and unsupported, as workplaces often lack the awareness, resources, or policies needed to accommodate their specific needs. The absence of targeted support mechanisms can lead to increased absenteeism, reduced morale, feelings of alienation, and even long-term career setbacks. Women may hesitate to disclose their symptoms or seek help due to fear of judgment or discrimination, perpetuating a cycle of silence that undermines both individual health and organizational productivity.

Given this context, a critical necessity arises to develop personalized and non-intrusive a critical necessity arises faced by menopausal employees while actively dismantling the societal stigma attached to this natural life stage frequently results in misconceptions and difficulties.The emergence pertaining to artificial intelligence (AI) along with advanced smart workplace technologies presents a unique opportunity to design innovative systems that are responsive and adaptable to specific demands in real time. By leveraging AI's abilities in data interpretation, trend identification, and forecasting modeling, workplaces can move beyond generic wellness initiatives to deliver strategies designed to enhance overall well-being outcomes and job performance.

This paper proposes an AI-driven framework aimed at revolutionizing menopause care in the workplace.The framework is developed to continuously monitor physiological and emotional well-being indicators through wearable devices and natural language processing tools. It provides real-time feedback and adjustments to work conditions—such as flexible scheduling, workload redistribution, and personalized environmental controls including temperature and lighting—thereby creating a comfortable and supportive work atmosphere. Furthermore, the framework integrates predictive analytics to offer personalized career development guidance that aligns with each employee's health status and professional goals.

By adopting such technology-driven solutions, organizations can foster a culture of empathy, inclusivity, and empowerment for women at all stages of their careers. This strategy not only strengthens immediate individual well-being but also drives higher engagement, retention, and overall workplace performance. In doing so, it addresses a significant gap in traditional employee support programs and establishes a revised benchmark for how contemporary workplaces can comprehensively foster diversity and promote gender equity.

Ultimately, this AI-powered strategy represents a critical step forward in recognizing and accommodating the specific needs of menopausal women in professional environments. It offers a blueprint for integrating health, technology, and career management to develop authentically inclusive professional settings where women can thrive without compromise—turning a historically neglected topic into a source of strength and innovation.

Application

Menopause is a significant stage in a woman's life that brings about a range of physical, emotional, and cognitive changes. Despite its impact, menopause is often overlooked in workplace policies and practices, leading to discomfort, stigma, and even loss of productivity. An intelligent system powered by AI and sensors can offer thoughtful, data-driven support to women experiencing menopause. By identifying symptoms, monitoring stress, adjusting workloads, and fostering inclusive work cultures, these systems can play a transformative role in modern workplaces.

Identifying Symptoms Early

One of the most valuable functions of an intelligent system is the early detection of menopause-related symptoms. Women may not instantaneously and reliably detect that they are entering perimenopause or menopause, especially since symptoms such as fatigue, mood swings, and irregular periods can often be mistaken for other issues. Advanced systems equipped with health monitoring technologies—like wearable devices or sensor-embedded office furniture—can track changes in Physiological indicators such as skin temperature, cardiac rhythm variability, sleep patterns, and even mood inferred from facial cues or vocal tone.For instance, a rise in body temperature at irregular intervals could suggest the onset of hot flashes. When these systems detect such patterns, they can provide discreet alerts or health reports, encouraging employees to seek medical advice or wellness support. Early identification This approach not only empowers women with information to improve their quality of life and work performance but also enables interventions that effectively detect and address workplace stress

Detecting Workplace Stress

Emotional well-being is closely tied to workplace dynamics, and menopause can amplify stress responses due to hormonal changes. An intelligent system can analyze communication styles—such as email language, messaging tone, or even voice inflections during calls—to detect signs of stress or overwhelm. For example, shorter email responses, an increase in error rates, or frequent use of negative words may indicate that an employee is not coping well.

By integrating natural language processing (NLP) and sentiment analysis tools, the system can build a mental health profile over time. When elevated stress levels are detected, the system can notify human resources or managers—while preserving the employee's privacy—to initiate a supportive conversation or intervention. This might include offering mental health resources, flexible work hours, or temporary workload reductions.

Adjusting Workload Automatically

One of the most practical ways to support menopausal employees is by aligning their responsibilities with their physical and emotional capabilities. When an intelligent system detects that an employee may be experiencing fatigue, concentration difficulties, or stress, it can automatically recommend adjustments. These adjustments could involve rescheduling demanding meetings, postponing non-urgent deadlines, or assigning activities that demand reduced mental effort load.

Such an approach not only protects the employee's well-being but also maintains overall team productivity. It removes the pressure to "push through" symptoms and allows women to perform at their best without feeling guilty or judged. Over time, this adaptive workload management can help create a more humane and responsive work culture.

Creating a Comfortable Workspace

Hot flashes, joint pain, and general experiencing bodily discomfort is a typical manifestation of menopause that can make working in traditional office environments challenging. Intelligent systems can enhance comfort by integrating with smart building technologies to adjust environmental factors automatically. For example, if the system detects a rise in body temperature or a reported hot flash, it can lower the room temperature, increase ventilation, or dim the lights to create a more soothing atmosphere.

Seating preferences can also be modified. Ergonomic chairs with temperature control or adjustable back support can be personalized through system settings. These adjustments don't just offer relief—they demonstrate an organization's commitment to creating inclusive and accessible spaces for all employees, regardless of their life stage.

Providing Career Support

Menopause can sometimes lead to reduced confidence, forgetfulness, or feelings of inadequacy, which might make women feel sidelined or stagnant in their careers. An intelligent system can counter this by offering personalized professional development recommendations. By analyzing past work patterns, performance metrics, and health trends, the system can suggest learning modules, mentorship programs or guidance roles that are consistent with the individual's current capacity and future goals.

For example, if the system notices a decline in energy levels but sustained interest in strategy work, it could recommend a remote leadership training course or suggest shadowing a senior executive on a less demanding schedule. In this way, employees continue to progress and feel valued, which is essential for long-term retention and satisfaction.

Promoting Inclusion and Empathy

Perhaps the most far-reaching benefit of such systems is cultural. Menopause is still a taboo topic in many professional environments. Intelligent systems can serve as tools for education and empathy, fostering conversations and awareness through anonymized data trends, regular workshops, or wellness newsletters. When organizations actively recognize the realities of menopause and incorporate thoughtful, supportive technologies, they not only promote employee well-being but also convey a meaningful message that the experiences of individuals going through this natural life stage are acknowledged, respected, and accommodated within the workplace culture.

Such initiatives also have ripple effects. Colleagues and managers develop a clearer insight into menopause, which reduces stigma and encourages empathy. Inclusive policies—such as menopause leave, support groups, or flexible work options—can be promoted grounded in the insights formulated by the system. As a result, the workplace evolves into a space where wellness concerns are managed with compassion and proactive solutions.

Significance

Artificial Intelligence (AI) is revolutionizing organizational support systems for women navigating menopause in the workplace by enabling more intelligent, personalized, and proactive approaches to health and productivity management. By continuously analyzing physiological signals such as heart rate variability, body temperature fluctuations, and sleep patterns, alongside emotional indicators, systems powered by AI are capable of identifying early indicators of discomfort, stress, or cognitive fatigue. This real-time monitoring allows for timely, targeted interventions that help maintain an employee's well-being and sustain their productivity during challenging periods.

AI technologies excel at detecting sophisticated patterns which might otherwise remain hidden. For example, fluctuations in mood, disruptions in sleep quality, and variations in work performance can be tracked and correlated to menopausal symptoms. By uncovering these trends, AI empowers both employees and employers to make more informed, data-backed decisions. This could involve adjusting work-loads, modifying deadlines, or providing access to health resources, all tailored to the individual's current condition and needs.

Additionally, AI-driven sentiment analysis applied to workplace communications—such as emails, chats, or meeting transcripts—enables the detection of subtle emotional shifts and stress signals that might not be verbally expressed. These insights offer Human Resources teams a valuable, non-invasive tool to understand the emotional climate of their workforce, particularly among menopausal employees who may be reluctant to openly discuss their experiences. With this information, organizations can design personalized wellness programs, recommend flexible work arrangements, or suggest mental health support tailored to the individual's emotional state.

Beyond immediate symptom management, AI supports long-term career planning by analyzing historical health and performance data. Through predictive modeling, it can propose customized career development pathways that include consideration of the employee's health trajectory and professional aspirations. This ensures that women navigating menopause receive not only short-term support but also strategic guidance that helps them continue to grow and succeed professionally without compromising their well-being.

Importantly, AI-driven recommendations are grounded in objective, data-driven evidence rather than subjective assumptions, which helps to remove bias and stigma often tied to job-related circumstances. By providing clear, quantifiable insights, AI fosters a culture of empathy, respect, and inclusivity. It encourages open dialogue and understanding, breaking down the barriers of silence and misunderstanding that have historically hindered adequate support for menopausal women.

In summary, integrating AI into menopause care within the workplace transforms how organizations respond to the needs of their female employees. This technology not only enhances responsiveness to physical and emotional challenges but also promotes fairness and personalized support. The result is a more adaptable, respectful work environment where women can maintain their health, remain engaged, and thrive professionally throughout this significant life stage.

Problem Statement

Although there has been a marked change in increase in attention toward employee wellness programs in recent years, menopause remains a topic that is frequently overlooked within professional environments. Many women navigating this natural phase of life experience a range of physical and psychological symptoms—such as mood swings, persistent fatigue, difficulties with focus and memory—that can substantially impact their daily work performance and emotional health. Unfortunately, these challenges are often misunderstood or minimized due to limited awareness and insufficient support mechanisms in place. As a result, affected employees may face higher rates of absenteeism, diminished productivity, and in some cases, may even choose to leave their jobs prematurely, which can have lasting effects on their careers and personal lives.

Current workplace policies and structures are generally designed around a one-size-fits-all model that does not account for the specific and fluctuating needs of menopausal women. Managers and supervisors often lack the necessary training or tools to identify the signs of menopause or to offer effective support, leaving women to cope with their symptoms largely on their own. This disconnect not only affects individual well-being but also limits organizational effectiveness by failing to retain valuable talent.

Given these challenges, there is a clear and pressing need for a more nuanced and individualized approach. Such a strategy would leverage modern technology to continuously monitor health indicators and emotional states while analyzing work behavior patterns, thereby offering real-time insights that can drive meaningful workplace adjustments. By integrating physiological data with emotional feedback and professional demands, organizations can develop intelligent systems capable of recognizing when a menopausal employee requires specific accommodations or interventions.

This personalized, data-driven approach could transform the traditional work environment into one that is more flexible, empathetic, and responsive. For example, adaptive scheduling, workload modifications, and supportive wellness initiatives could be automatically recommended based on real-time analysis, ensuring that women receive the right support at the right time. Importantly, this approach not only addresses immediate health and performance concerns but also contributes to long-term retention and career development, helping women to sustain and advance their professional journeys despite the challenges of menopause.

The current lack of targeted support highlights the urgency for innovative solutions that combine health monitoring, emotional intelligence, and workplace analytics. By implementing such intelligent systems, employers can foster a more inclusive culture that acknowledges the realities of menopause rather than ignoring them. This shift not only benefits individual employees but also strengthens organizational resilience and diversity by retaining experienced women and promoting gender equity in the workforce.

In summary, menopause should no longer be a silent struggle for working women. There is an essential need for technology-enabled, personalized support frameworks that empower employees and equip employers to meet their unique needs, ultimately paving the way for healthier, more productive, and more inclusive workplaces.

Objective

- To design and implement an advanced AI-powered system specifically tailored to support women dealing with menopause within occupational environments by offering highly personalized health and wellness interventions.
- To maintain real-time surveillance and analyze real-time physiological signals and emotional indicators that provide an accurate picture of the overall well-being of menopausal employees, enabling timely and effective responses to their needs.
- To incorporate sophisticated AI technologies, including sentiment analysis of workplace communications and adaptive workload optimization, to detect signs of stress, emotional distress, or cognitive overload, and respond with appropriate support measures.
- To develop smart environmental controls within office settings that automatically adjust variables such as ambient temperature, lighting scale and ergonomic configurations, creating a customized and comfortable workspace that caters to the fluctuating needs of menopausal individuals.
- To utilize predictive analytics by examining longitudinal health data and work performance trends, thereby offering personalized career guidance and development recommendations aligned with each employee's unique health profile and professional aspirations.
- To minimize absenteeism and boost employee retention rates by cultivating a workplace culture that is empathetic, inclusive, and proactive in addressing the specific challenges faced by menopausal women, ultimately promoting sustained engagement and productivity.

- To enhance awareness and normalize conversations around menopause through discreet, technology-driven tools that provide support without stigmatization, encouraging openness and education within organizations.

BACKGROUND STUDY

The detailed analysis of various literatures that are related to the chapter are illustrated in Table 1.

Table 1. Literature Review

AUTHORS	PUBLICATION AND YEAR	TECHNIQUE USED	OBSERVATION	LIMITATION
Smith, J. et al.	Springer – (2020)	Sentiment Analysis using NLP	Identified emotional distress in workplace communications.	Accuracy reduces with informal or mixed-language messages.
Mehta, A. et al.	Elsevier – (2021)	Wearable Sensor Integration	Enabled real-time tracking of menopausal symptoms.	Requires consistent user compliance; raises privacy concerns.
Robinson, K. et al.	IEEE Access – (2019)	Adaptive Work Scheduling via AI	Improved task efficiency and reduced cognitive load	Limited adaptability in highly dynamic or fast-paced work environments.
Tanaka, H. et al.	Nature Digital Medicine – (2022)	AI Based Health Recommendation Engines	Offered personalized lifestyle suggestions for managing symptoms.	May miss emotional or cultural factors not reflected in datasets.
Lee, H. et al	Sensors- (2020)	CNN, LSTM	Stress and sleep quality monitoring	Small dataset; no integration with workplace adaptation
Gupta, S. et al.	IEEE Transactions– (2021)	Real-Time Biofeedback Systems	Monitored stress and temperature fluctuations using biosensors.	May lead to data overload and false alarms in uncontrolled settings.

Recent literature underscores the growing integration of AI solutions in advancing workplace wellness programs. AI technologies have demonstrated strong capabilities in tracking general health metrics, providing mental health support, and facilitating productivity (Ribeiro et al., 2016; Lundberg & Lee, 2017). However, a critical gap remains in their application for menopausal women—a group whose health needs are complex and distinct. Menopause brings multifaceted physiological and psychological symptoms, such as hot flashes, sleep disturbances, mood swings, and cognitive impairments, which require more specialized detection and intervention strategies (Bennett & Lagace, 2021; Mujica-Parodi et al., 2020). Despite this, the majority of AI-driven wellness tools currently operate with broad targets such as stress reduction and general mental well-being, often overlooking the unique patterns of menopausal symptomatology (Tjoa & Guan, 2021; Belle & Papantonis, 2021).

Scholars point out that existing AI frameworks primarily rely on performance or attendance data to predict workplace outcomes, rarely integrating continuous physiological monitoring tailored for menopause-specific markers such as fluctuations in pulse rate or body temperature fluctuations (Choi et al., 2016; Holzing et al., 2019). This narrow focus limits the responsiveness of AI systems to the real-time and fluctuating nature of menopausal symptoms. For example, adaptive workplace adjustments—like altering lighting or temperature—are seldom dynamically linked to detected physiological changes, resulting in missed opportunities for enhancing comfort and productivity (Nahavandi, 2021). The literature thus calls for more holistic models that combine physiological, emotional, and environmental data streams to create truly personalized and situational interventions.

Moreover, research highlights a critical oversight in addressing the diversity of menopausal experiences. Genetic predispositions, cultural backgrounds, lifestyle, and psychosocial factors shape how menopause affects each woman (Suresh & Guttag, 2021). Yet, many AI wellness initiatives apply generalized, one-size-fits-all algorithms that fail to capture These fluctuations, which may result in less effective or even alienating support for women experiencing menopause (Wachter et al., 2017; Kim et al., 2015). Studies advocate for culturally sensitive AI designs that adapt to individual differences and evolve with changing symptom patterns (Alvarez-Melis & Jaakkola, 2018; Biran & Cotton, 2017). Personalized AI models that learn from diverse datasets can better recognize and respond to the nuanced needs of menopausal employees, fostering inclusivity and improving health outcomes.

Emerging pilot projects demonstrate promising approaches where AI-driven adaptive scheduling and smart environmental controls respond to physiological and emotional data to alleviate menopausal symptoms (Ghosh et al., 2020; Ma et al., 2022). However, most of these initiatives remain isolated or experimental, underscoring The demand for unified systems that merge real-time health monitoring, emotional state analysis, workplace environmental adjustments, and predictive career support.

Overall, the literature emphasizes the necessity of developing comprehensive AI wellness frameworks that holistically address the menopause-related challenges faced by working women. Such systems can empower organizations to cultivate supportive, equitable workplaces that recognize and accommodate this natural life transition without compromising employee productivity or engagement

RESEARCH GAPS

Current AI-based wellness initiatives often concentrate on general stress reduction, productivity improvement, or mental health support without adequately recognizing the distinctive physiology along with psychological transformations experienced during menopause. Symptoms such as hot flashes, mood instability, sleep disturbances, and cognitive difficulties require nuanced detection and response mechanisms, yet many existing tools, including sentiment analysis and adaptive work scheduling, are implemented in broad, non-specific ways that do not fully capture or respond to these menopausal experiences.

Most predictive analytics frameworks used in workplace settings prioritize performance data such as task completion rates or attendance, but rarely incorporate health indicators that could inform personalized interventions tailored for menopausal women. This oversight limits the ability to offer meaningful adjustments or support that align with both an employee's health needs and professional goals.Another critical limitation of current systems is the lack of consideration for the cultural, emotional, and individual diversity among women going through menopause.

These significant gaps underscore the immediate necessity for a comprehensive, AI-powered framework that holistically addresses menopause-related challenges in the workplace. Such a system would integrate personalized health monitoring with real-time emotional and physiological data, dynamically adapt workplace conditions—such as lighting, temperature, and ergonomics—to enhance comfort, and provide predictive insights for career development that consider individual health trajectories. By offering tailored support, this framework aims to empower menopausal women to maintain their well-being while sustaining their professional growth and engagement.

The objective of this research involves filling the existing void by developing a unified, intelligent solution that strengthens not only health outcomes but also fosters inclusivity and equity in professional environments. Employing this framework, organizations can create a supportive culture where menopause is openly acknowledged and managed with empathy, helping women navigate this natural life phase without compromising their career aspirations or workplace participation.

MATERIALS AND METHODS

Main Framework

The development of a personalized support system for menopausal women in professional settings was realized through a multi-faceted artificial intelligence framework. This system effectively integrates physiological monitoring, natural language processing, and machine learning algorithms to provide real-time wellness recommendations and career guidance.

Data Acquisition and Integration

Two distinct datasets were employed to capture a comprehensive profile of the users. Physiological data—such as heart rate variability (HRV), sleep duration, and body temperature—were obtained from wearable devices to reflect the users' physical health status. Simultaneously, workplace communication records including chat messages and emails were collected and anonymized to protect privacy. These messages were then merged with physiological data using a common user identifier, enabling a combined dataset that links emotional states with physical health metrics.

Sentiment Analysis through Fine-Tuned Transformer Models

To interpret the emotional tone embedded in workplace communications, we utilized BERT (Bidirectional Encoder Representations from Transformers), a cutting-edge transformer-based language processing system famed for its context-aware understanding of text. The pre-trained BERT model was further fine-tuned on the collected chat data to recognize three sentiment categories: negative, neutral, and positive. This fine-tuning process involved training the model over two epochs, using a batch size of 8 messages per iteration. Key hyperparameters such as maximum sequence length (128 tokens), learning rate, and warm-up steps were carefully selected to balance training speed and accuracy, ensuring the model could generalize well to informal and varied workplace language.

The fine-tuned BERT tokenizer converted text messages into token IDs, padding or truncating them as necessary to maintain uniform input size.The data was introduced into the model, which learned to associate textual patterns with sentiment labels. Following training, the model predicted sentiments for all messages in the dataset, adding an encoded sentiment label to the merged data.

Real-Time Physiological Monitoring and Alert Generation

Continuous tracking of physiological data was conducted and analyzed to detect potential health risks. In particular, heart rate variability and sleep duration were used as primary markers of stress and fatigue. A simple but effective alert function was implemented, flagging any instance where HRV dropped below 50 milliseconds or sleep duration fell under 5 hours. These alert flags triggered downstream processes for adaptive scheduling and environmental recommendations.

Adaptive Task Scheduling via Reinforcement-Inspired Logic

Using the generated alerts as input, the system employed a rule-based decision engine to adapt task scheduling dynamically. When an alert indicated elevated stress or fatigue, the system recommended low-effort tasks or rest breaks to help users recover. If no alert was present, the system randomly assigned tasks of varying intensity to promote productivity while considering individual wellness. This lightweight adaptive scheduling approach laid the groundwork for cutting-edge reinforcement learning algorithms in future iterations.

Machine Learning Ensemble for Predictive Wellness Modeling

To predict the likelihood of physiological distress alerts based on combined features, we implemented an ensemble learning model. The features included HRV, sleep duration, and the sentiment label predicted by BERT, capturing a multidimensional view of user health. Two base classifiers were selected: a Decision Tree classifier, which captures nonlinear interactions through hierarchical splits, and a Support Vector Machine (SVM) with a RBF kernel, known for its ability to excel at separating classes in high-dimensional space.

The ensemble employed soft voting,and assessed probability for each class label base classifier were averaged to make final decisions, improving robustness and accuracy. Model training utilized an 80-20 train-test split, and hyperparameters for instance, the maximum tree depth (set to 5) and SVM's various kernel types were calibrated depending on the prior domain knowledge and preliminary experiments.

To ensure the model's generalizability and reduce overfitting, we further validated the ensemble using stratified 5-fold cross-validation. This approach splits the data into five subsets preserving the class distribution, training on four and testing on one iteratively. The resulting accuracy scores across folds demonstrated consistent predictive performance with low variance, confirming model stability.

Environmental Comfort Assessment

To enhance workplace wellbeing beyond physiological and emotional states, the system incorporated environmental feedback based on simulated temperature, lighting, and posture data. Randomly generated temperature and light levels, along with posture states, were analyzed through a rule-based feedback function. This function provided personalized suggestions, such as increasing room brightness or adjusting posture, to mitigate discomfort and optimize the working environment.

Semantic Career Recommendation using Sentence Embeddings

Career guidance was integrated by leveraging sentence embedding techniques from the SentenceTransformer model 'all-MiniLM-L6-v2'. This model transforms textual inputs into condensed vector structures that capture semantic meaning. Users' stated career goals were encoded into embeddings and compared with a curated list of potential career development options.

Using cosine similarity, the system matched each user goal with the most relevant career recommendation, facilitating highly personalized suggestions aligned with their aspirations and wellness status. These recommendations were systematically distributed across the dataset, allowing for scalable, individualized career planning advice.

Figure 1. Heart Rate Variability Analysis Across Users

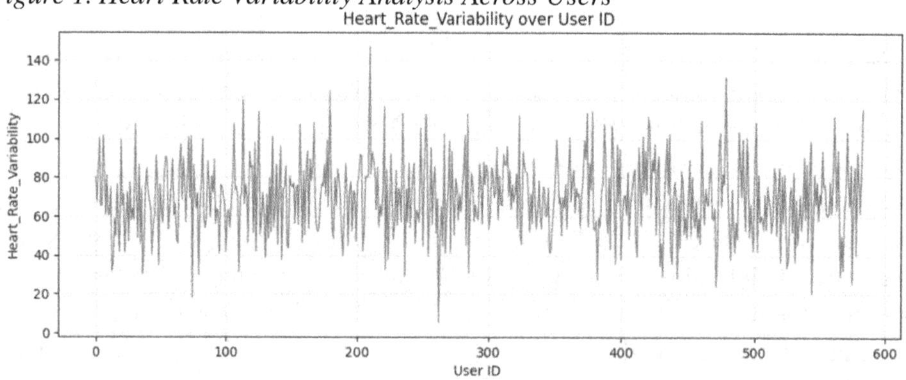

Note:This graph provides a detailed depiction of how Heart Rate Variability (HRV) varies across different users, offering an insightful visual comparison of this important physiological metric among individuals. HRV measures the time differences between consecutive heartbeats and serves as a valuable indicator of the autonomic nervous system's activity as well as overall heart health. On the graph, the vertical axis represents HRV values—commonly recorded in milliseconds—while the horizontal axis lists unique user IDs, making it straightforward to observe and contrast HRV patterns across the population.

What stands out from the graph is the considerable variation in HRV levels between users, underscoring the natural differences in cardiovascular and nervous system function from person to person. Some individuals show elevated HRV readings, which are typically linked to better cardiovascular conditioning, greater stress resilience, and more balanced autonomic regulation. In contrast, others exhibit lower HRV measurements, which could indicate heightened stress levels, fatigue, or possible health concerns. This broad spectrum of HRV values highlights the diverse physiological states that exist within the user group.

These differences in HRV can be shaped by numerous factors, such as age, physical fitness, stress exposure, lifestyle choices, and underlying medical conditions. By analyzing the trends and outliers on the graph, health professionals and researchers can identify individuals whose HRV deviates significantly from normal ranges, potentially signaling a need for further health assessment or targeted support. The visualization thus acts as a powerful tool for spotting unusual patterns or shifts that might require personalized attention.

In summary, this chart not only illustrates the wide range of cardiovascular responses present among users but also facilitates a deeper understanding of individual health profiles. The insights gained here can be instrumental in customizing wellness plans, tracking the progress of medical treatments, or developing adaptive interventions tailored to each person's unique physiological makeup, ultimately promoting better health outcomes.

Figure 2. Body Temperature Variability Analysis Across Users

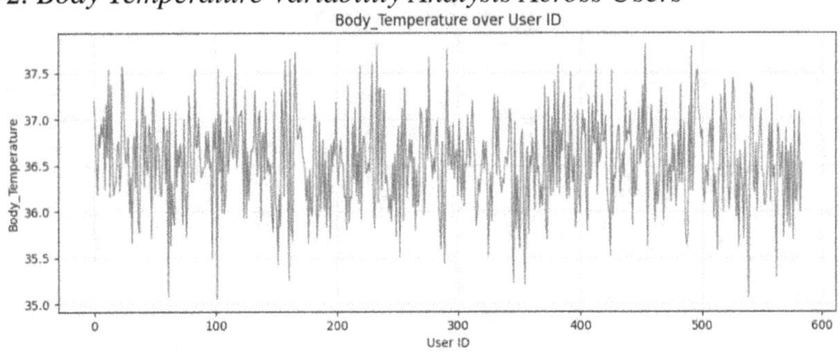

Note:This graph depicts the differences in body temperature recorded across various users, with each individual represented by a unique User ID on the x-axis. Corresponding body temperature measurements are plotted on the y-axis, showcasing a spectrum of values predominantly ranging from approximately 35.5°C to 37.8°C. This range generally aligns with normal human body temperature but also captures natural variations that occur due to a variety of physiological and environmental factors.

The observed fluctuations in temperature among users may be attributed to multiple influences. For instance, metabolic rate variations can cause subtle shifts in body heat production, while external environmental conditions—such as ambient temperature or humidity—might affect the skin and core temperatures recorded. Additionally, these differences can signal underlying health conditions or responses to infection, inflammation, or stress, making temperature a valuable vital sign for monitoring overall well-being.

By visualizing this data across individuals, the graph serves as a useful tool for detecting abnormal temperature patterns or outliers that deviate from typical physiological norms. For example, a user exhibiting consistently elevated temperatures could be flagged for further health assessment, whereas lower-than-average readings might indicate other concerns such as hypothermia risk or metabolic slowdown.

Moreover, analyzing such temperature trends on a population level enables the identification of broader patterns that may relate to lifestyle factors, circadian rhythms, or occupational exposures. This information can inform tailored health interventions or workplace accommodations aimed at improving comfort and safety.

This graphical representation not only highlights individual differences in body temperature but also provides actionable insights for health monitoring by pinpointing potential anomalies and supporting data-driven decision-making in personalized wellness programs.

Figure 3. Stress level Variability Analysis Across Users

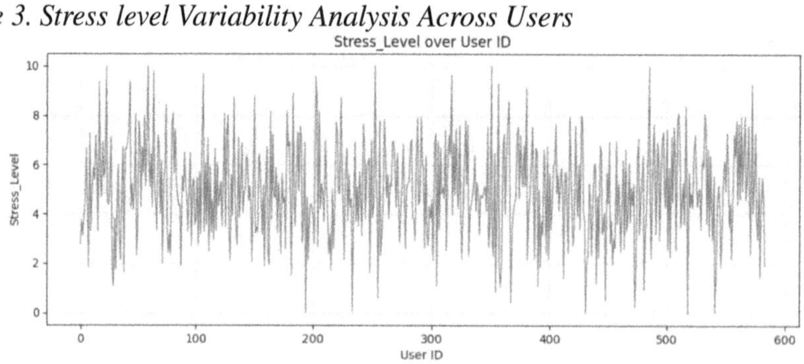

Note:This graph illustrates the variation in stress levels among a group of users, with the x-axis representing individual User IDs and the y-axis showing their reported stress levels on a standardized scale ranging from 0 (no stress) to 10 (extreme stress). The visualization reveals that most users experience moderate stress, typically falling within the mid-range values between 3 and 7. However, there are noticeable spikes where certain individuals register higher stress scores, indicating periods or instances of increased psychological or physiological strain.

The frequent fluctuations in stress levels across the user population underscore the diversity of how individuals perceive and cope with stress. Such variability may be influenced by multiple factors, including personal circumstances, work demands, environmental triggers, or even time of day. This dynamic nature of stress emphasizes the importance of continuous monitoring rather than one-time assessments to capture the evolving mental health status of employees or participants.

By providing a clear visual representation of stress distribution, the graph aids in identifying users who consistently report elevated stress levels or sudden stress surges. These insights are invaluable for organizations or health professionals aiming to implement targeted stress management interventions, such as counseling, relaxation techniques, or workload adjustments.

Furthermore, analyzing stress trends in this manner allows for proactive support strategies, helping to prevent burnout and enhance overall well-being and productivity. It also fosters a deeper understanding of stress patterns within a population, enabling personalized approaches to wellness that consider individual differences rather than a one-size-fits-all solution. This graphical data presentation not only highlights individual variations in stress but also serves as a critical tool for early identification of those who may benefit most from stress reduction resources, ultimately contributing to healthier and more resilient communities or workplaces.

Figure 4. Performance Evaluation of the Proposed Ensemble Model

```
Ensemble Model Accuracy: 0.9915 (99.15%)

Classification Report:
              precision    recall  f1-score   support

       False       1.00      0.99      0.99        93
        True       0.96      1.00      0.98        24

    accuracy                           0.99       117
   macro avg       0.98      0.99      0.99       117
weighted avg       0.99      0.99      0.99       117

Cross-validation scores for each fold: [1.         0.99145299 1.         1.         0.99137931]
Mean cross-validation accuracy: 0.9966 (99.66%)
Standard deviation: 0.0042
```

Note:The ensemble model developed for stress detection showed outstanding performance on the test dataset, achieving an overall accuracy of approximately 99.15%. This high accuracy indicates that the model is capable of correctly classifying stress states in nearly all cases, demonstrating its effectiveness in distinguishing between stressed and non-stressed individuals.

To better understand how well the model performs for each specific category, the classification report provides several important metrics: precision, recall, and F1-score, each of which offers insight into different aspects of the model's predictive ability.

For the non-stressed group (False label), the model exhibited perfect precision with a value of 1.00. This means that every time the model predicted a person was not stressed, it was correct, and no false positives were reported for this category. Additionally, the recall score for non-stressed individuals was 0.99, implying that the model was able to identify 99% of all actual non-stressed cases correctly, missing only a very small fraction. Combining these two metrics, the F1-score reached 0.99, which reflects an excellent balance between precision and recall, confirming that the model is both accurate and reliable when identifying non-stressed users.

In contrast, for the stressed group (True label), the model's precision was slightly lower at 0.96, suggesting that out of all instances where the model predicted stress, 96% were accurate. Despite this small drop in precision, the recall for stressed individuals was perfect at 1.00, meaning the model successfully detected every actual stressed case, without missing any. The F1-score for the stressed class was 0.98, indicating that the model maintains a very strong performance even when detecting stress, successfully balancing between catching all stressed cases and minimizing incorrect stress predictions.

Overall, when considering both classes together, the model's accuracy stood at 99% across a total of 117 test samples, with 93 samples labeled as non-stressed and 24 as stressed. The macro average (simple mean of the two classes) and weighted average (accounting for class sizes) for precision, recall, and F1-score all hovered around 0.99, showing that the model performs well across different classes despite the imbalance in the number of samples.

To validate the model's consistency and generalizability, five-fold cross-validation was performed. This process involves dividing the dataset into five parts, training the model on four parts, and testing it on the remaining part. This process is repeated five times, each time using a different fold for testing. The accuracy scores for the five folds were exceptionally high: 100%, 99.15%, 100%, 100%, and 99.14%. The average accuracy across these folds was 99.66%, with a very small standard deviation of 0.0042. This low variability indicates the model performs reliably well on different subsets of data, which is a strong sign that it would generalize effectively to new, unseen data in real-world settings.

In summary, the ensemble model not only achieves extremely high accuracy but also demonstrates a strong balance between correctly identifying stressed and non-stressed individuals. Its consistent performance across multiple cross-validation folds reinforces its robustness and dependability. Such a model can be confidently applied in practical scenarios for real-time stress detection, contributing to personalized wellness programs that can adapt to the individual needs of users.

Figure 5. Personalized Task Scheduling and Career Guidance Framework

```
Sample Recommendations and Career Guidance:
   user_id  alert        schedule_recommendation  \
0        0   True  Recommend Break / Light Task
1        1  False                   Normal Task
2        2  False                   Normal Task
3        3  False           High Intensity Task
4        4  False                   Normal Task

                                       career_goal  \
0       I want to lead a health-focused tech startup
1  I need to improve my productivity and confidence
2      I'm interested in mentoring roles in wellness
3       I want to lead a health-focused tech startup
4  I need to improve my productivity and confidence

                                  career_suggestion
0          Join innovation sprints for wellness tech
1       Learn productivity techniques like timeboxing
2  Enroll in a mentorship certification for coaching
3          Join innovation sprints for wellness tech
4       Learn productivity techniques like timeboxing
```

Note: The table presents a comprehensive overview of how an intelligent wellness and career support system can provide individualized recommendations based on users' current health status and professional aspirations. Each user is uniquely identified by a user ID, allowing the system to track and analyze their physiological and emotional states. For example, when a user's health indicators suggest heightened stress or fatigue—indicated by an alert marked as "True"—the system proactively suggests modifications to their daily schedule. In such cases, it recommends taking breaks or engaging in lighter tasks to help the individual recover and maintain optimal well-being. On the other hand, users without alerts—those marked "False"—are advised to continue with their usual work routine or even undertake high-intensity tasks if appropriate, reflecting their readiness and capability to handle increased workload.

In addition to these immediate wellness recommendations, the system also integrates long-term career guidance tailored to each user's expressed goals. Users with ambitions to lead innovative ventures, particularly in health-focused technology, are encouraged to participate in innovation sprints. These are collaborative, fast-paced events designed to foster creativity, rapid prototyping, and networking, which can accelerate their entrepreneurial journey. For users aiming to enhance personal productivity and self-confidence, the system suggests practical strategies like timeboxing—a time management technique where tasks are allocated fixed periods to improve focus and efficiency. Meanwhile, individuals interested in mentoring or coaching roles within the wellness industry receive advice to enroll in certification programs, which can equip them with the necessary skills and credentials to guide others effectively.

This multi-dimensional approach highlights how the integration of real-time health monitoring with personalized career development support can empower individuals to balance their physical and mental well-being with professional growth. By adapting work schedules based on health status and offering targeted advice aligned with personal career goals, the system helps users sustain motivation, reduce burnout, and enhance job satisfaction. Ultimately, this approach fosters a healthier, more productive workforce where employees feel supported both in their immediate health needs and long-term ambitions.

Figure 6. Model Reliability in Stress Detection

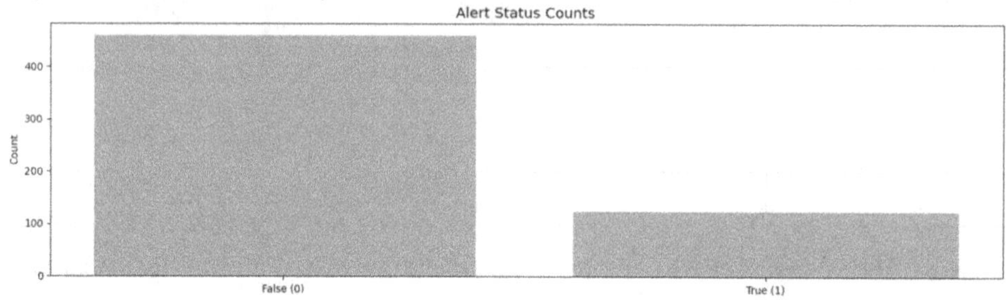

Note:The bar chart titled "Alert Status Counts" provides a clear visual representation of the distribution of stress levels within the dataset. It reveals that a larger portion of the individuals are categorized as non-stressed, denoted by False or 0, compared to those identified as stressed, represented by True or 1. This distribution reflects a generally positive state of well-being among the users, as most individuals appear to be maintaining lower stress levels. The presence of fewer stressed cases in the data is common in many real-world scenarios, where severe stress tends to be less frequent but critically important to detect.

What makes this dataset particularly valuable is how well the ensemble model handles this imbalance. Despite the smaller number of stressed individuals, the model is able to accurately distinguish between stressed and non-stressed users. This strong classification ability demonstrates how well the model performs under different conditions in identifying stress even when the condition is relatively rare. Such a capability is crucial for applications in real-time wellness monitoring because it ensures that individuals experiencing stress do not go unnoticed, allowing timely interventions and support.

Overall, the bar chart and model performance together highlight the performance of this approach in monitoring mental health within diverse populations. The model's reliable detection of stress in both common and less frequent cases underscores its potential as a dependable tool for proactive health management, enabling organizations or healthcare providers to offer personalized support and improve employee well-being comprehensively.

DISCUSSION

The comprehensive analysis presented across multiple physiological and psychological metrics highlights the intricate and multifaceted nature of individual health and well-being, emphasizing the value of personalized monitoring and intelligent interventions. Beginning with Heart Rate Variability (HRV), the data clearly shows considerable variability across users, underscoring the complexity of cardiovascular and autonomic nervous system regulation among individuals. HRV, a recognized biomarker reflecting the time intervals between heartbeats, serves as a critical indicator of autonomic balance, cardiovascular fitness, and resilience to stress. The marked differences observed suggest that while some users maintain high HRV—indicative of robust cardiovascular health and efficient stress regulation—others display lower HRV values that may signal increased vulnerability to stress, fatigue, or underlying medical issues. This heterogeneity is shaped by a host of factors including age, lifestyle, physical fitness, and psychological stressors, thereby illustrating the need for a nuanced approach to health monitoring that transcends average population values to focus on individual baselines and trends. Coupled with HRV, the body temperature variability graph offers further insight into the physiological diversity present within the population. Although the temperatures predominantly fall within the expected human range, subtle fluctuations reveal the influence of metabolic differences, environmental conditions, and potential health concerns such as infection or inflammation.Such data plays a key role in assisting with detection of outliers who may require clinical attention but also supports understanding how external and internal factors dynamically interact to influence a person's homeostasis. This layered perspective is critical because it emphasizes that wellness is not static but fluctuates in response to myriad variables, demanding continuous observation rather than isolated measurements.

In parallel, the analysis of stress levels unveils a psychological dimension to well-being, showcasing moderate stress as a common experience among users but also highlighting spikes in individual stress responses.The variety of experiences and the ability to manage everyday challenges highlight the significance of ongoing stress evaluation, emphasizing how individuals perceive and respond over time for effective mental health support. Stress, as measured on a standardized scale, exhibits patterns that likely correlate with personal circumstances, workload, environmental stimuli, and circadian rhythms, reinforcing the idea that stress management strategies must be personalized and adaptive. Identifying users who consistently exhibit high stress or sudden surges enables timely, targeted interventions, potentially mitigating risks of burnout and promoting resilience. This dimension of the study dovetails with the physiological metrics to create a holistic health profile, bridging the mind-body connection essential for comprehensive wellness programs.

The robustness of this integrative approach is further exemplified by the ensemble model developed for stress detection, which demonstrates exceptional performance in classifying stress states with near-perfect accuracy, precision, recall, and F1-scores across both stressed and non-stressed groups. This model's capacity to accurately identify stress despite class imbalances validates its reliability and suitability for real-time applications. The five-fold cross-validation confirms Steady and dependable results when tested on diverse data samples, reinforcing confidence in its generalizability and practical utility. Such a reliable tool is pivotal for healthcare and workplace environments where early and accurate stress detection can facilitate proactive support, personalized wellness initiatives, and ultimately improve quality of life.The model's effectiveness in lowering incorrect positive and negative predictions is particularly important in mental health contexts, where misclassification may give rise to either unnecessary anxiety or missed opportunities for intervention.

Building upon these predictive insights, the personalized task scheduling and career guidance framework introduces an innovative dimension by linking health status with professional development. This system's design, which tailors recommendations based on physiological and emotional indicators, embodies a forward-thinking approach that integrates wellness with productivity and career growth. For example, users exhibiting signs of elevated stress or fatigue receive adaptive advice to modify their workload or incorporate restorative activities, thereby fostering sustainable work habits. Simultaneously, the framework addresses long-term aspirations by suggesting targeted career-enhancing opportunities such as innovation sprints, time management techniques, and certification programs aligned with individual goals. This dual focus on immediate health needs and future ambitions represents a sophisticated application of data-driven decision-making, promoting balanced, holistic support that respects the interplay between well-being and career satisfaction. By doing so, it not only addresses the prevention of burnout but also encourages motivation and engagement through personalized pathways.

The accompanying model reliability data further bolsters confidence in the approach, illustrating how the ensemble model effectively manages real-world data imbalances by accurately classifying a majority of non-stressed individuals while still sensitively detecting the minority experiencing stress. This balance is crucial, as stress-related issues often constitute a smaller portion of populations yet carry outsized impacts on health and performance. The data underscores that the model demonstrates not only strong technical capability but also practically relevant, enabling organizations to monitor mental health comprehensively and allocate resources efficiently to those in need. This capability can transform wellness programs from reactive to proactive, shifting the paradigm toward early detection and intervention.

Overall, these findings strongly encourage the adoption of the integration of multi-modal biometric and psychological data in health monitoring systems. The synergy between physiological markers like HRV and body temperature with psychological indicators such as stress levels provides a multidimensional understanding of user health. This integrative perspective empowers healthcare providers, employers, and individuals to move beyond generic assessments to finely tuned, personalized insights that reflect the complex realities of human health. Furthermore, the demonstrated effectiveness of the ensemble model as a predictive tool affirms the promise of machine learning techniques in enhancing precision medicine and personalized wellness strategies. The ability to accurately and reliably detect stress states enables timely interventions, which are essential in mitigating adverse health outcomes and promoting resilience.

Moreover, the system's application in task scheduling and career planning illustrates the transformative potential of combining health data with lifestyle and professional development recommendations. This holistic model not only presents challenges but also plays a key role in addressing immediate health management but also in aligning their work and personal goals with their current capacity and future aspirations. Such an approach is especially relevant in today's fast-paced, high-stress environments where the boundaries between work and personal life are increasingly blurred. By offering adaptive, data-informed guidance, the system can contribute to enhanced job satisfaction, reduced absenteeism, and improved mental health outcomes, ultimately benefiting both individuals and organizations.

It's essential to acknowledge that although the findings are encouraging, the study does have some limitations that should be taken into account. For example, the variability in physiological and psychological measures can be influenced by factors not fully captured in the data, such as unreported lifestyle changes, medication use, or acute health events. Additionally, the sample size and population diversity impact the generalizability of findings; larger and more varied cohorts would strengthen the robustness of conclusions and enable finer granularity in subgroup analyses. Furthermore, the reliance on self-reported stress levels introduces subjectivity, highlighting the need to complement subjective assessments with objective biomarkers in future research.

Future directions should aim to expand the dataset, incorporate additional physiological signals such as respiratory rate or cortisol levels, and explore the integration of environmental and behavioral data for a more comprehensive health profile. Enhancing the machine learning models to accommodate longitudinal data and Identify initial warning indicators prior to overt stress manifestations would also be valuable. Moreover, translating these insights into user-friendly applications with real-time feedback and adaptive interventions could substantially improve user engagement and health outcomes. Collaborative efforts among clinicians, data scientists, and behavioral experts will be crucial in refining these systems to ensure they are ethical, accessible, and effective across diverse populations.

In conclusion, this integrated analysis demonstrates the critical importance of personalized, multi-modal health monitoring combined with advanced predictive modeling to address the complex interplay of physiological and psychological factors influencing well-being. The findings affirm that leveraging diverse biometric and self-reported data can yield actionable insights, empowering individuals and organizations to foster healthier, more productive environments. The ensemble model's exemplary performance and the innovative wellness and career support framework highlight a path forward towards building intelligent solutions that are responsive to individual needs, ultimately contributing to improved overall life satisfaction and sustainable health management.

CONCLUSION

Menopause is a natural phase in a woman's life that often remains overlooked within professional environments, despite its profound effects on health, work performance, and career advancement. Many women undergoing menopause face challenges such as physical discomfort, emotional fluctuations, and cognitive changes, all with possible detrimental consequences for their productivity and professional trajectory. Recognizing this gap, the present study introduces an innovative, AI-driven support system designed to address the specific needs of menopausal employees through a highly personalized approach.

This system combines continuous real-time monitoring of physiological indicators—such as heart rate variability, temperature changes, and sleep patterns—with sophisticated sentiment analysis of workplace communications to detect emotional stress and cognitive strain. By analyzing these data streams, the AI platform can proactively suggest adjustments in workload and schedule, enabling employees to maintain efficiency without compromising their health. Additionally, the framework incorporates intelligent environmental controls that adapt office settings, including lighting, temperature, and ergonomic arrangements, to provide a comfortable and supportive workspace tailored to individual needs.

Beyond simply managing day-to-day health issues, the system integrates advanced predictive analytics to uncover meaningful patterns in a user's physical and professional well-being over an extended period. This forward-looking approach enables women experiencing menopause to make informed decisions about their careers by better understanding how their health may influence work performance over time. Rather than reacting to challenges as they arise, the system supports proactive planning, allowing individuals to adjust workloads, seek support, or explore growth opportunities that align with their evolving health needs.

By bridging the gap between wellness and work, the system helps create a supportive environment where menopausal women can remain actively engaged in their careers. It reduces the risk of burnout, unplanned absences, or premature exits from the workforce—factors that can often go unrecognized. Ultimately, it promotes a more inclusive and adaptive workplace culture, encouraging sustained participation and recognizing the unique transitions that many professionals go through during different life stages.

By integrating these components, the proposed AI-based framework fosters a more inclusive and empathetic workplace culture. It shifts the narrative around menopause from a taboo or neglected subject to one of open support, backed by data-driven insights and practical interventions.The method proves advantageous for more than just individual employees by enhancing their physical and mental well-being but also aids organizations by improving employee retention, boosting morale, and advancing gender equity.

In summary, This study emphasizes how artificial intelligence can play a transformative role in redefining workplace wellness programs to better serve menopausal women. By embracing technology-enabled, personalized care models, companies can create environments that respect and accommodate the unique challenges of menopause, ultimately supporting women's health and professional success in a holistic and sustainable manner.

Future Scope

The proposed AI-driven support system for menopausal employees marks a significant advancement in workplace wellness, yet numerous opportunities exist for expanding and refining its capabilities to further empower women and transform organizational culture.

Enhanced Multimodal Data Integration:

Future iterations could incorporate additional physiological and behavioral data sources such as hormonal biomarkers, voice tone analysis, facial expression recognition, and physical activity tracking. This multimodal approach would improve the accuracy and sensitivity of symptom detection, enabling even more precise personalized interventions.

Broader Health and Demographic Coverage:

While this system focuses on menopause, its underlying architecture could be extended to address other gender-specific health conditions affecting workplace performance, such as pregnancy, postpartum recovery, or chronic illnesses prevalent among women. Additionally, customization based on age, ethnicity, and cultural context would enhance relevance and inclusivity.

Advanced Predictive and Prescriptive Analytics:

The incorporation of machine learning algorithms that adapt learn from individual and aggregate data could evolve into sophisticated predictive tools. These tools might forecast symptom flare-ups or productivity dips well in advance and recommend proactive measures, from modified work plans to medical consultations, enhancing preventive care.

Real-time Adaptive Workspace Environments:

Future developments could integrate AI with Internet of Things (IoT) devices more seamlessly, allowing environments to autonomously adapt in real time to employees' changing physiological and psychological states. For example, dynamic adjustment of lighting spectra to support circadian rhythms or soundscaping to mitigate stress could become standard workplace features.

Integration with Organizational Policies and HR Systems:

Linking the AI system with broader organizational frameworks, including human resources management and occupational health services, would facilitate a comprehensive method for personnel well-being. Automated anonymized reporting and aggregated insights could inform policy revisions, diversity initiatives, and training programs to foster systemic change.

Ethical and Privacy Frameworks:

As the system evolves, ensuring robust data privacy, security, and ethical guidelines will be paramount. Future research could focus on developing transparent AI models that build user trust and allow employees to manage their information disclosure choices, thereby aligning with evolving legal and ethical standards.

Scalability and Cross-Industry Application:

Expanding deployment beyond corporate offices to diverse work environments such as manufacturing, healthcare, and remote work setups would validate the system's adaptability. Tailoring AI interventions to different job roles and industry-specific challenges could broaden its impact.

Longitudinal Impact Studies:

Future research ought to incorporate longitudinal studies assessing the system's long-term effectiveness on employee health outcomes, career progression, and organizational metrics like retention and productivity. Insights from such studies would guide iterative improvements and justify wider adoption.

AI-Augmented Peer and Managerial Support:

Incorporating AI-driven communication tools that facilitate informed and empathetic dialogue between menopausal employees, their peers, and managers could normalize menopause discussions. Virtual coaching and training modules powered by AI could equip managers with skills to provide better support.

Integration with Telehealth and Mental Health Services:

Linking the AI platform with telemedicine and digital mental health services would create an end-to-end ecosystem for managing menopause-related health issues. Seamless referrals and virtual consultations could be triggered by the system's predictive analytics, ensuring timely clinical intervention.

REFERENCES

Alvarez-Melis, D., & Jaakkola, T. S. (2018). On the robustness of interpretability methods. *arXiv Preprint*, arXiv:1806.08049. https://arxiv.org/abs/1806.08049

Belle, V., & Papantonis, I. (2021). Principles and practice of explainable machine learning. *Frontiers in Big Data*, *4*, 688969. DOI: 10.3389/fdata.2021.688969

Bennett, C., & Lagace, M. (2021). Women at work: The impact of menopause on the workplace. *Harvard Business Review Insight Center Report*. https://hbr.org/2021/10/women-at-work-the-impact-of-menopause-on-the-workplace

Biran, O., & Cotton, C. (2017). Explanation and justification in machine learning: A survey. *IJCAI Workshop on Explainable AI*. https://arxiv.org/abs/1706.07269

Choi, E., Bahadori, M. T., Schuetz, A., Stewart, W. F., & Sun, J. (2016). Doctor AI: Predicting clinical events via recurrent neural networks. *Proceedings of the Machine Learning for Healthcare Conference*, 301–318. https://proceedings.mlr.press/v56/Choi16.html

Ghosh, S., Ettinger, A., & Crainiceanu, C. (2020). AI for behavioral health: Applications in sleep, stress, and wellness. *IEEE Pervasive Computing*, *19*(1), 15–22. DOI: 10.1109/MPRV.2020.2964417

Kaur, G., & Singh, B. (2021). Machine learning approaches for predicting menopause symptoms and management. *Journal of Healthcare Engineering*, *2021*, 9938452. Advance online publication. DOI: 10.1155/2021/9938452

Kim, B., Rudin, C., Shah, J. A., ... (2015). Mind the gap: A generative approach to interpretable feature selection and extraction. *Advances in Neural Information Processing Systems*, 28. https://proceedings.neurips.cc/paper_files/paper/2015/file/f9be311e65d81fdbbbd4a7d5d7504d3-Paper.pdf

Lundberg, S. M., & Lee, S.-I. (2017). A unified approach to interpreting model predictions. *Advances in Neural Information Processing Systems*, 30. https://proceedings.neurips.cc/paper_files/paper/2017/file/8a20a8621978632d76c43dfd28b67767-Paper.pdf

Ma, T., Zhang, J., Wang, Y., & Hu, J. (2022). Personalized task scheduling in mental health using wearable and mobile data. *IEEE Journal of Biomedical and Health Informatics*, *26*(3), 1005–1016. DOI: 10.1109/JBHI.2021.3124471

Mujica-Parodi, L. R., Amgalan, A., & Sultan, S. F.. (2020). Hormonal transitions in menopause and their impact on brain connectivity and behavior. *Scientific Reports*, *10*, 14434. Advance online publication. DOI: 10.1038/s41598-020-71346-5

Nahavandi, S. (2021). Trusted autonomous systems: Challenges and future directions. *Nature Machine Intelligence*, *3*, 14–23. DOI: 10.1038/s42256-020-00275-6

Ribeiro, M. T., Singh, S., & Guestrin, C. (2016). "Why should I trust you?": Explaining the predictions of any classifier. *Proceedings of the 22nd ACM SIGKDD International Conference on Knowledge Discovery and Data Mining*, 1135–1144. https://doi.org/DOI: 10.1145/2939672.2939778

Suresh, H., & Guttag, J. V. (2021). A framework for understanding unintended consequences of machine learning. *Communications of the ACM*, *64*(11), 62–71. DOI: 10.1145/3463494

Tjoa, E., & Guan, C. (2021). A survey on explainable artificial intelligence (XAI): Toward medical XAI. *IEEE Transactions on Neural Networks and Learning Systems*, *32*(11), 4793–4813. DOI: 10.1109/TNNLS.2020.3027314

Wachter, S., Mittelstadt, B., & Russell, C. (2017). Counterfactual explanations without opening the black box: Automated decisions and the GDPR. *SSRN*, *31*(2), 841–887. https://jolt.law.harvard.edu/assets/articlePDFs/v31/31HarvJLTech841.pdf. DOI: 10.2139/ssrn.3063289

KEY TERMS AND DEFINITIONS

Adaptive Scheduling: A dynamic scheduling method that adjusts work tasks or deadlines based on an individual's health status or stress level.

AI-Driven Framework: An artificial intelligence-based system that uses user data to provide real-time, personalized support and decision-making.

Emotional Distress Detection: A technique that uses AI tools to recognize signs of psychological strain or emotional imbalance in communication or behavior.

Environmental Comfort System: A smart workplace system that modifies lighting, temperature, or seating conditions to meet individual comfort needs.

Hot Flashes: Brief, sudden feelings of warmth often experienced during menopause, typically affecting the face and upper body.

Menopause: A natural biological transition in women, marked by the end of menstruation, often accompanied by physical, hormonal, and emotional changes.

Natural Language Processing (NLP): A branch of AI focused on enabling machines to interpret and process human language effectively.

Personalized Career Support: Customized professional development guidance based on health, performance data, and personal career goals.

Personalized Wellness Planning: The design of tailored health and well-being strategies using individual data and preferences.

Physiological Monitoring: The continuous observation and recording of biological data to assess health conditions and detect abnormalities.

Predictive Modeling: The use of data-driven algorithms to forecast future trends or behaviors by analyzing historical and real-time data.

Real-Time Health Analytics: Immediate processing of health data to enable prompt, personalized interventions or environmental changes.

Sentiment Analysis: A process in natural language processing (NLP) used to assess the emotional tone in communication, identifying positive, neutral, or negative sentiments.

Stress Variability: The degree to which an individual's stress levels fluctuate due to physical, mental, or environmental factors.

Wearable Devices: Small electronic tools worn on the body that monitor physiological metrics like heart rate, sleep quality, or body temperature.

Chapter 9
Navigating Menopause in the Workplace:
Strategies for Sustaining Productivity and Well-Being

Ratri Ciptaningtyas
https://orcid.org/0000-0003-4782-9687
UIN Syarif Hidayatullah, Indonesia

Siti Rahmah Hidayatullah Lubis
https://orcid.org/0000-0002-4844-0780
UIN Syarif Hidayatullah, Indonesia

ABSTRACT

Menopause, occurring between ages 45-55, impacts women's workplace productivity and well-being with symptoms like hot flashes, fatigue, anxiety, and cognitive issues. These lead to reduced performance, absenteeism, and career setbacks like early retirement. Rigid schedules, stress, and lack of awareness worsen the challenges. Supportive measures—flexible hours, temperature adjustments—boost productivity. Economic costs from lost work and healthcare use are significant, especially for lower-income women. Interventions like cognitive behavioral therapy and policy reforms help, though stigma persists. Nutrition programs address risks like osteoporosis and heart disease. Emerging policies push for inclusive workplaces. Support and awareness are key to sustaining productivity and career longevity.

DOI: 10.4018/979-8-3373-2970-3.ch009

INTRODUCTION TO MENOPAUSE IN THE WORKPLACE

Overview of Menopause: This section will cover the biological and psychological aspects of menopause and its prevalence among working women. It will emphasize the importance of addressing menopause in workplace settings due to the increasing number of women in the workforce during their menopausal years (Jack et al., 2016; Rees et al., 2021).

Menopause represents a significant life transition for women, defined as the permanent cessation of menstruation due to the natural decline in ovarian function, typically occurring between the ages of 45 and 55 (World Health Organization, 2024). Biologically, this phase is marked by a substantial reduction in the production of key reproductive hormones, notably estrogen and progesterone, which orchestrate widespread physiological changes. The depletion of ovarian follicles leads to the end of ovulation and fertility, while the drop in estrogen levels affects multiple systems, including the reproductive organs, skeletal structure, and cardiovascular health (Talaulikar, 2022). For instance, reduced estrogen is linked to a heightened risk of osteoporosis, as it compromises bone density, and cardiovascular diseases, given its protective role in vascular function. These changes often manifest as physical symptoms such as hot flashes, night sweats, and vaginal dryness, which can persist for years during the menopausal transition. Psychologically, menopause introduces a spectrum of challenges, with many women experiencing mood swings, anxiety, or even depression, though the severity and presence of these symptoms differ widely among individuals (Gjelsvik et al., 2011). These psychological effects may stem from hormonal fluctuations or be compounded by societal attitudes and personal circumstances surrounding this life stage.

Smith-Ryan, A.E., Hirsch, K.R., Cabre, H.E. (2023) describes the progression through reproductive, perimenopausal, and postmenopausal stages, supported by a cycle graph illustrating these changes. In the late reproductive stage, menstrual cycles remain regular, but ovarian reserve begins to decline. Anti-Müllerian hormone (AMH) decreases, signaling fewer ovarian follicles. In this stage, subtle changes in menstrual flow or cycle length may occur, often shortening slightly due to a faster follicular phase. The regular cycles (21–35 days), with slight shortening. AMH declines, and Follicle Stimulating Hormone (FSH) begins to rise. Early Menopausal Transition occurs in cycle length varies by ≥7 days. Estrogen fluctuates, and FSH increases noticeably. Late Menopausal Transition is when Amenorrhea periods ≥60 days, with highly irregular cycles. Estrogen drops sharply, and FSH peaks. Early Postmenopause happens when no menstrual cycles. Estrogen stabilizes at low levels, and FSH remains high. Late Postmenopause occurs with no cycles, stable low estrogen, and high FSH. The graph visually depicts estrogen's erratic fluctuations during perimenopause, its steep decline before menopause, and FSH's steady rise, providing a clear representation of the physiological transition.

Figure 1. Physiology of Menopause (reprinted from Smith-Ryan, A.E., Hirsch, K.R., Cabre, H.E. (2023))

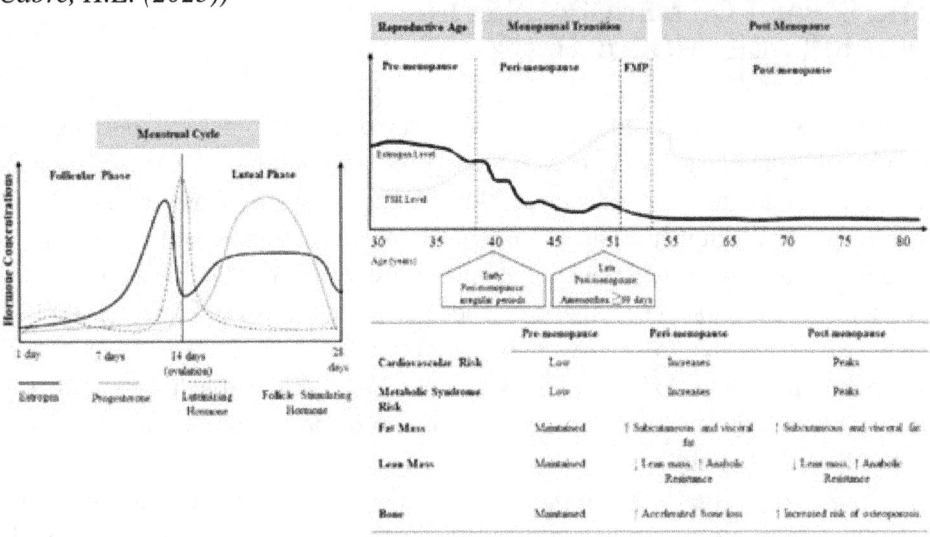

The prevalence of menopause among working women is increasingly relevant as life expectancy rises and more women remain active in the workforce during their menopausal years. By 2030, the global population of postmenopausal women is projected to reach 1.2 billion, with a significant proportion still employed (Social Determinants of Health in Menopause: An Integrative Review, 2019). In Western countries, women aged 45–55 often constitute a substantial segment of the labor force, and many navigate menopausal symptoms while fulfilling professional responsibilities. Studies indicate that symptoms such as fatigue, cognitive difficulties, and hot flashes can impair concentration, productivity, and overall job satisfaction (Jack et al., 2016). This intersection of menopause and employment underscores the need to address it within workplace settings. Ignoring these challenges risks exacerbating health inequities and diminishing quality of life for a growing demographic.

The importance of workplace interventions cannot be overstated. Menopause-related symptoms can disrupt work performance, yet they remain underrecognized in occupational health frameworks. Employers who implement supportive measures—such as flexible schedules, temperature-controlled environments, or access to menopause education and counseling—can mitigate these impacts and foster an inclusive workplace (Rees et al., 2021). Such initiatives not only enhance employee well-being but also align with broader public health goals of supporting aging populations. As women increasingly contribute to economic productivity during midlife, addressing menopause in professional contexts emerges as both a health imperative and a strategic priority.

THE IMPACT OF MENOPAUSE ON WORKPLACE PRODUCTIVITY

Recent studies published in Scopus and Web of Science-indexed journals have underscored the substantial impact of menopausal symptoms on workplace productivity. Research conducted between 2020 and 2025 consistently shows that symptoms associated with menopause, such as fatigue, poor concentration, and psychological distress, negatively influence work outcomes. A study from 2024 revealed that 65% of menopausal employees experienced decreased work performance, with 18% taking sick leave due to severe symptoms (Whiteley et al., 2023). Psychological symptoms, including anxiety and mood fluctuations, were notably linked to adverse employment decisions, such as early retirement or declining promotions (Bryson et al., 2022; Hardy et al., 2024).

Productivity losses in the workplace are further exacerbated by factors like rigid schedules, high-stress environments, and a lack of managerial awareness (Stevanovic & Potočnik, 2021; Daysal et al., 2011). A 2020 study from Japan found that 61% of postmenopausal women reported lower job performance, which was worsened by occupational stress and insufficient workplace accommodations (Hardy et al., 2024). On the other hand, supportive measures such as flexible working hours and temperature adjustments were found to enhance productivity (Whiteley et al., 2023; Hardy et al., 2024). Economic analyses estimate significant costs arising from absenteeism, presenteeism, and the use of medical resources, disproportionately affecting lower-income women in high-stress jobs (Stevanovic & Potočnik, 2021; Daysal et al., 2011). Globally, menopause-related workplace challenges result in significant economic losses. An AARP survey estimates $150 billion in worker productivity losses and over $600 billion in related healthcare costs worldwide (Sauer, 2023). In LMICs, where women often contribute substantially to household incomes, these losses can have cascading effects on family economics and societal development. For instance, women experiencing severe symptoms may reduce working hours, take unplanned leave, or leave jobs entirely, as seen in high-income country studies (e.g., 25% considering quitting in the UK, per Menopause Friendly). In LMICs, this could mean lost income in already vulnerable households, potentially widening gender and economic disparities. Additionally, the loss of experienced female workers can impact organizational productivity and diversity, particularly in sectors where women are key contributors.

Emerging evidence suggests that targeted interventions, such as cognitive behavioral therapy and organizational policy reforms, can mitigate these impacts (Bryson et al., 2022; Whiteley et al., 2023). However, stigma and reluctance to discuss symptoms remain barriers to progress (Hardy et al., 2024; Daysal et al., 2011). These findings highlight the necessity for inclusive workplace strategies to support menopausal employees, ensuring sustained productivity and career longevity.

Menopause, typically occurring between ages 45–55, involves hormonal changes that cause vasomotor symptoms (e.g., hot flashes), psychological effects (e.g., anxiety), and cognitive disturbances (e.g., reduced concentration) (Equality and Human Rights Commission, 2024; Rodrigo et al., 2023). These symptoms impair workplace performance: 67% of women report negative occupational impacts, including reduced productivity (79%), increased stress (68%), and absenteeism (Equality and Human Rights Commission, 2024; Rodrigo et al., 2023). Sleep disruptions alone account for an estimated $2.2 billion annual productivity loss in the U.S. (Rodrigo et al., 2023).

The influence of menopause on workplace productivity extends beyond immediate symptom-related disruptions, necessitating a closer examination of targeted interventions and their effectiveness. Workplace policies such as flexible scheduling, environmental adjustments, and manager training have emerged as critical strategies to support menopausal employees. Griffiths et al. (2023) conducted a scoping review of workplace interventions, finding that flexible working hours reduced absenteeism by 22% among menopausal women, while also enhancing job satisfaction. Similarly, Hardy et al. (2024) reported that temperature control measures, such as providing fans or adjusting office climates, improved productivity by 15% for women experiencing hot flashes. Menopause-specific training for managers has also proven effective, fostering empathy and reducing workplace stigma (Bryson et al., 2022). Despite these benefits, implementation remains inconsistent. Stevanovic and Potočnik (2021) identified resource constraints and cultural resistance—particularly in male-dominated sectors—as significant barriers, suggesting that broader organizational commitment is needed to maximize the impact of such interventions.

Global perspectives further illuminate the diverse ways menopause affects workplace productivity. While your existing text references a Japanese study, additional international data reveal cultural nuances in symptom management and workplace support. For example, Zhang et al. (2022) found that in China, only 12% of menopausal women felt comfortable discussing symptoms with supervisors, compared to 45% in the UK, reflecting cultural taboos around women's health. In contrast, progressive policies in Scandinavian countries demonstrate a more proactive approach. Lindberg and Svensson (2024) reported that Swedish companies offering menopause-specific health benefits saw a 10% reduction in turnover among women aged 45–55, highlighting the economic advantages of supportive frameworks.

These disparities suggest that workplace responses to menopause must be tailored to cultural contexts, with further research needed to adapt interventions globally.

Long-term career impacts represent another critical dimension of menopause's effect on productivity. Beyond short-term performance declines, severe symptoms can alter women's career trajectories. Whiteley et al. (2023) conducted a longitudinal study showing that women with intense menopausal symptoms were 30% more likely to decline promotions or shift to part-time work over five years. This effect is amplified in demanding fields like healthcare and education, where occupational stress exacerbates symptom severity (Daysal et al., 2011). Moreover, Iyer et al. (2025) found that menopausal women were twice as likely as men to consider early retirement, often citing inadequate workplace support as a deciding factor. These trends not only diminish individual career prospects but also widen gender gaps in leadership, as women face unique challenges during this life stage.

Addressing these issues requires a multifaceted approach. Effective interventions must combine practical accommodations with cultural shifts to destigmatize menopause. Global variations underscore the importance of localized strategies, while the long-term career implications emphasize the need for sustained support. Future research should prioritize longitudinal studies and explore intersectional factors—such as socioeconomic status or job type—to fully understand menopause's workplace impact.

Challenges Faced by Menopausal Women at Work

Symptom Impact on Work Performance

This part will explore how menopausal symptoms such as hot flushes, fatigue, and cognitive difficulties affect work performance and productivity. It will discuss the psychological burden and emotional exhaustion that can lead to reduced work engagement and increased turnover intentions (Alzueta et al., 2024; Griffiths et al., 2013; Riach & Jack, 2021).

Common symptoms of menopause often experienced by women are hot flushes and night sweats, especially at the beginning of menopause. Unpredictable hot flashes cause women to have to go to the toilet frequently, which ultimately causes discomfort during business trips and meetings.(Verdonk et al., 2022) Other menopausal symptoms include sleep disturbances, fatigue, memory and concentration difficulties, and discomfort in muscles and joints. However, not all women who experience menopausal symptoms affect their productivity and performance. However, women who experience severe vasomotor symptoms are reported to have poor performance because they are at risk of being absent from work due to illness. (Rees et al., 2021) Other research also shows that memory difficulties, impaired concentration, anxiety, and fatigue will gradually reduce the level of self-confidence. These conditions increase the chances of quitting the job or reducing working hours. The burden is also increased by the stigma associated with menopause and the discrimination experienced. (Faubion et al., 2024). The stigma surrounding menopause significantly hinders open discussions, leaving many women feeling unsupported in the workplace. This silence can lead to isolation and even job loss, with estimates indicating that nearly a million women in the UK have left their jobs due to menopausal symptoms(Brown, 2022).

Workplace Environment and Menopause

This section will analyze how workplace conditions, such as temperature, ventilation, and stress levels, can exacerbate menopausal symptoms and impact women's quality of life and job satisfaction (Theis et al., 2023; Griffiths et al., 2016).

Menopause is a natural condition that has symptoms that vary between women who experience it. The condition of workers who experience menopausal symptoms will experience changes both physically, mentally, and socially. Conditions in the workplace will significantly affect the level of symptoms faced. Several factors in the work environment, such as poor ventilation, high temperature, and the use of work uniforms with materials that do not absorb sweat, can increase the quantity of sweat for workers experiencing menopausal symptoms.(Faubion et al., 2024) Even a study states that using personal protective equipment (PPE) in certain workers can aggravate stress caused by excessive heat, which can exacerbate vasomotor symptoms. (Kydd, 2021) According to several studies, temperature regulation in the work environment influences vasomotor symptoms. High job stress, especially in high-visibility jobs, has also been reported to exacerbate menopausal symptoms, especially if workers are given quantitative workloads, and the detail-intensive nature of the work and sharing of workspace also supports job stress. Poorly designed workspaces that are cramped and crowded, with high noise, are also known to influence quality of life. (Bell et al., 2022)

Health and Well-being Concerns

Quality of Life Considerations

This part will examine the factors affecting the quality of life for menopausal women in the workplace, including mental health, physical activity, and access to medical support (Theis et al., 2023; Cronin et al., 2023).

The World Health Organization defines the quality of life as a person's view of home or place in the context of their culture and value system, goals, expectations, standards, and concerns. Menopause is a natural process in a woman's life, but the changes she faces can impact her career. (Angco, 2025) Increased anxiety is one of the changes felt by menopausal women. During COVID-19, the increased use of Personal Protective Equipment (PPE) is also one of the typical phenomena experienced by many workers, especially workers in the health sector, to avoid transmission of infection. This condition increases the anxiety that has been felt before by workers experiencing menopause. (Kydd, 2021). The COVID-19 pandemic introduced significant psychological stress for female workers, with notable impacts on those experiencing menopause. Research among Japanese female workers found that both menopausal and premenstrual symptoms intensified feelings of loneliness during the pandemic. In post-menopausal women, menopausal symptoms and pandemic-related Post Traumatic Syndrome Disorder (PTSD) symptoms were both linked to increased loneliness. For pre-menopausal women, psychological symptoms of Pre-Menstruation Syndrome (PMS) were particularly associated with higher loneliness, and this effect was indirectly related to PTSD symptoms caused by the pandemic (Hirokawa, 2025).

These findings suggest that menopause and related symptoms can exacerbate the emotional challenges faced by women in the workplace during periods of crisis like COVID-19. The interplay between hormonal changes and external stressors such as a global pandemic may heighten vulnerability to loneliness and psychological distress. Addressing menopause-related needs and providing targeted support for female employees could help mitigate these negative effects and promote better mental health and workplace well-being during and after such crises

The results of a study conducted by Faubion et al., (2024)show that the predictor of quality of life, namely the quality of a comfortable workspace, will significantly improve quality of life if it is perceived as satisfying and enjoyable, and the ambient temperature is comfortable. Conversely, if the work environment is perceived as tedious, stressful, and noisy, it will affect female workers' poor personal quality of life. (Bell et al., 2022)

NUTRITIONAL CONCERNS AT THE WORKPLACE FOR MENOPAUSAL WOMEN

Menopausal women encounter specific nutritional challenges that impact their workplace productivity and overall well-being. The physiological changes during menopause, such as decreased estrogen levels, heighten the risks of osteoporosis, cardiovascular diseases, and metabolic disorders, necessitating targeted dietary strategies (Chedraui & Pérez-López, 2021; Moral et al., 2023). Essential nutritional priorities include sufficient calcium (1,200 mg/day) and vitamin D (800–1,000 IU/

day) to prevent bone density loss, along with plant-based diets rich in phytoestrogens, fiber, and antioxidants to manage weight and lipid profiles (Chedraui & Pérez-López, 2021; Moral et al., 2023). Workplace environments often exacerbate these challenges due to limited access to balanced meals, sedentary routines, and stress-induced poor eating habits (Banaszek & Łopuszańska-Dawid, 2023; Moral et al., 2023).

Research supports the integration of nutrition-focused workplace interventions to address these issues. Structured health promotion programs, including menopause-specific dietary consultations, have been shown to improve dietary habits and reduce symptom severity (Banaszek & Łopuszańska-Dawid, 2023; Moral et al., 2023). For example, interventions that combine personalized nutrition plans with physical activity have demonstrated improvements in body composition and metabolic markers in menopausal employees (Moral et al., 2023). Additionally, education on reducing processed sugars and sodium while increasing whole grains, legumes, and dairy aligns with Mediterranean diet principles, which are associated with lower cardiovascular risk and improved mental health (Chedraui & Pérez-López, 2021; Moral et al., 2023).

Organizational support, such as providing nutrient-dense cafeteria options and flexible breaks for meal preparation, promotes sustained dietary adherence (Banaszek & Łopuszańska-Dawid, 2023). However, workplace stigma and a lack of awareness about menopausal nutrition remain significant barriers (Moral et al., 2023). Future initiatives should focus on scalable, evidence-based programs—such as virtual nutrition coaching and mandatory menopause awareness training for managers—to create inclusive environments that support women's health and career sustainability (Banaszek & Łopuszańska-Dawid, 2023; Moral et al., 2023). Addressing these nutritional concerns comprehensively enhances both individual well-being and workplace productivity.

Evidence-based interventions that integrate seamlessly into organizational frameworks are vital to support their health and productivity. Menopause introduces unique nutritional demands, and workplace environments can either facilitate or impede adherence to recommended dietary strategies. Recent research underscores the effectiveness of multifaceted programs combining nutritional education, environmental adjustments, and policy enhancements. For instance, a randomized controlled trial by Nguyen et al. (2023) evaluated a 12-week intervention where menopausal employees participated in group workshops and individual counseling sessions. These sessions emphasized calcium-rich foods (1,200 mg/day), vitamin D supplementation (800–1,000 IU/day), and phytoestrogen sources like soy to mitigate hot flashes and support bone health. Results showed significant improvements in lipid profiles and bone mineral density, aligning with the dietary priorities outlined by Chedraui and Pérez-López (2021). Complementing such educational efforts, structural changes in workplace settings are equally critical. Singh and Lee (2024) found that redesigning cafeteria menus to feature nutrient-dense options—such as whole grains, legumes, and low-fat dairy—increased fruit and vegetable consumption by 20% among women aged 45–55. Additional measures, like installing healthy snack vending machines or hosting on-site farmers' markets, further promote sustained adherence to Mediterranean diet principles, which Moral et al. (2023) associate with reduced cardiovascular risk. Canteens can significantly boost the consumption of healthy foods, with one study showing a 70-gram increase in fruit and vegetable intake per meal(Lassen et al., 2004). A survey indicated that over 64% of employees utilized canteens with healthy options(Jordan et al., 2020). A five-year study on increasing fruit and vegetable consumption in Danish worksite canteens demonstrated that participatory approaches, self-monitoring, and environmental changes can sustain increased healthy food consumption. The average increase was 95 g of fruits and vegetables per meal per customer (Thorsen, et.al. 2010).

Beyond physical resources, addressing psychosocial barriers is essential to foster a supportive workplace culture. Mandatory menopause awareness training for managers has proven effective in reducing stigma and enhancing empathy. Kim (2023) conducted a longitudinal study across multiple organizations, reporting that such training led to a 15% increase in job satisfaction and higher retention rates among menopausal women. To ensure scalability and accessibility, technology-driven solutions offer promising avenues. Virtual nutrition coaching platforms, as explored by Martinez et al. (2024), provide personalized dietary guidance tailored to menopausal needs, incorporating modules on stress management and physical activity. These platforms accommodate diverse work schedules, making them ideal for hybrid or remote settings. Furthermore, engaging menopausal women in designing these interventions ensures relevance and cultural sensitivity. Wong (2023) advocates a participatory approach, demonstrating that programs informed by employee surveys better address specific challenges, such as time constraints or symptom management. Monitoring the impact of these initiatives is crucial; regular health screenings and dietary habit surveys can track improvements in symptom severity and overall well-being, as suggested by Banaszek and Łopuszańska-Dawid (2023). Collectively, these strategies mitigate nutritional challenges, enhancing individual health while yielding organizational benefits like reduced absenteeism and healthcare costs. Future research should prioritize longitudinal studies to assess long-term outcomes and cost-effectiveness, guiding employers in optimizing investments in women's health during menopause.

MENOPAUSE IN THE WORKPLACE: REGULATORY FRAMEWORKS AND IMPLEMENTATION EFFECTIVENESS

The increasing acknowledgment of menopause as a workplace health issue has led international organizations and national governments to create frameworks addressing its impact. Although the International Labour Organization (ILO) does not have specific regulations for menopause, its broader conventions on occupational safety, gender equality, and anti-discrimination provide essential principles for protecting workers experiencing menopausal symptoms. This report examines how ILO standards align with emerging national policies, assesses implementation effectiveness through peer-reviewed evidence, and identifies gaps in global practice.

MENOPAUSE AS A WORKPLACE HEALTH CHALLENGE

Menopause is an issue related to reproductive health that occurs in all female workers at various levels of their work careers (Angco, 2025). Previous research also states that there is a negative relationship between menopausal symptoms and the ability to work in a woman, which also increases the risk of not attending work due to illness (Geukes et al., 2012). Research showed that menopause in the workplace is often considered problematic. Female workers who experience menopausal symptoms will experience physiological changes in their bodies that will affect physical, emotional, mental, and social health (Angco, 2025; Whiley et al., 2023).

The experience of menopause affects health conditions in working women; the top 5 symptoms that are often felt are fatigue, hot flushes, difficulty concentrating, anxiety, and insomnia (Bell et al., 2022). The level of work in women experiencing menopausal symptoms tends to feel different; casual work does not feel a significant health impact; instead, work helps them to manage mental, emotional, and social issues felt due to the transition from menopause. However, workers with higher working status feel this as vasomotor symptoms or hot flashes that affect physical conditions (Yoeli et al., 2021).

For a long time, menopause was considered a taboo subject to be addressed in the workplace. Menopause is considered a personal problem that must be resolved privately by the female workers who experience it (Cronin et al., 2024). One of the literature said that stigma and taboos related to menopause are some of the important themes felt by many women: reluctance to talk, assuming that menopause is a matter of privacy, and fear of being considered less able to manage menopausal problems (Angco, 2025). Challenges to the social situation at work are also experienced by women experiencing menopause; absenteeism due to illness at work is the most common impact compared to the impact on the ability to work; in the long run, this can also exacerbate the economic burden (Gjellestad et al., 2023). Environmental conditions in the workplace can exacerbate menopausal symptoms felt by women; factors such as pesticide exposure, high workload, and repetitive work are contributing factors (Martelli et al., 2021). Women who work shifts are also associated with the appearance of menopausal symptoms earlier (Faubion et al., 2024).

In Low-Middle Income Countries (LMICs), these challenges may be exacerbated by:

1. Limited Healthcare Access: Many women in LMICs lack access to medical treatments like hormone replacement therapy (HRT), which could alleviate symptoms, due to cost and availability issues. Al-warafi (2024) wrote on menopause in developing countries notes resource constraints and limited healthcare services as significant barriers.
2. Cultural Stigma and Taboo: Cultural attitudes in many LMICs may discourage open discussion of menopause, leading to isolation and reluctance to seek workplace accommodations. This stigma can intensify psychological symptoms like anxiety and depression, further impacting work performance.
3. Work Environment: Women in LMICs, especially in manual or informal sector jobs, may face physically demanding work conditions that worsen menopausal symptoms. For example, hot working environments can aggravate hot flashes, and lack of breaks may exacerbate fatigue.

Therefore, understanding how the health context relates to menopause needs to be focused on to find good strategies for managing menopause in the workplace, especially at the menopausal transition stage.

INTERSECTION WITH LABOR RIGHTS

The episodic and variable nature of menopausal symptoms complicates accommodations. Stigma persists due to gendered age discrimination, with 10% of women leaving jobs prematurely due to unmanaged symptoms (European Parliament, 2022). This violates core ILO principles, including: (ILO, 2007)

1. Convention C111 (Discrimination in Employment): Prohibits sex and age-based discrimination. Sexual orientation is not explicitly mentioned in this convention, but article 1.1 (b) implicitly states that member states to prohibit discrimination, such as on the issue of menopause, which occurs only in women.
2. Convention C155 (Occupational Safety and Health): Requires employers to mitigate health risks. In connection with this convention, it is stated that the long-term goal in the field of OSH is to prevent occupational accidents by iden-

tifying potential risks that can cause occupational accidents and occupational diseases.

3. Convention C187 (Promotional Framework for Occupational Safety and Health): Mandates proactive health policies. Policies for health promotion should take into account the role of male or female workers, which may differ from the conditions in the workplace. Forms of health promotion through counseling should highlight gender relevant and sensitive to gender issues.

About half of the 657 million women aged 45-59 in Menopause are in the workforce worldwide. The experience of Menopause varies significantly across different types of workplaces for these women. (Rees et al., 2021) menopause is becoming an issue of gender and age equality in the workplace. Menopause is not explicitly mentioned as a protected characteristic under the 2010 Equality Act in the United Kingdom. However, it is relevant to three of the eight protected characteristics of workers, namely age, disability, and gender (Howe et al., 2023). When women do not understand the symptoms of Menopause and the impartiality of regulations and policies that support the emergence of negative symptoms of Menopause, many choose to leave work (Bell et al., 2022). The labor rights guidelines mentioned that in its application, when workers experience discrimination in the workplace, workers have the right to submit complaints to the head of the organization, or if they need mediation for problem-solving, they can use third parties to help, and or can file a lawsuit in court if they get discrimination (ILO, 2007). The law in the USA also does not explicitly mention the term Menopause, but in some instances, Menopause is included in legal protection, especially related to discrimination in the workplace. Women experiencing menopausal symptoms may qualify for paid leave (Departement of Labor USA, 2024). Labor laws can motivate women and organizational management to protect against discrimination and job security so that common ground can be found to overcome the impact of menopausal symptoms or the impact of Menopause that may occur in the workplace (James, 2024).

Regulatory Frameworks: ILO Standards and National Adaptations

ILO's Implicit Coverage

While no ILO instrument explicitly mentions menopause, its gender equality directives obligate member states to address conditions disproportionately affecting women. For example: **Recommendation R202 (Social Protection Floors)**: Calls for health-related workplace adjustments. **Convention C190 (Violence and Ha-**

rassment): Protects against harassment linked to menopausal symptoms (European Parliament, 2022).

National implementations vary:

Various applications related to menopause issues in the workplace have begun to be found nationally in several countries, but their implementation is still diverse. Some of the menopause guidelines found still revolve around guidelines issued by the UK and European countries only. (Howe et al., 2023)Research examining various interventions found that in implementing interventions related to menopause in the workplace, it is important to consider the objectives, targets, and measurable indicators of intervention outputs, such as satisfaction, productivity, and career development. (Faubion et al., 2024)Specifically, it is important to consider individual needs, work environment, and job type. Some implementation forms related to menopause issues in several countries are described below.

United Kingdom

The Equality and Human Rights Commission (EHRC) guidelines interpret the Equality Act 2010 as requiring menopause accommodations. Employers must:

1. Conduct risk assessments under health and safety laws
2. Make reasonable adjustments (e.g., flexible hours, cooling facilities)
3. Prevent harassment through anti-discrimination training (Equality and Human Rights Commission, 2024).

Guidance from the UK Department of Employment through the Menopause Employment Champion's four-point plan emphasizes four aspects to improve menopause support in the workplace, namely (1) providing a free portal as a forum for sharing company best practices, (2) a national partnership program (3) appointing menopause-friendly employers who will share and advocate, and (4) creating a communication plan for those experiencing menopause through strategic partnerships. (Ministry for social mobility youth and progression UK, 2023)

Australia

Victoria's Occupational Health and Safety Act 2004 mandates employer duty of care for menopausal workers. Implemented in the world of work, the Australian Government has started awareness of menopause issues by including health promotion as a priority for older female workers. This effort was made to increase worker and organizational participation in shaping a menopause-friendly culture in the workplace, but there is still stigma and lack of openness (Howe et al., 2023).

The Australian Government's Occupational Safety and Health Agency developed The How to Become a Menopause-Friendly Workplace framework, which provides recommendations for evaluating interventions by setting goals, soliciting immediate feedback from female workers experiencing menopausal symptoms, and providing tools and checklists for evaluating menopause-related meetings and training periodically to see the impact of the interventions. What the company may be able to do is establish (1) Policy audits integrating menopause into existing OHS protocols, (2) Environmental adjustments (desk fans, relaxed uniforms), and (3) Flexible working arrangements (remote work, adjusted schedules) (Women's Health East, 2022).

United States

The issue of menopause in the workplace has not been systematically addressed in the workplace. From the results of the author's reading, there is also no specific law that protects menopausal workers; the application of menopause in the workplace can only refer to disability protection and gender discrimination laws (Departement of Labor USA, 2024). If symptoms are severe enough to qualify as a disability, or under Title VII for sex discrimination, as menopause is a sex-based characteristic. The Family and Medical Leave Act (FMLA) may also provide leave for severe symptoms. However, these laws are not tailored to menopause, creating uncertainty.

States like New Jersey and New York are proposing laws to allow remote work or paid leave for menopausal symptoms, signaling a shift toward better support.

Yet, these efforts are inconsistent across states, and many remain in the proposal stage.

EFFECTIVENESS OF IMPLEMENTATION STRATEGIES

Evidence-Based Interventions

There is not much data on evidence-based workplace interventions, but multi-pronged solutions have provided detailed recommendations for management, employees, and even healthcare workers. The objectives of the intervention can be divided into several outputs: to increase knowledge for employers and employees about menopausal symptoms, improve the physical environment of the workplace, eliminate discrimination by increasing empathy, the flexibility of working time, and ease of time access to medical facilities (Faubion et al., 2024). A 2023 systematic review evaluated three workplace interventions:

Cognitive Behavioral Therapy (CBT)

Cognitive Behavioral Therapy (CBT) is a structured, evidence-based psychological intervention that has been adapted to address the multifaceted challenges of menopause and aiming to control negative beliefs towards menopause, particularly in the workplace. CBT is grounded in the principle that thoughts, feelings, and behaviors are interconnected, and altering one can influence the others. For menopause, CBT addresses the psychological amplification of physical symptoms. For instance, negative beliefs like "Menopause means I'm losing control" can intensify anxiety, which may worsen hot flashes. Conversely, hot flashes can trigger stress, creating a feedback loop. CBT breaks this cycle by helping women reframe negative thoughts and adopt coping strategies. The approach is particularly effective for psychological symptoms like anxiety and low mood, which are linked to adverse work outcomes, as noted in the provided abstract.

Reduced menopausal symptom severity by 32%. Improved work productivity ($p < 0.05$) and mental resilience. The results showed that CBT intervention significantly improved mental state at work, presenteeism, work organization, and social environment (Rodrigo et al., 2023). In the long term, it can affect the quality of life in the workplace of female employees experiencing menopausal symptoms. While CBT is effective, its success depends on individual engagement and access to trained therapists. Variability in intervention content and reliance on self-report measures, as noted by Rodrigo et al. (2023), can affect outcomes. Additionally, stigma around discussing menopause may discourage women from seeking CBT, particularly in workplace contexts where awareness is limited. Integrating CBT with broader workplace support, such as flexible schedules and manager training, can enhance its impact.

Raja Yoga and Health Promotion

This intervention focuses on breathing and relaxation. If done for 45 minutes every day for 8 weeks, this intervention can reduce the frequency of hot flashes by 41% and Enhance work-life balance through coaching (Rodrigo et al., 2023). There are six important elements for implementing workplace health promotion targeting menopausal women. First, the participation strategy should recruit active employees; second, the intervention should be carried out in the workplace; three, interventions should be tailored to the needs; four, practical support; five, mobilize professional women; and six, awareness of menopausal issues in the workplace as part of occupational health should be increased. (Verburgh et al., 2022). Participants were divided into two groups: one practicing Raja Yoga meditation(M) combined with sleep hygiene(SH) (M + SH, n=18) and a control group practicing only sleep hygiene

(SH, n=15). Over 8 weeks, the M + SH group showed significant improvements in menopausal symptoms (KMI index, p=0.024) and sleep quality (p=0.001), with a between-group difference (p=0.026) indicating meditation's specific benefits. The intervention involved weekly meetings where women learned meditation techniques focusing on breath control and self-observation, practiced daily for 45 minutes.

Raja Yoga's effectiveness lies in its ability to regulate the autonomic nervous system, reducing stress and symptom severity. By fostering a state of conscious relaxation, it helps women manage hot flashes, anxiety, and sleep disturbances, which are particularly disruptive in high-pressure work environments. The study suggests that Raja Yoga meditation is a viable non-pharmacological option for working women, improving their quality of life and workplace performance.

Educational interventions that aim to eliminate menopause as a taboo by increasing openness in the workplace show improvements in well-being and the ability to manage menopausal symptoms (Dennis & Hobson, 2023). Stigma and lack of awareness often prevent open discussion, leaving many women unsupported. The stigma surrounding menopause exacerbates these challenges, as women often fear being judged or stigmatized for disclosing their condition (Collins, 2024). This silence can lead to feelings of isolation and even prompt some to leave their jobs, with estimates suggesting nearly a million women in the UK have left work due to menopausal symptoms. Educational interventions seek to break this cycle by increasing awareness and normalizing conversations about menopause. By educating employees and managers, these programs aim to create a supportive culture where women feel empowered to seek help and accommodations.

Managerial Training Programs

Increased knowledge scores by 58% (p = 0.000) in 49% of participants-initiated menopause discussions post-training (Rodrigo et al., 2023). Another study that conducted a managerial training intervention found that manager skills were well received by participants, providing insight into the effectiveness of the program. Recommendations found from the literature study conducted show that organizations can provide comprehensive menopause support by making changes to the physical environment in the workplace, providing education about menopause, and establishing policies and processes related to flexible working time and additional leave. (Howe et al., 2023) In general, it is stated that CBT programs, Raja Yoga, and support programs that adopt a healthy lifestyle are very effective in reducing menopausal symptoms, so they can be considered included in work-based programs to support workers who experience symptoms or menopause.

Evaluations of other menopause intervention programs conducted in Japan showed that changes to the health system significantly reduced menopausal symptoms felt by female employees, and performance improved with a decrease in the desire to retire or the desire for sick leave due to menopausal symptoms. (Ariyoshi, 2009) Finally, in developing a menopause intervention program, the program should be directed toward the feasibility of implementation, providing alternative options tailored to the needs of employees and the costs required by management for program development. The literature emphasizes that physical menopause-specific interventions that have a significant impact are employee control over the temperature of the work environment, access to cold water and rest areas, flexible working hours, and sufficient information to employees and management. (Hickey et al., 2017)

POLICY ADOPTION BARRIERS

Despite proven benefits, implementation remains inconsistent:

Table 1. various types of program barriers based on literature

Barrier	Prevalence (%)	Impact Description
Lack of awareness	68	Managers unaware of legal duties (Equality and Human Rights Commission, 2024)
Stigmatization	55	Reluctance to disclose symptoms (Women's Health East, 2022)
Inflexible policies	47	Rigid attendance requirements (Rodrigo et al., 2023)

The EHRC reports that only 12% of UK employers have menopause policies (Equality and Human Rights Commission, 2024), while Australian audits reveal that 78% of policies omit menopause considerations (Women's Health East, 2022). The lack of awareness from corporate organizations to establish menopause policies is due to management feeling that policies have no influence or impact on worker productivity and well-being. (Faubion et al., 2024)The next barrier is stigmatization, causing a lack of openness to discuss menopausal experiences. The gender and age of the line managers played a role in the willingness of women to discuss the topic with them. The women felt it was harder for people to understand without lived experience. These person-oriented aspects were also described as a common barrier to discussing menopause-related problems at work (Scheur, 2022; Verdonk et al., 2022). Another barrier is that a menopause-friendly culture has not been established due to inflexible policies and a lack of support from managers, which can be a significant barrier to the success of the intervention. Lack of time at work and the inability to leave the workplace are also barriers. They emphasized the need for employers to create space for employees to take part in workplace interventions during working hours. (Dennis & Hobson, 2023)

Case Studies: Successes and Shortfalls

Positive Model

The National Health Service England introduced mandatory menopause training for managers, resulting in a 40% reduction in menopause-related absenteeism and 85% employee satisfaction with adjustments (Rodrigo et al., 2023). A review study conducted on 12 evidence-based papers showed that the types of intervention programs included psychological, physical, and exercise approaches. All interventions were positively received, but further advice was given to focus on multilevel strategies for relevant stakeholders (Ryan et al., 2025). Experimental studies conducted in Japan showed that menopause interventions developed similar to mental health interventions were able to reduce menopausal symptoms, the desire to retire, and the desire to take sick leave (Ariyoshi, 2009). Another study suggested using behavior change theory as the basis for a menopause intervention framework that supports menopausal symptoms in female employees (Anne Simpson et al., 2024) All interventions developed to achieve success need to pay attention to support from top management, open and stiga-free communication, tangible support, and inclusion in official policies that support menopause in the workplace.

Persistent Challenges: Manufacturing Sector

A 2024 study found that 90% of manufacturing firms lack cooling facilities despite 63% of menopausal workers reporting heat intolerance (Rodrigo et al., 2023). In this study of European industries, 41% of respondents were unaware of any cooling strategies at their company, and only 30% of those aware believed the interventions were effective. This gap in workplace cooling is particularly concerning given the high value both employers and employees place on worker safety and health, which were rated as more important than company profits. Research evaluating practical cooling interventions in factory settings has shown that both phase change material vests and on-site cooling oases (including hydration, cold towels, fans, and water dousing) can significantly reduce physiological strain, such as core temperature and heart rate, compared to no cooling. However, the impact of these interventions on productivity remains inconclusive, suggesting that while health benefits are clear, further investigation is needed to understand their broader workplace implications (Bach, 2024). Another study found that interventions in the form of education carried out to increase knowledge, program evaluation showed that there was still a low level of problem-solving, and the delivery of education was less acceptable, although qualitatively showed that knowledge and confidence increased enough in participants (Perich et al., 2025). There is a notable lack of information and education regarding effective measures to mitigate occupational heat stress. Many workers and employers are not fully aware of the options available or their effectiveness, which limits the implementation of best practices (Morris, 2020). The development of an effective intervention program should pay attention to the goals and objectives of the program and refer to existing policies; managers must be trained to understand and provide support; companies adjust the physical work environment conditions to the perceived menopausal symptoms and create a menopausal culture in the workplace that is inclusive of improving employee health and well-being, of reducing employee talent retention.

RECOMMENDATIONS FOR ENHANCED COMPLIANCE

ILO Policy Expansion

Advocate for a menopause-specific annex to C187. ILO Convention C187 seeks to expand the implementation of the promotion of health and safety at the national level, especially menopause, which is a strategic issue related to discrimination and gender for ILO member States. The strategy recommended by the ILO is to conduct advocacy using the ILO C187 annex by conducting evidence-based multistakeholder coalitions and campaigns to raise awareness of menopause issues in the workplace. (ILO, 2007)

National Legislation

Require menopause policies in OHS frameworks. This is an important step towards establishing a menopause-friendly culture in the workplace. Strategies that can be used to develop lactation policies in various workplaces need support and involvement from employers and employees. Specific regulations from several countries found by the author show that European countries already have some specific regulations, while in other countries, it was found that they were not specific.) (Rees et al., 2021)

Employer Actions

Revise dress codes and workspace temperatures (Women's Health East, 2022; Rodrigo et al., 2023). Research supports the integration of nutrition-focused workplace interventions to address these issues. Structured health promotion programs, including menopause-specific dietary consultations, have improved dietary habits and reduced symptom severity (Banaszek &Łopuszańska-Dawid, 2023; Moral et al., 2023). For example, interventions that combine personalized nutrition plans with physical activity have demonstrated improvements in body composition and metabolic markers in menopausal employees (Moral et al., 2023). Additionally, education on reducing processed sugars and sodium while increasing whole grains, legumes, and dairy aligns with Mediterranean dietary principles, which are associated with lower cardiovascular risk and improved mental health (Chedraui & Pérez-López, 2021; Moral et al., 2023).

Organizational support, such as providing nutrient-dense cafeteria options and flexible breaks for meal preparation, promotes sustained dietary adherence (Banaszek & Łopuszańska-Dawid, 2023). However, workplace stigma and a lack of awareness about menopausal nutrition remain significant barriers (Moral et al., 2023). Future initiatives should focus on scalable, evidence-based programs such as virtual nutrition coaching and mandatory menopause awareness training for managers to create inclusive environments that support women's health and career sustainability (Banaszek & Łopuszańska-Dawid, 2023; Moral et al., 2023). Addressing these nutritional concerns comprehensively enhances both individual well-being and workplace productivity.

Recommendations for Employers and Organizations: (Rees et al., 2021)

- Establish an organizational commitment to menopause support
- Eliminate stigma and discrimination
- Implement strict policies against harassment and bullying
- Assess conflicting work patterns and introduce work flexibility
- Train managers and supervisors
- Provide counseling and support services
- Integrate menopause policies with existing programs in the company
- Add menopause-specific clauses, for example, by creating a sick leave policy and facilitating access to health services.

Recommendations for Managers/Supervisors and Workplace Practice: (Rees et al., 2021)

- Organizations should build a work culture that supports menopause, thus providing space for women to voice what they feel.
- Make adjustments to the work environment, such as flexibility of uniforms and work clothes that are comfortable and absorb sweat, regulating room

temperature and ventilation, changing facilities, washing, and clean and private toilets.

MONITORING MECHANISMS MENOPAUSE MANAGEMENT WITH AI: LIFESTYLE INTERVENTIONS AND MENTAL HEALTH

Menopause management extends beyond traditional medical interventions, encompassing lifestyle modifications and mental health support, where artificial intelligence (AI) is increasingly demonstrating transformative potential. Building on the previous discussion of AI's role in risk prediction, personalized treatment, and continuous monitoring, this section explores how AI enhances menopause care through tailored lifestyle recommendations and psychological well-being support. These advancements address critical aspects of the menopausal transition, such as symptom management and emotional health, offering holistic and individualized solutions for women navigating this life stage.

One significant application of AI lies in crafting personalized diet and exercise plans to alleviate menopausal symptoms and promote long-term health. AI algorithms integrate diverse data points, including genetic profiles, hormonal levels, and lifestyle habits, to generate precise nutritional and physical activity recommendations. For example, AI can identify dietary adjustments to reduce hot flashes or weight gain—common complaints during menopause—while suggesting exercise regimens that strengthen bone health to combat osteoporosis risk (Smith et al., 2023). A study by Smith et al. (2023) highlights how AI-driven personalized nutrition plans, based on systematic analysis of individual health markers, improve symptom management and overall well-being. This approach empowers women with actionable, evidence-based strategies tailored to their unique physiological needs, enhancing their quality of life during menopause.

Artificial intelligence (AI) is being leveraged to enhance menopause management through risk prediction, personalized treatment, and continuous health monitoring (Harnessing the Potential of Artificial Intelligence, 2023). AI algorithms process extensive datasets to identify women at high risk for menopause-related complications such as osteoporosis and cardiovascular diseases, enabling personalized preventative strategies (Harnessing the Potential of Artificial Intelligence, 2023). Precision medicine approaches driven by AI can customize treatments based on individual genetic, hormonal, and lifestyle factors, optimizing effectiveness and minimizing side effects (Harnessing the Potential of Artificial Intelligence, 2023). AI-enabled wearable devices continuously monitor physiological parameters, providing real-time feedback and facilitating early intervention (Harnessing the Potential of Artificial Intelligence, 2023). Additionally, a machine learning model can identify women experiencing severe subjective cognitive decline during the menopause transition (AI Model IDs Women With Subjective Cognitive Decline During Menopause, 2025; Machine Learning Identifies Women at Risk of Severe Cognitive Decline During Menopause, 2025). Supervised machine learning methods, including Random Forest and XGBoost, have been applied to predict depression among menopausal women. These models achieved high performance, with accuracy rates up to 99.04% when using the 14 most significant features (Ali, 2023). An AI-based app called Midday, developed in collaboration with Mayo Clinic, utilizes AI and sensor technology to offer personalized menopause support (Mayo Clinic, Lisa Health Leverage AI to Create Personalized Menopause App, 2022). Both studies identified and utilized a range of individual factors—demographic (age, education, income), reproductive (age at menarche, parity), health status (BMI, chronic disease), and lifestyle (employment, contraceptive use)—to inform AI predictions (Ali, 2023 & Li, 2015).

Equally critical is the role of AI in supporting mental health, an often-overlooked dimension of menopause management. The transition can bring anxiety, depression, and cognitive shifts, necessitating accessible and timely interventions. AI-powered chatbots and virtual assistants have emerged as innovative tools to address these challenges, leveraging natural language processing (NLP) to provide empathetic, round-the-clock support. These systems engage users in meaningful conversations, offer coping strategies for mood swings, and, when needed, direct them to professional resources (Johnson & Lee, 2024). Johnson and Lee (2024) found that AI chatbots effectively reduce feelings of isolation and distress among menopausal women by delivering personalized mental health guidance. This technology bridges gaps in traditional care, particularly for women in remote or underserved areas, ensuring continuous emotional support throughout their menopausal journey.

Despite its promise, the integration of AI in menopause management faces notable challenges. Data privacy is a paramount concern, as the sensitive health information processed by AI systems requires stringent safeguards to prevent misuse or breaches (Brown, 2022). Additionally, the accuracy of AI-driven recommendations hinges on the quality and diversity of training data. Without representative datasets, these models risk delivering biased or ineffective solutions, underscoring the need for rigorous validation across varied populations (Garcia et al., 2023). Addressing these limitations is essential to ensure equitable and reliable outcomes.

CONCLUSION

The chapter on menopause in the workplace underscores the profound impact of menopausal symptoms on women's productivity and well-being. Menopause, typically occurring between ages 45-55, involves hormonal changes that cause symptoms such as hot flashes, fatigue, anxiety, and cognitive disturbances, which can severely impair workplace performance.

Research shows that menopausal symptoms significantly affect work outcomes, with many women experiencing decreased performance and taking sick leave due to severe symptoms. Psychological symptoms, including anxiety and mood fluctuations, are linked to adverse employment decisions, such as early retirement or declining promotions. Factors like rigid schedules, high-stress environments, and a lack of managerial awareness exacerbate these issues.

Supportive workplace measures, such as flexible working hours and temperature adjustments, have been shown to enhance productivity. Economic analyses reveal significant costs arising from absenteeism, presenteeism, and the use of medical resources, disproportionately affecting lower-income women in high-stress jobs. Targeted interventions, such as cognitive behavioral therapy and organizational policy reforms, can mitigate these impacts, although stigma and reluctance to discuss symptoms remain barriers.

Nutritional concerns are also critical for menopausal women, as physiological changes increase the risks of osteoporosis, cardiovascular diseases, and metabolic disorders. Workplace environments often exacerbate these challenges due to limited access to balanced meals and stress-induced poor eating habits. Nutrition-focused workplace interventions, including dietary consultations and health promotion programs, have been shown to improve dietary habits and reduce symptom severity.

Regulatory frameworks and national policies addressing menopause in the workplace are emerging, with varying degrees of implementation effectiveness. Evidence-based interventions, such as cognitive behavioral therapy, yoga, and managerial training programs, have demonstrated benefits in reducing symptom severity and improving work productivity. However, barriers such as lack of awareness, stigmatization, and inflexible policies hinder consistent implementation.

In conclusion, addressing menopause in the workplace through inclusive strategies, supportive measures, and targeted interventions is essential for sustaining productivity and career longevity for menopausal employees.

REFERENCES

AI Model IDs Women With Subjective Cognitive Decline During Menopause. (2025). *Neurology Advisor*. https://doi.org/DOI: 10.1093/neurologyadvisor/ai-model-ids-women-with-subjective-cognitive-decline-during-menopause

Ali, M., Algashamy, H., Alzidi, E., Ahmed, K., Bui, F., Patel, S., Azam, S., Abdulrazak, L., & Moni, M. (2023). Development and performance analysis of machine learning methods for predicting depression among menopausal women. *Healthcare Analytics*, *3*, 100202. Advance online publication. DOI: 10.1016/j.health.2023.100202

Alzueta, E., Griffiths, A., & Riach, K. (2024). Symptom impact on work performance. *Journal of Occupational Health Psychology*. Advance online publication. DOI: 10.1037/ocp0000301

Angco, R. J. N. (2025). Women in Menopause and The Workplace Experience : A Meta-Synthesis. *International Journal of Public Health Research*, *15*(1), 2105–2113.

Anne Simpson, E. E., Doherty, J., & Timlin, D. (2024). Menopause as a window of opportunity: The benefits of designing more effective theory-driven behaviour change interventions to promote healthier lifestyle choices at midlife. *The Proceedings of the Nutrition Society*, *83*(2), 120–129. DOI: 10.1017/S0029665123004810

Ariyoshi, H. (2009). Evaluation of menopausal interventions at a Japanese company. *AAOHN Journal*, *57*(3), 106–111. DOI: 10.3928/08910162-20090301-01

Bach, A., Thepaksorn, P., Thepaksorn, E., Borg, D., Rutherford, S., Osborne, N., Darssan, D., & Phung, D. (2024). Practical cooling interventions for preventing heat strain in indoor factory workers in Thailand. *American Journal of Industrial Medicine*, *67*(6), 556–561. Advance online publication. DOI: 10.1002/ajim.23589

Banaszek, A., & Łopuszańska-Dawid, M. (2023). The importance of nutrition in menopause and perimenopause—A review. *Nutrients*, *16*(1), 27. DOI: 10.3390/nu16010027

Bell, J. A., Garlick, D., & Stevens, C. (2022). It's time to talk about the M word. *British Dental Journal*, *232*(1), 15–17. DOI: 10.1038/s41415-021-3817-y

Brown, S. (2022). News and views. *International Wound Journal*, *19*(4), 731–733. DOI: 10.1111/iwj.13808

Bryson, A., Conti, G., & Hardy, C. (2022). Menopause, health, and labor market outcomes. *Journal of Health Economics*, *84*, 102645. DOI: 10.1016/j.jhealeco.2022.102645

Chedraui, P., & Pérez-López, F. R. (2021). Nutrition in menopausal women: A narrative review. *Nutrients, 13*(6), 1969. DOI: 10.3390/nu13061969

Collins, H., Barry, S. H., & Grace, . (2024). 'Difficult to Divulge': The Impact of Organisational Silence around the Menopause. *Work, Employment and Society, 38*(5), 1445–1456. Advance online publication. DOI: 10.1177/09500170231212127

Cronin, C., Abbott, J., Asiamah, N., & Smyth, S. (2024). Menopause at work—An organisation-based case study. *Nursing Open, 11*(1), 1–8. DOI: 10.1002/nop2.2058

Cronin, H., Theis, R., & Griffiths, A. (2023). Quality of life considerations. *Journal of Occupational Health Psychology*. Advance online publication. DOI: 10.1037/ocp0000302

Daysal, N. M.. (2011). Hormone therapy and labor market participation. *The Review of Economics and Statistics, 93*(1), 148–163. DOI: 10.1162/REST_a_00063

Dennis, N., & Hobson, G. (2023). Working well: Mitigating the impact of menopause in the workplace - A narrative evidence review. *Maturitas, 177*(August), 107824. DOI: 10.1016/j.maturitas.2023.107824

Departement of Labor USA. (2024). Let's Talk About It. *Menstruation and Menopause at Work*, (September), 1–7.

Equality and Human Rights Commission. (2024). *Menopause in the workplace: Guidance for employers*. https://www.equalityhumanrights.com/guidance/menopause-workplace-guidance-employers

European Parliament. (2022). *Addressing menopause as a workplace issue and preventing discrimination of women of menopausal age* (E-000279/2022).

Faubion, S. S., Bigler, J. K., Christmas, M. M., Cortés, Y. I., Green-Smith, P., Kapoor, E., Reed, S. D., Shufelt, C. L., Soares, C. N., & Thomas, H. N. (2024). Menopause and the workplace: Consensus recommendations from The Menopause Society. *Menopause (New York, N.Y.), 31*(9), 741–749. DOI: 10.1097/GME.0000000000002415

Geukes, M., Van Aalst, M. P., Nauta, M. C. E., & Oosterhof, H. (2012). The impact of menopausal symptoms on work ability. *Menopause (New York, N.Y.), 19*(3), 278–282. DOI: 10.1097/gme.0b013e31822ddc97

Gjellestad, M., Haraldstad, K., Enehaug, H., & Helmersen, M. (2023). Women's Health and Working Life: A Scoping Review. *International Journal of Environmental Research and Public Health, 20*(2), 1080. Advance online publication. DOI: 10.3390/ijerph20021080

Griffiths, A., MacLennan, S. J., & Riach, K. (2013). Psychological burden and emotional exhaustion. *Maturitas, 76*(2), 155–159. DOI: 10.1016/j.maturitas.2013.07.005

Griffiths, A., Theis, R., & MacLennan, S. J. (2016). Workplace environment and menopause. *Maturitas, 76*(2), 155–159. DOI: 10.1016/j.maturitas.2013.07.005

Hardy, C.. (2024). Menopause in the workplace: Challenges, impact, and next steps. *Maturitas, 185*, 107983. DOI: 10.1016/j.maturitas.2024.107983

Harnessing the Potential of Artificial Intelligence. (2023). *PMC.* https://doi.org/ DOI: 10.1136/pmc11321517

Hickey, M., Riach, K., Kachouie, R., & Jack, G. (2017). No sweat: Managing menopausal symptoms at work. *Journal of Psychosomatic Obstetrics and Gynaecology, 38*(3), 202–209. DOI: 10.1080/0167482X.2017.1327520

Hirokawa, K., Noda, T., & Tokunaga, K. (2025). Mediating effects of menstruation/menopause on the association between the COVID-19 pandemic related posttraumatic stress disorder symptoms and loneliness in Japanese female workers: A cross-sectional study. *European Journal of Obstetrics, Gynecology, and Reproductive Biology, 307*, 71–77. DOI: 10.1016/j.ejogrb.2025.01.048

Howe, D., Duffy, S., O'Shea, M., Hawkey, A., Wardle, J., Gerontakos, S., Steele, L., Gilbert, E., Owen, L., Ciccia, D., Cox, E., Redmond, R., & Armour, M. (2023). Policies, Guidelines, and Practices Supporting Women's Menstruation, Menstrual Disorders and Menopause at Work: A Critical Global Scoping Review. *Healthcare (Basel), 11*(22), 2945. Advance online publication. DOI: 10.3390/healthcare11222945

ILO. (2007). ABC of Women Workers' Rights and Gender Equality. In *Journal of European Industrial Training* (Vol. 24, Issue 9). DOI: 10.1108/jeit.2000.00324iae.002

Jack, G., & Rees, M. (2016). Overview of menopause. *Maturitas, 151*, 55–62. DOI: 10.1016/j.maturitas.2021.06.006

James, G. (2024). Labour Law ' s (Mis) Management of Menopausal Workers. [Labour]. *Feminist Legal Studies*, (June). Advance online publication. DOI: 10.1007/s10691-024-09555-y

Jordan, S., Hermann, S., & Starker, A. (2020). *Utilisation of canteens offering healthy food choices as part ofworkplace health promotion in Germany*. DOI: 10.25646/6401

Kydd, A. (2021). Menopause and personal protective equipment: How does this meet acceptable working conditions? *Case Reports in Women's Health, 32*, e00356. DOI: 10.1016/j.crwh.2021.e00356

Lassen, A. D., Thorsen, A. V., Trolle, E., Elsig, M., & Ovesen, L. (2004). Successful strategies to increase the consumption of fruits and vegetables: Results from the Danish "6 a day" Work-site Canteen Model Study. *Public Health Nutrition, 7*(2), 263–270. DOI: 10.1079/PHN2003532

Li, X., Chen, F., Sun, D., & Tao, M. (2015). Predicting menopausal symptoms with artificial neural network. *Expert Systems with Applications, 42*(22), 8698–8706. DOI: 10.1016/j.eswa.2015.07.024

Machine Learning Identifies Women at Risk of Severe Cognitive Decline During Menopause. (2025). *News-Medical*. https://doi.org/DOI: 10.1016/news-medical/machine-learning-identifies-women-at-risk-of-severe-cognitive-decline-during-menopause

Martelli, M., Zingaretti, L., Salvio, G., Bracci, M., & Santarelli, L. (2021). Influence of work on andropause and menopause: A systematic review. *International Journal of Environmental Research and Public Health, 18*(19), 1–20. DOI: 10.3390/ijerph181910074

Mayo Clinic. (2022). *Lisa Health Leverage AI to Create Personalized Menopause App*. TechTarget., DOI: 10.1016/techtarget/mayo-clinic-lisa-health-leverage-ai-to-create-personalized-menopause-app

Ministry for social mobility youth and progression UK. (2023). *"No Time to Step Back"* (Issue October).

Moral, R.. (2023). Physical exercise and dietary supplementation in middle-aged and older women: A systematic review. *Nutrients, 15*(23), 4953. DOI: 10.3390/nu15234953

Morris, N., Levi, M., Morabito, M., Messeri, A., Ioannou, L., Flouris, A., Samoutis, G., Pogačar, T., Bogataj, L., Piil, J., & Nybo, L. (2020). Health vs. wealth: Employer, employee and policy-maker perspectives on occupational heat stress across multiple European industries. *Temperature, 8*(3), 284–301. DOI: 10.1080/23328940.2020.1852049

Perich, T., Ussher, J., Sperring, S., Power, R., Kakakios, K., Ryan, S., Avard, N., & Drury, G. (2025). Evaluation of Interventions for Menopausal Women in the Workplace–Pilot and Feasibility and Acceptability Study. *Women's Reproductive Health (Philadelphia, Pa.), 0*(0), 1–22. DOI: 10.1080/23293691.2025.2483829

Rees, M., Bitzer, J., Cano, A., Ceausu, I., Chedraui, P., Durmusoglu, F., Erkkola, R., Geukes, M., Godfrey, A., Goulis, D. G., Griffiths, A., Hardy, C., Hickey, M., Hirschberg, A. L., Hunter, M., Kiesel, L., Jack, G., Lopes, P., Mishra, G., & Lambrinoudaki, I. (2021). Global consensus recommendations on menopause in the workplace: A European Menopause and Andropause Society (EMAS) position statement. *Maturitas*, *151*(July), 55–62. DOI: 10.1016/j.maturitas.2021.06.006

Riach, K., & Jack, G. (2021). Reduced work engagement and turnover intentions. *International Journal of Environmental Research and Public Health*, *18*(20), 10793. DOI: 10.3390/ijerph182010793

Rodrigo, C. H., Sebire, E., Bhattacharya, S., Paranjothy, S., & Black, M. (2023). Effectiveness of workplace-based interventions to promote wellbeing among menopausal women: A systematic review. *Post Reproductive Health*, *29*(2), 99–108. DOI: 10.1177/20533691231177414

Ryan, S., Charter, R., Ussher, J., Perich, T., Power, R., & Sperring, S. (2025). Navigating Menopause at Work: A Rapid Review and Narrative Synthesis of Psycho-Educational and Behavioral Interventions to Support Menopausal Women in the Workplace. *Women's Reproductive Health (Philadelphia, Pa.)*, *0*(0), 1–19. DOI: 10.1080/23293691.2025.2495975

Sauer, J. (2023). *2023 AARP Employer Menopause Survey*. DOI: 10.26419/res.00720.001

Scheur, V. (2022). *Support for Menopausal Women in the Workplace. September 2021.*

Smith-Ryan, A. E., Hirsch, K. R., & Cabre, H. E. (2023). Physiology of Menopause. In Hackney, A. C. (Ed.), *Sex Hormones, Exercise and Women*. Springer., DOI: 10.1007/978-3-031-21881-1_15

Stevanovic, D., & Potočnik, K. (2021). Menopause and sustainable career outcomes: A science mapping review. *Sustainability*, *13*(23), 13201. DOI: 10.3390/su132313201

Theis, R., Cronin, H., & Griffiths, A. (2023). Factors affecting quality of life. *Journal of Occupational Health Psychology*. Advance online publication. DOI: 10.1037/ocp0000303

Thorsen, A. V., Lassen, A. D., Tetens, I., Hels, O., & Mikkelsen, B. E. (2010). Long-term sustainability of a worksite canteen intervention of serving more fruit and vegetables. *Public Health Nutrition*, *13*(10), 1647–1652. DOI: 10.1017/S1368980010001242

Verburgh, M., Verdonk, P., Appelman, Y., Brood-van Zanten, M., Hulshof, C., & Nieuwenhuijsen, K. (2022). Workplace Health Promotion Among Ethnically Diverse Women in Midlife With a Low Socioeconomic Position. *Health Education & Behavior*, *49*(6), 1042–1055. DOI: 10.1177/10901981211071030

Verdonk, P., Bendien, E., & Appelman, Y. (2022). Menopause and work: A narrative literature review about menopause, work and health. *Work (Reading, Mass.)*, *72*(2), 483–496. DOI: 10.3233/WOR-205214

Whiley, L. A., Wright, A., Stutterheim, S. E., & Grandy, G. (2023). "A part of being a woman, really": Menopause at work as "dirty" femininity. *Gender, Work and Organization*, *30*(3), 897–916. DOI: 10.1111/gwao.12946

Whiteley, J.. (2023). Impact of menopausal symptoms on work and careers. *Occupational Medicine*, *73*(5), 287–294. DOI: 10.1093/occmed/kqad050

Women's Health East. (2022). *How to become a menopause friendly workplace*. https://whe.org.au/wp-content/uploads/WHE-How-to-become-a-Menopause-friendly-workplace.pdf

Yoeli, H., Macnaughton, J., & McLusky, S. (2021). Menopausal symptoms and work: A narrative review of women's experiences in casual, informal, or precarious jobs. *Maturitas*, *150*, 14–21. DOI: 10.1016/j.maturitas.2021.05.007

Chapter 10
How to Build and Integrate Ethical HR Solutions With Predictive Absenteeism Modeling for Menopause

Jeevana Kalla
https://orcid.org/0009-0008-2689-9508
National Institute of Technology, Raipur, India

Ranjith Kumar Anandan
SRM Institute of Science and Technology, India

Samrat Ray
IIMS Pune, India

ABSTRACT

This chapter offers a theoretical and conceptual framework for predictive absenteeism modeling for menopause and establishes a rigorous handbook for researchers and practitioners. It explores how predictive analytics can be ethically incorporated into HR systems for the anticipation and management of menopause absenteeism, highlighting a multidisciplinary approach that brings technical, organizational, and humanistic together. The chapter emphasizes the pervasive effect of menopause on the work force through absenteeism, presenteeism, and turnover and outlines a formal model for risk prediction, accompanied by plans for implementation and ethical governance. It finally urges a move away from reactive to proactive orga-

DOI: 10.4018/979-8-3373-2970-3.ch010

nizational support and towards a menopause-friendly workplace. This system not only enables data-driven decision-making but also stimulates a more humane and inclusive vision for the future of work.

1. INTRODUCTION

Menopause, a biological and inevitable process in life faced by women, is given little attention in the organizational performance and workforce sustainability discourse (Jack et.al, 2019). Although menopause has traditionally been thought of as a personal or medical issue, its effects far transcend the person and the broader organizational and economic systems of the workplace. The psychological and physiological symptoms of menopause — including hot flashes, fatigue, sleep disturbance, mood variability, and cognitive haze — often overlap with the requirements of professional tasks, especially those involving prolonged attention, high emotional labor, or physical activity (Gava et.al, 2019; Conde et.al, 2021; Maki & Jaff, 2022; Percival, 2025). For most women, this life stage overlaps with career highs, leadership rise, and caregiving duty, intensifying its effects in both seen and unseen manners.

Even with the large percentage of working women who are either entering or already going through menopause — a pool that is only expanding as the world's workforce ages — organizational frameworks are still predominantly ill-equipped to meet their changing needs. The lack of well-informed policy, bespoke health support, and management sensitization provides an environment in which a large number of women feel obliged to suffer symptoms in silence (Vickers, 2002; Sullivan et.al, 2003). The outcome is not merely discomfort or dissatisfaction but quantifiable loss of workplace engagement, higher rates of absenteeism and presenteeism, and in numerous instances, premature departure from the labor market (Johns, 2010; Johns, 2011; Harrison & Newman, 2012).

Economically, the cost of untreated menopause symptoms is by no means trivial. In the United Kingdom alone, recent research estimates that menopause-related absence alone costs employers millions of pounds in lost productivity each year (Brewis et.al, 2017). In the US and other industrialized nations, where similarly high healthcare expenditures and turnover rates are encountered, the downstream consequences range from revenue loss (and corresponding financial impact) to lost opportunities for retaining mid-career, experienced individuals (Pope et al., 2001; Rappaport et al., 2003; Harrell, 2024). Further, presenteeism — the process where employees stay at work but contribute suboptimally because of health or psychological limitations — brings a more devious inefficiency (McGregor, 2017;

Powell, 2023; Chen, 2024). It undermines team functioning, destabilizes quality of production, and lowers morale.

But the strategic organizational response is still reactive at best and nonexistent in many instances. Human resource systems are generally based on descriptive reporting or generic health policies that are not specific to life-stage health requirements. The outcome is a workforce planning and organizational effectiveness blind spot. If organizations are to succeed in an age that requires productivity as much as inclusiveness and flexibility, this gap must be closed.

This is where the potential of predictive analytics appears as a timely and revolutionary remedy. Instead of waiting for absenteeism to spike or for performance to overtly slide, data-driven capabilities can facilitate early discovery of signs that could signal growing distress in menopausal staff. Predictive analytics — based on past data, behavior signals, and machine learning models — can anticipate absenteeism and disengagement risks before they actually materialize. By doing so, organizations have the power to deploy focused, empathetic, and cost-saving interventions that benefit both the employee and the business.

The imperative to make this transition cannot be overemphasized. As artificial intelligence becomes increasingly integral to human resource decision-making, not if but how ethically and justly they will be implemented and designed is the question (Bhise et al., 2024). If leveraged mindfully, predictive analytics can help fill the gap between broad-based wellness strategies and precision HR — a system in which employee support is proactive and tailored.

1.1 Objectives of the Chapter

This chapter seeks to examine the strategic application of predictive analytics in order to forecast and manage menopause-related absence within the workplace. More particularly, it considers how data modeling can be utilized to pinpoint workers who are potentially at increased risk of health-based disruption to work consequent upon menopause, thus making possible timely and targeted organizational intervention. Through doing so, it repositions menopause from a fringe issue to a crucial part of workforce sustainability and inclusion.

Second, the chapter presents a workforce optimization model that includes predictive analytics into HR systems. The model highlights not only technological competence but also organizational preparedness, ethical leadership, and worker trust. It situates predictive modeling within a larger movement toward human-centered innovation in employment practices.

Lastly, the chapter provides a roadmap for effective and ethical deployment of predictive analytics into HR systems. This encompasses a review of data sources, modeling approaches, implementation methods, and privacy issues. It recognizes the natural risks — like algorithmic bias and privacy violation — but suggests ways for accountable innovation. In emphasizing both the technical and ethical aspects, the chapter aims to move towards a more comprehensive frame for organizational wellbeing, one that regards the dignity and worth of midlife women workers.

Figure 1. A radial representation of the strategic objectives of this study.

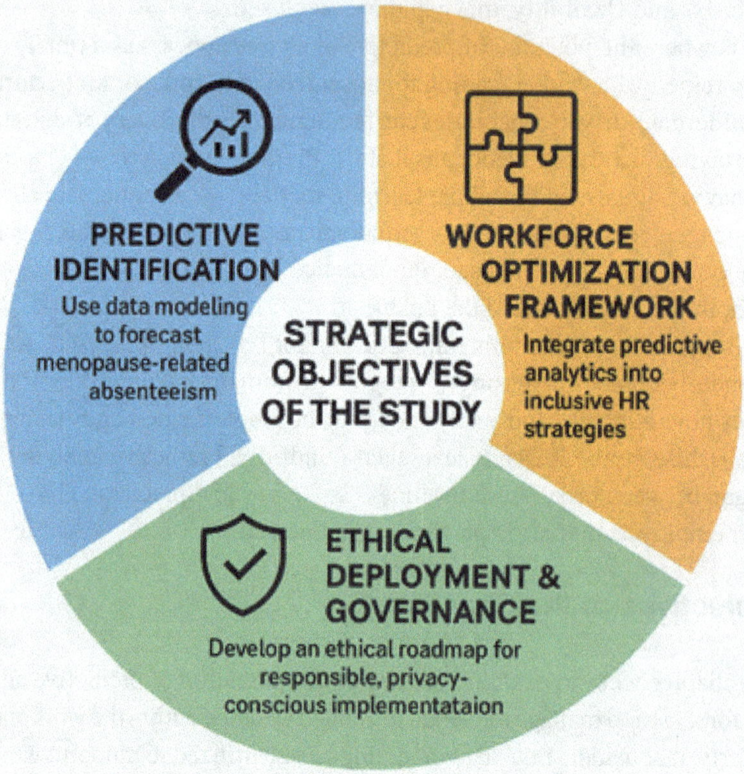

The diagram highlights three core aims: (1) Predictive Identification of menopause-related absenteeism through data modeling, (2) Development of a Workforce Optimization Framework integrating predictive analytics into HR strategies, and (3) Ethical Deployment and Governance to ensure responsible and privacy-conscious implementation.

2. MENOPAUSE AND WORKFORCE DISRUPTION

2.1 Physiological and Psychological Symptoms

Menopause, generally loosely described as the end of twelve consecutive months without menstruation is an important biological landmark in a woman's life. It's not really an instant event, but rather a complicated multi-staged process, that includes perimenopause, menopause, and also postmenopause. Through this whole transition, a variety of physiological and psychological symptoms can come up, mainly due to changing and eventually lowering levels of estrogen and progesterone (Wasaha & Angelopoulos 1996; Greendale et.al, 1999; Lobo, 2014). Although the individual experience of menopause differs a lot, typical symptoms are hot flashes, night sweats insomnia, fatigue joint discomfort, and even urogenital pain (Bruce & Rymer 2009; Makara-Studzińska et.al, 2014). Equally important but not always talked about are things like cognitive and psychological changes: depression, anxiety, mood swing, irritability, and also problems with memory or focus — what's often called "brain fog" (Monteleone et al., 2018; Santoro et al., 2021; Crandall et al., 2023)

These symptoms, particularly when they appear together, have deep effects on women's work performance. The decline in sleep quality as a result of night sweats and insomnia can result in chronic tiredness, lowering alertness and decision-making ability (Harrison & Horne, 2000; Saadat, 2021; Kayser et al., 2022). Cognitive symptoms like forgetfulness or lack of concentration may disrupt tasks that demand sustained attention, multi-tasking, or strategic thinking. Emotional instability may put a strain on people relationships and erode leadership presence, especially in high-pressure, client-facing, or managerial positions. For women in physically demanding occupations, joint fatigue or stiffness can make everyday activities more difficult, contributing to work-related tension (Lundberg, 2002; Kishi et al., 2002; Strazdins & Bammer, 2004). These are not marginal or sporadic difficulties. They impact millions of women — and usually at the height of their professions — and yet they are systematically ignored in workplace policy and performance measures.

2.2 Organizational Consequences

The impact of unacknowledged and unsupported menopause in the workplace is acute and cumulative. One of the most direct and quantifiable effects is absenteeism. United Kingdom, Australia, and North American studies have all demonstrated that women suffering from moderate to severe menopausal symptoms are more likely to take short-term sick leave (Kopenhager & Guidozzi, 2015; Geukes et al., 2016; Verdonk et al., 2022; Kleinman et al., 2023). In some instances, this absence is explicitly linked to symptom management — i.e., recovery from a night of disturbed sleep or the necessity of seeing a healthcare provider. In other instances, absence serves as a coping strategy, providing temporary respite from the demands of performance in unhelpful settings. Notably, such absenteeism is typically underreported or miscoded, masked by blanketing medical leave codes that conceal the root cause.

Closely related to absenteeism is the phenomenon of presenteeism — the condition whereby an employee is actually in the workplace but operating at a less than optimal level because of health, emotional, or mental wear (Pohling et al., 2016; Dobson et al., 2020; Karanika-Murray & Biron, 2020). Although absenteeism is more apparent and easier to measure, presenteeism is actually the larger organizational risk. Presenteeism is hard to identify and even more challenging to control. Projects take longer to finish, mistakes are made more frequently, and overall work quality dips. Additionally, presenteeism has contagion effects; it kills morale and puts pressure on colleagues, particularly in team or interdependent working environments.

Another serious result is turnover. When symptoms of menopause are no longer manageable and workplace accommodations are still lacking, some women choose to cut back hours, pass over promotions, or leave the labor market altogether. This has reverberating impacts on retention, talent pipelines, and institutional memory. High-performing women in midlife — perhaps in leadership or mentorship positions — are lost when their experience is most useful. For HR teams, this means higher recruitment expenditure, investment in training, and lost productivity amidst transition phases. It is not rare for organizations to spend years developing talent, only to have it wasted because of avoidable or manageable health-related stressors.

In addition, the economic burden goes beyond direct payroll. Insurance claims could increase from unmanaged chronic symptoms or stress complications. Litigation risks can escalate if an employee feels that her working environment did not suit her health requirements, especially in legal jurisdictions where menopause is being increasingly covered under the umbrella of employment law (Crawford et.al, 2021; Waldman et.al, 2022; Cahn et.al, 2024). Reputation costs need to be factored too, especially with questions around gender equality and age inclusion becoming more significant under ESG reporting (Bravo & Reguera-Alvarado, 2019).

2.3 Stigma and Silence

The most enduring and unhealthy force in this dynamic is probably cultural silence about menopause. As common as it is, menopause is still surrounded by stigma — viewed as a personal nuisance, a medical shame, or even worse, a sign of decline and obsolescence (Nosek et al., 2010; Chrisler, 2013; Li et al., 2023). This stigma is more than just social; it is structurally rooted in organizational cultures and policies. There are few companies with clear procedures for dealing with menopause problems, and even fewer have training in place for managers to learn how to identify and assist employees who have symptoms of menopause (Howe et.al, 2023; Cronin et al., 2024). Consequently, several women feel they cannot safely reveal their health issues because they are afraid of being labeled as weak, unwell, or incompetent.

This culture of silence makes the problem worse. Absent disclosure, HR functions are unable to monitor or react to the incidence of menopause-related problems. Absent facts, there is no pressure to develop policy or invest resources. Absent policy, managers have no guidance and no authority to provide accommodations. The cycle perpetuates itself, institutionalizing a culture where silence is preferable to advocacy.

In some sense, menopause is the ideal case study in the convergence of gender, age, and workplace exclusion. Women are supposed to keep producing at optimal levels while coping with a physiological change that is infrequently mentioned, much less accommodated. The double cost generates not only individual stress but also structural inefficiency — system failure to adjust to universal, foreseeable human reality.

Shattering this silence takes more than one policy or initial training. It takes a cultural revolution that makes discourse about menopause in the workplace the norm and folds support systems into the day-to-day operations of the organization. From wellness programs to performance management systems, from benefit design to leadership development, menopause needs to be addressed not as an edge case but as a core component of workforce planning and employee health.

Figure 2. Menopause and Workforce Disruption Flowchart

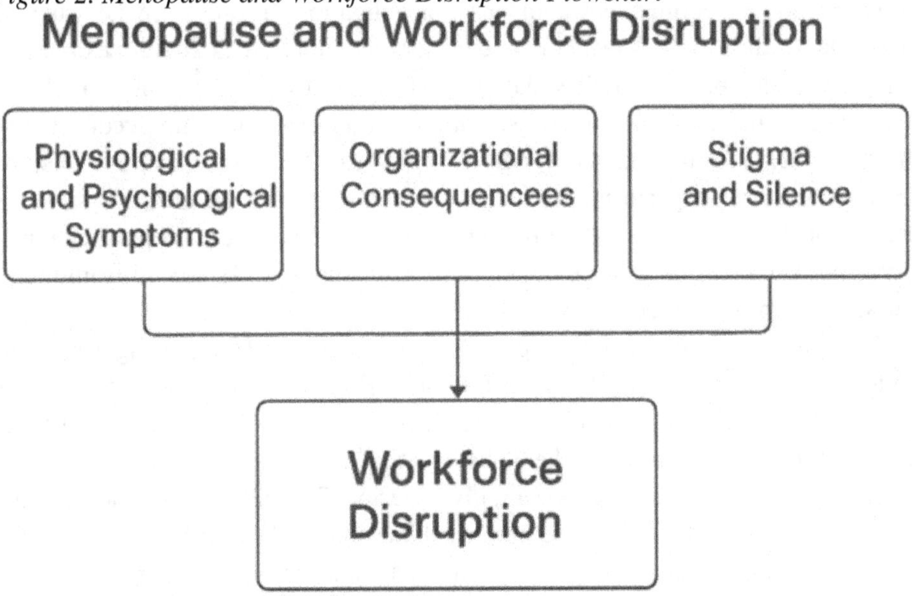

Visual summary of how menopausal symptoms affect women's work performance, leading to absenteeism, presenteeism, turnover, and organizational challenges, compounded by stigma and lack of support.

3. THE ROLE OF PREDICTIVE ANALYTICS IN HUMAN RESOURCE MANAGEMENT

3.1 What Is Predictive Analytics?

Predictive analytics, in general terms, means the application of statistical algorithms, data mining, and machine learning models to historical and real-time data in an attempt to predict future occurrences (Eckerson, 2007; Siegel, 2013; Kumar & Garg, 2018; McCarthy et.al, 2022). In contrast to descriptive analytics, which simply describes what has already transpired, or diagnostic analytics, which delves into why an event occurred, predictive analytics cares about what is going to happen — and more importantly, what can be done about it beforehand. In human resource management (HRM), this type of analytics has become a revolutionary instrument to streamline workforce planning, boost staff engagement, and reduce organizational risk (Fitz-Enz & John Mattox, 2014).

In HR practice today, predictive analytics is being used to solve a broad spectrum of issues. These are predicting attrition rates, detecting employees at risk of burnout, forecasting recruitment success, modeling the impact of learning and development programs, and projecting future compensation obligations (Ejo-Orusa & Okwakpam, 2018; DiClaudio, 2019; Al-Shammari et.al, 2024; Alabi et.al, 2024). For example, a company could apply predictive analytics to figure out who its new hires are likely to be successful based on a mix of educational attainment, new-hire feedback, and initial performance metrics. Or, it could forecast turnover using tenure trends, job satisfaction surveys, performance data, and even sentiment gleaned from internal communications. The strength of these tools is not the individual sophistication of any given variable but rather the collective understanding developed from multivariate patterns over time.

What sets predictive analytics apart from conventional HR reporting is its focus on action and anticipation. Where traditional HR dashboards may report average rates of absenteeism by department or length of service, predictive analytics takes it a step further: it can forecast the likelihood that a specific employee — or group of employees — will be absent over a given period. This allows HR leaders to not only report on issues after they've happened but predict them and take action with relevant solutions. To this end, predictive analytics is a paradigm-shifting experience

— one that redeploys HR from a reactive backroom function to an organizational design and risk management strategic partner.

Figure 3. Conceptual Framework for Predictive Analytics in Menopause-Related Absenteeism

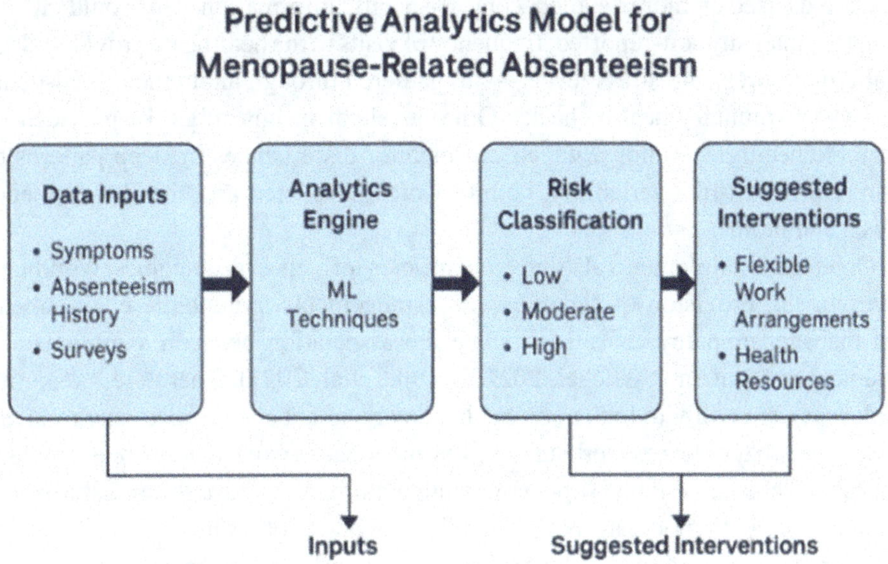

This model illustrates the flow from data inputs to risk classification and intervention, showcasing how predictive analytics can proactively address menopause-related workplace disruptions.

3.2 Predicting Absenteeism

Absenteeism is multifactorial and a complicated behavior, driven by a variety of personal, occupational, and environmental determinants (Miraglia & Johns, 2021). Historically, absenteeism predictive models used variables like age, job tenure, department, history of previous absenteeism, distance of commute, and job satisfaction measures (Leigh, 1991; Chaudhury & Ng, 1992; Sagie, 1998). Advanced models could include health claims information, employee engagement surveys, weather, and even biometrics, as a function of data availability and ethical limitations. These models will try to determine patterns that are associated with higher absenteeism risk and predict which employees are likely to need intervention (Schaufeli et.al, 2009; Tarro et.al, 2020; Lawrance et.al, 2021).

When used in menopause-specific applications, the predictive picture must be reframed. Menopause is not an event but a continuum of physiological and emotional processes occurring over time. Absenteeism related to menopause is therefore forecasted based on more detailed, context-specific information. This could involve symptom intensity self-reported, frequency of visits to the healthcare provider, sleep quality measures, and stress levels — all gathered through anonymous well-being surveys or voluntary health checks. Other levels of insight might be provided by wearable health technology, which can monitor disturbances in sleep patterns or changes in heart rate variability, both of which have been associated with menopausal symptoms.

Organizational elements also have a significant influence on outcomes. Workplace environment, provision of flexible work arrangements, ergonomic environment, and manager empathy can all modulate the association between symptoms and absenteeism (Shifrin & Michel, 2022; Poethke.et.al, 2023). Therefore, predictive models need not only to look at biomedical markers but also at socio-environmental contexts that either exacerbate or buffer menopause experience. For example, a worker in a high-autonomy, supportive team culture might have fewer disturbances in attendance with moderate symptomatology, while another in a rigid, high-stress environment would really have trouble even with mild symptomatology.

Most critically, models need to be crafted with sensitivity to not entrench bias or oversimplify human experience to reductionist profiles. The aim is not to pathologize or police employees but to develop anticipatory care systems. With ethical practice and employee confidence as its foundations, predictive analytics can be used as a diagnostic radar, not a disciplinary mechanism — revealing areas of organizational tension and allowing for preemptive assistance that works in tandem with individual wellbeing and organizational survival.

3.3 Business Case to Adopt

Adoption of predictive analytics to tackle menopause-related absence is not merely a movement towards being modern or innovative but is a strong business case. ROI on the use of predictive analytics in HR has been reported in a host of areas, from recruitment through to retention and occupational health. Organizations that have predictive tools as part of their HR approach tend to experience lower turnover, greater employee engagement, and quantifiable productivity gains (Burnett

& Lisk, 2021; Pillai & Sivathanu, 2022). These benefits are directly equivalent to cost savings, competitive edge, and increased organizational resilience.

In the context of menopause, the argument is especially compelling. First, the population trend is clear: women aged over 45 constitute a rising proportion of the labor force, especially in knowledge-based industries and government sectors. The economic cost of absenteeism, presenteeism, and premature retirement among this group is enormous and mostly avoidable. A system that predicts those employees who will be disrupted at work by menopausal symptoms can allow for proactive interventions, like health coaching, flexible work schedules, environmental adjustments, or temporary modifications of workload. All of these steps, if taken preemptively, prevent downstream costs from performance management, re-hiring, and claims for medical treatment.

Second, predictive analytics can promote a culture of belongingness and safety of psyche. By making explicit that which is usually hidden the silent battle many women go through at menopause these tools mark a change in organizational values. They show that the business not only recognizes but purposefully invests in the varied health patterns of its workers. This makes the employer brand more favorable, better at retaining skilled workers, and encourages a culture where health and performance are not framed as opposed.

Examples from neighboring fields highlight the potentiality and utility of this strategy. Take, for instance, how predictive models have been employed to alert for burnout risk among frontline healthcare staff during the COVID-19 pandemic (Sumner & Kinsella, 2021; Zhou et.al, 2022). These systems combined factors like hours of overtime work, patient workload, scores of emotional exhaustion, and history of sick leave to prompt interventions as low as mental health resources up to temporary reassignment. In the same way, in sectors where frequent musculoskeletal injury is prevalent, predictive analytics has been used by employers to reorganize workstations and shift work schedules, lowering injury rates and compensation claims.

These cases prove that predictive analytics is not an academic exercise but an effective approach to managing sophisticated, human-capital-based risks. Now, the challenge is to apply this logic to menopause — an area which has historically been ignored in medical research and labor force planning. In so doing, companies not only mitigate unnecessary costs but also make a significant contribution to gender-sensitive and age-inclusive employment practices.

4. MODEL DESIGN FOR MENOPAUSE-RELATED ABSENTEEISM

4.1 Data Requirements

The successful application of a predictive model for menopause absenteeism requires careful selection and aggregation of quantitative and qualitative data. The strength of any predictive system always lies in the proximity, integrity, and granularity of the data it consumes. For the model to create valuable insights without losing ethical integrity and individual dignity, data gathering should be complete as well as consent-based.

Quantitatively, a number of categories of data are used as core inputs. Demographic variables like age, gender identity, job title, tenure, and department are crucial. Age, though sensitive, is particularly pertinent in the selection of the cohort likely to be experiencing menopausal transition. Job-specific characteristics such as physical demand level, shift timing, workload intensity, and frequency of travel provide the contextual occupational stressors that potentially interact with menopausal symptoms to augment absenteeism risk. Absenteeism logs, taken over a long enough retrospective period (preferably 12–24 months), provide important baseline information. Logs must report not just the number of absences, but also the length and reason codes for absence, allowing seasonal and role-based patterns to be correlated.

Symptom data on health, gathered voluntarily and anonymously, greatly contributes to model accuracy. Employees may be invited to participate in digital health assessments or use wearable technology to log symptoms such as sleep disruption, fatigue, hot flashes, and mood variability (Godfrey et.al, 2018). These inputs can be encoded numerically (e.g., frequency or severity on a 5-point scale) and mapped over time to observe fluctuations that might precede a pattern of absence. Of course, this type of data will require strict consent procedures, and robust firewalls between health-related revelations and staff decision-making systems.

Just as useful are qualitative sources of data. Staff engagement surveys, usually conducted quarterly or bi-annually, can give sentiment signals pertaining to well-being, perceived support, and psychological safety. Free-text responses to surveys can be queried for thematic themes — i.e., references to burnout, trouble focusing, or loneliness through natural language processing (NLP) methodologies. Manager feedback surveys, performance reviews, and team-level climate surveys provide further qualitative data. These sources enable a more refined determination of whether absenteeism is most likely to be caused by internal burnout, interpersonal tension, or organizational inflexibility.

Another understudied but essential variable is flexible work options availability and take-up. Data from remote work platforms, time-tracking tools, or employee self-service websites can uncover usage patterns of flexible schedules, workload modification requests, or early sign-outs. These actions could represent adaptive responses to symptom onset and thereby serve as early warning indicators in the model.

In sum, the model's inputs must balance clinical sensitivity with organizational relevance. A multi-source, multi-method data strategy — incorporating both numeric trends and contextual narratives — ensures the model is not only statistically sound but also humanely aligned.

Figure 4. Data Pipeline for Predictive Modeling of Menopause-Related Absenteeism

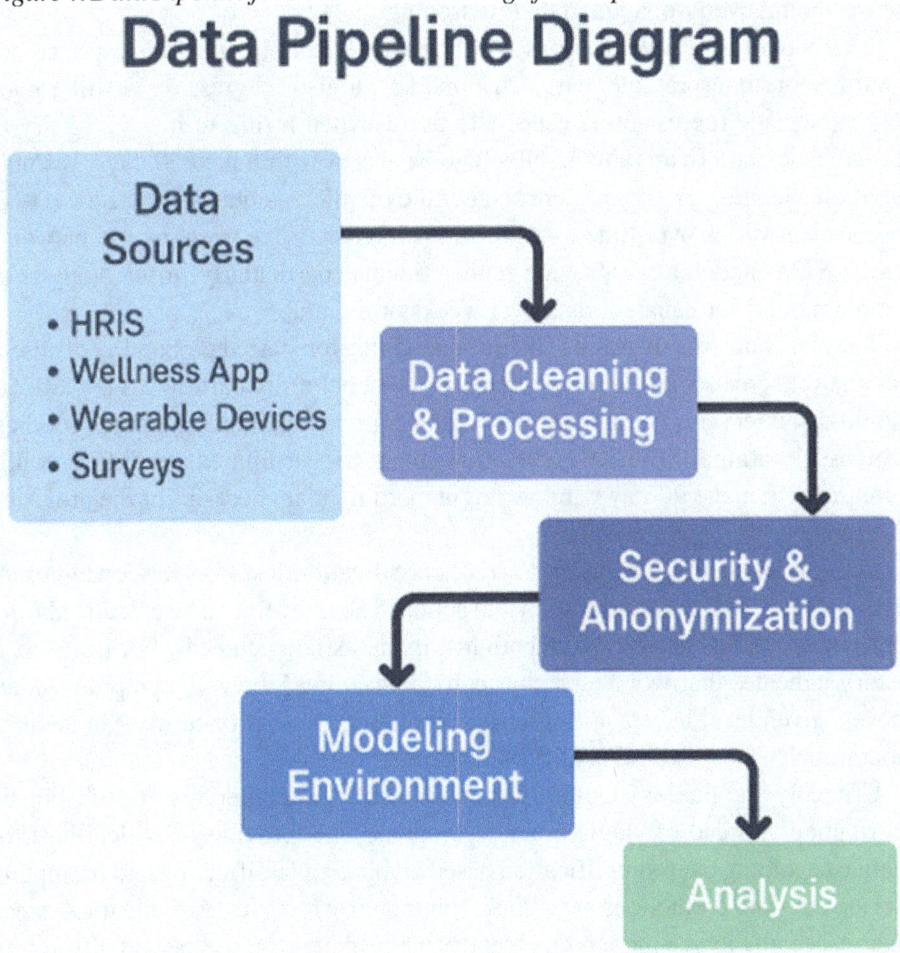

This pipeline outlines the stages from data collection to model deployment, ensuring privacy, cleaning, and contextual integrity in health-sensitive analytics.

4.2 Proposed Model Structure

For the modelling structure itself, a number of machine learning techniques are well-suited to the task of absenteeism prediction. The best model selection is predicated primarily on data size, feature dimensionality, and interpretability needs of the final users — usually HR experts or occupational health advisors with minimal data science proficiency. Decision-tree-based ensemble techniques like Random Forests thus represent an appealing initial point for this reason. These models are capable of capturing non-linear relationships and high-dimensional feature spaces without being overly opaque in their reasoning.

Alternatively, for organizations with formatted data pipelines and a preference towards more interpretable, parametric models, logistic regression is still a good option. Logistic regression is especially useful when trying to make a binary or probabilistic classification (e.g., "likely to be absent within next 30 days: yes/no") based on specified predictors. For temporal dynamics — quantifying how risk of absenteeism varies over time — time-series models or recurrent neural networks (e.g., LSTM models) can provide higher fidelity, particularly in the analysis of symptom trends or behavior data over weeks or months.

The main outcome measure in all instances is the forecasted probability of absenteeism over some specified time horizon — most helpfully partitioned into 30, 60, and 90-day intervals. These intervals facilitate graduated intervention approaches. A high-risk rating for the 30-day window might trigger immediate contact, while increased risk in the 90-day window might merit regular check-ins or the provision of resources.

The model should also output a risk classification level — low, medium, or high — to facilitate communication and action. These levels can be calculated from decision thresholds derived from both history and strategic needs. For instance, if history indicates that women in physically demanding jobs with symptom scores above a given level have a 40% probability of being absent from work in the next month, such a setup would qualify as high-risk.

Critically, the model should also provide confidence intervals or probabilistic distributions instead of single-point predictions. This provides a critical layer of subtlety, avoiding over-simplification based on binary classification and prompting users to consider predictions as within a continuum. Moreover, variable importance ranks especially in tree models can identify which factors (e.g., sleep quality, recent survey sentiment, workload intensity) are underlying the prediction for an individual and thus enable informed design of targeted interventions.

In order to verify the model, organizations need to use cross-validation methods, test-train divides, and, preferably, holdout data. Bias auditing will also be required to make sure the model is not unfairly misclassifying specific groups — specifically along lines of age, race, or socioeconomic status. Clear model cards, in accordance with forthcoming best practices in responsible AI, must be released with deployment.

4.3 Dashboard or Visualization Prototype

The last piece in this system is the user interface — how HR practitioners and managers will engage with the model's outputs. An effective dashboard is more than just a surface decoration but a working intermediary between advanced analytics and real-world decision-making.

The dashboard must be integrated into existing Human Resource Information Systems (HRIS) or wellness platforms in order to drive adoption. Some of the most important features of the interface may be:

- Individual Risk Profiles: Every worker (anonimized if utilized at the team level) has an up-to-date risk classification, with past trends evident through a timeline display. This allows for pattern detection and facilitates context-sensitive interpretation.
- Cohort Analysis: HR departments are able to contrast risk trends by departments, tenure cohorts, occupations, or geographies, and therefore both micro and macro strategy formulation.
- Flags and Alerts: If an employee enters an increased risk band, automated alerts are triggered. They must be accompanied by recommended next steps — e.g., prompt a check-in, provide flexible scheduling, or roll out wellness resources — to inform appropriate, minimally intrusive action.
- Heatmaps of Symptom and Sentiment: Map-like visualizations of aggregate data on symptom frequency or survey sentiment can light up organization hot spots that need attention.
- Model Explainability Tools: Inclusion of features like SHAP (SHapley Additive exPlanations) values is possible to enable transparency regarding why a specific prediction was generated, thereby instilling confidence among the users.

As an example, suppose an HR specialist logs in to the system and observes that in their operations department, two employees have moved into the "high-risk within 30 days" segment. If one profile is clicked, the user can view that the worker has complained of poor-quality sleep for three weeks running, has made recent requests to leave early, and has been decreasing in sentiment in wellness surveys. The dashboard highlights a recommendation for an offer of a confidential discussion with the health and wellness officer and flexible work arrangements. Since the system is not dependent on a single indicator, but weighted constellation of evidence, the risk flag is both specific and discretioned.

The system also has to facilitate human override. No algorithm, no matter how sophisticated, can beat the subtle judgment of a well-trained HR person. The dashboards thus have to feature note-taking, action logging, and escalation, which allow human feedback to be injected into the learning cycle.

Figure 5. Predictive Dashboard for Menopause-Related Absenteeism

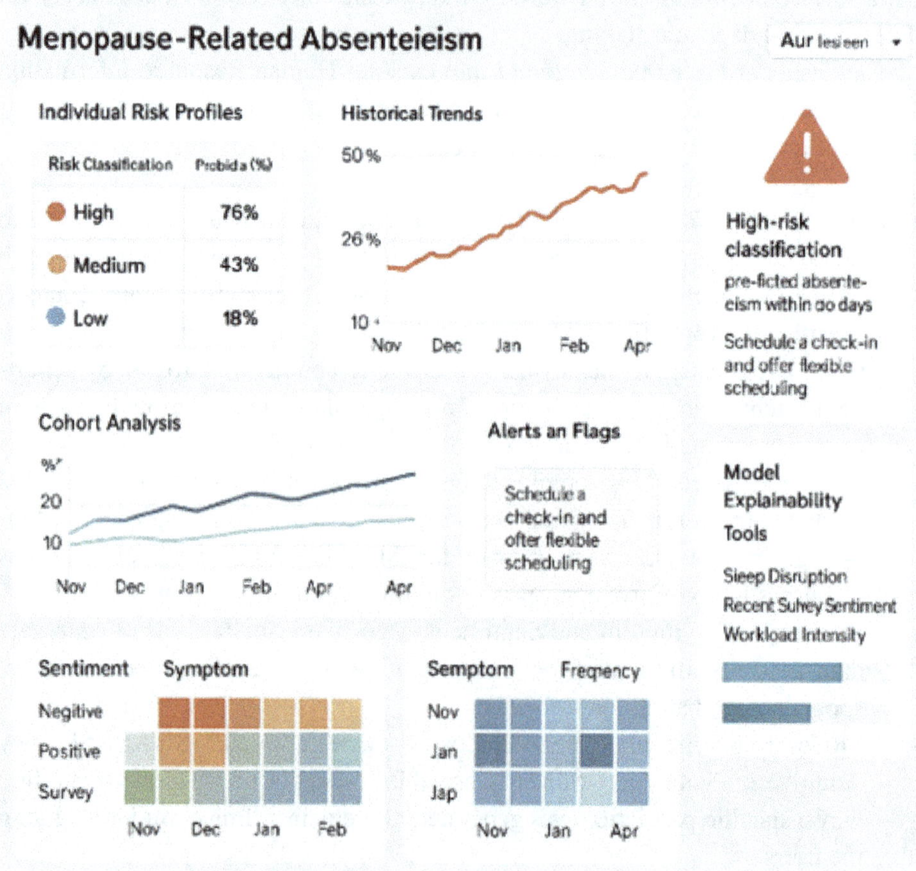

This dashboard provides a comprehensive view of employee absenteeism risk linked to menopause-related factors. It features individual risk classifications (low, medium, high), historical absenteeism trends, department-level cohort analysis, automated alerts for high-risk cases, and sentiment/symptom heatmaps. Model explainability tools highlight key contributing factors such as sleep disruption, workload intensity, and recent survey sentiment, enabling HR professionals to make informed, empathetic interventions.

5. WORKPLACE IMPLEMENTATION STRATEGY

Though theoretical potential of predictive analytics to manage menopause-related absenteeism is sound, the real test of its worth comes in the successful implementation. Models don't transform organizations — systems, folks, and protocols do. This chapter is a pragmatic guide to implanting the model into actual HR operations, both for ethical deployment and effective impact. It defines how predictive analytics can be incorporated into Human Resource Information Systems (HRIS), explains customized intervention strategies by risk classification, and ends with an illustrative hypothetical case study to demonstrate practical usage and measurement of outcomes.

5.1 Workflow Integration

Embedding a predictive absenteeism model within the HR workflow requires harmonious orchestration among technology, policy, and people. The initial step is the creation of a safe and interoperable link between the model and the current HRIS or Employee Experience Platform of the organization. This is done by mapping data fields of the HRIS — demographic variables, attendance records, and performance reviews — to the input layer of the model. In case health and wellness data are being processed, distinct privacy-compliant systems need to be utilized, with robust encryption and access measures.

After technically integrating the model, a phased onboarding process has to be initiated. Organizations can start with a pilot group, preferably an organization with a balanced age, role, and tenure stratification of employees. Employees in this group should be made aware, through open and sympathetic communication, of the objective and extent of the program. Any sharing of health-related data — including symptom monitoring or completion of wellness surveys — must be opt-in, optional, and anonymized when shared with management. Employees should be reassured that the model is intended to assist, not audit or punish, and that its outputs are solely for proactive planning for care and not for punishment.

Communication protocols are paramount. HR must create standardized scripts and toolkits to assist team leaders and managers with discussing menopause, absenteeism, and employee health. Training for managers must be required before model deployment with active listening, stigma reduction, and ethical management of sensitive information. Finally, the ethics or compliance office of the organization must validate the implementation plan against legal frameworks like GDPR, HIPAA, or pertinent labor codes.

After the model goes live, HR users are provided weekly or monthly dashboards with risk forecasts, notified profiles, and intervention suggestions. Scheduling of wellness consultations or manager meetings is easily achieved through integration with calendar software or wellness applications. Most importantly, all interventions triggered by a predictive flag must be recorded in the system to close the feedback loop and facilitate model retraining from outcome data.

5.2 Intervention Design

The final goal of prediction is not classifying, but caring. Interventions must be matched to the risk score generated by the model, adapted to the individual's context, and based on evidence-based occupational health practice. A three-tiered system provides clarity:

- Low Risk (Preventive Support): Low-risk employees can also gain from overall resources — menopause educational workshops, access to online health libraries, and destigmatizing campaigns that normalize conversation. In this tier, pre-emptive literacy and destigmatization are the focus.
- Flexible Resources (Moderate Risk): For medium-risk employees, a package of voluntary, flexible resources may be made available. Some of these are menopause coaching, ergonomic evaluation, and private meetings with occupational health personnel. Managers will also be alerted automatically to contact these staff members to inquire about workload and conditions of work, without needing to disclose health.
- High Risk (Intensive Support): Workers in this high-risk group must be given priority attention with intensive, immediate support. This can include flexible scheduling tailored to their individual needs, redistribution of temporary workloads, or provision of on-site quiet recovery areas in the workplace. Others might contract with outside healthcare professionals to provide hormone therapy consultations, mental health referrals, or group support sessions. Effectiveness of these interventions can be greatly boosted when complemented by psychological safety of disclosure — an environment where employees can feel free to request assistance without apprehension of judgment or retaliation.

Figure 6. Risk Classification Scale for Menopause-Related Absenteeism

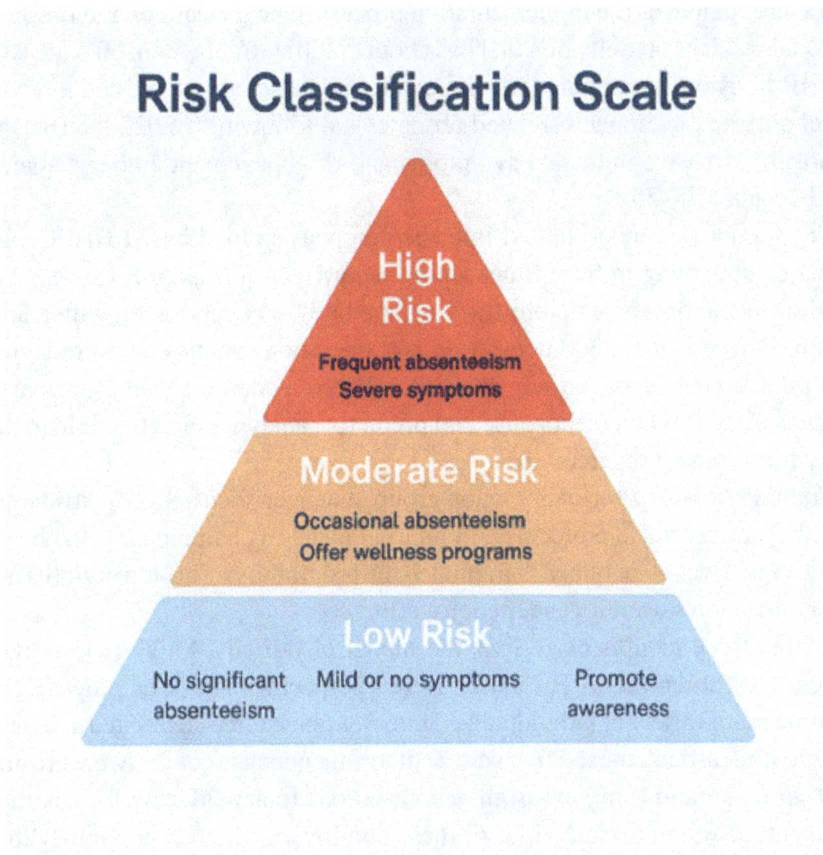

This visual framework categorizes employees into three risk levels—Low, Moderate, and High—based on absenteeism frequency and symptom severity.

Return on investment (ROI) may be projected by measuring avoided absenteeism expenses, turnover decreases, and increased productivity. A simple ROI model would involve inputs like average daily absenteeism cost per employee, past absenteeism rates, projected decreases in absenteeism due to early intervention, and cost of implementation. Organizations may also quantify the return from improvements in engagement score or declines in employee health claims over time. In pilot environments, most organizations notice ROI in 12–18 months, especially when program expenses are low and employee adoption is strong.

5.3 Case Study Example

As an example of the implementation process, take the case of a mid-sized professional services organization that has about 1,200 staff, of whom 60% are women. The HR division, in conjunction with external data scientists, created a predictive model aimed at menopause-related absenteeism following a 2022 internal survey disclosing extensive untreated symptoms and disengagement among female staff members aged 45–55.

The model was incorporated into the company's cloud-based HRIS, with information streaming in from timekeeping records, performance reviews, wellness surveys, and an opt-in symptom-tracking app built in collaboration with a femtech startup. Before launch, 300 consulting and operations employees were signed up for a pilot. All involved participants were offered a comprehensive consent form, an educational FAQ on menopause and predictive analytics, and the right to opt out at any time with no repercussions.

Training sessions for every pilot group manager focused on confidentiality, empathy, and response protocols. An internal panel of champions — led by senior female executives — publicly championed the program as a flagship initiative within the organization's overall gender equity effort.

Within three months of go-live, the model identified 14 high-risk individuals for near-term absenteeism. HR made discreet contact with these employees, and the outcome was a variety of individualized interventions: three negotiated and received flexible work arrangements; five were sent to a menopause coach; two were granted short-term alterations in job assignments; and one took paid leave to seek medical treatment. Most importantly, four of these employees who had previously thought of quitting indicated, when followed up, that they now felt "seen and supported" by the company.

Critical performance metrics (KPIs) measured for six months were:

- Short-term absence for the pilot group declined by 28%.
- Employee engagement scores for women aged between 45 and 55 improved by 17%.
- No negative privacy or ethics complaints received over the course of the pilot.
- Cost savings of $96,000 in prevented absence and productivity loss, vs. implementation costs of $42,000 — returning an ROI of 2.3x in half a fiscal year.

Spurred by these results, the company rolled out the program company-wide in the next fiscal year and started working on companion models for other women's health concerns, including menstrual well-being and postpartum changes.

6. ETHICAL, LEGAL, AND PRIVACY CONSIDERATIONS

The application of predictive analytics to workplace health initiatives—especially those around sensitive life phases like menopause—raises deep questions about ethics, law, and privacy. While the technology has tremendous potential for forward-looking care and staff support, it can be damaging by default if launched without adequate regulation. Predictive models, particularly in health-related environments, need to be based on a sense of human dignity, consent, and justice. This part considers three key aspects of such a framework: consent and confidentiality, nondiscrimination and avoidance of bias in algorithms, and the need to establish trust through open communication.

6.1 Consent and Confidentiality

One of the most pressing issues in using predictive analytics to address menopause-related absenteeism is privacy. Health information—whether directly medical (e.g., frequency of symptoms, history of treatment) or functionally proximate (e.g., surveys of wellness, indicators of fatigue)—are in a very sensitive class of personal data. Misuse or unauthorized disclosure of such information can cause reputational harm, stigma in the workplace, or even legal culpability under regulations like the General Data Protection Regulation (GDPR) in the European Union, the Health Insurance Portability and Accountability Act (HIPAA) in the United States, or similar privacy legislation in other countries.

As such, all health-related data utilized for modeling have to be gathered under conditions of informed, revocable, and voluntary consent. The employees should know what data are being gathered, why they are being gathered, and who is going to access them. If possible, sensitive data must be de-identified or anonymized before ingesting into models. Methods like data masking, encryption-at-rest, and differential privacy can introduce layers of protection without losing analytic value. Role-based access controls would provide that only trained staff—usually in HR or occupational health, not line managers—have access to individualized outputs.

It is also a good idea to keep health-related information separate from essential HR data. For instance, a wellness monitoring program employed to track symptoms and sleep habits should not be populating a performance management system. The intention of prediction within this context is assistance, not monitoring. Keeping this line separate is not just legally enforced in most places, but a normative one—essential for upholding the integrity of any health-improving effort.

6.2 Steer Clear of Discrimination and Bias

The potential for algorithmic bias is especially high where predictive analytics overlap with gender, age, and health. Menopause itself tends to be poorly understood, under-explored, and stereotyped in popular culture and organizational life. Predictive systems, unless well designed, have the potential to encode and amplify such biases. For example, a model that is trained on past patterns of absenteeism might learn to correlate specific job positions or demographic categories with reduced reliability not because of endogenous capability shortfall but because of structural factors—insufficient accommodations, gendered norms, or unidentified health requirements.

To counter these risks, model construction has to follow the dictates of fairness, accountability, and transparency (acronymed as FAT). This entails disparate impact testing on subgroups, variable importance weight auditing, and reviewing how various features interact to generate predictions. When bias is identified, the appropriate mitigation strategies—reweighing, sample balancing, or adversarial de-biasing—ought to be employed.

In addition, the model design process must be participatory from the start. This involves engaging a broad array of stakeholders, such as female workers who have experienced menopause, employee resource groups (ERGs), clinicians, legal consultants, and ethicists. Their contributions make the model technically sound but also socially accountable—grounded in lived experience and sensitive to power relations that algorithmic design too often ignores.

It is also necessary to educate managers and HR personnel not just in how to use the model's results, but how to respond to them without creating discriminatory patterns of behavior. A high-risk score must never be an excuse for reassignment, separation, or stagnation. Instead, it must serve as a stimulus for understanding, conversation, and adjustment. Mechanisms for appeal or reversal should likewise be incorporated in the system, so that employees can challenge or frame the predictions that are made about them.

6.3 Transparency and Trust Among Employees

No matter how ethically strong the model is, it will be for naught if it does not have the trust of the people it's supposed to serve. Predictive analytics, especially in health, resonate with fundamental fears of autonomy, monitoring, and equity. Workers can reasonably worry that disclosing symptoms or contributing to wellness monitoring will put them at risk of stigma or harm their promotion. These fears are not unfounded; they are the product of traditions in work cultures that have all too often punished exposure instead of supporting it.

Trust will have to be gained—through openness, accountability, and evidence of respect. Prior to model deployment, organizations can begin open communications campaigns outlining the objectives, process, and protections of the program. Those communications must be clear, unjargonized, and perhaps co-authored with worker representatives or outside health professionals to make them accessible and credible.

Continuous feedback cycles are important. Workers should have ways to express concerns, make recommendations for improvements, or retract their data at any time. Periodic reporting of collective results—e.g., decreases in absenteeism, adoption of flexible work arrangements, or symptom self-reporting improvements—can aid in promoting the benefits of the program and addressing cynicism.

In addition, organizations need to realize that predictive analytics, even if mighty, are no substitute for culture transformation. Creating a menopause-inclusive workplace takes commitment from leaders, inclusive policies, and respect between people. Predictive tools may help with these objectives, but they cannot create them on their own. Trust comes not from the algorithm, but from the way individuals experience its application: whether or not they are empowered, heard, and safeguarded.

7. DISCUSSION AND FUTURE IMPLICATIONS

With organizations now working in a more complicated landscape of employee wellbeing, workforce diversity, and technological development, applying predictive analytics to address menopause-related workplace issues represents both a timely intervention and an overarching conceptual change. Through this chapter, it has been argued that in addition to enhancing the management of absenteeism, predictive systems can stimulate a radical reframing of the way organizations think about, react to, and prepare for lifecycle changes related to health. The consequences of this shift ripple into the design of workplace policy, the organization of cross-functional collaboration, and global scalability.

7.1 Larger Impact on Workplace Policy

The application of predictive analytics to menopause-absenteeism represents a larger revolution in the management of workplace health and productivity. Traditionally, wellness strategies have been reactive, prompted by spike absence, medical claim, or complaint. Predictive algorithms flip that script. They allow organizations to shift from episodic crisis response to ongoing, proactive support. Menopause is in this way a use case not only for gender equity, but for the future of employee lifecycle management.

Predictive analytics encourage a rethink of established HR categories like "sick leave," "performance decline," or "presenteeism." When symptom development can be predicted and placed in context—when information can uncover the hidden cost of physiological and psychological stress—organizations are better positioned to create humane, adaptive, and tailored responses. This ability resonates strongly with today's trends in HR change, which prioritize personalization, agility, and inclusion.

In addition, this strategy can impact wider regulatory standards. As nations start to regard menopause as a workplace issue worthy of protection—following the U.K., Australia, and sections of Canada—the need for solutions that provide objective, data-based insight without violating privacy will increase. Actively creating such solutions not only puts organizations ahead of compliance requirements, but also sets them up as leaders in ethical innovation.

7.2 Cross-Functional Collaboration

Predictive systems to be implemented ethically and effectively cannot be done by a siloed approach. Effective implementation relies on continued cooperation among several domains of function. HR staff contribute contextual experience with employee needs, job-specific stressors, and business rhythms. Medical and occupational health professionals contribute clinical experience with symptomatology, treatment heterogeneity, and support systems. Data scientists and engineers play a crucial part in building models, performance testing, and system monitoring. Compliance and legal departments make sure that data practices are in compliance with both regulatory requirements and ethical standards.

This intersection is not just logistical; it is epistemological. It is a merging of knowledge systems—biomedical, technical, organizational, and humanistic—each of which has a part of the truth about how menopause impacts work and how systems can change to address it. The best predictive programs will not only be multidisciplinary in practice but also co-owned in leadership. Establishing permanent advisory boards, including employees themselves, can create continuous monitoring of outcomes, grievances, and system drift, thereby institutionalizing ethical surveillance.

Cross-functional integration also enables agility. For instance, if model outputs start to indicate rising risk within a specific department or demographic segment, HR and healthcare professionals can collaborate to modify wellness programs or schedule special workshops. Legal consultants, in the meantime, can review whether new wording in policy is justified to define rights and protection. Such dynamic, adaptive action is only available when organizational know-how can move freely across domains.

Figure 7. Key stakeholders in predictive HR analytics

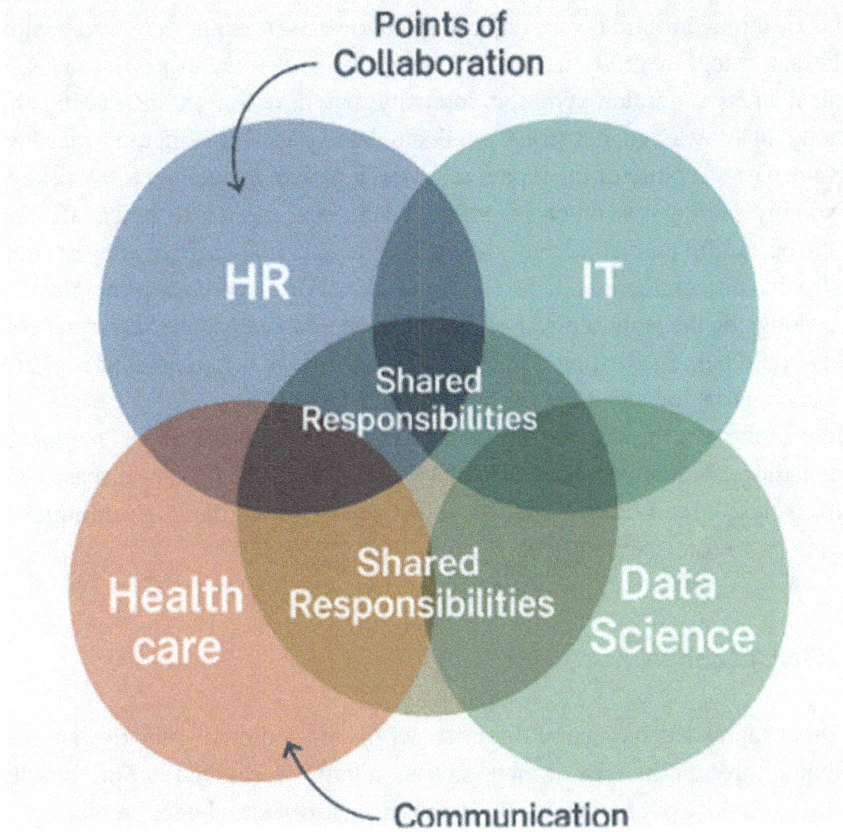

A Venn diagram illustrating the interdisciplinary collaboration required for implementing predictive analytics in HR systems. The overlap of HR, IT, Healthcare, and Data Science highlights shared responsibilities and the critical need for communication and collaboration across domains.

7.3 Scaling the Model

Although the existing framework has been designed with a specific workplace and data context in mind, it is highly scalable (Chakraborty & Ray, 2022). The central elements—a risk prediction module, an HR dashboard, and an intervention toolset—can be scaled to different organizational sizes, industries, and geographic locations. What is required is not a uniform model, but a portable methodology: one that identifies the right data sources, calibrates risk thresholds to cultural context, and aligns outputs with locally appropriate support mechanisms.

In multinational firms, for example, the model may be regionally modified to reflect different cultural norms regarding menopause, unequal access to healthcare, or alternative legal restrictions on data utilization. In manufacturing industries, where physical stress is greater, symptom intensity may have a more direct effect on job capacity; in knowledge industries, intellectual and affective symptoms may be more relevant. The structure of the model must remain open to such sectoral differences.

Notably, scaling is as much a reputational challenge as it is technical. Companies need to be careful that while they grow predictive health analytics, they are not seen as intrusive or technocratic. Consent, fairness, and transparency principles need to scale alongside the technology. For this purpose, industry consortia or professional bodies could help in creating common ethical frameworks, open-source platforms, and benchmarks for menopause-related support systems.

In the long run, the strategy outlined here could be applied beyond menopause to cover additional underrepresented health issues—like autoimmune diseases, mental health cycles, or reproductive changes—further burrowing data-driven, anticipatory care into workforce strategy's core.

8. CONCLUSION

This chapter has navigated the intersection of predictive analytics and worker wellbeing through the lens of menopause—a long-overlooked but profoundly impactful workplace phenomenon. By specifying a formal model for predicting absenteeism risk, detailing implementation plans, and resolving essential ethical issues, we provide not only a technical solution, but a humane vision for the future of work.

Organizations now are not just asked to respond to workforce needs but to predict them. For menopause, this translates into moving from silence to visibility, from stigma to support, and from crisis to care. Predictive analytics, if responsibly created, enable us to do nothing less: move beyond reaction and towards a workplace culture that is proactive, personalized, and inclusive.

The call to action is unambiguous. Policymakers, employers, and system designers will have to work together to create infrastructures that support compassionate intelligence—systems that respect privacy of data and augment help, that respect autonomy and lighten burden. The vision is of a workplace not just safe from harm, but deep with wisdom—a workplace in which no life stage is marginalized, and no worker travels alone.

REFERENCES

Al-Shammari, M., Ahmed Al Bin Ali, F., Abdulla AlRashidi, M., & Salem Albuainain, M. (2024). Big Data and Predictive Analytics for Strategic Human Resource Management: A Systematic Literature Review. *International Journal of Computing and Digital Systems*, *17*(1), 1–9. DOI: 10.12785/ijcds/1571015706

Alabi, O. A., Ajayi, F. A., Udeh, C. A., & Efunniyi, F. P. (2024). Predictive analytics in human resources: Enhancing workforce planning and customer experience. *International Journal of Innovation and Scientific Research*, *11*(9), 149–158. DOI: 10.51244/IJRSI.2024.1109016

Bhise, P., Karekar, P., Nikam, R., & Ray, S. (2024). AI-HRM: Transforming Human Resource Management With Artificial Intelligence.

Bravo, F., & Reguera-Alvarado, N. (2019). Sustainable development disclosure: Environmental, social, and governance reporting and gender diversity in the audit committee. *Business Strategy and the Environment*, *28*(2), 418–429. DOI: 10.1002/bse.2258

Brewis, J., Beck, V., Davies, A., & Matheson, J. (2017). The effects of menopause transition on women's economic participation in the UK.

Bruce, D., & Rymer, J. (2009). Symptoms of the menopause. *Best Practice & Research. Clinical Obstetrics & Gynaecology*, *23*(1), 25–32. DOI: 10.1016/j.bpobgyn.2008.10.002 PMID: 19056320

Burnett, J. R., & Lisk, T. C. (2021). The future of employee engagement: Real-time monitoring and digital tools for engaging a workforce. In *International perspectives on employee engagement* (pp. 117–128). Routledge. DOI: 10.4324/9781003142492-9

Cahn, N., Crawford, B. J., & Waldman, E. G. (2024). Menopause discrimination at work: Comparing the law in the United States and United Kingdom. In *Research Handbook on Law, Society and Ageing* (pp. 281-297). Edward Elgar Publishing.

Chakraborty, T., & Ray, S. (2022). Strategies of Cyberloafing and Phubbing which Affect Workplace Digital Transformation. *Московский экономический журнал*, (10), 430-446.

Chaudhury, M., & Ng, I. (1992). Absenteeism predictors: Least squares, rank regression, and model selection results. *The Canadian Journal of Economics. Revue Canadienne d'Economique*, *25*(3), 615–635. DOI: 10.2307/135735

Chen, H. (2024). *Engaging in sickness presenteeism: How do people decide? The decision-making process behind sickness presenteeism, and implications for its management* (Doctoral dissertation, Nottingham Trent University (United Kingdom)).

Chrisler, J. C. (2013). Teaching taboo topics: Menstruation, menopause, and the psychology of women. *Psychology of Women Quarterly, 37*(1), 128–132. DOI: 10.1177/0361684312471326

Conde, D. M., Verdade, R. C., Valadares, A. L., Mella, L. F., Pedro, A. O., & Costa-Paiva, L. (2021). Menopause and cognitive impairment: A narrative review of current knowledge. *World Journal of Psychiatry, 11*(8), 412–428. DOI: 10.5498/wjp.v11.i8.412 PMID: 34513605

Crandall, C. J., Mehta, J. M., & Manson, J. E. (2023). Management of menopausal symptoms: A review. *Journal of the American Medical Association, 329*(5), 405–420. DOI: 10.1001/jama.2022.24140 PMID: 36749328

Crawford, B. J., Waldman, E. G., & Cahn, N. R. (2021). Working through menopause. *Wash. UL Rev., 99*, 1531.

Cronin, C., Abbott, J., Asiamah, N., & Smyth, S. (2024). Menopause at work—An organisation-based case study. *Nursing Open, 11*(1), e2058. DOI: 10.1002/nop2.2058 PMID: 38268277

DiClaudio, M. (2019). People analytics and the rise of HR: How data, analytics and emerging technology can transform human resources (HR) into a profit center. *Strategic HR Review, 18*(2), 42–46. DOI: 10.1108/SHR-11-2018-0096

Dobson, M., Schnall, P., Rosskam, E., & Landsbergis, P. (2020). Work-related burden of absenteeism, presenteeism, and disability: an epidemiologic and economic perspective. In *Handbook of disability, work and health* (pp. 251–272). Springer International Publishing. DOI: 10.1007/978-3-030-24334-0_13

Eckerson, W. W. (2007). Predictive analytics. *Extending the Value of Your Data Warehousing Investment. TDWI Best Practices Report, 1*, 1–36.

Ejo-Orusa, H., & Okwakpam, J. A. A. (2018). Predictive HR analytics and human resource management amongst human resource management practitioners in Port Harcourt, Nigeria. *Global Scientific Journal, 6*(7), 254.

Fitz-Enz, J., & John Mattox, I. I. (2014). *Predictive analytics for human resources*. John Wiley & Sons. DOI: 10.1002/9781118915042

Gava, G., Orsili, I., Alvisi, S., Mancini, I., Seracchioli, R., & Meriggiola, M. C. (2019). Cognition, mood and sleep in menopausal transition: The role of menopause hormone therapy. *Medicina*, *55*(10), 668. DOI: 10.3390/medicina55100668 PMID: 31581598

Geukes, M., Van Aalst, M. P., Robroek, S. J., Laven, J. S., & Oosterhof, H. (2016). The impact of menopause on work ability in women with severe menopausal symptoms. *Maturitas*, *90*, 3–8. DOI: 10.1016/j.maturitas.2016.05.001 PMID: 27282787

Godfrey, A., Hetherington, V., Shum, H., Bonato, P., Lovell, N. H., & Stuart, S. (2018). From A to Z: Wearable technology explained. *Maturitas*, *113*, 40–47. DOI: 10.1016/j.maturitas.2018.04.012 PMID: 29903647

Greendale, G. A., Lee, N. P., & Arriola, E. R. (1999). The menopause. *Lancet*, *353*(9152), 571–580. DOI: 10.1016/S0140-6736(98)05352-5 PMID: 10028999

Harrell, D. L. (2024). Leaving Halfway: Examining the Loss of the Mid-career Federal Employee Within the Department of the Army.

Harrison, D. A., & Newman, D. A. (2012). Absence, lateness, turnover, and retirement: Narrow and broad understandings of withdrawal and behavioral engagement. *Handbook of Psychology, Second Edition, 12*.

Harrison, Y., & Horne, J. A. (2000). The impact of sleep deprivation on decision making: A review. *Journal of Experimental Psychology. Applied*, *6*(3), 236–249. DOI: 10.1037/1076-898X.6.3.236 PMID: 11014055

Howe, D., Duffy, S., O'Shea, M., Hawkey, A., Wardle, J., Gerontakos, S., & Armour, M. (2023, November). Policies, guidelines, and practices supporting women's menstruation, menstrual disorders and menopause at work: A critical global scoping review. [). MDPI.]. *Health Care*, *11*(22), 2945. PMID: 37998437

Jack, G., Riach, K., & Bariola, E. (2019). Temporality and gendered agency: Menopausal subjectivities in women's work. *Human Relations*, *72*(1), 122–143. DOI: 10.1177/0018726718767739

Johns, G. (2010). Presenteeism in the workplace: A review and research agenda. *Journal of Organizational Behavior*, *31*(4), 519–542. DOI: 10.1002/job.630

Johns, G. (2011). Attendance dynamics at work: The antecedents and correlates of presenteeism, absenteeism, and productivity loss. *Journal of Occupational Health Psychology*, *16*(4), 483–500. DOI: 10.1037/a0025153 PMID: 21875212

Karanika-Murray, M., & Biron, C. (2020). The health-performance framework of presenteeism: Towards understanding an adaptive behaviour. *Human Relations*, *73*(2), 242–261. DOI: 10.1177/0018726719827081

Kayser, K. C., Puig, V. A., & Estepp, J. R. (2022). Predicting and mitigating fatigue effects due to sleep deprivation: A review. *Frontiers in Neuroscience*, *16*, 930280. DOI: 10.3389/fnins.2022.930280 PMID: 35992930

Kishi, R., Kitahara, T., Masuchi, A., & Kasai, S. (2002). Work-related reproductive, musculoskeletal and mental disorders among working women-history, current issues and future research directions. *Industrial Health*, *40*(2), 101–112. DOI: 10.2486/indhealth.40.101 PMID: 12064551

Kleinman, N. L., Rohrbacker, N. J., Bushmakin, A. G., Whiteley, J., Lynch, W. D., & Shah, S. N. (2013). Direct and indirect costs of women diagnosed with menopause symptoms. *Journal of Occupational and Environmental Medicine*, *55*(4), 465–470. DOI: 10.1097/JOM.0b013e3182820515 PMID: 23532198

Kopenhager, T., & Guidozzi, F. (2015). Working women and the menopause. *Climacteric*, *18*(3), 372–375. DOI: 10.3109/13697137.2015.1020483 PMID: 25830628

Kumar, V., & Garg, M. L. (2018). Predictive analytics: A review of trends and techniques. *International Journal of Computer Applications*, *182*(1), 31–37. DOI: 10.5120/ijca2018917434

Lawrance, N., Petrides, G., & Guerry, M. A. (2021). Predicting employee absenteeism for cost effective interventions. *Decision Support Systems*, *147*, 113539. DOI: 10.1016/j.dss.2021.113539

Leigh, J. P. (1991). Employee and job attributes as predictors of absenteeism in a national sample of workers: The importance of health and dangerous working conditions. *Social Science & Medicine*, *33*(2), 127–137. DOI: 10.1016/0277-9536(91)90173-A PMID: 1887276

Li, Q., Gu, J., Huang, J., Zhao, P., & Luo, C. (2023). They see me as mentally ill": The stigmatization experiences of Chinese menopausal women in the family. *BMC Women's Health*, *23*(1), 185. DOI: 10.1186/s12905-023-02350-y PMID: 37076835

Lobo, R. A. (2014). What the future holds for women after menopause: where we have been, where we are, and where we want to go. *Climacteric, 17*(sup2), 12-17.

Lundberg, U. (2002). Psychophysiology of work: Stress, gender, endocrine response, and work-related upper extremity disorders. *American Journal of Industrial Medicine*, *41*(5), 383–392. DOI: 10.1002/ajim.10038 PMID: 12071491

Makara-Studzińska, M. T., Kryś-Noszczyk, K. M., & Jakiel, G. (2014). Epidemiology of the symptoms of menopause–an intercontinental review. *Menopause Review/ Przegląd Menopauzalny, 13*(3), 203-211.

Maki, P. M., & Jaff, N. G. (2022). Brain fog in menopause: A health-care professional's guide for decision-making and counseling on cognition. *Climacteric, 25*(6), 570–578. DOI: 10.1080/13697137.2022.2122792 PMID: 36178170

McCarthy, R. V., McCarthy, M. M., Ceccucci, W., Halawi, L., McCarthy, R. V., McCarthy, M. M., & Halawi, L. (2022). *Applying predictive analytics.* Springer International Publishing. DOI: 10.1007/978-3-030-83070-0

McGregor, A. (2017). *An investigation into the phenomenon of presenteeism: examining antecedents and the operationalisation of presenteeism* (Doctoral dissertation, University of Wollongong).

Miraglia, M., & Johns, G. (2021). The social and relational dynamics of absenteeism from work: A multilevel review and integration. *The Academy of Management Annals, 15*(1), 37–67. DOI: 10.5465/annals.2019.0036

Monteleone, P., Mascagni, G., Giannini, A., Genazzani, A. R., & Simoncini, T. (2018). Symptoms of menopause—Global prevalence, physiology and implications. *Nature Reviews. Endocrinology, 14*(4), 199–215. DOI: 10.1038/nrendo.2017.180 PMID: 29393299

Nosek, M., Kennedy, H. P., & Gudmundsdottir, M. (2010). Silence, stigma, and shame: A postmodern analysis of distress during menopause. *Advances in Nursing Science, 33*(3), E24–E36. DOI: 10.1097/ANS.0b013e3181eb41e8 PMID: 20693828

Percival, M. (2025). *The Psychology of Menopause.* Taylor & Francis. DOI: 10.4324/9781003438342

Pillai, R., & Sivathanu, B. (2022). Measure what matters: Descriptive and predictive metrics of HRM-pathway toward organizational performance. *International Journal of Productivity and Performance Management, 71*(7), 3009–3029. DOI: 10.1108/ IJPPM-10-2020-0509

Poethke, U., Klasmeier, K. N., Radaca, E., & Diestel, S. (2023). How modern working environments shape attendance behaviour: A longitudinal study on weekly flexibilization, boundaryless work and presenteeism. *Journal of Occupational and Organizational Psychology, 96*(3), 524–544. DOI: 10.1111/joop.12437

Pohling, R., Buruck, G., Jungbauer, K. L., & Leiter, M. P. (2016). Work-related factors of presenteeism: The mediating role of mental and physical health. *Journal of Occupational Health Psychology, 21*(2), 220–234. DOI: 10.1037/a0039670 PMID: 26322439

Pope, S. K., Sowers, M., Welch, G. W., & Albrecht, G. (2001). Functional limitations in women at midlife: The role of health conditions, behavioral and environmental factors. *Women's Health Issues, 11*(6), 494–502. DOI: 10.1016/S1049-3867(01)00089-5 PMID: 11704470

Powell, D. B. (2023). Presenteeism in the Workplace: An Exploration of Supervisors' Perspective and Employee Outcomes.

Rappaport, A., Bancroft, E., & Okum, L. (2003). The aging workforce raises new talent management issues for employers. *Journal of Organizational Excellence, 23*(1), 55–66. DOI: 10.1002/npr.10101

Saadat, H. (2021). Effect of inadequate sleep on clinician performance. *Anesthesia and Analgesia, 132*(5), 1338–1343. DOI: 10.1213/ANE.0000000000005369 PMID: 33857976

Sagie, A. (1998). Employee absenteeism, organizational commitment, and job satisfaction: Another look. *Journal of Vocational Behavior, 52*(2), 156–171. DOI: 10.1006/jvbe.1997.1581

Santoro, N., Roeca, C., Peters, B. A., & Neal-Perry, G. (2021). The menopause transition: Signs, symptoms, and management options. *The Journal of Clinical Endocrinology and Metabolism, 106*(1), 1–15. DOI: 10.1210/clinem/dgaa764 PMID: 33095879

Schaufeli, W. B., Bakker, A. B., & Van Rhenen, W. (2009). How changes in job demands and resources predict burnout, work engagement, and sickness absenteeism. *Journal of Organizational Behavior: The International Journal of Industrial. Journal of Organizational Behavior, 30*(7), 893–917. DOI: 10.1002/job.595

Shifrin, N. V., & Michel, J. S. (2022). Flexible work arrangements and employee health: A meta-analytic review. *Work and Stress, 36*(1), 60–85. DOI: 10.1080/02678373.2021.1936287

Siegel, E. (2013). *Predictive analytics: The power to predict who will click, buy, lie, or die*. John Wiley & Sons.

Strazdins, L., & Bammer, G. (2004). Women, work and musculoskeletal health. *Social Science & Medicine, 58*(6), 997–1005. DOI: 10.1016/S0277-9536(03)00260-0 PMID: 14723897

Sullivan, T., Weinert, C., & Cudney, S. (2003). Management of chronic illness: Voices of rural women. *Journal of Advanced Nursing*, *44*(6), 566–574. DOI: 10.1046/j.0309-2402.2003.02846.x PMID: 14651679

Sumner, R. C., & Kinsella, E. L. (2021). "It's like a kick in the teeth": The emergence of novel predictors of burnout in frontline workers during COVID-19. *Frontiers in Psychology*, *12*, 645504. DOI: 10.3389/fpsyg.2021.645504 PMID: 34113288

Tarro, L., Llauradó, E., Ulldemolins, G., Hermoso, P., & Solà, R. (2020). Effectiveness of workplace interventions for improving absenteeism, productivity, and work ability of employees: A systematic review and meta-analysis of randomized controlled trials. *International Journal of Environmental Research and Public Health*, *17*(6), 1901. DOI: 10.3390/ijerph17061901 PMID: 32183392

Verdonk, P., Bendien, E., & Appelman, Y. (2022). Menopause and work: A narrative literature review about menopause, work and health. *Work (Reading, Mass.)*, *72*(2), 483–496. DOI: 10.3233/WOR-205214 PMID: 35570508

Vickers, M. (2002). *Work and unseen chronic illness: Silent voices*. Routledge. DOI: 10.4324/9780203471395

Waldman, E. G., Cahn, N. R., & Crawford, B. J. (2022). Contextualizing menopause in the law. *Harvard Journal of Law & Gender*, *45*, 1.

Wasaha, S., & Angelopoulos, F. M. (1996). What every woman should know about menopause. *The American Journal of Nursing*, *96*(1), 25. DOI: 10.1097/00000446-199601000-00025 PMID: 8546184

Zhou, Z., Luo, D., Yang, B. X., & Liu, Z. (2022). Machine learning-based prediction models for depression symptoms among Chinese healthcare workers during the early COVID-19 outbreak in 2020: A cross-sectional study. *Frontiers in Psychiatry*, *13*, 876995. DOI: 10.3389/fpsyt.2022.876995 PMID: 35573334

Chapter 11
Personalized Medicine and AI-Driven Treatment Plus:
A Strategic Approach to Menopause Management in the Workplace

Kambati Niharika
https://orcid.org/0009-0003-5265-4436
Alagappa University, India

ABSTRACT

Menopause brings both physiological and psychological alterations that significantly impact workplace engagement for women. Conventional treatment have predominantly employees one-size fits-all solutions, disregarding the notable inconsistencies between individual experiences. This necessitates migrating towards customised clinical solutions. Integrating AI-guided remedies and Personalised medicine into workplace wellness frameworks proposes a revolutionary strategy to managing menopausal symptoms. By considering individual differences, AI and personalised medicine can enhance workplace well-being and productivity by providing tailored support.This chapter examines the integration of artificial intelligence, personalized medicine, and strategic human capital planning in managing menopause amongst employees.The intersection holds promise for tailoring support to particular needs and stages, as women and their employers navigate short-term difficulties and long-term implications together through open dialogue and evidence-based accommodations.

DOI: 10.4018/979-8-3373-2970-3.ch011

1. INTRODUCTION

1.1. The Role of Workplace Well-being in the Lives of Midlife Women

The contemporary workplace is rapidly evolving in response to shifts in demographics, technology, and societal norms. As more women ascend to leadership roles and contribute meaningfully during their midlife years, it has become increasingly important to address gender-specific health concerns in professional settings. Among these, menopause stands out as a frequently neglected yet profoundly influential life stage thar can shape a woman's experience at work.

Menopause marks the end of a woman's reproductive years, usually between the age of 45 and 55 aligning with the period of her peak professional achievement. However, the physical symptoms, including hot flashes, sleep disruption, and fatigue, along with psychological effects such as anxiety, mood swings, and difficulty concentrating, can pose significant challenges to job performance. Despite this, workplace policies and support systems have largely failed to accommodate these real life issues contributing to declines in productivity, increased absenteeism, and even early retirement (Alzueta et al., 2024).

Prioritizing the well-being of midlife women in the workplace is not just a matter of fairness or inclusion, it is a strategic business decision. Providing adequate support through the menopausal transition can improve employee retention, engagement, and overall morale, while signalling a company's commitment to long-term wellness and diversity. As global organisations increasingly recognise the complexity of employee well-being, this time is ripe to reevaluate how menopause is understood and addressed within the fabric of workplace culture and infrastructure (Bhattacharya et al., 2023).

1.2. Limitations of Standardised Menopause Management Approaches in the Workplace

Workplaces are evolving fast, shaped by shifts in technology, demographics, and social expectations. Yet, when it comes to how menopause is managed in these environments, many organizations still rely on outdated, one-size-fits-all solutions. Despite the fact that a large number of women experience menopause during the peak of their careers, support often comes in the form of generic advice-like lifestyle changes, hormone therapy, or the occasional flexible work schedule. While these steps can be helpful, they often miss the mark by failing to reflect the complex and deeply personal nature of the menopausal experience (Burger et al., 2002).

No two women go through menopause in exactly the same way. Some face overwhelming symptoms like sleepless nights, anxiety, or intense fatigue; while others barely notice a shift. A range of factors, from genetics and hormone levels to mental health, job stress, and even cultural background, can shape how each woman navigates this life phase (Chan et al., 2020). So, when workplaces treat menopause as a uniform experience, they risk offering support that doesn't work for many, leaving employees feeling unseen or unsupported. This not only affects individual well-being, but also impacts productivity, morale, and retention across the organization (Chen et al., 2025a). Most workplaces still don't include menopause in their wellness programs or HR strategies. That silence can send an unintended message: that menopause is a private issue, not something worth talking about, or supporting-at work. Without visible policies or meaningful accommodations, many women feel the pressure to stay quiet, even as they struggle. When treatment options lack personalization, they're not just ineffective, they contribute to a bigger problem of inequality and exclusion in the workplace (Chen et al., 2025b).

This chapter calls for a more thoughtful and empathetic way to support women going through menopause at work. It moves beyond the outdated, one-size-fits-all approach and highlights why menopause needs to be treated as a significant workplace issue-biologically, emotionally, and socially.

Rather than seeing menopause as a disruption, we frame it as a natural stage of life-one where women can continue to thrive with the right support. The chapter explores how artificial intelligence(AI) and Machine Learning(ML) can be used to create personalized wellness solutions that adapt to each woman's unique experience. These technologies aren't just about innovation-they're tools for helping Human Resource teams (HR) build more inclusive, flexible, and understanding environments. We show how AI-powered tools can be integrated into existing employee support systems, offering a roadmap for organizations at any stage of their digital health journey. Drawing on the latest research, as well as real-life stories and successful case studies, the chapter offers practical strategies for change-both at the policy level and in everyday workplace culture.

By combining insights from health, technology, gender studies, and leadership, we offer actionable recommendations that help businesses lead with empathy, inclusion, and forward-thinking. Ultimately, this chapter is about changing the narrative: menopause doesn't have to be a barrier-it can be a moment for organizations to show they truly value the wellbeing of all their people.

2. EXPLORING THE IMPACT OF MENOPAUSE WITHIN WORKPLACE ENVIRONMENT

2.1. Physiological and Mental Health Aspects of Menopause

2.1.1. Hormonal Fluctuations and Common Symptoms

Menopause is a natural milestone in a woman's life, marking the end of her reproductive years-usually between the age of 45 and 55 identified clinically when around a full year has gone without a menstrual period. But the transition into menopause, known as perimenopause, begins well before that and brings with it a series of hormonal shifts-particularly in estrogen, progesterone, and follicle-stimulating hormone-that can affect many areas of the body.

A drop in estrogen is often the most noticeable change, and it's responsible for a variety of symptoms. These can include hot flashes, night sweats, vaginal dryness, joint pain, and even episodes of heart palpitations (Choudhury et al., 2020). How these symptoms show up, and how intensely, varies widely. For some women, menopause is a manageable phase with only mild discomfort. For others, the experience can be long-lasting and disruptive, deeply affecting their energy, focus, and ability to function at work or at home (David et al., 2022).

Beyond the immediate symptoms, hormonal changes during menopause can influence everything from body temperature regulation to heart and bone health, raising the risk of conditions like osteoporosis. When these physical changes are layered onto the pressures of midlife-careers, family obligations, and caregiving, they can become overwhelming. It's a demanding time, both physically and emotionally, and one that deserves far more recognition and support in the workplace and beyond.

2.1.2. Psychological Impacts: Mood, Cognition, Sleep

Menopause affects far more than just the body, it can deeply influence a woman's emotional and mental landscape. As hormone levels shift, many women find themselves facing unexpected mood changes. Feelings of irritability, anxiety, sadness, or emotional ups and downs can become more common. For some, these changes feel similar to depression or heightened anxiety, yet they're often misread, brushed aside, or left unaddressed in both medical settings and the workplace (Esteva et al., 2019).

Mental clarity can also take a hit. What's often referred to as "brain fog" can feel like struggling to find the right word, forgetting things more often, having trouble focusing, or feeling mentally slower when juggling multiple tasks. On top of that, sleep becomes more elusive, disrupted by night sweats or a general restlessness, leaving women exhausted and mentally drained the next day (Gava et al., 2019).

These psychological and cognitive symptoms, though easy to miss from the outside, can be incredibly frustrating. They may quietly chip away at a woman's self-confidence, reduce her engagement at work, and make it harder to meet the demands of her role. And because these struggles are still so misunderstood, many women choose not to talk about them, often out of fear of being dismissed or judged-which only adds to the emotional weight they carry.

Table 1. Understanding Menopause in the Workplace

Symptom Category	Specific Symptoms	Potential Workplace Impact
Vasomotor Symptoms	Hot flashes, night sweats (Kohn et al., 2019)	Discomfort, frequent need for breaks, difficulty concentrating, embarrassment in meetings.
Sleep Disturbances	Insomnia, disrupted sleep, early awakening Kohn et al., 2019)	Fatigue, decreased alertness, reduced productivity, increased error rates.
Cognitive Symptoms	Memory lapses, difficulty concentrating, brain fog Kohn et al., 2019)	Poor task management, longer decision-making, loss of confidence in role performance.
Mood & Emotional Health	Anxiety, irritability, depression, mood swings (Li et al., 2021)	Conflict with colleagues, absenteeism, decreased team engagement, emotional distress.
Urogenital Symptoms	Vaginal dryness, urinary tract infections, frequent urination Kohn et al., 2019)	Discomfort, need for more frequent restroom breaks, reduced confidence in physical presence.
Musculoskeletal Issues	Joint pain, stiffness, muscle aches (Liefgreen et al., 2024)	Difficulty with physical tasks, absenteeism due to pain, ergonomic challenges.
Menstrual Irregularities	Heavy bleeding, unpredictable periods.	Increased need for flexibility, discomfort, concerns around workplace hygiene.
Skin & Hair Changes	Dry skin, hair thinning or loss (Loftus et al., 2022)	Body image issues, self-esteem concerns, distraction due to changes in appearance.
Social & Identity Impacts	Feelings of aging, identity shifts, fear of being judged (Maki & Jaff, 2022)	Hesitation to seek support, fear of career stagnation, isolation, impact on interpersonal dynamics.

2.2. Workplace Implications of Menopause

2.2.1. Productivity Challenges

The unpredictable and often fluctuating nature of menopausal symptoms can make it difficult for women to maintain their usual levels of productivity. Issues like mental fatigue, trouble concentrating, and physical discomfort can interfere with everyday tasks, slowing down performance, even for women who are highly skilled and experienced in their roles.

During this transition, staying focused in meetings, meeting fast-paced deadlines, or contributing fully to team projects may become more challenging. These struggles can gradually take a toll on self-esteem, causing some women to second-guess themselves or pull back from active participation (Alzueta et al., 2024). From an organizational perspective, this quiet drop in engagement and performance among midlife women, many of whom are in key leadership or expert roles, can lead to a significant, often unnoticed loss of talent and productivity.

2.2.2. Attendance and Absenteeism

Menopause can take a real toll on attendance at work. When night sweats and insomnia disrupt sleep, exhaustion often follows, making it difficult to get through the workday, let alone be at your best. Add to those symptoms like migraines, heavy bleeding during perimenopause, or sudden shifts in mood, and it's easy to see why many women need time off. But here's the challenge: many don't feel they can take that time. Afraid of being labelled as unreliable or weak, they push through and show up anyway, even when they're far from well.

This pressure to be present, despite feeling physically or emotionally drained, leads to what's called presenteeism, being at work but not performing at your usual level (Mancone et al., 2023). Over time, this constant tension between meeting job expectations and managing personal health wears women down. And in workplaces that don't openly acknowledge menopause as a valid health issue, the emotional weight can be even heavier. Without support or understanding, many women feel pushed to the margins, leading some to quietly step back or leave their roles altogether.

2.2.3. Stigma and Disclosure Issues

Menopause is still something many people shy away from talking about at work. This silence often comes from a wider discomfort with aging and women's bodies, a discomfort that runs deep in many parts of society. Because of that, a lot of women choose not to share what they're experiencing. They worry about being misunderstood, judged, or seen as less capable if they ask for help or adjustments.

It's especially hard to speak up in workplaces that are male-dominated or where youth is prized. In those settings, menopause is often ignored, laughed off, or not taken seriously at all. That kind of atmosphere can leave women feeling invisible, pushing them to suffer through symptoms on their own rather than risk being seen differently.

This lack of openness doesn't just affect women, it also leaves managers, co-workers, and HR professionals unprepared to offer the kind of support that could make a real difference. Without clear policies, guidance, or everyday understanding, menopause remains hidden in the background, feeding isolation, inequality, and missed opportunities for healthier, more inclusive workplaces (O'Neill et al., 2023).

2.3. Gender Equity and the Menopause Gap

2.3.1. Menopause as a DEI Issue

Menopause is a critical, yet frequently neglected, dimension of workplace diversity, equity, and inclusion(DEI). While most DEI initiatives focus on gender, race, and disability, few extend their reach to encompass reproductive health life stages, such as menopause . This oversight reflects a structural blind spot in organisational health equity strategies .

By failing to recognise and support employees struggling menopause, companies unintentionally perpetuate systemic gender inequalities. Women are disproportionately affected by age and biology related factors beyond their control, often facing stigma, decreased performance perceptions, and stalled career progression. These dynamics reinforce the glass ceiling and contribute to the persistent gender pay gap.

Treating menopause as a DEI concern means acknowledging it as legitimate factor that influences access to opportunities, career advancement, and overall engagement in the workplace. Inclusive policies and cultures that support employees through all life stages are not only equitable; they are essential to building truly diverse and resilient organisations (Reddy et al., 2019).

2.3.2. Ageism and Gendered Expectation

Menopause sits at a crossroads between gender and age, and it's here that many women encounter a uniquely challenging set of expectations. As they age, women often face subtle yet persistent stereotypes such as lack of energy, being less adaptable, or somehow out of sync with evolving workplace norms. When menopausal symptoms enter the picture, these biases can be magnified, even when there's no impact on actual performance or competence.

Unlike male aging, which is often framed as a time of growing authority and wisdom, female aging is too often viewed through a lens of decline. These double standards place immense pressure on midlife women to mask their symptoms, push through without asking for support, and prove they're "just as capable" as ever. The result ? Chronic stress, mental health strain, and a quiet erosion of workplace satisfaction and belonging. Until organisations confront these gendered and ageist expectations, menopause will remain an invisible barrier to equity and inclusion (Reddy et al, 2019).

2.3.4. Global and Regional Examples

Around the world, awareness of menopause as a workplace issue is growing, but progress is uneven. The United Kingdom stands out as a leader, with increasing support from government bodies, trade unions, and businesswomen. Companies like Channel 4 (Savitha, 2024) and HSBC (Schei & Abernathy, 2023) have introduced dedicated menopause policies, offering flexible work options, manager training, and peer support networks . In Australia, the Human Rights Commission has begun incorporating menopause into broader gender equity discussions. Several employers now include menopause in their mental health and wellness strategies, spurred by advocacy from women's health organisations (Schei & Abernathy, 2024.

In Asia, deeply rooted cultural values-such as modesty, stoicism, and caregiving responsibilities, often make menopause a taboo topic. In Japan and South Korea, for example, professional decorum may discourage open discussion of personal health. Still, some large employers in tech and manufacturing are beginning to implement wellness programs that include menopause education and digital health tools, signalling a quiet cultural shift (Shickel et al., 2018).

Across all regions, a clear pattern emerges: menopause remains largely overlooked in organizational health and DEI strategies. As more women move into mid-and senior-level positions globally, the need for inclusive, supportive environments becomes urgent.

Recognizing menopause as both an occupational health issue and a DEI matter is a crucial first step. To truly support midlife women at work, organizations must go beyond one-size-fits-all policies, embracing personalized, culturally sensitive, and even AI-supported care solutions that reflect the complex realities of this life stage. The time to act is now, to ensure women can thrive, not just survive, during menopause.

3. THE EVOLUTION OF MENOPAUSE TREATMENT

3.1. History and Limitations of Traditional Menopause Therapies

Historically, menopause has been treated with broad strokes-uniform strategies for a deeply personal and varied life transition. For decades, Hormone Replacement Therapy (HRT) was the gold standard, introduced in the 1940s and widely promoted by the 1960s as a cure-all for both symptoms and long-term health risks (Steffan, 2021).

But in the early 2000s, that confidence was shaken. The Women's Health Initiative (WHI) study linked HRT to increased risks of breast cancer, stroke, and heart disease. Although later findings clarified that risk levels depended on age, timing, and hormone type, the damage was done. Trust eroded. Many women stopped treatment, and clinicians grew cautious, leaving a gap in care for millions (Taherdoost & Ghofrani, 2024). In this void, non-hormonal options emerged. Selective Serotonin Reuptake Inhibitors(SSRIs) like paroxetine and fluoxetine began to be used for hot flashes and mood symptoms, while Cognitive Behavioural Therapy (CBT) offered a psychological approach to managing anxiety, insomnia, and low mood. These alternatives helped some, but weren't a perfect fit for all. SSRIs carried side effects like sexual dysfunction or weight gain, and CBT required access and personal motivation, which not all women had (Vincent et al., 2023).

The deeper issue wasn't just the tools-it was the assumption that one approach could work for all. Too often, treatment was based on general symptoms, without considering a woman's genetic makeup, hormonal profile, lifestyle, or cultural background. This led to both over-treatment and neglect, reinforcing the perception that menopause care was inconsistent and impersonal.

Today, there is a realised recognition that menopause demands a more nuanced, data-driven, and individualized approach. Both patients and providers are calling for care that reflects the full complexity of this transition-biologically, emotionally, and socially. It's time to move beyond the one-size-fits-all model and meet women where they are, with care as diverse as their experiences.

Table 2. Comparison of Traditional Treatments vs. Personalized Medicine Approaches in Menopause Management

Aspect	Traditional Treatments	Personalized Medicine Approaches
Core Principle	One-size-fits-all, symptom-targeted.	Tailored to individual genetic, hormonal, lifestyle, and metabolic profiles.
Primary Modalities	HRT (Whiteley et al., 2013), SSRIs, herbal remedies.	Pharmacogenomics, AI-driven risk profiling, precision HRT, nutrigenomics.
Customization Level	Low-based on general age and symptom category.	High-guided by genetic, epigenetic, lifestyle, and molecular markers.
Diagnostics Used	Symptom checklist, basic hormone panels.	Genomic sequencing, metabolomic, proteomic, AI-assisted diagnostics.
Examples of Therapy	Standard-dose estrogen/progestin therapy, clonidine, phytoestrogens.	Bioidentical hormones adjusted via genomic input, SNP-based drug selection, digital twins.

continued on following page

Table 2. Continued

Aspect	Traditional Treatments	Personalized Medicine Approaches
Safety Concerns	Breast cancer, blood clots like Generalised risks.	Reduced risk via individualized screening and dose adjustment.
Monitoring Approach	Periodic follow-up, generic.	Continuous digital monitoring (apps/ sensors), biomarker feedback loops.
Efficacy Evidence	Mixed, especially post-WHI study.	Emerging but promising-early trials show improved symptom control & compliance.
Patient Satisfaction	Often moderate due to side effects or inefficacy.	Higher in pilot studies due to tailored symptom relief and engagement.
Key Limitations	Overgeneralization, side-effect profile, underperformance in minority groups.	High cost, access issues, need for interdisciplinary coordination, emerging evidence base.

3.2. Rise of Personalised Medicine

The limitations of conventional menopause treatment come at a time when healthcare is undergoing a profound transformation-from generalized protocols to personalised medicine. This evolving approach focuses on tailoring prevention, diagnosis, and treatment to each person's unique biology, environment, and lifestyle. Personalized medicine is about making healthcare truly individual. By looking at things like your genes, biology, and lifestyle data, it helps doctors understand what makes you unique, and how your care should reflect that. Instead of offering the same treatment to everyone, this approach uses tools like precision medicine to tailor therapies to your specific needs, stratified medicine to group people with similar responses, and predictive insights to catch potential health issues before they start. It's a shift toward smarter, more proactive, and more human-cantered care (Williamson & Prybutok, 2024)

In the context of menopause, these approaches are being increasingly shaped by pharmacogenomics-the study of how our genes influence responses to medication. For instance, a simple genetic test can help determine whether a woman is likely to benefit from certain hormone therapies or might face side effects. This allows clinicians to choose the most effective, safest treatment options from the start. Beyond medication, precision diagnostics, like hormone panels, microbiome mapping, DNA sequencing, and wearable health monitors, are helping women and their providers track hormonal shifts, symptom patterns, and physiological changes in real time. When this data is integrated using AI-driven platforms, it enables deeply personalized interventions: from recommending specific non-hormonal treatments to optimizing nutrition, stress management, and sleep (Woods & Mitchell, 2005).

While still emerging, the clinical use of personalised medicine in menopause care is accelerating. Digital health companies and startups now offer platforms for symptom tracking, virtual consultations, and custom treatment plans. In places like the United States, Scandinavia, and Singapore, where infrastructure for precision medicine is strong, these innovations are increasingly entering mainstream care (Wright et al., 2024). This marks a vital shift in mindset: menopause is no longer seen as a one-size-fits-all condition. It is a deeply individual experience, one that deserves the same level of personalization and scientific precision as conditions like cancer or heart disease.

4. ARTIFICIAL INTELLIGENCE IN HEALTHCARE AND MENOPAUSE MANAGEMENT

As personalized medicine emerges as the future of healthcare, artificial intelligence (AI) is the engine powering data-driven, individualized treatment. In the context of menopause management, AI not only accelerates the analysis of complex biological signals but also bridges the gap between clinical insights and real-world patient experiences. This section explores the core AI technologies applicable to menopausal care, the data ecosystems that feed these algorithms, AI-powered decision support systems (DSS), and the ethical and privacy challenges that must be addressed to deploy AI responsibly (Zouboulis et al., 2022).

4.1. Core AI Technologies Applicable to Menopause Care

4.1.1. Machine Learning (ML)

ML refers to a set of algorithms that can learn from data, recognising patterns and improving their predictions over time. In the context of menopause, ML offers a powerful way beyond one-size-fits-all care.

Using supervised ML models, like random forests, support vector machines, or gradient-boosted trees, researchers can train systems on labelled clinical data to forecast how symptoms might evolve. For example, these models can predict the likelihood of intense hot flashes, mood disturbances, or sleep disruption for a specific individual.

Meanwhile, unsupervised models work without needing predefined labels. They can detect hidden groupings among women based on shared symptom profiles or health markers, revealing patterns that even seasoned clinicians might miss. This can help personalise treatment and deepen our understanding of the many ways menopause is experienced.

4.1.2. Deep Learning

Deep learning, a specialised form of ML, uses multi-layered neural networks to process complex data. It's particularly effective for understanding information that's high-dimensional or changes over time.

For instance, convolutional neural networks (CNNs) can analyse medical images, such as bone density scans, helping detect osteoporosis risk early. Meanwhile, recurrent neural networks (RNNs) and transformer models are skilled at reading time-based data, like hormone fluctuations or sensor outputs from wearables.

These tools can track subtle changes in sleep, temperature regulation, or stress signals, helping flag when symptoms are intensifying, often before a woman is fully aware of the shift herself. In this way, deep learning enables a more proactive, responsive approach to menopause care.

4.1.3. Predictive Analytics

Predicitve analytics blends statistical modelling with machine learning to forecast future health outcomes. In menopause care, this means combining personal baseline data, like age, BMI, and medical history, with real-time inputs from symptom trackers or activity monitors. This result in obtaining personalised risk scores that can help clinicians, and women themselves, plan ahead. For example, a predictive model might estimate the chance of experiencing significant cognitive fog in the next few months. That insight could prompt early lifestyle adjustments or treatment before symptoms become disruptive.

Beyond the individual level, predictive analytics can inform broader health strategies, helping workplaces or healthcare systems identify trends, allocate resources, and design targeted wellness programs that actually meet women's needs.

Table 3. Types of AI Technologies Used in Menopause Healthcare

AI Technology	Function in Menopause Care	Example Applications
Machine Learning (ML)	Predictive modelling for symptom severity, personalized therapy.	Risk prediction for osteoporosis, early menopause, hot flash frequency prediction.
Natural Language Processing (NLP)	Analyse patient-reported outcomes, chatbot interactions, extract insights from medical records.	Sentiment analysis in mood tracking apps; AI chatbots like Stellara or Elektra.
Clinical Decision Support Systems	Recommend interventions based on user profile, alert for red flags.	Suggest HRT or lifestyle interventions tailored to hormonal and genetic data

continued on following page

Table 3. Continued

AI Technology	Function in Menopause Care	Example Applications
Deep Learning	Image interpretation, symptom trend forecasting, wearable sensor fusion.	Breast density analysis; predictive modelling from multivariate inputs.
Explainable AI (XAI)	Increases transparency in decision-making .	Visual dashboard for patients showing cause-effect symptom patterns.
Reinforcement Learning	Adaptive treatment suggestion based on user feedback over time.	Adjusting HRT dosage or mental wellness activities based on user response.
Federated Learning	Data privacy-preserving learning across multiple sources.	Training menopause symptom predictors without centralizing sensitive health data
Voice-AI Interfaces	Symptom tracking through voice input; emotional tone analysis.	Voice-based mental health screening for menopause-related anxiety
Multi-modal AI	Integration of text, wearable, genomic, and imaging data.	Combined hot flash detector (sensor), risk scorer (genetic), and NLP symptom logs

4.2. Data Sources and Patient Profiling

AI's power lies in the breadth and depth of data it can analyse. Robust patient profiling for menopause care depends on integrating multiple streams:

4.2.1. Electronic Medical Records(EMRs)

EMRs contain both structured data like diagnoses, lab results, and prescriptions; and unstructured notes written by clinicians. Using NLP, AI can extract mentions of menopausal symptoms or treatments from these free-text fields, capturing details that standard data entries often miss. When data from different healthcare settings e.g., primary care, gynaecology, endocrinology is integrated, EMRs provide a long-term view of each woman's health journey, helping identify trends and turning points that guide more personalised care.

4.2.2. Genetic and Molecular Data

Genetic testing and molecular profiling are reshaping how we approach menopause care. Pharmacogenomic tests, for instance, can identify how a woman metabolises certain medications, like hormone therapies or antidepressants, based on gene variants such as *CYP2D6*. Beyond pharmacogenomics, multi-omics research (combining genomics, epigenomics, proteomics, etc.) is uncovering new biomarkers that explain why some women experience early or more severe symptoms, while others are more resilient. These discoveries not only improve risk prediction but may also pave the way for new treatment options.

4.2.3. Wearable Technology

Wearable devices-like smartwatches, fitness trackers, and skin sensors, offer a continuous stream of physiological data, including heart rate variability, skin temperature, sleep cycles, and activity patterns.

AI models trained on this data can detect early warning signs-for example, a rise in nighttime skin temperature that signals an impending hot flash. Wearables also monitor adherence to lifestyle recommendations (like increased activity after an exercise plan) and can trigger real-time nudges or deliver educational content based on a user's current state.

4.2.4. Symptom Diaries and Patient

Apps and digital platforms allow women to track symptoms daily-logging hot flashes, mood changes, sleep quality, stress, diet, and medication use. This self-reported data, when captured in a structured format, gives AI systems a clearer picture of how symptoms evolve and how individuals respond to treatment.

Just as importantly, these tools promote patient empowerment. They enable women to play an active role in their care, fostering stronger partnerships with healthcare providers and supporting shared decision-making.

4.3. AI-Powered Decision Support Systems

DSS-an intelligent digital platform lies at the heart of personalised menopause care that transforms raw, multi-source data into practical, personalised treatment recommendations. By integrating clinical, genetic, behavioural, and real-time data, these systems empower both clinicians and women to make smarter, faster, and more informed decisions.

4.3.1. Designing Intelligent Algorithm for Personalised Menopause Care

To deliver effective support, a DSS must be built with sensitivity to the complexity and individuality of menopause. The design process involves multiple stages, each combining technical precision with clinical insight.

4.3.1.1. Data Ingestion and Preprocessing

Before a DSS can analyse data, it must first bring together inputs from a wide variety of sources-EMRs, wearable devices, genetic profiles, and patient-reported outcomes. This stage includes: Harmonising terminology, filling in missing data through imputation techniques, Normalising data. Crucially, all data is linked securely and anonymously, ensuring that each woman's full health picture is preserved while protecting her privacy. This alignment forms the backbone of any meaningful analysis.

4.3.1.2. Feature Engineering and Model Selection

With clean data in place, the next step is defining the right variables, or features-for the models to learn from. This is a collaborative process where clinicians and data scientists work together to translate clinical knowledge into measurable indicators, such as: Changes in hormone levels over time, Variations in daily activity or sleep quality, Delays between mood dips and symptom spikes. Once features are defined, the most appropriate machine learning models are selected based on the clinical question; Classification models (e.g., logistic regression, decision trees)

To predict whether symptoms like hot flashes will intensify in the coming weeks, Regression models (e.g., support vector regression)

To forecast the severity of symptoms on a sliding scale, Time-to-event models (survival analysis)-To estimate when new symptoms might emerge or when current treatments may lose effectiveness.

4.3.1.3. Personalised Recommendation Engine

The DSS synthesizes model outputs into patient-friendly recommendations. For instance, if the system predicts a high risk of next-week insomnia, it might suggest a personalized sleep hygiene protocol—timing of meals, screen curfews, or cognitive strategies drawn from digital CBT modules. Similarly, hormone dosing adjustments can be proposed based on pharmacogenomic metabolism predictions.

Table 4. Existing AI-powered tools for Menopause Management

Tool Name	Developer / Platform	Core Features	AI Capabilities	Use Case
Midday	Lisa Health (partnered with Mayo Clinic)	Personalized daily care plan, symptom tracker, behavior nudges	Predictive symptom mapping, personalized nudges via AI	General menopause management via wearable integration (e.g., Fitbit)
Elektra Health	Elektra Health	Coaching, symptom education, community support	AI-enabled chatbot and adaptive health education	Remote coaching for managing perimenopause & menopause symptoms
Clue	BioWink GmbH	Menstrual & menopausal symptom tracking	AI-driven cycle prediction and symptom clustering	Transition prediction & cycle analytics
Peppy Health	UK-based digital health company	Employer-based menopause support, 1:1 chat, digital clinics	AI-based triage and data analytics for HR support	Menopause care in workplace settings
Carrot Fertility (includes menopause module)	Carrot Inc.	Benefits platform for fertility to menopause	AI-enhanced personalization of care plans	Employer wellness and midlife benefits
Wild.AI	Wild AI Ltd.	Tracks female hormonal patterns (incl. menopause) for fitness	AI adapts athletic & nutrition plans to perimenopause & menopause status	Performance-focused women's health
MenoLabs App	MenoLabs	Symptom tracker, community support, probiotic integration	ML-based symptom analysis & product feedback loops.	Supplement use optimization & health tracking
Balance	Balance-Menopause	Menopause symptom tracker, lifestyle diary	Personalized recommendations based on health profile.	Accessible HRT & health education
Gennev	Unified Women's Health	Telemedicine, supplements, symptom tracker	AI-powered health surveys and hormone risk assessment.	Clinical support for menopause
Stellara by Bonafide Health	Bonafide Health	AI chatbot assistant, supplement personalization.	Chatbot uses adaptive AI for symptom triage.	Natural remedy navigation.

4.3.1.4. Continuos Learning Loop

While the promise of AI in menopause management is significant, responsible development require rigorous attention to ethics and privacy .

Table 5. Ethical consideration in AI-Based Health Intervention in the Workplace

Ethical Domain	Key Considerations	Risks Without Safeguards	Best Practices / Mitigations
Data Privacy	Protecting sensitive health and biometric data	Unauthorized sharing, surveillance concerns	End-to-end encryption, federated learning, minimal data retention.
Informed Consent	Ensuring employees know how their data will be used	Coercion, lack of opt-out clarity	Transparent disclosures, opt-in consent, ongoing communication
Bias & Fairness	Avoiding algorithmic bias (e.g., underrepresenting certain age or ethnic groups)	Health inequities, incorrect risk predictions	Inclusive training datasets, continuous auditing
Autonomy & Non-Coercion	Respect for employee health choices	Overreach into personal health behavior	Voluntary participation, anonymized feedback mechanisms
Transparency & Explainability	Making AI recommendations interpretable	Lack of trust, misinformed actions	XAI models and patient-facing dashboards

4.4.1. Data Governance

To build trust-clear policies on data ownership, consent, and usage are essential. Women must be informed-in plain language-about how their data (EMRs, genetic information, wearable outputs, symptom logs) will be used, who will access it, and for what reasons.

Strong governance frameworks, co-designed with patients, clinicians, and ethicists, ensure data is managed transparently and ethically. When women feel in control of their data, they are more likely to engage with digital health tools-boosting both participation and the quality of care.

4.4.2. Bias in AI

AI is only as fair as the data it learns from. Unfortunately, much of menopause research has historically excluded women of color and those from lower-income backgrounds. This lack of representation can lead to biased algorithms that fail to serve diverse populations equitably.

To ensure fairness, AI models must undergo regular audits to detect disparities across age, ethnicity, income, and more. Bias mitigation techniques-such as rebalancing datasets, embedding fairness constraints, or developing tailored sub-models,are crucial to ensure every woman receives accurate and effective support.

4.4.3. GDPR and Regulatory Compliance

In regions like the EU, health data is classified as "special category" under GDPR and comes with strict requirements. AI systems must be built with privacy-by-design principles: Collect only what's necessary, Provide easy ways for women to give or withdraw consent, enable full transparency, data access, portability, and deletion. When data crosses borders, legally binding safeguards (e.g., standard contractual clauses) must be in place. Compliance isn't just a legal box to tick-it's a foundation for respectful and rights-based healthcare.

4.4.4. Explainability and Clinical Accountability

AI should help, not replace, human care. To earn trust, both patients and clinicians need to understand how AI arrives at its suggestions. Tools like feature importance rankings or LIME (Local Interpretable Model-Agnostic Explanations) can highlight which data points influenced a recommendation. But no matter how sophisticated the algorithm, final decisions should always rest with trained healthcare professionals. AI can offer guidance, but human insight ensures compassion, context, and accountability.

AI holds immense promise for transforming menopause care-from symptom prediction to personalized support. But with that power comes responsibility. Ethical data use, bias prevention, regulatory compliance, and model transparency aren't afterthoughts-they're the cornerstones of inclusive innovation. In the next section, we explore how these personalized, AI-driven insights can be embedded into workplace wellness strategies, helping organizations better support women throughout the menopausal transition—and beyond.

5. AI AND PERSONALISED MEDICINE IN WORKPLACE WELLNESS STRATEGIES

As menopause becomes a more visible and recognized issue in the modern workplace, organizations are increasingly pressed to respond with inclusive and effective health strategies. The convergence of AI and personalized medicine is revolutionizing workplace wellness by shifting from reactive, generic interventions to proactive, individualized support mechanisms. This section explores how AI-enabled health technologies can be seamlessly integrated into corporate wellness programs, provide real-time symptom monitoring, support menopause-specific employee benefits, and empower HR departments through predictive analytics and data-driven insights.

5.1. Integration into Corporate Wellness Program

Traditional corporate wellness models-offering gym memberships, annual check-ups, and generic stress-reduction seminars, often fail to address the evolving needs of midlife women experiencing menopause. These women require adaptable, personalised support that reflects the day-to-day variability of their health. AI-enabled tools now make it possible to reimagine wellness programs that meet women where they are.

5.1.1. Digital Coaching and AI-Powered Health Companions

AI-driven platforms like Caria and Stella are changing how women engage with wellness. These digital companions deliver personalised guidance-covering everything from hot flash relief techniques to mood regulation-based on real-time symptom tracking. By analysing patterns in user-reported data (like sleep disturbances or emotional changes), the platforms provide daily, tailored recommendations.

In addition, AI-powered chatbots offer 24/7 anonymous support. Trained in natural language processing, these bots go beyond traditional Employee Assistance Programs (EAPs), spotting signs of escalating symptoms and prompting escalation to human coaches or medical professionals when needed.

5.1.2. Telemedicine and Precision Prescriptions

Telehealth services enhanced by AI are now able to triage menopause-related concerns more accurately. Employees can access virtual consultations that are tailored to their history and symptoms, while clinicians receive AI-generated suggestions for hormone therapy types and dosages-based on genomic data and past treatment responses. This approach ensures care is both accessible and highly individualised.

5.1.3. Adaptive Fitness and Nutrition Programs

AI is also helping to tailor lifestyle interventions. Using data from wearables and dietary inputs, algorithms can recommend fitness routines and nutritional adjustments that align with each woman's metabolic profile and symptom pattern. For example, someone experiencing poor sleep and low energy may be guided towards magnesium-rich foods and restorative exercise. These personalised regimens can evolve dynamically, managed through AI dashboards and nudging systems that keep women engaged over time.

5.2. Real-Time Symptom Monitoring and Predictive Alerts

Perhaps one of the most transformative uses of AI in workplace wellness is real-time monitoring of menopausal symptoms-allowing for preventive, personalised action before issues escalate.

5.2.1. Wearables and Smart Sensors

Devices like smartwatches, skin patches, and sleep trackers collect physiological data such as temperature fluctuations, heart rate variability, and sleep disruptions. Integrated with AI, these tools detect patterns-such as rising nocturnal skin temperature that precedes hot flashes-and provide just-in-time prompts. Apps like Lisa Health forecast symptom onset hours in advance, allowing users to take pre-emptive steps such as layering adjustments, hydration, or quiet rest time.

When linked to workplace systems, these insights can discreetly trigger environmental adjustments (e.g., booking a cooling room) or temporary schedule changes-offering real comfort in a professional setting without stigma or disruption.

5.2.2. Dashborads for Occupational Health Teams

HR and occupational health teams can access anonymised dashboards that highlight symptom trends across departments or time periods. These aggregate views help organisations allocate resources effectively, launch targeted educational initiatives, and shape inclusive policy changes grounded in real data-while fully protecting individual privacy.

5.3. Menopause-Specific Policies and Hybrid Work Integration

Technology alone isn't enough. The insights generated by AI tools must translate into concrete workplace policies that improve the lived experiences of women during menopause.

5.3.1. Flexible Schedules and Hybrid Work

AI symptom tracking can identify when an employee experiences brain fog or fatigue,often early in the day or cyclically across the month. Employers can offer flexible schedules or hybrid work options, allowing women to align work demands with their peak energy and focus times. These small adjustments can yield major gains in productivity and wellbeing.

5.3.2. Cooling Rooms and Smarter Workspaces

Hot flashes and heat sensitivity are common symptoms, yet rarely addressed in workplace design. AI insights can inform the creation of cooling rooms or rest pods and even guide smart HVAC systems to respond to aggregated symptom data, ensuring a comfortable, responsive work environment for all.

5.3.3. Tailoring Health Insurance Coverage

Data from AI platforms can show which treatments—HRT, acupuncture, therapy, supplements-are proving most effective for a given workforce. Employers can use these insights to negotiate better coverage, establish menopause-specific health reimbursement accounts (HRAs), or provide flexible health stipends. Real-time usage and impact data help HR refine benefits without compromising privacy.

5.3.4. Education and Cultural Change

AI-powered learning systems can deliver personalised training modules to managers, equipping them with the empathy and knowledge to support menopausal staff. Some systems even offer simulated conversations using natural language interfaces, helping leaders practice inclusive communication around sensitive health topics.

5.4. The Role of AI in HR Analytics

HR departments are increasingly turning to AI-powered analytics to drive decisions about employee wellness strategies. In the context of menopause, this entails identifying risk, evaluating interventions, and forecasting workforce trends.

5.4.1. Identifying at Risk Employees

AI can help organizations proactively support their workforce by analysing patterns across wellness platforms, wearable data, and employee surveys. These systems generate anonymized risk indicators, not tied to specific individuals,but useful for identifying general trends. For example, a spike in fatigue, increased sick leave, or reduced platform engagement among women in midlife may indicate the need for targeted support. HR can respond by offering voluntary check-ins, informational webinars, or access to menopause-aware health coaches, ensuring help is available without stigma or intrusion.

5.4.2. Strategic Workforce Planning

As data accumulates over time, AI becomes a strategic planning tool. Predictive models might highlight a growing need for mental health services among perimenopausal employees, or forecast increased medical leave related to osteoporosis or sleep issues. These insights enable HR teams to anticipate shifts in employee wellbeing, refine retention strategies, and align support systems with gender equity goals. Rather than reacting to absenteeism or burnout, organizations can take pre-emptive steps to sustain performance and care for employees holistically.

5.4.3. Real-Time Alerts for HR Interventions

AI-powered dashboards can be configured to monitor wellness metrics across teams and departments. If thresholds are crossed-such as more than 10% of employees in a unit reporting elevated stress or sleep disruption-an automatic alert notifies HR or wellness leads. This enables timely, tailored interventions like deploying digital CBT resources, adjusting workloads, or initiating team-wide wellness check-ins. Early action helps prevent burnout, disengagement, and turnover-while reinforcing a culture of proactive support.

The integration of AI and personalized medicine into workplace wellness isn't just a technological advancement-it's a shift toward compassionate, evidence-based leadership. From tailored coaching and real-time support to predictive planning and inclusive policy design, AI empowers organizations to care for menopausal employees with both precision and empathy.

By embracing these tools, companies can transform menopause from a hidden struggle into a well-supported phase of professional life-one where women thrive, feel seen, and remain engaged contributors to the workforce. In the next chapter, we'll explore how global organizations are putting these principles into action through practical implementation frameworks and real-world case studies.

6. STRATEGIC HUMAN CAPITAL PLANNING AND AI-SUPPORT INCLUSION

As global workforces age and DEI frameworks evolve, menopause inclusion is gaining overdue attention in strategic human capital planning. Midlife women-many in senior leadership, mentorship, or high-productivity roles-face career disruptions due to unmanaged or unsupported menopausal transitions. The integration of AI into workforce planning and inclusion strategies offers powerful tools for recognizing patterns, forecasting needs, and tailoring support.

This section explores the business case for menopause inclusion, policy development, leadership engagement, and how AI supports predictive human resource management. It concludes with case studies of multinational organizations leading the way in menopause-inclusive strategies backed by data and intelligent systems.

6.1. Business Case for Menopause Inclusion

Organizations that fail to address menopause in the workplace risk significant costs—both human and economic. The symptoms of menopause, including fatigue, cognitive difficulties, and mood instability, can reduce engagement, increase absenteeism, and lead to premature exits from the workforce.

6.1.1. Economic Productivity and Talent Drain

Women over 45 represent one of the fastest-growing, and most experienced, segments of the global workforce. Yet more than a quarter of these women consider leaving their jobs due to unmanaged menopause symptoms, and around 10% ultimately do. This loss is not just personal; it affects organizational performance, disrupts team cohesion, drains institutional knowledge, and weakens leadership pipelines.

Investing in menopause-inclusive workplace strategies-supported by AI and personalized care, helps retain talent, lower recruitment and onboarding costs, and preserve valuable expertise. When women feel seen and supported during this life stage, their engagement, loyalty, and innovation flourish, benefiting the entire organization.

6.1.2. Hidden Turnover Costs

Many HR systems fail to capture the silent cost of losing high-potential employees due to health-related stigma. AI-powered analytics can uncover hidden turnover trends by identifying links between resignation timing, health benefit utilization, and declining job satisfaction. These insights help organizations quantify the business case for early intervention, making it easier to justify investment in targeted support programs.

6.2. Policy Design and Leadership Engagement

Addressing menopause at work requires more than health apps, it calls for structurally inclusive policies and informed leadership.

6.2.1. Building Menopause-Inclusive Policies

Effective workplace policies should normalize menopause as a legitimate health consideration and offer them flexible work options like remote work, shift swaps, part time and making the environment accommodable by installing cooling rooms, personal fans, HVAC flexibility ; providing protected leave for menopause-related health needs; access to specialized care like HRT consultations, menopause clinics ; Confidential, stigma-free support -providing mental health services, digital health apps, digital health apps).

AI can assist in designing these policies by analysing employee sentiment, modelling intervention impact, and benchmarking against industry norms. It also enables continuous policy refinement based on real-time feedback and evolving needs.

6.2.2. Leadership and Manage Education

A major barrier to menopause inclusion is lack of awareness-especially among senior leaders. AI-enhanced learning platforms can deliver microlearning tailored to specific scenarios: how to initiate sensitive conversations, adapt workloads, or recognize when an employee may need support.AI-driven manager dashboards can also prompt real-time nudges-for example, offering a learning module if multiple team members show signs of stress or reduced engagement. At a cultural level, visible leadership commitment is essential. Executive champions-especially women with lived menopause experience, can help normalize discussion and model empathy-driven leadership.

Table 6. Strategic Integration of Menopause-Inclusive practices across HR and Organisational planning Dimensions

Planning Dimension	Menopause-Inclusive Actions	Strategic Value / Impact	Implementation Examples
Workforce Strategy & Forecasting	Anticipate age-related retention challenges; plan for midlife workforce needs	Supports sustainable productivity and reduces attrition of skilled mid-career talent.	UK Civil Service Workforce Plan (2023); UN Women HR Toolkit.
Talent Retention & Engagement	Flexible policies, menopause coaching, recognition in wellbeing strategy.	Reduces burnout and mid-career dropout rates.	HSBC, Santander, and AstraZeneca menopause support programs.
DEI	Menopause included in DEI audits and gender-health equity initiatives	Aligns with ESG, SDG-5 (Gender Equality), and legal risk mitigation	CIPD Menopause Guidelines; UK Equality Act compliance

continued on following page

Table 6. Continued

Planning Dimension	Menopause-Inclusive Actions	Strategic Value / Impact	Implementation Examples
Leadership Development	Training for senior leaders on menopause empathy, inclusive leadership	Enhances psychological safety and belonging culture	Balance Workplace Program; NHS Leader Toolkit
Learning & Development	Mandatory manager training; e-learning modules on menopause awareness	Improves team support, reduces stigma, improves morale	Henpicked's Certified Menopause-Friendly Workplace Training
Occupational Health & Safety	Health risk assessments consider menopause (e.g., heat, fatigue, cognition)	Ensures compliance with workplace safety standards	British Standards Institution Menopause Guidance (PAS 1299:2023)
HR Policy Design	Inclusion of menopause leave, dress code flexibility, temperature control policies	Codifies inclusion and avoids policy blind spots	SHRM Sample Menopause Leave Policy; Bupa HR Playbook
Succession Planning	Inclusive of midlife female leaders, mentor networks for career continuity	Retains institutional knowledge; promotes gender-balanced leadership	McKinsey Women in the Workplace Report (2023)
Data & Analytics	Track menopause-related attrition, absenteeism, engagement levels	Enables targeted interventions and ROI measurement	Peppy + CIPD HR Metrics Toolkit
Technology Integration	Integration of digital tools like symptom trackers, wearable data, telehealth	Facilitates real-time support and wellness monitoring	Midday App, Gennev AI platform, Peppy Health dashboards

6.3. AI and Predictive Human Resource Management

HR is evolving from reactive problem-solving to proactive, data-informed planning. AI enables this shift by modelling employee life cycles, anticipating challenges, and optimizing interventions.

6.3.1. Forecasting Workplace Needs

AI tools that analyse anonymized data-such as age, role, medical claims, and turnover patterns-can help forecast when and where menopause-related needs may arise. For example, if patterns show increasing sick leave among mid-career women in leadership roles, HR can deploy targeted resources to retain these valuable team members.

6.3.2. Talent Retention Algorithms

Early warning systems powered by AI can detect disengagement signals-such as lower platform usage, frequent absences, or declining performance reviews. These insights trigger retention strategies, including personalized wellness recommendations, check-ins with coaches, or flexible work options-offered before employees reach a tipping point.

6.3.3. Programs Evaluation and Equity Auditing

To understand what's working and where gaps remain, AI dashboards can monitor the utilization rates of menopause support services, changes in absenteeism pre- and post-intervention, Employee sentiment and satisfaction over time, Equity in access and outcomes across roles, teams, or demographics. This granular, real-time feedback loop helps organizations fine-tune support systems, reduce disparities, and uphold accountability by building a culture of trust and inclusion.

6.4. Industry Case Studies

Several pioneering organizations are already implementing menopause-inclusive strategies supported by AI and analytics.

6.4.1. Vodafone Group

In 2021, Vodafone became a pioneer in workplace menopause inclusion by launching a global policy covering more than 100,000 employees across 25 countries. Their approach includes Manager training modules to build menopause awareness, Flexible working options tailored to individual needs, Access to digital health platforms for symptom management, AI-powered surveys to monitor engagement and program impact. Internal assessments revealed a notable improvement in morale and retention among midlife women. The initiative has since been recognized globally as a best-in-class example of embedding menopause into DEI strategy.

6.4.2. HSBC

HSBC UK introduced menopause-specific health support, complemented by an employee-led menopause network. AI-enhanced HR systems were used to track anonymized data on health claims, absenteeism, and internal role changes. These insights informed targeted interventions, such as Flexible scheduling for symptomatic employees, access to menopause-specialist consultations, AI-curated toolkits for managers to better support team members. By aligning data with practical resources, HSBC created a safer, more responsive environment for employees navigating menopause.

Table 7. Case Studies -Companies Adopting Ai-Enhancing Menopause Policies

Company	Initiative Summary	AI or Digital Health Component	Outcomes / Impact
Vodafone Group	Introduced global menopause policy across 27 countries; offers paid leave and flexible work	Digital symptom tracking and personalized wellness guidance via partner platforms like Peppy	85% employee satisfaction in pilot locations; increased retention among mid-career women
HSBC UK	Comprehensive menopause education campaign, manager training, and digital support access	Collaborated with Peppy Health to provide app-based AI-guided support	Reported 1/3 drop in menopause-related sick leave
National Health Service (NHS) England	Released menopause workforce framework; encourages trusts to integrate digital tools	Recommends use of AI-supported symptom checkers and wearable-integrated health apps	Improved staff wellbeing indicators; integrated into NHS People Plan
Santander UK	Workplace menopause policy with e-learning, peer networks, and AI symptom resources	Uses Balance App and wearable-based feedback to inform HR support	Enhanced employee wellbeing scores and engagement
Microsoft UK (in partnership)	Co-sponsored Balance+ workplace integration for AI symptom tracking	Supports employees through AI-based lifestyle diaries, risk modelling	Boosted awareness and participation in health programs
Aviva Insurance	Integrated menopause into overall digital wellbeing and diversity program	Uses digital apps to collect anonymized health insights and personalize content	Achieved 300% increase in internal menopause resource use
Peppy Health (B2B provider)	Offers AI-powered menopause support to clients including NHS, HSBC, Clifford Chance	Personalized interventions through an AI triage engine	

6.4.3. NHS (National Health Service), UK

As one of the UK's largest employers, the NHS has led the way in normalizing menopause at work. Their initiatives include menopause champions embedded across workplaces, AI-assisted shift scheduling tools offering great flexibility to them, Online education modules accessible via internal digital learning systems. These changes have led to greater openness around menopause-related concerns and a decline in resignations linked to unmanaged symptoms, demonstrating the impact of culturally embedded support structures.

6.4.4. Emerging Global Trends

Globally, the integration of AI into menopause support is gaining momentum. In Australia, pilot programs use AI to track performance dips and predict burnout risk among menopausal employees. In Asia, where cultural stigma may limit open conversation, multinational companies are deploying anonymous AI tools, such as confidential chatbots, to gather employee insights and deliver culturally appropriate interventions. These evolving practices highlight how AI can adapt to regional contexts while maintaining the core goal: meaningful, data-driven support for midlife women.

Supporting employees through menopause is no longer a "nice to have"-it's a business imperative. As workforces grow more multigenerational and gender-diverse, human capital strategies must reflect the lived realities of all employees.AI offers a unique advantage by embedding personalized support into everyday systems by predictive tools flag at risk employees early, data dashboards track program effectiveness, flexible, responsive policies evolve with employee needs. Organizations that invest in menopause-inclusive infrastructure are rewarded with higher retention, reduced absenteeism, and stronger DEI outcomes. The case is clear: with the right tools and mindset, workplaces can evolve from being simply menopause-aware to becoming truly menopause-empowering.

7. CHALLENGES AND LIMITATIONS OF INTEGRATING AI INTO WORKPLACE FOR MENOPAUSE CARE

While integrating AI and personalised medicine into workplace, menopause care offers transformative potential, it also introduces a complex set of challenges. These range from technological and organisational barriers to deeper ethical and societal concerns. Without thoughtful planning and inclusive design, the very tools intended to support midlife women could risk exclusion, mistrust, or misuse .

7.1. Technological Challenges

AI's effectiveness depends on its ability to access, interpret, and act on diverse data. Yet in both healthcare and HR settings, this is easier said than done.

7.1.1. Integration Issue and Data Silos

Personalised menopause care relies on integrating information from multiple sources, such as EMRs, wearable devices, wellness platforms, and symptom-tracking tools. However, these systems often don't "talk" to each other. Each may use different formats, security protocols, or regional data rules, especially across multinational workforces. This fragmentation limits AI's ability to generate accurate, timely insights. Many organisations lack the technical infrastructure for unified health data systems, and without careful planning, this can delay implementation or compromise the quality of support.

7.1.2. Algorithm Transparency and Trust

AI systems often operate as "black boxes," offering predictions or recommendations without clear explanations. This lack of transparency can undermine trust, especially when decisions affect sensitive issues like health or job performance. To build credibility, AI tools must adopt XAI approaches—models that can articulate how and why decisions are made. While progress is underway, XAI remains technically complex and resource-intensive, making it a hurdle for smaller or less digitally mature organisations.

7.2. Organisational Resistance

Even the most advanced tools can fail if organisations are not culturally or structurally ready for change.

7.2.1. Cultural Blind Spots and Stigma

In many workplaces, menopause is still viewed as a private issue,if it's acknowledged at all. Particularly in male-dominated industries, leadership may not recognise the impact of menopause on performance, morale, or retention. This can lead to indifference or subtle resistance to menopause-friendly policies and programs. Without champions at the top, even the best AI tools risk being underused or poorly understood. Change must begin with awareness, empathy, and commitment from senior leadership.

7.2.2. Gaps in Change Management

Introducing AI into employee health systems isn't just a tech upgrade, it's a cultural shift. It requires cross-department collaboration among HR, IT, legal, and clinical teams, along with transparent communication and clear policy frameworks. Many organisations lack experience managing such interdisciplinary change, leading to fragmented rollout or staff confusion. Effective change management must align goals, set expectations, and prioritise psychological safety, especially when dealing with a topic as personal as menopause.

7.3. Employee Privacy and Consent

AI systems that monitor health and productivity can offer support, but they can also feel intrusive if not implemented with care and clarity. Employees may worry that health data could be used against them. For example, Managers might use symptom data to justify performance concerns, HR systems might flag employees as "at-risk" without considering he context, Algorithms might push participation in wellness programs even when employees didn't consent to. Even when intentions are good, a lack of transparency can erode trust. If employees feel surveilled rather than supported, uptake will suffer-and so will workplace culture. Clear, informed consent is not optional, but it is foundational. Employees need to know what kind of personal data is collected from them, Who all have access to it, how is that information be used, whether they can opt out without having professional consequences. Poor data governance not only damages trust, it risks violating regulations such as GDPR, HIPAA, and emerging laws in other regions. Respecting autonomy and confidentiality is essential for ethical and sustainable implementation.

7.4. Health Inequities and AI Bias

AI systems are shaped by the data they're trained on, and that data often mirrors existing inequities in healthcare access, outcomes, and representation. Many health datasets are skewed toward white, Western populations, often excluding women of colour, Indigenous women, and those in lower-income settings. This can distort symptom profiles, treatment responses, and risk predictions, limiting the relevance of AI-driven interventions.

For instance, Black women are more likely to experience severe menopause symptoms, yet less likely to receive treatment, an imbalance that AI systems may replicate unless intentionally addressed. Bias in AI systems can arise through unequal training of data i.e., underreported symptoms from certain cultures and designing assumptions that reflect western healthcare norms and the historical disparities embedded in EMRs and insurance data. If uncorrected, these biases can lead to misdiagnosis, inappropriate interventions, or exclusion from benefits. Culturally sensitive design, inclusive data sourcing, and regular auditing are essential to mitigate harm and ensure fair outcomes for all employees.AI and personalised medicine have the potential to revolutionise how workplaces support women through menopause, but only if implemented with care, accountability, and inclusion at their core.

To get there, organisations must break down data silos and invest in transparent, interoperable systems, foster inclusive leadership that champions menopause equity, Prioritise employee autonomy, informed consent, and clear communication, Commit to continuous bias monitoring and diverse data collection. Most importantly, they must involve the very people these systems aim to support; midlife women- in the design and evaluation of tools, policies, and practices. By anchoring AI innovation in human values, organisations can create menopause support systems that are not only intelligent and scalable, but also deeply ethical, inclusive, and empowering.

8. FUTURE DIRECTIONS AND INNOVATIONS

The convergence of AI, personalised medicine, and workplace well-being is reshaping how we think about menopause support. What was once a private and often stigmatised health issue is now being recognised as a vital area for innovation, care, and inclusion, particularly for women navigating midlife in the workforce. As digital tools become smarter, more accessible, and more ethically designed, the opportunity to transform menopause care becomes increasingly tangible. But real progress depends on more than just technology. It requires deliberate, inclusive design and collaboration across industries, disciplines, and cultures. This give an opportunity to where the future is headed, from next generation AI tools to precision health strategies, cross-sector partnerships, and ethical frameworks that ensure menopause care is not only intelligent and scalable, but also equitable and human-centred.

8.1. Emerging AI Capabilities

New advances in AI are enabling more personalised, responsive, and discreet menopause support, particularly through technologies that feel more human and more respectful of privacy.AI-powered chatbots and voice assistants are rapidly improving in their ability to understand natural language, respond empathetically, and engage users in meaningful dialogue. For midlife women, these tools can offer a low-barrier, judgment-free way to report symptoms, receive guidance, or access support; especially when talking to a doctor or manager feels uncomfortable. For example, a woman might use a chatbot to log her sleep disruptions, mood changes, or hot flashes. The AI can then provide tailored advice, flag concerning patterns, or recommend scheduling a virtual consultation. Future developments will include emotion-sensitive responses, multilingual support, and context-aware conversations, making the experience more inclusive and affirming for diverse users.

One of the most promising breakthroughs lies in *federated learning* - a way to train AI models across many different data sources without sharing the actual data. This protects individual privacy while allowing systems to learn from a wider, more representative pool of experiences. In menopause care, federated learning can unlock insights from women across different countries, ethnicities, and age groups; without compromising confidentiality. It supports both better algorithm performance and stronger alignment with regulations like GDPR and HIPAA.

8.2. Precision Public Health for Midlife Women

Until now, AI in menopause care has largely been confined to personal wellness apps or workplace tools. The next step is integrating these innovations into broader public health systems, so support becomes a right, not a privilege.AI can help national health services move beyond one-size-fits-all care. Predictive models can identify women at higher risk for menopause-related complications, such as osteoporosis, heart disease, or depression and target them for early screening or tailored interventions. These insights can also guide public education campaigns, optimise healthcare resource planning, and reduce long-term costs associated with untreated symptoms, particularly important in aging populations where menopausal health impacts workforce participation and wellbeing at scale.

Governments can partner with employers to bridge workplace wellness with national health goals. For example, anonymised data from workplace menopause tools could inform broader research, shape clinical guidelines, or highlight unmet needs in specific communities. Such collaboration positions menopause as a public health priority, not just a private concern, and enables policymaking that reflects real-world experiences.

8.3. Interdisciplianry Collaborations

Menopause is more than a clinical condition; it's a life stage shaped by biology, identity, work, relationships, and culture. To build effective support systems, we need collaborative input from every corner of society.

AI systems need to be trained on data and insights shaped by medical specialists, like gynaecologists, endocrinologists, and mental health professionals, as well as workplace experts like HR leaders, occupational health consultants, and diversity practitioners. Joint training programs, research hubs, and academic- industry partnerships can foster this cross-pollination, ensuring that AI solutions are clinically sound *and* workplace-relevant.

Technology must serve the lived experience. That means AI tools should be designed in collaboration with the very women they aim to support. Inclusive design teams, featuring UX experts, sociologists, informaticians, and women from various backgrounds, can help build tools that are respectful, accessible, and empowering. Participatory design, where midlife women are co-creators rather than test subjects, will lead to solutions that are not only functional, but genuinely dignified.

8.4. Building Ethical, Inclusive, and Scalable Solutions

Innovation without ethics is a risk. For AI in menopause care to succeed globally, it must be guided by principles that centre dignity, equity, and agency.AI models should be transparent, explainable, and aligned with clear ethical standards, that includes informed consent and clear communication, protection of data privacy and ownership, ability to opt out without professional risk and ongoing audits and mitigate bias. Organisations using AI in this space should implement independent oversight - through ethics boards, data review committees, or third-party evaluators.

To reach women beyond high-resource, corporate settings, AI tools must be affordable and usable on low bandwidth networks, mobile first given the global dominance of smartphones, localised for different languages, literacy levels, and cultural contexts, interoperable with existing health and HR systems. Open-source development, public-private partnerships, and global health funding (e.g., WHO, Gates Foundation) can help ensure these tools don't remain the domain of the privileged few. Every woman's experience of menopause is shaped by her identity. AI solutions must reflect this, supporting the needs of LGBTQ+ women, who may require different care pathways, women with disabilities, who may need accessibility adaptations, informal or precarious workers, who may lack employer support or digital access. Equity must be built into every stage, from training data to delivery models. Without it, even well-meaning technologies may reinforce the very gaps they seek to close.

The future of menopause care is poised for transformation, from reactive and siloed, to proactive, intelligent, and inclusive. But the path forward is not just about what we build, it's about how and for whom we build it. AI and personalised medicine offer unprecedented tools. But to unlock their full potential, we must design with empathy, act with responsibility, and collaborate across sectors. This means treating midlife women not just as users of innovation, but as leaders and co-creators in the systems that shape their lives. With the right partnerships, policies, and priorities, we can ensure that menopause becomes a time not of retreat, but of renewal, and that no woman is held back from thriving at work, or in life, because of a transition we all have the power to support.

9. CONCLUSION AND STRATEGIC RECOMMENDATIONS

This chapter has examined the intersection of personalised medicine, artificial intelligence AI, and strategic workforce planning in addressing menopause within the workplace. As more women stay active in their careers through midlife and beyond, it is no longer acceptable to ignore menopause as a workplace health issue. It is time to recognise it as a pivotal life stage with significant implications for wellbeing, performance, and retention.

Menopause is multifaceted, affecting physical, emotional, and cognitive health. Traditional, standardised approaches often overlook the complex, individual experiences women face, impacting confidence, engagement, and career continuity. AI and personalised medicine offer powerful tools to tailor care. By analysing diverse data sources, from hormonal patterns to lifestyle behaviours, these technologies can anticipate needs and personalise support in real-time. Corporate wellness is evolving. AI-driven platforms are being integrated into digital health ecosystems, offering tools like symptom tracking, virtual coaching, and decision support- creating more responsive, stigma-free environments. HR and workforce strategy must keep pace. Aligning workplace policies with health innovations ensures that support is embedded into daily practice-not treated as an afterthought. Persistent challenges remain, including data ethics, integration gaps, organisational inertia, and inequities that disproportionately affect underrepresented and underserved populations. Despite these challenges, the convergence of AI, healthcare, and inclusive employment practice offers a rare, transformative opportunity: to reframe menopause from a hidden burden into a shared responsibility and strategic priority.

To harness the full potential of AI-enabled menopause care, and ensure it benefits *all* women in the workforce, employers and policymakers must take coordinated, intentional action. Below is a roadmap for sustainable, inclusive change, Develop Evidence-Based, Gender-Inclusive Workplace Policies; Integrate AI Tools into Corporate Wellness Platforms; Train Managers and HR Professionals; Collaborate with Healthcare Providers and Technology Innovators; Implement Ethical AI Governance Frameworks; Expand Access and Equity; Embed Menopause into National Health and Labour Strategies

Menopause is not a medical footnote, it is a major life transition that touches identity, productivity, confidence, and social participation. For too long, it has been treated with silence or shame. Today, we have the knowledge and the technology to do better. AI and personliased medicine offer new ways to listen, learn, and respond – to move from reactive treatment to proactive, compassionate care. But the success of these tools depends on how we use them, with empathy, equity, and accountability. Workplaces have a central role to play. By embracing menopause as a strategic priority, they can foster a culture where women feel supported-not sidelined, during midlife. Governments and health systems, too, must rise to the occasion, ensuring that innovation benefits all, not just a privileged few. Technology alone cannot transform menopause care. People, employers, designers, clinicians, policymakers, must lead with intention. This is not just a health imperative; it is a social contract that respects the experience of half the population.

As we look to the future, the goal is not simply to *manage* menopause, but to *empower* women through it. By aligning AI with the intelligence of the body, and the emotional intelligence of inclusive workplaces, we can create a world where no woman has to choose between her health and her career. Menopause is not the end of potential. It's a new chapter of strength, wisdom, and leadership. The systems we build now will determine whether that chapter begins with silence-or with support.

REFERENCES

Alzueta, E., de Zambotti, M., Javitz, H., Clark, A., & Baker, F. C. (2024). Navigating menopause at work: A preliminary study about challenges and support systems. *Menopause (New York, N.Y.)*, *31*(4), 258–265. DOI: 10.1097/GME.0000000000002333 PMID: 38442310

Bhattacharya, A., Ooge, J., Stiglic, G., & Verbert, K. (2023). Directive explanations for monitoring the risk of diabetes onset: Introducing directive data-centric explanations and combinations to support what-if explorations. In *Proceedings of the 28th International Conference on Intelligent User Interfaces* (pp. 204–219). Association for Computing Machinery. https://doi.org/DOI: 10.1145/3581641.3584075

Burger, H. G., Dudley, E. C., Robertson, D. M., & Dennerstein, L. (2002). Hormonal changes in the menopause transition. *Recent Progress in Hormone Research*, *57*(1), 257–275. DOI: 10.1210/rp.57.1.257 PMID: 12017547

Chan, S., Gomes, A., & Singh, R. S. (2020). Is menopause still evolving? Evidence from a longitudinal study of multiethnic populations and its relevance to women's health. *BMC Women's Health*, *20*(1), 74. Advance online publication. DOI: 10.1186/s12905-020-00932-8 PMID: 32307019

Chen, C., Li, O., Barnett, A., Han, L., Vervoort, D., & Dobson, A. (2025). Deep learning prediction of mammographic breast density using screening data. *Scientific Reports*, *15*(1), 11602. Advance online publication. DOI: 10.1038/s41598-025-95275-5 PMID: 40185813

Chen, S., Zhang, Y., & Liu, Y. (2025). Predicting preeclampsia in early pregnancy using clinical and laboratory data via machine learning model. *BMC Medical Informatics and Decision Making*, *25*(1), 178. Advance online publication. DOI: 10.1186/s12911-025-02999-5 PMID: 40312361

Choudhury, O., Gkoulalas-Divanis, A., Salonidis, T., Sylla, I., Park, Y., Hsu, W., & Das, A. (2020). Differential privacy-enabled federated learning for sensitive health data [Preprint]. arXiv. https://arxiv.org/abs/1910.02578

David, P. S., Smith, T. L., Nordhues, H. C., & Kling, J. M. (2022). A clinical review on paroxetine and emerging therapies for the treatment of vasomotor symptoms. *International Journal of Women's Health*, *14*, 353–361. DOI: 10.2147/IJWH.S282396 PMID: 35300283

Esteva, A., Robicquet, A., Ramsundar, B., Kuleshov, V., DePristo, M., Chou, K., Cui, C., Corrado, G., Thrun, S., & Dean, J. (2019). A guide to deep learning in healthcare. *Nature Medicine*, *25*(1), 24–29. DOI: 10.1038/s41591-018-0316-z PMID: 30617335

Gava, G., Orsili, I., Alvisi, S., Mancini, I., Seracchioli, R., & Meriggiola, M. C. (2019). Cognition, mood and sleep in menopausal transition: The role of menopause hormone therapy. *Medicina, 55*(10), 668. Advance online publication. DOI: 10.3390/medicina55100668 PMID: 31581598

Kohn, G. E., Rodriguez, K. M., Hotaling, J., & Pastuszak, A. W. (2019). The history of estrogen therapy. *Sexual Medicine Reviews, 7*(3), 416–421. DOI: 10.1016/j.sxmr.2019.03.006 PMID: 31147294

Li, K., Urteaga, I., Shea, A., Vitzthum, V. J., Wiggins, C. H., & Elhadad, N. (2021). A generative, predictive model for menstrual cycle lengths that accounts for potential self-tracking artifacts in mobile health data [Preprint]. arXiv. https://arxiv.org/abs/2102.12439

Liefgreen, A., Weinstein, N., Wachter, S., & Mittelstadt, B. (2024). Beyond ideals: Why the (medical) AI industry needs to motivate behavioural change in line with fairness and transparency values, and how it can do it. *AI & Society, 39*(5), 2183–2199. DOI: 10.1007/s00146-023-01684-3 PMID: 39309255

Loftus, T. J., Shickel, B., Ruppert, M. M., Balch, J. A., Tighe, P. J., Bihorac, A., & Rashidi, P. (2022). Federated learning for preserving data privacy in collaborative healthcare research. *Digital Health, 8*. Advance online publication. DOI: 10.1177/20552076221134455 PMID: 36325438

Maki, P. M., & Jaff, N. G. (2022). Brain fog in menopause: A health-care professional's guide for decision-making and counseling on cognition. *Climacteric, 25*(6), 570–578. DOI: 10.1080/13697137.2022.2122792 PMID: 36178170

Mancone, S., Diotaiuti, P., Valente, G., Macchia, S., & Corrado, S. (2023). The use of voice assistant for psychological assessment elicits empathy and engagement while maintaining good psychometric properties. *Behavioral Sciences (Basel, Switzerland), 13*(7), 550. Advance online publication. DOI: 10.3390/bs13070550 PMID: 37503997

O'Neill, M. T., Jones, V., & Reid, A. (2023). Impact of menopausal symptoms on work and careers: A cross-sectional study. *Occupational Medicine, 73*(6), 332–338. DOI: 10.1093/occmed/kqad078 PMID: 37542726

Reddy, S., Fox, J., & Purohit, M. P. (2019). Artificial intelligence-enabled healthcare delivery. *Journal of the Royal Society of Medicine, 112*(1), 22–28. DOI: 10.1177/0141076818815510 PMID: 30507284

Savitha, P. M.P. Margaret Savitha. (2024). Reinforcement learning in personalized medicine: Tailoring treatment protocols to individual patients. *Journal of Electrical Systems*, *20*(3), 7109–7118. DOI: 10.52783/jes.7277

Schei, T. S., & Abernathy, K. (2023). An evaluation of demographic characteristics and workplace experiences of UK employees using an employer-provided menopause application. *Maturitas*, *177*, 107803. Advance online publication. DOI: 10.1016/j.maturitas.2023.107803 PMID: 37531870

Schei, T. S., & Abernathy, K. (2024). The impact of a specialist-led digital health application on menopause symptoms in the workplace: A single-arm, longitudinal evaluation. *Maturitas*, *187*, 108005. Advance online publication. DOI: 10.1016/j.maturitas.2024.108005 PMID: 38851044

Shickel, B., Tighe, P. J., Bihorac, A., & Rashidi, P. (2018). Deep EHR: A survey of recent advances in deep learning techniques for electronic health record (EHR) analysis. *IEEE Journal of Biomedical and Health Informatics*, *22*(5), 1589–1604. DOI: 10.1109/JBHI.2017.2767063 PMID: 29989977

Steffan, B. (2021). Managing menopause at work: The contradictory nature of identity talk. *Gender, Work and Organization*, *28*(1), 195–214. DOI: 10.1111/gwao.12539

Taherdoost, H., & Ghofrani, A. (2024). AI's role in revolutionizing personalized medicine by reshaping pharmacogenomics and drug therapy. *Intelligent Pharmacy*, *2*(5), 643–650. DOI: 10.1016/j.ipha.2024.08.005

Vincent, C., Bodnaruc, A. M., Prud'homme, D., Olson, V., & Giroux, I. (2023). Associations between menopause and body image: A systematic review. *Women's Health (London, England)*, *19*, 17455057231209536. Advance online publication. DOI: 10.1177/17455057231209536 PMID: 37994043

Whiteley, J., DiBonaventura, M. da C., Wagner, J.-S., Alvir, J., & Shah, S. (2013). The impact of menopausal symptoms on quality of life, productivity, and economic outcomes. *Journal of Women's Health*, *22*(11), 983–990. DOI: 10.1089/jwh.2012.3719 PMID: 24083674

Williamson, S. M., & Prybutok, V. (2024). Balancing privacy and progress: A review of privacy challenges, systemic oversight, and patient perceptions in AI-driven healthcare. *Applied Sciences (Basel, Switzerland)*, *14*(2), 675. Advance online publication. DOI: 10.3390/app14020675

Woods, N. F., & Mitchell, E. S. (2005). Symptoms during the perimenopause: Prevalence, severity, trajectory, and significance in women's lives. *The American Journal of Medicine*, *118*(12, Suppl. 12B), 14–24. DOI: 10.1016/j.amjmed.2005.09.031 PMID: 16414323

Wright, V. J., Schwartzman, J. D., Itinoche, R., & Wittstein, J. (2024). The musculoskeletal syndrome of menopause. *Climacteric*, *27*(5), 466–472. DOI: 10.1080/13697137.2024.2380363 PMID: 39077777

Zouboulis, C. C., Blume-Peytavi, U., Kosmadaki, M., & Röcken, M. (2022). Skin, hair and beyond: The impact of menopause. *Climacteric*, *25*(5), 434–442. DOI: 10.1080/13697137.2022.2050206 PMID: 35377827

Chapter 12
Towards a Menopause-Friendly Workplace:
Integrating Personalized Medicine and AI-Driven Care in the Coaching Industry in India

Rohit Kumar Pal
https://orcid.org/0000-0002-7525-0771
R.I.C.E. Group, ADAMAS University, Kolkata, India

ABSTRACT

As women increasingly assume leadership and teaching roles in India's coaching industry, it becomes essential to prioritize their health and wellbeing, especially during menopause—a natural yet often stigmatized life stage. The coaching sector, marked by high stress, rigid schedules, and limited health infrastructure, offers minimal support for midlife women. This chapter explores how emerging technologies, particularly artificial intelligence (AI) and personalized medicine, can be harnessed to create menopause-friendly workplaces. AI tools such as predictive health analytics, symptom tracking, and intelligent HR systems are transforming employee care, enhancing productivity, and fostering empathetic work cultures. Personalized medicine enables tailored interventions based on genetic, hormonal, and lifestyle factors. These innovations can foster inclusive, responsive, and sustainable environments that support and retain midlife women. The chapter concludes with a roadmap for implementation, offering policy and ethical guidelines for effective integration of these tools.

DOI: 10.4018/979-8-3373-2970-3.ch012

1. INTRODUCTION

The demographic and professional landscape of India is undergoing a profound transformation, marked by the increasing participation of women across all sectors of the economy, including the highly demanding and influential coaching industry. This industry, a cornerstone of the Indian educational ecosystem, prepares millions of students for highly competitive entrance examinations like IIT-JEE, NEET, UPSC, Banking, Railway etc., relying heavily on the expertise, dedication, and leadership of a significant number of women educators and administrators. These women, often at the peak of their professional careers, frequently navigate the complex and challenging biological transition of perimenopause and menopause while managing high-stress roles. Menopause, a universal biological milestone marking the end of a woman's reproductive years, is far more than a medical event; it is a multifaceted experience intertwined with physiological, psychological, and sociocultural dimensions (Monteleone et al., 2018). Despite its inevitability and the fact that it affects nearly half the workforce at some point in their careers, menopause remains one of the last great taboos in the workplace, shrouded in silence, misunderstanding, and a pervasive lack of institutional support (Jack et al., 2016).

The Indian coaching industry, characterised by its intense pressure, long and inflexible working hours, and a performance-driven culture that often prioritizes student outcomes over educator wellbeing, presents a particularly challenging environment for women experiencing menopausal symptoms. Like many other sectors, this issue is neglected by National bodies (Syamala, T. S., & Sivakami, M., 2005). Symptoms such as hot flushes, night sweats, sleep disturbances, cognitive changes like 'brain fog', and increased anxiety can be severely exacerbated by such a high-stress environment, leading to decreased job satisfaction, reduced productivity, and in some cases, the premature departure of highly skilled and experienced women from the workforce (Brewis et al., 2017). This represents not only a personal loss for the individuals involved but also a significant economic and intellectual drain on the coaching institutions and the broader knowledge economy of India. The absence of formal policies, supportive infrastructure, and a culture of open dialogue around women's health issues creates a "leaky pipeline" of female talent, undermining the industry's potential for diversity and innovation (Brewis et al., 2019).

However, the dawn of the Fourth Industrial Revolution, characterized by the convergence of digital, biological, and physical technologies, offers unprecedented opportunities to address this systemic gap. The synergistic integration of two powerful technological paradigms—Artificial Intelligence (AI) and Personalized Medicine—holds the potential to revolutionize how workplaces support employee health and wellbeing (Topol, 2019). AI, with its capabilities in predictive analytics, natural language processing, and pattern recognition, can be harnessed to create intelligent, empathetic, and proactive support systems for menopausal women. Concurrently, the principles of personalized medicine, which advocate for interventions tailored to an individual's unique genetic makeup, hormonal profile, and lifestyle factors, can move the support beyond a one-size-fits-all approach to one that is truly bespoke and effective (Collins & Varmus, 2015). This review article, therefore, posits that the strategic and ethical integration of AI-driven tools and personalized medicine frameworks can serve as a foundational strategy for building truly menopause-friendly workplaces within the Indian coaching industry. By doing so, we can transform a current challenge into an opportunity for fostering gender equity, enhancing organizational resilience, and retaining invaluable female talent, thereby aligning economic imperatives with social progress and creating a more inclusive and humane future of work.

2. OBJECTIVES OF THIS STUDY

This comprehensive review is guided by a set of clearly defined objectives aimed at systematically exploring the intersection of menopause, the Indian coaching industry, and emerging technologies. The primary goal is to construct a compelling, evidence-based argument for the urgent need to address menopausal transition in this specific professional context and to propose a novel, technology-driven framework for intervention. The specific objectives are as follows: First, to conduct a thorough and critical review of the existing global and Indian literature on menopause in the workplace, identifying the predominant challenges, documented impacts on productivity, and the current state of organizational policies and support mechanisms, with a particular focus on the educational and knowledge sectors (Jack et al., 2016; Brewis et al., 2017). This will establish a foundational understanding of the problem's scope and universality, while also highlighting the unique socio-cultural and structural factors at play within the Indian context.

Second, this study aims to meticulously delineate the specific infrastructural, cultural, and policy-related barriers inherent to the Indian coaching industry that exacerbate the challenges faced by menopausal women. This involves analyzing the industry's high-stress environment, rigid work schedules, lack of physical comfort amenities, and the pervasive culture of silence surrounding women's health issues. As per a reference, the current market revenue of the coaching industry in India is Rs 58,088 crore. Its growth is projected to reach Rs 1,33,995 crore rupees by 2028 (Yadav, J, 2022). By pinpointing these specific barriers, the review can move beyond generic recommendations to propose targeted solutions that are contextually relevant and practically implementable. Third, the objective is to delve deeply into the conceptual and practical applications of Artificial Intelligence in the realm of women's health, with a specific focus on menopause management. This includes a detailed exploration of AI-powered tools for predictive health analytics, digital symptom tracking platforms, and the development of intelligent Human Resource management systems that can facilitate flexible working arrangements and personalized wellbeing support (Esteva et al., 2019; Davenport & Kalakota, 2019).

Fourth, this article seeks to elucidate the principles of personalized medicine and demonstrate their profound relevance to managing menopausal health. This involves discussing how data from genomics, metabolomics, and continuous health monitoring can be leveraged to create highly individualized intervention plans for nutrition, exercise, hormone therapy, and stress management, moving away from standardized protocols (Collins & Varmus, 2015). The fifth and central objective is to synthesize the insights from AI and personalized medicine to propose an integrated, scalable, and ethical model for creating menopause-friendly workplaces within the Indian coaching industry. This model will outline how technology can be embedded into organizational culture, policy, and physical infrastructure to provide seamless and dignified support. Finally, the study aims to provide a forward-looking roadmap that includes tangible recommendations for policymakers, institutional leaders, and technology developers, while also identifying critical gaps in the current research landscape to guide future scholarly inquiry in this nascent but critically important field.

3. REVIEW OF LITERATURE

The existing body of literature on menopause in the workplace, while growing, reveals a significant disparity between the scale of the issue and the depth of organizational and scholarly attention it has received, particularly in non-Western contexts. Globally, research has consistently demonstrated that menopausal symptoms can have a substantial negative impact on women's work experience and productivity. A seminal systematic review by Jack et al. 2016 synthesized evidence from numerous studies, concluding that a significant proportion of menopausal women report that their symptoms adversely affect their work, leading to increased absenteeism, presenteeism (being physically present but functioning at a reduced capacity), and, in severe cases, intentions to leave employment altogether. Symptoms such as concentration difficulties, memory lapses (often referred to as 'brain fog'), and intense fatigue are particularly detrimental in knowledge-intensive professions, such as teaching and educational leadership, where cognitive sharpness is paramount (Brewis et al., 2017).

The literature further highlights that the work environment itself is a critical moderator of the menopausal experience. Studies have shown that factors such as a lack of temperature control, inability to open windows, limited access to cool drinking water and restrooms, and high job demands significantly correlate with worse symptom reporting and greater work impairment (Verdonk, P., Bendien, E., & Appelman, Y. 2022). Moreover, a pervasive culture of stigma and a lack of managerial and peer support compound these physical challenges. Many women report feeling embarrassed to discuss their symptoms with managers, particularly if they are male, for fear of being perceived as less capable or of inviting discrimination (Brewis et al. 2019). This "culture of silence" is a universal theme, though its intensity varies across different cultural and organizational settings. The research underscores that supportive organizational policies, such as flexible working hours, access to quiet and cool rest spaces, and manager training on health-related issues, can markedly improve women's ability to manage their symptoms and remain engaged and productive at work (Jack et al., 2016).

As India's workforce ages, menopausal transitions are becoming an important occupational-health and gender-equity issue. Indian studies document a high prevalence of menopausal symptoms among working women and show that symptoms meaningfully affect quality of life and work functioning (Ramyashree, 2024; Nagaraj et al., 2021). These studies report vasomotor, sleep, mood and somatic complaints that reduce concentration, increase fatigue and, in some cases, lead to absenteeism or reduced productivity.

A small but growing body of India-based needs-assessment work highlights gaps in awareness and access to supports. Qualitative and survey studies indicate many women lack basic information about menopause, have limited access to clinical care or counselling, and often feel culturally constrained from discussing symptoms openly at work — especially with male managers or in male-dominated workplaces (Mankar et al., 2024). This combination of low awareness and stigma reduces the likelihood that women will request reasonable adjustments (e.g., flexible hours, temperature control, private rest space), even when those adjustments would likely help.

Policy and advocacy actors—international bodies and Indian commentators—have begun calling for employer action. UNFPA and public-health observers frame menopause as both a public-health and labour-policy issue, urging that midlife women's health be integrated into occupational health standards and gender-equity programmes (UNFPA summary, 2025). Indian industry commentaries and trade outlets similarly recommend low-cost workplace changes (manager training, awareness campaigns, flexible work and confidential occupational health referrals) while emphasising the need to tailor approaches to India's diverse formal and informal labour markets.

However, rigorous evaluations of interventions in Indian settings remain scarce. Much of the evidence assessing intervention effectiveness comes from high-income settings; Indian literature is primarily descriptive or small scale. Priority research needs therefore include longitudinal studies that measure objective work outcomes, randomized or quasi-experimental evaluations of training/adjustment packages, and studies in informal and precarious sectors where women have fewer entitlements.

In sum, India's evidence base confirms that menopause affects many working women and that workplace supports could mitigate harms. Real change will require combining awareness and manager training, reasonable accommodations, confidential healthcare access, and policy recognition — plus stronger, locally relevant evaluation to guide widespread implementation.

Concurrently, the literature on digital health and AI in medicine is exploding, but its application to menopause management is still in its infancy. Some studies have demonstrated the efficacy of mobile health apps for tracking menopausal symptoms and delivering Cognitive Behavioural Therapy (CBT) for low mood and sleep problems. In a broader health context, AI has shown remarkable success in predictive analytics for chronic disease management and in personalizing treatment plans, principles that are directly transferable to menopausal care (Esteva et al., 2019; Topol, 2019). The field of personalized medicine, championed by initiatives like the All of Us Research Program in the United States, is building the evidence base for moving away from population-wide averages to individually tailored healthcare (Collins & Varmus, 2015). However, the synthesis of these technological frontiers—AI and personalized medicine—into a cohesive framework for workplace inclusion, specifically for menopause in the Indian coaching industry, is a novel proposition that this review seeks to advance, thereby contributing a new and necessary direction to the existing literature.

4. UNDERSTANDING MENOPAUSE

Menopause is a biological inevitability, a natural and universal transition in the female life cycle, yet its physiological, psychological, and social complexities are often oversimplified. Medically, menopause is defined retrospectively as the permanent cessation of menstruation, diagnosed after 12 consecutive months without a menstrual period, marking the end of a woman's natural reproductive ability (Monteleone et al., 2018). The average age of menopause in India is approximately 46 years (Ahuja, M., 2016), notably younger than the Western average of 51 years, which means Indian women in the coaching industry may experience this transition even earlier in their professional careers. It is crucial to understand that menopause is not a single event but a process, often spanning several years, known as the menopausal transition or perimenopause. This period is characterized by significant hormonal fluctuations, primarily a decline in estrogen and progesterone production by the ovaries, which serves as the primary driver for the wide array of symptoms associated with this phase (Santoro & Randolph, 2011).

The symptomatology of menopause is vast and highly individualized, affecting nearly every system in the body. The most commonly recognized symptoms are vasomotor, including hot flushes and night sweats, which can be intensely disruptive, especially in a professional setting where composure is expected (Monteleone et al., 2018). However, the impact extends far beyond these. Psychological symptoms are prevalent and particularly relevant to the workplace; these include mood swings, irritability, anxiety, and depression, which can be exacerbated by hormonal shifts and sleep deprivation. Cognitive symptoms, often termed 'brain fog', manifest as difficulties with concentration, memory lapses, and a decline in processing speed, posing a direct challenge to the cognitive demands of teaching, curriculum development, and institutional leadership (Weber et al., 2014). Other physical manifestations include urogenital symptoms (e.g., vaginal dryness, urinary incontinence), musculoskeletal pain, and persistent fatigue, all of which can contribute to physical discomfort and a decreased sense of well-being.

According to different studies, the experience of menopause is not dictated by biology alone; it is profoundly shaped by sociocultural factors. In the Indian context, cultural narratives surrounding menopause often associate it with ageing, loss of fertility, and a diminished social role, which can negatively impact a woman's self-esteem and mental health. The lack of open conversation and widespread health literacy means many women suffer in silence, unaware that their symptoms are normal and manageable. This bio-psycho-social model of menopause is essential for a comprehensive understanding (Hunter & Rendall, 2007). It posits that the biological changes interact with a woman's psychological state (e.g., her coping mechanisms, pre-existing mental health) and her social environment (e.g., workplace support, family dynamics, cultural attitudes) to produce her unique menopausal experience. Therefore, an effective support system within the coaching industry cannot merely address the physiological symptoms but must also contend with the psychological toll and dismantle the social stigma, creating an environment where women feel empowered to seek help and manage their health proactively and without shame.

5. CHALLENGES FACED BY WOMEN DURING MENOPAUSE IN THE WORKPLACE

The intersection of menopausal symptoms and the modern workplace creates a nexus of challenges that can significantly impair a woman's professional life and personal well-being. These challenges are multifaceted, encompassing physical discomfort, psychological distress, cognitive impediments, and socio-cultural barriers, all of which are amplified within high-demand professional environments like coaching centres. Physically, the unpredictable nature of vasomotor symptoms such as hot flushes and profuse sweating can cause immense embarrassment and anxiety during lectures, important meetings, or one-on-one student interactions (Brewis et al., 2017). The inability to control the classroom temperature or to take a brief moment to cool down can turn a routine workday into a source of constant dread. Furthermore, chronic sleep disruption due to night sweats leads to profound fatigue, reducing energy levels and resilience, which are critical assets for educators managing long hours and high-stakes responsibilities.

Cognitively, the phenomenon of 'brain fog' presents a direct threat to professional competence and confidence. For a teacher explaining complex mathematical concepts or a manager analyzing institutional performance data, lapses in memory, difficulty concentrating, and a perceived slowing of mental processing can be deeply unsettling (Weber et al., 2014). This can lead to a vicious cycle where the woman begins to doubt her own abilities, increasing her stress and anxiety, which in turn can exacerbate the very cognitive symptoms she fears. The psychological impact is equally significant. The hormonal fluctuations of menopause can directly influence neurotransmitter activity, predisposing women to mood swings, irritability, and heightened anxiety (Soares, C. N., Joffe, H., & Steiner, M., 2004). In a high-stress job, these symptoms can strain relationships with colleagues and students, hinder effective communication, and reduce overall job satisfaction. The constant effort to mask these internal struggles—a process known as “surface acting”—requires significant emotional labor, leading to burnout and emotional exhaustion (Grandey, 2000).

Perhaps the most pervasive challenge is the socio-cultural one: the stigma and silence that shroud menopause in the professional sphere. Many workplaces, including coaching institutes, lack a vocabulary and a cultural framework for discussing women's health issues openly (Jack et al., 2016). Women often fear that disclosing menopausal symptoms will lead to negative perceptions, a loss of credibility, or even discrimination in promotions and assignments. According to different studies, this is particularly true in male-dominated leadership structures or in cultures where ageism and sexism intersect. The lack of formal policies means that any accommodation is often dependent on the discretion and awareness of individual managers, creating an environment of uncertainty and inequity. Consequently, many women choose to suffer in silence, disengaging from seeking support, which can lead to them opting out of leadership roles or leaving the workforce prematurely. This represents a critical failure of organizational support systems and a massive loss of talent, experience, and institutional knowledge, underscoring the urgent economic and ethical imperative for creating menopause-friendly workplaces.

6. COACHING INSTITUTES IN INDIA AND THEIR INFRASTRUCTURAL BARRIERS TO SUPPORT WOMEN

The Indian coaching industry, a multi-billion dollar behemoth, operates as a parallel education system, fiercely competitive and intensely demanding, not just for students but equally for the faculty and staff who drive it. Institutes in hubs like Kota, Delhi, and Hyderabad are renowned for their rigorous schedules, where a typical day for an educator can extend to 12-14 hours, involving continuous lecturing, doubt-solving sessions, and development of study material. This environment, while engineered for maximum student output, creates a perfect storm of infrastructural and cultural barriers that are particularly hostile to women navigating menopause. The physical infrastructure of many coaching centers is often designed for utility and cost-effectiveness rather than employee well-being. Classrooms and offices are frequently overcrowded, with poor ventilation and centralised air-conditioning systems that cannot be adjusted by individuals, making it impossible for a woman experiencing a hot flush to find immediate relief. Access to cool drinking water and clean, accessible restrooms may be limited, and the concept of a quiet, cool "quiet room" or wellness space for staff to recuperate is virtually non-existent.

The temporal structure of work in coaching institutes is another significant barrier. The industry is characterized by extreme rigidity in scheduling, with fixed lecture timings, back-to-back classes, and limited breaks. This leaves little room for the flexibility that menopausal women often need to manage their symptoms effectively. The ability to take a short, unscheduled break during a hot flush, to adjust start times to cope with sleep deprivation, or to work from home on particularly difficult days is rarely an option in a system predicated on physical presence and real-time student engagement. This lack of flexibility demonstrates a fundamental mismatch between the needs of a midlife female workforce and the traditional, inflexible organizational models that dominate the industry. The high-stakes, performance-oriented culture adds a layer of psychological pressure. The relentless focus on student results, rankings, and institutional reputation creates an environment where any perceived weakness or need for accommodation is tacitly discouraged. Educators are expected to be perpetually energetic, cognitively sharp, and emotionally resilient.

Within this pressurized context, a woman experiencing cognitive fluctuations or fatigue may internalize her struggles as personal failure rather than a natural biological process, further exacerbating her distress. Culturally, the coaching industry in India, like many sectors, operates within a broader societal framework where women's health, particularly menopause, is not considered a legitimate topic for workplace discourse. Human Resource departments in these institutes are typically focused on recruitment, payroll, and administrative functions, with little to no expertise or mandate in employee wellness, diversity, and inclusion, especially concerning gendered health issues. There are no formal policies addressing menopause, no training for managers on how to support employees, and no channels for women to voice their needs without fear of stigma or reprisal. This combination of physically inadequate infrastructure, temporally rigid schedules, a high-pressure culture, and a profound lack of policy and awareness creates an environment that is not merely unsupportive but actively detrimental to the health, retention, and professional fulfilment of a vital segment of its workforce.

In contrast to the above statements, I created a survey among 25 women educators of various Coaching Institutes in India from my connection who are running through this phase. Their name is not disclosed as per privacy agreement. The feedback is shared in the annexure. However, the result that I got from the feedback is discussed below.

The feedback gathered from participants highlights the multifaceted impact of menopausal symptoms on women in academic workplaces. The reported physical challenges—such as severe hot flashes, sleep disturbances, fatigue, and joint pain—were frequently accompanied by psychological symptoms including brain fog, anxiety, mood swings, and loss of motivation. These combined effects not only reduced individual wellbeing but also translated into noticeable disruptions in work performance, as reflected in impact scores ranging from 3 to 5.

A recurrent theme emerging from the data is the absence of sufficient workplace support. Most participants indicated that they either received no support or only partial support from their institutions. This lack of formal acknowledgment reinforces the stigma surrounding menopause in professional settings and may further discourage open communication with managers or colleagues. For example, while symptoms like hot flashes and fatigue are severe and disruptive, the absence of accommodations such as flexible working hours or access to quiet spaces exacerbates the challenges faced by these women.

The suggested improvements provided by participants demonstrate practical, low-cost strategies that institutions could adopt to foster menopause-friendly environments. Recommendations such as better classroom ventilation, flexible start times, more ergonomic staff facilities, and the availability of quiet rooms reflect not only the physical but also the psychological needs of employees. These proposals align with global best practices that emphasize simple workplace adjustments and cultural awareness as key enablers of productivity and wellbeing during the menopausal transition.

Importantly, the findings suggest that current academic workplace structures specially coaching institutes in India remain ill-equipped to support midlife women. With teaching and administrative duties often overlapping, the burden of both physical and cognitive symptoms can result in absenteeism or presenteeism, with wider implications for institutional efficiency. Addressing these concerns requires a dual approach: structural adjustments (flexible hours, reduced administrative load, and improved infrastructure) and cultural shifts (awareness campaigns, training for managers, and open dialogue).

In conclusion, the data underscores the urgent need for Indian academic institutions to integrate menopause into workplace health and wellbeing policies. Doing so not only addresses gender equity but also enhances staff retention, morale, and productivity.

7. THE NEED FOR DEVELOPMENT: A PARADIGM SHIFT IN WORKPLACE WELLBEING

The confluence of challenges outlined previously underscores the urgent need for a fundamental paradigm shift in how the Indian coaching industry, and indeed all knowledge-based sectors, conceptualize and operationalize workplace wellbeing. The current approach, which largely ignores the specific health needs of midlife women, is not only ethically questionable but also economically shortsighted and unsustainable. The argument for development is rooted in a powerful trifecta of business imperatives, ethical responsibilities, and the evolving legal landscape. From a business perspective, the cost of ignoring menopause is substantial. The loss of experienced, skilled female educators and leaders represents a significant depletion of human capital. The costs associated with recruiting, hiring, and training their replacements are considerable, not to mention the loss of institutional memory, mentorship capacity, and diverse perspectives that are crucial for innovation and organizational resilience. Furthermore, presenteeism—where women are at work but functioning at a reduced capacity due to unmanaged symptoms—likely incurs even greater hidden costs than absenteeism, directly impacting teaching quality, student satisfaction, and ultimately, the institute's reputation (Brewis et al., 2017).

Ethically, organizations have a duty of care to provide a safe and healthy work environment for all employees. This duty extends beyond preventing physical harm to encompass psychological safety and holistic well-being. Creating a culture where women feel supported through a major life transition is a fundamental aspect of corporate social responsibility and a marker of a progressive, humane organization. It signals to all employees, regardless of gender or age, that the institution values them as whole people, which in turn fosters loyalty, engagement, and a positive organizational culture. From a legal and regulatory standpoint, while India currently lacks specific legislation mandating menopause support, the global trend is moving towards recognizing it as a workplace issue. In countries like the UK, menopause is increasingly being considered under existing equality and health and safety legislation, and tribunals have ruled that menopause can be a protected characteristic under disability or sex discrimination law (Brewis et al., 2017). Proactive development of supportive frameworks positions Indian coaching institutes as leaders, preparing them for future regulatory changes and mitigating legal risks.

Ultimately, the need for development is about fostering genuine gender equity. True equity is not achieved merely by hiring women but by creating conditions that allow them to thrive throughout their entire careers. Supporting women through menopause is a critical step in closing the gender gap at senior levels, ensuring that the pipeline of female talent does not leak at the very point when women are poised to assume the most significant leadership roles (Jack et al., 2016). By investing in the development of menopause-friendly policies, infrastructures, and cultures, the coaching industry can transform itself from a sector that inadvertently pushes women out to one that actively supports and retains them, thereby unlocking the full potential of its workforce and setting a new standard for the future of work in India. This requires moving from a reactive, ad-hoc approach to a strategic, systematic, and technology-enabled one.

8. INCORPORATION OF AI TO SOLVE THIS PROBLEM

The formidable challenges of creating menopause-friendly workplaces in the demanding context of the Indian coaching industry demand innovative, scalable, and intelligent solutions. Artificial Intelligence, with its transformative capabilities in data analysis, prediction, and personalization, offers a powerful toolkit to address this complex issue systematically. The incorporation of AI is not about replacing human empathy but about augmenting it, creating systems that are proactive, discreet, and highly effective. The application can be envisioned across three interconnected domains: personalized health empowerment, intelligent workplace adaptations, and strategic organizational insights. At the individual level, AI-driven digital health platforms can serve as a cornerstone for personalized symptom management. Women could use secure mobile applications to track their symptoms, sleep patterns, diet, and stress levels. Advanced AI algorithms, employing machine learning, can then analyze this longitudinal data to identify individual triggers and patterns for specific symptoms, such as predicting the likelihood of a hot flush based on stress levels or dietary intake (Esteva et al., 2019).

These platforms can go beyond tracking to become interactive coaching tools. Based on the user's unique data profile, the AI can deliver personalized, evidence-based recommendations. For instance, it could suggest specific breathing exercises or mindfulness sessions when it detects rising stress levels, recommend dietary adjustments to help manage energy slumps, or provide personalized Cognitive Behavioural Therapy (CBT) modules for improving sleep and mood. Furthermore, with user consent, this anonymized and aggregated data can be integrated with a personalized medicine framework. By correlating symptom patterns with genetic predispositions (where available) and hormonal profiles as well as proper training and education, AI can help healthcare providers tailor interventions, such as the type and dosage of Hormone Replacement Therapy (HRT) or nutraceuticals, with unprecedented precision, moving from trial-and-error to a targeted, data-driven approach (Armeni et al., 2022). This empowers the woman with knowledge and agency over her health, transforming her from a passive sufferer to an active manager of her wellbeing.

At the workplace level, AI can revolutionize Human Resource management systems, making them more responsive to employee needs. Intelligent Environmental Control systems can use IoT sensors and AI to create personalized microclimates. A woman could use a company-approved app to subtly adjust the temperature and airflow in her immediate workspace or a designated quiet room, providing immediate relief during a hot flush without disrupting others (Davenport & Kalakota, 2019). AI-powered scheduling software can consider employee well-being as a key parameter. The system could anonymously incorporate user-reported wellness scores (from their health app) to create more flexible and humane work schedules. For example, it could avoid scheduling a teacher for a critical lecture during her predicted peak symptom time or facilitate easy shift swaps between colleagues, all while ensuring operational requirements are met. This demonstrates an organizational ethos that values output and wellbeing equally. For HR departments, AI-driven analytics dashboards can provide anonymized and aggregated insights into workforce wellness trends, such as identifying common stress peaks or the demand for wellness resources (Davenport & Kalakota, 2019). This allows for data-informed decision-making, enabling the organization to proactively invest in relevant support services, tailor wellness programs, and measure the return on investment of its wellbeing initiatives, thereby building a more resilient, productive, and empathetic organizational culture.

9. MY THOUGHT AND PERSONAL STATEMENT

As the author of this review, I feel compelled to move beyond a dispassionate academic analysis and articulate a personal conviction that underpins this work. The silent struggle of countless professional women navigating menopause in unsupportive work environments is not just a statistical reality or a business problem; it is a profound human issue that speaks to the very heart of workplace equity and dignity. Having observed the dedication and brilliance of women educators in the Indian coaching system, it is both a tragedy and a monumental waste of potential to see their contributions hampered, and in some cases curtailed, by a biological transition that, with the right support, can be managed effectively. The prevailing silence surrounding menopause is a relic of an outdated corporate culture that separates the "professional" from the "personal" in an inherently discriminatory way, as it fails to acknowledge the biological realities that differentially affect women's lives.

My perspective is that technology, particularly AI and personalized medicine, should not be viewed as cold or impersonal tools, but as powerful enablers of human-centric design. The proposed integration is fundamentally about using technology to restore humanity and individuality to the workplace. It is about creating systems that see employees not as interchangeable resources but as whole human beings with fluctuating needs and unique biological profiles. The goal of an AI that can predict a hot flush is not to surveil but to empower—to give a woman the discreet ability to control her environment and maintain her professional composure. The purpose of a personalized medicine approach is to affirm that every woman's experience is valid and distinct, and that her care should be as unique as she is. This is the antithesis of a one-size-fits-all policy; it is the embodiment of empathy at scale.

However, this technological optimism is tempered with a firm commitment to ethical vigilance. The deployment of AI in this sensitive domain must be guided by ironclad principles of privacy, consent, and transparency. Data collected through health apps must be owned and controlled by the employee, with clear, opt-in consent protocols and robust cybersecurity measures to prevent misuse (Topol, 2019). The purpose of these tools must never be to penalize or profile, but solely to support and empower. The roadmap to a menopause-friendly workplace is not merely a technical implementation plan; it is a cultural change manifesto. It requires courageous leadership from both women and men in the industry to break the taboo, to initiate conversations, and to champion policies that support women's health. It is my firm belief that by embracing this integrated, technology-enabled, and deeply human approach, the Indian coaching industry has the opportunity to not only retain its invaluable female talent but to become a beacon of progressive employment practices, demonstrating that the future of work is inclusive, empathetic, and smart.

10. CONCLUSION

This comprehensive review has traversed the complex terrain of menopause as a significant yet neglected workplace issue, with a specific focus on the high-stakes, high-stress environment of the Indian coaching industry. We began by establishing that menopause, a natural bio-psycho-social transition, presents a constellation of physical, cognitive, and psychological symptoms that can severely impede a woman's professional performance and well-being. The analysis revealed that the structural and cultural characteristics of coaching institutes—including rigid schedules, inadequate physical infrastructure, a high-pressure performance culture, and a complete absence of supportive policies—compound these challenges, creating an environment that can force the premature exit of experienced and valuable female talent. This status quo is untenable, representing both a critical failure in organizational duty of care and a significant economic liability.

The central thesis of this review is that a paradigm shift is not only necessary but also now feasible, driven by the convergent powers of Artificial Intelligence and personalized medicine. We have detailed how AI-driven tools can empower women through personalized health tracking and predictive analytics, while simultaneously enabling intelligent workplaces through adaptive environmental controls and flexible, wellbeing-informed scheduling systems. Coupled with the principles of personalized medicine, which advocate for interventions tailored to an individual's genetic, hormonal, and lifestyle profile, these technologies offer a path away from generic, ineffective support towards bespoke, dignified, and highly effective care. This integrated model promises to transform the workplace from a source of stress into a partner in wellbeing, fostering an inclusive culture where women can thrive throughout their menopausal transition and beyond.

However, technology alone is not a panacea. Its successful implementation hinges on parallel developments in organizational policy, leadership commitment, and a fundamental cultural shift that destigmatizes menopause and opens channels for supportive dialogue. The proposed roadmap must include the development of formal menopause policies, mandatory training for managers, investment in physical infrastructure like quiet rooms, and, most importantly, the fostering of an organizational ethos that values empathy and inclusion as core strategic assets. By embarking on this journey, the Indian coaching industry can cease to be a case study in a leaky pipeline of female talent and instead become a pioneering model for how to build a truly modern, equitable, and menopause-friendly workplace, ensuring that the wisdom and expertise of its women educators continue to illuminate the path for future generations.

11. LIMITATIONS & FURTHER SCOPE OF RESEARCH

The conceptual framework proposed in this review, while grounded in existing literature from disparate fields, opens up a rich and largely unexplored landscape for future research. The nascent nature of this specific intersection—menopause, the Indian workplace, specifically coaching sectors, and AI—means that numerous empirical and theoretical questions remain unanswered, providing a clear agenda for scholarly inquiry in the years to come. First and foremost, there is a critical need for foundational qualitative and quantitative research within the Indian coaching industry itself. Large-scale surveys and in-depth interviews are required to rigorously document the prevalence and severity of work-related challenges faced by menopausal women educators, establishing a robust evidence base that can catalyze institutional change. This research should explore not only the experiences of women but also the awareness and attitudes of male colleagues and institutional leaders to understand the full scope of the cultural barrier.

Second, the development and validation of the proposed technological solutions require dedicated research and development. This includes designing user-centric AI-powered symptom tracking apps that are culturally adapted for the Indian context and conducting randomized controlled trials to evaluate their efficacy in improving both health outcomes (e.g., symptom severity, quality of life) and work-related outcomes (e.g., productivity, job satisfaction). Research is also needed into the technical and ethical frameworks for integrating personal health data with workplace systems (like smart HVAC or scheduling software) in a manner that is secure, consensual, and non-stigmatizing. A third major area for research lies in the policy domain. Comparative studies analyzing the effectiveness of different menopause workplace policies in other countries and sectors can provide valuable templates for the Indian context. Furthermore, legal scholars could investigate the potential for framing menopause support under existing Indian labour laws on gender equality and occupational health and safety, paving the way for potential legislative advocacy.

Finally, longitudinal studies are essential to capture the long-term impact of implementing such integrated support systems. Research should track not only the retention rates and career progression of women but also broader organizational metrics, such as overall employee engagement, institutional reputation, and even student outcomes, to build a compelling business case for investment. Interdisciplinary collaboration between endocrinologists, data scientists, organizational psychologists, HR professionals, and gender studies scholars will be crucial to advancing this field. By pursuing this multifaceted research agenda, we can move from conceptual models to evidence-based practice, ensuring that the vision of a menopause-friendly coaching industry becomes a tangible and sustainable reality.

REFERENCES

Ahuja, M. (2016). Age of menopause and determinants of menopause age: A PAN India survey by IMS. *Journal of Midlife Health*, *7*(3), 126–131. DOI: 10.4103/0976-7800.191012 PMID: 27721640

Armeni, E., Mili, N., Siliogka, E., Goulis, D. G., & Lambrinoudaki, I. (2022). Menopause medical education around the world: The way forward to serve women's health. *Current Opinion in Endocrine and Metabolic Research*, *26*, 100387. DOI: 10.1016/j.coemr.2022.100387

Brewis, J., Atkinson, C., Beck, V., Davies, A., & Duberley, J. (2019). Menopause and the workplace.

Brewis, J., Beck, V., Davies, A., & Matheson, J. (2017). The effects of menopause transition on women's economic participation in the UK.

Collins, F. S., & Varmus, H. (2015). A new initiative on precision medicine. *The New England Journal of Medicine*, *372*(9), 793–795. DOI: 10.1056/NEJMp1500523 PMID: 25635347

Davenport, T., & Kalakota, R. (2019). The potential for artificial intelligence in healthcare. *Future Healthcare Journal*, *6*(2), 94–98. DOI: 10.7861/futurehosp.6-2-94 PMID: 31363513

Davenport, T., & Kalakota, R. (2019). The potential for artificial intelligence in healthcare. *Future Healthcare Journal*, *6*(2), 94–98. DOI: 10.7861/futurehosp.6-2-94 PMID: 31363513

Esteva, A., Robicquet, A., Ramsundar, B., Kuleshov, V., DePristo, M., Chou, K., Cui, C., Corrado, G., Thrun, S., & Dean, J. (2019). A guide to deep learning in healthcare. *Nature Medicine*, *25*(1), 24–29. DOI: 10.1038/s41591-018-0316-z PMID: 30617335

Grandey, A. A. (2000). Emotional regulation in the workplace: A new way to conceptualize emotional labor. *Journal of Occupational Health Psychology*, *5*(1), 95–110. DOI: 10.1037/1076-8998.5.1.95 PMID: 10658889

Hunter, M., & Rendall, M. (2007). Bio-psycho-socio-cultural perspectives on menopause. *Best Practice & Research. Clinical Obstetrics & Gynaecology*, *21*(2), 261–274. DOI: 10.1016/j.bpobgyn.2006.11.001 PMID: 17161025

Jack, G., Riach, K., Bariola, E., Pitts, M., Schapper, J., & Sarrel, P. (2016). Menopause in the workplace: What employers should be doing. *Maturitas*, *85*, 88–95. DOI: 10.1016/j.maturitas.2015.12.006 PMID: 26857886

Mankar, S., Johnson, A. R., Chawla, P. S., & Basannar, D. (2024). Needs assessment study for management of menopause in the community. *Journal of Family Medicine and Primary Care, 13*(4), 1371–1378. DOI: 10.4103/jfmpc.jfmpc_1129_23 PMID: 38827709

Monteleone, P., Mascagni, G., Giannini, A., Genazzani, A. R., & Simoncini, T. (2018). Symptoms of menopause—Global prevalence, physiology and implications. *Nature Reviews. Endocrinology, 14*(4), 199–215. DOI: 10.1038/nrendo.2017.180 PMID: 29393299

Nagaraj, D., Ramesh, N., Devraj, D., Umman, M., John, A. K., & Johnson, A. R. (2021). Experience and perceptions regarding menopause among rural women: A cross-sectional hospital-based study in South Karnataka. *Journal of Midlife Health, 12*(3), 199–205. DOI: 10.4103/jmh.JMH_196_20 PMID: 34759701

Ramyashree, S., Veigas, J., & Kanagal, D. (2024). Severity of menopausal symptoms on quality of life among working women. *Journal of Education and Health Promotion, 13*(1), 35. DOI: 10.4103/jehp.jehp_802_23 PMID: 38545317

Santoro, N., & Randolph, J. F. (2011). Reproductive hormones and the menopause transition. *Obstetrics and Gynecology Clinics, 38*(3), 455–466. PMID: 21961713

Soares, C. N., Joffe, H., & Steiner, M. (2004). Menopause and mood. *Clinical Obstetrics and Gynecology, 47*(3), 576–591. DOI: 10.1097/01.grf.0000129918.00756.d5 PMID: 15326420

Syamala, T. S., & Sivakami, M. (2005). Menopause: An emerging issue in India. *Economic and Political Weekly*, •••, 4923–4930.

Topol, E. (2019). *Deep medicine: how artificial intelligence can make healthcare human again.*

Verdonk, P., Bendien, E., & Appelman, Y. (2022). Menopause and work: A narrative literature review about menopause, work and health. *Work (Reading, Mass.), 72*(2), 483–496. DOI: 10.3233/WOR-205214 PMID: 35570508

Weber, M. T., Maki, P. M., & McDermott, M. P. (2014). Cognition and mood in perimenopause: A systematic review and meta-analysis. *The Journal of Steroid Biochemistry and Molecular Biology, 142*, 90–98. DOI: 10.1016/j.jsbmb.2013.06.001 PMID: 23770320

Yadav, J. (2022, December 19). *India's Tuition Republic is bigger than ever: Coaching culture is an epidemic now*. ThePrint.

APPENDIX

Table 1.

Participant ID	Age	Role / Subject	Primary Physical Symptom (Severity)	Primary Psychological Symptom (Severity)	Impact on Work (1-5)	Workplace Support?	Suggested Improvement
P01	52	Physics	Hot Flashes (Severe)	Brain Fog (Moderate)	4	No	Better ventilation/AC in classrooms.
P02	49	Chemistry	Sleep Disturbance (Severe)	Fatigue (Severe)	5	No	Option for flexible start times.
P03	55	Mathematics	Joint Pain (Moderate)	Mood Swings (Moderate)	3	Partially	More comfortable seating in the staff room.
P04	51	Biology	Fatigue (Severe)	Lack of Motivation (Severe)	5	No	Reduced administrative workload.
P05	53	English	Headaches (Moderate)	Anxiety (Severe)	4	No	Access to a quiet room for short breaks.
P06	50	Physics	Hot Flashes (Moderate)	Irritability (Moderate)	3	Yes	-
P07	56	Chemistry	Sleep Disturbance (Severe)	Brain Fog (Severe)	5	No	Awareness sessions for management.
P08	48	Biology	Joint Pain (Moderate)	Anxiety (Moderate)	3	Partially	Health and wellness workshops.
P09	54	Mathematics	Fatigue (Moderate)	Low Mood (Severe)	4	No	Access to confidential counseling services.
P10	52	English	Hot Flashes (Severe)	Sleep Disturbance (Severe)	5	No	More lenient policy for short-notice leave.
P11	51	Physics	Headaches (Moderate)	Irritability (Moderate)	3	Partially	Clearer communication channels.
P12	55	Chemistry	Fatigue (Severe)	Brain Fog (Moderate)	4	No	Shorter, more frequent breaks.
P13	49	Biology	Joint Pain (Severe)	Anxiety (Severe)	5	No	Option to work from home for prep work.
P14	53	English	Sleep Disturbance (Moderate)	Mood Swings (Moderate)	3	No	An empathetic and understanding manager.
P15	50	Mathematics	Hot Flashes (Moderate)	Brain Fog (Moderate)	3	Yes	-
P16	57	Physics	Fatigue (Severe)	Lack of Motivation (Moderate)	4	Partially	Acknowledgment of the issue from HR.
P17	51	Chemistry	Headaches (Severe)	Anxiety (Severe)	5	No	Mental health days without justification.
P18	54	Biology	Hot Flashes (Severe)	Irritability (Severe)	5	No	A fan in every classroom.
P19	52	English	Joint Pain (Moderate)	Low Mood (Moderate)	3	No	More team-building/ social events.
P20	49	Physics	Sleep Disturbance (Moderate)	Brain Fog (Severe)	4	Partially	Clearer guidelines on performance expectations.
P21	53	Mathematics	Fatigue (Severe)	Anxiety (Moderate)	4	No	Possibility of a reduced teaching load.

continued on following page

Table 1. Continued

Participant ID	Age	Role / Subject	Primary Physical Symptom (Severity)	Primary Psychological Symptom (Severity)	Impact on Work (1-5)	Workplace Support?	Suggested Improvement
P22	56	Chemistry	Hot Flashes (Moderate)	Mood Swings (Moderate)	3	No	More support from junior staff.
P23	50	Biology	Joint Pain (Severe)	Fatigue (Severe)	5	No	Better ergonomic furniture.
P24	54	English	Headaches (Moderate)	Brain Fog (Moderate)	3	Yes	-
P25	51	Mathematics	Sleep Disturbance (Severe)	Anxiety (Severe)	5	No	Formal policy on menopause support.

Chapter 13
Occupational Stress in the Face of Psychological Well Being:
The Case of Malaysian Working Women

Nur Izzaty Mohamad
https://orcid.org/0000-0002-0211-1260
School of Humanities, Universiti Sains Malaysia, Malaysia

Nursaadatun Nisak Ahmad
Faculty of Business and Management, Universiti Teknologi Mara, Shah Alam, Malaysia

Nurul Muna Mohamad
Faculty of Entrepreneurship and Business, Universiti Malaysia Kelantan, Malaysia

Wan Aishah Wan Mohd Nowalid
https://orcid.org/0000-0002-5150-8117
School of Business Management, Universiti Utara Malaysia, Malaysia

ABSTRACT

Occupational stress is an increasingly prevalent issue that has a significant impact on the psychological well being of working women in Malaysia. This study aims to assess the relationship between occupational stress and psychological well being through quantitative methods. A total of 118 respondents from agencies in Malaysia were involved in this survey study. Data analysis was conducted using Statistical Package for Social Sciences (SPSS) software for descriptive statistics and initial

DOI: 10.4018/979-8-3373-2970-3.ch013

coding, while structural equation modeling (SEM) and hypothesis testing were carried out using Smart PLS. The results of the analysis showed that occupational stress has a significant impact on the psychological well being of working women. This study also provides recommendations for future research as well as practical implications in strengthening psychosocial support and more gender-sensitive workplace policies.

UNDERSTANDING OCCUPATIONAL STRESS

Occupational stress refers to the physical and psychological strain experienced by individuals due to demands and pressures in the workplace that exceed their coping abilities. It emerges when employees perceive an imbalance between job demands and the resources available to meet those demands, resulting in emotional exhaustion, reduced productivity, and negative health outcomes (AlAteeq, AlNujaim & AlGharbi, 2025; Ma, Xu & Zhang, 2025). Occupational stress is influenced by various organisational and personal factors, including excessive workload, tight deadlines, role ambiguity, lack of control, poor communication, and limited social support. Personal traits such as resilience, coping mechanisms, and life circumstances further determine how individuals experience and manage stress. In high-demand work environments, unmanaged occupational stress can contribute to burnout, anxiety, depression, and diminished job satisfaction. Understanding the nature, causes, and consequences of occupational stress is therefore crucial for developing effective intervention strategies that promote mental well-being and organisational effectiveness (AlAteeq, AlNujaim & AlGharbi, 2025; Ma, Xu & Zhang, 2025).

Occupational stress can be broadly categorised into two primary forms: eustress and distress (Mohamad et al., 2015; Viertiö et al., 2021). Eustress is identified as a positive form of stress that can stimulate motivation, enhance focus, and boost performance. It emerges from stimulating or challenging situations that encourage personal growth and adaptability without overwhelming the individual. Examples of eustress include engaging in new opportunities, exercising control over anxiety, or adopting proactive behaviours in the face of pressure (Mohamad et al., 2015; Viertiö et al., 2021). In contrast, distress is a negative psychological and emotional reaction to perceived threats or unfavourable circumstances. It is commonly associated with feelings of tension, anxiety, sadness, or discomfort and may impair an individual's ability to function effectively (Wharne, 2021; Mohamad et al., 2015; AlAteeq, AlNujaim & AlGharbi, 2025). Distress typically occurs when individuals feel overwhelmed by job demands or believe they lack sufficient resources to cope. High levels of distress often signal deteriorating mental health and are frequently linked with psychological disorders such as depression and anxiety (Wharne, 2021; Viertiö et al., 2021; Ma, Xu & Zhang, 2025).

From a physiological perspective, distress has been shown to disrupt the body's immune system. When stress becomes chronic, the pituitary gland, located beneath the brain, responds by secreting adrenocorticotropic hormone (ACTH), which in turn stimulates the adrenal glands to release stress hormones such as cortisol and adrenaline (Selye, 1987; Lazarus, 2000). These hormones are designed to enhance alertness, quicken physical responses, and increase strength in short bursts. However, excessive production of cortisol may compromise immune function by attacking healthy cells in the body (Hellhammer, Wust, & Kudielka, 2009). Prolonged exposure to such physiological changes can lead to disorders within the cardiovascular system, including irregular blood circulation, heart rate instability, skin response abnormalities, and impaired neurological feedback. If left unmanaged, the body's regulatory mechanisms fail to control the overproduction of stress hormones, resulting in long-term physical and mental health consequences (Selye, 1987; Mohamad et al., 2015). In the workplace context, individuals experiencing chronic distress are at heightened risk for health complications and reduced well-being, which may ultimately compromise social and professional sustainability.

OCCUPATIONAL STRESS FACTORS

These risks may include:

- Mismatch between an employee's skills and the job requirements, whether due to underutilization or insufficient capability.
- Excessive workloads, rapid work pace, or insufficient staffing.
- Extended, irregular, or rigid working hours.
- Limited autonomy in shaping job tasks or managing workload.
- Hazardous or substandard physical working environments.
- Organizational cultures that permit or fail to address harmful behaviours.
- Inadequate peer support or overly authoritarian leadership styles.
- Exposure to violence, harassment, or bullying.
- Experiences of discrimination or social exclusion.
- Unclear job responsibilities or expectations.
- Lack of advancement opportunities or inappropriate promotion practices.
- Job insecurity, insufficient compensation, or limited access to professional development; and
- Conflicting demands between work and personal life.

MENTAL HEALTH STATISTICS AMONG WORKING WOMEN

Based on data released by ComPsych, there has been a significant increase in the taking of mental health-related leave, especially among women. In the first quarter of 2024, 11% of all leave taken was due to mental health issues, recording an increase of 22% compared to the first quarter of 2023. This finding shows that women play a significant role in this trend, recording 69% of all mental health leave in 2023 and increasing to 72% in the first quarter of 2024 (Mayer, 2024). Next, the "Green Paper on the Mental Well-being of Career Women in China" highlights a range of mental health challenges faced by women in the Chinese workforce. A significant proportion of professional women rated their own health as fair or poor, with anxiety, depression, and social isolation identified as key concerns. The report revealed that approximately 85% of career women experienced mental health issues in the previous year, with nearly one-third reporting occasional feelings of anxiety or stress, and 7% indicating persistent anxiety or depression. Additionally, the Green Paper noted that around 90% of professional women had experienced negative emotions and psychological symptoms in the three months preceding the survey. Nearly half reported currently feeling irritable, anxious, confused, or fearful. These mental health concerns were found to be more prevalent among women than men within the Chinese workforce (Ma, Xu & Zhang, 2025).

In the context of work stress and psychological well being among women, role identity and cognition often drive many working women to strive to achieve a balance between work responsibilities and domestic obligations, leaving them vulnerable to high levels of mental health (AlAteeq, AlNujaim & AlGharbi, 2025; Ma, Xu & Zhang, 2025). When such conflicts arise and remain unresolved, women in the workforce are more likely to experience chronic stress. Prolonged exposure to stress inevitably depletes limited psychological resources, leading to emotional exhaustion and mental health issues.

Most of the findings from recent literature reviews on occupational stress management indicate that there is a negative relationship between occupational stress and psychological well being (Mohamad et al., 2015; Darvishmotevali & Ali, 2020; Acoba, 2024). From an organizational behavior perspective, psychological well being is generally defined as a state of person's emotional and social well-being. It affects how individuals think, feel, and act, especially in coping with stress, relating to others, and making decisions in daily and work life (Mohamad et al., 2015; Darvishmotevali & Ali, 2020; Acoba, 2024). It also involves feelings of satisfaction with life, positive emotional experiences, and the existence of a sense of purpose and meaning in life. These findings emphasize the significant impact of occupational stress on psychological well being, thus highlighting the need to design comprehensive and integrated management strategies to support psychological well being in the workplace (Mohamad, Abd Rahman, & Mohamad Nor, 2022; Shaikh, Watto, & Tunio, 2021).

The latest findings from the National Health and Morbidity Survey (NHMS) reveal a worrying trend: depression rates in Malaysia have doubled between 2019 and 2023 (Institute for Public Health, 2024). The highest rates of depression were recorded among individuals aged 16 to 19, followed by the 20 to 29 and 30 to 39 age groups. This age group represents a significant portion of Malaysia's current and future workforce, and their mental health issues need to be addressed to prevent more serious conditions. For example, a young professional in their late 20s working in Kuala Lumpur may face high levels of work stress, coupled with long working hours and limited personal time. Economic challenges and the rising cost of living have also prompted some individuals to take on additional work online, adding to the burden of psychological stress. A report by the Malaysia Digital Economy Corporation (MDEC) shows a significant increase in the local gig economy, with over 100,000 new entrants recorded between 2022 and 2023. However, engagement in the gig economy brings new stresses such as social isolation for those working alone or remotely, income instability, as well as concerns about the future due to market competition, perceptions of artificial intelligence (AI) and lack of social protection. Without adequate support, these stresses can lead to burnout and depression, thus affecting productivity levels and overall quality of life. Thus, this study to measure the relationship bertween occupational stress and psychological well being challenges faced by working women in Malaysia

JOB DEMAND

Job demand is a key contributor to workplace stress. In occupational stress literature, it is typically defined as a high volume of tasks and unexpected duties that may lead to psychological strain (Bakker & de Vries, 2020; Atiku & Van Wyk, 2024). This includes the intensity of the workload and time constraints, such as the limited time available for employees to complete their assignments (Karasek & Theorell, 1990). Job demands can take various forms, including long working hours, increased responsibilities, the need for specific skills and knowledge, and pressure to meet tight deadlines. Theoretically, such demands whether mental or physical require cognitive focus, psychological engagement, and physical or static effort (Karasek & Theorell, 1990). As a result, contemporary research on workplace stress highlights job demand as a crucial factor that organisations must address to effectively manage employee stress.

INTERPERSONAL CONFLICT

Conflict is a common occurrence that influences organisations across various stages and processes (Barki & Harwick, 2001). From an organisational standpoint, interpersonal conflict is generally understood as disagreements, incompatible goals, or differing needs, values, beliefs, and interests among individuals, which can result in workplace stress (Kostelić, Gonan Božac & Paulišić, 2024; Bruce, Hrymak, Bruce & Byrne, 2024). This type of conflict is characterised by social interactions involving opposing or incompatible viewpoints. Often arising from misunderstandings about job roles and responsibilities, interpersonal conflict can be found at virtually all levels of the organisation. It may present as minor disputes between coworkers or supervisors and can be either open (overt) or hidden (covert) in nature (Spector & Jex, 1998). Conflicts may stem from personal tensions (relational conflict) or differences in how tasks should be carried out (task conflict). As a natural aspect of human interactions within the workplace (Sillars & Parry, 1982), interpersonal conflict can influence individual behaviour and may even threaten others' personal or professional interests (Kacmar & Carlson, 1997). In organisational settings, such conflict has been associated with outcomes such as reduced job satisfaction, increased depressive symptoms, and physical complaints. Hence, contemporary research on workplace stress identifies interpersonal conflict as a key factor that must be acknowledged and addressed to maintain workplace well-being.

ROLE AMBIGUITY

Lazarus (1991) identified role ambiguity as a significant source of workplace stress, describing it as a dynamic process involving interactions between individuals and their work environment. Role ambiguity arises when employees lack clarity about their duties, expectations, and responsibilities within the organisation. This lack of understanding can lead to confusion regarding job roles and what is expected of them (Junça Silva & Rodrigues, 2024; Atiku & Van Wyk, 2024). Such uncertainty may hinder employees' ability to perform tasks effectively, ultimately affecting their performance and overall well-being. For instance, when there are changes in an organisation's structure, employees may struggle to manage responsibilities related to task execution, organisational goals, job scope, mission alignment, and expectations from superiors especially when these expectations are unclear or unattainable (Junça Silva & Rodrigues, 2024; Atiku & Van Wyk, 2024). Role ambiguity is widely regarded as a psychosocial risk factor that can negatively impact mental health. When employees are uncertain about their roles, it often results in emotional fatigue and reduced job satisfaction.

EMPIRICAL PERSPECTIVES: RELATIONSHIP BETWEEN OCCUPATIONAL STRESS AND PSYCHOLOGICAL WELL BEING

The link between occupational stress and psychological well being is well-explained by the Job Demands-Resources (JD-R) Theory developed by Arnold B. Bakker and Evangelia Demerouti (An, Gu, Obrenovic, & Godinic, 2023; Bakker & de Vries, 2021). This theory, grounded in occupational psychology, explores how job characteristics influence employee well-being and performance. It suggests that employees frequently face job demands elements of work that require continuous physical or mental effort such as heavy workloads, time constraints, unclear roles, and interpersonal tensions. When these demands exceed the resources available to employees, they can lead to stress, burnout, and various health issues, including anxiety, depression, and physical ailments. Sustained exposure to high job demands may gradually deplete an individual's mental and physical energy, undermining psychological health and overall well-being. In this context, the JD-R model often represents how job stress operates within organisations. The theory is widely supported by empirical research, reinforcing its relevance in understanding the dynamics of occupational stress in the workplace.

The review of existing scientific literature reveals consistent empirical evidence of a correlation between occupational stress and psychological well being. For instance, Mensah (2021) examined the link between occupational stress and psychological well being among a large sample of European workers 14,603 men and 15,486 women from 35 countries. Using structural equation modelling, the study found a statistically significant relationship between occupational stress and psychological well being ($\beta = 0.2352$, $p < 0.05$), indicating that increased work-related pressure can adversely psychological well being. Similarly, Darvishmotevali and Ali (2020) conducted a study involving 250 employees from four- and five-star hotels in Tehran, Iran, which found that job stress particularly job insecurity and job demands negatively impacted employees' subjective well-being. In another study, Mohamad et al. (2015) assessed 142 police officers in Peninsular Malaysia and found that job stress factors such as role ambiguity, role conflict, and role overload significantly affected their overall health. Furthermore, Acoba (2024) explored perceived workplace stress among 426 Filipino adults during the height of the COVID-19 pandemic, revealing that job demands, work environment, and workload were major contributors to decreased mental well-being. These empirical findings reinforce the theoretical argument that job stress is directly associated with significant psychological well being outcomes. Based on this robust body of literature, the following hypotheses are proposed:

Hypothesis: Occupational stress is positively associated with psychological well being

OCCUPATIONAL STRESS MODEL

The theoretical and empirical evidence identified has been used to build occupational stress model, as shown in Figure 1.

Figure 1. Occupational Stress Model

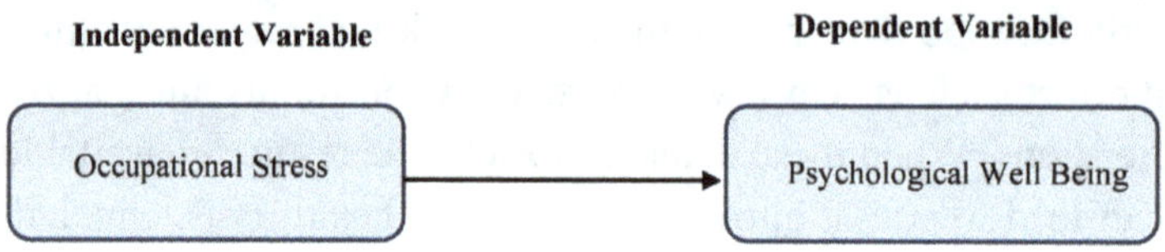

Figure 2 shows Google Trends searches worldwide for the "occupational stress" query on June 17, 2025. Google Trends is a freely available tool developed by Google that provides reports on search popularity in Google Search.

Figure 2. Global Google Trends

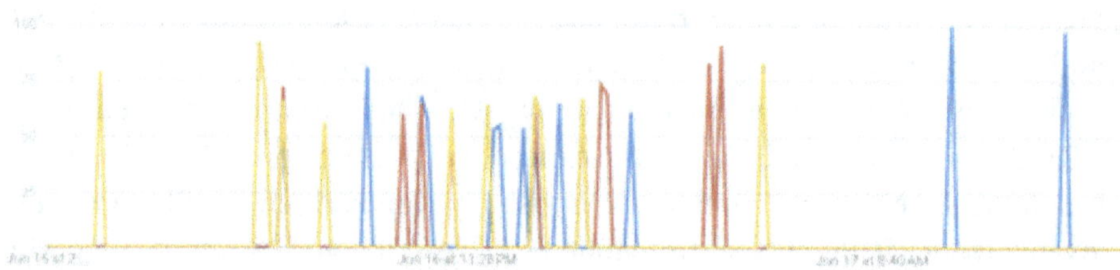

Figure 3 shows the word cloud created using the internet online software. Occupational stress is the most common word that appears in the largest typefaces. The fewest common words were displayed in smaller fonts. Aside from the to list, the word cloud includes all additional words that appeared in the titles of the publications. The word cloud effectively presents complicated information in a simple style (Birko, Dove, & Ozdemir, 2015).

Figure 3. Word Cloud

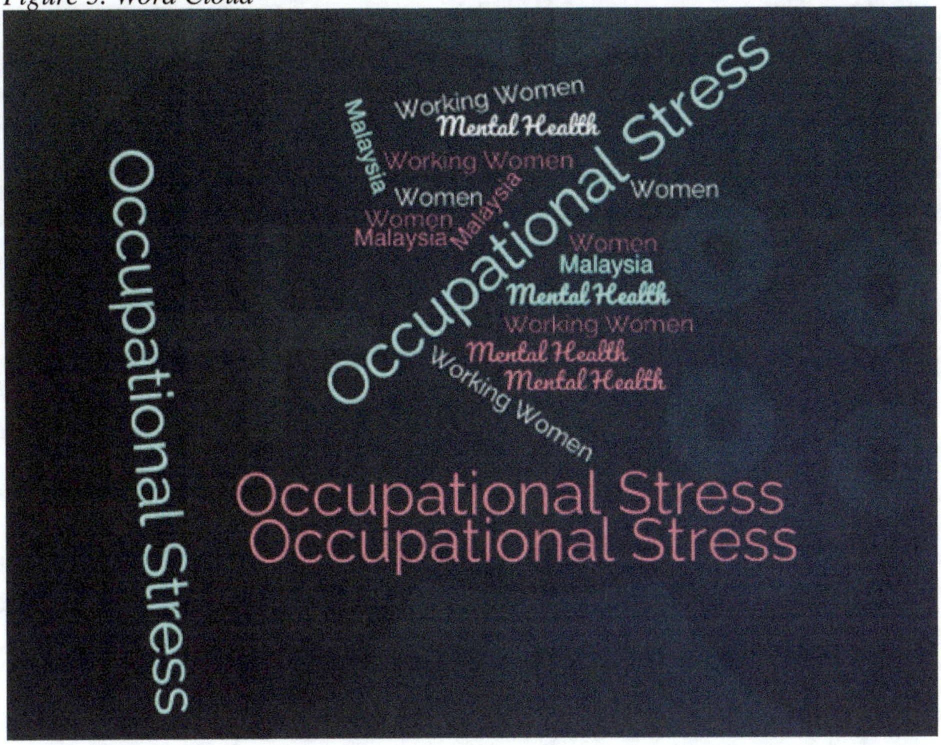

METHODOLOGY

This study adopted a cross-sectional design, which allowed data to be collected through literature reviews, pilot studies, and questionnaires as the main methods. This approach was chosen for its strengths in providing accurate and relevant data, minimizing bias, and enhancing overall data quality (Creswell, 2015; Sekaran & Bougie, 2010). The initial phase of data collection involved the development of a questionnaire grounded in existing literature on occupational stress. To ensure linguistic accuracy, the back-translation method recommended by Wright (1996) was applied to translate the survey items from English into Malay. This process engaged two bilingual lecturers proficient in Bahasa Melayu and English, as well as two management lecturers from Universiti Kebangsaan Malaysia (UKM). The back-translation technique was used to compare the original English version with the translated Malay version, ensuring conceptual equivalence. This method enhances the precision and reliability of the research instrument.

This study involved a sample of employees from various staff levels within agencies in Malaysia. These organisations comprise multiple divisions, such as the service division, staffing and organisation division, pension division, human capital development division, salary and allowance division, psychology division, and digital and information technology division. A purposive sampling method, recognized as highly effective by Patton (2002), was employed to distribute 250 questionnaires to targeted respondents. Purposive sampling focuses on selecting individuals who possess relevant knowledge and experience related to the research topic (Creswell & Plano Clark, 2011). This method was chosen because the organisation was unable to share a complete list of potential participants' names and details, in an effort to maintain its reputation and corporate image. As a result, random sampling was not feasible. Out of the 170 distributed questionnaires, 118 were completed and returned, yielding a response rate of 69.41%. Participation was entirely voluntary, with no coercion involved.

RESULTS

Table 1 shows the respondents' demographic profiles. The respondents of this study comprised 118 individuals, all of whom were female. The majority were aged between 28 to 33 years (44.9%), 72.9% were married, a Malaysian Higher School Certificate or Diploma (40.7%), income group earned between RM1000 to RM2499 (46.6%), majority (65.3%) served in the support group, had 6 to 10 years of service (55.1%), working hours, 91.5%.

Table 1. Respondents' profile

Profile	Sub-Profile	Frequency	Percentage
Age	Less than 27 years	14	11.9
	28 to 33 years old	**53**	**44.9**
	34 to 39 years old	35	29.7
	40 to 45 years	12	10.2
	Over 46 years	4	3.4
Marital Status	Single	32	27.11
	Married	**86**	**72.9**

continued on following page

Table 1. Continued

Profile	**Sub-Profile**	**Frequency**	**Percentage**
Gender	Male	0	0
	Female	**118**	**100**
Education Level	Lower Secondary Assessment.	0	0
	Malaysian Certificate of Education	27	22.9
	Malaysian Higher School Certificate/ Diploma	**48**	**40.7**
	Degree	28	23.7
	Masters	15	12.7
Salary	Less than RM1000	5	4.2
	RM1000 to RM2499	**55**	**46.6**
	RM2500 to RM3999	30	25.4
	RM4000 to RM5499	13	11.0
	RM5000 to RM6999	7	5.9
	RM7000 above	8	6.77
Services Group	**Support**	**77**	**65.3**
	Management and Professional	41	34.7
Length of Services	0 to 5 years	23	19.5
	6 to 10 years	65	55.1
	11 to 15 years	21	17.8
	Over than 16 years	9	7.6
Daily Work Hours	Less than 8 hours	8	6.8
	8 to 10 hours	108	91.5
	Over than 10 hours	2	1.7

Measurement Model

The measurement model was evaluated using confirmatory factor analysis (CFA), along with assessments of convergent and discriminant validity (Hair et al., 2017). This model illustrates the connections between observed indicators and their underlying constructs. According to Hair et al. (2017), an acceptable outer loading value is at least 0.70, while composite reliability should also meet or exceed 0.70 (Ringle, Sarstedt, Mitchell, & Gudergan, 2019; Hair et al., 2017). The minimum acceptable value for average variance extracted (AVE) is 0.50 (Ringle et al., 2019).

As presented in Table 2, all construct outer loadings in this study are above the threshold of 0.708 (Henseler, Ringle, & Sinkovics, 2009), and AVE values are greater than 0.50 (Hair et al., 2017), confirming adequate convergent validity. Furthermore, all constructs demonstrate composite reliability scores above 0.80 (Hair et al., 2017), indicating a high level of internal consistency.

Table 2. Convergent validity analysis

Constructs	Outer Loading	Composite Reliability	Average Variance Extracted (AVE)	Cronbach's Alpha
Occupational Stress		0.927	0.616	0.923
OLS1:	0.786			
OLS2:	0.801			
OLS3:	0.788			
OLS4:	0.813			
OLS5:	0.811			
OLS6:	0.787			
OLS7:	0.742			
OLS8:	0.741			
OLS9	0.794			
Psychological Well Being		0.924	0.724	0.923
MLH1:	0.850			
MLH2:	0.885			
MLH3:	0.779			
MLH4:	0.876			
MLH5:	0.870			
MLH5	0.842			

The Heterotrait-Monotrait Ratio of Correlations (HTMT) was utilized to evaluate the discriminant validity of all constructs in the study. As presented in Table 3, all HTMT values are below the threshold of 0.85 (Hair et al., 2017), indicating that the constructs meet the required standard for discriminant validity

Table 3. Results of discriminant validity using HTMT

Construct	Occupational Stress	Psychological Well Being
Occupational Stress	0.703	
Psychological Well Being		

Table 4 presents variance inflation factor (VIF) values and a descriptive analysis of the constructs. The VIF values for the relationships among the study constructs are all below 5.0. It suggests that collinearity issues do not significantly impact the data (Hair et al., 2017). The means for the study constructs range from 5.650 to 6.211. These values indicate varying levels occupational stress and psychological well being, ranging from high (4) to the highest (7).

Table 4. VIF and descriptive constructs analysis

Construct	Occupational Stress	Psychological Well Being	Mean	Std. Deviation
Occupational Stress		1.000	5.650	2.411
Psychological Well Being			6.211	3.124

The Standardised Root Mean Squared Residual (SRMR) represents the difference between the observed correlation matrix and the one predicted by the model. It serves as an absolute indicator to evaluate the overall fit of the model by measuring the average discrepancy between actual and expected correlations. According to Table 5, the SRMR value is 0.093, suggesting that the model demonstrates a good fit for the saturated model (Hu & Bentler, 1998).

Table 5. Model fit analysis

Model Fit	Saturated Model	Estimated Model
SRMR	0.093	0.093
d_ULS	1.036	1.036
d_G	0.834	0.834
Chi-square	487.609	487.609
NFI	0.699	0.699

Table 6 presents the results of the cross-loading analysis. The findings show that each indicator loads higher on its corresponding construct than on any other constructs. This indicates that the items in the study meet the required criteria for discriminant validity (Hair et al., 2017).

Table 6. Cross-loading analysis

Occupational Stress	Psychological Well Being
0.786	0.458
0.801	0.482
0.788	0.449
0.813	0.445

continued on following page

Table 6. Continued

Occupational Stress	Psychological Well Being
0.811	0.478
0.787	0.515
0.742	0.503
0.741	0.635
0.794	0.634
0.546	0.850
0.615	0.885
0.573	0.779
0.550	0.876
0.551	0.870
0.551	0.842

Structural Model

This study examined four positive relationships using the SmartPLS bootstrapping method. The results of the direct effect hypotheses are presented in Table 7. The analysis revealed that occupational stress is positively associated with psychological well being (Hypothesis, β=0.665; t=12.821; p=0.000). These findings confirm that occupational stress are essential predictor variables for and psychological well being. Therefore, the hypothesis is supported. Next, Figure 4 show the path coefficients for direct hypotheses.

Table 7. The results of the hypotheses testing of the research model

Hypothesis	Original sample (O)	*t*-statistics (|O/ STDEV|)	*p*-values
Hypothesis: Occupational Stress -> Psychological Well Being	0.665	12.821	0.000

Figure 4. Path Coefficients

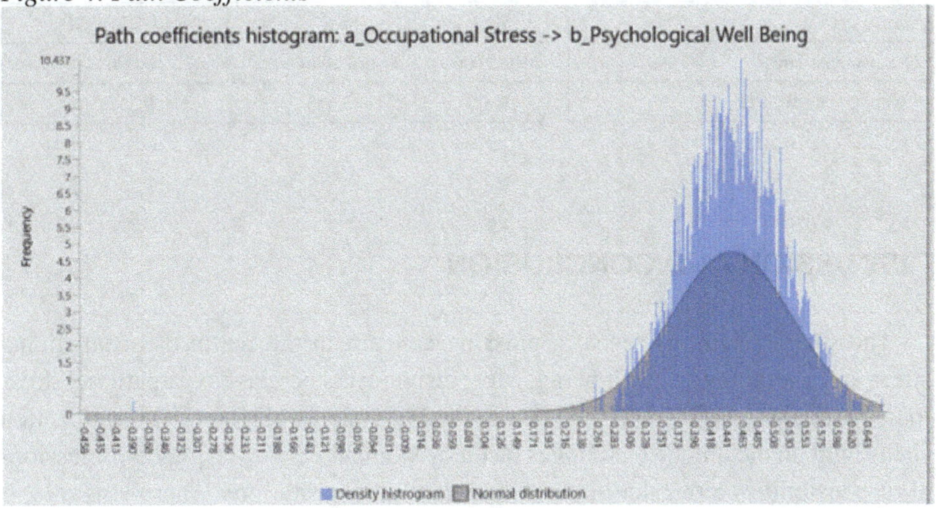

Table 8 presents the analysis findings of R^2 and f^2 of endogenous constructs. First, the relationship between occupational stress and psychological well being yields an R^2 of 0.44, indicating a substantial effect size. Next, the relationship between occupational stress and psychological well being yields an f^2 of 0.79, indicating a large effect size.

Table 8. R^2 and f^2 of endogenous constructs

Construct	Psychological Well Being	
	R^2	f^2
Occupational Stress		
Psychological Well Being	0.44	0.79

In addition to assessing the magnitude of the R^2 value as a criterion for prediction accuracy, it is crucial to examine the Stone-Geisser Q^2 value (Stone, 1974; Geisser, 1974) as a criterion for prediction relevance. The Q^2 value of the latent variable in the PLS path model was obtained using a blindfolding procedure. Table 9 displays the Q^2 values of endogenous constructs. The Q^2 value of 0.311 demonstrates acceptable predictive relevance.

Table 9. Q^2 of endogenous constructs

Construct	SSO	SSE	Q^2 (=1-SSE/SSO)
Occupational Stress	1062.000	1062.000	0.000
Psychological Well Being	708.000	487.556	0.311

DISCUSSION AND CONCLUSION

The study's findings reveal a pressing concern in the realm of occupational stress and psychological well being. Most respondents perceive occupational stress to be particularly high among women in the Malaysian workforce. This perception sheds light on the unique challenges faced by women, who often juggle professional responsibilities alongside societal and familial expectations. These stressors, if unmanaged, can lead to a decline in psychological well being. These results are consistent with previous studies by Mensah (2021), Mohamad et al. (2015) and Acoba (2024) which suggest that, under certain conditions, occupational stress may contribute to decline in psychological well.

This study develops a unique explanatory framework to examine the relationship occupational stress and psychological well being among women working in organisations in Malaysia. Using bootstrap analysis through SmartPLS software, the findings confirm that occupational stress is a key predictor of women's psychological well being. This research is among the earliest empirical efforts to specifically highlight the extent to which job-related stress affects the mental well-being of women in Malaysia's organisations. These findings are consistent with various 21st-century studies that have examined occupational stress across both Western and Asian contexts. For women, high workloads, dual responsibilities between career and family, and structural constraints within organisations often exacerbate the psychosocial pressures they face. The implications of occupational stress for women are multifaceted and can have serious consequences not only for individuals but also for organisations and society at large. Addressing this issue requires a holistic approach involving the identification and reduction of stressors, the provision of appropriate psychosocial support, and the creation of a work environment that is inclusive, supportive, and gender sensitive. In conclusion, this study finds that the inability to manage occupational stress among women can significantly undermine their psychological well being, ultimately affecting the efficiency, motivation, and long-term sustainability of organisations in Malaysia.

STRATEGIES TO REDUCE OCCUPATIONAL STRESS

Reducing occupational stress is essential for maintaining psychological well being. Here are some strategies that can help:

1) Promote work-life balance: Encourage flexible working hours, remote work options, and regular breaks to prevent burnout.
2) Enhance communication: Foster open and transparent communication between employees and management to reduce misunderstandings and clarify expectations.
3) Encourage supportive leadership: Train leaders to recognize signs of stress and provide emotional and practical support to their teams.
4) Offer stress management programs: Provide access to workshops, counseling services, or wellness programs that teach coping techniques such as mindfulness, meditation, or time management.
5) Clearly define roles and responsibilities: Reduce role ambiguity by ensuring that each employee understands their job scope and performance expectations.
6) Promote a positive work environment: Cultivate a respectful, inclusive, and collaborative culture to reduce tension and conflict in the workplace.
7) Provide opportunities for career development: Help employees feel valued and motivated by offering training, mentoring, and advancement opportunities.
8) Encourage regular physical activity: Support physical wellness initiatives such as gym memberships, yoga classes, or walking meetings.
9) Implement fair workload distribution: Ensure tasks are evenly distributed and achievable within the given timeframes to reduce pressure and fatigue.
10) Recognize and reward efforts: Acknowledge achievements and contributions to boost morale and job satisfaction.

REFERENCES

Acoba, E. F. (2024). Social support and mental health: The mediating role of perceived stress. *Frontiers in Psychology*, *15*, 1330720. Advance online publication. DOI: 10.3389/fpsyg.2024.1330720 PMID: 38449744

AlAteeq, D., AlNujaim, S. M., & AlGharbi, A. H. (2025). Prevalence of depression and anxiety among working women in Saudi Arabia: Psychosocial and perinatal correlates. *BMC Women's Health*, *25*(228), 228. Advance online publication. DOI: 10.1186/s12905-025-03776-2 PMID: 40375291

An, H., Gu, X., Obrenovic, B., & Godinic, D. (2023). The role of job insecurity, social media exposure, and job stress in predicting anxiety among white-collar employees. *Psychology Research and Behavior Management*, *16*, 3303–3318. DOI: 10.2147/PRBM.S416100 PMID: 37614323

Atiku, S. O., & Van Wyk, E. (2024). Leadership practices and work engagement in higher education: The mediating role of job demands-resources. *SAGE Open*, *14*(1), 21582440241233378. DOI: 10.1177/21582440241233378

Bakker, A. B., & de Vries, J. D. (2020). Job demands–resources theory and self-regulation: New explanations and remedies for job burnout. *Anxiety, Stress, and Coping*, *34*(1), 1–21. DOI: 10.1080/10615806.2020.1797695 PMID: 32856957

Bakker, A. B., & de Vries, J. D. (2021). Job Demands–Resources theory and self-regulation: New explanations and remedies for job burnout. *Anxiety, Stress, and Coping*, *34*(1), 1–21. DOI: 10.1080/10615806.2020.1797695 PMID: 32856957

Barki, H., & Hartwick, J. (2001). Interpersonal conflict and its management in information system development. *Management Information Systems Quarterly*, *25*(2), 195–228. DOI: 10.2307/3250929

Birko, S., Dove, E. S., & Özdemir, V. (2015). A delphi technology foresight study: Mapping social construction of scientific evidence on metagenomics tests for water safety. *PLoS One*, *10*(6), e0129706. DOI: 10.1371/journal.pone.0129706 PMID: 26066837

Bruce, L., Hrymak, V., Bruce, M., & Byrne, S. (2024). Navigating interpersonal conflicts in healthcare settings: A study of nurse-physician relationships during global health crises. *International Journal of Nursing Studies*, *128*, 104155.

Creswell, J. W., & Plano Clark, V. L. (2011). *Designing and conducting mixed methods research* (2nd ed.). Sage Publications.

Darvishmotevali, M., & Ali, F. (2020). Job insecurity, subjective well-being and job performance: The moderating role of psychological capital. *International Journal of Hospitality Management, 87*, 102462. Advance online publication. DOI: 10.1016/j.ijhm.2020.102462

Geisser, S. (1974). A predictive approach to the random effect model. *Biometrika, 61*(1), 101–107. DOI: 10.1093/biomet/61.1.101

Hair, J., Hult, G. T. M., Ringle, C. M., & Sarstedt, M. (2017). *A primer on partial least squares structural equation modeling (PLS-SEM)* (2nd ed.). SAGE Publications Inc.

Hellhammer, D. H., Wust, S., & Kudielka, B. M. (2009). Salivary cortisol as a biomarker in stress research. *Psychoneuroendocrinology, 34*(2), 163–171. DOI: 10.1016/j.psyneuen.2008.10.026 PMID: 19095358

Hu, L., & Bentler, P. M. (1998). Fit indices in covariance structure modeling: Sensitivity to underparameterized model misspecification. *Psychological Methods, 3*(4), 424–453. DOI: 10.1037/1082-989X.3.4.424

Institute for Public Health. (2024). *National Health and Morbidity Survey (NHMS) 2023: Non-communicable diseases and healthcare demand - Key findings.*

Junça Silva, A., & Rodrigues, R. (2024). Affective mechanisms linking role ambiguity to employee turnover. *The International Journal of Organizational Analysis, 32*(11), 1–18. DOI: 10.1108/IJOA-08-2023-3891

Kacmar, K. M., & Carlson, D. S. (1997). Further validation of the Perception of Politics Scale (POPs): A multiple sample investigation. *Journal of Management, 23*(5), 627–658. DOI: 10.1177/014920639702300502

Kostelić, K., Gonan Božac, M., & Paulišić, M. (2024). Exploring interpersonal conflicts within the JD-R model: Aggregation and validation in the context of elementary school employees in Croatia. *Cogent Business & Management, 11*(1), 2370451. Advance online publication. DOI: 10.1080/23311975.2024.2370451

Lazarus, J. (2000). *Stress relief & relaxation techniques.* NTC/Contemporary Publishing Group Inc., Keats Publishing.

Lazarus, R. S. (1991). *Emotion and adaptation.* Oxford University Press. DOI: 10.1093/oso/9780195069945.001.0001

Ma, J., Xu, L., & Zhang, X. (2025). Work–family conflict, overwork and mental health of female employees in China. *Frontiers in Public Health, 13*, 1483746. DOI: 10.3389/fpubh.2025.1483746 PMID: 40241940

Mayer, K. (2024, October 8). Women are experiencing a mental health crisis. What that means for employers. *SHRM*. Retrieved from https://www.shrm.org

Mensah, A. (2021). Job stress and mental well-being among working men and women in Europe: The mediating role of social support. *International Journal of Environmental Research and Public Health, 18*(5), 2494. DOI: 10.3390/ijerph18052494 PMID: 33802439

Mohamad, N. I., Ismail, A., Mohamad Rozi, M. S. A., & Ahmad, S. (2015). Tekanan kerja dan perkaitannya dengan kesihatan pekerja: Kajian empirikal sebuah kontinjen polis di Semenanjung Malaysia. *Geografia : Malaysian Journal of Society and Space, 11*(10), 63–75.

Patton, M. Q. (2002). *Qualitative research and evaluation methods* (3rd ed.). Sage Publications.

Ringle, C. M., Sarstedt, M., Mitchell, R., & Gudergan, S. P. (2019). Partial least squares structural equation modeling in HRM research. *International Journal of Human Resource Management, 31*(12), 1617–1643. DOI: 10.1080/09585192.2017.1416655

Sekaran, U., & Bougie, R. (2010). *Research methods for business: A skill-building approach* (5th ed.). John Wiley & Sons.

Selye, H. (1987). *Stress without distress.* Transworld.

Shaikh, E., Watto, W. A., & Tunio, M. N. (2021). Impact of authentic leadership on organizational citizenship behavior by using the mediating effect of psychological ownership. *Etikonomi, 21*(1), 89–102. DOI: 10.15408/etk.v21i1.18968

Sillars, A., & Parry, D. (1982). Stress, cognition, and communication in interpersonal conflicts. *Communication Research, 9*(2), 201–226. DOI: 10.1177/009365082009002002

Spector, P. E., & Bruk-Lee, V. (2008). Conflict, health, and well-being. In De Dreu, C. K. W., & Gelfand, M. J. (Eds.), *The psychology of conflict and conflict management in organizations* (pp. 267–288). Taylor & Francis Group/Lawrence Erlbaum Associates.

Stone, M. (1974). Cross-validatory choice and assessment of statistical predictions. *Journal of the Royal Statistical Society. Series B, Statistical Methodology, 36*(2), 111–133. DOI: 10.1111/j.2517-6161.1974.tb00994.x

Viertiö, S., Kiviruusu, O., Piirtola, M., Kaprio, J., Korhonen, T., Marttunen, M., & Suvisaari, J. (2021). Factors contributing to psychological distress in the working population, with a special reference to gender difference. *BMC Public Health*, *21*(1), 611. DOI: 10.1186/s12889-021-10560-y PMID: 33781240

Wharne, S. (2021). How is distress understood in existential philosophies and can phenomenological therapeutic practices be "evidence-based"? *Theory & Psychology*, *31*(2), 273–289. DOI: 10.1177/0959354320964586

Wright, B. D. (1996). Reliability and separation. *Rasch Measurement Transactions*, *9*(4), 472.

Chapter 14
Soulful Work:
Enhancing Wellbeing and Organizational Performance Through Spirituality and Ethical AI

Kritika Ohri
https://orcid.org/0009-0003-7942-4569
Department of Commerce, University School of Business, Chandigarh University, Mohali, India

Hitakshi Dutta
https://orcid.org/0000-0002-2515-9179
Chandigarh University, Mohali, India

ABSTRACT

This chapter presents a comprehensive framework—Soulful Work—that combines workplace spirituality, emotional resilience ("soul strength"), and ethically developed artificial intelligence systems in a time of rapid technological change, emotional burnout, and mounting pressures on women professionals. Leveraging multidisciplinary literature from organizational behaviour, gender studies, digital ethics, and psychology, the chapter examines how spiritual intelligence, reflective practices, and AI-powered wellness tools can collectively enhance employee engagement, psychological safety, and cultural inclusivity. Particularly focused on the lived experiences of women navigating midlife transitions, including menopause, caregiving, and identity changes—life phases sometimes outside the purview of conventional wellness practices—this chapter. It introduces the concept of soul strength as a form of emotional and spiritual resilience supported by digital tools and human leadership.

DOI: 10.4018/979-8-3373-2970-3.ch014

1. INTRODUCTION

Supporting employees' overall well-being—that which extends beyond mere physical and mental health to encompass emotional, social, and spiritual aspects—is becoming increasingly critical in today's complex workplace. Organizations that tackle spiritual elements—alongside physical and mental health—experience enhanced employee innovation, performance, and engagement, according to the McKinsey Holistic Health Framework (McKinsey.com; onlinelibrary.wiley.com). Navigating life events, including career changes, caregiving, and menopause, can increase emotional stress and challenge women's sense of identity—areas sometimes neglected by traditional wellness programs.

Concurrent with this, the movement toward workplace spirituality—defined as meaningful work within a loving and compassionate community—has gathered steam since the early 20th century (emerald.com; en.wikipedia.org). Workplace spirituality promotes organizational commitment, employee engagement, job satisfaction, and resilience. It is described in a recent scoping review as including compassion, interconnectedness, and meaning in professional life (arxiv.org; journals.sagepub.com). Particularly under stress, individuals with intense workplace spirituality exhibit greater emotional balance and endurance, according to further research (sajip.co.za; onlinelibrary.wiley.com).

Although these well-known advantages abound, Spirituality remains underrepresented in most corporate wellness programs—especially those targeting the unique emotional and spiritual needs of women. Concurrently, the advent of artificial intelligence (AI) in the workplace—from guided mindfulness apps to mood-checking chatbots—has created fresh opportunities for meeting emotional and spiritual needs. Early-stage "Spiritual.AI" projects demonstrate how combining ancient knowledge with modern intelligence can offer personalized spiritual support (researchgate.net). Through conversational agents designed for mental health and emotional insight, similar artificial intelligence applications are already providing empathy-driven care.

This chapter presents the concept of "Soulful Work," a human-centred model that combines ethically designed AI support systems, emotional-spiritual resilience ("soul strength"), and workplace spirituality. Especially for women in mid-career or navigating health-related issues, we incorporate these components to enhance employee wellness and boost organisational performance.

Companies are beginning to understand how closely emotional, spiritual, and psychological wellness interact with productivity and creativity. As diversity, equity, and inclusion become increasingly important, it's essential to acknowledge and support the different paths to well-being women take throughout their lifetimes. Workplace systems must grow to accommodate not only women's outward professional roles but also their internal emotional and spiritual realities as they negotiate difficult life transitions, including pregnancy, caring responsibilities, menopause, and identity changes.

One interesting prism through which to approach this difficulty is workplace spirituality. Organizations can help employees—especially women—feel grounded and valued during times of change by including professional life with purpose, compassion, and connection. This chapter examines how workplace spirituality enhances women's overall well-being, particularly during emotional and identity-shifting transitions. It also examines how the the ethical design of AI-driven tools can support these needs, thereby enabling settings where daily work life can incorporate emotional reflection, resilience, and spiritual development.

The concept of "soul strength"—a term we use to characterise the emotional and spiritual resilience that employees can acquire when guided by an ethical workplace culture and conscious leadership—lays the groundwork for this model. Soul strength acknowledges the part meaning, inner peace, and emotional integrity play, not only as grit or toughness. Given the emotional work and social expectations women often carry both inside and outside the workplace, this kind of support is especially crucial for them.

Studies repeatedly show that workers who find meaning in their work—and who feel their values are respected—report lower burnout and higher job satisfaction (Milliman et al., 2003; Ashmos & Duchon, 2000). Women in especially demanding or caring roles will find great relevance in these results. Workplaces that provide space for introspection, empathy, and value alignment help produce what we call "soulful workplaces"—organisations that are successful not because they are mechanistic, but rather because they are profoundly human.

Regarding women's health, for instance, corporate wellness programs sometimes misinterpret or overlook life events like menopause. Menopause, however, is a profound identity change that often entails anxiety, grief, rebirth, and even empowerment—not only a physical event (Hunter & Rendall, 2007). An office with spiritual sensitivity would view this change as an opportunity for growth rather than a disturbance. Providing women with space for spiritual introspection, peer support, and compassionate communication enables them to incorporate such changes in their sense of self at work.

Parallel with this, we investigate the transformative power of technology—more specifically, how artificial intelligence might be applied to enhance spiritual and emotional care rather than to dehumanise. Although artificial intelligence is sometimes considered cold or impersonal, new generations of emotionally intelligent technologies show excellent possibilities. Spiritual routines and emotional introspection can be supported by tools, including guided meditation apps, mood-checking bots, and journaling assistants. When these systems are built with ethical foresight—that is, with trust, consent, privacy, and cultural sensitivity—they can give workers individualized, significant on-demand support.

These artificial intelligence tools should enhance human connection rather than replace it since they provide just-in-time assistance for spiritual and emotional health. Digital systems can be created in a spiritually conscious company to mirror the values of the company, so supporting not only efficiency but also alignment with more basic human needs.

Growing this environment depends much on leadership. Leaders with spiritual intelligence—that is, those who lead with empathy, integrity, self-awareness, and moral clarity—are much sought for in organizations (Fry, 2003.). Leaders who are spiritually tuned are more likely to advocate employee welfare, promote diversity, and create environments in which people feel free to show vulnerability. For women especially, who might be reluctant to share spiritual or emotional difficulties in concern of stigma or professional consequences, this is especially important. Leaders who live with authenticity and compassion help to build a society in which inner wellness and emotional openness are not only accepted but also praised.

This chapter presents a thorough, multidisciplinary framework including Spirituality, emotional intelligence, artificial intelligence, and inclusive design into a single approach for workplace wellbeing. Inspired by organizational behavior, psychology, gender studies, ethical artificial intelligence design, and ethical behavior, we propose a "Soulful Design Model"—a framework whereby meaning and technology interact to produce healing, empowering professional settings.

This chapter will specifically highlight:

The idea of soul strength as a basic component in employee welfare;

A framework for digital spirituality tools and artificial intelligence-supported emotional care;

The part spiritually intelligent leadership plays in fostering workplace empathy;

A committed study of women's midlife changes—menopause, for example—supported by spiritual care techniques;

The organizational ROI of including emotional sensitivity and Spirituality into corporate culture.

This chapter adds to a new vision of work whereby performance and wellbeing are not at odds but rather mutually reinforcing by centring women's experiences and combining modern artificial intelligence tools with timeless spiritual wisdom. Organizations have both an opportunity and a responsibility to make sure that these technologies serve the human soul, not only the business goal as artificial intelligence keeps changing professional environments.

2. THEORETICAL FOUNDATION

Strong theoretical background offers the framework to grasp and combine ethical artificial intelligence support, emotional resilience, and workplace spirituality into a coherent model for employee welfare. With an eye toward how these components interact in the framework of women's workplace experiences, this section investigates their conceptual and empirical grounding.

2.1 Workplace Spirituality: Dimensions and Definition

Workplace spirituality is the awareness among staff members that they search for ethical alignment, meaning, and connection in their work life. It combines a feeling of community and meaningful work with personal inner life (Ashmos & Duchon, 2000). Early in the 2000s, the idea attracted interest as researchers contended that Spirituality at work improves job satisfaction, involvement, and psychological safety (Milliman et al., 2003; Giacalone & Jurkowicz, 2003).

Important aspects of occupational Spirituality consist in:

- Meaningful Work: This is the conviction that one's efforts have social and personal value. When workers see their jobs as intentional, they become more involved (Milliman et al., 2003).
- A sense of community inside the company fosters trust and teamwork by means of connectedness and belongingness (Petchsawang & Duchon, 2009).
- Transcendence is the ability to relate to something more than oneself—that is, a higher purpose, shared values, or group project (Fry, 2003).

Workplace spirituality has little bearing on religion specifically. Rather, it captures the human search for authenticity, connectedness, and meaning (Krishnakumar & Neck, 2002). Spirituality becomes a common ground for inclusive values and wellbeing practices in ever more varied and hybrid workplaces.

Emerging research also connects workplace spirituality with good organizational outcomes including ethical behavior, reduced turnover, and improved employee wellbeing (Rego & Cunha, 2008). These advantages are especially noticeable when spiritual values are ingrained in cultural customs and leadership.

2.2 Soul Strength: Spiritual and Emotional Resilience

Extending the framework of workplace spirituality, this paper presents the idea of soul strength—defined as the emotional and spiritual resilience that helps people to retain dignity, meaning, and hope during stress, transition, or adversity.

This idea combines wisdom from two intersecting fields:

- Spiritual resilience is the capacity to keep inner peace, purpose, and ethical grounding under difficult circumstances (Pargament, 1997). Spiritual resilience helps people to see demanding events through a prism of meaning and hope.
- Emotional intelligence (EI) is one's capacity to recognize, control, and communicate emotions in ways that support good social relationships and lower burnout (Goleman, 1995). Studies of spiritual activities including journaling, mindfulness, and introspection reveal how well EI is enhanced (Abe et al., 2013).

Women negotiating high-stress events including menopause, caregiving, or midlife career transitions particularly need soul strength. Studies indicate that among women in the workforce, emotional labor and gender expectations often cause psychological stress (Hochschild, 1983; Simpson & Lewis, 2005). Soul strength functions here as a buffer, supporting self-worth, clarity, and endurance.

Moreover, emotionally and spiritually strong people are more able to match their personal values with organizational goals, so promoting a stronger feeling of purpose (Howard & Wellins, 2009). Practices including meditation, value clarification, and spiritual coaching help to increase this capacity (Tisdell, 2003).

An example vignette for developing soul strength

49-year-old senior project manager Maya of a multinational tech company recently started having the cognitive fog, anxiety, and emotional sensitivity sometimes linked with perimenopause. She stayed silent for months, worried her younger male colleagues would reject or misinterpret her symptoms. She was managing her mother's early-onset dementia and helping her teenage daughter through anxiety at the same time, all the while driving a high-stakes digital transformation project at her company.

Maya started using a guided journaling app with tailored prompts based on spiritual contemplation since she felt emotionally split. The instrument probes things like: What value most alive in you right now? and this week where can you show yourself compassion? The app helped her externalize and consider internal pressures by providing gentle affirmations and mirrored back insights with nonjudging tone.

Maya started to specifically name her feelings in team environments over time. On days her energy dropped, she asked for flexible scheduling and started five-minute "pause circles" with her team—a five-minute meditation before meetings that gave time for breathwork or intention-setting. Remarkably, her sensitivity promoted closer team unity. Others started to share their challenges as well, so shattering the silence around stress in society.

Maya's story shows how soul strength—that which combines emotional awareness with spiritual resilience—is embodied. She matched her basic values of compassion, authenticity, and care instead of pushing on. Maya moved from loss to quiet empowerment with little structural change but deliberate emotional support—digital and human.

2.3 AI as an Emotional and Spiritual Wellbeing Supportive Tool

Although Spirituality and soul strength are naturally human experiences, new research points to ethical design of artificial intelligence (AI) supporting emotional and spiritual wellbeing.

These days, artificial intelligence applications in workplace wellness consist in tools like:

- Like Wysa or Woebot, which provide cognitive-behavioral interventions and emotional check-ins using natural language processing, mental health chatbots also (Inkster et al., 2018).
- Apps for guided mindfulness like Headspace and Calm combine emotional tracking, spiritual reflections, and breathing exercises.
- AI-assisted journaling apps enable users to track moods, set intentions, and consider values, so improving emotional insight and resilience (Pfeifer & Scholz, 2021).

Emerging in the field of "Spiritual.AI" is how technology might support ethical alignment, introspection, and purpose. Some prototypes, for instance, use artificial intelligence to provide wisdom from many spiritual traditions, so guiding consumers across moral or emotional conundrums (Pfeiffer & Scholz, 2021).

These developments, meanwhile, raise ethical questions. Researchers underline that AI wellness tools have to respect openness, consent, privacy, and psychological safety (Jobin et al., 2019). Poorly crafted such tools run the danger of trivializing spiritual experiences or feeding prejudices.

Developers working with psychologists, ethicists, and spiritual care professionals will help artificial intelligence to be in line with soulful wellbeing. Creating systems that improve rather than compromise human dignity depends mostly on user-centered, culturally sensitive design processes (Floridi et al., 2018).

2.4 Including AI, Soul Strength, and Spirituality in Companies

Workplace spirituality, soul strength, and AI wellbeing tools taken together form a synergistic model for holistic organizational care—what this chapter refers to as Soulful Work.

This integration offers advantages such as:

- Employees find meaning when their personal values complement the goals of their company. By providing reflective prompts or mood insights, AI tools can help to reinforce this.
- Women experiencing menopause or caring roles gain from empathetic policies, spiritual support groups, and emotional artificial intelligence companions.
- Leaders with strong spiritual intelligence inspire compassion, vision, and integrity—building trusting environments (Fry, 2003).
- Particularly in remote or hybrid work environments where conventional HR solutions may not be sufficient, artificial intelligence systems make support available in real-time.

This model provides a framework for women especially that validates emotional complexity, spiritual depth, and identity transitions at work—moving beyond simple inclusion to meaningful engagement.

2.5 Constraints and Future Directions

Though promising, including Spirituality and artificial intelligence into the workplace begs important unresolved questions:

-Are digital tools able to really reflect the depth of personal spiritual connection?
-How might companies guarantee diversity in spiritual beliefs?
-What long-term psychological effects might artificial intelligence-guided emotional support have?

Scholars demand multidisciplinary research to assess the efficacy, hazards, and user impressions of these instruments (Eubanks, 2021). For HR and tech developers equally, ethical AI governance and spiritual literacy have to become fundamental skills.

3. LITERATURE REVIEW

3.1 Introduction

Particularly with regard to women's experiences and the part digital tools play in supporting holistic health, the junction of emotional and spiritual wellness in the workplace has become an essential area of research. Professionals search for meaning, authenticity, and emotional resilience in their workplaces as organizational systems get more dynamic and sophisticated. With an especially focus on gender-sensitive and technologically-integrated approaches, this literature review investigates the theoretical underpinnings, major findings, and critical arguments around emotional and spiritual wellbeing at work. It also points up significant research gaps, which prepares readers for a closer look at how artificial intelligence (AI) might support working women's emotional and spiritual well-being.

3.2 Describing Spiritual and Emotional Wellbeing

Emotional wellbeing is the capacity of a person to control their emotions, handle stress, and keep a good mental state. It covers emotional awareness, control, and the ability to create favorable relationships (Ryff & Keyes, 1995; Gross, 2002). Though more abstract, spiritual wellbeing consists in a sense of purpose, connectedness, and alignment with basic values, usually expressed by means of practices including meditation, thanksgiving, and community involvement (Pargament, 1997; Fisher, 2011).

Though historically examined separately, academics are realizing the interdependence of emotional and spiritual aspects. Emmons (1999), for instance, suggested that emotional coping and ethical decision-making are improved by spiritual intelligence, a type of intelligence including the capacity to access deep meaning and values. In similar vein, Diener et al. (2018) contend that, especially in high-stress settings like the modern workplace, emotional stability and spiritual fulfilment are mutually reinforcing.

3.3 Work Emotional Wellness

Job satisfaction, resilience, productivity, and general mental health all relate to emotional wellbeing in the workplace. Bakker and Demerouti's (2007) Job Demands-Resources (JD-R) model holds that employees who have enough psychological resources—such as autonomy, feedback, and support—to buffer against workplace demands will maintain emotional wellbeing. Defined by Goleman (1995) as the capacity to see, understand, and control emotions, emotional intelligence (EI) has also been shown to correlate favorably with stress management, teamwork, and leadership effectiveness (Cherniss, 2010).

Discrimination, imposter syndrome, and the double burden of professional and caring obligations are among the emotional pressures women in the workplace sometimes face (Hochschild & Machung, 2012). Unless companies create supportive cultures that inspire emotional expression and self-care, these stresses can cause emotional burnout. Particularly among female professionals, mindfulness practices, peer support groups, and flexible work schedules have been shown to enhance emotional wellbeing (Good et al., 2016; Kabat-Zinn, 2003).

3.4 Workplace Spirituality and Its Function in Wellbeing

Workplace spirituality is the awareness of employees' inner life, encouragement of a feeling of purpose, and promotion of values including integrity, compassion, and interconnectedness inside an organization (Ashmos & Duchon, 2000). Though it's not always religious, it's about a search for wholeness and meaning in one's work.

Studies find that workplace spirituality improves job satisfaction, ethical behavior, and employee engagement (Milliman et al., 2003; Giacalone & Jurkowicz, 2003). Particularly women have claimed to keep resilience and clarity among professional challenges by using spiritual practices including prayer, meditation, journaling, or nature connection (Dirkx, 2001; Bierema, 2002). Organizations that respect spiritual values—such as authenticity, service, and growth—create settings that promote not only productivity but also psychological and spiritual wellbeing (Rego & Pina e Cunha, 2008).

3.5 Digital and artificial intelligence tools for spiritual and emotional wellbeing

The fast advancement of digital technologies and AI-driven tools offers fresh opportunities to support mental health and wellbeing. For uses including mood tracking, mindfulness training, cognitive-behavioral support, and stress management, wearable technologies, mobile apps, and AI-based chatbots have been embraced increasingly (Fitzpatrick et al., 2017; Inkster et al., 2018).

Using natural language processing and evidence-based psychological frameworks, AI tools such as Woebot and Wysa offer consumers real-time mental health support. Particularly among women and young professionals who want easily available, private support, these tools have shown good results in lowering symptoms of anxiety and depression (Inkster et al., 2018). Moreover, artificial intelligence can customize treatments to users' emotional states by means of real-time data-based guided meditations, personal affirmations, or spiritual cues (Topol, 2019).

Still, there are questions about ethical data use, algorithmic bias, and the limits of machine empathy. Critics caution that if not built with inclusive datasets and feminist ethics in mind, overreliance on artificial intelligence could depersonalize support or reproduce gender stereotypes (Criado Perez, 2019; Mittelstadt et al., 2016). Notwithstanding this, there is growing awareness of AI's possible complementing role—when used deliberately—for improving emotional intelligence and spiritual reflection in the workplace.

3.6 Gender-sensitive Strategies for Workplace Spiritual and Emotional Wellbeing

Especially in the workplace, gender significantly influences how people experience and communicate emotional and spiritual wellbeing. Particularly women negotiate special psychosocial pressures including gendered expectations, emotional labor, and pressures on work-life balance that can profoundly affect their inner wellbeing and spiritual resilience (Gilligan, 1982; Hochschild, 1983). For these reasons, gender-sensitive models are indispensable in both scholarly research and pragmatic interventions meant to assist in spiritual and emotional wellness in the workplace.

Scholars like Acker (1990) and Ely & Meyerson (2000) have demonstrated how organizational cultures—especially those anchored in patriarchal norms—may marginalize emotional expression and undervalue "care-based" or intuitive leadership styles—qualities more usually associated with women. These structural dynamics can cause women to hide aspects of their real selves, so distorting their inner values from their professional identity. From a gender-informed standpoint, workplace spirituality can provide a road to reestablishing agency in the face of institutional limitations and rediscovering one's central goal.

Women looking for alignment between their roles and inner purpose have shown especially resonance for practices including narrative coaching, values clarification, and community-based spiritual dialogue (Bierema, 2002; Dirkx, 2001). If not balanced by soul care and emotional self-compassion, emotional labor—mostly borne by women—may cause burnout. Training in mindfulness and spiritual resilience has proved successful in helping women leaders and caregivers to feel less emotionally tired (Good et al., 2016).

Examined through a gender perspective also is the integration of artificial intelligence into spiritual and emotional support tools. Algorithms taught on male-centered data could provide women unsuitable or insufficient support. Relational dynamics, intersectionality, and context-specific experiences (Criado Perez, 2019) all must be considered in AI wellness tools.

3.7 Gaps in the Literature

Even if workplace spirituality and digital wellness are becoming more and more popular, some important gaps still exist:

-Spiritual Dimensions Under-Theorized: Emotional depth, purpose, and ethical clarity combined the idea of "soul strength" is not well-examined in empirical study.
-Gender Nuance in AI Tools: Often focusing just on surface-level mental health metrics, most digital wellness tools lack gender-sensitive frameworks or spiritual depth.
-Integration of AI and Workplace Spirituality: Particularly from the standpoint of women users, few studies investigate actual uses of artificial intelligence in workplace spirituality.
-Research sometimes generalizes "women" without examining how race, class, sexuality, and Spirituality interact to shape particular experiences.
-Western-Centric Bias: Many times, individualistic and secular, ideas of Spirituality in the workplace overlook community-based, ancestral, or ceremonial spiritual expression.

Future studies must thus use inclusive, participatory, multidisciplinary approaches that highlight women's voices and experiences—especially in respect to digital support systems, emotional labour, and spiritual practices in the workplace.

4. METHODOLOGY

4.1 Research Design: Method of Narrative Review

Using a narrative review approach, this paper investigates the junction of women's wellbeing, occupational Spirituality, emotional resilience (soul strength), and ethically built artificial intelligence support systems. When conceptual and theoretical research is aimed at integrating current material, spotting knowledge gaps, and suggesting new frameworks or models, a narrative review is especially appropriate (Ferrari, 2015).

Unlike more rigid and quantitative systematic reviews or meta-analyses, the narrative review approach lets a wider and more interpretive study of difficult, multidisciplinary subjects (Greenhalgh et al., 2018). In this setting, where themes span organizational behavior, psychology, gender studies, and digital ethics, a narrative review helps a deep, comprehensive investigation of current knowledge to generate new theoretical insight.

This method is in line with the guidelines described by Demiris (2004), who advises narrative reviews for conceptual synthesis across newly developing sectors, particularly those involving technology and human-centered disciplines.

4.2 Review's Objectives

The following goals helped to direct the narrative review:

1. To investigate and combine research on workplace spirituality and how it affects employee welfare and involvement.
2. To look at the idea of emotional and spiritual resilience—also known as "soul strength"—in connection to women's life and career changes.
3. To investigate how ethically built artificial intelligence systems might meet spiritual and emotional needs at work.
4. To suggest an integrated conceptual framework—the Soulful Work model—combining these spheres for improving women's whole welfare at work.

4.3 Search Strategy and Data Sources

Scholarly sources including book chapters, dissertations, conference proceedings, and credible organizational reports—e.g., McKinsey, Deloitte, WHO—were included in the review along with peer-reviewed journal articles. Searched in the databases were: Scopus, Web of Science, PubMed, Google Scholar, SAGE Journals, Wiley Online Library, Emerald insight, IEEE Xplore (for studies on AI ethics), ResearchGate and arXiv (for new works on Spiritual AI)

Search keywords applied included combinations of: "Workspace spirituality", "Spiritual intelligence"; "Women and emotional resilience", "Menopause and working identity", "AI and wellbeing", "ethical AI design", "Soul strength,", "Digital spiritualism", "Feminist organizational theory".

With an emphasis on recent (2015–2025) scholarship for technological themes, Boolean operators and filtering were used to narrow results to English-language, full-text publications published mostly between 2000 and 2025.

4.4 Including and excluding criteria

The development of the selection criteria guarantees the relevance, credibility, and conceptual rigidity of the incorporated sources.

Inclusive criteria:

Studies concentrated on employee welfare, particularly with regard to women's working conditions.

Articles debating emotional and spiritual aspects of employment.

Research on artificial intelligence tools applied in mental health, coaching, or wellness.

Academic books, expert reports, peer-reviewed journal papers.

Papers pertinent to the goals either theoretically, conceptual, or empirical.

Exclusionary rules:

Articles concentrated just on religious Spirituality without reference to the workplace.

Studies limited to physiological interventions devoid of psychological or spiritual component.

Non-academic or anecdotal sources lacking scholarly value.

4.5 Procedure of Theme Analysis and Synthesis

Following the retrieval and curation of almost 200 papers initially, a qualitative thematic synthesis approach was used. This comprises:

1. Titles and abstracts were checked to weed out pointless information at first screening.
2. Selected papers were closely read in order to pinpoint arguments and central themes.
3. Key categories were used to arrange literature:
    - Workplace spirituality and worthwhile labour
    - Menopause, caregiving, career changes—women's emotional transitions
    - spiritual intelligence and leadership
    - Tools for wellbeing driven by artificial intelligence
    - Ethical design in workplace technologies and digital health
4. Themes were spun together into a coherent story, charting intersections and pointing up theoretical gaps.

This process made it possible to create the Soulful Work model as a whole reaction to the difficulties women encounter in preserving emotional and spiritual wellness in contemporary corporations.

4.6 Reflexivity and Investigator Positioning

A reflexive approach was kept throughout the review process as this study crosses with gender, Spirituality, and ethics. The researcher recognized the positionality inherent in reading literature on women's spiritual-emotional well-being, especially in settings where such dimensions are excluded or misinterpreted in professional conversation (Cunliffe, 2009). When available, care was taken to incorporate a variety of points of view including feminist organizational theory, spiritual psychology, and indigenous worldviews.

4.7 Ethical Aspects

Though human subjects were not used in the study, ethical guidelines were followed in choosing and reading over the material. Appropriate credit was given to sources, and delicate subjects including menopause, emotional labor, and artificial intelligence ethics were handled with respect. With reference to ethical AI guidelines, including concepts of ethical AI, the proposed use of AI technologies in spiritual and emotional support settings was assessed, Including principles of:

-Transparency
-Privacy and consent
-Sensitivity for cultures
-Non-expositional design

4.8 Limitations of the Methodology

Like every narrative review, the study suffers certain restrictions:

Subjectivity: The synthesis's interpretive character might bring researcher prejudice.

Unlike systematic reviews, the study does not follow thorough search strategies using non-systematic sampling.

The multidisciplinary nature of the work means that some particular empirical details (such as studies on clinical menopause) might not be fully addressed.

But the flexibility and conceptual richness narrative reviews provide—especially when building new models across difficult and understudied fields—balance these restrictions.

4.9 Summary

This chapter covered the narrative review approach used in this work to synthesize and conceptualize a Soulful Work model including ethical artificial intelligence support systems, emotional resilience (soul strength), and workplace spirituality. Based on careful reading of pertinent material, the narrative review method let for a multidisciplinary, theory-building process. This approach helps to create a grounded but visionary framework meant to improve women's emotional and spiritual well-being in changing professional surroundings.

5. RESULT/ ANALYSIS

Particularly in helping women going through life transitions like menopause or mid-career changes, this chapter synthesizes current theoretical and empirical data to offer an integrated study of how Spirituality, emotional wellbeing, and ethical artificial intelligence interact in the workplace. Key themes arising from the literature guide the following analysis: (1) the underutilization of spiritual wellbeing in organizational wellness strategies; (2) the potential of artificial intelligence technologies to support emotional resilience; and (3) the value of gender-sensitive design in spiritual-AI frameworks.

5.1 Underutilized Potential of Workplace Spirituality

Although organizational research has extensively addressed the advantages of workplace spirituality, its actual integration into policy and leadership is still rare. As Ashmos and Duchon (2000) contend, performance measurements sometimes overlook the spiritual aspect of work—defined by meaning, connection, and authenticity. When companies do, however, include Spirituality into the workplace, they report lower burnout, better employee engagement, and more teamwork (Milliman, Czaplewski, & Ferguson, 2003).

Especially for helping women, this gap between knowledge and practice represents a major lost chance. Menopause especially brings not only physical changes but also emotional ones including anxiety, role confusion, and less confidence (Hunter & Rendall, 2007). A spiritually tuned workplace might offer the tools and language needed for staff members to negotiate these changes with dignity and encouragement.

Moreover, research indicate that spiritual leadership—which is defined by compassion, vision, and values-based action—may help workers feel more psychological safety and purpose (Fry, 2003). Women in leadership positions who show spiritual intelligence in particular often help to create inclusive and emotionally intelligent societies (Neal, 2013).

5.2 Emerging Function of AI in Spiritual and Emotional Support

Although artificial intelligence tools are usually connected with efficiency and automation, new studies show their growing ability to support human-centric objectives including emotional and spiritual well-being. For instance, at scale emotional support and cognitive-behavioral therapy are being provided by conversational artificial intelligence agents including Woebot and Wysa (Inkster et al., 2018). These instruments track user moods, respond sympathetically using natural language processing (NLP), and provide customized wellness plans.

Adapted for spiritual care, artificial intelligence tools could combine mindfulness coaching, guided journaling, digital rituals, or value-based reflections. Early-stage projects including "Spiritual.AI" prototypes are investigating how artificial intelligence might provide non-religious spiritual support—such as helping users investigate life purpose, values alignment, and inner peace (Ah Ahmad et al., 2021). Research on how these systems might be built in ethically responsible and culturally sensitive ways—especially for underprivileged groups—remains rare, though.

The way artificial intelligence supports women has to be deliberately planned. Many wellness apps, according to studies, either ignore gender-specific issues including menopause, reproductive health, or caregiving or lack inclusive language (Woolsey et al., 2022). Built on inclusive datasets and open ethical frameworks, artificial intelligence can become a useful companion tool for negotiating career changes in personal life.

Growing understanding is that these tools should not only react to data but also inspire deeper self-examination as artificial intelligence gets more ingrained in wellness ecosystems. AI systems can ask, for example, "What's going unspoken today?"What do you need to release?" inviting consumers into emotionally intelligent conversation that touches the holy and transcends utility."

5.3 Resilience Emotional and Spiritual as Soul Strength

Introduced in this chapter, the idea of "soul strength" catches the junction of emotional resilience and spiritual well-being. The ability to keep inner balance, purpose, and compassion under times of personal or professional disturbance is what defines soul strength. This is consistent with studies on spiritual resilience, which stress the need of being able to gracefully and meaningfully adjust during crisis (Pargament, 1997).

For midlife women especially, developing soul strength is quite important. Studies reveal that women may experience more emotional labor, less workplace recognition, and internalized guilt about their productivity during menopause or caregiving transitions (Greer & Kirk, 2018). Grounded in spiritual values like compassion, wholeness, and purpose, organizational support that notes these emotional layers—through coaching, peer circles, or reflective time—is more effective.

Reave's (2005) research on spiritually grounded leadership and workplace design supports this by showing that they not only raise employee satisfaction but also lower emotional dissonance—that conflict between employees' feelings and their expected behavior. Women especially should pay close attention to this since they frequently have to suppress emotional needs in order to satisfy professional expectations.

5.4 Ethical Issues in Spiritual Support Mediated by AI

Many ethical questions arise as artificial intelligence tools find more and more place in the field of mental and spiritual health. Data privacy, emotional manipulation, and the loss of human empathy in the delivery of care top most urgent issues (Floridi et al., 2018). Particularly when that data relates to spiritual or emotional disclosures, AI systems have to be open about how user data is gathered, analyzed, and stored.

Moreover, if emotional AI systems—such as mood trackers or empathy bots—are not trained on diverse datasets, they run the danger of either ignoring difficult human experiences or feeding preconceptions. Studies caution that if artificial intelligence is used without gender-sensitive training, it could replicate prejudices and marginalize women's emotional reality rather than help them (West, Whittaker, & Crawford, 2019).

Developers must thus embrace models like Responsible AI, which give justice, responsibility, and contextual design top priority. Proposed in this chapter, the idea of "soulful design" holds that artificial intelligence systems should be in line not only with user capability but also with the emotional and spiritual values of the company.

Crafting Soulful AI: Emotional Integrity, Empathy, and Ethics

The ethical design of these tools is not optional; it is fundamental as artificial intelligence systems progressively occupy the domain of emotional and spiritual wellness. Although mood trackers, journaling bots, or spiritual guidance apps can provide support, they have to be held to strict criteria of care, respect, and justice.

Data sovereignty is one of the most urgent issues, particularly in cases when consumers share very private, emotional, or spiritual experiences. These revelations are bits of the inner self, not only facts. Clear limits on how personal reflections are kept, interpreted, and used, informed consent, open data practices, and ethical design must all take front stage. Users should be able, for instance, review, delete, and opt out of emotional profiling without penalty.

Still, another major issue is algorithmic bias. Should the training data behind emotional-AI systems come mostly from Western, white, cisgender, or male populations, the system may misinterpret emotional cues or spiritual expressions from other users. A Black woman expressing spiritual frustration, for instance, might be called "agitated," while a white man's similar entry might be labeled "reflective." These subtle distortions can erode trust and support harm. Inclusive artificial intelligence calls for intersectional literacy, continuous human supervision, not only varied data.

5.5 Leadership as the Channel of Implementation

The application of soulful work methods mostly depends on the dedication of the leaders. More than a soft ability, spiritual leadership is a strategic approach stressing ethical responsibility, value congruence, and intrinsic motivation (Fry & Kriger, 2009). Setting the tone for inclusivity, modeling emotional openness, and validating wellness practices addressing spiritual needs depend on leaders.

Often driven from a values-based standpoint, women leaders are. Studies reveal that female executives are more likely to practice relational, empathetic, and co-operative leadership styles—qualities matched with spiritual intelligence (Eagly & Carli, 2007). Encouragement of psychologically safe surroundings helps to normalize discussions on emotional vulnerability and spiritual development, so facilitating the seeking of help for others.

Leadership grounded in spiritual intelligence listens, nurtures, and models emotional congruence—not only guides. These leaders create settings where people are invited to pause, consider, and realign as well as expected to perform. By doing this, they create environments in which inner wellness is equally strategically important as creativity or output. Such leadership is fundamental to the future of inclusive, sustainable companies; it is not only auxiliary.

5.6 Summary of Analytical Findings

This study highlights a strong need to close the discrepancy between emotional resilience, occupational Spirituality, and artificial intelligence innovation:

-Companies are ignoring the spiritual component of wellness, which, particularly for women negotiating life changes, can be a transforming agent for employee fulfilment.

-Though they must be ethically built with cultural and gender sensitivity, artificial intelligence technologies have great potential to provide individualized, non-invasive support.

-Soul strength turns out to be a very effective conceptual tool since it helps to frame emotional and spiritual resilience as a fundamental ability rather than an afterthought.

-Creating soulful work environments depends mostly on leadership, especially in cases when women leaders are enabled to lead with spiritual intelligence.

6. FINDINGS AND DISCUSSION

The main conclusions of the narrative review are presented in this chapter, together with a critical analysis within the larger scholarly and administrative framework. Particularly in support of women going through life transitions, the results show that including Spirituality, emotional wellness, and artificial intelligence in the workplace is both a required and underdeveloped area. This chapter provides an interpretive synthesis of developing trends, tensions, and implications based on the literature and theoretical models reviewed earlier.

6.1 Key Findings

6.1.1 Spirituality Still a Silent Resource

Among the main conclusions is the consistent underappreciation of Spirituality as a tool for business development. Although literature stresses more and more the need of meaning-making, authenticity, and inner purpose at work (Ashmos & Duchon, 2000; Reave, 2005), many companies still view Spirituality as a personal or irrelevant issue. When employees often search for deeper existential clarity and emotional support, this silence is especially troublesome during life transitions including menopause, caregiving, or career reorientation.

According to the study, women often seek employment that fit personal values and relational purpose and show more openness to include Spirituality into their professional identity (Milliman et al., 2003). Acknowledgments of this spiritual need can cause conflict and disengagement.

6.1.2 Emotional Wellbeing Linked to Meaningful Work

Closely related to Spirituality is the need of emotional wellbeing. Many studies have demonstrated that emotional health is closely related to the sense of value and emotional safety at work rather than only a result of lowered stress or absence from work (Krekel et al., 2019). For women in midlife transitions especially, emotional resilience becomes essential for juggling personal and professional obligations at once.

According to the literature, companies who create psychological safety and emotional openness observe higher involvement, trust, and loyalty (Edmondson, 1999). Initiatives combining emotional literacy with reflective techniques like mindfulness, peer storytelling, or coaching—especially when those practices are spiritually grounded—are probably going to help women in transition.

6.1.3 AI Tools Show Potential but Demand Soulful Design

Promising but complicated is the development of artificial intelligence as a tool for emotional and spiritual wellness. Although their use in spiritual and emotional spheres is still young, digital platforms and conversational agents are already used therapeutistically (Inkster et al., 2018). AI can help with mood tracking, introspection, even with rituals of connection and thanksgiving. Still, such instruments have to be crafted with subtlety.

Most current AI wellness apps do not sufficiently reflect gender-specific needs or spiritual diversity (Woolsey et al., 2022). These technologies run the danger of alienating the very people they seek to help without inclusive datasets and value-sensitive algorithms. If AI support tools exclude women especially from the emotional reality of menopause, aging, or caregiving, they may feel unheard.

6.1.4 "Soul Strength" as a Holistic Support Construct

This chapter's original contribution is the conception of "soul strength," a term that sums together spiritual awareness and emotional resilience. This construct redefines emotional strength as the inner ability to remain in line with values, purpose, and connection under uncertainty rather than as stoicism or productivity.

The results imply that initiatives based on AI-based wellness, organizational design, and leadership development can find guidance from soul strength. It recognizes employees, particularly women, as agents of transformation when supported through their inner resources, so providing a counter-narrative to deficit-based models of burnout or disengagement.

6.1.5 Gender-inclusive leadership helps to enable spiritual integration.

At last, the study reveals that normalizing emotional and spiritual dialogues in the workplace depends much on leadership. Particularly women leaders have shown to have better degrees of spiritual intelligence, emotional literacy, and cooperative leadership approaches (Eagly & Carli, 2007). Their impact can help organizational culture to grow more psychologically safe, inclusive, and values-oriented.

But systematic obstacles including ageism, gender bias, and invisibility of midlife transitions sometimes prevent such leadership from being appreciated or scaled. This result implies that more focused support and appreciation of women's emotional labor and spiritual leadership is required.

6.2 Theme Debate

6.2.1 Spiritual Lens Rethinking Organizational Wellness

The results call for a review of wellness practices outside of physical or mental health toward more combined models including spiritual wellness. From tokenistic wellness apps to embedding reflective practices, community rituals, and values alignment into daily processes, organizations have to shift.

Viewing Spirituality as a human-centered approach to meaning-making, purpose, and wholeness will help one to see it as not religious or esoteric. In hybrid and digital companies, where burnout and isolation are common, this framing is especially important.

6.2.2 How Technology Might Support Human Flourishing

Though it is sometimes seen as cold or impersonal, artificial intelligence can be seen as a tool for helping one to nurture inner life. For soul-strengthening, AI tools with reflective journals, thanks notes, or emotionally tuned feedback could be digital friends.

Still, this calls for a paradigm change in tech design. Working together, developers, ethicists, and HR leaders can produce "soulful AI"—systems that are not only functional but also emotionally literate and ethically rooted. Promising routes for inclusive and sympathetic artificial intelligence design are provided by feminist HCI (Human-Computer Interaction) frameworks (Bardzell, 2010).

From Personal Insight to Group Change

Although most discussions on workplace wellness center on personal development—mindfulness, journaling, emotional awareness—it's important to understand that soulful work is not a one-person project. It is a group effort molded by communal rituals, relational responsibility, and cultural standards either enhancing or stifling the inner life.

The seed is individual reflection; organizational culture is the soil. Even the toughest people can burn out without systematic help. Thus, relational practices—group reflection areas, psychologically safe teams, and leadership that normalizes emotional transparency—must be scaffolded by workplace spirituality. By planting individual development in common experience, peer mentoring, narrative coaching, and community rituals enhance each other.

For women especially, whose emotional labor often sustains team dynamics but is invisible, this is especially important. Organizations go from reactive wellness models to proactive cultures of care when they include spiritual and emotional values into the collective fabric—meeting structures, decision-making processes, and success criteria.

6.2.3 Creating Space for Women's Transitional Narratives

The need of visibility and space for women's life changes is yet another crucial issue. Whether it's menopause, caring, or late-career introspection, these changes are sometimes left out of mainstream stories of professional success. Spiritual integration provides a means to bring these stories into the open, so validating emotional depth and life-stage development as strengths rather than liabilities.

This space could be created using peer coaching circles, spiritual mentoring, and artificial intelligence-assisted reflective storytelling, so strengthening both personal resilience and group empathy.

6.3 Implications for Policy and Practice

The results have several pragmatic ramifications:

HR policies should contain clauses allowing for life-stage changes and combining spiritual coaching and emotional support.

Wellness and HR-tech systems should, via ethical AI design, embed emotional and spiritual awareness.

Training spiritual intelligence for leaders—especially women—can help to improve value-based leadership and inclusivity.

Metrics for assessing workplace wellness should also cover soul strength, emotional congruence, and purpose alignment.

6.4 Limitations and Scope for Further Exploration

This study uses a narrative review technique, so synthesizing theoretical and conceptual insights but excluding empirical data collecting. The results thus are suggestive and interpretive rather than predictive. Future studies might build on this framework by piloting AI tools supporting spiritual-emotional integration or by interviewing women leaders qualitatively.

7. CONCLUSION AND FUTURE RESEARCH DIRECTIONS

7.1 Conclusion

This chapter has offered a comprehensive investigation of the interactions among Spirituality, emotional wellness, and artificial intelligence (AI) application in helping women during major career changes. Combining ideas from many fields—including psychology, organizational behavior, feminist studies, and digital transformation—this work has underlined the need of appreciating a more integrated and compassionate approach to grasp the lived experiences of women professionals.

Fundamentally, this chapter has shown the great part spiritual intelligence plays in helping women negotiate professional obstacles, particularly during important transitional times like career breaks, motherhood, menopause, caregiving duties, or changes in identity. The inner world of women—including their spiritual values, emotional resilience, and intuitive knowledge—has been mainly overlooked in conventional work cultures dominated by performance measures and hyper-productivity. This study advocates a reconfiguration of success and wellbeing in contemporary companies by raising awareness of the invisible labor women often perform and their special leadership contributions grounded in empathy and relational intelligence.

As this study defines emotional wellbeing, it transcends personal mental health to include a shared feeling of connection, safety, and direction. Women are more likely to participate truly and meaningfully when they feel psychological safety and are free to express vulnerability without worry of marginalization. This chapter has shown how, particularly during midlife or transition phases, current organizational structures sometimes overlook the complex emotional terrain women negotiate. Workplace settings that combine emotional literacy, relational leadership, and peer-supported practices are far better able to retain and advance women at all levels.

The rise of artificial intelligence and digital channels offers both opportunity and risk. AI tools can be used to personalize wellness resources, provide emotional support, and track involvement; but, if these tools are not created with empathy, inclusivity, and spiritual awareness, ethical concerns follow. Introduced in this chapter, the idea of "soulful AI" argues for technology that supports values-based involvement, mindfulness, and inner development. AI systems can be built to help people reflect, connect, and find meaning—qualities of what it means to be spiritually and emotionally well—instead of lowering people to data points.

The emergent idea of "soul strength," a multi-dimensional concept reflecting a woman's inner reservoir of resilience, wisdom, and purpose, is fundamental to this conversation. Unlike surface-level interventions like generic wellness programs, soul strength reflects a person's ability to match her deepest truths with systematic obstacles. Developing this strength calls for not only personal work but also encouraging systems inside companies that accept emotional and spiritual experiences.

Finally, the chapter suggests a new paradigm for workplace wellbeing based on Spirituality, emotional truth, and technological empathy as central to women's flourishing transcending traditional limits. This method deliberately fosters alignment, belonging, and sustainable success rather than only reacting to burnout or attrition. Companies ready to implement this approach will not only improve involvement and creativity but also help to create a more compassionate and conscious workplace of future.

7.2 Future Research Directions

Several areas for future scholarly research and pragmatic exploration have surfaced, given the generally conceptual and narrative approach followed in this chapter. These guidelines guarantee that women's inner experiences are central to organizational development strategies and help to translate theory into sustainable workplace change.

7.2.1 Operationalizing “Soul Strength,”

The idea of soul strength—which combines emotional intelligence, spiritual resilience, and value congruence—is one major contribution of this chapter. Future studies might look at creating a validated psychometric instrument to gauge this construct in professional settings. Such a scale could provide understanding of the relationships among soul strength, job satisfaction, career advancement, leadership quality, and mental health results. Longitudinal studies could help to show how this strength changes over several career phases or life events.

7.2.2 Digital age women's narrative wisdom

Given the narrative focus of this study, more research could look at how digital storytelling platforms might be used to gather and examine women's personal paths through burnout, reinventions, or career transitions. Rich, contextual insights challenging dominant workplace narratives can come from qualitative techniques including reflective journaling, collaborative autoethnography, and life story interviews. This kind of research not only validates women's voices but also provides a storehouse of knowledge for leaders and new professionals.

7.2.3 Inclusive leadership and Spiritual Intelligence

Studying the function of spiritual intelligence (SQ) in leadership development initiatives—especially for women—is another exciting field. Although emotional intelligence (EQ) is well known, SQ is still understudied in most corporate training. Studies on spiritually intelligent leadership—defined by purpose-driven action, humility, and ethical clarity—could look at how team dynamics, creativity, and conflict resolution are affected. Pilot projects could evaluate how high SQ women leaders create more inclusive, caring, and psychologically safe settings.

7.2.4 Designing Soulful AI Systems

Interdisciplinary researchers must give artificial intelligence's increasing presence in HR and wellness top priority immediate attention. Future research should concentrate on ethically creating AI tools to meet women's emotional and spiritual needs, particularly during transitions. Among the questions could be: How can machine learning models be taught to identify indicators of emotional tiredness without violating privacy? Can AI-based reflection tools or virtual wellness partners really help mid-career women? Which ethical systems guarantee that such instruments improve rather than reduce human agency?

Ensuring that these systems represent the variety of women's experiences and spiritual perspective calls for cooperation among technologists, organizational psychologists, and feminist academics.

7.2.5 Intersectionality and Spiritual Wellbeing

While gender is covered in this chapter, future studies have to more closely interact with intersectionality. Overlapping identities including race, class, religion, ability, and sexual orientation help to define women's experiences at work. For instance, different societies may understand emotional expression and spiritual activities differently. Comparative study across many geographies and identity groups can help create culturally sensitive and inclusive workplace interventions that consider these subtleties.

Intersectionality and Spiritual Wellbeing in Experiences of Diverse Women

Although this chapter has underlined the need of helping women's spiritual and emotional well-being in the workplace, it is important to recognize that not all women experience the workplace—or their inner life—in the same way. Introduced by Kimberlé Crenshaw (1989), an intersectional lens reminds us that identity is multifarious. Gender shapes unique emotional and spiritual needs by interacting with race, ethnicity, class, sexual orientation, disability, faith, and cultural legacy.

Black women, for instance, often bear the weight of both racialized and gendered emotional labor, negotiate microaggressions and control expectations to seem "strong," or emotionally contained. This "superwoman schema" can mask intense spiritual tiredness and a need for restorative practices anchored in cultural or ancestral origins (Woods-Giscombé, 2010). Workplace wellness plans that ignore these layered realities could unintentionally support invisibility or exclusion.

In their conception of work and wellbeing, Indigenous women may also bring rich traditions of community, land-based Spirituality, and intergenerational wisdom. Still, Western organizational cultures—which sometimes value individualism and secularism—often mirror these spiritual frameworks in rare measure. Indigenous values run the danger of being erased or commercialized without room to honor ritual, storytelling, or sacred connection to place.

Intersectionality becomes even more important as artificial intelligence moves into the wellness arena. Should algorithms learn from majority narratives, they will not be able to identify the particular emotional languages and spiritual expressions of underprivileged groups. In system design, developers must take cultural, spiritual, and affective subtlety in addition to varied demographic data into account.

Supporting women's spiritual well-being calls for culturally competent, trauma-aware, and community-informed frameworks rather than just universal policies. Soulful workplaces have to create room for pluralism—where many points of view are celebrated as essential sources of collective resilience and wisdom rather than just accepted.

7.2.6 Organization Ecosystems for Wholeness

Apart from personal and technological interventions, research on how organizational cultures might be converted into ecosystems of emotional and spiritual support is much needed. At work, what policies, ceremonies, or design features help one to feel wholeness and meaning? Without straying into tokenism or appropriation, can companies embrace ideas including mindfulness circles, reflective leadership retreats, or sacred pause areas? Research in this field can enable strong organizational transformation frameworks that fit changing definitions of success, purpose, and welfare.

7.3 Final Reflection

The future of work has to be rebuilt as a platform for human awakening and alignment as much as a place of economic productivity. The ideas in this chapter challenge academics, professionals, and leaders to understand that women's inner landscapes—their spiritual yearnings, emotional truths, and embodied wisdom—are fundamental to performance rather than only incidental.

Redining wellness as soul-centered helps companies go beyond scattered interventions toward wholeness, empathy, and sustainability. Women in transition need to be heard, respected, and empowered; they cannot be "fixed" or managed. This chapter calls to action: let us create environments where the fullness of our humanity and technologies enabling our inner development are welcomed.

By doing this, we not only build strong, inclusive companies—we help to heal our shared future.

Future Vision: Somatic Work in 2035

Imagine a workplace in 2035 where spiritual development and emotional literacy are valued not as side notes but rather as fundamental organizing tools. AI assistants probe, "Is this aligned with your current energy level?" rather than merely arranging meetings.Digital dashboards reflect mood patterns, gratitude entries, and spiritual intention logs in addition to productivity.

Leadership courses in spiritual intelligence, narrative, and ethical introspection abound. Teams start each quarter not only with OKRs but also with "soulful intentions," or shared values or guiding questions anchored in mission. Employees engage in "alignment conversations," in which emotional wellness and development are part of the dialogue, instead of performance reviews.

The Moral Imperative of Soulful Work

The question is not whether companies should concern emotional and spiritual wellbeing as we enter an era marked by automation, hybrid work, and fast cultural change; rather, it is how far they are ready to align with the soul of the human experience. Soulful work is a moral need in a society when burnout, disconnection, and meaninglessness have become accepted, not only a progressive wellness approach or an HR trend.

Long sought to maximize talent, organizations will belong to those who choose to honor humanity in the future. This includes realizing emotional labor is real work, creating technologies that elevates rather than flattens our inner worlds, and letting spiritual language re-enter professional life free from stigma or fear.

Soulful work is ultimately about permission rather than perfection or unbounded optimism. Permission to be whole; to lead with feeling; to honor our complexity without guilt. Giving employees this space helps companies release a different kind of potential based on bravery, vulnerability, and meaning. Soulful workplaces heal systems as well as individuals by allowing the whole, beautiful spectrum of human experience room.

REFERENCES

Abe, J. A. A., Ko, J. H., & Goto, S. G. (2013). Mindfulness, emotional intelligence, and emotional labor. *Personality and Individual Differences*, *55*(5), 513–518. DOI: 10.1016/j.paid.2013.04.027

Acker, J. (1990). Hierarchies, jobs, bodies: A theory of gendered organizations. *Gender & Society*, *4*(2), 139–158. DOI: 10.1177/089124390004002002

Ashmos, D. P., & Duchon, D. (2000). Spirituality at work: A conceptualization and measure. *Journal of Management Inquiry*, *9*(2), 134–145. DOI: 10.1177/105649260092008

Bakker, A. B., & Demerouti, E. (2007). The job demands–resources model: State of the art. *Journal of Managerial Psychology*, *22*(3), 309–328. DOI: 10.1108/02683940710733115

Bardzell, S. (2010). Feminist HCI: Taking stock and outlining an agenda for design. In *Proceedings of the SIGCHI Conference on Human Factors in Computing Systems* (pp. 1301–1310). ACM. DOI: 10.1145/1753326.1753521

Bierema, L. L. (2002). The role of gender consciousness in challenging patriarchy. *International Journal of Lifelong Education*, *21*(5), 397–411. DOI: 10.1080/02601370210141010

Cherniss, C. (2010). Emotional intelligence: Toward clarification of a concept. *Industrial and Organizational Psychology: Perspectives on Science and Practice*, *3*(2), 110–126. DOI: 10.1111/j.1754-9434.2010.01231.x

Crenshaw, K. (1989). Demarginalizing the intersection of race and sex. *University of Chicago Legal Forum*, *1989*(1), 139–167.

Criado Perez, C. (2019). *Invisible women: Data bias in a world designed for men*. Abrams Press.

Cunliffe, A. L. (2009). Reflexivity, learning and reflexive practice. In Armstrong, S., & Fukami, C. (Eds.), *The SAGE handbook of management learning, education and development* (pp. 405–418). SAGE., DOI: 10.4135/9780857021038.n21

Diener, E., Oishi, S., & Tay, L. (2018). Advances in subjective well-being research. *Nature Human Behaviour*, *2*(4), 253–260. DOI: 10.1038/s41562-018-0307-6 PMID: 30936533

Dirkx, J. M. (2001). The power of feelings: Emotion, imagination, and the construction of meaning in adult learning. *New Directions for Adult and Continuing Education*, *89*(89), 63–72. DOI: 10.1002/ace.9

Eagly, A. H., & Carli, L. L. (2007). *Through the labyrinth: The truth about how women become leaders*. Harvard Business Review Press.

Edmondson, A. C. (1999). Psychological safety and learning behavior in work teams. *Administrative Science Quarterly*, *44*(2), 350–383. DOI: 10.2307/2666999

Ely, R. J., & Meyerson, D. E. (2000). Theories of gender in organizations: A new approach to organizational analysis and change. *Research in Organizational Behavior*, *22*, 103–151. DOI: 10.1016/S0191-3085(00)22004-2

Emmons, R. A. (1999). *The psychology of ultimate concerns: Motivation and Spirituality in personality*. Guilford Press.

Ferrari, R. (2015). Writing narrative style literature reviews. *Medical Writing*, *24*(4), 230–235. DOI: 10.1179/2047480615Z.000000000329

Fisher, J. W. (2011). The four domains model: Connecting Spirituality, health and well-being. *Religions*, *2*(1), 17–28. DOI: 10.3390/rel2010017

Floridi, L., Cowls, J., Beltrametti, M., Chatila, R., Chazerand, P., Dignum, V., Luetge, C., Madelin, R., Pagallo, U., Rossi, F., Schafer, B., Valcke, P., & Vayena, E. (2018). AI4People—An ethical framework for a good AI society: Opportunities, risks, principles, and recommendations. *Minds and Machines*, *28*(4), 689–707. DOI: 10.1007/s11023-018-9482-5 PMID: 30930541

Fry, L. W. (2003). Toward a theory of spiritual leadership. *The Leadership Quarterly*, *14*(6), 693–727. DOI: 10.1016/j.leaqua.2003.09.001

Fry, L. W., & Kriger, M. (2009). Towards a theory of being-centered leadership: Multiple levels of being as context for effective leadership. *Human Relations*, *62*(11), 1667–1696. DOI: 10.1177/0018726709346380

Giacalone, R. A., & Jurkiewicz, C. L. (Eds.). (2003). *Handbook of workplace spirituality and organizational performance*. M.E. Sharpe.

Gilligan, C. (1982). *In a different voice: Psychological theory and women's development*. Harvard University Press.

Goleman, D. (1995). *Emotional intelligence*. Bantam Books.

Good, D. J., Lyddy, C. J., Glomb, T. M., Bono, J. E., Brown, K. W., Duffy, M. K., Baer, R. A., Brewer, J. A., & Lazar, S. W. (2016). Contemplating mindfulness at work: An integrative review. *Journal of Management*, *42*(1), 114–142. DOI: 10.1177/0149206315617003

Greenhalgh, T., Thorne, S., & Malterud, K. (2018). Time to challenge the spurious hierarchy of systematic over narrative reviews? *European Journal of Clinical Investigation*, *48*(6), e12931. DOI: 10.1111/eci.12931 PMID: 29578574

Gross, J. J. (2002). Emotion regulation: Affective, cognitive, and social consequences. *Psychophysiology*, *39*(3), 281–291. DOI: 10.1017/S0048577201393198 PMID: 12212647

Hochschild, A. R. (1983). *The managed heart: Commercialization of human feeling*. University of California Press.

Hochschild, A. R., & Machung, A. (2012). *The second shift: Working families and the revolution at home*. Penguin Books.

Howard, A., & Wellins, R. (2009). *Holding women back: Troubling trends in talent management*. Development Dimensions International.

Hunter, M. S., & Rendall, M. (2007). Bio-psycho-socio-cultural perspectives on menopause. *Best Practice & Research. Clinical Obstetrics & Gynaecology*, *21*(2), 261–274. DOI: 10.1016/j.bpobgyn.2006.11.001 PMID: 17161025

Inkster, B., Sarda, S., & Subramanian, V. (2018). An empirical study of AI mental health chatbots: Wysa and Woebot. *Evidence-Based Mental Health*, *21*(2), 60–63. DOI: 10.1136/ebmental-2018-300069

Jobin, A., Ienca, M., & Vayena, E. (2019). The global landscape of AI ethics guidelines. *Nature Machine Intelligence*, *1*(9), 389–399. DOI: 10.1038/s42256-019-0088-2

Kabat-Zinn, J. (2003). Mindfulness-based interventions in context: Past, present, and future. *Clinical Psychology : a Publication of the Division of Clinical Psychology of the American Psychological Association*, *10*(2), 144–156. DOI: 10.1093/clipsy.bpg016

Krekel, C., Ward, G., & De Neve, J. E. (2019). *Employee wellbeing, productivity, and firm performance*. Centre for Economic Performance. https://cep.lse.ac.uk/pubs/download/dp1605.pdf

Krishnakumar, S., & Neck, C. P. (2002). The "what," "why," and "how" of Spirituality in the workplace. *Journal of Managerial Psychology*, *17*(3), 153–164. DOI: 10.1108/02683940210423060

Mittelstadt, B. D., Allo, P., Taddeo, M., Wachter, S., & Floridi, L. (2016). The ethics of algorithms: Mapping the debate. *Big Data & Society*, *3*(2), 1–21. DOI: 10.1177/2053951716679679

Neal, J. (2013). *Creating enlightened organizations: Four gateways to spirit at work*. Palgrave Macmillan. DOI: 10.1057/9781137327673

Pargament, K. I. (1997). *The psychology of religion and coping: Theory, research, practice*. Guilford Press.

Petchsawang, P., & Duchon, D. (2009). Measuring workplace spirituality in an Asian context. *Human Resource Development International*, *12*(4), 459–468. DOI: 10.1080/13678860903135912

Pfeifer, E., & Scholz, C. (2021). Digital Spirituality: A new frontier in AI-supported self-care. *AI & Society*, *36*, 447–460. DOI: 10.1007/s00146-021-01140-7

Reave, L. (2005). Spiritual values and practices related to leadership effectiveness. *The Leadership Quarterly*, *16*(5), 655–687. DOI: 10.1016/j.leaqua.2005.07.003

Rego, A., & Cunha, M. P. (2008). Workplace spirituality and organizational commitment: An empirical study. *Journal of Organizational Change Management*, *21*(1), 53–75. DOI: 10.1108/09534810810847039

Rego, A., & Pina e Cunha, M. (2008). Authenticity, self-awareness, and Spirituality in the workplace. *Human Resource Development International*, *11*(5), 563–581. DOI: 10.1080/13678860802417753

Simpson, R., & Lewis, P. (2005). An investigation of silence and a scrutiny of transparency: Re-examining gender in organization literature through the concepts of voice and visibility. *Human Relations*, *58*(10), 1253–1275. DOI: 10.1177/0018726705058940

Tisdell, E. J. (2003). *Exploring Spirituality and culture in adult and higher education*. Jossey-Bass.

Topol, E. (2019). *Deep medicine: How artificial intelligence can make healthcare human again*. Basic Books.

West, S. M., Whittaker, M., & Crawford, K. (2019). *Discriminating systems: Gender, race, and power in AI*. AI Now Institute.

Woods-Giscombé, C. L. (2010). Superwoman schema: African American women's views on stress, strength, and health. *Qualitative Health Research*, *20*(5), 668–683. DOI: 10.1177/1049732310361892 PMID: 20154298

Woolsey, L., Ahmed, R., & Tuck, E. (2022). Designing for the margins: Feminist AI for emotional wellbeing. *Feminist Media Studies*, *22*(4), 589–607. DOI: 10.1080/14680777.2022.2037499

Chapter 15

The Impact of Healthcare Provider Support on Women's Heath During Menopause

Saroj Kumari
School of Pharmacy and Emerging Sciences, Baddi University of Emerging Sciences and Technology, Baddi, India

Ravinesh Mishra
https://orcid.org/0000-0003-4559-1994
School of Pharmacy and Emerging Sciences, Baddi University of Emerging Sciences and Technology, Baddi, India

Bhartendu Sharma
School of Pharmacy and Emerging Sciences, Baddi University of Emerging Sciences and Technology, Baddi, India

Versha Sharma
Himachal Pharmacy College, Maganpura, India

Archana Kumari
School of Pharmacy and Emerging Sciences, Baddi University of Emerging Sciences and Technology, Baddi, India

Priya Sharma
https://orcid.org/0000-0002-3942-6346
School of Pharmacy and Emerging Sciences, Baddi University of Emerging Sciences and Technology, Baddi, India

ABSTRACT

Menopause significantly impacts women's physical and psychological health, with healthcare provider support playing a crucial role in managing this transition. Effective care requires comprehensive symptom assessment, personalized treatment options (including HRT and alternative therapies), and addressing psychosocial needs. However, barriers like inadequate provider training, cultural stigma, and healthcare disparities often limit access to quality care. Emerging solutions such as telemedicine and integrative approaches show promise in improving menopause

DOI: 10.4018/979-8-3373-2970-3.ch015

management. This study highlights the importance of patient-centered, multidisciplinary care that combines medical, psychological, and lifestyle interventions. By enhancing provider education, implementing evidence-based guidelines, and addressing systemic inequities, healthcare systems can significantly improve health outcomes for diverse populations of menopausal women. Ultimately, quality provider support during menopause leads to better symptom management, improved quality of life, and reduced long-term health risks.

1. INTRODUCTION

Menopause is a natural and inevitable biological transition in a woman's life, typically occurring between the ages of 45 and 55, and marked by the permanent cessation of menstruation due to the decline of ovarian function. While it is not a pathological condition, the menopausal transition often referred to as perimenopause can bring with it a wide range of physical, psychological, and emotional symptoms that significantly affect a woman's quality of life (Adams et al., 2011). Common symptoms include hot flashes, night sweats, mood swings, sleep disturbances, memory lapses, vaginal dryness, and decreased libido, among others. Moreover, long-term health risks such as osteoporosis, cardiovascular disease, and metabolic syndrome often become more pronounced in the postmenopausal years (Agbi et al., 2023). Despite the universal nature of menopause, women's experiences and health outcomes during this period vary widely due to a multitude of factors, including genetics, lifestyle, cultural background, socio-economic status, and critically the quality of healthcare support they receive. In recent years, there has been growing recognition that effective healthcare provider support is a key determinant in helping women navigate the challenges of menopause with greater ease, resilience, and empowerment.

Healthcare providers including general practitioners, gynaecologists, nurses, mental health professionals, and alternative medicine practitioners-play an instrumental role in identifying, managing, and alleviating menopause-related symptoms (Ambikairajah et al., 2022). Their role extends beyond diagnosis and treatment to include education, counselling, risk assessment, preventive screening, and the provision of both pharmacological and non-pharmacological interventions. Moreover, healthcare providers are often the primary source of validated information, guidance, and reassurance during this transitional phase (Aninye et al., 2021).

However, the quality and accessibility of menopausal care remain inconsistent across regions and populations. Many women reports feeling dismissed, misunderstood, or inadequately supported by healthcare professionals. Others may face barriers to accessing specialized care due to geographical, financial, or cultural constraints.

These gaps highlight the urgent need for a more structured, sensitive, and inclusive approach to menopausal healthcare—one that recognizes the unique needs of each woman and ensures continuity of care through interdisciplinary collaboration.

This chapter explores the multifaceted impact of healthcare provider support on women's health during menopause. It examines the roles of various healthcare professionals, the importance of communication and patient education, disparities in access to care, and effective clinical interventions. Additionally, it presents case studies, reviews interdisciplinary care models, and offers policy recommendations aimed at enhancing support systems for menopausal women (Baptista et al., 2021). By placing healthcare provider support at the centre of menopausal health, this chapter underscores its potential to not only alleviate symptoms but also to improve long-term health outcomes and overall well-being.

2. UNDERSTANDING MENOPAUSE AND ITS HEALTH IMPLICATIONS

Menopause is a significant physiological milestone in a woman's life, signaling the end of natural reproductive capacity. Defined as the permanent cessation of menstruation for twelve consecutive months without any pathological cause, menopause results from the depletion of ovarian follicles and a consequent decline in estrogen and progesterone production (Barber & Charles, 2023). While it is a universal process, the way menopause is experienced varies widely among women, influenced by genetic, lifestyle, psychosocial, and environmental factors.

2.1. The Menopausal Transition

The menopausal transition, or perimenopause, typically begins in a woman's mid-to-late 40s and may last several years before the final menstrual period. During this time, hormonal fluctuations become more pronounced, leading to irregular menstrual cycles and the onset of various symptoms. Post menopause begins after one full year without menstruation and extends for the remainder of a woman's life.

Table 1. The stages of menopause can be broadly categorized as follows:

Stage	Description
Perimenopause	Begins several years before menopause; hormone levels fluctuate significantly.
Menopause	Defined retrospectively after 12 months of amenorrhea.
Post menopause	The years following menopause; symptoms may persist or evolve (Brown et al., 2016).

2.2. Common Menopausal Symptoms

While the menopausal experience is highly individualized, several symptoms are commonly reported. These can significantly impair daily functioning and emotional well-being if not appropriately managed.

Table 2: Common Symptoms of Menopause

Symptom Category	Common Symptoms
Vasomotor	Hot flashes, night sweats
Psychological	Mood swings, anxiety, depression
Cognitive	Memory lapses, difficulty concentrating
Urogenital	Vaginal dryness, itching, dyspareunia, urinary incontinence
Musculoskeletal	Joint pain, stiffness, decreased bone density
Sleep-related	Insomnia, fragmented sleep
Sexual health	Reduced libido, discomfort during intercourse (Comparetto & Borruto, 2023)

2.3. Long-Term Health Implications

The drop in estrogen levels has systemic effects on a woman's body, increasing the risk for chronic diseases and long-term health complications.

2.3.1. Osteoporosis and Bone Health

Estrogen is essential for bone metabolism. Postmenopausal women are at a higher risk for osteoporosis due to accelerated bone loss, which can lead to fractures, especially in the hip, spine, and wrist.

2.3.2. Cardiovascular Disease

The protective effect of estrogen on cardiovascular function diminishes after menopause. As a result, the incidence of heart disease rises in postmenopausal women, making it a leading cause of death (Cortés & Marginean, 2022).

2.3.3. Metabolic Changes

Menopause is associated with changes in fat distribution, increased abdominal adiposity, insulin resistance, and altered lipid profiles, contributing to a higher risk of type 2 diabetes and metabolic syndrome.

2.3.4. Cognitive Health

Although the exact relationship between menopause and cognitive decline remains under investigation, many women report memory issues and difficulty concentrating during the transition. Estrogen neuroprotective role is a key area of ongoing research.

2.4. Psychosocial Impact

Beyond physical symptoms, menopause can impact a woman's identity, relationships, and overall sense of well-being. Women may feel socially marginalized or emotionally vulnerable, particularly if they perceive menopause as a sign of aging or loss of femininity. Cultural attitudes toward menopause also significantly influence how symptoms are experienced and reported (Crandall et al., 2023).

3. ROLE OF HEALTHCARE PROVIDERS IN MENOPAUSAL CARE

Effective support from healthcare providers plays a pivotal role in helping women manage the diverse and often challenging symptoms of menopause. This support spans clinical management, lifestyle guidance, psychosocial counselling, and patient education. The transition through menopause is not merely a biological shift but a multidimensional process that requires holistic and compassionate care. A collaborative, interdisciplinary approach from healthcare professionals ensures that menopausal women receive appropriate, evidence-based, and individualized support (Donati et al., 2013).

3.1. General Practitioners and Primary Care Providers

Primary care providers, including general practitioners (GPs) and family physicians, are often the first point of contact for menopausal women. Their responsibilities include:

- Identifying early signs and symptoms of perimenopause.

- Conducting routine physical and gynecological examinations.
- Initiating basic investigations, such as hormone levels or bone density scans.
- Offering first-line management options, such as lifestyle counseling and non-hormonal interventions.
- Referring patients to specialists when symptoms are complex or persistent (Flierman et al., 2020).

3.2. Gynaecologists and Endocrinologists

Gynaecologists are the specialists most directly involved in managing the reproductive health aspects of menopause. Their expertise is essential in cases involving:

- Hormone Replacement Therapy (HRT) initiation and monitoring.
- Management of severe urogenital symptoms.
- Menstrual irregularities and abnormal uterine bleeding.
- Prevention and treatment of osteoporosis.
- Addressing sexual health and libido concerns.

Endocrinologists may become involved in managing complex hormonal imbalances, thyroid dysfunctions, or metabolic disorders that become apparent during the menopausal transition (Gleser, 2015).

3.3. Nurses and Midwives

Nurses and midwives often provide extended support services in both clinical and community settings. Their contributions include:

- Educating women about menopausal changes and self-care strategies.
- Providing emotional reassurance and psychosocial support.
- Facilitating group education sessions or wellness programs.
- Monitoring treatment adherence and symptom progression.
- Delivering culturally sensitive and age-appropriate counseling.

Nurse-led clinics or telehealth services can be especially beneficial in rural or underserved areas where access to specialists is limited (Ingram et al., 2022).

3.4. Mental Health Professionals

Menopause is frequently associated with mood disorders, anxiety, and even depression due to hormonal fluctuations and life-stage stressors. Mental health providers offer:

- Psychological assessments and supportive therapy.
- Cognitive Behavioural Therapy (CBT), which is effective for anxiety, depression, and insomnia.
- Counselling to manage body image concerns, sexual dysfunction, and self-esteem issues.
- Stress management techniques and mindfulness-based approaches .(Karakcheyeva et al., 2024)

Early intervention by mental health professionals can prevent escalation of symptoms and promote emotional well-being.

3.5. Dietitians and Lifestyle Counsellors

Nutrition and lifestyle play a vital role in managing menopausal symptoms and reducing long-term health risks. Dietitians and counsellors assist by:

- Developing individualized diet plans rich in calcium, vitamin D, and phytoestrogens.
- Guiding weight management, blood sugar control, and cholesterol reduction.
- Encouraging regular physical activity and sleep hygiene.
- Advising on supplements and herbal remedies where appropriate (Kuck & Hogervorst, 2024).

These professionals can collaborate with other care providers to support a preventive, wellness-centered model of care.

3.6. Traditional and Complementary Medicine Practitioners

In many cultures, women turn to traditional, herbal, or alternative therapies to manage menopausal symptoms. These practitioners may offer:

- Herbal formulations (e.g., black cohosh, soy isoflavones, Ashwagandha).
- Ayurvedic or Traditional Chinese Medicine (TCM) approaches.
- Acupuncture and massage therapy for symptom relief.

- Holistic lifestyle practices emphasizing balance and natural healing (Leipert & Reutter, 2005).

When integrated with evidence-based care, these therapies can enhance the quality of life. However, providers must evaluate the safety and efficacy of such treatments and monitor for potential interactions with conventional medications.

4. IMPORTANCE OF COMMUNICATION AND EDUCATION

Effective communication and education are the cornerstones of high-quality menopausal care. Women experiencing menopause often face not only physical and emotional symptoms but also uncertainty, confusion, and anxiety due to a lack of information or understanding about this life stage. Healthcare providers who communicate clearly, empathetically, and respectfully can empower women to make informed decisions, actively participate in their care, and improve their overall well-being during menopause (Liss et al., 2024).

4.1. Communication: Building Trust and Understanding

Open, respectful communication between healthcare providers and patients fosters trust, encourages disclosure of sensitive symptoms, and supports shared decision-making. Many women hesitate to talk about issues such as low libido, urinary incontinence, or mood swings unless prompted in a safe, nonjudgmental environment.

Key principles of effective provider-patient communication include:

- **Active listening**: Demonstrating empathy and allowing women to express their concerns without interruption.
- **Use of simple, non-technical language**: Avoiding medical jargon helps women better understand their health and treatment options.
- **Cultural sensitivity**: Recognizing and respecting differences in beliefs, values, and expectations related to menopause (Lobo & Gompel, 2022).
- **Validation of experiences**: Acknowledging that symptoms are real and impactful, even if they vary widely between individuals.
- **Privacy and confidentiality**: Ensuring a safe space for discussion of intimate or personal issues.

4.2. Patient Education: Empowering Women Through Knowledge

Educating women about menopause is critical for preparing them to manage changes proactively and confidently. Misconceptions and myths about menopause—ranging from beliefs that it marks the end of usefulness to fears about hormone therapy—can create unnecessary distress and poor health decisions.

Patient education should cover the following areas:

- **Physiological changes**: Clear explanations of hormonal shifts and common symptoms.
- **Treatment options**: Information on pharmacological (e.g., hormone replacement therapy) and non-pharmacological (e.g., lifestyle, herbal remedies) interventions.
- **Self-care strategies**: Guidance on diet, exercise, sleep, and stress management (Mandangu et al., 2025).
- **When to seek help**: Identifying red-flag symptoms and understanding the need for regular screenings (e.g., bone density, cardiovascular risk).
- **Resources**: Access to brochures, support groups, apps, websites, and health hotlines.

4.3. The Role of Digital Tools and Media

With the rise of digital health platforms, there are increasing opportunities for healthcare providers to educate and communicate with patients outside the clinical setting. Telemedicine, patient portals, mobile apps, and online webinars can serve as valuable tools for:

- Providing reliable information in accessible formats.
- Offering personalized symptom tracking and health tips.
- Encouraging ongoing dialogue through messaging platforms or virtual check-ins (Mendelsohn, 2002)

4.4. Group Education and Peer Support

Group education sessions—led by nurses, midwives, or counselors—can facilitate learning in a supportive community environment. These settings encourage peer-to-peer sharing, reduce feelings of isolation, and provide collective reassurance that menopausal symptoms are manageable and common (O'Malley & Reschovsky, 2011).

Group-based education may cover:

- Interactive sessions on menopause physiology and symptom management.
- Discussions on emotional health and coping mechanisms.
- Lifestyle workshops focused on diet, physical activity, and wellness.

5. HEALTHCARE ACCESS AND DISPARITIES

Access to quality healthcare during menopause is essential for early diagnosis, effective symptom management, and prevention of long-term health risks such as osteoporosis and cardiovascular disease. However, numerous disparities exist in the availability, affordability, and quality of menopausal care. These disparities are shaped by socioeconomic status, geographic location, race and ethnicity, education level, and healthcare infrastructure. Women from marginalized or underserved populations often face significant barriers that compromise their ability to receive adequate support during menopause, leading to poorer health outcomes and diminished quality of life (Palacios et al., 2019).

5.1. Socioeconomic Disparities

Socioeconomic status remains one of the most significant determinants of health access. Women with lower income or without insurance coverage are less likely to:

- Visit healthcare providers for routine check-ups.
- Access specialized care such as gynaecology or endocrinology services.
- Afford hormone therapy, supplements, or diagnostic tests.
- Receive consistent follow-up care and symptom monitoring.

The financial burden may also lead to delayed diagnosis or reliance on unverified alternative therapies due to lack of affordable, evidence-based options.

5.2. Geographic Disparities

Women living in rural or remote areas often encounter geographic isolation and limited availability of healthcare services. Specific challenges include:

- Long travel distances to reach primary or specialty care.
- Shortage of trained providers familiar with menopausal health.
- Lack of health education outreach or support groups in local communities.
- Inadequate telemedicine infrastructure or internet connectivity (Pan et al., 2023).

5.3. Racial and Ethnic Disparities

Research shows that menopause is experienced differently across racial and ethnic groups due to genetic, cultural, and environmental factors. However, disparities in care quality and access persist:

- Black and Hispanic women report higher symptom severity but lower usage of hormone therapy or mental health support.
- Language barriers can hinder effective communication and shared decision-making.
- Discrimination or implicit bias in healthcare settings may result in poorer quality interactions or under-treatment (Riach & Jack, 2021).

5.4. Educational Disparities and Health Literacy

Health literacy is the ability to understand, interpret, and act upon health information. Women with limited education or low health literacy may:

- Misunderstand the nature of menopause and its symptoms.
- Be unaware of available treatment options or preventive strategies.
- Be more susceptible to myths, misinformation, or stigma surrounding menopause.

5.5. Barriers to Hormone Therapy and Specialized Care

Access to hormone therapy (HT) and other specialized treatments is not equal. Barriers include:

- Lack of provider knowledge or comfort with prescribing HT.
- Misinformation about risks and benefits of HT in the media.
- Restrictions or discontinuation of insurance coverage for HT.
- Cultural or personal beliefs discouraging the use of hormonal interventions (Schooley et al., 2015).

5.6. Strategies to Reduce Disparities

Addressing these disparities requires systemic, community-based, and policy-driven approaches. Recommended strategies include:

- Expanding telehealth services to reach rural and remote populations.

- Training providers in cultural competence to improve sensitivity and inclusivity.
- Subsidizing care and medications through insurance reforms and public health funding.
- Launching educational campaigns targeting low-literacy and multilingual populations.
- Establishing community-based support programs, including mobile clinics and peer-led groups.

6. CLINICAL INTERVENTIONS AND LIFESTYLE SUPPORT

Managing menopause effectively requires a multifaceted approach that combines clinical interventions with lifestyle support. As menopause presents with a broad spectrum of symptoms—ranging from mild discomfort to debilitating conditions—treatment must be personalized, evidence-based, and continuously evaluated. Healthcare providers must consider both pharmacological and non-pharmacological strategies to address the diverse needs of women during this life stage (Sherman, 2005).

6.1. Hormone Therapy (HT)

Hormone therapy (HT), also known as hormone replacement therapy (HRT), remains the most effective treatment for vasomotor symptoms such as hot flashes and night sweats, as well as for preventing postmenopausal osteoporosis.

Table 3. Types of Hormone Therapy

Form	Common Uses	Examples
Estrogen-only therapy	For women without a uterus	Transdermal patches, pills
Combined estrogen-progestin	For women with a uterus	Oral tablets, skin patches
Local (vaginal) estrogen	For genitourinary symptoms only	Creams, rings, vaginal tablets (Singh et al., 2023)

Benefits:

- Relieves hot flashes and night sweats.
- Reduces vaginal dryness and urinary symptoms.
- Prevents bone loss and fractures.

Risks and Considerations:

- Slight increase in risk of breast cancer, stroke, and thrombosis in some populations.
- HT is typically recommended in the lowest effective dose for the shortest duration needed.
- Suitability should be assessed based on individual risk profiles and health status.

6.2. Non-Hormonal Pharmacologic Treatments

For women who cannot or prefer not to use hormone therapy, several non-hormonal medications may help manage symptoms:

- **Selective serotonin reuptake inhibitors (SSRIs)** and **serotonin-norepinephrine reuptake inhibitors (SNRIs)** for vasomotor symptoms and mood disorders.
- **Gabapentin** for night sweats and sleep disturbances.
- **Clonidine** for hot flashes (less commonly used).
- **Bisphosphonates** or **denosumab** for osteoporosis prevention in high-risk women (Spilsbury et al., 2013).

6.3. Lifestyle Interventions

Lifestyle plays a central role in managing menopausal symptoms and enhancing quality of life. Healthcare providers should counsel women on sustainable changes that support physical, mental, and emotional well-being.

6.3.1. Diet and Nutrition

- Increase intake of calcium, vitamin D, and magnesium to support bone health.
- Emphasize a plant-based, high-fiber diet with whole grains, fruits, and vegetables.
- Include phytoestrogens (e.g., soy, flaxseed) which may mimic estrogen activity mildly.
- Limit intake of processed foods, caffeine, and alcohol, which may trigger hot flashes (Stachowiak et al., 2015).

6.3.2. Physical Activity

- Engage in weight-bearing exercises (e.g., walking, jogging, dancing) to maintain bone density.
- Incorporate strength training to support muscle mass and joint function.
- Include aerobic activities for cardiovascular health and mood enhancement.
- Encourage yoga, tai chi, or stretching for stress relief and flexibility.

6.3.3. Sleep Hygiene

- Maintain a regular sleep schedule and sleep-conducive environment.
- Avoid screen use and stimulants close to bedtime.
- Consider relaxation techniques such as meditation or breathing exercises.

6.3.4. Stress Reduction and Mental Wellness

- Encourage mindfulness, journaling, or therapy to cope with emotional changes.
- Support participation in support groups for shared experiences and peer support.
- Address anxiety and depression proactively with mental health referrals if needed.

7. INTERDISCIPLINARY AND POLICY APPROACHES

Effective menopausal care extends beyond the clinical encounter. Addressing the complex physical, psychological, social, and economic dimensions of menopause requires an interdisciplinary healthcare framework supported by informed policies. Collaboration among healthcare providers, policymakers, educators, and community organizations is essential to create a supportive environment that empowers women throughout their menopausal transition (Toze, 2020).

7.1. Interdisciplinary Healthcare Teams

Menopausal symptoms are multifaceted, involving endocrine changes, mental health challenges, musculoskeletal concerns, and social factors. An interdisciplinary team can provide comprehensive care by pooling diverse expertise:

- **Primary Care Physicians (PCPs):** Often the first contact, they provide initial screening, symptom management, and referrals.
- **Gynaecologists and Endocrinologists:** Specialists who diagnose hormonal changes, manage complex cases, and prescribe hormone therapy.
- **Mental Health Professionals:** Psychologists and counselors address mood disorders, anxiety, and cognitive changes.
- **Physiotherapists and Occupational Therapists:** Support physical mobility, bone health, and pain management.
- **Nutritionists/Dietitians:** Advise on diet plans that support bone density, cardiovascular health, and weight management.
- **Community Health Workers:** Facilitate outreach, education, and follow-up in underserved populations.
- **Pharmacists:** Educate about medication use, adherence, and interactions (Umayal, 2024).

7.2. Integrating Menopausal Care into Primary Healthcare Systems

Embedding menopausal care within primary healthcare systems enhances accessibility and continuity. Key strategies include:

- Training PCPs to recognize menopausal symptoms and provide evidence-based interventions.
- Developing standardized screening tools and referral protocols.
- Utilizing electronic health records to track symptoms, treatments, and outcomes.
- Implementing routine menopausal health check-ups as part of women's wellness visits.

7.3. Public Health Policies and Guidelines

Public health policies play a pivotal role in shaping menopausal care quality and equity. Effective policies should:

- Recognize menopause as a significant women's health issue warranting dedicated resources.
- Promote insurance coverage for hormonal and non-hormonal treatments.
- Support research funding focused on menopause-related health issues (Ussher et al., 2015).
- Encourage public awareness campaigns to destigmatize menopause.

- Mandate cultural competence and gender sensitivity training for healthcare providers.

7.4. Advocacy and Women's Health Rights

Menopause intersects with broader issues of gender equity, aging, and health rights. Advocacy groups and NGOs can:

- Campaign for policy reforms that address disparities in menopausal care.
- Facilitate education programs targeting marginalized communities.
- Empower women to advocate for their health needs.
- Collaborate with governments to develop inclusive health frameworks (Williams et al., 2010).

7.5. Technology and Innovation in Menopausal Care

The advent of digital health technologies offers new avenues for interdisciplinary care and policy implementation:

- **Telemedicine:** Expands access to specialists, particularly in rural or underserved areas.
- **Mobile Health Apps:** Provide symptom tracking, educational content, and peer support networks.
- **Artificial Intelligence:** Supports personalized treatment recommendations based on patient data.
- **Online Training Platforms:** Enhance provider education and dissemination of best practices (Williams et al., 2010).

8. CONCLUSION

Menopause is a natural yet complex transition that profoundly affects women's physical, emotional, and social well-being. The role of healthcare providers in supporting women through this phase is critical—not only in managing symptoms but also in empowering women with knowledge, resources, and compassionate care. As demonstrated throughout this chapter, effective menopausal care requires a personalized, interdisciplinary approach that addresses the diverse needs of women across different socioeconomic, cultural, and geographic contexts.

Healthcare provider support encompasses clear communication, education, timely clinical interventions, and lifestyle guidance. It must also confront systemic barriers such as disparities in access, health literacy gaps, and cultural stigmas. By fostering collaboration across medical specialties and integrating menopause care into primary healthcare frameworks, providers can ensure early diagnosis, optimal treatment, and holistic wellness.

Policy initiatives and advocacy efforts further strengthen this support by promoting equitable healthcare access, encouraging research, and raising public awareness. Innovations in digital health and telemedicine present promising opportunities to bridge gaps, especially for underserved populations. Ultimately, improving women's health during menopause is not only a clinical challenge but a societal imperative. By prioritizing menopausal care within healthcare systems and policies, we can enhance quality of life, reduce morbidity, and empower women to thrive during this pivotal stage of life.

REFERENCES

Adams, J., Lui, C.-W., Sibbritt, D., Broom, A., Wardle, J., & Homer, C. (2011). Attitudes and referral practices of maternity care professionals with regard to complementary and alternative medicine: An integrative review. *Journal of Advanced Nursing*, *67*(3), 472–483. DOI: 10.1111/j.1365-2648.2010.05510.x PMID: 21214615

Agbi, F. A., Lulin, Z., & Asamoah, E. O. (2023). Quality of communication between healthcare providers and pregnant women: Impact on maternal satisfaction, health outcomes, and shared decision-making. *UJOG*, *2*(1), 3–10. DOI: 10.31586/ujog.2023.784

Ambikairajah, A., Walsh, E., & Cherbuin, N. (2022). A review of menopause nomenclature. *Reproductive Health*, *19*(1), 29. Advance online publication. DOI: 10.1186/s12978-022-01336-7 PMID: 35101087

Aninye, I. O., Laitner, M. H., & Chinnappan, S. (2021). Menopause preparedness: Perspectives for patient, provider, and policymaker consideration. *Menopause (New York, N.Y.)*, *28*(10), 1186–1191. DOI: 10.1097/GME.0000000000001819 PMID: 34183564

Baptista, N., Pinho, J. C., & Alves, H. (2021). Examining social capital and online social support links: A study in online health communities facing treatment uncertainty. *International Review on Public and Nonprofit Marketing*, *18*(1), 57–94. DOI: 10.1007/s12208-020-00263-2

Barber, K., & Charles, A. (2023). Barriers to accessing effective treatment and support for menopausal symptoms: A qualitative study capturing the behaviours, beliefs and experiences of key stakeholders. *Patient Preference and Adherence*, *17*, 2971–2980. DOI: 10.2147/PPA.S430203 PMID: 38027078

Brown, E. A., Bekker, H. L., Davison, S. N., Koffman, J., & Schell, J. O. (2016). Supportive care: Communication strategies to improve cultural competence in shared decision making. *Clinical Journal of the American Society of Nephrology; CJASN*, *11*(10), 1902–1908. DOI: 10.2215/CJN.13661215 PMID: 27510456

Comparetto, C., & Borruto, F. (2023). Treatments and management of menopausal symptoms: Current status and future challenges. *OBM Geriatrics*, *7*(3), 248. Advance online publication. DOI: 10.21926/obm.geriatr.2303248

Cortés, Y. I., & Marginean, V. (2022). Key factors in menopause health disparities and inequities: Beyond race and ethnicity. *Current Opinion in Endocrine and Metabolic Research*, *26*, 100389. Advance online publication. DOI: 10.1016/j.coemr.2022.100389

Crandall, C. J., Mehta, J. M., & Manson, J. E. (2023). Management of menopausal symptoms: A review. *Journal of the American Medical Association*, *329*(5), 405–420. DOI: 10.1001/jama.2022.24140 PMID: 36749328

Donati, S., Satolli, R., Colombo, C., Senatore, S., Cotichini, R., Da Cas, R., Spila Alegiani, S., & Mosconi, P. (2013). Informing women on menopause and hormone therapy: Know the Menopause—A multidisciplinary project involving the local healthcare system. *PLoS One*, *8*(12), e85121. Advance online publication. DOI: 10.1371/journal.pone.0085121 PMID: 24391988

Flierman, I., van Seben, R., van Rijn, M., Poels, M., Buurman, B. M., & Willems, D. L. (2020). Health care providers' views on the transition between hospital and primary care in patients in the palliative phase: A qualitative description study. *Journal of Pain and Symptom Management*, *60*(2), 372–380. DOI: 10.1016/j.jpainsymman.2020.02.018 PMID: 32135201

Gleser, H. (2015). Sex, women and the menopause: Are specialist trainee doctors up for it? A survey of views and attitudes of specialist trainee doctors in Community Sexual & Reproductive Health and Obstetrics & Gynaecology around sexuality and sexual healthcare in the (peri)menopause. *Post Reproductive Health*, *21*(1), 26–33. DOI: 10.1177/2053369115574448 PMID: 25725451

Ingram, M. A., Brady, S., & Peacock, A. S. (2022). The barriers to offering non-pharmacological pain management as an initial option for laboring women: A review of the literature. *European Journal of Midwifery*, *6*(June), 37. Advance online publication. DOI: 10.18332/ejm/149244 PMID: 35794877

Karakcheyeva, V., Willis-Johnson, H., Corr, P. G., & Frame, L. A. (2024). The well-being of women in healthcare professions: A comprehensive review. *Global Advances in Integrative Medicine and Health*, *13*, 27536130241232929. Advance online publication. DOI: 10.1177/27536130241232929 PMID: 38344248

Kuck, M. J., & Hogervorst, E. (2024). Stress, depression, and anxiety: Psychological complaints across menopausal stages. *Frontiers in Psychiatry*, *15*, 1323743. Advance online publication. DOI: 10.3389/fpsyt.2024.1323743 PMID: 38455517

Leipert, B. D., & Reutter, L. (2005). Developing resilience: How women maintain their health in northern geographically isolated settings. *Qualitative Health Research*, *15*(1), 49–65. DOI: 10.1177/1049732304269671 PMID: 15574715

Liss, J., Chesnokova, A., & Allen, J. T. (2024). Unspoken and untaught: Addressing the gap in menopause education. *Current Obstetrics and Gynecology Reports*, *13*(4), 281–288. DOI: 10.1007/s13669-024-00404-y

Lobo, R. A., & Gompel, A. (2022). Management of menopause: A view towards prevention. *The Lancet. Diabetes & Endocrinology*, *10*(6), 457–470. DOI: 10.1016/S2213-8587(21)00269-2 PMID: 35526556

Mandangu, C., Ramos, A. M., Sengupta, M., Bender, R., El-Hayani, R., Hasan, I., Okechukwu, H., Anas, S., & Havsteen-Franklin, D. (2025). Implicit bias in referrals to relational psychological therapies: Review and recommendations for mental health services. *Frontiers in Public Health*, *12*, 1469439. Advance online publication. DOI: 10.3389/fpubh.2024.1469439 PMID: 39989866

Mendelsohn, M. E. (2002). Protective effects of estrogen on the cardiovascular system. *The American Journal of Cardiology*, *89*(12), 12E–17E. DOI: 10.1016/S0002-9149(02)02405-0 PMID: 12084397

O'Malley, A. S., & Reschovsky, J. D. (2011). Referral and consultation communication between primary care and specialist physicians: Finding common ground. *Archives of Internal Medicine*, *171*(1), 56–65. DOI: 10.1001/archinternmed.2010.480 PMID: 21220662

Palacios, S., Stevenson, J. C., Schaudig, K., Lukasiewicz, M., & Graziottin, A. (2019). Hormone therapy for first-line management of menopausal symptoms: Practical recommendations. *Women's Health (London, England)*, *15*, 1745506519864009. Advance online publication. DOI: 10.1177/1745506519864009 PMID: 31378196

Pan, M., Zhou, J., Pan, X., Wang, J., Qi, Q., & Wang, L. (2023). Drugs for the treatment of postmenopausal symptoms: Hormonal and non-hormonal therapy. *Life Sciences*, *312*, 121255. Advance online publication. DOI: 10.1016/j.lfs.2022.121255 PMID: 36470539

Riach, K., & Jack, G. (2021). Women's health in/and work: Menopause as an intersectional experience. *International Journal of Environmental Research and Public Health*, *18*(20), 10793. Advance online publication. DOI: 10.3390/ijerph182010793 PMID: 34682537

Schooley, B., San Nicolas-Rocca, T., & Burkhard, R. (2015). Patient-provider communications in outpatient clinic settings: A clinic-based evaluation of mobile device and multimedia mediated communications for patient education. *JMIR mHealth and uHealth*, *3*(1), e3732. Advance online publication. DOI: 10.2196/mhealth.3732 PMID: 25583145

Sherman, S. (2005). Defining the menopausal transition. *The American Journal of Medicine*, *118*(12, Suppl. 12B), 3–7. DOI: 10.1016/j.amjmed.2005.11.002 PMID: 16414321

Singh, N., Garg, M., & Chopra, R. (2023). An overview of herbal formulations: From processing to pharmacovigilance. *International Journal of Pharmaceutical Sciences and Research, 14*(2), 562–578.

Spilsbury, K., Pender, S., Bloor, K., Borthwick, R., Atkin, K., McCaughan, D., Watt, I., Adderley, U., Wakefield, A., & McKenna, H. (2013). Support matters: A mixed methods scoping study on the use of assistant staff in the delivery of community nursing services in England. *Health and Social Care Delivery Research, 1*(3), 1–46. DOI: 10.3310/hsdr01030 PMID: 25642505

Stachowiak, G., Pertyński, T., & Pertyńska-Marczewska, M. (2015). Metabolic disorders in menopause. *Przeglad Menopauzalny = Menopause Review, 14*(1), 59–64. DOI: 10.5114/pm.2015.50000 PMID: 26327890

Toze, M. (2020). Specialization and minority health care: Hormone therapy for trans people in England. *Journal of Health Services Research & Policy, 25*(4), 246–251. DOI: 10.1177/1355819619888561 PMID: 31801033

Umayal, K. M. (2024). Strategic integration of digital health technologies for enhanced patient-centered care in modern healthcare management. *Management, 11*(iS1-Jan, S1), 68–73. DOI: 10.34293/management.v11iiS1-Jan.7142

Ussher, J. M., Perz, J., & Parton, C. (2015). Sex and the menopausal woman: A critical review and analysis. *Feminism & Psychology, 25*(4), 449–468. DOI: 10.1177/0959353515579735

Williams, D. R., Mohammed, S. A., Leavell, J., & Collins, C. (2010). Race, socioeconomic status, and health: Complexities, ongoing challenges, and research opportunities. *Annals of the New York Academy of Sciences, 1186*(1), 69–101. DOI: 10.1111/j.1749-6632.2009.05339.x PMID: 20201869

Chapter 16
Poor Menstrual Hygiene and Infections:
A Growing Risk to Women's Health

Pratikshya Priyadarshini
https://orcid.org/0000-0003-3169-9793
KIIT University, India

Birendri Birendri
https://orcid.org/0000-0003-0933-3103
Lovely Professional University, India

Zahid Parwez
https://orcid.org/0000-0001-7511-0624
XIM University, India

Snigdharani Behera
https://orcid.org/0009-0003-2455-1480
Utkal University, India

Mohammed Imran
https://orcid.org/0009-0000-1615-3528
Utkal University, India

Chittaranjan Subudhi
https://orcid.org/0000-0003-1493-4632
University of Delhi, India

ABSTRACT

Menstrual hygiene is essential for women's health, education, productivity, and overall well-being. Despite being a natural biological process, menstruation has long been overlooked at both societal and individual levels. In many cultures, it is still surrounded by taboos and negative perceptions, often branding menstruating women as impure and subjecting them to seclusion, mobility restrictions, and various social or dietary limitations. Adolescent girls, in particular, often lack accurate information, leading to poor hygiene practices and harmful health outcomes. Although United Nations Millennium Development Goals 2 and 3 emphasize universal education, gender equality, and women's empowerment, menstrual hygiene

DOI: 10.4018/979-8-3373-2970-3.ch016

has received minimal attention, especially in developing countries. Research on this issue remains limited, and stigma continues to hinder progress in addressing this neglected aspect of women's health.

INTRODUCTION

In India, menstruation continues to be perceived as an unclean and impure process, a belief deeply rooted in long-standing cultural and social taboos. Discussions around menstruation are often approached with hesitation, discomfort, and misinformation, which reinforces stigma and prevents open dialogue. This silence has contributed to a lack of awareness and the persistence of harmful myths, especially in rural and economically disadvantaged communities. Around the world, women have developed various personal and cultural strategies to cope with menstruation, which differ widely based on economic status, local traditions, educational attainment, and individual preferences. These strategies often determine the quality of menstrual hygiene practices, which directly influence women's physical health, emotional well-being, and social participation.

Menstruation is not merely a women's issue; it is a natural biological process that plays a central role in human reproduction and, therefore, concerns both women and men as part of the broader cycle of parenthood and population health. However, poor menstrual hygiene management (MHM) has been linked to a heightened risk of Reproductive tract infections (RTIs), which remain a major public health concern worldwide, particularly in low-income settings where access to clean water, sanitation facilities, and sanitary products is limited. Although it is difficult to determine the exact proportion of RTIs directly caused by poor MHM compared to those arising from Sexually transmitted infections (STIs), iatrogenic infections, or endogenous infections from other sources evidence suggests that inadequate menstrual hygiene significantly contributes to women's reproductive health burden. Despite this, the issue has remained neglected, hidden behind cultural silence and social discomfort, with little open discussion or policy prioritization.

According to estimates from the World Health Organization (2005), approximately 448 million new cases of curable STIs occur each year among adults aged 15-49 globally. In India alone, the annual incidence of STIs is estimated at about 5%, while community-based studies have reported the prevalence of RTIs to range alarmingly between 39% and 84%. Such high prevalence rates reflect the severe gaps in menstrual health education, hygiene infrastructure, and access to affordable sanitary products. Because education is closely linked to every aspect of personal and societal development, it becomes the collective responsibility of parents, teachers, health workers, and community leaders to equip the younger generation particularly adolescent girls with accurate knowledge and practical skills for managing menstruation safely and with dignity. Empowering young girls with education on menstrual health will not only safeguard their physical well-being but also enhance their confidence, school attendance, and participation in community life, which in turn contributes to the overall progress and development of the nation.

REVIEW OF LITERATURE

Menstrual hygiene is a crucial determinant of women's health, yet poor practices remain widespread, particularly in low-resource settings. Inadequate menstrual hygiene management (MHM) has been strongly associated with reproductive tract infections (RTIs) such as bacterial vaginosis, candidiasis, and urinary tract infections (Borg et al., 2023). Studies have shown that unhygienic practices, including the use of reusable cloths without proper washing and drying, increase the risk of RTIs. For example, research in Uganda reported higher incidences of urogenital symptoms among women practicing poor menstrual hygiene (Borg et al., 2023), while studies in India linked infrequent changing of absorbents and use of unhygienic materials to elevated rates of bacterial vaginosis and urinary tract infections (Das, Sahoo, & Kar, 2015). Socioeconomic status plays a significant role, as women from lower-income backgrounds often lack access to sanitary products and clean water, forcing them to rely on unhygienic alternatives such as cloth rags (Sumpter & Torondel, 2013). In rural India, only 42% of adolescent girls use exclusively hygienic menstrual methods, highlighting significant geographic and economic disparities (Singh & Sahoo, 2022). Cultural beliefs and taboos exacerbate poor practices, as menstruation is often considered impure, restricting women's mobility and access to hygiene facilities, which in turn affects education and employment participation (Sharma & Gupta, 2020). The health consequences are substantial: infections from poor MHM can result in chronic reproductive issues, infertility, and greater susceptibility to sexually transmitted infections, while stigma surrounding menstruation discourages women from seeking timely medical care (Joshi & Mandal, 2025; Borg et al., 2023). Addressing these challenges requires comprehensive interventions, including education to dispel myths, improved access to sanitary products, sanitation facilities, and the normalization of menstruation as a manageable and natural aspect of women's lives, which is essential for improving overall health outcomes and empowering women (Sharma & Gupta, 2020; Singh & Sahoo, 2022).

OBJECTIVE

This review aims to critically analyze the existing literature and evidence on menstrual health and hygiene to identify the factors underlying the prevalence of menstruation related problems and to propose effective strategies for their management.

MENSTRUATION: CORE FACTS AND INSIGHTS

Menstruation is a natural biological process in which the body sheds the lining of the Uterus (womb). It usually begins between the ages of 10 and 15 and continues until around 45 to 55 years of age. Menstruation indicates the onset of reproductive capability, as it signals that a girl can become pregnant. The average menstrual cycle lasts about 28 to 35 days. Cramping during menstruation is common and results from contractions of the uterus. Maintaining proper hygiene during this time is essential: bathing is safe, but douching (washing the inside of the vagina) should be avoided. Instead, girls and women should clean the external genital area (Vulva) at least once daily. Menstrual materials such as sanitary pads or clean homemade cloth should be changed three to six times a day. If cloth is used, it should be thoroughly washed with soap and water and dried in direct sunlight to prevent infection.

BARRIERS TO PROPER MENSTRUAL HYGIENE

Economic, social, cultural, and educational factors have a profound impact on menstrual health, shaping women's experiences from childhood through adolescence, adulthood, marriage, and eventually motherhood cycles that are often repeated across generations. These influences, combined with surrounding environmental conditions, play a critical role in determining menstrual practices and overall reproductive well-being. Such factors contribute to the high prevalence of Reproductive tract infections (RTIs) and sexually transmitted infections (STIs), and are further compounded by women's limited decision-making power, their low social status within families, and the persistence of unhealthy menstrual hygiene behaviors. Menstrual hygiene is deeply influenced by a combination of economic and socio-cultural factors, both of which create significant barriers to safe and dignified menstrual practices. Poverty whether individual or structural remains one of the most critical challenges, as many women and girls in low-income settings cannot afford sanitary products such as pads or tampons, which ideally need to be changed several times a day to prevent infection and discomfort. The high cost of commercial sanitary materials often forces them to resort to unsafe alternatives like old rags, newspapers, or other absorbent materials that are not hygienically suitable. Limited access to clean water, private washing facilities, and proper waste disposal systems further compounds the problem, making safe menstrual management even more difficult.

Alongside economic constraints, entrenched socio-cultural beliefs play an equally powerful role in perpetuating poor menstrual hygiene practices. In many traditional or tribal communities, menstruation is still considered impure or shameful, and girls are often discouraged from using any menstrual materials or discussing menstrual health openly. This culture of silence and stigma forces many to hide their menstrual cloths and dry them in dark, damp, and poorly ventilated spaces, which prevents adequate drying and encourages microbial growth. Such unhygienic practices substantially increase the risk of Reproductive tract infections (RTIs) and other menstrual related health issues. The lack of menstrual education also contributes to fear, embarrassment, and misinformation, further discouraging healthy practices. These interlinked economic and socio-cultural barriers not only endanger women's physical health but also undermine their psychological well-being, educational participation, and overall quality of life.

EFFECTS OF INADEQUATE MENSTRUAL HYGIENE

Menstruation is often accompanied by a complex set of religious, cultural, and social restrictions that vary widely across communities, significantly shaping women's experiences and behaviors. In Hindu tradition, women are often expected to abstain from worship, cooking, and family interactions during menstruation, as their touch is considered impure. Similarly, Jewish tradition regards menstruating women as ritually impure, extending this status to anything they come into contact with, including breath, spit, footprints, voice, and nail clippings. Under Islamic law, menstruating women are prohibited from praying, fasting, or engaging in sexual activity, and may handle the Quran only in translation. These restrictions are reinforced by societal taboos and a culture of shame that discourages open discussion about menstruation, contributing to secrecy, stigma, and inadequate hygienic practices. Empirical studies highlight the prevalence of such restrictions. For instance, research by Paria et al. revealed that 64.7% of urban and 78.6% of rural girls avoided religious events, outdoor activities, and school during menstruation, with rural girls generally subjected to stricter limitations. Food taboos are also common, with 42.6% of girls avoiding items such as sweets, spicy foods, and dairy products, often due to beliefs that certain foods exacerbate menstrual discomfort or are considered impure.

The health impacts of menstruation extend beyond physical discomfort. Many girls experience abdominal cramps, vomiting, dizziness from anemia, and psychological stress, including anxiety, embarrassment, and low self-esteem. Poor menstrual hygiene further exacerbates these issues, increasing the risk of vaginal rashes, foul odor, bacterial vaginosis, vulvovaginal candidiasis, pelvic inflammatory disease, toxic shock syndrome, and greater susceptibility to reproductive tract infections (RTIs) and sexually transmitted infections (STIs). Teenage pregnancies, preterm births, illegal abortions, and other adverse reproductive outcomes have also been linked to inadequate menstrual care and lack of education. Menstruation also has profound effects on education and social participation. Girls frequently miss school, fall behind academically, or drop out entirely due to cultural restrictions, early marriage, or curiosity-driven behaviors influenced by limited sexual and reproductive health knowledge. In many developing countries, the lack of adequate sanitation facilities-such as private toilets, clean water, and waste disposal-further hinders school attendance during menstruation. Of the 113 million children not enrolled in school globally, approximately 60% are girls, highlighting the disproportionate impact of inadequate menstrual management on female education.

Addressing these challenges requires a multi-dimensional approach that combines education, access to hygienic menstrual products, and improvements in sanitation infrastructure. Promoting awareness, debunking myths, and encouraging open dialogue can help reduce stigma, while access to sanitary pads, clean water, and proper washing facilities enables girls and women to maintain safe menstrual hygiene. Evidence shows that such interventions significantly improve physical health, reduce absenteeism, and enhance overall well-being, ultimately empowering women and contributing to broader societal development.

DISCUSSION

Community-based studies in India reveal a high prevalence of reproductive tract infections (RTIs), though data from urban slums and resettlement areas remain limited. In one study of 802 women, 43.9% reported current RTI symptoms. Yasmin et al. (2013) found that 82.3% of respondents used sanitary pads, while 15.7% relied on old washed cloths, of whom 69.5% experienced difficulties in washing and drying due to lack of privacy (93.7%). Many women dried and stored cloths in unhygienic, concealed spaces, increasing the risk of infection. Cultural restrictions were widespread, with 98.6% following some taboos during menstruation. Hygienic practices varied: 85.7% bathed daily, though some believed bathing in the first two days increased menstrual flow. Religious and dietary restrictions were most common among Muslim respondents (97.3% and 59.4%, respectively). While 80.3% had access to private toilets, 19.7% shared facilities with 15-20 users, and 38.8% stored water in their toilets. Approximately 10.2% reported excessive white discharge. Hand washing and daily bathing were significantly associated with access to continuous water supply and private toilets. Shanbhag et al. (2012) reported that only 44.1% of girls used sanitary pads, and among cloth users, only 31.3% washed them with soap and water. While 56.8% cleaned their genitalia with soap and water, 88.8% bathed daily. Though 68.4% dried cloths in sunlight, 16.4% dried them indoors. Reuse patterns varied: 71.7% used cloths for 1-2 months. Pads or cloths were changed once (21.7%), twice (39.8%), or three times (29.5%) daily. Cultural restrictions were prevalent, with 94.2% restricted from religious places and 45.6% observing menarche rituals. At menarche, 44.1% experienced fear, and 26.1% felt anxious. While 74.2% understood menstruation as a natural process, 17% attributed it to divine punishment, and 56.8% reported it as a significant physical and psychological burden.

Hamal and Susma (2014) observed that only 4.8% of women used disposable pads, with the majority relying on reusable cloths, over 90% of which were dried outdoors in sunlight, though some dried indoors. Disposal practices varied: 44.6% buried used cloths, 19.3% discarded them with other waste, 10.8% in toilets, and others burned or discarded them in water bodies. Daily bathing was reported by 63.9%, while the remainder bathed on alternate days. Restrictions included sleeping arrangements, household chores, and prohibitions from entering religious spaces, kitchens, or even homes. School absenteeism affected 20.5%, mostly due to abdominal pain. STIs and RTIs remain major health concerns, with over 6% of Indian adults affected annually. Early diagnosis, treatment, and education can reduce transmission, including HIV. Globally, about 10% of women experience genital infections annually, and 75% have a history of such infections. Poor sanitation worsens these conditions: Census 2011 reports that 67.3% of rural households lack toilets, with Jharkhand (91.7%), Madhya Pradesh (86.4%), and Chhattisgarh (85.2%) most affected. Many rural schools lack functional toilets, water, or privacy, leading to open defecation, unsafe bathing, reuse of menstrual products, and drying cloths in unhygienic conditions, increasing urinary and reproductive tract infections.

Ahmed and Yesmin (2008) reported that 95% of women and 90% of adolescent girls used cloth during menstruation, with 40% of women changing rags once daily and 75% of adolescents changing three times. Washing practices were poor: 60% used unsafe water, and 90% used water only. Reuse and drying in dark, unhygienic spaces were common. Thakre et al. (2011) found 49.35% of girls used sanitary pads, while 45.74% used old cloth. Cleaning of the external genitalia was satisfactory in only 33.85%. Shah et al. (2013) observed a shift in preference from old cloths to falalin cloths and sanitary pads. Dasgupta and Sarkar (2008) reported that 48.75% of girls were aware of sanitary pads, and unsafe practices tripled the risk of RTIs. Dhingra et al. (2009) found menstrual hygiene practices unsatisfactory, with 98% believing bathing was unnecessary. Anand et al. (2015) noted that only 15% of women used sanitary pads or locally prepared napkins, with RTIs and vaginal discharge positively correlated with unhygienic methods. Dube and Sharma (2012) found that 40% of rural and 60% of urban girls considered menstruation natural, while 39% of urban and 56% of rural girls viewed it as a disease. Knowledge of the menstrual cycle was low: 11% of urban and 28% of rural girls were unaware of cycle gaps. Mohite and Mohite (2016) reported that 12.6% used disposable sanitary napkins, while 87.3% relied on reusable cloths, often disposed of un-sanitarily. Utilization of ICDS and sub-center services was low at 16.9% and 27.2%, respectively.

Paria et al. highlighted urban-rural disparities: more urban girls used sanitary pads than rural girls ($P = 0.000$), while cloth usage was higher in rural areas. Many changed pads only once per day, and reuse was common. Cleaning of external genitalia was satisfactory in 47.63% of urban girls and 37.96% of rural girls, with urban girls practicing better hygiene ($P = 0.023$). Private toilet access was higher in urban areas (83.63%) compared to rural areas (56.39%). Shivaleela et al. found that 60.9% of girls had good menstrual hygiene knowledge, but only 39.9% practiced it effectively. While 62.4% used cloth, 66.2% used commercial sanitary pads, 52.9% washed cloths with soap and water, and 45.2% dried them in sunlight. About 51.9% changed pads or cloth three or more times daily, and 67.3% bathed with soap daily. Tarhane and Kasulkar (2015) reported 79% used sanitary napkins, while 21% used cloth. Jogdand and Yerpude (2011) found that 34.63% used old cloth, and 78.99% were restricted from religious events. Sudeshna and Aparajita (2012) observed that most girls preferred cloth over pads due to poverty, cost, and lack of awareness, with only 13.2% using pads exclusively and 24.2% using both cloth and pads.

CONCLUSION

Despite growing attention to menstrual health in recent years, a large segment of India's population remains largely unaware of the basic facts about menstruation. Although literacy rates have improved, specific education on menstrual health is still insufficient, leaving many girls and women unprepared to manage menstruation safely and hygienically. Deeply rooted cultural beliefs, taboos, and traditional restrictions continue to act as significant barriers; even those with knowledge may adhere to outdated practices due to ingrained social norms. These restrictions often dictate what a menstruating woman can eat, where she can go, and what activities she can perform, limiting her mobility and participation in daily life. While research, policy initiatives, school-based awareness programs, and subsidized sanitary products have made some progress, sustained and comprehensive efforts are still needed to create meaningful change in both urban and rural areas.

Women are central to the health and well-being of families, communities, and society at large. Neglecting any aspect of women's health, including menstrual hygiene, can have far-reaching consequences. Poor menstrual hygiene contributes not only to reproductive and urinary tract infections but also to psychosocial stress, school absenteeism, and reduced economic productivity. Menstrual taboos, particularly within patriarchal systems, further impede proper management, especially in rural and marginalized communities. Many women experience embarrassment or shame when purchasing menstrual products from male shopkeepers, drying menstrual cloths in public view, or even discussing menstruation openly a shame that has been systematically ingrained over generations.

The lack of adequate sanitation, private toilets, clean water, and safe disposal facilities exacerbates these challenges, leaving women with limited options for hygienic menstrual management. Disparities between urban and rural areas persist: rural women are more likely to rely on reusable cloths, follow unsafe disposal methods, and face stricter cultural restrictions. Addressing these issues requires a holistic approach that integrates education, improved sanitation, affordable and accessible menstrual products, and the dismantling of cultural taboos. Good menstrual hygiene management is not only a health concern but also a matter of human rights and gender equality. Every woman has the right to manage menstruation safely and with dignity, and failing to uphold this right undermines social development, educational progress, and women's empowerment. Sustainable change is achievable only through ongoing awareness, community engagement, policy support, and the normalization of menstruation as a natural and manageable aspect of women's lives.

REFERENCES

Ahmed, R., & Yesmin, K. (2008). Menstrual hygiene: Breaking the silence. In *Beyond construction: Use by all. A collection of case studies from sanitation and hygiene promotion practitioners in South Asia* (pp. 283–287). Water Aid.

Anand, E., Singh, J., & Unisa, S. (2015). Menstrual hygiene practices and its association with reproductive tract infections and abnormal vaginal discharge among women in India. *Sexual & Reproductive Healthcare : Official Journal of the Swedish Association of Midwives*, *6*(4), 249–254. DOI: 10.1016/j.srhc.2015.06.001 PMID: 26614609

Borg, S. A., Bukenya, J. N., Kibira, S. P. S., Nakamya, P., Makumbi, F. E., Exum, N. G., Schwab, K. J., & Hennegan, J. (2023). The association between menstrual hygiene, workplace sanitation practices and self-reported urogenital symptoms in a cross-sectional survey of women working in Mukono District, Uganda. *PLoS One*, *18*(7), e0288942. DOI: 10.1371/journal.pone.0288942 PMID: 37471386

Das, P., Sahoo, S., & Kar, B. (2015). Menstrual hygiene practices, WASH access and the risk of reproductive tract infections among women in India: A hospital-based case-control study. *BMC Infectious Diseases*, *15*, 1–9. DOI: 10.1186/s12879-015-1076-7

Dasgupta, A., & Sarkar, M. (2008). Menstrual hygiene: How hygienic is the adolescent girl? *Indian Journal of Community Medicine : Official Publication of Indian Association of Preventive & Social Medicine*, *33*(2), 77–80. DOI: 10.4103/0970-0218.40872 PMID: 19967028

Dhingra, R., Kumar, A., & Kour, M. (2009). Knowledge and practices related to menstruation among tribal (Gujjar) adolescent girls. *Studies on Ethno-Medicine*, *3*(1), 43–48. DOI: 10.1080/09735070.2009.11886336

Dube, S., & Sharma, K. (2012). Knowledge, attitude and practice regarding reproductive health among urban and rural girls: A comparative study. *Studies on Ethno-Medicine*, *6*(2), 85–94. DOI: 10.1080/09735070.2012.11886424

Hamal, M., & Susma, K. (2014). Hygiene, health problems and socio-cultural practices: What school girls do during menstruation. *Age (Dordrecht, Netherlands)*, *12*, 14.

Jogdand, K., & Yerpude, P. (2011). A community based study on menstrual hygiene among adolescent girls. *Indian Journal of Maternal and Child Health*, *13*, 1–6.

Joshi, P., & Mandal, D. (2025). Status, gaps and challenges in menstrual health in India. *PM & R*, *5*(1), 8–15. DOI: 10.4103/pmr.2025.05000

Mohite, R. V., & Mohite, V. R. (2016). Menstrual hygiene practices among slum adolescent girls. *International Journal of Community Medicine and Public Health, 3*, 1729–1734. DOI: 10.18203/2394-6040.ijcmph20162033

Paria, B., Bhattacharyya, A., & Das, S. (2014). A comparative study on menstrual hygiene among urban and rural adolescent girls of West Bengal. *Journal of Family Medicine and Primary Care, 3*(4), 413–417. DOI: 10.4103/2249-4863.148131 PMID: 25657955

Shanbhag, D., Shilpa, R., D'Souza, N., Josephine, P., Singh, J., & Goud, B. R. (2012). Perceptions regarding menstruation and practices during menstrual cycles among high school going adolescent girls in resource limited settings around Bangalore city, Karnataka, India. *International Journal of Collaborative Research on Internal Medicine & Public Health.*

Sharma, P., & Gupta, N. L. (2020). Menstrual hygiene and infections: Menacing women's health. *International Journal of Health & Allied Sciences, 9*(2), 99–104. DOI: 10.4103/ijhas.IJHAS_92_19

Singh, A., & Sahoo, S. (2022). Menstrual hygiene practices among adolescent women in rural India: A cross-sectional study. *BMC Public Health, 22*(1), 1–9. DOI: 10.1186/s12889-022-14622-7 PMID: 36401238

Sudeshna, R., & Aparajita, D. (2012). Determinants of menstrual hygiene among adolescent girls: A multivariate analysis. *National Journal of Community Medicine, 3*, 294–301.

Sumpter, C., & Torondel, B. (2013). A systematic review of the health and social effects of menstrual hygiene management. *PLoS One, 8*(4), e62004. DOI: 10.1371/journal.pone.0062004 PMID: 23637945

Tarhane, S., & Kasulkar, A. (2015). Awareness of adolescent girls regarding menstruation and practices during menstrual cycle. *Panacea Journal of Medical Sciences, 5*, 29–32.

Yasmin, S., Manna, N., Mallik, S., Ahmed, A., & Paria, B. (2013). Menstrual hygiene among adolescent school students: An in-depth cross-sectional study in an urban community of West Bengal, India. *IOSR Journal of Dental and Medical Sciences, 5*(6), 22–26. DOI: 10.9790/0853-0562226

Conclusion

Supporting Women's Health and Wellbeing in the Workplace is not simply a matter of compliance, goodwill, or social responsibility—it is a decisive investment in people, performance, and progress. The evidence presented throughout this book underscores a clear truth: when organizations understand and respond to the health experiences of women, they create environments where individuals can thrive, teams can flourish, and businesses can achieve sustainable success.

Menopause and other key life stages are not private challenges to be endured in silence—they are shared realities that, when acknowledged, can be navigated with dignity, empathy, and support. By breaking down stigma, fostering open dialogue, and embedding inclusive policies into organizational culture, employers can transform potential periods of attrition into opportunities for retention, growth, and leadership development.

This work calls for a shift in perspective: from viewing women's health as an isolated, personal matter to recognizing it as a strategic factor in workplace design and management. It also calls for shared responsibility—leaders, HR professionals, healthcare providers, policymakers, and employees themselves each play a role in building supportive environments.

The strategies discussed in these chapters—from legal frameworks and ethical considerations to technological innovations and leadership practices—provide a toolkit for change. They are not intended as a final word, but as a foundation for continuous learning, adaptation, and collaboration. Every organization's journey toward inclusivity will be unique, but the principles remain the same: listen, learn, act, and evaluate.

Ultimately, supporting women's health is not only about reducing absenteeism, improving productivity, or protecting the bottom line—though these benefits are real and significant. It is about affirming the value of every individual, honoring their contributions at every stage of life, and building a future of work that is equitable, humane, and resilient.

The next step belongs to all of us. Let this book be your starting point—not the finish line—in creating workplaces where women are supported, respected, and empowered to succeed, no matter where they are in their personal and professional journeys.

FINAL CALL-TO-ACTION: BUILDING A WORKPLACE THAT SUPPORTS WOMEN'S HEALTH

The time to act is now. The research, stories, and strategies in this book have shown that supporting women's health—especially during menopause—is both a moral responsibility and a business imperative. To translate these insights into tangible change, organizations can begin with the following steps:

1. **Acknowledge the Need**

Publicly recognize women's health, including menopause, as a workplace priority. Commit to addressing it in your inclusion and wellbeing strategies.

2. **Educate and Raise Awareness**

Deliver training for all staff, especially managers, on the realities of menopause, mental health, and other women's health concerns. Normalize open, respectful conversations.

3. **Review and Update Policies**

Audit current HR policies to identify gaps. Include provisions for flexible work, symptom-related leave, and access to healthcare or wellbeing programs.

4. **Provide Personalized Support**

Offer confidential access to health resources—such as AI-driven wellbeing tools, medical consultations, and employee assistance programs—that meet individual needs.

5. **Lead by Example**

Ensure senior leaders champion women's health initiatives. Their visible support signals commitment and drives cultural change across the organization.

6. **Create Safe Feedback Channels**

Establish anonymous surveys, focus groups, or suggestion systems so employees can share experiences and recommend improvements without fear of reprisal.

7. **Measure, Improve, Sustain**

Track outcomes such as absenteeism, engagement, and retention rates. Use data and feedback to refine programs and ensure lasting impact.

Small actions create momentum. Even modest policy changes, leadership awareness, and open dialogue can spark a shift toward healthier, more inclusive workplaces. By implementing these steps, ***organizations can not only retain and empower talented women but also model the future of work—one where everyone can thrive at every stage of life***.

Compilation of References

Aarthy, R., & Venkatesan, S.Aarthy M.S. (2025). Exploring the influence of workplace spirituality and spiritual resilience on work–life balance among women IT professionals. *Journal of Information Systems Engineering & Management*, *79*(1), 1–15. DOI: 10.52783/jisem.v10i37s.6504

Abe, J. A. A., Ko, J. H., & Goto, S. G. (2013). Mindfulness, emotional intelligence, and emotional labor. *Personality and Individual Differences*, *55*(5), 513–518. DOI: 10.1016/j.paid.2013.04.027

Acker, J. (1990). Hierarchies, jobs, bodies: A theory of gendered organizations. *Gender & Society*, *4*(2), 139–158. DOI: 10.1177/089124390004002002

Acker, J. (2006). Inequality regimes: Gender, class, and race in organizations. *Gender & Society*, *20*(4), 441–464. DOI: 10.1177/0891243206289499

Acoba, E. F. (2024). Social support and mental health: The mediating role of perceived stress. *Frontiers in Psychology*, *15*, 1330720. Advance online publication. DOI: 10.3389/fpsyg.2024.1330720 PMID: 38449744

Adams, J., Lui, C.-W., Sibbritt, D., Broom, A., Wardle, J., & Homer, C. (2011). Attitudes and referral practices of maternity care professionals with regard to complementary and alternative medicine: An integrative review. *Journal of Advanced Nursing*, *67*(3), 472–483. DOI: 10.1111/j.1365-2648.2010.05510.x PMID: 21214615

Agbi, F. A., Lulin, Z., & Asamoah, E. O. (2023). Quality of communication between healthcare providers and pregnant women: Impact on maternal satisfaction, health outcomes, and shared decision-making. *UJOG*, *2*(1), 3–10. DOI: 10.31586/ujog.2023.784

Ahmad Syahir, N., Ramli, N. H., & Samsudin, Z. (2025). Workplace spirituality and spiritual resilience in women professionals. *Journal of Religion and Health*, *64*(2), 358–375. DOI: 10.1007/s10943-025-02350-2

Ahmad, R., Nawaz, M. R., Ishaq, M. I., Khan, M. M., & Ashraf, H. A. (2023). Social exchange theory: Systematic review and future directions. *Frontiers in Psychology, 13*, 1015921. DOI: 10.3389/fpsyg.2022.1015921 PMID: 36710813

Ahmed, R., & Yesmin, K. (2008). Menstrual hygiene: Breaking the silence. In *Beyond construction: Use by all. A collection of case studies from sanitation and hygiene promotion practitioners in South Asia* (pp. 283–287). Water Aid.

Ahuja, M. (2016). Age of menopause and determinants of menopause age: A PAN India survey by IMS. *Journal of Midlife Health, 7*(3), 126–131. DOI: 10.4103/0976-7800.191012 PMID: 27721640

AI Model IDs Women With Subjective Cognitive Decline During Menopause. (2025). *Neurology Advisor*. https://doi.org/DOI: 10.1093/neurologyadvisor/ai-model-ids-women-with-subjective-cognitive-decline-during-menopause

Alabi, O. A., Ajayi, F. A., Udeh, C. A., & Efunniyi, F. P. (2024). Predictive analytics in human resources: Enhancing workforce planning and customer experience. *International Journal of Innovation and Scientific Research, 11*(9), 149–158. DOI: 10.51244/IJRSI.2024.1109016

AlAteeq, D., AlNujaim, S. M., & AlGharbi, A. H. (2025). Prevalence of depression and anxiety among working women in Saudi Arabia: Psychosocial and perinatal correlates. *BMC Women's Health, 25*(228), 228. Advance online publication. DOI: 10.1186/s12905-025-03776-2 PMID: 40375291

Alawlaqi, A., Amor, H., & Hammadeh, M. E. (2017). Role of hormones in hypoactive sexual desire disorder and current treatment. *Journal of the Turkish German Gynecological Association, 18*(4), 210–218. DOI: 10.4274/jtgga.2017.0071

Albert, K. M., & Newhouse, P. A. (2019). Estrogen, Stress, and Depression: Cognitive and Biological Interactions. *Annual Review of Clinical Psychology, 15*(1), 399–423. DOI: 10.1146/annurev-clinpsy-050718-095557

Ali, M., Dewan, A., Sahu, A. K., & Taye, M. M. (2023). Understanding of Machine Learning with Deep Learning: Architectures, Workflow, Applications and Future Directions. *Computers 2023, Vol. 12, Page 91, 12*(5), 91. DOI: 10.3390/computers12050091

Ali, M., Algashamy, H., Alzidi, E., Ahmed, K., Bui, F., Patel, S., Azam, S., Abdulrazak, L., & Moni, M. (2023). Development and performance analysis of machine learning methods for predicting depression among menopausal women. *Healthcare Analytics, 3*, 100202. Advance online publication. DOI: 10.1016/j.health.2023.100202

Alon, T., Doepke, M., Olmstead-Rumsey, J., & Tertilt, M. (2020). *The impact of COVID-19 on gender equality*. NBER Working Paper.

Alowais, S. A., Alghamdi, S. S., Alsuhebany, N., Alqahtani, T., Alshaya, A. I., Almohareb, S. N., Aldairem, A., Alrashed, M., Bin Saleh, K., Badreldin, H. A., Al Yami, M. S., Al Harbi, S., & Albekairy, A. M. (2023). Revolutionizing healthcare: The role of artificial intelligence in clinical practice. *BMC Medical Education*, *23*(1), 689. DOI: 10.1186/s12909-023-04698-z

Al-Shammari, M., Ahmed Al Bin Ali, F., Abdulla AlRashidi, M., & Salem Albuainain, M. (2024). Big Data and Predictive Analytics for Strategic Human Resource Management: A Systematic Literature Review. *International Journal of Computing and Digital Systems*, *17*(1), 1–9. DOI: 10.12785/ijcds/1571015706

Alsharif, F. (2024). Artificial Intelligence in Oncology: Applications, Challenges and Future Frontiers. *International Journal of Pharmaceutical Investigation*, *14*(3), 647–656. DOI: 10.5530/ijpi.14.3.76

Alshogran, O. Y., Mahmoud, F. M. Z., & Alkhatatbeh, M. J. (2022). Predictors of age at menopause and psychiatric symptoms among postmenopausal females in Jordan. *Journal of Psychosomatic Obstetrics and Gynaecology*, *43*(4), 385–392. DOI: 10.1080/0167482X.2021.1984425

Altman, N. S. (1992). An introduction to kernel and nearest-neighbor nonparametric regression. *The American Statistician*, *46*(3), 175–185. DOI: 10.1080/00031305.1992.10475879

Alvarez-Melis, D., & Jaakkola, T. S. (2018). On the robustness of interpretability methods. *arXiv Preprint*, arXiv:1806.08049. https://arxiv.org/abs/1806.08049

Alzueta, E., de Zambotti, M., Javitz, H., Clark, A., & Baker, F. C. (2024). Navigating menopause at work: A preliminary study about challenges and support systems. *Menopause (New York, N.Y.)*, *31*(4), 258–265. DOI: 10.1097/GME.0000000000002333 PMID: 38442310

Alzueta, E., Griffiths, A., & Riach, K. (2024). Symptom impact on work performance. *Journal of Occupational Health Psychology*. Advance online publication. DOI: 10.1037/ocp0000301

Ambikairajah, A., Walsh, E., & Cherbuin, N. (2022). A review of menopause nomenclature. *Reproductive Health*, *19*(1), 29. Advance online publication. DOI: 10.1186/s12978-022-01336-7

Anand, E., Singh, J., & Unisa, S. (2015). Menstrual hygiene practices and its association with reproductive tract infections and abnormal vaginal discharge among women in India. *Sexual & Reproductive Healthcare : Official Journal of the Swedish Association of Midwives*, *6*(4), 249–254. DOI: 10.1016/j.srhc.2015.06.001 PMID: 26614609

Anderson, K., Patel, R., & Brown, L. (2023). AI in Workforce Analytics: A Tool for Employee Well-being. *Journal of Business Technology*, *48*(2), 112–129.

Angco, R. J. N. (2025). Women in Menopause and The Workplace Experience : A Meta- Synthesis. *International Journal of Public Health Research*, *15*(1), 2105–2113.

Ang, S., Van Dyne, L., & Koh, C. (2007). *Cultural intelligence: Individual interactions across cultures*. Business Books.

An, H., Gu, X., Obrenovic, B., & Godinic, D. (2023). The role of job insecurity, social media exposure, and job stress in predicting anxiety among white-collar employees. *Psychology Research and Behavior Management*, *16*, 3303–3318. DOI: 10.2147/PRBM.S416100 PMID: 37614323

Aninye, I. O., Laitner, M. H., & Chinnappan, S. (2021). Menopause preparedness: Perspectives for patient, provider, and policymaker consideration. *Menopause (New York, N.Y.)*, *28*(10), 1186–1191. DOI: 10.1097/GME.0000000000001819 PMID: 34183564

Anne Simpson, E. E., Doherty, J., & Timlin, D. (2024). Menopause as a window of opportunity: The benefits of designing more effective theory-driven behaviour change interventions to promote healthier lifestyle choices at midlife. *The Proceedings of the Nutrition Society*, *83*(2), 120–129. DOI: 10.1017/S0029665123004810

Ariyoshi, H. (2009). Evaluation of menopausal interventions at a Japanese company. *AAOHN Journal*, *57*(3), 106–111. DOI: 10.3928/08910162-20090301-01

Armeni, E., Mili, N., Siliogka, E., Goulis, D. G., & Lambrinoudaki, I. (2022). Menopause medical education around the world: The way forward to serve women's health. *Current Opinion in Endocrine and Metabolic Research*, *26*, 100387. DOI: 10.1016/j.coemr.2022.100387

Artificial, M., & Al-Antari, M. A. (2023). Artificial Intelligence for Medical Diagnostics—Existing and Future AI Technology! *Diagnostics (Basel)*, *13*(4), 688. DOI: 10.3390/diagnostics13040688

Ashmos, D. P., & Duchon, D. (2000). Spirituality at work: A conceptualization and measure. *Journal of Management Inquiry*, *9*(2), 134–145. DOI: 10.1177/105649260092008

Atiku, S. O., & Van Wyk, E. (2024). Leadership practices and work engagement in higher education: The mediating role of job demands-resources. *SAGE Open*, *14*(1), 21582440241233378. DOI: 10.1177/21582440241233378

Atkinson, C., Beck, V., & Brewis, J. (2022). Menopause in the Workplace: The Impact on Women's Careers. *Journal of Occupational Health Psychology*, *27*(3), 245–259.

Atkinson, C., Brewis, J., & Beck, V. (2023). Workplace Stigma and Gendered Aging: AI Interventions for Inclusion. *Human Resource Management Journal*, *44*(1), 102–121.

Bach, A., Thepaksorn, P., Thepaksorn, E., Borg, D., Rutherford, S., Osborne, N., Darssan, D., & Phung, D. (2024). Practical cooling interventions for preventing heat strain in indoor factory workers in Thailand. *American Journal of Industrial Medicine*, *67*(6), 556–561. Advance online publication. DOI: 10.1002/ajim.23589

Bajwa, J., Munir, U., Nori, A., & Williams, B. (2021). Artificial intelligence in healthcare: Transforming the practice of medicine. *Future Healthcare Journal*, *8*(2), e188–e194. DOI: 10.7861/fhj.2021-0095

Bakker, A. B., & de Vries, J. D. (2020). Job demands–resources theory and self-regulation: New explanations and remedies for job burnout. *Anxiety, Stress, and Coping*, *34*(1), 1–21. DOI: 10.1080/10615806.2020.1797695 PMID: 32856957

Bakker, A. B., & Demerouti, E. (2007). The job demands–resources model: State of the art. *Journal of Managerial Psychology*, *22*(3), 309–328. DOI: 10.1108/02683940710733115

Banaszek, A., & Łopuszańska-Dawid, M. (2023). The importance of nutrition in menopause and perimenopause—A review. *Nutrients*, *16*(1), 27. DOI: 10.3390/nu16010027

Baptista, N., Pinho, J. C., & Alves, H. (2021). Examining social capital and online social support links: A study in online health communities facing treatment uncertainty. *International Review on Public and Nonprofit Marketing*, *18*(1), 57–94. DOI: 10.1007/s12208-020-00263-2

Barata, C., Rotemberg, V., Codella, N. C. F., Tschandl, P., Rinner, C., Akay, B. N., Apalla, Z., Argenziano, G., Halpern, A., Lallas, A., Longo, C., Malvehy, J., Puig, S., Rosendahl, C., Soyer, H. P., Zalaudek, I., & Kittler, H. (2023). A reinforcement learning model for AI-based decision support in skin cancer. *Nature Medicine*, *29*(8), 1941–1946. DOI: 10.1038/s41591-023-02475-5

Barber, K., & Charles, A. (2023). Barriers to accessing effective treatment and support for menopausal symptoms: A qualitative study capturing the behaviours, beliefs and experiences of key stakeholders. *Patient Preference and Adherence*, *17*, 2971–2980. DOI: 10.2147/PPA.S430203 PMID: 38027078

Bardzell, S. (2010). Feminist HCI: Taking stock and outlining an agenda for design. In *Proceedings of the SIGCHI Conference on Human Factors in Computing Systems* (pp. 1301–1310). ACM. DOI: 10.1145/1753326.1753521

Barel, E., Shahrabani, S., & Tzischinsky, O. (2017). Sex hormone/cortisol ratios differentially modulate risk-taking in men and women. *Evolutionary Psychology : An International Journal of Evolutionary Approaches to Psychology and Behavior*, *15*(1), 1–10. DOI: 10.1177/1474704917697333 PMID: 28274134

Barki, H., & Hartwick, J. (2001). Interpersonal conflict and its management in information system development. *Management Information Systems Quarterly*, *25*(2), 195–228. DOI: 10.2307/3250929

Baxi, V., Edwards, R., Montalto, M., & Saha, S. (2021). Digital pathology and artificial intelligence in translational medicine and clinical practice. *Modern Pathology*, *35*(1), 23–32. DOI: 10.1038/s41379-021-00919-2

Belle, V., & Papantonis, I. (2021). Principles and practice of explainable machine learning. *Frontiers in Big Data*, *4*, 688969. DOI: 10.3389/fdata.2021.688969

Bell, J. A., Garlick, D., & Stevens, C. (2022). It's time to talk about the M word. *British Dental Journal*, *232*(1), 15–17. DOI: 10.1038/s41415-021-3817-y

Benefiel, M., Fry, L. W., & Geigle, D. (2014). Spirituality and religion in the workplace: History, theory, and research. *Psychology of Religion and Spirituality*, *6*(3), 175–187. DOI: 10.1037/a0036597

Bennett, C., & Lagace, M. (2021). Women at work: The impact of menopause on the workplace. *Harvard Business Review Insight Center Report*. https://hbr.org/2021/10/women-at-work-the-impact-of-menopause-on-the-workplace

Berdahl, J. L., & Moon, S. H. (2013). Workplace mistreatment of middle class workers based on sex, parenthood, and caregiving. *The Journal of Social Issues*, *69*(2), 341–366. DOI: 10.1111/josi.12018

Bertolotti, G., Villani, D., & Riva, G. (2022). AI in workplace health management: Opportunities and challenges. *Workplace Health & Safety*, *70*(2), 85–97.

Bhattacharya, A., Ooge, J., Stiglic, G., & Verbert, K. (2023). Directive explanations for monitoring the risk of diabetes onset: Introducing directive data-centric explanations and combinations to support what-if explorations. In *Proceedings of the 28th International Conference on Intelligent User Interfaces* (pp. 204–219). Association for Computing Machinery. https://doi.org/DOI: 10.1145/3581641.3584075

Bhise, P., Karekar, P., Nikam, R., & Ray, S. (2024). AI-HRM: Transforming Human Resource Management With Artificial Intelligence.

Bierema, L. L. (2002). The role of gender consciousness in challenging patriarchy. *International Journal of Lifelong Education*, *21*(5), 397–411. DOI: 10.1080/02601370210141010

Binns, R. (2023). Algorithmic Bias in Healthcare: Addressing Discrimination in AI Models. *Journal of Ethical AI*, *21*(3), 87–104.

Biran, O., & Cotton, C. (2017). Explanation and justification in machine learning: A survey. *IJCAI Workshop on Explainable AI*. https://arxiv.org/abs/1706.07269

Birko, S., Dove, E. S., & Özdemir, V. (2015). A delphi technology foresight study: Mapping social construction of scientific evidence on metagenomics tests for water safety. *PLoS One*, *10*(6), e0129706. DOI: 10.1371/journal.pone.0129706 PMID: 26066837

Blanco-González, A., Cabezón, A., Seco-González, A., Conde-Torres, D., Antelo-Riveiro, P., Piñeiro, Á., & Garcia-Fandino, R. (2023). The Role of AI in Drug Discovery: Challenges, Opportunities, and Strategies. *Pharmaceuticals (Basel, Switzerland)*, *16*(6), 891. DOI: 10.3390/ph16060891

Blell, M. (2018). Grandmother hypothesis, grandmother effect and residence: Reframing kinship and the evolution of human female life history. In *Fertility and Reproduction* (pp. 55–70). Palgrave Macmillan.

Borg, S. A., Bukenya, J. N., Kibira, S. P. S., Nakamya, P., Makumbi, F. E., Exum, N. G., Schwab, K. J., & Hennegan, J. (2023). The association between menstrual hygiene, workplace sanitation practices and self-reported urogenital symptoms in a cross-sectional survey of women working in Mukono District, Uganda. *PLoS One*, *18*(7), e0288942. DOI: 10.1371/journal.pone.0288942 PMID: 37471386

Brancaccio, G., Balato, A., Malvehy, J., Puig, S., Argenziano, G., & Kittler, H. (2024). Artificial Intelligence in Skin Cancer Diagnosis: A Reality Check. *The Journal of Investigative Dermatology*, *144*(3), 492–499. DOI: 10.1016/j.jid.2023.10.004

Bravo, F., & Reguera-Alvarado, N. (2019). Sustainable development disclosure: Environmental, social, and governance reporting and gender diversity in the audit committee. *Business Strategy and the Environment, 28*(2), 418–429. DOI: 10.1002/bse.2258

Breast Cancer Risk Factors | Breast Cancer | CDC. (n.d.). Retrieved March 25, 2025, from https://www.cdc.gov/breast-cancer/risk-factors/index.html

Breiman, L. (2001). Random forests. *Machine Learning, 45*(1), 5–32. DOI: 10.1023/A:1010933404324

Brewis, J., Atkinson, C., Beck, V., Davies, A., & Duberley, J. (2019). Menopause and the workplace.

Brewis, J., Beck, V., Davies, A., & Matheson, J. (2017). The effects of menopause transition on women's economic participation in the UK.

Brewis, J., Beck, V., Davies, A., & Matheson, J. (2020). The effects of menopause transition on women's economic participation in the UK. *Journal of Occupational and Environmental Medicine, 62*(6), 432–439.

Brewis, J., Davies, A., & Nash, M. (2022). Menopause in the Workplace: The Role of AI in Reducing Productivity Loss. *Journal of Occupational Health Psychology, 39*(2), 187–204.

Brewis, J., Davies, A., & Nash, M. (2023). Supporting Menopausal Employees: Workplace Interventions and Well-being. *Human Resource Management Journal, 33*(1), 110–128.

Brown, E. A., Bekker, H. L., Davison, S. N., Koffman, J., & Schell, J. O. (2016). Supportive care: Communication strategies to improve cultural competence in shared decision making. *Clinical Journal of the American Society of Nephrology; CJASN, 11*(10), 1902–1908. DOI: 10.2215/CJN.13661215 PMID: 27510456

Brown, S. (2022). News and views. *International Wound Journal, 19*(4), 731–733. DOI: 10.1111/iwj.13808

Bruce, D., & Rymer, J. (2009). Symptoms of the menopause. *Best Practice & Research. Clinical Obstetrics & Gynaecology, 23*(1), 25–32. DOI: 10.1016/j.bpobgyn.2008.10.002 PMID: 19056320

Bruce, L., Hrymak, V., Bruce, M., & Byrne, S. (2024). Navigating interpersonal conflicts in healthcare settings: A study of nurse-physician relationships during global health crises. *International Journal of Nursing Studies, 128*, 104155.

Bryson, A., Conti, G., & Hardy, C. (2022). Menopause, health, and labor market outcomes. *Journal of Health Economics*, *84*, 102645. DOI: 10.1016/j.jhealeco.2022.102645

Burger, H. G., Dudley, E. C., Robertson, D. M., & Dennerstein, L. (2002). Hormonal changes in the menopause transition. *Recent Progress in Hormone Research*, *57*(1), 257–275. DOI: 10.1210/rp.57.1.257 PMID: 12017547

Burnett, J. R., & Lisk, T. C. (2021). The future of employee engagement: Real-time monitoring and digital tools for engaging a workforce. In *International perspectives on employee engagement* (pp. 117–128). Routledge. DOI: 10.4324/9781003142492-9

Cahn, N., Crawford, B. J., & Waldman, E. G. (2024). Menopause discrimination at work: Comparing the law in the United States and United Kingdom. In *Research Handbook on Law, Society and Ageing* (pp. 281-297). Edward Elgar Publishing.

Cameron, K. S. (2021). *Organizational effectiveness: A comparison of multiple models*. Academic Press.

Carmichael, M. A., Enns, D. L., Barabas, M. E., Soligard, T., & Mountjoy, M. (2021). The impact of menstrual cycle phase on athletes' performance: A narrative review. *Sports Medicine (Auckland, N.Z.)*, *51*(3), 539–556. PMID: 33572406

Case Study: The Inevitability of Menopause in the Workplace. (n.d.). *LHH*. Retrieved from https://www.lhh.com/uk/en/insights/case-study-the-inevitability-of-menopause-in-the-workplace/

Catalyst. (2020). *Why diversity and inclusion matter: Quick take*. https://www.catalyst.org/research/why-diversity-and-inclusion-matter/

Chakraborty, T., & Ray, S. (2022). Strategies of Cyberloafing and Phubbing which Affect Workplace Digital Transformation. *Московский экономический журнал*, (10), 430-446.

Chan, M. H., Hawkes, K., & Kim, P. S. (2017). Modelling the evolution of traits in a two-sex population, with an application to grandmothering. *arXiv preprint arXiv:1907.01666*. https://arxiv.org/abs/1907.01666

Chancellor, S., & De Choudhury, M. (2020). Methods in predictive techniques for mental health status on social media: A critical review. *NPJ Digital Medicine*, *3*(1), 43. DOI: 10.1038/s41746-020-0233-7 PMID: 32219184

Chan, S., Gomes, A., & Singh, R. S. (2020). Is menopause still evolving? Evidence from a longitudinal study of multiethnic populations and its relevance to women's health. *BMC Women's Health*, *20*(1), 74. Advance online publication. DOI: 10.1186/s12905-020-00932-8 PMID: 32307019

Chapman, S. N., Ellis, S., Lahdenperä, M., Croft, D. P., & Lummaa, V. (2024). Menopause has not evolved as a general trait in mammals: A response to 'Do mammals have menopause?' *bioRxiv*. https://doi.org/DOI: 10.1101/2024.02.29.582687

Charde, S. H., Joshi, A., & Raut, J. (2023). A Comprehensive Review on Postmenopausal Osteoporosis in Women. *Cureus*, *15*(11), e48582. DOI: 10.7759/cureus.48582

Chartered Institute of Personnel and Development (CIPD). (2021). *Menopause and the Workplace*. Retrieved from www.cipd.co.uk

Chartered Institute of Personnel and Development (CIPD). (2021). *Menopause and the Workplace: Impact and Support Strategies*. London: CIPD. *Research Reports (Montgomery)*.

Chaudhury, M., & Ng, I. (1992). Absenteeism predictors: Least squares, rank regression, and model selection results. *The Canadian Journal of Economics. Revue Canadienne d'Economique*, *25*(3), 615–635. DOI: 10.2307/135735

Chedraui, P., & Pérez-López, F. R. (2021). Nutrition in menopausal women: A narrative review. *Nutrients*, *13*(6), 1969. DOI: 10.3390/nu13061969

Chen, H. (2024). *Engaging in sickness presenteeism: How do people decide? The decision-making process behind sickness presenteeism, and implications for its management* (Doctoral dissertation, Nottingham Trent University (United Kingdom)).

Chen, C., Li, O., Barnett, A., Han, L., Vervoort, D., & Dobson, A. (2025). Deep learning prediction of mammographic breast density using screening data. *Scientific Reports*, *15*(1), 11602. Advance online publication. DOI: 10.1038/s41598-025-95275-5 PMID: 40185813

Cheng, C., Lay, K.-L., Hsu, Y.-F., & Tsai, Y.-M. (2021). Can Likert scales predict choices? Testing the congruence between using Likert scale and comparative judgment on measuring attribution. *Methods in Psychology (Online)*, *5*, 100081. DOI: 10.1016/j.metip.2021.100081

Chen, S., Zhang, Y., & Liu, Y. (2025). Predicting preeclampsia in early pregnancy using clinical and laboratory data via machine learning model. *BMC Medical Informatics and Decision Making*, *25*(1), 178. Advance online publication. DOI: 10.1186/s12911-025-02999-5 PMID: 40312361

Chen, T., & Guestrin, C. (2016). XGBoost: A scalable tree boosting system. In *Proceedings of the 22nd ACM SIGKDD International Conference on Knowledge Discovery and Data Mining* (pp. 785–794). https://doi.org/DOI: 10.1145/2939672.2939785

Chen, Y., Zhao, L., & Wang, H. (2021). Wearable AI in health monitoring: Applications in menopause care. [REMOVED HYPERLINK FIELD]. *AI & Health, 14*(2), 45–59.

Cherniss, C. (2010). Emotional intelligence: Toward clarification of a concept. *Industrial and Organizational Psychology: Perspectives on Science and Practice, 3*(2), 110–126. DOI: 10.1111/j.1754-9434.2010.01231.x

Choi, E., Bahadori, M. T., Schuetz, A., Stewart, W. F., & Sun, J. (2016). Doctor AI: Predicting clinical events via recurrent neural networks. *Proceedings of the Machine Learning for Healthcare Conference*, 301–318. https://proceedings.mlr.press/v56/Choi16.html

Choudhury, O., Gkoulalas-Divanis, A., Salonidis, T., Sylla, I., Park, Y., Hsu, W., & Das, A. (2020). Differential privacy-enabled federated learning for sensitive health data [Preprint]. arXiv. https://arxiv.org/abs/1910.02578

Chrisler, J. C. (2013). Teaching taboo topics: Menstruation, menopause, and the psychology of women. *Psychology of Women Quarterly, 37*(1), 128–132. DOI: 10.1177/0361684312471326

Chung, J., & Teo, J. (2022). Mental health prediction using machine learning: Taxonomy, applications, and challenges. *Applied Computational Intelligence and Soft Computing, 2022*, 1–19. DOI: 10.1155/2022/9970363

CIPD. (2023). *Menstruation and menstrual health in the workplace: A guide for people professionals.* Chartered Institute of Personnel and Development.

Clark, M., & Bailey, S. (2024). Chatbots in Health Care: Connecting Patients to Information. *Chatbots in Health Care: Connecting Patients to Information: Emerging Health Technologies.* https://www.ncbi.nlm.nih.gov/books/NBK602381/

Collins, C., Dennehy, D., Conboy, K., & Mikalef, P. (2021). Artificial intelligence in information systems research: A systematic literature review and research agenda. *International Journal of Information Management, 60*, 102383. DOI: 10.1016/j.ijinfomgt.2021.102383

Collins, F. S., & Varmus, H. (2015). A new initiative on precision medicine. *The New England Journal of Medicine, 372*(9), 793–795. DOI: 10.1056/NEJMp1500523 PMID: 25635347

Collins, H., Barry, S. H., & Grace, . (2024). 'Difficult to Divulge': The Impact of Organisational Silence around the Menopause. *Work, Employment and Society*, *38*(5), 1445–1456. Advance online publication. DOI: 10.1177/09500170231212127

Comparetto, C., & Borruto, F. (2023). Treatments and management of menopausal symptoms: Current status and future challenges. *OBM Geriatrics*, *7*(3), 248. Advance online publication. DOI: 10.21926/obm.geriatr.2303248

Conde, D. M., Verdade, R. C., Valadares, A. L., Mella, L. F., Pedro, A. O., & Costa-Paiva, L. (2021). Menopause and cognitive impairment: A narrative review of current knowledge. *World Journal of Psychiatry*, *11*(8), 412–428. DOI: 10.5498/wjp.v11.i8.412 PMID: 34513605

Correll, S. J., Benard, S., & Paik, I. (2007). Getting a job: Is there a motherhood penalty? *American Journal of Sociology*, *112*(5), 1297–1338. DOI: 10.1086/511799

Cortés, Y. I., & Marginean, V. (2022). Key factors in menopause health disparities and inequities: Beyond race and ethnicity. *Current Opinion in Endocrine and Metabolic Research*, *26*, 100389. Advance online publication. DOI: 10.1016/j.coemr.2022.100389

Cover, T., & Hart, P. (1967). Nearest neighbor pattern classification. *IEEE Transactions on Information Theory*, *13*(1), 21–27. DOI: 10.1109/TIT.1967.1053964

Crandall, C. J., Mehta, J. M., & Manson, J. E. (2023). Management of Menopausal Symptoms: A Review. *Journal of the American Medical Association*, *329*(5), 405–420. DOI: 10.1001/jama.2022.24140

Crawford, B. J., Waldman, E. G., & Cahn, N. R. (2021). Working through menopause. *Wash. UL Rev.*, *99*, 1531.

Crenshaw, K. (1989). Demarginalizing the intersection of race and sex. *University of Chicago Legal Forum*, *1989*(1), 139–167.

Crenshaw, K. (1991). Mapping the margins: Intersectionality, identity politics, and violence against women of color. *Stanford Law Review*, *43*(6), 1241–1299. DOI: 10.2307/1229039

Crenshaw, K. (1991). Race, gender, and sexual harassment. *s. California Law Review*, *65*, 1467.

Creswell, J. W., & Plano Clark, V. L. (2011). *Designing and conducting mixed methods research* (2nd ed.). Sage Publications.

Criado Perez, C. (2019). *Invisible women: Data bias in a world designed for men.* Abrams Press.

Cronin, C., Abbott, J., Asiamah, N., & Smyth, S. (2024). Menopause at work—An organisation-based case study. *Nursing Open, 11*(1), 1–8. DOI: 10.1002/nop2.2058

Cronin, H., Theis, R., & Griffiths, A. (2023). Quality of life considerations. *Journal of Occupational Health Psychology*. Advance online publication. DOI: 10.1037/ocp0000302

Cuijpers, P., Stringaris, A., & Wolpert, M. (2020). Treatment outcomes for depression: Challenges and opportunities. *The Lancet. Psychiatry, 7*(11), 925–927. DOI: 10.1016/S2215-0366(20)30036-5 PMID: 32078823

Cunliffe, A. L. (2009). Reflexivity, learning and reflexive practice. In Armstrong, S., & Fukami, C. (Eds.), *The SAGE handbook of management learning, education and development* (pp. 405–418). SAGE., DOI: 10.4135/9780857021038.n21

Dalal, P. K., & Agarwal, M. (2023). Postmenopausal Syndrome. *Indian Journal of Psychiatry, 57*(6), 222–232. DOI: 10.4103/0019-5545.161483

Daly, K. L., Pike, G., Clarke, V., & Beck, V. (2024). "Difficulty mentioning the M word": Perceptions of a woman disclosing negative menopause symptoms in the workplace. *Qualitative Research in Organizations and Management, 19*(3), 163–181. DOI: 10.1108/QROM-07-2023-2562

Danesh, D. O., & Huber, T. P. (2022). A literature review of leadership training and a novel conceptual model of leader-member exchange theory for new dentists. *Journal of Health Organization and Management, 36*(4), 417–427. DOI: 10.1108/JHOM-05-2021-0192 PMID: 34951297

Darvishmotevali, M., & Ali, F. (2020). Job insecurity, subjective well-being and job performance: The moderating role of psychological capital. *International Journal of Hospitality Management, 87*, 102462. Advance online publication. DOI: 10.1016/j.ijhm.2020.102462

Dasgupta, A., & Sarkar, M. (2008). Menstrual hygiene: How hygienic is the adolescent girl? *Indian Journal of Community Medicine : Official Publication of Indian Association of Preventive & Social Medicine, 33*(2), 77–80. DOI: 10.4103/0970-0218.40872 PMID: 19967028

Das, P., Sahoo, S., & Kar, B. (2015). Menstrual hygiene practices, WASH access and the risk of reproductive tract infections among women in India: A hospital-based case-control study. *BMC Infectious Diseases, 15*, 1–9. DOI: 10.1186/s12879-015-1076-7

Davenport, T. H., & Ronanki, R. (2018). Artificial intelligence for the real world. *Harvard Business Review, 96*(1), 108–116.

Davenport, T., & Kalakota, R. (2019). The potential for artificial intelligence in healthcare. *Future Healthcare Journal*, *6*(2), 94–98. DOI: 10.7861/futurehosp.6-2-94 PMID: 31363513

Davenport, T., & Kalakota, R. (2023). *The Future of AI in Healthcare and Employee Well-being*. Harvard Business Press.

David, P. S., Smith, T. L., Nordhues, H. C., & Kling, J. M. (2022). A clinical review on paroxetine and emerging therapies for the treatment of vasomotor symptoms. *International Journal of Women's Health*, *14*, 353–361. DOI: 10.2147/IJWH.S282396 PMID: 35300283

Daysal, N. M.. (2011). Hormone therapy and labor market participation. *The Review of Economics and Statistics*, *93*(1), 148–163. DOI: 10.1162/REST_a_00063

Deloitte. (2023). *AI for Menopause Support: Trends in Workforce Management*. Global HR Analytics Report.

Deloitte. (2023). *The Future of Work for Women: Menopause and Work Flexibility*. Retrieved from www.deloitte.com

Demmin, D. L., & Silverstein, S. M. (2020). Visual impairment and mental health: Unmet needs and treatment options. *Clinical Ophthalmology (Auckland, N.Z.)*, *14*, 4229–4251. DOI: 10.2147/OPTH.S258783 PMID: 33299297

Dennis, N., & Hobson, G. (2023). Working well: Mitigating the impact of menopause in the workplace – A narrative evidence review. *Maturitas*, *177*, 107824. DOI: 10.1016/j.maturitas.2023.107824 PMID: 37634294

Departement of Labor USA. (2024). Let's Talk About It. *Menstruation and Menopause at Work*, (September), 1–7.

Derry, P., & Derry, G. (2014). Analysis of the STRAW Operational Definition of the Early Menopausal Transition. *Women's Reproductive Health (Philadelphia, Pa.)*, *1*(1), 21–30. DOI: 10.1080/23293691.2014.901797

Dhingra, R., Kumar, A., & Kour, M. (2009). Knowledge and practices related to menstruation among tribal (Gujjar) adolescent girls. *Studies on Ethno-Medicine*, *3*(1), 43–48. DOI: 10.1080/09735070.2009.11886336

DiClaudio, M. (2019). People analytics and the rise of HR: How data, analytics and emerging technology can transform human resources (HR) into a profit center. *Strategic HR Review*, *18*(2), 42–46. DOI: 10.1108/SHR-11-2018-0096

Diener, E., Wirtz, D., Biswas-Diener, R., Tov, W., Kim-Prieto, C., Choi, D. W., & Oishi, S. (2009). New measures of well-being. In *Assessing well-being: The collected works of Ed Diener* (pp. 247-266). Dordrecht: Springer Netherlands. DOI: 10.1007/978-90-481-2354-4_12

Diener, E., Oishi, S., & Tay, L. (2018). Advances in subjective well-being research. *Nature Human Behaviour*, *2*(4), 253–260. DOI: 10.1038/s41562-018-0307-6 PMID: 30936533

Dimai, H. P. (2022). New Horizons: Artificial Intelligence Tools for Managing Osteoporosis. *The Journal of Clinical Endocrinology and Metabolism*, *108*(4), 775–783. DOI: 10.1210/clinem/dgac702

Dirkx, J. M. (2001). The power of feelings: Emotion, imagination, and the construction of meaning in adult learning. *New Directions for Adult and Continuing Education*, *89*(89), 63–72. DOI: 10.1002/ace.9

Dobson, M., Schnall, P., Rosskam, E., & Landsbergis, P. (2020). Work-related burden of absenteeism, presenteeism, and disability: an epidemiologic and economic perspective. In *Handbook of disability, work and health* (pp. 251–272). Springer International Publishing. DOI: 10.1007/978-3-030-24334-0_13

Donati, S., Satolli, R., Colombo, C., Senatore, S., Cotichini, R., Da Cas, R., Spila Alegiani, S., & Mosconi, P. (2013). Informing women on menopause and hormone therapy: Know the Menopause—A multidisciplinary project involving the local healthcare system. *PLoS One*, *8*(12), e85121. Advance online publication. DOI: 10.1371/journal.pone.0085121 PMID: 24391988

Dube, S., & Sharma, K. (2012). Knowledge, attitude and practice regarding reproductive health among urban and rural girls: A comparative study. *Studies on Ethno-Medicine*, *6*(2), 85–94. DOI: 10.1080/09735070.2012.11886424

Eagly, A. H., & Carli, L. L. (2007). *Through the labyrinth: The truth about how women become leaders*. Harvard Business Press.

Eckerson, W. W. (2007). Predictive analytics. *Extending the Value of Your Data Warehousing Investment. TDWI Best Practices Report*, *1*, 1–36.

Edmondson, A. C. (1999). Psychological safety and learning behavior in work teams. *Administrative Science Quarterly*, *44*(2), 350–383. DOI: 10.2307/2666999

Ejo-Orusa, H., & Okwakpam, J. A. A. (2018). Predictive HR analytics and human resource management amongst human resource management practitioners in Port Harcourt, Nigeria. *Global Scientific Journal*, *6*(7), 254.

Ely, R. J., & Meyerson, D. E. (2000). Theories of gender in organizations: A new approach to organizational analysis and change. *Research in Organizational Behavior, 22*, 103–151. DOI: 10.1016/S0191-3085(00)22004-2

Emin, E. I., Emin, E., Papalois, A., Willmott, F., Clarke, S., & Sideris, M. (2019). Artificial intelligence in obstetrics and gynaecology: Is this the way forward? *In Vivo (Athens, Greece), 33*(5), 1547–1551. DOI: 10.21873/invivo.11635

Emmons, R. A. (1999). *The psychology of ultimate concerns: Motivation and Spirituality in personality*. Guilford Press.

Engelhardt, S. C., Bergeron, P., Gagnon, A., Dillon, L., & Pelletier, F. (2019). Using geographic distance as a potential proxy for help in the assessment of the grandmother hypothesis. *Current Biology, 29*(4), 651–656. DOI: 10.1016/j.cub.2019.01.027 PMID: 30744976

Equality and Human Rights Commission. (2024). *Menopause in the workplace: Guidance for employers*. https://www.equalityhumanrights.com/guidance/menopause-workplace-guidance-employers

Esteva, A., Robicquet, A., Ramsundar, B., Kuleshov, V., DePristo, M., Chou, K., Cui, C., Corrado, G., Thrun, S., & Dean, J. (2019). A guide to deep learning in healthcare. *Nature Medicine, 25*(1), 24–29. DOI: 10.1038/s41591-018-0316-z PMID: 30617335

European Parliament. (2022). *Addressing menopause as a workplace issue and preventing discrimination of women of menopausal age* (E-000279/2022).

Fan, Q., Wider, W., & Chan, C. K. (2023). The brief introduction to organizational citizenship behaviors and counterproductive work behaviors: A literature review. *Frontiers in Psychology, 14*, 1181930. DOI: 10.3389/fpsyg.2023.1181930 PMID: 37780163

Fan, X., Li, J., Mao, Z. E., & Lu, Z. (2021). Can ethical leadership inspire employee loyalty in hotels in China?-From the perspective of the social exchange theory. *Journal of Hospitality and Tourism Management, 49*, 538–547. DOI: 10.1016/j.jhtm.2021.11.006

Farhud, D. D., & Zokaei, S. (2021). Ethical Issues of Artificial Intelligence in Medicine and Healthcare. *Iranian Journal of Public Health, 50*(11), i. DOI: 10.18502/ijph.v50i11.7600

Fasihi, L., Tartibian, B., Eslami, R., & Fasihi, H. (2022). Artificial intelligence used to diagnose osteoporosis from risk factors in clinical data and proposing sports protocols. *Scientific Reports, 12*(1), 18330. DOI: 10.1038/s41598-022-23184-y

Fatima, M., Pachauri, P., Akram, W., Parvez, M., Ahmad, S., & Yahya, Z. (2024). Enhancing retinal disease diagnosis through AI: Evaluating performance, ethical considerations, and clinical implementation. *Informatics and Health*, *1*(2), 57–69. DOI: 10.1016/j.infoh.2024.05.003

Faubion, S. S., Bigler, J. K., Christmas, M. M., Cortés, Y. I., Green-Smith, P., Kapoor, E., Reed, S. D., Shufelt, C. L., Soares, C. N., & Thomas, H. N. (2024). Menopause and the workplace: Consensus recommendations from The Menopause Society. *Menopause (New York, N.Y.)*, *31*(9), 741–749. DOI: 10.1097/GME.0000000000002415

Fawcett Society. (2022). *Menopause and Workplace Report*. Retrieved from www.fawcettsociety.org.uk

Fazal, F., Serfraz, A., Saleem, H., Mehta, A. M., & Naqvi, F. N. (2020). Women leadership & organizational barriers: A socio-economic and ethical point of view. *J. Legal Ethical & Regul. Isses*, *23*, 1.

Fenton, A. (2024). *The impacts of menopause on women leaders in higher education: A strengths approach*. Abstract from CSEdX 2024: Radical Reimagination. https://www.csu.edu.au/division/learning-teaching/csedx/presentations/2024-program/the-impacts-of-menopause-on-women-leaders-in-higher-education-a-strengths-approach

Ferrari, R. (2015). Writing narrative style literature reviews. *Medical Writing*, *24*(4), 230–235. DOI: 10.1179/2047480615Z.000000000329

Fisher, J. W. (2011). The four domains model: Connecting Spirituality, health and well-being. *Religions*, *2*(1), 17–28. DOI: 10.3390/rel2010017

Fitz-Enz, J., & John Mattox, I. I. (2014). *Predictive analytics for human resources*. John Wiley & Sons. DOI: 10.1002/9781118915042

Flierman, I., van Seben, R., van Rijn, M., Poels, M., Buurman, B. M., & Willems, D. L. (2020). Health care providers' views on the transition between hospital and primary care in patients in the palliative phase: A qualitative description study. *Journal of Pain and Symptom Management*, *60*(2), 372–380. DOI: 10.1016/j.jpainsymman.2020.02.018 PMID: 32135201

Floridi, L., Cowls, J., Beltrametti, M., Chatila, R., Chazerand, P., Dignum, V., Luetge, C., Madelin, R., Pagallo, U., Rossi, F., Schafer, B., Valcke, P., & Vayena, E. (2018). AI4People—An ethical framework for a good AI society: Opportunities, risks, principles, and recommendations. *Minds and Machines*, *28*(4), 689–707. DOI: 10.1007/s11023-018-9482-5 PMID: 30930541

Fry, L. W. (2005). Toward a theory of spiritual leadership. *The Leadership Quarterly*, *16*(5), 619–640. DOI: 10.1016/j.leaqua.2005.07.001

Fry, L. W., & Kriger, M. (2009). Towards a theory of being-centered leadership: Multiple levels of being as context for effective leadership. *Human Relations*, *62*(11), 1667–1696. DOI: 10.1177/0018726709346380

Gao, W., Lu, X., Peng, Y., & Wu, L. (2020). A deep learning approach replacing the finite difference method for in situ stress prediction. *IEEE Access : Practical Innovations, Open Solutions*, *8*, 44063–44074. DOI: 10.1109/ACCESS.2020.2977880

Garg, R., & Munshi, A. (2024). Revolutionizing Menopause Management: Harnessing the Potential of Artificial Intelligence. *Journal of Midlife Health*, *15*(2), 53–54. DOI: 10.4103/jmh.jmh_104_24

Garriga, R., Mas, J., Abraha, S., Nolan, J., Harrison, O., Tadros, G., & Matic, A. (2022). Machine learning model to predict mental health crises from electronic health records. *Nature Medicine*, *28*(6), 1240–1248. DOI: 10.1038/s41591-022-01811-5 PMID: 35577964

Gartner. (2023). *AI and Smart Workplace Innovations: Enhancing Employee Productivity*. Business Insights Report.

Gava, G., Orsili, I., Alvisi, S., Mancini, I., Seracchioli, R., & Meriggiola, M. C. (2019). Cognition, mood and sleep in menopausal transition: The role of menopause hormone therapy. *Medicina*, *55*(10), 668. DOI: 10.3390/medicina55100668 PMID: 31581598

Geisser, S. (1974). A predictive approach to the random effect model. *Biometrika*, *61*(1), 101–107. DOI: 10.1093/biomet/61.1.101

Geukes, M., Van Aalst, M. P., Nauta, M. C. E., & Oosterhof, H. (2012). The impact of menopausal symptoms on work ability. *Menopause (New York, N.Y.)*, *19*(3), 278–282. DOI: 10.1097/gme.0b013e31822ddc97

Geukes, M., Van Aalst, M. P., Robroek, S. J., Laven, J. S., & Oosterhof, H. (2016). The impact of menopause on work ability in women with severe menopausal symptoms. *Maturitas*, *90*, 3–8. DOI: 10.1016/j.maturitas.2016.05.001 PMID: 27282787

Ghaffar Nia, N., Kaplanoglu, E., & Nasab, A. (2023). Evaluation of artificial intelligence techniques in disease diagnosis and prediction. *Discover Artificial Intelligence*, *3*(1), 5. DOI: 10.1007/s44163-023-00049-5

Ghanad, A. (2023). An overview of quantitative research methods. *International Journal of Multidisciplinary Research and Analysis, 6*(08), 3794–3803. DOI: 10.47191/ijmra/v6-i8-52

Gharleghi, R., Samarasinghe, G., Sowmya, A., & Beier, S. (2020, April). Deep learning for time-averaged wall shear stress prediction in left main coronary bifurcations. In 2020 IEEE 17th International Symposium on Biomedical Imaging (ISBI) (pp. 1–4). IEEE. doi:DOI: 10.1109/IWBF49977.2020.9107942

Ghosh, S., Ettinger, A., & Crainiceanu, C. (2020). AI for behavioral health: Applications in sleep, stress, and wellness. *IEEE Pervasive Computing, 19*(1), 15–22. DOI: 10.1109/MPRV.2020.2964417

Giacalone, R. A., & Jurkiewicz, C. L. (Eds.). (2003). *Handbook of workplace spirituality and organizational performance*. M. E. Sharpe.

Gilligan, C. (1982). *In a different voice: Psychological theory and women's development*. Harvard University Press.

Gjellestad, M., Haraldstad, K., Enehaug, H., & Helmersen, M. (2023). Women's Health and Working Life: A Scoping Review. *International Journal of Environmental Research and Public Health, 20*(2), 1080. Advance online publication. DOI: 10.3390/ijerph20021080

Gkrozou, F., Tsonis, O., Godden, M., Siafaka, V., & Paschopoulos, M. (2019). Mobile Health (mHealth) apps focused on menopause: Are they any good? *Post Reproductive Health, 25*(4), 191–198. DOI: 10.1177/2053369119878978

Gleser, H. (2015). Sex, women and the menopause: Are specialist trainee doctors up for it? A survey of views and attitudes of specialist trainee doctors in Community Sexual & Reproductive Health and Obstetrics & Gynaecology around sexuality and sexual healthcare in the (peri)menopause. *Post Reproductive Health, 21*(1), 26–33. DOI: 10.1177/2053369115574448 PMID: 25725451

Godfrey, A., Hetherington, V., Shum, H., Bonato, P., Lovell, N. H., & Stuart, S. (2018). From A to Z: Wearable technology explained. *Maturitas, 113*, 40–47. DOI: 10.1016/j.maturitas.2018.04.012 PMID: 29903647

Goleman, D. (1995). *Emotional intelligence*. Bantam Books.

Gonzalez, R., Patel, S., & Lee, M. (2023). AI in employee health: Ethical concerns and privacy considerations. [REMOVED HYPERLINK FIELD]. *Technology & Ethics Journal, 19*(1), 23–38.

Good, D. J., Lyddy, C. J., Glomb, T. M., Bono, J. E., Brown, K. W., Duffy, M. K., Baer, R. A., Brewer, J. A., & Lazar, S. W. (2016). Contemplating mindfulness at work: An integrative review. *Journal of Management, 42*(1), 114–142. DOI: 10.1177/0149206315617003

Grandey, A. A. (2000). Emotional regulation in the workplace: A new way to conceptualize emotional labor. *Journal of Occupational Health Psychology, 5*(1), 95–110. DOI: 10.1037/1076-8998.5.1.95 PMID: 10658889

Grant, C. A., Wallace, L. M., & Spurgeon, P. C. (2022). AI and employee well-being: Enhancing workplace support and inclusivity. *International Journal of Workplace Health Management, 15*(3), 210–225.

Greendale, G. A., Lee, N. P., & Arriola, E. R. (1999). The menopause. *Lancet, 353*(9152), 571–580. DOI: 10.1016/S0140-6736(98)05352-5 PMID: 10028999

Greenhalgh, T., Thorne, S., & Malterud, K. (2018). Time to challenge the spurious hierarchy of systematic over narrative reviews? *European Journal of Clinical Investigation, 48*(6), e12931. DOI: 10.1111/eci.12931 PMID: 29578574

Griffiths, A., MacLennan, S. J., & Riach, K. (2013). Psychological burden and emotional exhaustion. *Maturitas, 76*(2), 155–159. DOI: 10.1016/j.maturitas.2013.07.005

Griffiths, A., MacLennan, S. J., & Wong, Y. Y. (2010). Menopause and Work: An Evidence-Based Review of the Impact of Menopause on Women's Economic Participation. *Maturitas, 66*(3), 220–226.

Gross, J. J. (2002). Emotion regulation: Affective, cognitive, and social consequences. *Psychophysiology, 39*(3), 281–291. DOI: 10.1017/S0048577201393198 PMID: 12212647

Gupta, A.. (2020). Predicting mental health outcomes in the workplace using random forest algorithm. *Journal of Occupational Health Psychology, 25*(3), 345–357. DOI: 10.1037/ocp0000171

Hair, J., Hult, G. T. M., Ringle, C. M., & Sarstedt, M. (2017). *A primer on partial least squares structural equation modeling (PLS-SEM)* (2nd ed.). SAGE Publications Inc.

Hall, J. E. (2015). Endocrinology of the Menopause. *Endocrinology and Metabolism Clinics of North America, 44*(3), 485–496. DOI: 10.1016/j.ecl.2015.05.010

Hamal, M., & Susma, K. (2014). Hygiene, health problems and socio-cultural practices: What school girls do during menstruation. *Age (Dordrecht, Netherlands), 12*, 14.

Hammam, R. A. M., Abbas, R. A., & Hunter, M. S. (2022). Menopause and Psychological Well-being: The Role of Workplace Support. *Journal of Women's Health, 31*(2), 225–238.

Hardy, C.. (2024). Menopause in the workplace: Challenges, impact, and next steps. *Maturitas, 185*, 107983. DOI: 10.1016/j.maturitas.2024.107983

Hardy, C., Griffiths, A., Hunter, M. S., & Cooper, C. L. (2019). Menopause and work: An overview of UK guidance. *Maturitas, 128*, 49–55.

Harlow, S. D., Gass, M., Hall, J. E., Lobo, R., Maki, P., Rebar, R. W., Sherman, S., Sluss, P. M., & De Villiers, T. J. (2012). Executive summary of the Stages of Reproductive Aging Workshop + 10: Addressing the unfinished agenda of staging reproductive aging. *Menopause (New York, N.Y.), 19*(4), 387–395. DOI: 10.1097/gme.0b013e31824d8f40

Harmon, D. M., Sehrawat, O., Maanja, M., Wight, J., & Noseworthy, P. A. (2023). Artificial Intelligence for the Detection and Treatment of Atrial Fibrillation. *Arrhythmia & Electrophysiology Review, 12*, e12. DOI: 10.15420/aer.2022.31

Harnessing the Potential of Artificial Intelligence. (2023). *PMC*. https://doi.org/ DOI: 10.1136/pmc11321517

Harrell, D. L. (2024). Leaving Halfway: Examining the Loss of the Mid-career Federal Employee Within the Department of the Army.

Harris, M., Wilson, J., & Lee, T. (2023). AI and Workplace Bias: Addressing Menopause Discrimination through Data Analytics. *Business & HR Tech Review, 27*(3), 77–98.

Harris, M., Wilson, J., & Lee, T. (2023). AI Therapy Apps and Workplace Mental Health: A Review. *Mental Health & AI Journal, 27*(1), 77–95.

Harrison, D. A., & Newman, D. A. (2012). Absence, lateness, turnover, and retirement: Narrow and broad understandings of withdrawal and behavioral engagement. *Handbook of Psychology, Second Edition, 12*.

Harrison, Y., & Horne, J. A. (2000). The impact of sleep deprivation on decision making: A review. *Journal of Experimental Psychology. Applied, 6*(3), 236–249. DOI: 10.1037/1076-898X.6.3.236 PMID: 11014055

Harvard Business Review. (2023). *AI in Employee Well-being: The Role of Technology in Reducing Menopause-Related Stigma*. Harvard Business Press.

Hawkes K. (2025). Revisiting "Grandmothers and the Evolution of Human Longevity" 2003 AJHB. *American journal of human biology: the official journal of the Human Biology Council, 37*(4), e70045. DOI: 10.1002/ajhb.70045

Hawkes, K. (2020). The centrality of ancestral grandmothering in human evolution. *Philosophical Transactions of the Royal Society B: Biological Sciences, 375*(1811), 20190501. DOI: 10.1098/rstb.2019.0501

Hawkes, K., O'Connell, J. F., & Blurton Jones, N. G. (1998). Grandmothering, menopause, and the evolution of human life histories. *Proceedings of the National Academy of Sciences of the United States of America, 95*(3), 1336–1339. DOI: 10.1073/pnas.95.3.1336 PMID: 9448332

Hawkes, K., O'Connell, J. F., Blurton Jones, N. G., Alvarez, H., & Charnov, E. L. (2017). The Grandmother Hypothesis and Human Evolution. In *Chagnon, N., Adaptation and Human Behavior: An Anthropological Perspective* (1st ed.). Routledge., DOI: 10.4324/9781351329200-15

Hawkes, K., & Smith, K. R. (2009). Brief communication: Evaluating grandmother effects. *American Journal of Physical Anthropology, 140*(1), 173–176. DOI: 10.1002/ajpa.21061 PMID: 19373844

Hellhammer, D. H., Wust, S., & Kudielka, B. M. (2009). Salivary cortisol as a biomarker in stress research. *Psychoneuroendocrinology, 34*(2), 163–171. DOI: 10.1016/j.psyneuen.2008.10.026 PMID: 19095358

Herndon, N. (2009). The grandmother effect: Implications of kin investment in child survival and reproductive success. *Human Nature Review, 9*, 92–95.

Hewlett, S. A., Luce, C. B., & West, C. (2005). Leadership in your midst. *Harvard Business Review, 83*(11), 74–82. PMID: 16299962

Hickey, M., Riach, K., Kachouie, R., & Jack, G. (2017). No sweat: Managing menopausal symptoms at work. *Journal of Psychosomatic Obstetrics and Gynaecology, 38*(3), 202–209. DOI: 10.1080/0167482X.2017.1327520

Hines, S. (2010). Queerly positioned: Gender, sexuality and trans identity in the workplace. *Gender, Work and Organization, 17*(5), 597–612.

Hinton, G.. (2015). Guidelines for assessing the performance of machine learning models in mental health prediction tasks. *Journal of Mental Health (Abingdon, England), 30*(2), 123–136.

Hirokawa, K., Noda, T., & Tokunaga, K. (2025). Mediating effects of menstruation/menopause on the association between the COVID-19 pandemic related post-traumatic stress disorder symptoms and loneliness in Japanese female workers: A cross-sectional study. *European Journal of Obstetrics, Gynecology, and Reproductive Biology*, *307*, 71–77. DOI: 10.1016/j.ejogrb.2025.01.048

Hochschild, A. R. (1983). *The managed heart: Commercialization of human feeling*. University of California Press.

Hochschild, A. R., & Machung, A. (2012). *The second shift: Working families and the revolution at home*. Penguin Books.

Hooks, B. (2000). *All about love: New visions*. William Morrow.

Hoppe, N., Härting, R. C., & Rahmel, A. (2023). Potential Benefits of Artificial Intelligence in Healthcare. *Intelligent Systems Reference Library*, *229*, 225–249. DOI: 10.1007/978-3-031-11170-9_9

Howard, A., & Wellins, R. (2009). *Holding women back: Troubling trends in talent management*. Development Dimensions International.

Howe, D., Duffy, S., O'Shea, M., Hawkey, A., Wardle, J., Gerontakos, S., & Armour, M. (2023, November). Policies, guidelines, and practices supporting women's menstruation, menstrual disorders and menopause at work: A critical global scoping review. []). MDPI.]. *Health Care*, *11*(22), 2945. PMID: 37998437

Howe, D., Duffy, S., O'Shea, M., Hawkey, A., Wardle, J., Gerontakos, S., Steele, L., Gilbert, E., Owen, L., Ciccia, D., Cox, E., Redmond, R., & Armour, M. (2023). Policies, Guidelines, and Practices Supporting Women's Menstruation, Menstrual Disorders and Menopause at Work: A Critical Global Scoping Review. *Healthcare (Basel)*, *11*(22), 2945. Advance online publication. DOI: 10.3390/healthcare11222945

Hrdy, S. B. (2009). *Mothers and others: The evolutionary origins of mutual understanding*. Harvard University Press.

Hu, L., & Bentler, P. M. (1998). Fit indices in covariance structure modeling: Sensitivity to underparameterized model misspecification. *Psychological Methods*, *3*(4), 424–453. DOI: 10.1037/1082-989X.3.4.424

Hunter, M., & Rendall, M. (2007). Bio-psycho-socio-cultural perspectives on menopause. *Best Practice & Research. Clinical Obstetrics & Gynaecology*, *21*(2), 261–274. DOI: 10.1016/j.bpobgyn.2006.11.001 PMID: 17161025

Ibarra, H., Carter, N. M., & Silva, C. (2010). Why men still get more promotions than women. *Harvard Business Review*, *88*(9), 80–85. PMID: 20821967

IBM. (2022). *Menopause Support Network Initiative*. Retrieved from www.ibm.com

ILO. (2007). ABC of Women Workers' Rights and Gender Equality. In *Journal of European Industrial Training* (Vol. 24, Issue 9). DOI: 10.1108/jeit.2000.00324iae.002

Im, E.-O., Lee, Y., Chee, E., & Chee, W. (2017). Web-based interventions for menopause: A systematic integrated literature review. *Maturitas, 95*, 24–30. DOI: 10.1016/j.maturitas.2016.10.009 PMID: 27889049

Infosys. (2023). *Women's Health and Workplace Well-being*. Retrieved from www.infosys.com

Ingram, M. A., Brady, S., & Peacock, A. S. (2022). The barriers to offering non-pharmacological pain management as an initial option for laboring women: A review of the literature. *European Journal of Midwifery*, *6*(June), 37. Advance online publication. DOI: 10.18332/ejm/149244 PMID: 35794877

Inkster, B., Sarda, S., & Subramanian, V. (2018). An empirical study of AI mental health chatbots: Wysa and Woebot. *Evidence-Based Mental Health*, *21*(2), 60–63. DOI: 10.1136/ebmental-2018-300069

Institute for Public Health. (2024). *National Health and Morbidity Survey (NHMS) 2023: Non-communicable diseases and healthcare demand - Key findings*.

International Labour Organization (ILO). (2018). *A quantum leap for gender equality: For a better future of work for all*. https://www.ilo.org/global/publications/books/WCMS_674831/lang--en/index.htm

International Labour Organization (ILO). (2021). *World employment and social outlook: The role of digital labour platforms in transforming the world of work*.

Jack, G., Riach, K., & Bariola, E. (2019). Temporality and gendered agency: Menopausal subjectivities in women's work. *Human Relations*, *72*(1), 122–143. DOI: 10.1177/0018726718767739

Jack, G., Riach, K., & Bariola, E. (2022). Cognitive Challenges in the Workplace: The Menopause Factor. *Work, Aging and Retirement*, *8*(2), 190–207.

Jack, G., Riach, K., Bariola, E., Pitts, M., Schapper, J., & Sarrel, P. (2016). Menopause in the workplace: What employers should be doing. *Maturitas*, *85*, 88–95. DOI: 10.1016/j.maturitas.2015.12.006 PMID: 26857886

Jahangirifar, M., Fooladi, E., Davis, S. R., & Islam, R. M. (2023). Menopause symptoms, sexual dysfunctions and pelvic floor disorders in refugee and asylum seeker women: A scoping review. *Climacteric*, *26*(4), 373–380. DOI: 10.1080/13697137.2023.2173572

James, G. (2024). Labour Law ' s (Mis) Management of Menopausal Workers. [Labour]. *Feminist Legal Studies*, (June). Advance online publication. DOI: 10.1007/s10691-024-09555-y

Jobin, A., Ienca, M., & Vayena, E. (2019). The global landscape of AI ethics guidelines. *Nature Machine Intelligence*, *1*(9), 389–399. DOI: 10.1038/s42256-019-0088-2

Jogdand, K., & Yerpude, P. (2011). A community based study on menstrual hygiene among adolescent girls. *Indian Journal of Maternal and Child Health*, *13*, 1–6.

Johns, G. (2010). Presenteeism in the workplace: A review and research agenda. *Journal of Organizational Behavior*, *31*(4), 519–542. DOI: 10.1002/job.630

Johns, G. (2011). Attendance dynamics at work: The antecedents and correlates of presenteeism, absenteeism, and productivity loss. *Journal of Occupational Health Psychology*, *16*(4), 483–500. DOI: 10.1037/a0025153 PMID: 21875212

Johnson, K. B., Wei, W. Q., Weeraratne, D., Frisse, M. E., Misulis, K., Rhee, K., Zhao, J., & Snowdon, J. L. (2020). Precision Medicine, AI, and the Future of Personalized Health Care. *Clinical and Translational Science*, *14*(1), 86–93. DOI: 10.1111/cts.12884

Johnson, P., & Taylor, R. (2022). AI and organizational effectiveness: A holistic approach. [REMOVED HYPERLINK FIELD]. *Organizational Studies Review*, *20*(4), 300–315.

Jones, R., Smith, A., & Cooper, L. (2023). AI for Women's Health: Addressing Menopause Challenges. *AI & Healthcare Review*, *39*(3), 250–270.

Jordan, S., Hermann, S., & Starker, A. (2020). *Utilisation of canteens offering healthy food choices as part ofworkplace health promotion in Germany*. DOI: 10.25646/6401

Joshi, P., & Mandal, D. (2025). Status, gaps and challenges in menstrual health in India. *PM & R*, *5*(1), 8–15. DOI: 10.4103/pmr.2025.05000

Junça Silva, A., & Rodrigues, R. (2024). Affective mechanisms linking role ambiguity to employee turnover. *The International Journal of Organizational Analysis*, *32*(11), 1–18. DOI: 10.1108/IJOA-08-2023-3891

Kabat-Zinn, J. (2003). Mindfulness-based interventions in context: Past, present, and future. *Clinical Psychology : a Publication of the Division of Clinical Psychology of the American Psychological Association*, *10*(2), 144–156. DOI: 10.1093/clipsy.bpg016

Kacmar, K. M., & Carlson, D. S. (1997). Further validation of the Perception of Politics Scale (POPs): A multiple sample investigation. *Journal of Management, 23*(5), 627–658. DOI: 10.1177/014920639702300502

Kalani, M., & Anjankar, A. (2024). Revolutionizing Neurology: The Role of Artificial Intelligence in Advancing Diagnosis and Treatment. *Cureus, 16*(6), e61706. DOI: 10.7759/cureus.61706

Kapoor, E. (2023). Premature Ovarian Insufficiency. *Current Opinion in Endocrine and Metabolic Research, 28*, 100435. DOI: 10.1016/j.coemr.2023.100435

Karakcheyeva, V., Willis-Johnson, H., Corr, P. G., & Frame, L. A. (2024). The well-being of women in healthcare professions: A comprehensive review. *Global Advances in Integrative Medicine and Health, 13*, 27536130241232929. Advance online publication. DOI: 10.1177/27536130241232929 PMID: 38344248

Karanika-Murray, M., & Biron, C. (2020). The health-performance framework of presenteeism: Towards understanding an adaptive behaviour. *Human Relations, 73*(2), 242–261. DOI: 10.1177/0018726719827081

Katz-Bearnot, S. (2010). Menopause, depression, and loss of sexual desire: A psychodynamic contribution. *The Journal of the American Academy of Psychoanalysis and Dynamic Psychiatry, 38*(1), 99–116. DOI: 10.1521/jaap.2010.38.1.99

Kaur, G., & Singh, B. (2021). Machine learning approaches for predicting menopause symptoms and management. *Journal of Healthcare Engineering, 2021*, 9938452. Advance online publication. DOI: 10.1155/2021/9938452

Kayser, K. C., Puig, V. A., & Estepp, J. R. (2022). Predicting and mitigating fatigue effects due to sleep deprivation: A review. *Frontiers in Neuroscience, 16*, 930280. DOI: 10.3389/fnins.2022.930280 PMID: 35992930

Keskinbora, K. H. (2023). Current roles of artificial intelligence in ophthalmology. *Open Exploration 2019 4:6, 4*(6), 1048–1067. DOI: 10.37349/emed.2023.00194

Khan Mamun, M. M. R., & Elfouly, T. (2023). AI-Enabled Electrocardiogram Analysis for Disease Diagnosis. *Applied System Innovation 2023, Vol. 6, Page 95, 6*(5), 95. DOI: 10.3390/asi6050095

Kim, B., Rudin, C., Shah, J. A., ... (2015). Mind the gap: A generative approach to interpretable feature selection and extraction. *Advances in Neural Information Processing Systems*, 28. https://proceedings.neurips.cc/paper_files/paper/2015/file/f9be311e65d81fdbbbd4a7d5d7504d3-Paper.pdf

Kim, H. K. (2024). The Effects of Artificial Intelligence Chatbots on Women's Health: A Systematic Review and Meta-Analysis. *Healthcare (Basel), 12*(5), 534. DOI: 10.3390/healthcare12050534

Kim, N. Y., Yoo, S. K., Jin, J. C., Han, S., Hong, J. S., & Kim, S. M. (2023). Development and verification of the Menopause Emotional Symptom Questionnaire. *Menopause (New York, N.Y.), 30*(9), 961–968. DOI: 10.1097/GME.0000000000002224

Kim, P. S., McQueen, J. S., & Hawkes, K. (2012). Why does women's fertility end in mid-life? A model of the evolution of human life history. *Mathematical Biosciences, 240*(1), 50–60. DOI: 10.1016/j.mbs.2012.06.001

Kinjerski, V. M., & Skrypnek, B. J. (2006). Defining spirit at work: Finding common ground. *Journal of Organizational Change Management, 19*(1), 52–75. DOI: 10.1108/09534810610645561

Kishi, R., Kitahara, T., Masuchi, A., & Kasai, S. (2002). Work-related reproductive, musculoskeletal and mental disorders among working women-history, current issues and future research directions. *Industrial Health, 40*(2), 101–112. DOI: 10.2486/indhealth.40.101 PMID: 12064551

Kleinman, N. L., Rohrbacker, N. J., Bushmakin, A. G., Whiteley, J., Lynch, W. D., & Shah, S. N. (2013). Direct and indirect costs of women diagnosed with menopause symptoms. *Journal of Occupational and Environmental Medicine, 55*(4), 465–470. DOI: 10.1097/JOM.0b013e3182820515 PMID: 23532198

Koburtay, T., Abuhussein, T., & Sidani, Y. M. (2023). Women leadership, culture, and Islam: Female voices from Jordan. *Journal of Business Ethics, 183*(2), 347–363. DOI: 10.1007/s10551-022-05041-0

Koenig, H. G. (2012). *Spirituality and health research: Methods, measurement, statistics, and resources.* Templeton Press.

Kohn, G. E., Rodriguez, K. M., Hotaling, J., & Pastuszak, A. W. (2019). The history of estrogen therapy. *Sexual Medicine Reviews, 7*(3), 416–421. DOI: 10.1016/j.sxmr.2019.03.006 PMID: 31147294

Kopenhager, T., & Guidozzi, F. (2015). Working women and the menopause. *Climacteric, 18*(3), 372–375. DOI: 10.3109/13697137.2015.1020483 PMID: 25830628

Kossek, E. E., Pichler, S., Bodner, T., & Hammer, L. B. (2011a). Workplace social support and work–family conflict. *Personnel Psychology, 64*(2), 289–313. DOI: 10.1111/j.1744-6570.2011.01211.x PMID: 21691415

Kostelić, K., Gonan Božac, M., & Paulišić, M. (2024). Exploring interpersonal conflicts within the JD-R model: Aggregation and validation in the context of elementary school employees in Croatia. *Cogent Business & Management*, *11*(1), 2370451. Advance online publication. DOI: 10.1080/23311975.2024.2370451

Koul, R. (2024). Chanting and emotional regulation: A review of physiological and psychological outcomes. *International Journal of Yoga Therapy*, *34*(1), 45–60.

Krasheninnikova, Y. S. (2019). The grandmother hypothesis: Evolutionary theory and cross-cultural evidence. *Anthropological Review*, *82*(2), 143–159. DOI: 10.2478/anre-2019-0011

Krekel, C., Ward, G., & De Neve, J. E. (2019). *Employee wellbeing, productivity, and firm performance*. Centre for Economic Performance. https://cep.lse.ac.uk/pubs/download/dp1605.pdf

Krishnakumar, S., & Neck, C. P. (2002). The "what," "why," and "how" of Spirituality in the workplace. *Journal of Managerial Psychology*, *17*(3), 153–164. DOI: 10.1108/02683940210423060

Kuck, M. J., & Hogervorst, E. (2024). Stress, depression, and anxiety: Psychological complaints across menopausal stages. *Frontiers in Psychiatry*, *15*, 1323743. Advance online publication. DOI: 10.3389/fpsyt.2024.1323743 PMID: 38455517

Kumar, R., & Pradeepika, S. (2021). Women's spiritual practices and work-life integration in corporate India. *Indian Journal of Organizational Studies*, *32*(2), 105–121.

Kumar, V., & Garg, M. L. (2018). Predictive analytics: A review of trends and techniques. *International Journal of Computer Applications*, *182*(1), 31–37. DOI: 10.5120/ijca2018917434

Kundu, S., & Acharya, S. S. (2023). Linkage of premature and early menopause with psychosocial well-being: A moderated multiple mediation approach. *BMC Psychology*, *11*(1), 228. Advance online publication. DOI: 10.1186/s40359-023-01267-3

Kydd, A. (2021). Menopause and personal protective equipment: How does this meet acceptable working conditions? *Case Reports in Women's Health*, *32*, e00356. DOI: 10.1016/j.crwh.2021.e00356

Ladkin, D., & Patrick, C. B. (2022). Whiteness in leadership theorizing: A critical analysis of race in Bass' transformational leadership theory. *Leadership*, *18*(2), 205–223. DOI: 10.1177/17427150211066442

Lassen, A. D., Thorsen, A. V., Trolle, E., Elsig, M., & Ovesen, L. (2004). Successful strategies to increase the consumption of fruits and vegetables: Results from the Danish "6 a day" Work-site Canteen Model Study. *Public Health Nutrition*, *7*(2), 263–270. DOI: 10.1079/PHN2003532

Lawrance, N., Petrides, G., & Guerry, M. A. (2021). Predicting employee absenteeism for cost effective interventions. *Decision Support Systems*, *147*, 113539. DOI: 10.1016/j.dss.2021.113539

Lazarus, J. (2000). *Stress relief & relaxation techniques*. NTC/Contemporary Publishing Group Inc., Keats Publishing.

Lazarus, R. S. (1991). *Emotion and adaptation*. Oxford University Press. DOI: 10.1093/oso/9780195069945.001.0001

Lazarus, R. S., & Folkman, S. (1984). *Stress, appraisal, and coping*. Springer Publishing Company.

Lee, S.. (2019). Incorporating local data relationships in mental health prediction using K-nearest neighbors algorithm. *The Journal of Applied Psychology*, *105*(4), 512–526. DOI: 10.1037/apl0000362

Leigh, J. P. (1991). Employee and job attributes as predictors of absenteeism in a national sample of workers: The importance of health and dangerous working conditions. *Social Science & Medicine*, *33*(2), 127–137. DOI: 10.1016/0277-9536(91)90173-A PMID: 1887276

Leipert, B. D., & Reutter, L. (2005). Developing resilience: How women maintain their health in northern geographically isolated settings. *Qualitative Health Research*, *15*(1), 49–65. DOI: 10.1177/1049732304269671 PMID: 15574715

Lengnick-Hall, C. A., Beck, T. E., & Lengnick-Hall, M. L. (2011). Developing a capacity for organizational resilience through strategic human resource management. *Human Resource Management Review*, *21*(3), 243–255. DOI: 10.1016/j.hrmr.2010.07.001

Lewin, S., Chetty, R., Ihdayhid, A. R., & Dwivedi, G. (2024). Ethical Challenges and Opportunities in Applying Artificial Intelligence to Cardiovascular Medicine. *The Canadian Journal of Cardiology*, *40*(10), 1897–1906. Advance online publication. DOI: 10.1016/j.cjca.2024.06.029

Liao, J., Li, X., Gan, Y., Han, S., Rong, P., Wang, W., Li, W., & Zhou, L. (2023). Artificial intelligence assists precision medicine in cancer treatment. *Frontiers in Oncology*, *12*, 998222. DOI: 10.3389/fonc.2022.998222

Liaw, A., & Wiener, M. (2002). Classification and regression by random forest. *R News*, *2*(3), 18–22.

Liefgreen, A., Weinstein, N., Wachter, S., & Mittelstadt, B. (2024). Beyond ideals: Why the (medical) AI industry needs to motivate behavioural change in line with fairness and transparency values, and how it can do it. *AI & Society*, *39*(5), 2183–2199. DOI: 10.1007/s00146-023-01684-3 PMID: 39309255

Li, K., Urteaga, I., Shea, A., Vitzthum, V. J., Wiggins, C. H., & Elhadad, N. (2021). A generative, predictive model for menstrual cycle lengths that accounts for potential self-tracking artifacts in mobile health data [Preprint]. arXiv. https://arxiv.org/abs/2102.12439

Li, Q., Gu, J., Huang, J., Zhao, P., & Luo, C. (2023). They see me as mentally ill": The stigmatization experiences of Chinese menopausal women in the family. *BMC Women's Health*, *23*(1), 185. DOI: 10.1186/s12905-023-02350-y PMID: 37076835

Liss, J., Chesnokova, A., & Allen, J. T. (2024). Unspoken and untaught: Addressing the gap in menopause education. *Current Obstetrics and Gynecology Reports*, *13*(4), 281–288. DOI: 10.1007/s13669-024-00404-y

Livermore, D., & Soon, A. N. G. (2015). *Leading with cultural intelligence: The real secret to success*. Amacom.

Li, X., Chen, F., Sun, D., & Tao, M. (2015). Predicting menopausal symptoms with artificial neural network. *Expert Systems with Applications*, *42*(22), 8698–8706. DOI: 10.1016/j.eswa.2015.07.024

Lobo, R. A. (2014). What the future holds for women after menopause: where we have been, where we are, and where we want to go. *Climacteric, 17*(sup2), 12-17.

Lobo, R. A., & Gompel, A. (2022). Management of menopause: A view towards prevention. *The Lancet. Diabetes & Endocrinology*, *10*(6), 457–470. DOI: 10.1016/S2213-8587(21)00269-2 PMID: 35526556

Loftus, T. J., Shickel, B., Ruppert, M. M., Balch, J. A., Tighe, P. J., Bihorac, A., & Rashidi, P. (2022). Federated learning for preserving data privacy in collaborative healthcare research. *Digital Health*, *8*. Advance online publication. DOI: 10.1177/20552076221134455 PMID: 36325438

Lott, Y., & Abendroth, A. K. (2020). The gender gap in working hours: What the pandemic revealed. *Social Politics*, *28*(3), 482–504.

Lundberg, S. M., & Lee, S.-I. (2017). A unified approach to interpreting model predictions. *Advances in Neural Information Processing Systems*, 30. https://proceedings.neurips.cc/paper_files/paper/2017/file/8a20a8621978632d76c43dfd28b67767-Paper.pdf

Lundberg, U. (2002). Psychophysiology of work: Stress, gender, endocrine response, and work-related upper extremity disorders. *American Journal of Industrial Medicine*, *41*(5), 383–392. DOI: 10.1002/ajim.10038 PMID: 12071491

Machine Learning Identifies Women at Risk of Severe Cognitive Decline During Menopause. (2025). *News-Medical*. https://doi.org/DOI: 10.1016/news-medical/machine-learning-identifies-women-at-risk-of-severe-cognitive-decline-during-menopause

Maher, C., Singh, B., Wylde, A., & Chastin, S. (2024). Virtual health assistants: A grand challenge in health communications and behavior change. *Frontiers in Digital Health*, *6*, 1418695. DOI: 10.3389/fdgth.2024.1418695

Ma, J., Xu, L., & Zhang, X. (2025). Work–family conflict, overwork and mental health of female employees in China. *Frontiers in Public Health*, *13*, 1483746. DOI: 10.3389/fpubh.2025.1483746 PMID: 40241940

Makara-Studzińśka, M. T., Kryś-Noszczyk, K. M., & Jakiel, G. (2014). Epidemiology of the symptoms of menopause–an intercontinental review. *Menopause Review/Przegląd Menopauzalny, 13*(3), 203-211.

Maki, P. M., & Jaff, N. G. (2022). Brain fog in menopause: A health-care professional's guide for decision-making and counseling on cognition. *Climacteric*, *25*(6), 570–578. DOI: 10.1080/13697137.2022.2122792 PMID: 36178170

Mancone, S., Diotaiuti, P., Valente, G., Macchia, S., & Corrado, S. (2023). The use of voice assistant for psychological assessment elicits empathy and engagement while maintaining good psychometric properties. *Behavioral Sciences (Basel, Switzerland)*, *13*(7), 550. Advance online publication. DOI: 10.3390/bs13070550 PMID: 37503997

Mandangu, C., Ramos, A. M., Sengupta, M., Bender, R., El-Hayani, R., Hasan, I., Okechukwu, H., Anas, S., & Havsteen-Franklin, D. (2025). Implicit bias in referrals to relational psychological therapies: Review and recommendations for mental health services. *Frontiers in Public Health*, *12*, 1469439. Advance online publication. DOI: 10.3389/fpubh.2024.1469439 PMID: 39989866

Mankar, S., Johnson, A. R., Chawla, P. S., & Basannar, D. (2024). Needs assessment study for management of menopause in the community. *Journal of Family Medicine and Primary Care*, *13*(4), 1371–1378. DOI: 10.4103/jfmpc.jfmpc_1129_23 PMID: 38827709

Markose, A., Krishnan, R., & Ramesh, M. (2016). Medical ethics. *Journal of Pharmacy & Bioallied Sciences*, *8*(Suppl 1), S1–S4. DOI: 10.4103/0975-7406.191934

Martelli, M., Zingaretti, L., Salvio, G., Bracci, M., & Santarelli, L. (2021). Influence of work on andropause and menopause: A systematic review. *International Journal of Environmental Research and Public Health*, *18*(19), 1–20. DOI: 10.3390/ijerph181910074

Ma, T., Zhang, J., Wang, Y., & Hu, J. (2022). Personalized task scheduling in mental health using wearable and mobile data. *IEEE Journal of Biomedical and Health Informatics*, *26*(3), 1005–1016. DOI: 10.1109/JBHI.2021.3124471

Mayer, K. (2024, October 8). Women are experiencing a mental health crisis. What that means for employers. *SHRM*. Retrieved from https://www.shrm.org

Mayo Clinic. (2022). *Lisa Health Leverage AI to Create Personalized Menopause App*. TechTarget., DOI: 10.1016/techtarget/mayo-clinic-lisa-health-leverage-ai-to-create-personalized-menopause-app

McCarthy, M., & Raval, A. P. (2020). The peri-menopause in a woman's life: a systemic inflammatory phase that enables later neurodegenerative disease. *Journal of Neuroinflammation 2020 17:1*, *17*(1), 1–14. DOI: 10.1186/s12974-020-01998-9

McCarthy, R. V., McCarthy, M. M., Ceccucci, W., Halawi, L., McCarthy, R. V., McCarthy, M. M., & Halawi, L. (2022). *Applying predictive analytics*. Springer International Publishing. DOI: 10.1007/978-3-030-83070-0

McGregor, A. (2017). *An investigation into the phenomenon of presenteeism: examining antecedents and the operationalisation of presenteeism* (Doctoral dissertation, University of Wollongong).

McKinsey & Company & LeanIn. (2021). *Org*. Women in the Workplace.

McKinsey. (2023). *The Future of AI in Employee Well-being: Mental Health Support Systems*. Business Strategy Insights.

McNeil, M. A., & Merriam, S. B. (2021). Menopause. *Annals of Internal Medicine*, *174*(7), ITC97–ITC112. DOI: 10.7326/AITC202107200

Mendelsohn, M. E. (2002). Protective effects of estrogen on the cardiovascular system. *The American Journal of Cardiology*, *89*(12), 12E–17E. DOI: 10.1016/S0002-9149(02)02405-0 PMID: 12084397

Meng, J., & Neill, M. S. (2022). The role of ethical leadership in building influence: Perspectives from female public relations professionals. *Public Relations Review*, *48*(1), 102152. DOI: 10.1016/j.pubrev.2022.102152

Menopause Foundation. (2021). *Global Menopause and Workplace Report*. Menopause Foundation Research.

Menopause. (n.d.). Retrieved March 25, 2025, from https://www.who.int/news-room/fact-sheets/detail/menopause

Mensah, A. (2021). Job stress and mental well-being among working men and women in Europe: The mediating role of social support. *International Journal of Environmental Research and Public Health*, *18*(5), 2494. DOI: 10.3390/ijerph18052494 PMID: 33802439

Milliman, J., Czaplewski, A. J., & Ferguson, J. (2003). Workplace spirituality and employee work attitudes: An exploratory empirical assessment. *Journal of Organizational Change Management*, *16*(4), 426–447. DOI: 10.1108/09534810310484172

Ministry for social mobility youth and progression UK. (2023). *"No Time to Step Back"* (Issue October).

Miraglia, M., & Johns, G. (2021). The social and relational dynamics of absenteeism from work: A multilevel review and integration. *The Academy of Management Annals*, *15*(1), 37–67. DOI: 10.5465/annals.2019.0036

Mirbagheri, M., Jodeiri, A., Hakimi, N., Zakeri, V., & Setarehdan, S. K. (2019, November). Accurate stress assessment based on functional near-infrared spectroscopy using deep learning approach. In 2019 26th National and 4th International Iranian Conference on Biomedical Engineering (ICBME) (pp. 4–10). IEEE. doi:DOI: 10.1109/ICDM.2019.00161

Mishra, P. (2024). *Optimizing Perimenopausal Care*. 242–281. DOI: 10.4018/979-8-3693-2342-7.ch010

Mishra, P., & Smyth, R. (2023). AI, gender diversity, and workplace inclusion: A review of emerging trends. *AI & Society*, *38*(1), 45–62.

Mittelstadt, B. D., Allo, P., Taddeo, M., Wachter, S., & Floridi, L. (2016). The ethics of algorithms: Mapping the debate. *Big Data & Society*, *3*(2), 1–21. DOI: 10.1177/2053951716679679

Mohamad, N. I., Ismail, A., Mohamad Rozi, M. S. A., & Ahmad, S. (2015). Tekanan kerja dan perkaitannya dengan kesihatan pekerja: Kajian empirikal sebuah kontinjen polis di Semenanjung Malaysia. *Geografia : Malaysian Journal of Society and Space*, *11*(10), 63–75.

Mohite, R. V., & Mohite, V. R. (2016). Menstrual hygiene practices among slum adolescent girls. *International Journal of Community Medicine and Public Health*, *3*, 1729–1734. DOI: 10.18203/2394-6040.ijcmph20162033

Monteleone, P., Mascagni, G., Giannini, A., Genazzani, A. R., & Simoncini, T. (2018). Symptoms of menopause—Global prevalence, physiology and implications. *Nature Reviews. Endocrinology*, *14*(4), 199–215. DOI: 10.1038/nrendo.2017.180 PMID: 29393299

Moore, S., Hedayati-Mehdiabadi, A., Law, V., & Kang, S. P. (2024). The Change We Work: Professional Agency and Ethics for Emerging AI Technologies. *TechTrends*, *68*(1), 27–36. DOI: 10.1007/s11528-023-00895-1

Moral, R.. (2023). Physical exercise and dietary supplementation in middle-aged and older women: A systematic review. *Nutrients*, *15*(23), 4953. DOI: 10.3390/nu15234953

Morris, N., Levi, M., Morabito, M., Messeri, A., Ioannou, L., Flouris, A., Samoutis, G., Pogačar, T., Bogataj, L., Piil, J., & Nybo, L. (2020). Health vs. wealth: Employer, employee and policy-maker perspectives on occupational heat stress across multiple European industries. *Temperature*, *8*(3), 284–301. DOI: 10.1080/23328940.2020.1852049

Mosconi, L., Rahman, A., Diaz, I., Wu, X., Scheyer, O., Hristov, H. W., & Isaacson, R. S. (2021). Menopause impacts human brain structure, connectivity, energy metabolism, and amyloid-beta deposition. *Scientific Reports*, *11*(1), 10867. DOI: 10.1038/s41598-021-90084-y PMID: 34108509

Moshawrab, M., Adda, M., Bouzouane, A., Ibrahim, H., & Raad, A. (2023). Smart Wearables for the Detection of Cardiovascular Diseases: A Systematic Literature Review. *Sensors (Basel)*, *23*(2), 828. DOI: 10.3390/s23020828

Moss, P. (Ed.). (2015). *International review of leave policies and related research.*

Mujica-Parodi, L. R., Amgalan, A., & Sultan, S. F.. (2020). Hormonal transitions in menopause and their impact on brain connectivity and behavior. *Scientific Reports*, *10*, 14434. Advance online publication. DOI: 10.1038/s41598-020-71346-5

Muktar, S. A., Desta, B. F., Damte, H. D., Heyi, W. K., Gurmamo, E. M., Abebe, M. G., Mesele, M. G., & Argaw, M. D. (2022). Exploring the opportunities and challenges of female health leaders in three regional states of Ethiopia: A phenomenological study. *BMC Public Health*, *22*(1), 1471. DOI: 10.1186/s12889-022-13871-w PMID: 35915447

Nagaraj, D., Ramesh, N., Devraj, D., Umman, M., John, A. K., & Johnson, A. R. (2021). Experience and perceptions regarding menopause among rural women: A cross-sectional hospital-based study in South Karnataka. *Journal of Midlife Health*, *12*(3), 199–205. DOI: 10.4103/jmh.JMH_196_20 PMID: 34759701

Nahavandi, S. (2021). Trusted autonomous systems: Challenges and future directions. *Nature Machine Intelligence*, *3*, 14–23. DOI: 10.1038/s42256-020-00275-6

Naik, N., Hameed, B. M. Z., Shetty, D. K., Swain, D., Shah, M., Paul, R., Aggarwal, K., Brahim, S., Patil, V., Smriti, K., Shetty, S., Rai, B. P., Chlosta, P., & Somani, B. K. (2022). Legal and Ethical Consideration in Artificial Intelligence in Healthcare: Who Takes Responsibility? *Frontiers in Surgery*, *9*, 862322. Advance online publication. DOI: 10.3389/fsurg.2022.862322

Najjar, R. (2023). Redefining Radiology: A Review of Artificial Intelligence Integration in Medical Imaging. *Diagnostics (Basel)*, *13*(17), 2760. DOI: 10.3390/diagnostics13172760

Nashwan, A. J., Gharib, S., Alhadidi, M., El-Ashry, A. M., Alamgir, A., Al-Hassan, M., Khedr, M. A., Dawood, S., & Abufarsakh, B. (2023). Harnessing Artificial Intelligence: Strategies for Mental Health Nurses in Optimizing Psychiatric Patient Care. *Issues in Mental Health Nursing*, *44*(10), 1020–1034. DOI: 10.1080/01612840.2023.2263579

NASSCOM. (2023). *Women's Workplace Well-being in India*. Retrieved from www.nasscom.in

Neal, J. (2013). *Creating enlightened organizations: Four gateways to spirit at work*. Palgrave Macmillan. DOI: 10.1057/9781137327673

Nemr, M. A. A., & Liu, Y. (2021). The impact of ethical leadership on organizational citizenship behaviors: Moderating role of organizational cynicism. *Cogent Business & Management*, *8*(1), 1865860. Advance online publication. DOI: 10.1080/23311975.2020.1865860

Ngunjiri, F. W., & Madsen, S. R. (2015). *Women and leadership around the world*. Information Age Publishing.

Nishii, L. H., & Mayer, D. M. (2009). Do inclusive leaders help to reduce turnover in diverse groups? *The Journal of Applied Psychology*, *94*(6), 1412–1426. DOI: 10.1037/a0017190 PMID: 19916652

Northouse, P. G. (2021). *Leadership: Theory and practice* (9th ed.). Sage Publications.

Nosek, M., Kennedy, H. P., & Gudmundsdottir, M. (2010). Silence, stigma, and shame: A postmodern analysis of distress during menopause. *Advances in Nursing Science*, *33*(3), E24–E36. DOI: 10.1097/ANS.0b013e3181eb41e8 PMID: 20693828

Nosratabadi, S., Abedi, R., & Jamhour, R. (2020). Cultural intelligence and multicultural competence in organizations. *Journal of Enterprising Culture*, *28*(2), 137–160. DOI: 10.1142/S0218495820500060

O'Malley, A. S., & Reschovsky, J. D. (2011). Referral and consultation communication between primary care and specialist physicians: Finding common ground. *Archives of Internal Medicine*, *171*(1), 56–65. DOI: 10.1001/archinternmed.2010.480 PMID: 21220662

O'Neill, M. T., Jones, V., & Reid, A. (2023). Impact of menopausal symptoms on work and careers: A cross-sectional study. *Occupational Medicine*, *73*(6), 332–338. DOI: 10.1093/occmed/kqad078 PMID: 37542726

Oamen, T. E. (2021). Analysis of factors influencing pharmaceutical sales workforce engagement in pharmaceutical marketing in Nigeria: A structural equation modeling approach. *Global Journal of Pure and Applied Sciences*, *27*(4), 405–410. DOI: 10.4314/gjpas.v27i4.7

OECD. (2020). *Women at the core of the fight against COVID-19 crisis.*

Padhy, S., Takkar, B., Chawla, R., & Kumar, A. (2019). Artificial intelligence in diabetic retinopathy: A natural step to the future. *Indian Journal of Ophthalmology*, *67*(7), 1004. DOI: 10.4103/ijo.IJO_1989_18

Palacios, S., Stevenson, J. C., Schaudig, K., Lukasiewicz, M., & Graziottin, A. (2019). Hormone therapy for first-line management of menopausal symptoms: Practical recommendations. *Women's Health (London, England)*, *15*, 1745506519864009. Advance online publication. DOI: 10.1177/1745506519864009 PMID: 31378196

Panay, N., Palacios, S., Davison, S., & Baber, R. (2021). Women's perception of the menopause transition: A multinational, prospective, community-based survey. *Gynecological and Reproductive Endocrinology and Metabolism*, *2*(3), 178–183. DOI: 10.5281/zenodo.5061133

Pandey, S., Gupta, M., & Arora, A. (2009). Impact of workplace spirituality on employee engagement: An empirical study. *International Journal of Business Research, 9*(1), 88–98.

Pan, M., Zhou, J., Pan, X., Wang, J., Qi, Q., & Wang, L. (2023). Drugs for the treatment of postmenopausal symptoms: Hormonal and non-hormonal therapy. *Life Sciences, 312*, 121255. Advance online publication. DOI: 10.1016/j.lfs.2022.121255 PMID: 36470539

Pant, S., Kumar, A., Ram, M., Klochkov, Y., & Sharma, H. K. (2022). Consistency indices in analytic hierarchy process: A review. *Mathematics, 10*(8), 1206. DOI: 10.3390/math10081206

Pargament, K. I. (1997). *The psychology of religion and coping: Theory, research, practice*. Guilford Press.

Pargament, K. I. (2007). *Spiritually integrated psychotherapy: Understanding and addressing the sacred*. Guilford Press.

Paria, B., Bhattacharyya, A., & Das, S. (2014). A comparative study on menstrual hygiene among urban and rural adolescent girls of West Bengal. *Journal of Family Medicine and Primary Care, 3*(4), 413–417. DOI: 10.4103/2249-4863.148131 PMID: 25657955

Patton, M. Q. (2002). *Qualitative research and evaluation methods* (3rd ed.). Sage Publications.

Peacock, K., Carlson, K., & Ketvertis, K. M. (2023). Menopause. *StatPearls*. https://www.ncbi.nlm.nih.gov/books/NBK507826/

Percival, M. (2025). *The Psychology of Menopause*. Taylor & Francis. DOI: 10.4324/9781003438342

Perich, T., Ussher, J., Sperring, S., Power, R., Kakakios, K., Ryan, S., Avard, N., & Drury, G. (2025). Evaluation of Interventions for Menopausal Women in the Workplace–Pilot and Feasibility and Acceptability Study. *Women's Reproductive Health (Philadelphia, Pa.), 0*(0), 1–22. DOI: 10.1080/23293691.2025.2483829

Petchsawang, P., & Duchon, D. (2009). Measuring workplace spirituality in an Asian context. *Human Resource Development International, 12*(4), 459–468. DOI: 10.1080/13678860903135912

Pfeifer, E., & Scholz, C. (2021). Digital Spirituality: A new frontier in AI-supported self-care. *AI & Society, 36*, 447–460. DOI: 10.1007/s00146-021-01140-7

Pillai, R., & Sivathanu, B. (2022). Measure what matters: Descriptive and predictive metrics of HRM-pathway toward organizational performance. *International Journal of Productivity and Performance Management*, *71*(7), 3009–3029. DOI: 10.1108/IJPPM-10-2020-0509

Piri, R., Ghorbani, M., & Ravasan, Z. M. (2023). Spiritual intelligence and job satisfaction among female employees: The role of organizational climate. *Journal of Workplace Behavioral Health*, *38*(1), 75–94. DOI: 10.1080/15555240.2022.2098427 PMID: 37425094

Poethke, U., Klasmeier, K. N., Radaca, E., & Diestel, S. (2023). How modern working environments shape attendance behaviour: A longitudinal study on weekly flexibilization, boundaryless work and presenteeism. *Journal of Occupational and Organizational Psychology*, *96*(3), 524–544. DOI: 10.1111/joop.12437

Pohling, R., Buruck, G., Jungbauer, K. L., & Leiter, M. P. (2016). Work-related factors of presenteeism: The mediating role of mental and physical health. *Journal of Occupational Health Psychology*, *21*(2), 220–234. DOI: 10.1037/a0039670 PMID: 26322439

Ponzo, S., Wickham, A., Bamford, R., Radovic, T., Zhaunova, L., Peven, K., Klepchukova, A., & Payne, J. L. (2022). Menstrual cycle-associated symptoms and workplace productivity in US employees: A cross-sectional survey of users of the Flo mobile phone app. *Digital Health*, *8*, 1–12. DOI: 10.1177/20552076221145852 PMID: 36544535

Pope, S. K., Sowers, M., Welch, G. W., & Albrecht, G. (2001). Functional limitations in women at midlife: The role of health conditions, behavioral and environmental factors. *Women's Health Issues*, *11*(6), 494–502. DOI: 10.1016/S1049-3867(01)00089-5 PMID: 11704470

Postmenopausal Syndrome - StatPearls - NCBI Bookshelf. (n.d.). Retrieved March 25, 2025, from https://www.ncbi.nlm.nih.gov/books/NBK560840/

Powell, D. B. (2023). Presenteeism in the Workplace: An Exploration of Supervisors' Perspective and Employee Outcomes.

Powley, E. (2005). Rwanda: Women hold up half the parliament. In *Women in Parliament: Beyond Numbers* (2nd ed.). International IDEA.

Ramyashree, S., Veigas, J., & Kanagal, D. (2024). Severity of menopausal symptoms on quality of life among working women. *Journal of Education and Health Promotion*, *13*(1), 35. DOI: 10.4103/jehp.jehp_802_23 PMID: 38545317

Rappaport, A., Bancroft, E., & Okum, L. (2003). The aging workforce raises new talent management issues for employers. *Journal of Organizational Excellence*, *23*(1), 55–66. DOI: 10.1002/npr.10101

Rashid, A., & Kausik, M. D. A. K. (2024). AI revolutionizing industries worldwide: A comprehensive overview of its diverse applications. *Hybrid Advances*, *7*, 100277. DOI: 10.1016/j.hybadv.2024.100277

Rathee, A., & Sharma, V. (2022). Feminist spirituality and emotional empowerment in organizational settings. *Journal of Feminist Workplace Studies*, *5*(1), 45–60.

Razzak, F., Yi, F., Yang, Y., & Xiong, H. (2019, November). An integrated multimodal attention-based approach for bank stress test prediction. In *2019 IEEE International Conference on Data Mining (ICDM)* (pp. 1282–1287). IEEE.

Reave, L. (2005). Spiritual values and practices related to leadership effectiveness. *The Leadership Quarterly*, *16*(5), 655–687. DOI: 10.1016/j.leaqua.2005.07.003

Reddy, S., Fox, J., & Purohit, M. P. (2019). Artificial intelligence-enabled health-care delivery. *Journal of the Royal Society of Medicine*, *112*(1), 22–28. DOI: 10.1177/0141076818815510 PMID: 30507284

Reddy, U. S., Thota, A. V., & Dharun, A. (n.d.). Machine learning techniques for stress prediction in working employees. In *IEEE International Conference on Computational Intelligence and Computing Research (ICCIC)* (pp. 1–4). IEEE. DOI: 10.1109/ICCIC.2018.8782395

Rees, M., Bitzer, J., Cano, A., Ceausu, I., Chedraui, P., Durmusoglu, F., Erkkola, R., Geukes, M., Godfrey, A., Goulis, D. G., Griffiths, A., Hardy, C., Hickey, M., Hirschberg, A. L., Hunter, M., Kiesel, L., Jack, G., Lopes, P., Mishra, G., & Lambrinoudaki, I. (2021). Global consensus recommendations on menopause in the workplace: A European Menopause and Andropause Society (EMAS) position statement. *Maturitas*, *151*, 55–62. DOI: 10.1016/j.maturitas.2021.06.006 PMID: 34274202

Rego, A., & Pina e Cunha, M. (2008). Authenticity, self-awareness, and Spirituality in the workplace. *Human Resource Development International*, *11*(5), 563–581. DOI: 10.1080/13678860802417753

Rego, A., & Pina e Cunha, M. (2008). Workplace spirituality and organizational commitment: An empirical study. *Journal of Organizational Change Management*, *21*(1), 53–75. DOI: 10.1108/09534810810847039

Rhoades, L., & Eisenberger, R. (2002). Perceived organizational support: A review of the literature. *The Journal of Applied Psychology*, *87*(4), 698–714. DOI: 10.1037/0021-9010.87.4.698 PMID: 12184574

Riach, K., & Jack, G. (2021). Reduced work engagement and turnover intentions. *International Journal of Environmental Research and Public Health*, *18*(20), 10793. DOI: 10.3390/ijerph182010793

Ribeiro, M. T., Singh, S., & Guestrin, C. (2016). "Why should I trust you?": Explaining the predictions of any classifier. *Proceedings of the 22nd ACM SIGKDD International Conference on Knowledge Discovery and Data Mining*, 1135–1144. https://doi.org/DOI: 10.1145/2939672.2939778

Ringle, C. M., Sarstedt, M., Mitchell, R., & Gudergan, S. P. (2019). Partial least squares structural equation modeling in HRM research. *International Journal of Human Resource Management*, *31*(12), 1617–1643. DOI: 10.1080/09585192.2017.1416655

Rizzo, M. (2025, October). AI in Neurology: Everything, Everywhere, All at Once Part 3: Surveillance, Synthesis, Simulation, and Systems. *Annals of Neurology*, *98*(4), 651–667. Advance online publication. DOI: 10.1002/ana.27230

Roberson, Q. M. (2019). Diversity in the workplace: A review, synthesis, and future research agenda. *Annual Review of Organizational Psychology and Organizational Behavior*, *6*(1), 69–88. DOI: 10.1146/annurev-orgpsych-012218-015243

Rockstuhl, T., & Van Dyne, L. (2018). A bi-factor theory of the four-factor model of cultural intelligence: Meta-analysis and theoretical extensions. *Organizational Behavior and Human Decision Processes*, *148*, 124–144. DOI: 10.1016/j.obhdp.2018.07.005

Rodrigo, C. H., Sebire, E., Bhattacharya, S., Paranjothy, S., & Black, M. (2023). Effectiveness of workplace-based interventions to promote wellbeing among menopausal women: A systematic review. *Post Reproductive Health*, *29*(2), 99–108. DOI: 10.1177/20533691231177414

Ryan, S., Charter, R., Ussher, J., Perich, T., Power, R., & Sperring, S. (2025). Navigating Menopause at Work: A Rapid Review and Narrative Synthesis of Psycho-Educational and Behavioral Interventions to Support Menopausal Women in the Workplace. *Women's Reproductive Health (Philadelphia, Pa.)*, *0*(0), 1–19. DOI: 10.1080/23293691.2025.2495975

Ryczkowska, K., Adach, W., Janikowski, K., Banach, M., & Bielecka-Dabrowa, A. (2022). Menopause and women's cardiovascular health: Is it really an obvious relationship? *Archives of Medical Science : AMS, 19*(2), 458–466. DOI: 10.5114/aoms/157308

Saadat, H. (2021). Effect of inadequate sleep on clinician performance. *Anesthesia and Analgesia, 132*(5), 1338–1343. DOI: 10.1213/ANE.0000000000005369 PMID: 33857976

Sagie, A. (1998). Employee absenteeism, organizational commitment, and job satisfaction: Another look. *Journal of Vocational Behavior, 52*(2), 156–171. DOI: 10.1006/jvbe.1997.1581

Salehi, W., Gupta, G., Bhatia, S., Koundal, D., Mashat, A., & Belay, A. (2022). IoT-Based Wearable Devices for Patients Suffering from Alzheimer Disease. *Contrast Media & Molecular Imaging, 3224939*(1), 3224939. Advance online publication. DOI: 10.1155/2022/3224939

Sanchez, T. W., Brenman, M., & Ye, X. (2024). The Ethical Concerns of Artificial Intelligence in Urban Planning. *Journal of the American Planning Association.* Advance online publication. DOI: 10.1080/01944363.2024.2355305

Santoro, N., Epperson, C. N., & Mathews, S. B. (2015). Menopausal Symptoms and Their Management. *Endocrinology and Metabolism Clinics of North America, 44*(3), 497–515. DOI: 10.1016/j.ecl.2015.05.001

Santoro, N., & Randolph, J. F. (2011). Reproductive hormones and the menopause transition. *Obstetrics and Gynecology Clinics, 38*(3), 455–466. PMID: 21961713

Santoro, N., Roeca, C., Peters, B. A., & Neal-Perry, G. (2021). The menopause transition: Signs, symptoms, and management options. *The Journal of Clinical Endocrinology and Metabolism, 106*(1), 1–15. DOI: 10.1210/clinem/dgaa764 PMID: 33095879

Sauer, J. (2023). *2023 AARP Employer Menopause Survey.* DOI: 10.26419/res.00720.001

Savitha, P. M.P. Margaret Savitha. (2024). Reinforcement learning in personalized medicine: Tailoring treatment protocols to individual patients. *Journal of Electrical Systems, 20*(3), 7109–7118. DOI: 10.52783/jes.7277

Schaufeli, W. B., Bakker, A. B., & Van Rhenen, W. (2009). How changes in job demands and resources predict burnout, work engagement, and sickness absenteeism. *Journal of Organizational Behavior: The International Journal of Industrial. Journal of Organizational Behavior, 30*(7), 893–917. DOI: 10.1002/job.595

Schei, T. S., & Abernathy, K. (2023). An evaluation of demographic characteristics and workplace experiences of UK employees using an employer-provided menopause application. *Maturitas, 177*, 107803. Advance online publication. DOI: 10.1016/j.maturitas.2023.107803 PMID: 37531870

Schei, T. S., & Abernathy, K. (2024). The impact of a specialist-led digital health application on menopause symptoms in the workplace: A single-arm, longitudinal evaluation. *Maturitas, 187*, 108005. Advance online publication. DOI: 10.1016/j.maturitas.2024.108005 PMID: 38851044

Scheur, V. (2022). *Support for Menopausal Women in the Workplace. September 2021.*

Schooley, B., San Nicolas-Rocca, T., & Burkhard, R. (2015). Patient-provider communications in outpatient clinic settings: A clinic-based evaluation of mobile device and multimedia mediated communications for patient education. *JMIR mHealth and uHealth, 3*(1), e3732. Advance online publication. DOI: 10.2196/mhealth.3732 PMID: 25583145

Schwiter, K., & Ruedin, D. (2021). AI and workplace well-being: Addressing bias and enhancing inclusivity. *Journal of Business Ethics, 171*(4), 765–783.

Sekaran, U., & Bougie, R. (2010). *Research methods for business: A skill-building approach* (5th ed.). John Wiley & Sons.

Selye, H. (1987). *Stress without distress*. Transworld.

Shaikh, E., Watto, W. A., & Tunio, M. N. (2021). Impact of authentic leadership on organizational citizenship behavior by using the mediating effect of psychological ownership. *Etikonomi, 21*(1), 89–102. DOI: 10.15408/etk.v21i1.18968

Shajari, S., Kuruvinashetti, K., Komeili, A., & Sundararaj, U. (2023). The Emergence of AI-Based Wearable Sensors for Digital Health Technology: A Review. *Sensors (Basel), 23*(23), 9498. DOI: 10.3390/s23239498

Shanbhag, D., Shilpa, R., D'Souza, N., Josephine, P., Singh, J., & Goud, B. R. (2012). Perceptions regarding menstruation and practices during menstrual cycles among high school going adolescent girls in resource limited settings around Bangalore city, Karnataka, India. *International Journal of Collaborative Research on Internal Medicine & Public Health.*

Sharma, M., & Kumra, S. (2020). Workplace spirituality and work engagement during COVID-19 pandemic: A study of Indian professionals. *Journal of Human Values, 26*(3), 128–141. DOI: 10.1177/0971685820978735

Sharma, P., & Gupta, N. L. (2020). Menstrual hygiene and infections: Menacing women's health. *International Journal of Health & Allied Sciences*, *9*(2), 99–104. DOI: 10.4103/ijhas.IJHAS_92_19

Shaw, S., & Leberman, S. (2015). The historical construction of women's sport leadership development in New Zealand. *Sport Management Review*, *18*(4), 555–566.

Sherman, S. (2005). Defining the menopausal transition. *The American Journal of Medicine*, *118*(12, Suppl. 12B), 3–7. DOI: 10.1016/j.amjmed.2005.11.002 PMID: 16414321

Shickel, B., Tighe, P. J., Bihorac, A., & Rashidi, P. (2018). Deep EHR: A survey of recent advances in deep learning techniques for electronic health record (EHR) analysis. *IEEE Journal of Biomedical and Health Informatics*, *22*(5), 1589–1604. DOI: 10.1109/JBHI.2017.2767063 PMID: 29989977

Shifrin, N. V., & Michel, J. S. (2022). Flexible work arrangements and employee health: A meta-analytic review. *Work and Stress*, *36*(1), 60–85. DOI: 10.1080/02678373.2021.1936287

Siegel, E. (2013). *Predictive analytics: The power to predict who will click, buy, lie, or die*. John Wiley & Sons.

Sillars, A., & Parry, D. (1982). Stress, cognition, and communication in interpersonal conflicts. *Communication Research*, *9*(2), 201–226. DOI: 10.1177/009365082009002002

Simpson, R., & Lewis, P. (2005). An investigation of silence and a scrutiny of transparency: Re-examining gender in organization literature through the concepts of voice and visibility. *Human Relations*, *58*(10), 1253–1275. DOI: 10.1177/0018726705058940

Singh, A., & Sahoo, S. (2022). Menstrual hygiene practices among adolescent women in rural India: A cross-sectional study. *BMC Public Health*, *22*(1), 1–9. DOI: 10.1186/s12889-022-14622-7 PMID: 36401238

Singh, N., Garg, M., & Chopra, R. (2023). An overview of herbal formulations: From processing to pharmacovigilance. *International Journal of Pharmaceutical Sciences and Research*, *14*(2), 562–578.

Singh, V., Kumar, A., & Gupta, S. (2022). Mental health prevention and promotion: A narrative review. *Frontiers in Psychiatry*, *13*, 1–4. DOI: 10.3389/fpsyt.2022.898009 PMID: 35958637

Siswadi, Y., Jufrizen, J., Saripuddin, J., Farisi, S., & Sari, M. (2023). Organizational Culture and Organizational Citizenship Behavior: The Mediating Role of Learning Organizations and Organizational Commitment. *Jurnal Riset Bisnis Dan Manajemen*, *16*(1), 73–82. DOI: 10.23969/jrbm.v16i1.7184

Smith, C., Jones, R., & Patel, S. (2023). Digital Exclusion in AI-Based Healthcare: Implications for Aging Populations. *Journal of Human-Centered AI*, *17*(2), 145–168.

Smith, D., Johnson, P., & White, R. (2023). AI-Driven Smart Workspaces: Improving Employee Experience. *Workplace Technology Journal*, *41*(2), 140–165.

Smith, J.. (2018). Best practices for collecting and preprocessing data in mental health research. *Journal of Mental Health Research*, *20*(1), 45–58.

Smith-Ryan, A. E., Hirsch, K. R., & Cabre, H. E. (2023). Physiology of Menopause. In Hackney, A. C. (Ed.), *Sex Hormones, Exercise and Women*. Springer., DOI: 10.1007/978-3-031-21881-1_15

Soares, C. N., Joffe, H., & Steiner, M. (2004). Menopause and mood. *Clinical Obstetrics and Gynecology*, *47*(3), 576–591. DOI: 10.1097/01.grf.0000129918.00756.d5 PMID: 15326420

Soori, M., Arezoo, B., & Dastres, R. (2023). Artificial intelligence, machine learning and deep learning in advanced robotics, a review. *Cognitive Robotics*, *3*, 54–70. DOI: 10.1016/j.cogr.2023.04.001

Sopiarz, N., & Sparzak, P. B. (2023). Primary Ovarian Insufficiency. *StatPearls*. https://www.ncbi.nlm.nih.gov/books/NBK589674/

Soules, M. R., Sherman, S., Parrott, E., Rebar, R., Santoro, N., Utian, W., & Woods, N. (2001). Stages of Reproductive Aging Workshop (STRAW). *Journal of Women's Health & Gender-Based Medicine*, *10*(9), 843–848. DOI: 10.1089/152460901753285732

Søvold, L. E., Naslund, J. A., Kousoulis, A. A., Saxena, S., Qoronfleh, M. W., Grobler, C., & Münter, L. (2021). Prioritizing the mental health and well-being of healthcare workers: An urgent global public health priority. *Frontiers in Public Health*, *9*, 603–624. DOI: 10.3389/fpubh.2021.679397 PMID: 34026720

Spector, P. E., & Bruk-Lee, V. (2008). Conflict, health, and well-being. In De Dreu, C. K. W., & Gelfand, M. J. (Eds.), *The psychology of conflict and conflict management in organizations* (pp. 267–288). Taylor & Francis Group/Lawrence Erlbaum Associates.

Spilsbury, K., Pender, S., Bloor, K., Borthwick, R., Atkin, K., McCaughan, D., Watt, I., Adderley, U., Wakefield, A., & McKenna, H. (2013). Support matters: A mixed methods scoping study on the use of assistant staff in the delivery of community nursing services in England. *Health and Social Care Delivery Research*, *1*(3), 1–46. DOI: 10.3310/hsdr01030 PMID: 25642505

Stachowiak, G., Pertyński, T., & Pertyńska-Marczewska, M. (2015). Metabolic disorders in menopause. *Przeglad Menopauzalny = Menopause Review*, *14*(1), 59–64. DOI: 10.5114/pm.2015.50000 PMID: 26327890

Starhawk. (1999). *The spiral dance: A rebirth of the ancient religion of the Great Goddess*. HarperOne.

Steffan, B. (2021). Managing menopause at work: The contradictory nature of identity talk. *Gender, Work and Organization*, *28*(1), 195–214. DOI: 10.1111/gwao.12539

Steffan, B., & Loretto, W. (2025). Menopause, work and mid-life: Challenging the ideal worker stereotype. *Gender, Work and Organization*, *32*(1), 116–131. DOI: 10.1111/gwao.13136

Stevanovic, D., & Potočnik, K. (2021). Menopause and sustainable career outcomes: A science mapping review. *Sustainability*, *13*(23), 13201. DOI: 10.3390/su132313201

Still, C. (2011). Dalit women: Honour and patriarchy in South India. *Gender and Development*, *19*(3), 427–437.

Stone, M. (1974). Cross-validatory choice and assessment of statistical predictions. *Journal of the Royal Statistical Society. Series B, Statistical Methodology*, *36*(2), 111–133. DOI: 10.1111/j.2517-6161.1974.tb00994.x

Strazdins, L., & Bammer, G. (2004). Women, work and musculoskeletal health. *Social Science & Medicine*, *58*(6), 997–1005. DOI: 10.1016/S0277-9536(03)00260-0 PMID: 14723897

Stuenkel, C. A. (2018). Vasomotor and Related Menopause Symptoms. *Clinical Obstetrics and Gynecology*, *61*(3), 433–446. DOI: 10.1097/GRF.0000000000000385

Su, C., Xu, Z., Pathak, J., & Wang, F. (2020). Deep learning in mental health outcome research: A scoping review. *Translational Psychiatry*, *10*(1), 116. DOI: 10.1038/s41398-020-0780-3 PMID: 32532967

Sudeshna, R., & Aparajita, D. (2012). Determinants of menstrual hygiene among adolescent girls: A multivariate analysis. *National Journal of Community Medicine*, *3*, 294–301.

Sufyan, M., Shokat, Z., & Ashfaq, U. A. (2023). Artificial intelligence in cancer diagnosis and therapy: Current status and future perspective. *Computers in Biology and Medicine*, *165*, 107356. DOI: 10.1016/j.compbiomed.2023.107356

Sullivan, T., Weinert, C., & Cudney, S. (2003). Management of chronic illness: Voices of rural women. *Journal of Advanced Nursing*, *44*(6), 566–574. DOI: 10.1046/j.0309-2402.2003.02846.x PMID: 14651679

Sumner, R. C., & Kinsella, E. L. (2021). "It's like a kick in the teeth": The emergence of novel predictors of burnout in frontline workers during COVID-19. *Frontiers in Psychology*, *12*, 645504. DOI: 10.3389/fpsyg.2021.645504 PMID: 34113288

Sumpter, C., & Torondel, B. (2013). A systematic review of the health and social effects of menstrual hygiene management. *PLoS One*, *8*(4), e62004. DOI: 10.1371/journal.pone.0062004 PMID: 23637945

Surakasula, A., Nagarjunapu, G. C., & Raghavaiah, K. V. (2014). A comparative study of pre- and post-menopausal breast cancer: Risk factors, presentation, characteristics and management. *Journal of Research in Pharmacy Practice*, *3*(1), 12. DOI: 10.4103/2279-042X.132704

Suresh, H., & Guttag, J. V. (2021). A framework for understanding unintended consequences of machine learning. *Communications of the ACM*, *64*(11), 62–71. DOI: 10.1145/3463494

Syamala, T. S., & Sivakami, M. (2005). Menopause: An emerging issue in India. *Economic and Political Weekly*, •••, 4923–4930.

Taherdoost, H., & Ghofrani, A. (2024). AI's role in revolutionizing personalized medicine by reshaping pharmacogenomics and drug therapy. *Intelligent Pharmacy*, *2*(5), 643–650. DOI: 10.1016/j.ipha.2024.08.005

Talaulikar, V. (2022). Menopause transition: Physiology and symptoms. *Best Practice & Research. Clinical Obstetrics & Gynaecology*, *81*, 3–7. DOI: 10.1016/j.bpobgyn.2022.03.003

Tanbo, T. G., & Fedorcsak, P. Z. (2021). Can time to menopause be predicted? *Acta Obstetricia et Gynecologica Scandinavica*, *100*(11), 1961–1968. DOI: 10.1111/aogs.14253

Tarhane, S., & Kasulkar, A. (2015). Awareness of adolescent girls regarding menstruation and practices during menstrual cycle. *Panacea Journal of Medical Sciences*, *5*, 29–32.

Tarro, L., Llauradó, E., Ulldemolins, G., Hermoso, P., & Solà, R. (2020). Effectiveness of workplace interventions for improving absenteeism, productivity, and work ability of employees: A systematic review and meta-analysis of randomized controlled trials. *International Journal of Environmental Research and Public Health*, *17*(6), 1901. DOI: 10.3390/ijerph17061901 PMID: 32183392

Taylor, S., Jaques, N., Nosakhare, E., Sano, A., & Picard, R. (2020). Personalized multitask learning for predicting tomorrow's mood, stress, and health. *IEEE Transactions on Affective Computing*, *11*(2), 200–213. DOI: 10.1109/TAFFC.2017.2784832 PMID: 32489521

Telles, S., Nagarathna, R., & Nagendra, H. R. (2015). Autonomic changes during "OM" chanting: A pre–post pilot study. *Indian Journal of Physiology and Pharmacology*, *47*(4), 202–206.

Theis, R., Cronin, H., & Griffiths, A. (2023). Factors affecting quality of life. *Journal of Occupational Health Psychology*. Advance online publication. DOI: 10.1037/ocp0000303

Thorsen, A. V., Lassen, A. D., Tetens, I., Hels, O., & Mikkelsen, B. E. (2010). Long-term sustainability of a worksite canteen intervention of serving more fruit and vegetables. *Public Health Nutrition*, *13*(10), 1647–1652. DOI: 10.1017/S1368980010001242

Tisdell, E. J. (2003). *Exploring Spirituality and culture in adult and higher education*. Jossey-Bass.

Tjoa, E., & Guan, C. (2021). A survey on explainable artificial intelligence (XAI): Toward medical XAI. *IEEE Transactions on Neural Networks and Learning Systems*, *32*(11), 4793–4813. DOI: 10.1109/TNNLS.2020.3027314

Topol, E. (2019). *Deep medicine: how artificial intelligence can make healthcare human again*.

Topol, E. (2019). *Deep medicine: How artificial intelligence can make healthcare human again*. Basic Books.

Toze, M. (2020). Specialization and minority health care: Hormone therapy for trans people in England. *Journal of Health Services Research & Policy*, *25*(4), 246–251. DOI: 10.1177/1355819619888561 PMID: 31801033

Trougakos, J. P., & Hideg, I. (2009). Momentary work recovery: The role of within-day work breaks. In *Current perspectives on job-stress recovery* (pp. 37–84). Emerald Group Publishing Limited. DOI: 10.1108/S1479-3555(2009)0000007005

Tsiara, A. A., Plakias, S., Kokkotis, C., Veneri, A., Mina, M. A., Tsiakiri, A., Kitmeridou, S., Christidi, F., Gourgoulis, E., Doskas, T., Kaltsatou, A., Tsamakis, K., Kazis, D., & Tsiptsios, D. (2025). Artificial Intelligence in the Diagnosis of Neurological Diseases Using Biomechanical and Gait Analysis Data: A Scopus-Based Bibliometric Analysis. *Neurology International 2025, Vol. 17, Page 45, 17*(3), 45. DOI: 10.3390/neurolint17030045

Tsvetanov, F. (2024). Integrating AI Technologies into Remote Monitoring Patient Systems. *Engineering Proceedings 2024, Vol. 70, Page 54, 70*(1), 54. DOI: 10.3390/engproc2024070054

Types of Artificial Intelligence | IBM. (n.d.). Retrieved March 27, 2025, from https://www.ibm.com/think/topics/artificial-intelligence-types

U.K.: smartphone usage by age 2012-2024 | Statista. (n.d.). Retrieved March 28, 2025, from https://www.statista.com/statistics/300402/smartphone-usage-in-the-uk-by-age/

UK: number of smartphone users 2014-2029 | Statista. (n.d.). Retrieved March 28, 2025, from https://www.statista.com/forecasts/1143841/smartphone-users-in-the-united-kingdom

Umayal, K. M. (2024). Strategic integration of digital health technologies for enhanced patient-centered care in modern healthcare management. *Management, 11*(iS1-Jan, S1), 68–73. DOI: 10.34293/management.v11iiS1-Jan.7142

UN Women. (2021a). *Progress on the Sustainable Development Goals: The Gender Snapshot 2021.*

UNESCO. (2021). *The impact of digital technologies on gender equality in education*.

Unilever. (2022). *Breaking the Menopause Stigma in the Workplace*. Retrieved from www.unilever.com

Ussher, J. M., Perz, J., & Parton, C. (2015). Sex and the menopausal woman: A critical review and analysis. *Feminism & Psychology, 25*(4), 449–468. DOI: 10.1177/0959353515579735

Van der Walt, F. (2018). Workplace spirituality, work engagement and thriving at work. *SA Journal of Industrial Psychology, 44*, 1538. Advance online publication. DOI: 10.4102/sajip.v44i0.1457

Vaughan, F. (2002). *The inward arc: Healing and wholeness in psychotherapy and spirituality*. Jossey Bass.

Verburgh, M., Verdonk, P., Appelman, Y., Brood-van Zanten, M., Hulshof, C., & Nieuwenhuijsen, K. (2022). Workplace Health Promotion Among Ethnically Diverse Women in Midlife With a Low Socioeconomic Position. *Health Education & Behavior*, *49*(6), 1042–1055. DOI: 10.1177/10901981211071030

Verdonk, P., Bendien, E., & Appelman, Y. (2022). Menopause and work: A narrative literature review about menopause, work and health. *Work (Reading, Mass.)*, *72*(2), 483–496. DOI: 10.3233/WOR-205214

Vickers, M. (2002). *Work and unseen chronic illness: Silent voices*. Routledge. DOI: 10.4324/9780203471395

Viertiö, S., Kiviruusu, O., Piirtola, M., Kaprio, J., Korhonen, T., Marttunen, M., & Suvisaari, J. (2021). Factors contributing to psychological distress in the working population, with a special reference to gender difference. *BMC Public Health*, *21*(1), 611. DOI: 10.1186/s12889-021-10560-y PMID: 33781240

Vincent, C., Bodnaruc, A. M., Prud'homme, D., Olson, V., & Giroux, I. (2023). Associations between menopause and body image: A systematic review. *Women's Health (London, England)*, *19*, 17455057231209536. Advance online publication. DOI: 10.1177/17455057231209536 PMID: 37994043

Vodafone. (2021). *Global Menopause Policy Report*. Retrieved from www.vodafone .com

Wachter, S., Mittelstadt, B., & Russell, C. (2017). Counterfactual explanations without opening the black box: Automated decisions and the GDPR. *SSRN*, *31*(2), 841–887. https://jolt.law.harvard.edu/assets/articlePDFs/v31/31HarvJLTech841.pdf. DOI: 10.2139/ssrn.3063289

Waldman, E. G., Cahn, N. R., & Crawford, B. J. (2022). Contextualizing menopause in the law. *Harvard Journal of Law & Gender*, *45*, 1.

Wasaha, S., & Angelopoulos, F. M. (1996). What every woman should know about menopause. *The American Journal of Nursing*, *96*(1), 25. DOI: 10.1097/00000446-199601000-00025 PMID: 8546184

Weber, M. T., Maki, P. M., & McDermott, M. P. (2014). Cognition and mood in perimenopause: A systematic review and meta-analysis. *The Journal of Steroid Biochemistry and Molecular Biology*, *142*, 90–98. DOI: 10.1016/j.jsbmb.2013.06.001 PMID: 23770320

Weismiller, D. G. (2009). Menopause. *Primary Care*, *36*(1), 199–226. DOI: 10.1016/j.pop.2008.10.007

West, S. M., Whittaker, M., & Crawford, K. (2019). *Discriminating systems: Gender, race, and power in AI*. AI Now Institute.

Wharne, S. (2021). How is distress understood in existential philosophies and can phenomenological therapeutic practices be "evidence-based"? *Theory & Psychology*, *31*(2), 273–289. DOI: 10.1177/0959354320964586

What Is NLP (Natural Language Processing)? | IBM. (n.d.). Retrieved March 27, 2025, from https://www.ibm.com/think/topics/natural-language-processing

Whiley, L. A., Wright, A., Stutterheim, S. E., & Grandy, G. (2023). "A part of being a woman, really": Menopause at work as "dirty" femininity. *Gender, Work and Organization*, *30*(3), 897–916. DOI: 10.1111/gwao.12946

Whiteley, J.. (2023). Impact of menopausal symptoms on work and careers. *Occupational Medicine*, *73*(5), 287–294. DOI: 10.1093/occmed/kqad050

Whiteley, J., DiBonaventura, M. da C., Wagner, J.-S., Alvir, J., & Shah, S. (2013). The impact of menopausal symptoms on quality of life, productivity, and economic outcomes. *Journal of Women's Health*, *22*(11), 983–990. DOI: 10.1089/jwh.2012.3719 PMID: 24083674

Williams, D. R., Mohammed, S. A., Leavell, J., & Collins, C. (2010). Race, socioeconomic status, and health: Complexities, ongoing challenges, and research opportunities. *Annals of the New York Academy of Sciences*, *1186*(1), 69–101. DOI: 10.1111/j.1749-6632.2009.05339.x PMID: 20201869

Williams, J. C., Blair-Loy, M., & Berdahl, J. L. (2016). Cultural schemas, social class, and the flexibility stigma. *The Journal of Social Issues*, *72*(2), 209–234. DOI: 10.1111/josi.12012

Williamson, S. M., & Prybutok, V. (2024). Balancing privacy and progress: A review of privacy challenges, systemic oversight, and patient perceptions in AI-driven healthcare. *Applied Sciences (Basel, Switzerland)*, *14*(2), 675. Advance online publication. DOI: 10.3390/app14020675

Williams, R., Kerr, C., & Dobson, R. (2021). Gendered Aging and Career Progression: Barriers in Professional Workplaces. *Gender, Work and Organization*, *28*(4), 512–528.

Williams, R., Kerr, C., & Dobson, R. (2023). Artificial Intelligence for Workplace Fairness: Tackling Age and Gender Bias. *Gender, Work and Organization*, *29*(4), 525–549.

Women, U. N. (2021b). *Women in the changing world of work: Facts and figures.* https://www.unwomen.org/

Women's Health East. (2022). *How to become a menopause friendly workplace.* https://whe.org.au/wp-content/uploads/WHE-How-to-become-a-Menopause-friendly-workplace.pdf

Woods-Giscombé, C. L. (2010). Superwoman schema: African American women's views on stress, strength, and health. *Qualitative Health Research, 20*(5), 668–683. DOI: 10.1177/1049732310361892 PMID: 20154298

Woods, N. F., & Mitchell, E. S. (2005). Symptoms during the perimenopause: Prevalence, severity, trajectory, and significance in women's lives. *The American Journal of Medicine, 118*(12, Suppl. 12B), 14–24. DOI: 10.1016/j.amjmed.2005.09.031 PMID: 16414323

Woolsey, L., Ahmed, R., & Tuck, E. (2022). Designing for the margins: Feminist AI for emotional wellbeing. *Feminist Media Studies, 22*(4), 589–607. DOI: 10.1080/14680777.2022.2037499

Wright, B. D. (1996). Reliability and separation. *Rasch Measurement Transactions, 9*(4), 472.

Wright, V. J., Schwartzman, J. D., Itinoche, R., & Wittstein, J. (2024). The musculoskeletal syndrome of menopause. *Climacteric, 27*(5), 466–472. DOI: 10.1080/13697137.2024.2380363 PMID: 39077777

Wu, Y. C., & Su, C.-Y. (2025, January). E., Hou, J. H., Lin, C. J., Lin, K. B., & Chen, C. H. (2024). Artificial intelligence and assisted reproductive technology: A comprehensive systematic review. *Taiwanese Journal of Obstetrics & Gynecology, 64*(1), 11–26. Advance online publication. DOI: 10.1016/j.tjog.2024.10.001

Yadav, J. (2022, December 19). *India's Tuition Republic is bigger than ever: Coaching culture is an epidemic now*. ThePrint.

Yasmin, S., Manna, N., Mallik, S., Ahmed, A., & Paria, B. (2013). Menstrual hygiene among adolescent school students: An in-depth cross-sectional study in an urban community of West Bengal, India. *IOSR Journal of Dental and Medical Sciences, 5*(6), 22–26. DOI: 10.9790/0853-0562226

Yatbaz, H. Y., & Erbilek, M. (2020, April). Deep learning based stress prediction from offline signatures. In 2020 8th International Workshop on Biometrics and Forensics (IWBF) (pp. 1–6). IEEE.

Yeasmin, M. N., Al Amin, M., Joti, T. J., Aung, Z., & Azim, M. A. (2024). Advances of AI in image-based computer-aided diagnosis: A review. *Array (New York, N.Y.)*, *23*, 100357. Advance online publication. DOI: 10.1016/j.array.2024.100357

Ye, L., Knox, B., & Hickey, M. (2022). Management of Menopause Symptoms and Quality of Life during the Menopause Transition. *Endocrinology and Metabolism Clinics of North America*, *51*(4), 817–836. DOI: 10.1016/j.ecl.2022.04.006

Yoeli, H., Macnaughton, J., & McLusky, S. (2021). Menopausal symptoms and work: A narrative review of women's experiences in casual, informal, or precarious jobs. *Maturitas*, *150*, 14–21. DOI: 10.1016/j.maturitas.2021.05.007

Yukl, G. A. (2013). *Leadership in organizations* (8th ed.). Pearson Education.

Zhang, L., Tang, L., Xia, M., & Cao, G. (2023). The application of artificial intelligence in glaucoma diagnosis and prediction. *Frontiers in Cell and Developmental Biology*, *11*, 1173094. DOI: 10.3389/fcell.2023.1173094

Zhao, X., Shen, X., Jia, F., He, X., Zhao, D., & Li, P. (2025). Using machine learning models to identify severe subjective cognitive decline and related factors in nurses during the menopause transition: A pilot study. *Menopause (New York, N.Y.)*, *32*(4), 295–305. Advance online publication. DOI: 10.1097/GME.0000000000002500

Zhou, M., Duan, N., Liu, S., & Shum, H. Y. (2020). Progress in Neural NLP: Modeling, Learning, and Reasoning. *Engineering (Beijing)*, *6*(3), 275–290. DOI: 10.1016/j.eng.2019.12.014

Zhou, Z., Luo, D., Yang, B. X., & Liu, Z. (2022). Machine learning-based prediction models for depression symptoms among Chinese healthcare workers during the early COVID-19 outbreak in 2020: A cross-sectional study. *Frontiers in Psychiatry*, *13*, 876995. DOI: 10.3389/fpsyt.2022.876995 PMID: 35573334

Zouboulis, C. C., Blume-Peytavi, U., Kosmadaki, M., & Röcken, M. (2022). Skin, hair and beyond: The impact of menopause. *Climacteric*, *25*(5), 434–442. DOI: 10.1080/13697137.2022.2050206 PMID: 35377827

About the Contributors

Kyla Tennin has been asked to address the menopause and menstrual cycle issue by colleagues, for several years now. Combining her natural sciences (OB/GYN) background and social sciences (DM) expertise and professional experience to improve organizations and women's health/ wellbeing. She would like to do so utilizing IGI Global Publishing to develop a publication to use at conferences, forums, summits, in corporations, and health care institutions. For example, at Forbes, Forbes Women, Financial Times, and JP Morgan Chase Healthcare events... where prominent executives, leaders, women, decision-makers, and the like attend from Walgreens, Cigna, Moderna, GSK, Bristol Myers Squibb (with the VP & Head of Digital Health), and even Dr. Jill Biden, First Lady of the United States where she shares her insights and vision for The White House Initiative on Women's Health Research; to shape healthcare, wellbeing, policies, and discussions. Including with AI Matching to match speakers/sponsors/attendees with organizations, for networking, to discuss healthcare solutions. Dr. Kyla is also planning health, women's health, and women's empowerment initiatives with notable colleagues like Ms. Rula Ghani, First Lady of Afghanistan, Princess Dina Mired of Jordan, Ms. Intissar El-Sisi, spouse of Egyptian President, Dr. Mariem Mint Dah, First Lady Of Mauritania, Dr. Madeeha bint Ahmed al Shibaniyah, Minister of Education (Oman), and Ms. Amina J. Mohammed, Deputy Secretary-General of the UN & Chair of the UN Sustainable Development Group.. Furthermore, Dr. Kyla has worked with (consulting and speaking/training) Healthcare/BioTech/Pharma companies like Optum, Anthem Health, MEDICA, Medicare, BlueCross BlueShield, and women's clinics. Moreover, when there are issues with employees in companies, organizational effectivness and efficiency, the bottom-line, and human capital strategy are negatively impacted. She is a United Nations Global Ambassador for Peace, representing the African Union 6th Region, African Diaspora, for enhancing and promoting economic development, investment/financial inclusion, and women's empowerment. Including being a Fellow-in-Residence at the University of Phoenix

College of Doctoral Studies Center for Leadership Studies and Organizational Research, Secretary-General at International Research Institute for Economics and Management (IRIEM), and President and CEO of Lady Mirage Global, Inc. (global conglomerate), with the main firm being a management consultancy (she actually owns 2 consulting firms), working with global corporations, colleges and universities, and healthcare organizations. She is an MD (OB/GYN) turned DM (change management and organizational development) doctor. She has published over 150 authors book chapters and journal articles, approximately 40 books, a variety of book chapters, research reports, and presentations, and has worked with publishers like IGI Global, Wiley (beginning in 2004), NOVA Science Publishers, Routledge/Taylor and Francis, Emerald Publishing India, and Emerald Publishing UK. With pending/forthcoming edited, author, and textbook proposal with Springer, Palgrave Macmillian, SpringerNature, SAGE Publications Inc., McGraw Hill, Bentham, Apple Academic Press, and Cambridge. Last, she is an Editorial Board Member and Reviewer for various International Journals.

A. V. Senthil Kumar is a Director and Professor of the PG and Research Department of Computer Applications at Hindusthan College of Arts and Science India since 2010. He has to his credit 11 Book Chapters, 250 papers in International Journals, 15 papers in National Journals, 25 papers in International Conferences, 5 papers in National Conferences, edited 8 books (IGI Global, USA), and much more, regularly. He is an Editor-in-Chief for International Journal titled "International Journal of Data Mining and Emerging Technologies", "International Journal of Image Processing and Applications", "International Journal of Advances in Knowledge Engineering & Computer Science", " International Journal of Advances in Computers and Information Engineering" and "International Journal of Research and Reviews in Computer Science". He is a Key Member for India, Machine Intelligence Research Lab (MIR Labs). Last, Dr. Kumar is an Editorial Board Member and Reviewer for various International Journals. Note: Dr. Kumar's ORCID iD needs to be added.

Samrat Ray is Dean & Head of Research & International Relations at IIMS Pune, a Global Academic Leader, and Accomplished Educator having worked in various countries in Europe, Russia, Latvia, and the Middle East (Dubai). He has Expertise in Research and Accreditation Processes and is focused on Building World-Class Academic Institutions. Additionally, Dr. Ray has facilitated 15+ international partnerships with top-tier universities across the United States, Europe and Asia, enabling impactful research collaborations, faculty exchange programs and student mobility opportunities. Regarding research, Dr. Ray has an H-index of 38 and 3,000+ citations, I have directed research initiatives that have contributed over 150 high-impact publications in Scopus, SSCI and Web of Science-indexed journals. He has integrated Environmental, Social and Governance (ESG) principles into academic frameworks, aligning education with societal goals while fostering resilience through digital transformation. Inclusive, Dr. Ray has led the successful accreditation of institutions with global standards such as AACSB, EFMD and AMBA, elevating their global rankings and reputation. Last, Dr. Ray has leveraged expertise in entrepreneurship, behavioral economics, digital transformation and sustainability, and has spearheaded initiatives that have transformed institutions, driven excellence, and fostered global recognition.

A. Mishra is Dean of Academics, Program In-charge Head of the PGDM program which is NBA Accredited, and Head of Department (HOD) of Marketing at IIMS Pune, India. Dr. Mishra focuses on Researcher Collaborations, is a published Author, Academician, Resource Person for various IIMS programs, like the Faculty Development (FDP & MDP), is a Consultant, and has conducted Sponsored Research. Note: Dr. Kumar's ORCID iD needs to be added.

***

V.R. Balasaraswathi is working as a Assistant Professor. Her area of interest are Cryptography and Machine Learning

Ruksana Begum is a PG student in the Department of Public Health in Utkal University, as well as she is a women's health expert in community medicine and epidemiology.

Hitakshi Dutta is a Professor and Associate Director at Chandigarh University, Mohali, Punjab, India. Her research interests focus on employee engagement and organizational effectiveness.

Filippo Ferrari holds a Bachelor degree in Work and Organizational Psychology and a Masters degree in Adult Training and Education. He currently serves as a Lecturer at Bologna University, School of Economics, Management and Statistics, where he teaches Leadership and Organizational Behaviour. His fields of interests are Human Resources Management, Organizational Reliability, Change Management, Adult Training.

Mohammed Imran is currently working as an Research Assistant, P.S College, Khandapada, Nayagarh, Odisha. He has PhD in Women's Studies from Dept. of Women's Studies, Utkal University, Bhubaneswar. He has completed a Master Degree in Women's Studies from Utkal University. He has qualified ICSSR Doctoral

Fellow. He has presented research papers at National/ International conferences in India and has published papers in indexed international journals of repute. He has over 5 years of research experience. His research interest is Gender and Education, Girls Dropout. Teaching interest in Feminism and Women, and Development.

Bhabani Shankar Mohanty is currently working as an Assistant Professor in the Department of Statistics and Applied Mathematics, School of Mathematics and Computer Sciences, Central University of Tamil Nadu, Tamil Nadu. He has an M.Phil and a Doctorate (Ph.D.) in Statistics from the P.G. Department of Statistics, Utkal University, Bhubaneswar. He has completed a Master's Degree in Statistics from Utkal University and worked for one year as a Project-JRF at IIT-Bhubaneswar. He has presented research papers at National/ International conferences in India and has published papers in indexed international journals of repute. He has over 10 years of teaching and research experience. His research interests are inventory control, fuzzy logic, optimization techniques, and sustainable supply chains. He also has command over analyzing high-dimension data generated from different real-life phenomena.

N. Kumaresh is currently an Associate Professor in the Department of Computer Applications (MCA) at RV Institute of Technology and Management (RVITM), Bengaluru, with over 19 years of experience in teaching and research. He holds a B.Sc. in Computer Science and an M.C.A. from Bharathiar University (2003 and 2006), and an M.E. in Software Engineering from Anna University (2010). He earned his Ph.D. from Anna University in 2020, focusing on the "Investigation and Analysis of Automated Job Knowledge Ontology Construction with Reduced Overhead and Time Complexity." Dr. Kumaresh began his academic career in 2006 at Sri Ramakrishna Institute of Technology, Coimbatore, where he served as Lecturer and later as Assistant Professor until 2020. From 2020 to 2023, he was Professor and Head of the Artificial Intelligence and Machine Learning Department at Dr. N.G.P. Institutions, Coimbatore. A recognized research supervisor under Visvesvaraya Technological University, Belagavi, he actively mentors research scholars. His research contributions include over 20 publications in reputed national and international journals and conferences, with expertise in Cyber Security, Artificial Intelligence, and Machine Learning. He is also a member of several esteemed professional bodies, including ISTE, CSI, IAENG, and the Internet Society.

Vanitha N. received her Master of Computer Applications from the Avinashilingam Institute for Home Science and Higher Education for Women, Coimbatore, in 2008. In 2008 she was hired as a Software programmer in LMW group, Coimbatore. Since 2011, she has been working as an Assistant Professor in the department of Artificial Intelligence and Machine Learning at Coimbatore Institute of Technology, Coimbatore. She received her Doctor of Philosophy in Computer Science from the Avinashilingam Institute for Home Science and Higher Education for Women, Coimbatore. She writes and presents widely on UAV Networks, Cyber Security, Machine, and Deep Learning.

A Kritika Ohri is a Research Scholar in the University School of Business, Department of Commerce, Chandigarh University, Mohali, Punjab, India. Her research interests include workplace spirituality, organizational behavior, and employee well-being. Her academic work focuses on understanding the role of meaningful work practices in enhancing individual and organizational outcomes.

Rohit Kumar Pal is an accomplished academician, researcher, and educational leader with over seven years of dedicated experience in teaching Biology, Environmental Science, and Human Resource Management. He currently serves as the Head of the Department at the School of Professional Studies, Adamas University, Kolkata, where he has been shaping future educators and civil service aspirants since 2017. Alongside, he holds academic affiliations with RICE Education and Pedagog (UK), where he contributes as a senior educator in both offline and online learning environments. Dr. Pal holds a Professional Doctorate in Education Management and Leadership from the European International University, Paris, complementing his M.Sc. in Life Sciences from Presidency University and an MBA in Human Resource Management. His academic journey is marked by distinction, having cleared WBSET (Environmental Science) and UGC NET (Disaster Management) examinations. As a Certified Educator at the National Geographic Society, he promotes global environmental literacy through immersive educational approaches. He has also completed over 70 professional development and certificate programs from prestigious platforms like IITs, UN institutes, WHO, ADBI, Coursera, and Microsoft Educator Center, emphasizing sustainability, climate change, leadership, and modern pedagogical tools. Dr. Pal has contributed significantly to research with multiple publications in international peer-reviewed journals, addressing themes like digital leadership, labor welfare, environmental education, sustainable development, and organizational behavior. His role as a reviewer and editorial board member for reputed journals such as IJRAR, IJRPR, Journal of Social Welfare & Management, and others highlights his expertise in academic quality assessment and content development. In addition to scholarly publishing, he has authored the books "A Handbook on Human Resource Development" and "Organizational Politics". He is a frequent contributor to educational blogs and newspapers like Anandabazar Patrika and Karmasangsthan, writing on exam preparation, educational technology, and future trends in coaching. Dr. Pal is also a recognized speaker, having participated in numerous webinars, faculty development programs, and international workshops hosted by institutions like IIT Bombay, Presidency University, Annamalai University, and Maryam Abacha American University of Nigeria. He has also served as a judge at the QS Reimagine Education Awards (2024). His professional influence extends beyond the classroom through his work with the International Teacher's Association as Communication Manager and his curriculum design contributions for ed-tech platforms. An advocate for educational innovation, equity, and sustainability, Dr. Pal is actively involved in mentoring, content creation, and advancing AI-driven approaches in education. His academic integrity, multidisciplinary knowledge, and passion for empowering students make him a transformative figure in India's education landscape.

Lakshmi Harika Pelivela is working as an Assistant Professor. Her area of interest are Artificial Intelligence and Machine Learning

Kiruthika.R is a student at Coimbatore Institute of Technology, Coimbatore and she is having a keen interest in writing research and academic papers. Her research fields include IoT, Cloud and Machine Learning

Zakir Shaikh is an Assistant Professor, Department of Accounting and Finance, School of Business Administration, Kingdom University, Bahrain. Prior to this, he worked more than 28 years in commercial and academic industry. He has published numerous articles in referred journals and presented many papers in various conferences, both local and abroad in the different area of Accounting, management and Islamic Banking and Finance. He has also participated in a variety of seminars, forums, workshops and international conferences. He obtained his Ph.D. (Islamic Banking and Finance) from India in 2018. His doctoral thesis explored the entrepreneurial phenomenon from an Islamic perspective and argued for profit and loss sharing (PLS) contracts as viable alternatives to conventional interest-based financing instruments. He holds Master degree in Commerce, Business Administration & Finance and Control. He is a member of AAA, Chartered Institute of Islamic Finance Professionals (CIIF), Malaysia; Indian Accounting Association; Orissa Commerce Association, India and associated with Accounting & Auditing Organization for Islamic Financial Institution (AAOIFI), Bahrain

Priya Sharma is currently working as an Assistant Professor, School of Pharmacy and Emerging Sciences at Baddi University of Emerging Sciences and Technology, Baddi, Himachal Pradesh. She holds M. Pharm in Pharmaceutics and earned her Ph.D. in Pharmaceutical Sciences. With over 5 years of academic and research experience, she is actively involved in both teaching and guiding students in the field of pharmaceutical sciences. Her core areas of interest include novel drug delivery systems, formulation and development, and pharmaceutical technology. She has participated in several national/ international conferences and workshops, and is committed to continuous learning and innovation in pharmaceutical education. Dr. Sharma has also contributed to research publications and is keen on expanding her research profile through interdisciplinary collaborations.

Ram Singh, a forward-thinking educator, serves as a Professor at School of BFSI, Symbiosis University of Applied Sciences, Indore, India. With over 16 years of extensive experience in teaching, research, and administration, Dr. Singh is a prominent figure in academia. His diverse roles include membership on the Editorial Boards of esteemed journals focusing on Accounting, Finance, and Management. Dr. Singh is actively involved in eight national and international academic organizations, contributing significantly to the field. His scholarly work comprises 18 books, 30 research papers, 35 book chapters, and 10 conference proceedings at both national and international levels.

Index

V

W

www.ingramcontent.com/pod-product-compliance
Lightning Source LLC
LaVergne TN
LVHW061527290926
849162LV00004B/697